WESTERN CIVILIZATIONS

THEIR HISTORY AND THEIR CULTURE

VOLUME I / THIRTEENTH EDITION

WESTERN CIVILIZATIONS

THEIR HISTORY AND THEIR CULTURE

ROBERT E. LERNER

STANDISH MEACHAM

EDWARD MCNALL BURNS

VOLUME I / THIRTEENTH EDITION

W · W · NORTON & COMPANY  NEW YORK · LONDON

PRINTED IN THE UNITED STATES OF AMERICA

The Library of Congress has catalogued the one-volume edition as follows:

Lerner, Robert E.
Western civilizations, their history and their culture / Robert E.
Lerner, Standish Meacham, Edward McNall Burns.—13th ed.
p. cm.
Includes bibliographical references and index.
ISBN 0-393-97192-9
1. Civilization, Western. 2. Europe—Civilization. I. Meacham,
Standish. II. Burns, Edward McNall, 1897– . III. Title.
CB245.L47 1998
909′.09812—dc21 97–32338

The text of this book is composed in ITC Stone Serif with the display set in Optima.
Composition by TSI Graphics and manufacturing by Quebecor Hawkins County.
Book design by Jack Meserole.

ISBN 0-393-97200-3 (Volume 1)

W. W. Norton & Company, Inc., 500 Fifth Avenue, New York, N.Y. 10110
W. W. Norton & Company Ltd., 10 Coptic Street, London WC1A 1PU

http://www.wwnorton.com

1 2 3 4 5 6 7 8 9 0

For Dietlind and Olivia;
Edith, Louisa, and Samuel

Contents

List of Maps

PREFACE

George Orwell once remarked that "keeping the past up to date is a full-time job." This insight seems particularly telling as a result of the startling rush of events during the last few years. "Trends" that seemed so clear only yesterday have turned out to be no trends at all. In addition, dramatic advances in historical scholarship have cast new light on old problems and have placed into prominence subject matters that historians previously had all but ignored. Accordingly we have worked hard to keep the past up to date for this thirteenth edition of *Western Civilizations*. Yet we have always worked within the framework of authorial principles bequeathed to us by E. M. Burns—principles that may have served to make this book a "textbook classic." We offer a history of civilizations—an evolving account of the ways in which human beings have organized their lives in response to changing environments and persistent needs. Thus we complement narrative passages with discussions of ideas and societal institutions, and we draw heavily on pictorial material to give our readers the best impression possible of how our civilizations really looked. We try as well to avoid a tone of disembodied truth, both because we do not believe there is such a thing and because we want to engage and maintain our readers' attention. Our urgent desire is to demonstrate without resorting to cheapness that "first-year history" need not be viewed as a chore but might be welcomed as a source of intellectual excitement, even delight.

Although we have gone over *Western Civilizations* line by line in our effort to keep the past up to date, teachers will wish to know where the most significant changes occur. This bright new edition features full-color maps and illustrations throughout the text and, as an additional pedagogical aid for students, highlighted summary points at the end of each chapter. Toward the goal of keeping the volume within manageable limits we have deleted the material on fossils and paleoanthropology in Chapter 1; rather than beginning with *Homo habilis,* we now begin with *Homo sapiens* and the Ice-Age cave murals. The remainder of Chapter 1 has been substantially rewritten, with revised treatments of cave art, the emergence of food production, and the birth of cities in western Asia. In addition, a prominent new feature of Chapter 1 is a discussion of the central place of cloth production by women in early villages. Another means for holding down the length of the volume has been to reduce the amount of space (hitherto generous) devoted to the details of early religions and wars: the treatment of these subjects has been streamlined in Chapters 2 (Mesopotamia) and 3 (Egypt). In Chapter 4 the narrative of Hebrew political history now opens with the entrance of the Hebrews into Canaan, the period when the biblical account begins to be corroborated by independent evidence.

Chapter 4 also contains a new treatment of Minoan society, with special attention to women's dress.

The major changes in Chapter 5 are as follows: the section on early Greek religion has been shortened; Greek "colonization" is now called Greek expansion; erroneous statements about the electoral system under Clisthenes have been corrected; and there is a revised treatment of the poetess Sappho. In Chapter 6 we have deleted the coverage of the Cynics, Menander, and Hellenistic utopias as being too specialized for an introductory text, and we have revised the discussion of the Hellenistic pastoral. Chapter 7 contains changes in coverage and interpretation in the sections concerning the Roman republican constitution, Roman religion, Roman policy in granting citizenship, and Roman art and architecture. Throughout Parts One and Two we now use the abbreviation B.C.E. (before common era) for designating the time before the birth of Christ.

In Chapter 11 we have added a paragraph on Hildegard of Bingen, and in Chapter 13 we offer substantially revised treatments of Machiavelli, Botticelli, and Michelangelo's *David.* Chapter 14 presents corrected dates for early Portuguese sailings and colonizations of the Atlantic islands, and Chapter 15 contains a new approach to the problem of defining Mannerism.

The principal addition to the chapters on the nineteenth and twentieth centuries has been the introduction of considerable new material on nationalism. Chapter 19, on the French Revolution, now includes a discussion of the way in which warfare—and the idea of an enemy "other"—encouraged a nationalistic spirit throughout Europe. The chapter concludes with an assessment of nationalism as one of the lasting legacies of the revolutionary movement. Chapter 23, "Nationalism and Nation-Building," addresses the subject at considerable length. We argue, as do most recent scholars, that nationalism must be understood as policy as well as sentiment. It was manufactured by governments, "invented" as a way of encouraging loyalty to emerging and increasingly powerful state systems. In Chapter 24, we link nationalism to the rise of imperialism. And in Chapters 26 and 28, we demonstrate the manner in which nationalism fostered xenophobia and the rise of anti-Semitism, fascism, and Nazism.

We have also added material on the history of women, particularly in Chapter 21, where we explore the way in which women defined the public and private spheres of their daily existence. We take note also of the critical role that women played in the success of various early reform movements such as the abolition of slavery. Finally, material in Chapters 31 and 32 has been thoroughly updated, and includes a discussion of such topics as the fragmentation of Eastern Europe following the collapse of the Soviet Union, as well as recent changes on the continent of Africa.

Robert Lerner has been responsible for Chapters 1 through 15 and Chapter 18; Standish Meacham for the rest. As in the past, we have relied on the helpful criticisms and suggestions of fellow teachers. For this edition, we are indebted for reviews provided by George K. Behlmer (University of Washington), Ronald M. Berger (SUNY Oneonta), Michael D. Bess (Vanderbilt University), Maryann E. Brink, James M. Brophy (University of Delaware), Phyllis Culham (U.S. Naval Academy), Jeffrey W. Merrick (University of Wisconsin, Milwaukee), Phillip C. Naylor (Marquette University), John F. Robertson (Central Michigan University), and David R. Shearer (University of Delaware). Robert Lerner is grateful for suggestions from Stephen Harris, Laura May (Northwestern University), Tammy Ruen, Alauddin Samarrai (St. Cloud State University), Nancy Spatz (University of Northern Colorado), and Stephen Wessley (York College of Pennsylvania). Standish Meacham acknowledges the valuable assistance of Steven M. Salzman. At W. W. Norton Steven Forman and Jon Durbin have guided this edition along. Kate Nash resolved crises, gathered illustrations with efficiency and flair, and proved a superb consultant on a wide range of issues. Our editor, Traci Nagle, has throughout provided us with gentle but firm guidance in a way that has made working with her a genuine pleasure.

Robert Lerner
Standish Meacham

WESTERN CIVILIZATIONS

PART ONE

THE DAWN OF HISTORY

OUR STORY begins about 40,000 years ago with the completed evolution of the human species to which we all belong. The earliest humans, who lived in an "Ice Age," fashioned tools for hunting and handicrafts, and some of them painted beautiful murals on the walls of western European caves. With the invention of agriculture in western Asia about 10,000 years ago came a dramatic change in the entire nature of human existence, for humans engaged in agriculture stopped being wanderers and settled instead in villages. Sedentary life led "rapidly" (over the course of about 5,000 years) to civilization—government, writing, arts, and sciences on the one hand; war, social inequalities, and oppression on the other. The earliest Western civilizations emerged in Mesopotamia around 3200 B.C.E. Thereafter, until about 600 B.C.E., the most prominent civilizations outside of eastern Asia and America were those of the Mesopotamians, Egyptians, Hebrews, Minoans, and Mycenaeans.

Egyptian Bronze Cat. This elegant creature from roughly a millennium before the birth of Christ prefers a style in earrings that has regained popularity in the late twentieth century.

ANCIENT CIVILIZATIONS OF WESTERN ASIA, EGYPT, AND THE AEGEAN WORLD

	Political	Economic	Religious	Cultural
5000 B.C.E.	Age of villages in western Asia (c. 6500–c. 3500)			
	First cities in Mesopotamia (c. 4000–c. 3200)	Weaving with wool in western Asia (c. 4000)	Emergence of priestly caste in Mesopotamia (c. 4000–c. 3200)	
				Sumerian cuneiform writing (c. 3500–c. 2500)
		First evidence of wheel-made pottery in Sumeria (c. 3400)		
3200 B.C.E.	Supremacy of Sumerian cities in Mesopotamia (c. 3200–c. 2335)	Development of wheeled transport in Mesopotamia (c. 3200)		Lunar calendar in Mesopotamia (c. 3200) Sumerian temple architecture (c. 3200–c. 2000)
	Unification of Egypt (c. 3100) Archaic period in Egypt (c. 3100–c. 2680) Old Kingdom in Egypt (c. 2680–c. 2200)			Egyptian hieroglyphic writing (c. 3100)
				Construction of first pyramid in Egypt and first monumental columnar forms in architectural history (c. 2670)
	Dominance of Akkadian Empire in Mesopotamia (2335–c. 2130) Sumerian revival (c. 2130–c. 2000) Middle Kingdom in Egypt (c. 2050–1786)			
2000 B.C.E.	Old Babylonian Empire in Mesopotamia (c. 2000–c. 1600) Height of Minoan civilization under leadership of Knossos (c. 2000–c. 1500)	Extended commerce between Egypt and Crete (c. 2000) Horses introduced into western Asia (c. 2000)	Minoan worship of mother goddess (c. 2000) Growth of personal religion in Mesopotamia (c. 2000–c. 1600)	Solar calendar in Egypt (c. 2000) Mathematical advances in Old Babylonia (c. 2000–c. 1800) Minoan art on Crete (c. 2000–c. 1500) Epic of Gilgamesh (c. 1900)
			Egyptian belief in personal immortality (c. 1800)	
				Code of Hammurabi (c. 1790)

ANCIENT CIVILIZATIONS OF WESTERN ASIA, EGYPT, AND THE AEGEAN WORLD

Political	Economic	Religious	Cultural	
Mycenaean civilization on mainland Greece (c. 1600–c. 1200)				
			Egyptian temple architecture (c. 1580–c. 1090)	
New Kingdom in Egypt (c. 1560–1087)				
Mycenaean dominance on Crete (c. 1500–c. 1400)				1500 B.C.E.
Hittite Empire in Asia Minor (c. 1450–c. 1300)				
Destruction of Knossos and end of Minoan civilization (c. 1400)				
		Religious revolution of Akhenaton (c. 1375)	Naturalistic art in Egypt under Akhenaton (c. 1375)	
	Increasing use of iron throughout western Asia (c. 1300–c. 1100)			
	In Egypt, use of papyrus, pen, and ink for writing (c. 1300)			
Trojan War (c. 1250)				
		Hebrew exclusive worship of Yahweh (c. 1220)		
Collapse of Mycenaean civilization in Greece (c. 1200–c. 1100)				
			First alphabetic system of writing developed by Phoenicians (c. 1100)	
Unified Hebrew monarchy under Saul, David, and Solomon (c. 1025–933)				
				1000 B.C.E.
Kingdom of Israel (933–722)				
Kingdom of Judah (933–586)				
Height of Assyrian Empire (c. 750–612)		Hebrew prophetic revolution (c. 750–c. 550)	Astronomical observation and record-keeping by New Babylonians (c. 750–c. 400)	
			Earliest Greek settlement in Egypt's Nile delta (c. 700)	
New Babylonian Empire (612–539)				
		Hebrew ethical commandments (c. 600)	Deuteronomic Code (c. 600)	
Nebuchadnezzar conquers Jerusalem (586)				
Conquest of Babylon by Persians (539)				
Conquest of Egypt by Persians (525)				
				500 B.C.E.
			Hebrew Song of Songs (c. 450)	
		Eschatological phase of Hebrew religious development (c. 400 B.C.E.–70 C.E.)	Book of Job (c. 400)	

CHAPTER 1

FROM THE ICE AGE TO THE EARLIEST CITIES

THE NATURE OF HISTORY

History more than battles and treaties

CATHERINE MORLAND, the heroine of Jane Austen's novel *Northanger Abbey,* complained that history "tells me nothing that does not either vex or weary me. The quarrels of popes and kings, with wars or pestilences in every page; the men all so good for nothing, and hardly any women at all, it is very tiresome." Although Jane Austen's heroine said this around 1800, she might have lodged the same complaint until quite recently, for until deep into the twentieth century most historians considered history to be little more than "past politics"—and a dry chronicle of past politics at that. The content of historical study was restricted primarily to battles and treaties, the personalities and politics of statesmen, the laws and decrees of rulers. But important as such data are, they by no means constitute the whole substance of history. Especially within the last few decades historians have come to recognize that history comprises a record of past human activities in every sphere—not just political developments, but also social, economic, and intellectual ones. Women as well as men, the ruled as well as the rulers, the poor as well as the rich, are part of history. So too are the social and economic institutions that women and men have created and that in turn have shaped their lives: family and social class; manorialism and city life; capitalism and industrialism. Ideas and attitudes, too, not just of intellectuals, but also of people whose lives may have been virtually untouched by "great books," are all part of the historian's concern. And most important, history includes an inquiry into the causes of events and patterns of human organization and ideas—a search for the forces that impelled humanity toward its great undertakings, and the reasons for its successes and failures.

New historical methods

As historians have extended the scope of their work, they have also equipped themselves with new methods and tools, the better to practice their craft. No longer do historians merely pore over the same old chronicles and documents to ask whether Charles the Fat was at Ingelheim or Lustnau on July 1, 887. To evaluate quantitative data, they learn the methods of the statistician. To interpret the effect of a rise in the cost of living, they study economics. To deduce marriage patterns or evaluate the effect upon an entire population of wars and plagues, they master the skills of the demographer. To explore the phenomenon of cave-dwelling or modern urbanization, they become archeologists, studying fossil remains, fragments of pots, or modern city landscapes. To understand the motives of the men and women who have acted in the past, they draw on the insights of social psychologists and cultural anthropologists. To illuminate the lives and thoughts of those who have left few or no written records, they look for other cultural remains such as folk songs, folk tales, and funerary monuments.

Limited evidence and the quest for valid reconstructions

Of course with all their ingenuity historians cannot create evidence. An almost infinite number of past events are not retrievable because they transpired without leaving any traces; many others are at best known imperfectly. Thus some of the most fundamental questions about "how things were" in the past either can never be answered or can be answered only on the grounds of highly qualified inferences. Questions regarding motives and causes may not have definite answers for other reasons. Since individual humans often hardly understand their own motives, it is presumptuous to think that anyone can ever be entirely certain about establishing the motives of others. As for the causes of collective developments such as wars, economic growth trends, or changes in artistic styles, these are surely too complex to be reduced to a science. Nonetheless, the more evidence we have, the closer we come to providing valid reconstructions and explanations of what happened in the past. Moreover, the difficulties inherent in assembling and interpreting all sorts of data for the purposes of historical analysis should not be regarded with despair but looked upon as stimulating intellectual challenges.

Approaches to history

Should we go to the past to celebrate one or another lost age or seek to learn how we got to be the way we are now? Obviously neither one of these extremes is satisfactory, for nostalgia almost invariably leads to distortion, and at any rate is useless, whereas extreme "present-mindedness" also leads to distortion, and at any rate is foolish in its assumption that everything we do now is better than whatever people did before. It seems best, then, to avoid either revering the past or condescending to it. Instead, many historians seek to understand how people of a given era strove to solve their problems and live their lives fruitfully in terms appropriate to their particular environments and stages of development. Other historians look for change over time without postulating a march of progress to a current best of all possible worlds. Such historians believe (and let us hope they may be right) that identifying patterns and mechanisms of change will allow a better understanding of the present and a greater possibility of plotting prudent strategies for coping with the future.

Early Human Art and Early Human Survival

Long duration of human life on earth

People celebrating the advent of the third millennium since the birth of Christ seldom pause to consider that 2,000 years make up the tiniest fraction of the total length of time our ancestors have walked on this globe.

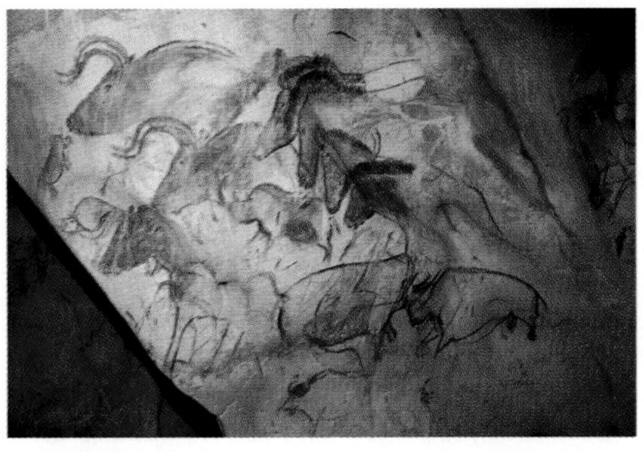

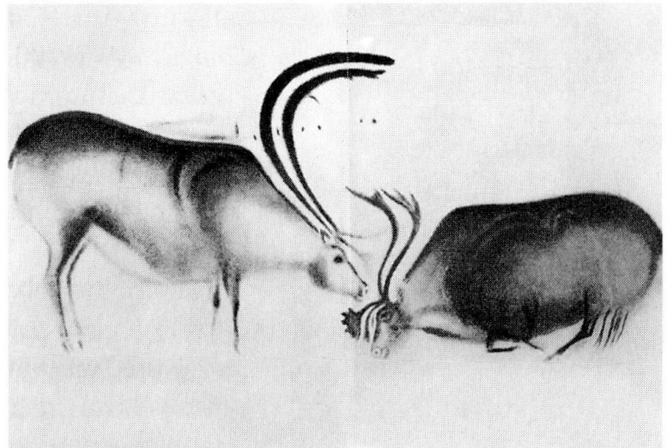

Cave Paintings from Southern France. On the left, one of the many cave paintings discovered in 1994. On the right, a stylized depiction of reindeer by an inspired artist "of the French school" who worked about 15,000 years ago.

The earliest humanlike species originated in Africa about four and a half million years ago, the earliest forms of our own species, *Homo sapiens,* originated about 150,000 years ago, and fully developed *Homo sapiens* crossed from the Eastern to the Western Hemisphere a "mere" 40,000 years ago. Put in other terms, the time since Christ constitutes just one four-hundredth of the total time since humanlike beings learned how to control fire for the purpose of keeping warm.

Early human art: cave murals

Scholars are limited in charting the details of early human social evolution because of the loss of evidence from natural causes. But owing to the fortunate "airtight" atmospheric conditions in numerous caves of France and Spain we know that between 33,000 and 12,000 years ago humans produced some of the most stunning paintings in the entire history of human art. In more than two hundred caves so far discovered (some as recently as 1991 and 1994), the earliest known artists painted breathtaking murals of prancing animals—bison, bulls, horses, stags, and even rhinoceroses. The emphasis in this cave art was on movement. Almost all of the murals depict game species running, leaping, chewing their cud, or facing the hunter at bay. An ingenious device for giving the impression of motion was the drawing of additional outlines to indicate the areas in which the leg or the head of the animal had moved. The cave painters sometimes achieved startling three-dimensional effects by using the natural bumps and indentations of their cave surfaces. All in all, visitors today who are lucky enough to see the cave murals usually find them as evocative as any paintings hanging in the world's foremost art museums.

The most convincing explanation for this striking cave art is that it aimed at working sympathetic magic—accomplishing a desired result by imitating it. When cave painters depicted bison with arrows piercing their flanks, the very act of representing such scenes was meant to ensure that arrows really would pierce bison. Granted that only about 10 percent of

Cave Bison. Although not all the experts agree, it seems reasonably clear that this bison has been wounded with arrows or spears. If so, this representation from a cave wall in southern France supports the theory that cave artists were attempting to employ sympathetic magic.

Cave Artist's Lamp. Found in a French cave site in 1960, this prehistoric receptacle was used for burning wood saturated with animal fat by underground artists as they went about their work.

all known cave murals show killing scenes, it is likely that sympathetic magic was practiced additionally by striking the painted animals while pronouncing incantations. Further support for this view is found in the fact that archeologists have discovered traces of ritualistic practices in some of the cave areas where murals are located. It may be that those who cast spells on painted animals were "specialists"—the earliest ancestors of priests, who perhaps even stayed behind to practice the supernatural while the hunt was on. Although this is just a theory, it is all but certain that the cave painters themselves were specialists. This can be deduced from the fact that their work called for considerable expertise: it not only entailed the use of charcoal sticks for drawing black outlines and lumps of claylike ores (ochres) for tones of yellow, red, and brown, but also drew on the mixing of earthen pigments with fat (as in the later production of tempera paints) and the use of feathers or bracken for "brushes."

Differentiation of labor

Cave painting is only one example of the earliest differentiation of labor. Hunters between about 30,000 and 12,000 years ago needed specialized training since artful new techniques were being added to their repertory. They brought down birds with darts and arrows, caught fish with harpoons and fishhooks, and trapped game herds by anticipating their instinctive movements. Others in these early human societies, possibly women as well as men, became handicraft workers, skilled in fashioning tools from stones, bones, and antlers. Whether or not women made tools, they certainly made clothes: the period of the cave paintings is also the period from which archeologists have found the first needles—presupposing the use of gut or thread to sew together animal skins—and the earliest known string made from plant fibers. Such division of labor would have called for orderly cooperation. Moreover, masses of charred bones found regularly at archeological sites dating from this period indicate that huge quantities of game were roasted in community feasts, proving that the peoples in question not only knew how to paint, hunt, and sew, but also knew how to share.

Bison Carved from a Reindeer Horn. Perhaps the most graceful of all known European prehistoric carvings, this bison was carved from a piece of antler between 15,000 and 12,000 years ago. Whatever its use might have been no one quite knows.

The Origins of Food Production

Around 12,000 years ago (i.e., 10,000 B.C.E.*), hunting feasts occurred ever more rarely because herds were vanishing. The era between 35,000 and 12,000 years ago had been an "Ice Age": daytime temperatures in the Mediterranean regions of Europe and western Asia averaged about 60°F (16°C) in the summer and about 30°F (–1°C) in the winter. Accordingly, cold-loving game species such as reindeer, elk, wild boar, bison, and mountain goats roamed the hills and valleys. But as the last glaciers receded northward such species retreated with them. Some humans may have moved north with the game, but others stayed behind, creating an extremely different sort of world.

*In this edition we have shifted from "B.C." to the abbreviation "B.C.E." to indicate dates before the birth of Christ. B.C.E. stands for "before common era." "A.D." has been changed to "C.E.," for "common era."

Specifically, within about 3,000 to 4,000 years after the end of the Ice Age humans in western Asia had accomplished one of the most momentous revolutions ever accomplished by any humans: a switch from subsistence by means of food-gathering to subsistence by means of food-producing. For roughly two million years humanlike species and humans had gained their sustenance either by foraging or by combined foraging and hunting. These modes of existence meant that such peoples could never stay very long in one place because they continually ate their way through local supplies of plant food, and, if they were hunters, they were forced to follow the movements of herds. But then substantial numbers of humans began to domesticate animals and raise crops, thereby settling down. As soon as this shift was accomplished villages were founded, trade developed, and populations in areas of sedentary habitation started increasing by leaps and bounds. When villages began evolving into cities, civilization was born.

Bronze Stag. A statuette combining naturalistic and stylized qualities, dating from about 2300 B.C.E. It was found in Asia Minor.

To term the change from food-gathering to food-producing a "revolution" is fully legitimate, in terms of both the momentous effects of the change and the comparatively small amount of time the change took compared to the length of time humans had existed. Yet from the perspective of today, when dramatic technological revolutions occur within a few years, the move to food production was very gradual. Not only did the transition take place over the course of some 3,000 to 4,000 years (c. 10,000 to c. 7000/6000 B.C.E.), but it was so gradual that the peoples involved did not know themselves what was happening.

The story is roughly as follows. Around 10,000 B.C.E. most of the larger game herds had left western Asia. Yet people in territories that today lie in Turkey, Syria, and Israel were not starving because the warmer climate and raised water levels from melting glaciers had created a nurturing environment for plentiful fields of wild grain. Since food was so easy to obtain, humans for the first time became sedentary for at least part of the year, no longer trekking regularly from place to place to forage or follow herds. Then, in the succeeding three millennia, they slowly began to produce their own food. Pressures would have been created by a growing population, for the birthrate of sedentary humans is much higher than that of trekkers. What came first in what region is by no means always clear, but by roughly 7000 B.C.E. people throughout most of western Asia were growing their own crops and raising farm animals.

Spread of agriculture

The systematic production of plant food required a crucial intermediary step: stockpiling. Even when plentiful, grain does not grow during the winter. Hence, roughly about 9,000 B.C.E., people learned how to preserve their grain by digging storage pits. This reinforced their sedentary way of life: moving away from "home" for the parts of the year when grain was not ripening was now less necessary. Once they had pits they probably also began to notice how grain began sprouting and rooting in or near the pits at the start of the spring rains. Maybe a single person was the genius who realized that she could "help nature out" by clearing some soil and planting, or maybe the discovery transpired more or less concurrently in similar environments. In any case, the discoverer or discoverers of planting affected our own modern existence much more than Columbus or Newton did, even though it may have taken hundreds of years more for humans to advance to the step of clearing large fields for the purpose of agriculture.

Domestication of animals

The first farm animals were sheep and goats, the most suitable species for driving in small flocks while people might still be traveling. For millennia wild animals had been slaughtered on the spot, but then some bright person realized that sheep and goats could be captured and driven home, thereby saving the effort of dragging their carcasses. Evidently once the animals were alive at home it became clear that they could be kept alive for longer periods to serve as dietary insurance policies—ready meat on the hoof. In time it became clear that stocks of sheep and goats could be kept alive to reproduce so that one might have a continuous supply without hunting. Thus, little by little, humans came to own and breed "livestock."

Settled agriculture as the dominant form of human existence

The earliest archeological evidence for fully sedentary agriculture comes from eastern Anatolia (modern-day Turkey), Syria, Iraq, and Iran and dates from roughly 7500 to roughly 7000 B.C.E. By 6000 B.C.E. the entire western Asian region had adopted agriculture as the central mode of survival. In all these areas agriculture was supplemented by raising livestock, and by 6000 B.C.E. that livestock included cattle and pigs as well as sheep and goats. Moreover, farming peoples continued to engage in some hunting and gathering on the side. (Even today many farmers look forward to using their rifles from time to time, and families in Europe until recently counted on foraging in the woods for wild berries and mushrooms.) Yet not only had settled agriculture become the dominant form of human existence in western Asia, but by around 5000 B.C.E. it had reached southeastern Europe (the Balkans), whence it spread over the entire European continent. "Amber waves of grain" have played a central role in European—and by extension American—history ever since.

The Age of Villages

Villages, trade, warfare, and the emergence of civilization

Concentrating here on developments in western Asia after the transition from food-gathering to food production, the next steps in the region's accelerating evolution toward civilization were the emergence of villages and the concurrent rise of handicrafts, long-distance trade, and warfare. Villages constituted the most advanced form of human organization in western Asia from about 6500 to about 3500/3000 B.C.E., when some villages evolved into cities. The typical village numbered about one thousand inhabitants. At first almost all of the able-bodied men and women engaged in field work, and all the women additionally in cloth production, but gradually there came to be full-time specialists in other handicrafts, as well as a few full-time traders.

"Women's work"

Why should women, and women alone, have been responsible for cloth production not only in the earliest villages but in all known human communities the world over until the invention of mechanical looms about two hundred years ago? The answer lies in the compatibility of cloth production with child care. Since women typically gave birth at least once every two or three years and breast-fed their babies during the intervals, child-rearing fell exclusively to them. In consequence their supplemental labors were addressed to repetitive jobs, such as sewing, spinning, and weaving, that could easily be interrupted to attend to children and that kept them near home. The only saving grace of such monotony was that much of this work could be done communally and hence allowed socializing.

Progress in cloth-making

Sewing and spinning (making thread from fibers) were known as early as the Ice Age, and weaving on looms followed next—no later than about 7000 B.C.E. For roughly 3,000 years the threads used for weaving came from plant fibers, but around 4000 B.C.E. came the innovation, probably in the area of modern Iraq, of weaving with wool. This change itself was related to another momentous change in human activity: until then domesticated animals had been kept alive only for their meat, but now they began to be exploited for their secondary products, such as wool, hair, hides, milk, and their power to drag farm implements. (The new use of animals for heavy farm labors would have reinforced the assignment of women to the home.)

Pottery

In addition to weaving, the most important village handicrafts were pottery and tool-making. The emergence of pottery was an immediate result of the shift to a sedentary existence. Once humans became settled they obviously became particularly interested in storing and no longer needed to worry about how well any storage receptacle might be suited for travel. Although humans may have known how to make clay pots in much earlier periods, they did not bother to make them because such pots were too fragile to carry on treks. But when they built villages they immediately built pots because they found them ideal for storing grain and other foods. Moreover, clay pots could also be used to haul and store water. Thus with pottery people could keep drinking water in their homes, a step toward luxury perhaps comparable to the modern invention of indoor plumbing.

Stone Foundation of a Sedentary Dwelling. Once people in western Asia became agriculturalists, they began to build homes for year-round habitation. This stone foundation for a prehistoric house was found at the site of the village of Jarmo (in Iraq) and dates from about 6000 B.C.E.

Advances in tool-making were spurred by the need for sharp and durable agricultural implements, especially sickles and plows. Early villagers, accustomed to working with rocks, discovered that certain "rocks" had particularly desirable qualities. Obsidian, actually a volcanic glass, could make sharp and almost indestructible cutting edges, and copper, actually a metal, could be pounded for making pointed tips and pounded again when blunted. Because freestanding copper came only in small supplies, it was employed between about 6500 and 4500 B.C.E. only for making tips and very small implements. But then someone, perhaps as the result of accidentally dropping a metallic rock into a pottery kiln, discovered that certain "rocks" (ore stones) would ooze copper under high heats. Whoever this person was, he or she discovered smelting, and thereafter, for roughly the next millennium, smelted copper was used in western Asia for manufacturing all sorts of containers, tools, and weapons.

Early Village Pottery. A shallow bowl from a western Asian village site dating from about 5000 B.C.E.

Development of long-distance trade

Reference to the use of obsidian and copper inevitably introduces the subject of trade, for these items did not grow in gardens and almost always had to be acquired from afar. Trade itself presupposes the existence of surpluses: if you want something other people have you must offer them something you yourself do not need. Villagers who were accustomed to storing thus became the first systematic traders since they could barter with foodstuffs and later with surplus products such as cloths and hides. Trade in western Asia from as early as about 6500 B.C.E. already extended over remarkably long distances. In particular, villages in Iran and Iraq had found the means of acquiring supplies of obsidian from sources near the Black Sea, 400 to 500 miles away, and the same villages were also acquiring small pieces of copper from central Anatolia, about twice as far away. Thereafter trade in all sorts of goods became ever more brisk, and by 3500 B.C.E. cargoes were being transported by boat as well as being moved over land.

Warfare not biologically determined

But trade was not the only means of acquiring goods, for successful pillaging could serve the acquisitive even better. No one knows exactly when human warfare began, but more and more experts are coming to doubt that aggressiveness is biologically "programmed" into us. Rather, it seems that humans have no strictly biological propensity for either peace or war and that before the switch to sedentary agriculture bands of roving humans were peaceable. At the very least it is certain that there are no depictions of humans fighting humans in the Ice Age cave paintings and that the earliest known representations of warfare appear together with settled village life. Even more dramatic is the fact that many of the earliest known villages in western Asia were fortified villages. Evidently, whatever humanity's past had been, its future was to fight and kill.

Links between village life and warfare

Settled life would have inspired ongoing warfare for obvious reasons. Members of roving bands needed to cooperate with each other in hunting and gathering, and they seldom even saw members of other bands. Assuming that one band did occasionally run into another, there would have been little reason to fight since there was little loot to be gained. In contrast, there was loot in a village, and villagers under attack would have tended to stand and fight rather than cut and run, not only to protect their belongings, but to preserve their fields, which invariably had cost them great effort to clear and cultivate. Endemic fighting probably began during the period of transition between wandering and settlement when some bands of wanderers became bands of pillagers. Then, by the time there were many villages, one settlement definitely started fighting another to attain more property and wealth.

The onset of warfare stimulated the progress of technology and trade. Whether for defensive or offensive reasons, early villagers in western Asia achieved great technological advances in weaponry, experimenting in the manufacture of daggers, battle-axes, spears, slings, and maces. Moreover, an area-wide village "arms race" stimulated the advance of metallurgy because copper made better spear points and daggers than stone or bone, and bronze, an alloy of copper and tin whose manufacture was perfected between 3500 and 3000 B.C.E., made vastly better weapons of all sorts than copper. Since metals from far away had to be acquired by trade, villagers caught in an arms race were forced to enhance their efficiency in producing surpluses of village products so that they could acquire metals. And so the search for more and better weapons stimulated economic life even while causing death and destruction.

Flint Dagger. Discovered in Anatolia and dating from about 7000 B.C.E., this dagger made from flint-stone with an elaborately carved bone handle was a weapon worthy of a commander-in-chief.

The Birth of Cities in Western Asia

The last major development in western Asian history before the time when archeology becomes supplemented by the existence of written records was the emergence of cities. As with all the changes we have examined so far, this one too was gradual: the evolution began around 4000 B.C.E. and was completed only by around 3200 B.C.E. The fully developed city would still have had much in common with the village. For example, the city was not necessarily much larger—perhaps two to three thousand

Early Representations of Warfare. On the left is a cave painting from Spain; on the right is a rock carving from Sweden. Although both representations are very difficult to date, it is almost certain that neither predated the establishment of settled agriculture in their respective regions.

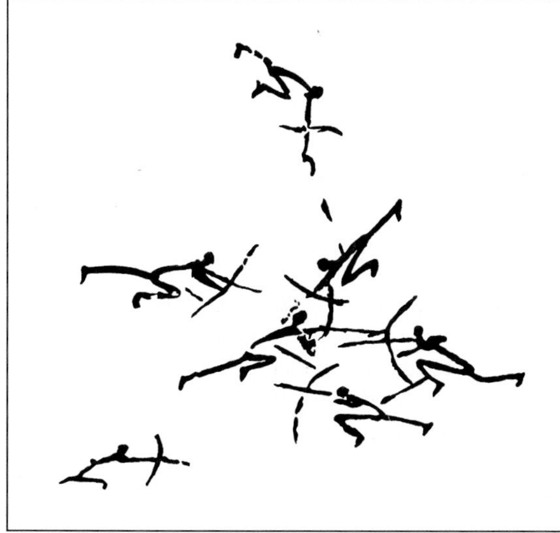

inhabitants compared to the village's one thousand. Moreover, its population was still made up predominantly of agriculturalists who worked in th nearby fields. But what marked a fundamental qualitative difference was the presence in cities of three new social groups: administrators, priests, and professional warriors.

Irrigation and division into ruler and ruled

The earliest cities arose in Mesopotamia, a region in modern-day Iraq lying between the Tigris and Euphrates Rivers. Although the soil in Mesopotamia is extremely fertile, humans had avoided settling there much before 4000 B.C.E. because of a lack of adequate rainfall to provide the moisture necessary for growing crops. Apparently, however, starting around 4000 population pressures drove people from neighboring regions into Mesopotamia to try to make a living as best they could, and once there they found that they could do this by constructing irrigation systems. Building and maintaining irrigation systems in turn called for a degree of planning and coordinated labor that was unprecedented in human societies until that time. The irrigation in question had to be accomplished by leading canals and channels from the two big rivers in crisscrossing patterns over the dry lands, and the work was never completed because the canals and channels had to be cleared constantly when they began silting up. Such labors required that people be organized in force, that provisions be assembled to support them, that pots be mass-produced to serve as their food receptacles, and so forth. Obviously, therefore, planners were needed to determine how, when, and where to work, overseers were needed to direct and coerce laborers, and governors were needed to plan and oversee the overseers. Accordingly society became divided into the rulers and the ruled.

Novelty of a full-time priesthood

The planners and overseers in the centuries after 4000 B.C.E. lived in villages that were becoming cities, and so did another new element in society, priests. Of course religion was not invented in Mesopotamia. Many millennia earlier humans had placed provisions next to their dead, evidently because they believed in an afterlife, and we have seen that cave art was probably meant to call upon supernatural forces. What was new in Mesopotamia was the emergence of a full-time priesthood—people attached to centers of ritual practice, temples—whose performance of incantations and rites was supported by the labors of others.

Explanations for the emergence of a priestly caste

Why such a social grouping first arose in Mesopotamia is a speculative question, but it seems likely that during the period between 4000 and 3200 B.C.E. the stresses of life were becoming so great that people in effect needed priests. Wandering bands had no difficulty in maintaining social cohesiveness because there was little property to fight over, because occupational functions were more or less equal, and because the bands were small enough for members to feel united by mutual familiarity. But such conditions started changing in villages. There, communal labor and distribution were still the rule, but inequalities in possessions would have become more pronounced over time, and the growth of populations would have made it harder for people to recognize each other on, so to speak, a first-name basis. Attacks from the outside probably provided a motive for sufficient cohesiveness among villagers to keep them from fighting each

Mesopotamian Archeological Mound. Several thousand years' worth of successive human building activities will often result in a mound of debris looking like this. Many decades of hard labor and intensive study by a team of archeologists would be necessary to recover all the historical information hidden in this mound, dating from about 5000 B.C.E. at the base and 500 C.E. at the top.

other, but during the stressful beginnings of irrigation in Mesopotamia still more cohesiveness would have been needed. On this admittedly conjectural reconstruction, religion inspired people in large groups to feel loyal to a common cause and to work hard in the belief that their labors were serving the local gods. And religion on this scale called for priests to define the faith and to preside over elaborate rituals in impressive temples.

Professional warriors

The third new element in society that defined the life of the city was that of the professional warrior. At first the leading warriors in Mesopotamia may have also served as the leading planners, but during the centuries in question the evolution of the economy and of military technology led inevitably to the emergence of full-time warriors. These mighty men would then have become the coercive rulers and would have made the planners their assistants. Military power would have led to governmental power and ever more military power by a spiraling process. Metal weapons were superior to stone ones but much more costly; those who had acquired wealth by subduing and exploiting others were thus the only ones who could have afforded to acquire metal weapons that allowed them to subdue and exploit still more people. A clay impression dating from about 3400 B.C.E. shows bound captives being smitten with rods and kneeling before a military ruler holding a spear. This was to be the wave of the future.

Cities as the manifestation of civilization

Discussing the origins of cities is really the same as discussing the origins of civilization, which may be defined as the stage in human organization when governmental, social, and economic institutions have developed sufficiently to manage (however imperfectly) the problems of order, security, and efficiency in a complex society. Around 3200 B.C.E. Mesopotamia was "civilized." That is, at least five cities existed, which all included among their inhabitants warrior-rulers, administrators, and priests; which all encompassed several monumental temples; and which all boasted in addition elaborate private residences, communal workshops, public storage facilities, and large marketplaces. Rudimentary forms of record-keeping were being mastered, and writing was on its way. Herewith the story of civilizations begins, and herewith we may begin following a story that is based on interpreting written evidence as well as archeological artifacts.

SUMMARY POINTS

- The realm of history comprises the whole of past human activities, encompassing political, social, economic, and intellectual developments.
- The technical sophistication of early human cave art is evidence that between 30,000 and 12,000 years ago humans had begun the differentiation of labor.
- Once humans had moved from migratory hunting to sedentary farming as their primary means of sustenance between 12,000 and 8,000 years ago, villages, trade, and warfare soon developed.
- The emergence of specialized administrators, priests, and warriors signaled the birth of cities in Mesopotamia.

SELECTED READINGS

Barber, Elizabeth Wayland, *Women's Work: The First 20,000 Years: Women, Cloth, and Society in Early Times,* New York, 1994. A fascinating and delightfully written account of the early history of cloth manufacture. Highly recommended.

Binford, Lewis, *In Pursuit of the Past: Decoding the Archaeological Record,* London, 1983. A prominent archeologist offers this readable and personalized description of how one can analyze artifacts scientifically in order to describe past social behavior and processes of change.

Chauvet, Jean-Marie, et al., *Dawn of Art: The Chauvet Cave: The Oldest Known Paintings in the World,* New York, 1996. Describes a major discovery of 1994.

Lamberg-Karlovsky, C. C., and Jeremy Sabloff, *Ancient Civilizations: The Near East and Mesoamerica,* 2d ed., Prospect Heights, Ill., 1995. A lucid discussion of how the earliest civilizations became increasingly complex over time.

Mauss, Marcel, *The Gift: Forms and Functions of Exchange in Archaic Societies,* New York, 1967. Originally written in 1927, this book offers enduring insights into the nature of social interaction.

Redman, Charles L. *The Rise of Civilization: From Early Farmers to Urban Society in the Ancient Near East,* San Francisco, 1978. A standard account.

Sandars, Nancy K., *Prehistoric Art in Europe,* rev. ed., Baltimore, 1985. A short survey emphasizing artistic techniques.

CHAPTER 2

MESOPOTAMIAN CIVILIZATION

The farmer watches. What can he do? The day became dark but it did not rain. It rained but he did not need to take off his shoes.

—Old Babylonian inscription, c. 1700 B.C.E.

In my school-days I learned the hidden treasure of writing. I solved complex mathematical reciprocals and products with no apparent solution. I read tables whose Sumerian is obscure and whose Akkadian is hard to construe. Then I advanced to the skills of archery and chariot-driving.

—A tablet of Assurbanipal, King of Assyria, c. 650 B.C.E.

UNTIL ONLY a little more than 5,000 years ago humans left behind many things but no words. Around 3200 B.C.E., however, in a region of Mesopotamia known as Sumer, the earliest forms of writing were invented and "history began" in the sense that words were recorded that help current scholars understand what people were doing.

A rich and diverse record of achievement

Obviously the invention of writing alone would earn the ancient Mesopotamians a prominent place among the most inventive and influential peoples who ever contributed to the forward movement of humankind. But amazingly the peoples who inhabited Mesopotamia in the centuries between roughly 3200 and roughly 500 B.C.E. contributed much more. We sometimes forget that somebody had to have invented the wheel, but somebody did, and he or she was a Mesopotamian who lived around 3000 B.C.E. Somebody had to invent the calendar too, and somebody had to invent the mathematical functions of multiplication and division, and those persons also were ancient Mesopotamians. Aside from arriving at such inventions, the Mesopotamians were profound thinkers who pioneered in the life of the mind to such an extent that their innovations in theology, jurisprudence, astronomy, and narrative literature all became fundamental for subsequent developments in these areas of thought and expression. Assuredly the ancient Mesopotamians had their unattractive qualities: for example, their rulers were usually ruthless militarists, and their art often seems frigid or fierce. Nevertheless, the "first chapter of history," which the Mesopotamians wrote by their exploits and their documents, was surely one of the most important chapters in the entire book of human events.

Ancient Sumer: The World of the First Cities

Sargon. A bronze head thought to depict the mighty warrior who united Akkad and Sumer.

Between 4000 and 3200 B.C.E., Mesopotamia, the land between the Tigris and Euphrates Rivers, became the first civilized territory on the globe in the sense that its society and culture rested on the existence of cities. We may call the historical period that ensued, lasting from about 3200 B.C.E. to about 2000 B.C.E., the "Sumerian era" because the most advanced part of Mesopotamia was then its southernmost territory, Sumer, a region of mud flats that was roughly the size of Massachusetts. During the first nine centuries of the Sumerian era no unified government existed in Sumer; instead, the region was dotted with numerous independent city-states, the most important of which were Uruk, Ur, and Lagash. Then, around 2335 B.C.E., all Sumer was conquered by a mighty warrior from Akkad, the part of Mesopotamia lying directly to the north. This warrior's birth name does not survive, but we know that he took the title of "Sargon," which means "true king." Mesopotamian chronicles record that Sargon gained control of Sumer by winning thirty-four battles; when his victories finally brought him to "the lower sea" (the Persian Gulf), he washed his weapons in its waters to signify the end of struggle. Sargon was history's first identifiable empire-builder; for almost two centuries his dynasty ruled an empire consisting of Akkad and Sumer. But around 2130 B.C.E. Sumer regained its independence and enjoyed a "revival" that lasted until roughly 2000 B.C.E., during which time most of the region was ruled by kings who resided in Ur.

Sumer's accomplishments were preponderantly influenced by its climate and geography. Although the soil between the southern Tigris and

Ancient Mesopotamia

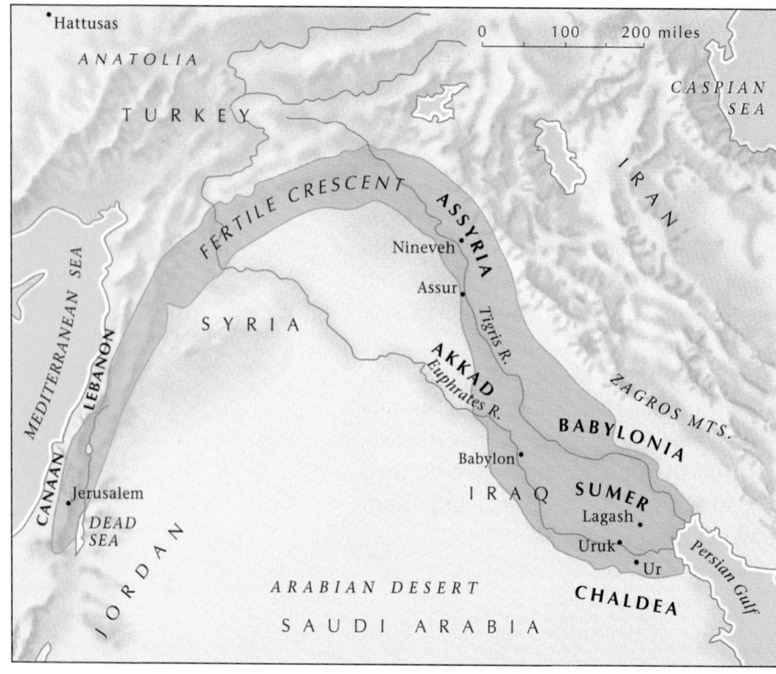

the southern Euphrates was extremely fertile, irrigation was essential because there was almost no rainfall for eight months of each year and torrential spring showers came too late to water the main crops that had to be harvested in April. (The summer months were not productive in Sumer because temperatures then rose to a soil-parching 125°F.) As we have seen, collective work on irrigation projects demanded careful planning and assertive leadership, which in turn led to social stratification, professional specialization, and the emergence of cities. The situation in Sumer was further determined by the fact that southern Mesopotamia was entirely lacking in natural resources such as stone, minerals, and even trees. This meant that Sumer's inhabitants were forced to rely heavily on trade and to be alert to any possible means of redressing economic imbalances to their advantage. In other words, the Sumerians had to subdue nature rather than live off its plenty.

Sumerians forced to subdue nature

One of the Sumerians' most remarkable inventions, which they perfected about the time the Sumerian era was opening (around 3200 B.C.E.), was wheeled transport. To appreciate how advanced this invention was from a comparative perspective, it should be noted that wheeled transport was unknown in Egypt until about 1700 B.C.E. and that wheels were unknown in the Western Hemisphere (except for Peruvian children's toys) until they were introduced by Europeans. Probably the first Sumerian to think of employing a circular device turning on an axis for purposes of conveyance drew on the potter's wheel, in use in Sumeria by about 3500 B.C.E. The process of extending the principle of the wheel from pottery-making to transport was by no means obvious: the Egyptians knew the potter's wheel by at least 2700 B.C.E., but they did not use the wheel for transport until a millennium later, and even then they probably did not "reinvent the wheel" but learned of it from contacts with Mesopotamia. Thus the unknown Sumerian who first attached wheels to a sled to make a better transportation vehicle really does have to be counted among the greatest technological geniuses of all time.

Wheeled transport

An Akkadian Soldier Leads Away Sumerian Captives. A fragment of a victory monument probably dating from the time of Sargon.

The earliest Sumerian wheeled vehicles were two-wheeled chariots and four-wheeled carts. Both were drawn by donkeys (horses were unknown in western Asia until they were introduced by Eastern invaders sometime between 2000 and 1700 B.C.E.), and both were mounted on wheels that were solid, not spoked: two or three slabs of wood were shaped into a circle and fastened together with studs or braces. Wheeled chariots appear to have contributed to an advance in phalanx warfare, for surviving illustrations dating from about 2600 B.C.E. depict them trampling the enemy. Carts meant for hauling freight had less need for speed and must have aided the Sumerians immeasurably in their numerous irrigation and urban building projects.

Along with the wheel, the Sumerians devised another of humanity's most crucial early inventions, the lunar (moon) calendar. In a perilous climate such as that of Mesopotamia it was absolutely essential to begin planting or harvesting at exactly the proper time; thus it was necessary to find some reliable way of marking the passage of days until the proper

Lunar calendar

Sumerian War Chariots. The earliest known representation of the wheel, dating from about 2600 B.C.E., shows how wheels were carpentered together from slabs of wood. (For a later Mesopotamian wheel with spokes, see the illustration on p. 33.) One can also observe that at the dawn of recorded history, military aims stimulated technological innovation, as they have ever since.

times for agricultural work came around. The simplest way of doing this was to utilize the cycles of the moon. Since the moon moves from the thinnest crescent and back over the course of twenty-nine and a half days, one could consider the completion of such a cycle to be a basic timekeeping unit (we would call it a month—originally "moonth") and then count those units until the seasons themselves had made a complete revolution. Hence the Sumerians concluded that when the moon had passed through twelve such units (half assigned twenty-nine days and half thirty), a "year" had passed and it was time to start planting again. Unfortunately they did not know that a "year" is really determined by the completion of the earth's rotation around the sun and that twelve lunar cycles or months fall eleven days short of the solar year. Over the centuries they learned that they had to add a month to their calendars every few years in order to predict the recurrence of the seasons with sufficient accuracy. The Sumerian lunar reckonings were the first known human steps in the direction of what we now understand to be exact, predictive science. The fact that the lunar calendar itself is indeed usable if days are added from time to time is confirmed by the modern Jewish and Islamic calendars, both of which are based on lunar cycles that the Jews and Muslims inherited from ancient Mesopotamia.

Development of writing

Ranking together with the wheel and the calendar as one of Sumer's three most precious gifts to succeeding civilizations was the invention of writing. To say that writing was "invented" is slightly misleading inasmuch as the emergence of writing in Sumer was gradual, evolving over the course of a millennium (c. 3500 to c. 2500 B.C.E.) from the representation of ideas by means of pictorial conventions to writing (albeit not alphabetic writing) as we currently know it. Around 3500 B.C.E. Sumerians had begun to carve pictures in stone or to stamp them on clay as ownership marks: a picture might have stood for a person's nickname (perhaps a rock for "Rocky") or dwelling (a house by a tree). Some five centuries later the evolution toward writing had advanced vastly farther. By then Sumerian temple administrators were using many standardized schematic pictures in combination with each other to preserve records of temple property and business transactions. Although the script of this period was still pictographic, it had advanced beyond pictures standing for people and tangible things to pictures standing for abstractions: a bowl meant any kind of food and a head with a bowl conveyed the concept of eating. After five more centuries full-fledged writing had taken over, for by then the original pictures had become so schematized that they were no longer recognizable as pictures but had to be learned purely as signs, and many of these signs no longer represented specific words but had become symbols of syllables that turned into words when combined with other such signs.

Cuneiform

The writing system that reached its fully developed form in Sumer around 2500 B.C.E. is known as *cuneiform* because it was based on wedge-shaped characters (*cuneus* is Latin for "wedge") impressed on wet clay by a reed stylus with a triangular point. In total there were about 500 characters, and many of these had multiple meanings (the "right one" could be identified only in context), making the system much more difficult to learn than subsequent writing systems based on alphabets. Nonetheless, cuneiform served well enough to be used as the sole writing system of Mesopotamia for two millennia and even to become the standard medium of commercial transactions throughout most of western Asia until about 500 B.C.E.

Sumerian literature and religion

About 90 percent of the cuneiform texts surviving from the Sumerian era are business or administrative records, and the other 10 percent fall roughly into the category of literature—proverbs, hymns, and fragments of mythic tales. A charming example of a worldly Sumerian proverb is "where cosmeticians are, there is slander," showing that the gossipy hairdresser has been known to human civilization for millennia. Hymns and

Early Pictorial Writing. On the left, a carving from about 3200 B.C.E. recording a commercial transaction. The signs above stand for "fifty-four" and those below for "cow": thus "fifty-four cows." On the right, Mesopotamian carvings on a piece of shale, dating from about 3100 B.C.E., depict two men engaged in a business deal, with pictographs around them specifying what they were trading.

Cuneiform Writing. On the left, a Sumerian clay tablet from about 3000 B.C.E. Here standardized pictures were beginning to represent abstractions. On the right, carvings on limestone from about 2600 B.C.E. The evolution of standardized cuneiform writing is now complete: the inscription proclaims that a king of Ur has built a temple.

mythic tales surviving on Sumerian clay tablets (supplemented by Sumerian texts copied by later Mesopotamians) reveal that assumptions concerning the gods underwent a process of evolution. For purposes of simplicity we may note a main trend from viewing the gods as being part of nature to imagining them acting like guardians of various spheres (sky, earth, underworld) or mighty overlords of different cities.

Dominating presence of the ziggurat

However the gods were conceived, Sumerian temples loomed mightily over Sumerian society throughout the period from 3200 to 2000 B.C.E. The temples literally dominated both the cities and the entire flat skyline because they were built on huge platforms intended solely to lend them height. All were constructed out of slabs and bricks made from sun-dried clay because stone and wood were unavailable, and most were built in the form known as the *ziggurat,* a terraced (stepped) tower topped by a shrine.

Sumerian Ziggurat. This edifice, built in Ur around 2100 B.C.E., is the best-preserved surviving ziggurat. As can be seen from the diagram of its original form at right, a shrine, reached by climbing four stories and passing through a massive portal, was the goal of the worshiper's ascent and the most sacred part of the temple.

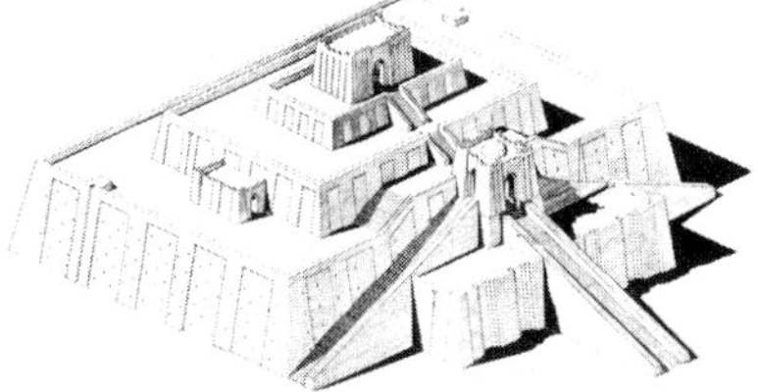

Sumerian Praying Figures. These statues dating from about 2700 B.C.E. show Sumerians praying for the gods to bring them prosperity.

So massive was the typical ziggurat and so arduous the work necessary for building it that, according to modern estimates, 1,500 laborers would have had to work on one for ten hours a day uninterruptedly for five years before it was finished. (Moreover, mud-brick edifices, once built, required constant large-scale repair, so building must have been nearly continuous.) Yet apparently such work was accomplished primarily in shifts by volunteers, as acts of religious devotion.

Temple schools

Sumerian priests did not live in the temples but rather in buildings that were part of the temple precincts. Also dwelling within the precincts were temple administrators, craftsmen, and slaves. Since priests and administrators (the two terms may often have been synonymous) needed to learn cuneiform, temple precincts included schools for teaching it and other knowledge necessary for the priestly caste. These Sumerian schools were the earliest known schools in the history of human civilization.

The wide-ranging role of the temple

Invariably the temple complexes owned huge stretches of land outside the cities, for without the income provided by such agricultural holdings they could not have supported their vast enterprises. Usually the temple complexes also engaged in trade, selling the goods that were manufactured or stored within their precincts to buyers within their respective cities or shipping them for sale over long distances. Thus the temples were virtually "states within the state." Furthermore, before the time of Sargon they frequently were "the state" insofar as the priests of the Sumerian cities were often their cities' rulers. After the liberation from Sargon's dynasty secular kings customarily took over the rulership of Sumerian cities, but even then the king and his family would have intermarried with the families of the foremost priests.

Sumerian social structure

Aside from priests, kings, and prominent warriors (who would have been members of the families of priests and/or kings), Sumerian society knew three ranks: the "specialists" in the temple complexes, the free farmers, and the slaves. The specialists were administrators, merchants,

Sumerian Headdress. The face is an artist's conception, but the floral headdress is copied from a genuine artifact, unearthed by archeologists in 1934. Fashioned from gold and gems, it was worn by a Sumerian queen who lived around 2500 B.C.E.

and artisans, all of whom were reasonably well off but dependent on the priests. The free farmers seem to have been left with the worst land and often found it necessary to place themselves in financial debt to the temples in order to survive. As for the slaves, we know very little about them because their very existence was hardly noted in the records, but it is virtually certain that their lives were supremely miserable.

Old Babylonian Developments

Sumer's economic eclipse: salinization

Although the Sumerians achieved marvels in mastering their physical environment, an ecological problem they were unable to master was the steady deterioration of their soil caused by mounting salt content, a process technically known as salinization. The irrigation of the dry soil of Sumer from the nearby rivers brought moisture, but it also brought salt, and the salt remained when the river water evaporated. On a year-by-year basis the quantities of salt thus introduced into Sumer's soil were insignificant, but on a century-by-century basis they became deleterious to its fertility. Study of surviving cuneiform tablets has shown that arable lands were becoming less productive in parts of Sumer by as early as 2350 B.C.E. By roughly 2000 B.C.E. the region had sunk into full economic eclipse. Unable to produce agricultural surpluses, Sumer's cities could no longer support their priests, administrators, and armies, and the area gradually yielded primacy in Mesopotamia to territories lying farther north.

Gradual transition to Old Babylonian dominance

The Sumerian era of Mesopotamian history was followed by the Old Babylonian era, which lasted from about 2000 to about 1600 B.C.E. It must be emphasized that the first date is chosen arbitrarily, for nothing happened in the year 2000 to mark a break from one era to another. Indeed, not only was the transition from Sumerian to Old Babylonian dominance in Mesopotamia gradual, but even when the Old Babylonian era had come to its fullest flowering around 1770 B.C.E., its culture was not dramatically different from the Sumerian culture that had preceded it. Two criteria alone allow for drawing distinctions between Sumerians and Old Babylonians: geography and language. We have seen that the most prosperous and culturally advanced cities in Mesopotamia during the Sumerian era were those that lay farthest to the south; during the succeeding 400 years, on the other hand, the weight of civilization shifted northward to Akkad, where for much of the time it became centered on the newly founded city of Babylon. In addition, unlike the Sumerians who had spoken a language unrelated to any other, the peoples who held sway in Mesopotamia during the Old Babylonian era spoke languages that belonged to the Semitic language group.

Influx of Semitic-language peoples

Semitic-language peoples (today including Arabs, Israelis, and Ethiopians) trace their descent to a point of origin in the Arabian peninsula. Exactly why or when Semitic tribes headed toward Mesopotamia remains unknown. What is known is that Sargon and his armies were Semites and that consequently Sumer had already undergone a period of Semitic dominance toward the end of the third millennium. The Sumerian revival occurring between 2130 and about 2000 B.C.E. had only been an interlude in this regard because even during that time other Semitic tribes were infiltrating Mesopotamia and taking over pockets of territory in Akkad and Sumer. Ultimately the most successful of these proved to be the Amorites, who advanced into Mesopotamia around 2000 B.C.E. and settled in parts of Akkad. Around this time the Semitic dialect they spoke replaced Sumerian as the language of Mesopotamia. Yet the very same Amorites adopted all other aspects of the Sumerian cultural inheritance.

Hammurabi: greatest Amorite ruler

Because the Amorites made the city of Babylon in Akkad the capital of their empire, they are commonly called the Babylonians, or, more often, the Old Babylonians, to distinguish them from the Chaldeans, who ruled Mesopotamia more than a millennium later. The founder of the Old Babylonian Empire and unquestionably the greatest Amorite ruler was Hammurabi (1792–1750 B.C.E.).* At the time of his accession the Amorites were still no more than one of several warring powers in southern Mesopotamia, but in 1763 B.C.E. Hammurabi conquered all of Sumer, and by 1755 he had subdued all the rest of Mesopotamia to its northern extremes. As his victories mounted, Hammurabi called himself "King of Akkad and Sumer," and then "King of the Four Quarters of the World." Despite this magniloquence his empire was short-lived (political events in Mesopotamia after the reign of Hammurabi will be treated in the next section), but another of his chosen titles, "King of Justice," refers to the source of his lasting fame, for Hammurabi was the promulgator of the earliest extensive collection of laws surviving in the human record.

* Here, and throughout, dates following a ruler's name refer to dates of reign.

"Code of Hammurabi"

Scholars agree that the "Code of Hammurabi," a stone document containing 282 laws, was based on Sumerian legal principles with an admixture of Semitic innovations, but since they seldom agree as to which principles were Sumerian and which Semitic it is wisest to consider the entire text as being simply the fullest-known document recording "Mesopotamian jurisprudence." Before considering some of the code's main premises it must be said that it was devoid of the modern notion of "equality before the law." In the Code of Hammurabi slaves have no rights whatsoever and are subject to frightful mutilations for trivial offenses. Otherwise, two legal classes appear: "men," clearly understood to be aristocrats; and all others neither "men" nor slaves, whom the law treated poorly but to whom it offered some rights. Crimes of "men" against their nonslave inferiors were punished less severely than crimes of "men" against "men," and crimes of "men" against slaves were punished only to the extent that they resulted in "property damage" to a slave owner.

Two legal principles

The two most famous principles underlying Hammurabi's code are "an eye for an eye" and "let the buyer beware." At first both seem dreadfully primitive. In offering the recompense of exact retaliation ("if a man destroy the eye of another, his eye shall be destroyed"; "if a man breaks another's bone, his bone will be broken"), the code never considers whether the initial injury may have been accidental and is chillingly insistent on inflicting pain and humiliation. The "buyer beware" principle is less chilling but hardly seems like law. Why should the state announce in a legal code that the seller is free to get away with trickeries? Hammurabi's code becomes more intelligible only if we recognize that it aimed at different ends than modern jurisprudence. The Mesopotamians promulgated laws primarily to stop fights. Thus they thought—and by no means without reason—that a person tempted to act violently might refrain from such behavior if he remembered that whatever wound he inflicted on another would probably be inflicted upon himself. They clearly also thought that punishments would exercise a deterrent effect only if they were executed swiftly and without hope of mercy, a point of view that made it necessary for them to dismiss motive as irrelevant because investigating circumstances and motives would have taken time and opened the possibility that truly willful crimes might go unpunished if the criminal knew how to defend himself. As for the "buyer beware" principle, that too was meant to stop fights because a buyer knew that he had no rights and would be swiftly punished if he tried to assert any.

Hammurabi: King of Babylon and Lawgiver

Concepts of justice in Hammurabi's code

Having considered these practical dimensions of Mesopotamian jurisprudence, it must be added that Hammurabi's code was not entirely indifferent to the notion of justice. Although the insistence on exact retaliation is surely cruel, it is not entirely lacking in a concept of fairness inasmuch as "an eye for an eye" is surely fairer than a head for an eye or an eye for a fingernail. Secondly, abstract ethical principles are embedded in Hammurabi's code in certain instances. For example, since the Mesopotamians believed that children should be deferential to their parents, law 195 of the code stated, "if a son has struck his father, his hand shall be cut off." Finally, the state is called upon occasionally to provide social well-being rather than merely to judge and punish. The most elevated aspect of this "welfare state" dimension to the code appears in law 23, wherein it is announced that if a man is robbed and the robber cannot be found, "the city . . . in whose territory the robbery was committed shall make good to the victim his lost property." We have seen that Hammurabi did wish to be known as "King of Justice," and by the measures of his time he was entirely that; moreover, although Western concepts of justice were to develop greatly thereafter, most of the principles inherent in the Code of Hammurabi were to become points of departure for much of that future development.

Code of Hammurabi. The entire code of Hammurabi survives on an eight-foot column made of basalt. The top quarter of the column depicts the Babylonian king paying homage to the seated god of justice. Directly below one can make out the cuneiform inscriptions that are the law code's text.

Old Babylonian literature: Epic of Gilgamesh

Equal in fame to Hammurabi's code as a monument of Old Babylonian civilization is the poem known as the Epic of Gilgamesh. Like the code, this work was a Sumerian-Babylonian hybrid. Its hero, Gilgamesh, was a real historical figure—a Sumerian king who ruled around 2600 B.C.E.—whose exploits so excited the imaginations of contemporaries that they began to tell fanciful stories about him. Retold over the centuries in the Sumerian tongue, the stories grew ever more fanciful until they became almost pure fiction. So entertaining were these stories that late in the third millennium the various Semitic conquerors of Sumer began to translate them into their own dialects. The surviving Epic of Gilgamesh represents a late stage in this evolutionary process. Sometime around 1900 B.C.E. a Semitic speaker wove four or five of the Gilgamesh stories into a loosely structured "epic," and this version is the marvelous poem we know today.

The most remarkable qualities of the epic are its sheer poetic forcefulness and its startling secularity, for it recounts nothing but the adventures and aspirations of a human hero in a world governed by the inevitability of death. After engaging in mighty battles and amorous encounters Gilgamesh, terrified of death, seeks the secret of immortality from an old man and his wife who had been saved by taking refuge in an ark when the gods had decided to destroy the world by a flood. The aged couple assure him that immortality is unobtainable, but they do disclose the location of a plant that at least will restore his lost youth. Unfortunately, after gaining this plant by heroic effort from the floor of the sea, Gilgamesh leaves it unguarded while asleep and a snake eats it. (According to the poem, this is why snakes gain new life every year when they shed their skins.) Thus the aspirant to immortality is finally forced to acknowledge that he should enjoy each day as it comes without worrying about the morrow: "Gilgamesh, whither art thou wandering?/ Life, which thou seekest, thou wilt never find,/ For when the gods created man, they let death be his share./. . . Gilgamesh, put on clean clothes, and wash thine head and bathe./ Gaze at the child that holdeth thine hand, /and let thy wife delight in thine embrace./ These things alone are men's concerns."

Old Babylonian religion

Despite these secular teachings, it would be a mistake to think that Old Babylonian culture was irreligious, for all Old Babylonians (the Gilgamesh poet included) assumed that the gods held omnipotent sway over humans. Indeed, surviving prayers show that the Old Babylonians had arrived at a hitherto unprecedented variety of religious commitment: personal religion. During the Old Babylonian period it came to be assumed that in addition to the "political gods" who looked over human collectivities, there existed other deities who looked over the daily affairs of individuals, and that it was necessary to pray to these personal deities for success and forgiveness of misdeeds. For example, an Old Babylonian would plead to a goddess: "I have cried to thee as a suffering, distressed servant./ See me, O my lady; accept my prayers." This development among the Old Babylonians is of particular interest to students of religious history because personal invocation to God and religious introspectiveness are basic features of the Judeo-Christian tradition. Additionally, the fact that individual Old Babylonians were praying fervently to personal gods is noteworthy in its own terms because it shows that Old Babylonian culture was tolerating a certain degree of individualism within a society that was otherwise intent on conformism.

Sumerian Bronze Figure

Mathematics

A final remarkable aspect of Old Babylonian culture lies in a very different area: mathematics. Old Babylonian temple scribes around 1800 B.C.E. were employing tables for multiplication and division, and also for calculating square roots, cube roots, reciprocals, and exponential functions. So impressive were these achievements that if only a single Old Babylonian mathematical tablet had survived it would still allow the conclusion that the Old Babylonians were the most accomplished arithmeticians in antiquity. (The Greeks were adept at geometry but not in mathematics of number.) A basic aspect of modern daily life that derives from Old Babylonian mathematical precedents is our division of the day into two sets of twelve hours, the hour into sixty minutes, and the minute into sixty seconds. When one stops to think of it, working with multiples of ten would be easier, but the Old Babylonians based their arithmetic on multiples of twelve (apparently because their most fundamental reckoning was that of twelve lunar cycles to a year), and all Western civilizations have adhered to Old Babylonian "duodecimal" time reckonings (those based on units of twelve) ever since.

The Kassite and Hittite Interlude

Decline of the Old Babylonian Empire

The Old Babylonian Empire lasted only a century and a half after Hammurabi's death in 1750 B.C.E., and throughout that time it was on the defensive. For reasons historians do not understand because the evidence is inadequate, the Babylonians gradually abandoned control over some of the major southern cities. In addition they were faced with the challenge of a foreign people, the Kassites, who had arrived in the region from central Asia and had introduced a new technique of fighting with light horse-driven chariots. (These chariots had spoked wheels rather than ones made from attached slabs.) During the period from roughly 1650 to roughly 1600 B.C.E. the Kassites began to take ever-greater portions of Mesopotamia by force. The last nail on the Old Babylonian coffin, however, was driven in not by the Kassites but by a related people, the Hittites. In a lightning raid from the north in 1595 B.C.E. a chariot-driven Hittite army demolished the city of Babylon itself and thereby destroyed the last remnants of the Old Babylonian Empire.

Mesopotamia's "dark age" under the Kassites

Retiring northward as quickly as they came, the Hittites left the Mesopotamian field clear for Kassite domination. But the Kassites did not take full advantage of this opportunity, apparently because they lacked a binding sense of political or cultural identity. For roughly the next three centuries Mesopotamia experienced a "dark age," during which most of the south (Akkad and Sumer) was ruled by the Kassites, while the north was divided among other warring peoples. The main reason this period is called a "dark age" is that historians simply know very little about what transpired; it is clear only that no noteworthy contributions were made to the history of civilization.

The Hittite Empire

Consequently, historians' interest centers on the Hittites. Originating from the steppes of central Asia and speaking an Indo-European tongue (the Indo-European linguistic family includes Hindi, Persian, Greek, Latin, and all the Romance, Slavic, and Germanic languages of today), the Hittites had occupied most of Anatolia (modern-day Turkey) by 1600 B.C.E. and within the next two centuries extended their empire southward along the eastern Mediterranean to include Syria and Lebanon. Having destroyed Babylon in 1595 B.C.E., they immediately decided not to overextend their lines of communication by attempting to rule directly in Mesopotamia. (The Bible states accurately that Hittite rule extended "even unto the great river, the river Euphrates" [Joshua 1:4].) The Hittite Empire reached its geographical and economic peak between about 1450 and 1300 B.C.E., but in the thirteenth century B.C.E. the Hittites faced invasions arising separately out of Egypt and northern Mesopotamia. In 1286 B.C.E. they staved off a mighty Egyptian onslaught into Syria, and later in the century they still were able to defend themselves against incursions from northern Mesopotamia launched by Semitic Assyrians. But exhaustion finally overcame them. In the years around 1185 B.C.E. successive waves of maritime attacks from the west (the exact origin of the "Sea Peoples" who briefly appeared in western Asia has not yet been identified) resulted in the utter destruction of the Hittites' power.

Misconceptions concerning the Hittites

Virtually nothing was known about the Hittites until their Anatolian capital, Hattusas (meaning "Hittite city"), was excavated in 1907, bringing to light an archive of 20,000 clay tablets. In 1915 a Czech scholar deciphered the language of these tablets, announcing that it was Indo-European, and thereupon a rush of scholarly interest in the Hittites ensued. Unfortunately some of this scholarship was racially biased or ill-informed and hence introduced some misconceptions about the Hittites, including the notion that they were great because they were Indo-European. This is a mistake on two counts, first because it assumes that all the Hittites belonged to an Indo-European race, and second because it assumes that all members of the Indo-European race possess superior intelligence. Although a homogeneous tribe of Indo-European-speaking

Hittites may once have migrated from central Asia into Anatolia, as soon as its members settled down they intermingled with native peoples so thoroughly that whatever "racial purity" they once may have had became lost. (The same would have been true of the Semitic tribes that settled in Mesopotamia.) In any case, biology demonstrates that there is no correspondence between intelligence and race. Another myth about the Hittites is that they owed their long-term success to monopolizing a secret weapon, the manufacture of iron, which they zealously kept beyond the ken of foreigners for centuries. Strange as it may seem, this belief rests on the misreading of a single Hittite document. The truth of the matter is that the Hittites did start making and using iron in the fourteenth century B.C.E., but so did all their contemporaries; so far as is known, the use of iron weaponry did not give any western Asian nation an advantage over any other.

Sources of Hittite strength

If the Hittites were not supremely smart or supremely well armed, how can one explain their might? Part of the answer lies in the resources that lay at their disposal, for Anatolia, in contrast to Mesopotamia, was rich in metallic ores, especially those of copper, iron, and silver. Dwelling at the source of such metals, the Hittites could trade some of them advantageously in their raw state, and they also were well positioned to experiment in metallurgy, hence excelling first in bronze and then in iron manufacture. Although the manufacture of iron did not give the Hittites any exclusive military advantage, it did bring them wealth because iron was as useful in peace as in war (it was particularly useful for making or reinforcing agricultural implements), and because in the earliest years of iron production (from roughly 1400 to roughly 1200 B.C.E.) anything made from iron had great prestige value. Accordingly, the Hittites grew rich

Hittite Sculpture. Perhaps the most highly conventionalized sculpture of the ancient world is found in Hittite reliefs.

from trade in a way that would have been impossible had they inhabited another region. To this must be added the fact that they devised an efficient governmental system, whereby a "great king" theoretically ruled supreme but actually delegated much authority to regional representatives. Aside from their metallurgy and their law, the Hittites were not particularly given to experimentation; they adopted cuneiform from their neighbors, their art was conventional, and they seem to have had no independent literature. Nonetheless, endowed with sufficient wealth and governmental skill, the Hittites were able to preserve their empire and their national identity longer than was typical in the ebb and flow of western Asian peoples and kingdoms.

The Might of the Assyrians

The evolution of Assyrian supremacy

Returning to the narrative of events in Mesopotamia, we find that the Kassite dark age was succeeded by the period of the Assyrian Empire, which lasted from roughly 1300 until exactly 612 B.C.E. The Assyrians were a people of the Semitic language group who had settled on the Tigris in northernmost Mesopotamia. During the dark age they had established a small state centered on their city of Assur, yet they did not begin to extend their power until the opening of the thirteenth century B.C.E., when they came to acquire skills in chariot warfare. By around 1250 the Assyrians had become masters of the entire Mesopotamian north, and soon after they dedicated themselves to subduing the Kassites in Akkad and Sumer. Since the Kassite kingdom was moribund, they had no trouble making such conquests. In 1225 B.C.E. an Assyrian monarch took Babylon and ordered his scribes to record, "I captured Babylon's king and trod his proud neck as if it were a footstool. . . . Thus I became lord of all Sumer and Akkad and fixed the boundary of my realm at the Lower Sea."

Masters of western Asia under Sennacherib

Direct Assyrian rule over Sumer and Akkad lasted for only eight years because the Assyrians did not have the resources to maintain a costly occupation of a region whose inhabitants resented their rule. Yet they did succeed in maintaining indirect overlordship over southern Mesopotamia for six centuries (with some interludes), preserving their trading interests in the region and making sure that no political counterweights would rise to challenge them. Moreover, shortly after 900 B.C.E. the Assyrians began to expand in other directions, apparently seeking control over natural resources and access to trade routes. In the first half of the ninth century they conquered Syria and reached the Mediterranean, and around 840 B.C.E. they annexed southeastern Anatolia. Temporary internal political divisions kept them from advancing immediately any farther, but one hundred years later they were on the march again until conquests culminating in the reign of Sennacherib (705–681 B.C.E.) made them masters of almost all the inhabitable territory of western Asia.

The splendor of Nineveh

Sennacherib's reign displays the Assyrians at their most magnificent and their most frightful. To seal his military victories Sennacherib built a splendid capital, Nineveh, on the banks of the upper Tigris. No city remotely so splendid had ever been seen in Mesopotamia before. Within walls whose circumference was seven and a half miles lay magnificent temples and a royal palace with at least seventy-one chambers. Outside the walls were orchards and zoos with rare trees and exotic animals that Sennacherib ordered to be brought from great distances. Dissatisfied with the quality of the local water supply, the mighty king supervised an extraordinary engineering project whereby water was led to Nineveh by channels and aqueducts from fresh mountain springs fifty miles distant. To commemorate the successful completion of the project, rock carvings at the source depicted the gods flanked by inscriptions listing all of Sennacherib's military victories.

Derivative nature of Assyrian culture

Among the chambers in Sennacherib's palace at Nineveh was a library of clay tablets amounting to a vast repository of practical knowledge and religious lore. This learning came from southern Mesopotamia, for the Assyrians were entirely in the debt of ancient Sumer and Old Babylonia when it came to the life of the mind. Intent on gaining whatever practical knowledge they could for the sake of administration and commerce, and willing to worship all of Old Babylonia's gods (along with "Assur," the Assyrians' own local deity), the Assyrians began carrying off cuneiform tablets from Babylon as early as their sack of that city in 1225 B.C.E. Hence when Sennacherib's learned successor Assurbanipal (668–627 B.C.E.) rounded out the holdings of the library at Nineveh, it

Assyrian Winged Human-Headed Bull. This relief was found in the palace of King Sargon II (722–705 B.C.E.). It measures 16 feet wide by 16 feet high and weighs approximately 40 tons.

contained virtually the entire available store of Sumerian and Old Babylonian learning and literature.

Assyrian frightfulness

A traveler through Nineveh in the seventh century B.C.E. would thus have concluded that the Assyrian Empire's ruling class was not only mighty but technologically proficient and very cultivated in certain respects. On the other hand, he would have seen ample evidence of what history has taken to be the Assyrians' most distinctive trait, their "calculated frightfulness." To be fair to the Assyrians, frightfulness was no more characteristic of their culture than it was of any other until the time of Sennacherib. Although frightfulness implies a culture's unrelenting emphasis on the virtues of brutal masculinity ("machismo"), it was the Assyrians, rather than any other Mesopotamian people, who once accepted the rule of a queen, Sammuramat (known to the Greeks and later Europeans as Semiramis). Indeed, her reign from 810 to 805 B.C.E. seemed so extraordinary to other peoples that it became the subject of legend.

Brutality in art and policy

Beginning with the reign of Sennacherib, however, the Assyrians began to display traits of extraordinary brutality in both their artwork and their actual policies. In the sculptured reliefs that adorned Nineveh, they celebrated war and slaughter. Scenes of lion-hunting were their favorites: men with the coolest bravery yet also the coolest cruelty are shown hunting leaping lions, with special attention being paid to the death agonies of wounded beasts. Meanwhile the Assyrians were slaughtering humans just as pitilessly. One of Sennacherib's military exploits was the quelling in 689 B.C.E. of a revolt against Assyrian hegemony in Babylon. Once he accomplished this he commanded his troops to pillage and destroy with the utmost thoroughness, thereupon boasting in an inscription, "I made Babylon's destruction more complete than that by a flood. . . . I demolished it with torrents of water and made it like a meadow."

Assyrian Relief Sculptures. These panels, representative of Assyrian "frightfulness," depict the emperor Assurbanipal on the hunt.

Uprisings against Assyrian domination

The Assyrian policy of frightfulness in military campaigns was meant above all to strike abject terror into the hearts of the nation's enemies. No doubt it did this, but it also succeeded in making the Assyrians more intensely hated than any western Asian conquerors had been until their time. Since the conquered peoples' hatred for the Assyrians often overcame their fear of them, uprisings against Assyrian domination flickered on and off throughout the seventh century B.C.E., with the most frequent center of resistance being the area around Babylon. Although Sennacherib had seen to Babylon's destruction in 689 B.C.E., his son undertook the city's rebuilding for motives of prestige, and by 651 B.C.E. the city had once more become the focal point of southern Mesopotamian revolt. In order to quell the unrest, Sennacherib's grandson Assurbanipal laid siege to Babylon in that year and forced its surrender in 648 B.C.E., once more unleashing Assyrian frightfulness. As he proclaimed in one of the most inhumane accounts of methodical carnage ever recorded, "I tore out the tongues of many who plotted against me and then had them murdered. The others I smashed to death with the statues of their local gods. . . . Then I fed their corpses, cut into small pieces, to the dogs, to the pigs, to the vultures, and to all the birds of the sky."

The Babylonian-Median vengeance

One might have thought that the southern Mesopotamians would have remained submissive for a long time after that, but in fact they continued to seek any possible opportunity to throw off the Assyrian yoke. In 614 B.C.E. this opportunity finally came in the form of an alliance with an Indo-European tribe, the Medes, who had recently consolidated their power in Iran, directly to the east. Two years of warfare were all it took to destroy the Assyrian Empire: in 612 B.C.E. Nineveh fell to a united Babylonian-Median force, was leveled, and unlike Babylon never rose again. The rejoicing of all the conquered nations is well reflected in the Old Testament Book of Nahum: "Woe to the bloody city! . . . There is no end of their corpses, they stumble upon their corpses. . . . Nineveh is laid waste, and who will bemoan her?"

The New Babylonian Revival

The Chaldeans as the New Babylonians

Throughout the century of southern Mesopotamian resistance to Assyrian domination, the peoples most prominently engaged in that resistance were Semitic speakers called Chaldeans (pronounced Kaldeeans), who, with the Medes, laid waste to Nineveh. Since the Medes used their victory of 612 B.C.E. as a springboard for invading Anatolia, the Chaldeans were left as masters of all Mesopotamia, and since they located their capital in Babylon, they are usually referred to by historians as the New Babylonians. The most famous New Babylonian ruler was Nebuchadnezzar (604–562 B.C.E.), who conquered Jerusalem, transported large numbers of Judeans to Babylon, and made his empire the foremost power in western

Asia. Soon after his death New Babylonian might was challenged by an Indo-European people from Iran, the Persians (closely allied and ultimately intermingled with the Medes, giving rise to the historians' joke that "one man's Mede is another man's Persian"). In 539 B.C.E. one of Nebuchadnezzar's successors, Belshazzar, failed to understand "the handwriting on the wall" (Daniel 5), and before he knew it the Persians had rushed into Mesopotamia so quickly that Babylon fell to them without a fight.

The wonders of Babylon

The city of Babylon during the era of the New Babylonians is the Babylon best known to us today, partly because of familiarity brought by early-twentieth-century excavations and partly because of surviving descriptions from eyewitness Greek travelers. Babylon's size alone during this period was astounding, for it extended to 2,100 acres, in comparison to the 1,850 acres of Sennacherib's Nineveh and the 135 acres of the typical Sumerian city. (One of western Europe's largest cities, Paris, had only about twice Babylon's acreage until the early twentieth century.) More astounding still was Babylon's color, for the New Babylonians had learned to build their major monuments in brightly colored glazed brick. The most famous example, so splendid that it was counted by the ancient Greeks as one of the "seven wonders of the world," was the city wall built by Nebuchadnezzar. Against a background of brilliant blue, lions, bulls, and dragons in shades of white and yellow promenaded the entire length of the wall and strutted in tiers along the entire height of the "Ishtar Gate" (so called because the gate was dedicated to the goddess Ishtar). German archeologists digging in the ruins of Babylon in 1902 were the first since ancient times to see this marvel, and they must have felt as thrilled as if they had walked on the moon. Had Nebuchadnezzar built no more than this, his fame as one of history's most magnificent builders would have been secure, but he also constructed another of the "seven ancient wonders": Babylon's "Hanging Gardens." This feat was so extraordinary that truth about it merges into legend. Apparently Nebuchadnezzar really did build ascending terraces of gardens from the Euphrates outward, each with splendid plants and trees, but it may be legendary that he did this to gratify his wife, a princess from Iran, who loathed southern Mesopotamia's flatness and longed for her homeland's rolling hills.

Accomplishments in astronomy

Aside from construction feats, New Babylonia's cultural accomplishments were greatest in the realm of astronomy. We have seen that in the earliest Sumerian times Mesopotamian peoples had observed the phases of the moon in order to make predictions about the recurrence of the seasons. Two thousand years later Mesopotamians were still carefully studying the night skies, but now they were concentrating on the movements of the planets and the stars because they had come to believe that some of their gods resided in the heavens and that by plotting and predicting the motions of the planets and stars they could predict which divinity was gaining power and how that might affect the course of human affairs.

Reconstruction of the Ishtar Gate. Visitors to the Near Eastern Museum in Berlin can see this impressive reconstruction of the gate built in Babylon by King Nebuchadnezzar around 575 B.C.E. rising to a height of fifty feet. About half of the reconstruction is original.

Such study of the heavens was brought to its perfection by the New Babylonians, who identified five "wandering stars" (we would say "planets") and linked them with the powers of five different gods. (If this sounds strange, we should remember that we still call the five viewable planets by the names of Roman gods—Mercury, Venus, Mars, Jupiter, and Saturn—because the Greeks and Romans inherited this system.) Going further, the New Babylonians concluded that when a given planet appeared in a particular part of the night sky or in close proximity to another planet its movement would portend war or famine, or the victory of one nation over another. Fully developed, these systems amounted to astrology, although New Babylonian astrology concerned itself exclusively with predictions about cosmic events such as floods and famines and the fortunes of nations rather than the fortunes of individual people. (The Greeks and Romans took the next step of casting personal horoscopes dependent on the configuration of the skies at the time of a person's birth.)

Efforts to measure and interpret the universe

Today it is recognized that all astrology is superstition, but the New Babylonians' search for correspondences between heavenly events and earthly ones was scientific in terms of their time. In other words, for humans to believe that they can measure and interpret their universe and thereby learn how to benefit from it is more scientific than cowering in ceaseless fear of inexplicable mysteries. Moreover, dedicated to this belief, the New Babylonians observed celestial phenomena more closely than any other ancient peoples before them, and recorded their observations so meticulously that they later could be used and supplemented by astronomers of other civilizations. Most notably, starting in 747 B.C.E. Chaldean court astronomers kept "diaries" on a monthly basis in which they recorded all planetary movements and eclipses, together with reports of earthly affairs such as price changes, shifting river levels, storms, and temperatures. Continued without interruption until Greek scientists gained knowledge of them, these records became a direct point of departure for astronomical science in the Greco-Roman world.

The Mesopotamian Legacy

Babylon fades into obscurity

The Hanging Gardens of Babylon are no more. Although the city of Babylon was not damaged when it was taken by the Persians in 539 B.C.E., the Persian conquest marked the end of Mesopotamian civilization insofar as native peoples and dynasties would never rule in Mesopotamia again. Gradually, as Greeks replaced Persians, Romans replaced Greeks, and Arabs replaced Romans, cuneiform ceased to be used, foreign artistic and building styles were introduced, and the old cities fell into ruins, to be supplanted by new ones. (The most magnificent city to arise in the Tigris-Euphrates region after the decay of Babylon was Baghdad, founded by the Arabs.) Entirely abandoned two centuries after the birth of Christ, Babylon became so covered up by the nearby shifting waters and sands that nobody knew for sure where it was until excavations accomplished shortly after 1900.

Lion from the Ishtar Gate. One of the many fierce animals striding across Nebuchadnezzar's "wonder of the world."

Influence on the Hebrews

Yet the Mesopotamian legacy endures in different ways. One is by means of the Hebrew Bible. Since the earliest Hebrew peoples dwelled somewhere in Mesopotamia before they migrated to Palestine and since they spoke a language closely related to that of the Old Babylonians, it is not surprising that the earliest chapters of the Bible often allude to Mesopotamia. According to the book of Genesis King Nimrod ruled "Babel (Babylon), Erech (Uruk), and Akkad," and Abraham came to Palestine from "Ur of the Chaldees"; the "Tower of Babel," built out of "brick for stone and slime for mortar" (Genesis 11:1–9), is surely a reference to an Old Babylonian ziggurat. Ancient Hebrew and Mesopotamian points of contact are further displayed by the appearance in the Epic of Gilgamesh of a flood story very similar to the ark narrative in Genesis: not only is a human couple saved in both by floating in an ark, but they learn in both of the waters' ebbing when a bird they send forth no longer returns. More noteworthy still is the fact that fundamental Hebrew religious concepts bear relationships to ancient Mesopotamian ones. This is to not say that the Hebrews were unoriginal in their theology. Quite to the contrary, the Hebrews were the most original religious thinkers in the ancient world. Yet Old Testament theological formulations emerged from an ancient Mesopotamian matrix, and specific Hebrew religious innovations may well have been adaptations of Mesopotamian precedents. By the time of Sennacherib and Nebuchadnezzar, the Hebrews came to hate the Assyrians and Babylonians because those peoples were constantly attacking them, and thereafter the invectives of the Hebrew prophets were passed on so effectively to Christians that the name Babylon even today remains a term for the essence of sinfulness. But the insults should not be allowed to obscure the kinships and the debts.

Technological and intellectual legacy

Mesopotamia also handed down a technological and intellectual legacy. We have seen that the wheel was first used for transportation in ancient Sumer, that the earliest known writing appeared there, and that the Old Babylonians pioneered in mathematical functions such as square and cube roots. Scholars find it difficult to determine whether all of these early Mesopotamian inventions were transmitted to other peoples by diffusion or whether some (writing above all) were invented independently elsewhere. In either case, however, the Mesopotamian inventions led step by step to modern practices taken for granted in Europe and America today. Mesopotamian jurisprudence and natural science similarly stand behind much that we today customarily take for granted. The visual world around us looks entirely different from that of ancient Mesopotamia because we have borrowed next to nothing from ancient Mesopotamian art and architecture, yet in fundamental aspects of technology and thought we owe a great debt to the ingenious people of five thousand years ago who resolved to wrest power and glory from a land of mud flats.

SUMMARY POINTS

- The first cities emerged in the Mesopotamian region of Sumer. The most remarkable accomplishments of Sumerian civilization were the invention of wheeled transport, the lunar calendar, and writing.
- The next civilization to arise in Mesopotamia was that of the Old Babylonians, who formulated the Code of Hammurabi (the earliest known extensive collection of laws), composed the Epic of Gilgamesh, and made impressive advances in mathematics.
- After the Old Babylonians were overthrown by the Kassites and the Hittites, Mesopotamia and much of western Asia came under the control of the Assyrians, a brutal empire that was finally destroyed by a Babylonian-Median alliance.
- The Chaldeans, or New Babylonians, rebuilt Babylon into a magnificent city and attempted to understand the universe by studying the stars.
- The Mesopotamian legacy endures through stories in the Bible and in mathematics, jurisprudence, transportation, and the natural sciences.

SELECTED READINGS

Cambridge Ancient History (3d ed., vols. I–III), Cambridge, 1971–1996.

Gurney, O. R., *The Hittites,* rev. ed., Baltimore, 1980. The standard survey in English.

Jacobsen, Thorkild, *The Treasures of Darkness: A History of Mesopotamian Religion,* New Haven, 1976.

Kramer, Samuel N., *The Sumerians: Their History, Culture, and Character,* Chicago, 1963. A still-useful account by a pioneer in the field.

Macqueen, J. G., *The Hittites and Their Contemporaries in Asia Minor,* rev. ed., London, 1986. Topical coverage.

Neugebauer, Otto, *The Exact Sciences in Antiquity,* 2d ed., New York, 1969. Includes the basic account of Mesopotamian mathematical accomplishments.

Oates, Joan, *Babylon,* rev. ed., London, 1986. A well-illustrated narrative that concentrates on Akkad from Sargon to the Persians and Greeks.

Postgate, J. N., *Early Mesopotamia: Society and Economy at the Dawn of History,* London, 1992. The best new social and economic history through the period of Old Babylonia. Somewhat technical.

Roux, Georges, *Ancient Iraq,* 3d ed., New York, 1992. The best one-volume introduction to the entire sweep of developments in ancient Mesopotamia.

Sasson, Jack M., ed., *Civilizations of the Ancient Near East,* 4 vols., New York, 1995. A collection of specialized articles communicating the results of the most up-to-date research.

Woolley, Sir Leonard, and P. R. S. Moorey, *Ur "of the Chaldees,"* London, 1982. An account of Woolley's excavations at Ur, which took place between 1922 and 1934.

Source Materials

Ferry, David, *Gilgamesh: A New Rendering in English Verse,* New York, 1992.

Foster, Benjamin R., *From Distant Days: Myths, Tales, and Poetry of Ancient Mesopotamia,* Bethesda, Md., 1995.

Pritchard, James B., *Ancient Near Eastern Texts Relating to the Old Testament,* 3d ed., Princeton, 1969.

CHAPTER 3

EGYPTIAN CIVILIZATION

Thou makest the Nile in the Nether World,
Thou bringest it as thou desirest,
To preserve alive the people of Egypt.
For thou hast made them for thyself,
Thou lord of them all. . . .

—Hymn to Aton, from reign of the Pharaoh Akhenaton

MODERN CROWDS that flood museums to view fabled treasures of Egyptian art are still captivated by the spell of one of the oldest and most alluring civilizations in history. Almost as old as the civilization founded in Mesopotamia during the fourth millennium B.C.E., Egyptian civilization provides a fascinating comparison to that of Mesopotamia because it was characterized by stability and serenity in contrast to the turmoil and tension of Mesopotamia. Not only were the Egyptians peaceful for long periods of their ancient history, but surviving Egyptian statuary and painted human figures often seem to smile and bask in the sun as if they were on summer vacation.

Environmental basis of differences between Egypt and Mesopotamia

Environmental factors best explain the striking differences. Since the Mesopotamian climate was harsh, and since the Tigris and Euphrates flooded irregularly, the Mesopotamians could not view nature as dependably life-enhancing. Furthermore, since Mesopotamia, located on an open plain, was not geographically protected from foreign incursions, its inhabitants were necessarily on continual military alert. Egyptian civilization, on the other hand, was centered on the dependably life-enhancing Nile. Not only did the richly fertile soil of the Nile valley provide great agricultural wealth, but the Nile flooded regularly year after year during the summer months and always receded in time for a bountiful growing season, offering Egyptians the feeling that nature was predictable and benign. In addition, since the Nile valley was surrounded by deserts and the Red Sea, Egypt was comparatively free from threats of foreign invasion. The centrality of the Nile in ancient Egyptian life is well illustrated by the fact that the Egyptians had two words for travel: either *khed,* which meant "to go downstream," or *khent,* which meant "to go upstream." All in all, the Greek historian Herodotus surely had warrant to designate Egypt as "the gift of the river."

POLITICAL HISTORY UNDER THE PHARAOHS

Foundation of Egypt's advanced civilization

The ancient history of Egypt is usually divided into six eras: the archaic period (c. 3100–c. 2770 B.C.E.), the Old Kingdom (c. 2770–c. 2200 B.C.E.), the first intermediate period (c. 2200–c. 2050 B.C.E.), the Middle Kingdom (c. 2050–1786 B.C.E.), the second intermediate period (c. 1786–c. 1560 B.C.E.), and the New Kingdom (c. 1560–1087 B.C.E.). Even before the beginning of the archaic period, the Egyptians had taken some fundamental steps in the direction of creating an advanced civilization. Above all, they had begun to engage in settled farming; they had learned to use copper tools in addition to stone ones; and shortly before 3100 B.C.E., they had developed a system of writing known as *hieroglyphic* (Greek for "priestly carving"). Experts are uncertain whether the Egyptians arrived at the idea of writing on their own, or whether the idea came to them from Mesopotamia. The strongest argument for the former position is that the hieroglyphic system is very different from Mesopotamian cuneiform, but the sudden appearance of hieroglyphic suggests that certain Egyptian administrator-priests decided to work out a record-keeping system on the basis of their knowledge of a foreign precedent. Whatever the case, writing surely allowed for greater governmental efficiency and apparently was a precondition for the greatest event in ancient Egyptian political history, the unification of the north and the south.

Narmer Palette. Dating from about 3100 B.C.E., this stone carving shows Narmer subduing an enemy from the north with a mace. The falcon probably represents the god Horus, who looks with approval on the birth of Egyptian unification in violence.

Egyptian unification, and therewith the beginning of the archaic period, occurred around 3100 B.C.E. Until then separate powers had ruled in Upper (or southern) Egypt, and Lower (or northern) Egypt, but unity was essential for Egypt's future because a single government was necessary to ensure the free flow of traffic along the entire length of the Nile, as well as to provide centralized direction of irrigation projects. The unification of Egypt was achieved by a warrior from the south called Narmer, the first of the *pharaohs* (kings), who brought all of Egypt north to the Mediterranean delta under his control. It may be that the process was somewhat more gradual, but there is little doubt that for roughly four hundred years after about 3100 B.C.E. a succession of two ruling dynasties held sway over a united Egypt.

Zoser and the founding of the Old Kingdom

The first two Egyptian dynasties were succeeded around 2680 B.C.E. by the rule of the mighty Zoser, the first king of the Third Dynasty and the founder of the Old Kingdom. While the details of how the governmental system of the Old Kingdom differed from that of the archaic period will never be known, it is certain that Zoser's reign initiated a period of vastly greater state power and royal absolutism, best witnessed by the fact that Zoser presided over the building of the first pyramid. Under Zoser and his leading successors of the Old Kingdom the power of the pharaoh was virtually unlimited. The pharaoh was considered to be the child of the sun god, and by custom married one of his sisters to keep the divine blood from becoming contaminated. No separation of religious and political life existed. The pharaoh's chief subordinates were priests, and he himself was the chief priest.

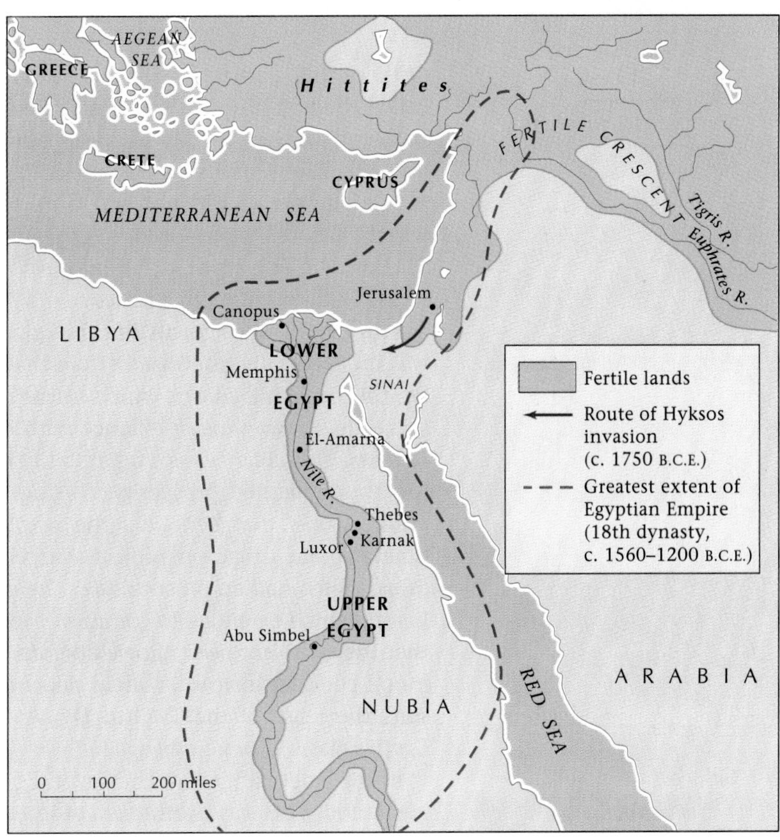

Ancient Egypt

The government of the Old Kingdom was founded upon a policy of peace. In this respect it was virtually unique among ancient states. The pharaoh had no standing army. Each local area had its own militia, but militias were commanded by civil officials and when called into active service generally devoted their energies to labor on the public works. In case of a threat of invasion the various local units were assembled at the call of the pharaoh and placed under the command of one of his civil subordinates. The Egyptians of the Old Kingdom were content for the most part to work out their own destinies and to let other nations alone. The reasons for this attitude lie in the protected position of their country, in their possession of land of inexhaustible fertility, and in the fact that their state was a product of cooperative need instead of being grounded in exploitation.

The nonmilitaristic character of the Old Kingdom

After centuries of peace and relative prosperity the Old Kingdom came to an end with the downfall of the Sixth Dynasty about 2200 B.C.E. Several causes were responsible. Governmental revenues became exhausted because the pharaohs invested heavily in such grandiose projects as pyramid-building. To make matters worse, overall Egyptian prosperity was adversely affected by climatic disasters that caused crop failures. In the meantime provincial strongmen usurped more and more power

End of the Old Kingdom

until central authority virtually disappeared. The era that followed is called the first intermediate period. Disunity now prevailed. The strongmen created their own rival principalities, and political chaos was aggravated by internal brigandage and invasion by desert tribes. The first intermediate period did not end until the rise of the Eleventh Dynasty, which restored centralized rule around 2050 B.C.E. from its base in Thebes (Upper Egypt). The next great stage of Egyptian history, known as the Middle Kingdom, ensued.

The Middle Kingdom

Throughout most of its life the government of the Middle Kingdom was more socially responsible than that of the Old Kingdom. In particular, the Twelfth Dynasty, which ruled from about 1990 until 1786 B.C.E., succeeded in forging an alliance with officials, merchants, artisans, and farmers. This alliance kept the nobility in check and laid the foundations for unprecedented prosperity. During the rule of the Twelfth Dynasty public works that benefited the whole population, such as extensive drainage and irrigation projects, largely replaced the building of pyramids, which had no practical use. There was also a democratization of religion, which extended to common people a hope for life in the hereafter that they had not been allowed before. Religion now emphasized proper moral conduct instead of ritual dependent on wealth. For all these reasons the reign of the Twelfth Dynasty is commonly considered to be Egypt's classical or golden age.

The invasion of the Hyksos

Immediately afterward, however, Egypt entered its second intermediate period. This was another era of internal division and foreign invasion lasting for more than two centuries, or from 1786 to about 1560 B.C.E. The contemporary records are scanty, but they seem to show that the internal disorder was the result of a counterrevolt of the provincial strongmen. The pharaohs were reduced to impotence, and much of the social progress of the Twelfth Dynasty was nullified. About 1750 B.C.E. the land was invaded by the Hyksos, or "rulers of foreign lands," peoples originating in western Asia. Their military prowess is commonly ascribed to the fact that they possessed horses and war chariots, but their victory was certainly made easier by dissension among the Egyptians themselves. Their rule had profound effects upon Egyptian history. Not only did they introduce the Egyptians to new methods of warfare, but by providing them with a common grievance in the face of alien rule they also enabled them to forget their differences and unite in a common cause.

The New Kingdom

Near the end of the seventeenth century B.C.E. the rulers of southern (Upper) Egypt launched a revolt against the Hyksos, a movement that was eventually joined by all of Egypt. By about 1560 B.C.E. the last conquerors who had not been killed or enslaved had been driven from the country. The hero of this victory, Ahmose, founder of the Eighteenth Dynasty, thereafter established a regime that was more highly consolidated than any that had hitherto existed. In this he was helped by the fact that the great outpouring of patriotism that had accompanied the struggle against the Hyksos succeeded in overcoming local loyalties. The period that followed is called the New Kingdom, and by some, the period of the Empire. It lasted from about 1560 to 1087 B.C.E., during which time Egypt was ruled by three dynasties: the Eighteenth, Nineteenth, and Twentieth. No longer was the state policy pacific and isolationist; a spirit of aggressive imperialism prevailed, for the military ardor generated by the successful war against the Hyksos whetted an appetite for further victories. Moreover, the military machine that had been created to expel the invader proved to be too valuable an adjunct to the pharaoh's power to be discarded. Indeed, the government of this period relied heavily on the ruler's ability to overawe both foreigners and his own subjects with his army.

Ramses II (19th Dynasty)

The first steps in the direction of the new policy were taken by the immediate successors of Ahmose in making extensive raids into Palestine. With one of the most formidable armies of ancient times, succeeding pharaohs eventually made themselves masters of a vast domain extending from the Euphrates in western Asia to the southern parts of the Nile, including the rich territory of Nubia. But they never succeeded in molding the conquered peoples into loyal subjects, and this weakness was the signal for revolt in Syria. Although their successors suppressed the uprising and managed to hold the Empire together for some time, ultimate disaster could not be averted. More territory had been annexed than could be managed successfully. The influx of wealth into Egypt fostered corruption, and the constant revolts of the vanquished eventually sapped the strength of the state. By the twelfth century B.C.E. most of the conquered provinces had been lost.

The end of Egyptian independence

The last of the great pharaohs was Ramses III, who ruled from 1182 to 1151 B.C.E. He was succeeded by a long line of nonentities who inherited his name but not his ability. By the end of the twelfth century B.C.E. Egypt had fallen prey to renewed barbarian invasions. The process of decline was hastened by the growing power of the priests, who usurped the royal prerogatives and dictated the pharaoh's decrees. From the middle of the tenth century B.C.E. until the end of the eighth century B.C.E. a dynasty of Libyan invaders held sway. They were followed briefly by a line of Nubians, who overran Egypt from the southern deserts. In 671 B.C.E. Egypt was conquered by the Assyrians, but they held their ascendancy for only eight years. After the collapse of Assyrian rule Egypt regained its independence, and a revival of traditionalism ensued. This was doomed to an untimely end, however, for in 525 B.C.E. Persian invaders overcame a defending Egyptian army in pitched battle. Egypt thence was absorbed into the Persian Empire and subsequently was ruled by Greeks and Romans.

Egyptian Religion

The early religious evolution

Religion played a dominant role in the life of the ancient Egyptians, leaving its impress on politics, literature, architecture, art, and the conduct of daily affairs. Egyptian religion went through stages of simple polytheism to the earliest known expression of monotheism, and then back to polytheism. In the beginning each city or district appears to have had its local

The Gods Isis, Osiris, and Horus

deities, who were guardian gods of the locality or personifications of nature powers. The unification of the country resulted in a fusion of divinities. All of the guardian deities were merged into the great sun god Re. Under the Theban rulers of the Middle Kingdom, this deity was called Amon or Amon-Re, from the name of the chief god of Thebes. The gods who personified the vegetative powers of nature were fused into a deity called Osiris, who was also the god of the Nile. Thereafter these two great powers who ruled the universe, Amon and Osiris, were Egypt's supreme gods. Other deities, as we shall see, were recognized also, but they occupied a distinctly subordinate place.

During the period of the Old Kingdom the solar faith prevailed, embodied in the worship of Re. It served as an official religion whose chief function was to give immortality to the state and to the people collectively. Re was not simply a guardian deity; he was the god of righteousness, justice, and truth, but he offered no spiritual blessings or material rewards to people as individuals. The solar faith was not a religion for the masses, except insofar as their welfare coincided with that of the state.

The cult of Osiris, as already observed, began its existence as a nature religion. His career was marked by elaborate legend. In the remote past, according to belief, he had been a benevolent ruler, who taught his people agriculture and other practical arts and gave them laws. After a time he was treacherously slain by his wicked brother Seth, and his body cut into pieces. His wife Isis, who was also his sister, went in search of the pieces, put them together, and miraculously restored his body to life. The risen god regained his kingdom and continued his beneficent rule for a time, but eventually he descended to the underworld to serve as judge of the dead. Then his son Horus avenged his father's death.

Significance of the Osiris legend

Originally this legend seems to have been little more than a nature myth. The death and resurrection of Osiris symbolized the drying of the Nile in the autumn and the coming of the flood in the spring. But during the period of the Middle Kingdom the Osiris legend began to take on a deeper significance. The human qualities of the deities concerned—the paternal care of Osiris for his subjects, the faithful devotion of his wife and son—appealed to the emotions of average Egyptians, who were now able to see their own tribulations and triumphs mirrored in the lives of the gods. More important, the death and resurrection of Osiris came to be regarded as offering a promise of personal immortality. As the god had triumphed over death, so might the individual who worshiped him inherit everlasting life. Finally, the victory of Horus appeared to foreshadow the ultimate ascendancy of good over evil.

Egyptian ideas of the hereafter

Because of their belief in an afterlife, Egyptians of the Middle Kingdom made elaborate preparations to prevent the loss of their earthly remains. Not only were bodies mummified, but the wealthy left rich endowments to provide their mummies with food and other essentials. The dead were believed to appear before Osiris to be judged according to their deeds on earth. All of the departed who met the tests entered a realm of physical delights. In marshes of lotus-flowers they would hunt geese and quail

Funerary Papyrus. The scene shows the heart of a princess of the Twenty-first Dynasty being weighed in a balance before the god Osiris. On the other side of the balance are the symbols for life and truth.

with never-ending success. Or they might build houses in the midst of orchards with luscious fruits. They would find lily-lakes on which to sail, pools of sparkling water in which to bathe, and shady groves inhabited by singing birds. But the unfortunate ones whose hearts revealed their vicious lives were utterly destroyed.

Akhenaton's religious revolution

Soon after the establishment of the Empire, people started preferring magical practices in a search for personal rewards. Priests sold magical charms that were supposed to prevent the heart of the deceased from betraying his or her real character. They also sold formulas that were alleged to be effective in facilitating the passage of the dead to the realm of the blessed. This trend toward the predominance of magical practices finally resulted in a great religious upheaval. The leader of this movement was the Pharaoh Amenhotep IV, who began his reign about 1375 B.C.E. and died or was murdered about fifteen years later. He drove the priests from the temples, effaced the names of the traditional deities from the public monuments, and initiated the worship of a new god whom he called "Aton," an ancient designation for the physical sun. He changed his own name from Amenhotep ("Amon rests") to Akhenaton, which meant "Aton is satisfied." His wife Nefertiti became Nefer-nefru-aton, which meant "beautiful is the beauty of Aton." In keeping with his desire to begin all over, Akhenaton built a new capital, El-Amarna, which he dedicated to the worship of the new deity.

Akhenaton. A life-sized, weathered bust.

More important than these physical changes was the set of doctrines enunciated by the reforming pharaoh. He taught first of all a religion of qualified monotheism. Aton and Akhenaton himself were the only gods in existence. Unprecedentedly, Aton had no human or animal shape but was conceived in terms of the life-giving, warming rays of the sun. He was the creator of all, and thus god not merely of Egypt but of the whole universe. Akhenaton deemed himself to be Aton's heir and co-regent; while the pharaoh and his wife worshiped Aton, others were to worship Akhenaton as a living deity. Aside from this important qualification, Akhenaton emphasized the ethical quality of religion by insisting that Aton was the author of the moral order of the world and the rewarder of human integrity. He envisaged the new god as the sustainer of all that is beneficial and as a heavenly father who watches with benevolent care over all his creatures. Conceptions like these of the unity, righteousness, and benevolence of a god were not attained again until the time of the Hebrew prophets 600 years later.

Akhenaton, His Wife Nefertiti, and Their Children. The god Aton is depicted here as a sundisk, raining down his power on the royal family.

Despite the energy with which Akhenaton pursued his religious program it gained little popular following. Most people remained devoted to their old gods because the new religion was too strange for them and lacked the greatest attraction of the older faith: the promise of an afterlife. Moreover, the pharaohs who followed Akhenaton were allied with the priests of Amon and accordingly restored the older modes of worship. Akhenaton's successor, the pharaoh whom we refer to as "King Tut," changed his name from Tutankhaton to Tutankhamen, abandoned El-

A Pharaoh of the New Kingdom: King Tutankhamen Fighting the Nubians. This painting depicts the pharaoh using war chariots, which were to be employed to great effect against the Syrians by his successor, Ramses II.

Amarna for the old capital of Thebes, and presided over a return to all the old ways. His own burial was a lavish demonstration of commitment to the old rituals and belief in life after death.

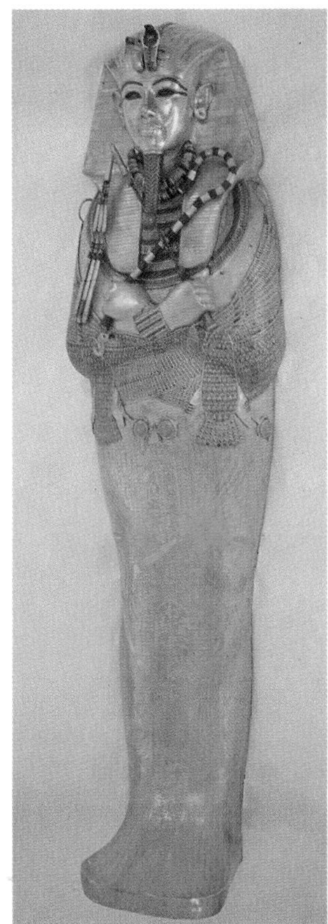

Tomb of Tutankhamen. Inside this solid-gold coffin weighing 2,500 pounds was the mummified body of King Tut.

Egyptian Intellectual Achievements

Aside from the varied richness of their religious thought, the greatest intellectual accomplishments of the Egyptians lay in their system of writing and in the realm of certain practical sciences. We have seen that Egyptian writing, hieroglyphic, emerged after the appearance of cuneiform writing in Mesopotamia, perhaps even with an awareness of the Mesopotamian precedent. Thus it is not so much the idea of writing as the particular nature of Egyptian writing that is worth consideration here. Specifically, as early as the time of the Old Kingdom, Egyptian hieroglyphic was based on three types of characters: the pictographic, the syllabic, and the alphabetic. The first two were already components of cuneiform, but the last was a crucially significant innovation. Had the Egyptians taken the step of separating their alphabetic characters—twenty-four symbols, each representing a single consonant sound of the human voice—from their nonalphabetic ones and using the former exclusively in their written communication they would have developed a writing system that was fully modern. Since a cultural conservatism kept them from doing this, it was left for a Semitic people of the eastern Mediterranean shore, the Phoenicians, to devise the first exclusively alphabetical system around 1100 B.C.E. The Phoenician alphabet in turn became the model for the alphabets of the Hebrews, Arabs, Greeks, and Romans. Nevertheless, since the Phoenicians definitely borrowed the idea of using single symbols for denoting single sounds from the Egyptians, and since they even modeled many of their letters on Egyptian exemplars, there is warrant for viewing the Egyptian alphabetical system as the parent of every alphabet that has been used in the Western world.

Writing on papyrus

Blessed with a plant, the papyrus reed, that grew abundantly in the Nile delta region (papyrus in Lower Egypt was so plentiful that it was the pictographic symbol in hieroglyphic for "Lower Egypt"), the Egyptians possessed a cheap material on which to write. Strips of the papyrus reed, when flattened and dried, could be used for setting down hieroglyphic and then rolled up into scrolls for storage or transport. The advantage of writing on papyrus over writing on clay tablets was that papyrus rolls were less cumbersome and vastly lighter: hence their use spread from the Egyptians to the civilizations of ancient Greece and Rome. (Could the Roman Empire have established its vast administrative system on clay tablets? It is doubtful.)

Practical nature of Egyptian science: (1) astronomy and the calendar

As for science, the Egyptians were most interested in those branches that aimed particularly at practical ends—astronomy, medicine, and mathematics. In the realm of astronomy the Egyptians' greatest achievement was their discovery of a way to avoid the imprecisions of a lunar calendar. We have seen that the peoples of ancient Mesopotamia remained limited in marking the passage of seasons and years to working with the cycles of the moon. In contrast, by around 2000 B.C.E. the Egyptians noticed that the brightest star in the sky, Sirius, rose in the morning once a year in direct alignment with the sun. Constructing a calendar on this observation, wherein "New Year's Day" began with Sirius's solar alignment, they could foretell the coming of the Nile's floods and produced the best calendar in antiquity before that devised by Julius Caesar. Indeed, Caesar's calendar itself rested on the Egyptian precedent.

(2) Medicine and a nature-based view of disease

Ancient Egyptian medical practice was distinguished by the view that diseases came from natural rather than supernatural causes and hence that physicians should provide accurate diagnoses and predictably reliable treatments. Among diagnostic methods was the taking of the pulse and the listening to the heartbeat. As for therapeutics, surviving papyrus documents show that some treatments must have been predictably reliable and others not. For example, Egyptian doctors prescribed castor oil as a cathartic but offered whipped ostrich eggs mixed with tortoise shells and thorns to cure internal ulcers. Concerned with hygiene as well as health, they proposed the following remedy for sweaty feet: "take uadu-plant-of-the-Fields and eel-from-the-Canal, warm in oil, and smear both feet therewith." While it is easy to smile at such prescriptions, the Egyptian attempt to alleviate pain and enhance health by natural means deserves respect, not to mention the fact that some Egyptian medicinal remedies, carried to Europe by the Greeks, are still employed today.

(3) Mathematics and measurement

In mathematics the Egyptians excelled in methods of measurement. For example, they were the first to mark off 360 degrees to a circle and the first to notice that the ratio of the circumference of a circle to its diameter is the same for all circles (today this is known as the "pi" ratio). They also devised means for computing the areas of triangles and the volumes of pyramids, cylinders, and hemispheres. Such accomplishments obviously were interrelated with the Egyptians' spectacular building projects, to which we will now turn.

The Splendor of Egyptian Art

The pyramids

The most famous of all Egyptian visual monuments are of course the pyramids—vast constructions of towering simplicity, built at the dawn of recorded time to serve as tombs of the pharaohs. Awe for the pyramids must extend from amazement at their stark beauty to astonishment regarding the circumstances of their construction. The earliest pyramid, the step-pyramid of the pharaoh Zoser, was erected around 2670 B.C.E. at a time when nothing remotely resembling its scale had ever been attempted by humanity. Whereas contemporary Sumerians built solely with mud bricks and prior Egyptians had gone no further than building floors and perhaps walls from a few tons of limestone, all of a sudden, under the guidance of Zoser's chief builder, Imhotep, one million tons of limestone were quarried, hauled without wheeled vehicles, and fitted precisely into place to a summit about 200 feet high. And that was just the

The Pyramids of Gizeh, built between 2600 and 2500 B.C.E. For thousands of Egyptians, pyramid-building was an interminable occupation passed on from generation to generation.

beginning. Soon after, in the century from roughly 2600 to roughly 2500 B.C.E., a total of some 25 million tons of limestone were hewn out of rock cliffs, dressed, hauled, and piled into a series of pyramids that are the most famous and beautiful of all. Of these the gem of gems is the pyramid of Khufu (a pharaoh known to the Greeks as Cheops), which rose to a height of 482 feet at the "perfect" angle of 52°, making its pinnacle stand in relation to its circumference as in the "pi" ratio of circles. When the Greeks decided to count the seven wonders of the world, they unhesitatingly ranked the pyramid of "Cheops" as the first.

The perennial summer's work

While the great pyramids remain for us to see, many questions arise as to how and why they were built. About seventy thousand laborers were needed to put up a pyramid. This work was almost certainly seasonal. During the summer months, when the Nile was at its flood stage, there was little for farmers to do, so they could be employed on massive building projects without detriment to the Egyptian agricultural economy. But one summer does not make a pyramid. Rather, it has recently been concluded that pyramid laborers must have worked summer after summer, starting on a new pyramid after the last one was finished, without reference to whether a reigning pharaoh had died or not, because that is the only way to account for the transformation of twenty-five million tons of stone into several enormous pyramids during the course of one century. Thus for thousands of people, hewing and hauling limestone in the raging heat of an Egyptian summer was a yearly way of life without prospect of termination.

The laborer's motivation: religious psychology and group dynamics

Why did seventy thousand laborers endure this? Brute coercion is surely not the answer, for Egypt at this time did not know slavery (aside from a small number of war captives); moreover, it is impossible to imagine that a handful of rulers could have forced tens of thousands of subjects to labor against their wills year after year without cowing them by any extraordinary weaponry. Religious psychology and group dynamics instead seem to provide the best explanations. The Egyptian laborers who built the pyramids apparently believed that their pharaohs were living gods who could ascend to eternal life upon their earthly exits solely by means of proper burial. Zoser's step-pyramid was thus in a literal sense a "stairway to heaven" and the later pyramids were simply straight-angle embodiments of the same ascent-to-heaven conception. The laborers who sweated to build these enormous monuments on the hot sands believed their own well-being was inextricably tied to that of their god-rulers: if the pharaohs journeyed well to their eternal glory, life on earth would flourish. In addition, collaborative labor must have given the individual toiler a sense of uplifting comradeship and team accomplishment. This point seems borne out by marks found on various pyramid stones reading "vigorous team," "enduring team," and so forth. Farmers who were relatively isolated during most of the year must have found teamwork on the most prestigious and exalted projects of the day to be a source of pride and emotional reward that made their heaving and sweating seem worthwhile.

The Great Sphinx at Gizeh.

Egyptian temples

Ultimately pyramid-building was recognized by Egyptian rulers to be a wasteful occupation. Since concern for personal salvation became the major religious trend during the time of the Middle Kingdom, the temple, then and afterwards, replaced the pyramid as Egypt's leading architectural form. The most noted Egyptian temples are those of Karnak and Luxor, built during the period of the New Kingdom. Many of their gigantic, richly carved columns still stand as silent witness to a splendid architectural talent. Egyptian temples were characterized by massive size. The temple at Karnak, with a length of about 1,300 feet, covered the largest area of any religious edifice ever built. Its central hall alone could contain almost any of the cathedrals of Europe. The columns used in the temples

The Temple at Karnak. Most of this building has collapsed or been carried away, but the huge columns give an idea of the massiveness of Egyptian temples.

had stupendous proportions. The largest were seventy feet high, with diameters in excess of twenty feet. It has been estimated that the capitals surmounting them could furnish standing room for a hundred people.

Egyptian sculpture served primarily as an adjunct to architecture. Sculpture was characterized by conventions governing its style and meaning. Statues of pharaohs were commonly of colossal size. Those produced during the New Kingdom ranged in height from seventy-five to ninety feet. Some of them were colored to enhance the portrait, and the eyes were frequently inlaid with rock crystal. The figures were nearly always rigid, with the arms folded across the chest or fixed to the sides of the body, and with the eyes staring straight ahead. Countenances were generally represented as slightly smiling but otherwise devoid of emotional expression. Anatomical distortion was customary: the natural length of the thighs might be increased, the squareness of the shoulders accentuated, or all of the fingers of the hand made equal in length. A familiar example of nonnaturalistic sculpture was the Sphinx, of which there were thousands in Egypt; the best-known example was the Great Sphinx at Gizeh. This represented the head of a pharaoh on the body of a lion. The purpose was probably to symbolize the notion that the pharaoh possessed the lion's qualities of strength and courage.

The meaning of Egyptian sculpture is not hard to perceive. The colossal size of the statues of pharaohs was doubtless intended to symbolize their power and the power of the state they represented. It is significant that the size of these statues increased as the Empire expanded and the government became more absolute. The conventions of rigidity and impassiveness were meant to express the timelessness and stability of the national life. Here was an empire that was not to be torn loose from its moorings by the uncertain mutations of fortune but was to remain fixed and imperturbable. The portraits of its rulers consequently must betray no anxiety, fear, or triumph, but an unvarying calmness throughout the ages.

An intriguing exception to the mainstream of Egyptian artistic development is the art produced during the reign of Akhenaton. Because the pharaoh wished to break with all manifestations of the ancient Egyptian religion, including its artistic conventions, he presided over an artistic revolution. The new style he patronized was naturalistic because his new religion revered nature as the handiwork of Aton. Accordingly portrait busts of the pharaoh himself and his queen Nefertiti abandoned the earlier stately impassivity and distortion in favor of more realistic detail. A surviving bust of Nefertiti that reveals her slightly quizzical and haunting femininity is one of the greatest monuments in the history of art. For the same reasons painting under the patronage of Akhenaton also emerged as a highly expressive art form. Murals of this period display the world of experience above all in terms of movement. They catch the instant action of the wild bull leaping in the swamp, the headlong flight of the frightened stag, and the effortless swimming of ducks in a pond. But just as Akhenaton's religious reform was not lasting, neither was the more naturalistic art of his reign.

Pharaoh Menkaure and His Queen. Above: A sculpture from the Fourth Dynasty, c. 2500 B.C.E.—an example of the impassive, stately style. Below: A comparison of their profiles leaves little doubt that they were brother and sister as well as husband and wife.

Social and Economic Life

Nefertiti. The famous portrait bust executed in Akhenaton's studios at El-Amarna.

During the greater part of the history of Egypt the population was divided into five classes: the royal family; the priests; the nobles; the middle class of scribes, merchants, artisans, and wealthy farmers; and the peasants, who comprised by far the bulk of the population. During the New Kingdom a sixth class, the professional soldiers, was added. Thousands of slaves were also captured in this period, and for a time they formed a seventh class. Despised by all, they were forced to labor in the government quarries and on the temple estates. Gradually, however, they were allowed to enlist in the army and even in the personal service of the pharaoh. With these developments they ceased to constitute a separate class. The position of the various ranks of society shifted from time to time. Most remarkable was the high social standing of merchants and artisans during the Middle Kingdom.

The gulf that separated the standards of living of the upper and lower classes of Egypt was enormous. The wealthy lived in splendid villas that opened onto fragrant gardens and shady groves. Their meals included many kinds of meat, poultry, cakes, fruit, wine, and sweets. They ate from vessels of alabaster, gold, and silver, and adorned themselves with costly jewels. In contrast, the life of the poor was wretched. Laborers in towns lived in mud-brick hovels whose only furnishings were stools, boxes, and a few crude pottery jars. A surviving verse from the Middle Kingdom tells of the "weaver in the workshop, with knees against his chest," who "cannot breathe air," and who is "beaten fifty strokes" if he does not keep up with his work.

Women

Compared to women in most other ancient societies, Egyptian women were not entirely subordinated to men. Although polygamy was permitted, it was not common; the basic social unit was the monogamous family. Even the pharaoh, who could keep secondary wives and concubines, had a chief wife. Women were not secluded. They could own and inherit property and engage in business. The Egyptians of the New Kingdom also permitted queens to act as royal regents: Queen Hatshepsut of the Eighteenth Dynasty "controlled the affairs of the land." In monumental statuary from the Eighteenth Dynasty some queens were depicted on an identical scale as their husbands.

Agriculture, trade, and industry

The Egyptian economy rested primarily upon an agrarian basis. Agriculture was diversified and highly developed, and the soil yielded excellent crops of wheat, barley, millet, vegetables, fruits, flax, and cotton. Theoretically the land was the property of the pharaoh, but in the earlier periods he granted most of it to his subjects, so that in actual practice it was largely in the possession of individuals. Commerce grew steadily after about 2000 B.C.E. to a position of primary importance. A flourishing trade was carried on with the island of Crete and with Lebanon on the eastern Mediterranean shore. Gold mines in Nubia controlled by Egypt were an important source of wealth. The chief articles of export consisted of gold, wheat, and linen fabrics, with imports being confined primarily to silver,

Throne of "King Tut." Dating from about 1360 B.C.E., this relief in gold and silver is part of the back of the young pharaoh's throne. The relaxed lounging position of the pharaoh's right arm is typical of the stylistic informality of the period.

ivory, and lumber. Of no less significance than commerce was manufacturing. As early as 3000 B.C.E. large numbers of people were engaged in artisanal crafts. Later, factories were established, employing twenty or more persons under one roof, and with some degree of division of labor. The leading industries were shipbuilding and the manufacture of pottery, glass, and textiles.

The development of instruments of business

From an early date the Egyptians made progress in the development of instruments of business. They knew the elements of accounting and

Fishing and Fowling: Wall Painting, Thebes, Eighteenth Dynasty. Most of the women appear to belong to the prosperous classes, while the simple garb and insignificant size of the men indicate that they are probably slaves.

Egyptian Slaves at Work. A wall painting done around 1550 B.C.E. displays slave-laborers making bricks.

bookkeeping. Their merchants issued orders and receipts for goods. They invented deeds for property, written contracts, and wills. While they had no system of coinage, they had rings of copper or gold of set weight circulated as exchange, in effect the oldest known currency in the history of civilizations. The simple dealings of the peasants and poorer townsfolk, however, were doubtless based on barter.

Economic collectivism

The Egyptian economic system was primarily collective. From the very beginning the energies of the people had been drawn into socialized channels. The interests of the individual and the interests of society were conceived as identical. The productive activities of the entire nation revolved around huge state enterprises, and the government remained by far the largest employer of labor. But this collectivism was not all-inclusive; a considerable sphere was left for private initiative. Merchants conducted their own businesses; many of the craftsmen had their own shops; and as time went on, larger and larger numbers of peasants gained the status of independent farmers. The government continued to operate the quarries and mines, to build pyramids and temples, and to farm the royal estates.

The Egyptian Achievement

Peace and self-sufficiency

When a party of Greeks visited the Nile valley about 500 B.C.E. a dignified Egyptian priest supposedly told them, "You Greeks are always children; there is not an old man among you." The point of course is that members of a civilization that had lasted for two and a half millennia considered the Greeks to be mere whippersnappers: Egypt was into its Twenty-sixth Dynasty when the Greeks were just beginning to organize their thoughts. Seen from today's perspective, the relatively untroubled longevity of Egyptian civilization still commands respect. Apparently the ancient Egyptians had found a way to cooperate with nature and each other in order to live in peace and self-sufficiency for centuries at a stretch. The Greeks, who conquered the Egyptians in 332 B.C.E., were vastly more experimental and creative, but they also introduced continual upheaval into an Egyptian world that until then had been characterized by stability.

Egypt's unique circumstances

The ancient Egyptian success formula was so closely bound to the annual flooding of the Nile that it could not easily be transported. Hence, aside from a few specific accomplishments such as the solar calendar or the calculation of cubic volumes, the Egyptian achievement is not best estimated by the directness of its influence on subsequent thought or events. Rather, Egyptian patterns of living, thinking, sculpting, painting, and building are fascinating for their own sake. There is something in all of us that makes us wish we could go back in time to view Nefertiti, listen to King Tut's priests intone their timeless hymns, or float on a barge down the Nile past lotus-flowers while the pyramids are rising. This is understandable awe for a civilization that found its place in the sun when history's sun was still at its dawn.

SUMMARY POINTS

- After the unification of Lower and Upper Egypt around 3100 B.C.E., ancient Egypt was ruled by a succession of pharaoh dynasties, divided into three "kingdoms." Although the three kingdoms were characterized by stability, the interspersed "intermediate" periods brought invasion, warfare, and foreign rule.
- For the most part, Egyptian religion was polytheistic; the major gods were the sun god, variously called Re, Amon, or Amon-Re, and the nature god Osiris. During the New Kingdom, the Pharaoh Akhenaton attempted to institute a monotheistic religion, but it did not supplant the devotion of the people to their old gods.
- Egyptian achievements in architecture are wondrous even today: the pyramids that served as tombs for the pharaohs and the great temples that served the religious needs of the Egyptian people. In addition, Egyptian civilization developed a system of writing and excelled in geometry and measurement.
- The relative stability of ancient Egypt and the lush fertility of the Nile valley gave rise to a rich social and economic life, with diversified agriculture and commerce.

Selected Readings

Aldred, Cyril, *Akhenaten: Pharaoh of Egypt,* London, 1968. The standard treatment in English.

Butzer, Karl W., *Early Hydraulic Civilization in Egypt: A Study in Cultural Ecology,* Chicago, 1976. A careful analysis of the Nile valley as an ecosystem. Downplays grandeur in favor of examining the conditions of daily existence.

Cambridge Ancient History (3d ed., vols. I–III), Cambridge, 1971–1996.

Cottrell, Leonard, *Life under the Pharaohs,* New York, 1960. Fascinating account of life under the Empire.

Mendelssohn, Kurt, *The Riddle of the Pyramids,* London, 1974. A lucid account of how the pyramids were built and a persuasive interpretation of why they were built.

Redford, Donald B., *Akhenaten: The Heretic King,* Princeton, 1984. Takes a more negative view of the controversial pharaoh than that offered by Aldred.

Rice, Michael, *Egypt's Making: The Origins of Ancient Egypt, 5000–2000 BC,* London, 1990. An engaging account of earliest Egypt, through the end of the Old Kingdom.

Robins, Gay, *Women in Ancient Egypt,* Cambridge, Mass., 1993. Authoritative and accessible.

Trigger, B. G., et al., *Ancient Egypt: A Social History,* London, 1983. The standard guide; difficult reading.

Wilson, John A., *The Burden of Egypt: An Interpretation of Ancient Egyptian Culture,* Chicago, 1951. (Paperback edition under title of *The Culture of Ancient Egypt.*) Still the best book to read if the student wishes to read just one. Scintillating and masterful.

Source Materials

Grayson, A. Kirk, and D. B. Redford, eds., *Papyrus and Tablet,* Englewood Cliffs, N.J., 1973. The best short collection.

Lichtheim, M., *Ancient Egyptian Literature,* 3 vols., Berkeley, 1973–1980. The standard selection.

Parkinson, R. B., *Voices from Ancient Egypt: An Anthology of Middle Kingdom Writings,* Norman, Okla., 1991.

CHAPTER 4

THE HEBREW AND EARLY GREEK CIVILIZATIONS

I am the Lord thy God, which brought thee out of the land of Egypt from the house of bondage.
Thou shalt have none other gods before me. . . .
Thou shalt not take the name of the Lord thy God in vain.

—Deuteronomy 5:6–11

Then Agamemnon awoke from slumber . . . and put on a soft tunic, fair and new, and he threw a great cloak about him; about his shining feet he bound fair sandals. . . . Then he grasped his ancestral sceptre, indestructible forever.

—HOMER, *The Iliad*

DWARFED BY THE GREAT EMPIRES of Mesopotamia and Egypt in territory and military prowess, the civilizations of the Hebrews and the early Greeks nonetheless merit full consideration. The extraordinary historical significance of the Hebrews lies beyond challenge, for despite their political insignificance, the Hebrews exerted the greatest influence of any ancient western Asian peoples on the thought and life of the modern world. As for the ancient Greek civilizations (as will be seen in this chapter, there were two of them), they are memorable for their grace and sophistication and for being the earliest civilizations of Europe.

THE RECORD OF POLITICAL HOPES AND FRUSTRATIONS

Hebrews enter Canaan

Students of the earliest history of the Hebrews tend to disregard the biblical narratives of events transpiring between Abraham and Moses on the grounds that these were set down many hundreds of years after the events they describe and may have been entirely legendary. The earliest mention of "Israelites"—another name for the Hebrews—in a nonbiblical source comes from an Egyptian inscription of about 1220 B.C.E. Since this has been interpreted to apply to a time when the Hebrews had begun fighting to win the land of Canaan, it is with this set of events that we

A Canaanite Deity. Thought to be an image of Baal, a god of storms and fertility, this statuette was discovered in a thirteenth-century B.C.E. temple in northern Palestine.

will begin. Whether or not the Hebrews, members of a Semitic language family, had been enslaved in Egypt (some archeological evidence suggests this is likely), they surely entered the "promised land" of Canaan (southern Syria) by crossing the River Jordan from the east. Their intent was to conquer as much of Canaan, in their eyes a "land flowing with milk and honey," as they could, but they were not easily able to do this because they were a pastoral people, divided into tribes, with no centralized leadership. Above all, they lacked the equipment and organization necessary to reduce the well-fortified Canaanite cities by siege warfare. Although the walls of Jericho may have come "a-tumbling down," not many followed, and it took more than a century, that is until about 1100 B.C.E., for the Hebrews to gain full control of the region.

Hardly had the Hebrews become masters of Canaan than they had to defend themselves against the Philistines, a non-Semitic people of uncertain origins, who quickly conquered so much of the region around 1050 B.C.E. that it became known as Palestine, meaning "the Philistine country." Faced with the threat of extinction, the Hebrews now put up desperate resistance. Whereas hitherto they had practiced a form of organization whereby tribal leaders known as judges were elected to lead the armies of their respective tribes in times of war, it now became clear that a tighter, "national" form of government was necessary to meet the Philistine challenge. Accordingly, around 1025 B.C.E., Samuel, a tribal judge with the force of personality to gain adherence from all the Hebrew tribes, selected for them a king who would make them a united people.

The reign of King Saul

Although the reign of this king, Saul, marked the beginning of Hebrew national unity, it was problematic. Saul asserted himself so much as a ruler that he provoked the resentment of Samuel, who had expected to remain the power behind the throne. So Samuel began to support a young warrior, David, who carried out skillful maneuvers to draw popular support away from Saul. Waging his own military campaigns, David achieved one triumph over the Philistines after another. (His victory over "Goliath" would have been accomplished with more than a slingshot.) In contrast, the armies of Saul met frequent reverses. Finally the king, being critically wounded, ended the rivalry by slaying himself. The date would have been roughly 1005 B.C.E.—close enough to the millennium marker to make it easy to remember.

David as absolute monarch

With Saul in his grave, David became king and initiated the most glorious period in Hebrew political history—at least until modern times. Advancing relentlessly against the Philistines, he reduced their territory to a narrow strip of coast in the south. He incorporated the native Canaanites under his dominion to such a degree that during the next few generations they lost their separate identity and became fully merged with the Hebrew people. As this process of amalgamation progressed, the Hebrews increasingly put aside pastoralism and took up either farming or urban occupations. Once David fully established his position as absolute monarch, he exacted forced labor from some of his subjects, instituted a census as a basis for collecting taxes, and then actually started to collect taxes. His ultimate goal was to build a splendid capital and religious center at Jerusalem, but although he made some progress in this enterprise he died before the work was completed.

Solomon, Jerusalem, and the Temple

David was succeeded by his son Solomon, who ruled from 973 to 933 B.C.E., the last of the three kings of the united Hebrew monarchy. Solomon was determined to finish his father's work in building Jerusalem. The purpose was twofold. First, if the Hebrews were to take their place among the great nations of western Asia, they had to have a magnificent capital as a visual manifestation of their greatness. And second, they also needed a splendid temple to reaffirm their national religious commitment. Until then the "Ark of the Covenant," the biblical name for the chest containing the stone tablets supposedly given by the Hebrew god Yahweh (Jehovah) to Moses on Mount Sinai, had been carried by them in their wanderings in a "tabernacle," actually no more than a portable tent. To house an exalted shrine in a tent may have been barely satisfactory for a nomadic people, but not for settled agriculturalists of a great nation. Instead, the ark, the physical token of a special relationship with Yahweh, had to be located in a mighty capital and housed properly in the innermost precincts of a splendid temple. For these reasons Solomon spared no expense in building his capital, and especially in building the temple that would be the central monument of Hebrew national and religious life. In the long run this policy contributed fundamentally to the survival of the Hebrews, for Solomon indeed succeeded in erecting a splendid temple, and Solomon's Temple thereafter served as an inspiring symbol whenever they were faced with the possibility of national and cultural obliteration. But in the short term the king's lavish building projects caused trouble because Palestine was poor in the resources needed for basic building materials, not to mention lacking in the gold and gems needed to adorn these projects. When, despite mountingly oppressive taxation, Solomon found himself unable to pay his construction debts, he first ceded territory to his main supplier, the bordering country (to the north) of Phoenicia, and then he drafted and deported Hebrews to work in Phoenicia's forests and mines.

Northern antagonism and secession

Not surprisingly, such tyrannical behavior provoked bitter antagonism among many of Solomon's subjects, especially those of the north. The northerners were the ones who saw their sons forcibly sent to Phoenicia, and they were least sympathetic to the building projects in Jerusalem, which lay more to the south of the Hebrew kingdom. (Apparently the northerners were also less ardent in exclusive dedication to Yahweh than the southerners, still another reason why they would have been less enthusiastic about making personal sacrifices to import gold for the Ark of the Covenant.) While Solomon remained alive his northern subjects remained obedient to him, but his death was the signal for open revolt. Refusing to pay taxes to Solomon's son Rehoboam, the northerners quickly seceded from the united Hebrew state and set up their own kingdom.

The fragility and fate of the kingdoms of Israel and Judah

The northern kingdom came to be known as the Kingdom of Israel, having its capital in Samaria, while the remnant in the south was the

Kingdom of Judah, with its capital in Jerusalem. Even as a united state the Hebrew realm would not have been impressively strong, but split in half it became pitifully weak. More by luck and the forbearance of its neighbors than by intrinsic viability the Kingdom of Israel managed to survive (usually paying tribute) for two centuries until 722 B.C.E., when it was annihilated by the Assyrians. Since the Assyrians followed a policy of leveling all the important buildings of conquered nations and scattering their populations, the Kingdom of Israel never rose again. As for the Kingdom of Judah, it just barely eluded the Assyrian menace, partly because of its very insignificance, but in 586 B.C.E. it was conquered by the Babylonians under Nebuchadnezzar, who plundered and burned Jerusalem and its Temple, deporting Judah's leading citizens to Babylon. For a half-century

Palestine after the Death of King Solomon

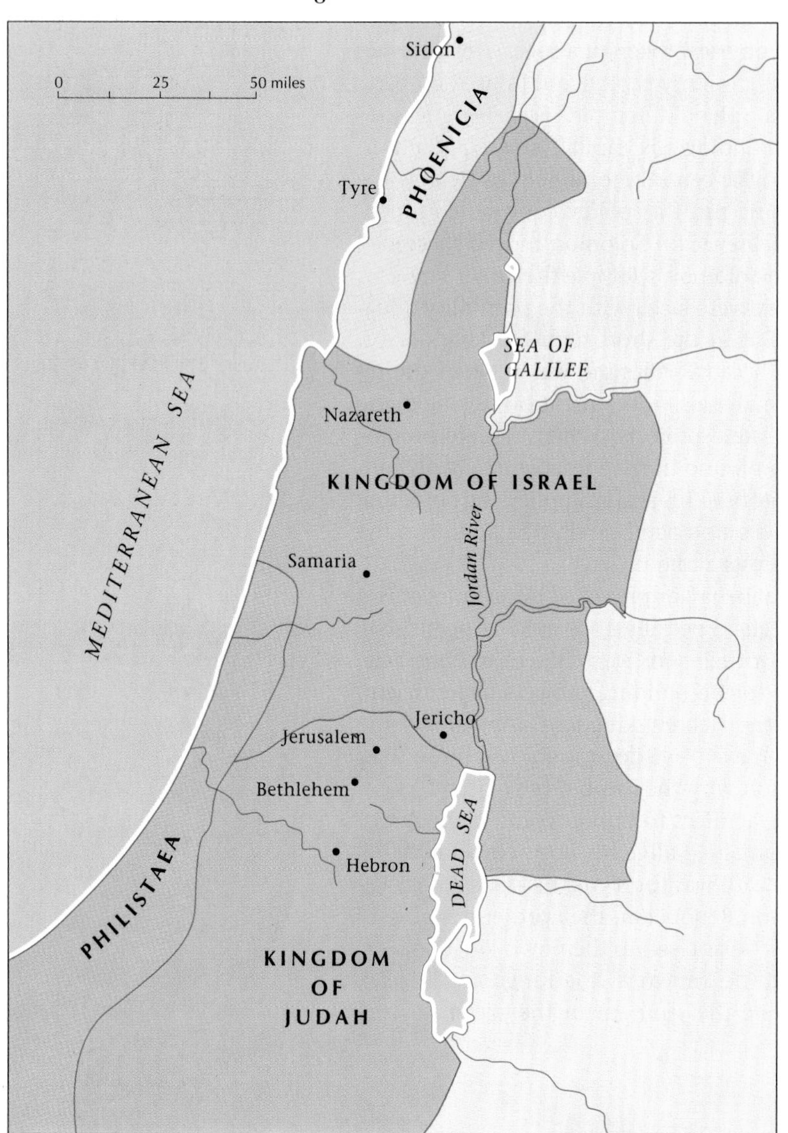

thereafter the Judeans—from this point customarily called the Jews by historians—suffered their "Babylonian Captivity," fearing that they would never again see their homeland.

Palestine: from Persian overlordship to Roman annexation

They were mistaken. Upon conquering Babylon in 539 B.C.E. Cyrus the Persian magnanimously allowed the Jews to return to Palestine and to establish their rule there semi-independently under Persian overlordship. The returnees wasted no time in rebuilding the Jerusalem Temple (accomplished from 520 to 516 B.C.E.), and their heirs lived more or less peacefully within the Persian sphere of influence until 332 B.C.E., when Palestine was conquered by the Greek Alexander the Great. Since Alexander died soon afterwards the Jews passed under the rule of successive Greek-speaking overlords. In 168 B.C.E., one of them, Antiochus Epiphanes, attempted to destroy the Jewish faith by desecrating the Temple and prohibiting all worship in it, but this ruthlessness provoked a Jewish revolt led by the inspiring fighter Judas Maccabeus. After two decades of struggle the Jews of Palestine finally succeeded in gaining political independence under the rule of a native Maccabean dynasty, but that situation lasted only until 63 B.C.E., when the Roman general Pompey took advantage of the dynasty's internal feuding to turn Palestine into a Roman protectorate. Resentful of Roman rule, the Jews revolted in 66 C.E. in a desperate attempt to recreate the victory over Antiochus. But this time they faced the mightiest of all ancient empires and lost all they had. In 70 C.E. the Roman emperor Titus put down the Jewish uprising mercilessly and razed the Temple, which has never been rebuilt since. Palestine then was annexed outright by the Romans, and the Jews gradually left for other parts of the vast Roman Empire, including Egypt. The diaspora, or migration of the Jews away from Palestine to country after country through the centuries, became the central fact of Jewish existence from then until the twentieth century.

Roman Coin Celebrating the Destruction of Jerusalem. The inscription IVDAEA CAPTA means "Judea captured," and "S. C." is a standard abbreviation for "with consent of the Senate." A triumphant Roman soldier lords it over a female personification of the Jews shown in an attitude of dejection.

Hebrew Religious Development

Jewish religion a product of evolution

Even during King David's time the ancient Hebrews were no more than a second-rate political power, and after Solomon's reign they were not even that. Hence the Hebrews would not be worth more than passing consideration here were it not for their achievements in religion. Today Judaism, the religion of the Jews, is a coherent body of beliefs, customs, and liturgical practices, all of which are founded in passages from the Jewish Bible (known to Christians as the Old Testament). The student of history, however, must recognize that Judaism did not spring suddenly into place in one moment but was the product of a long process of change.

Stage of national monolatry

Four stages can be distinguished in the growth of the Hebrew religion. In the first, known only by inference, the Hebrews were *polytheists* (worshipers of many gods), like all other contemporary western Asian peoples. Then came the stage of national *monolatry*, initiated around 1220 B.C.E. and lasting until about 750 B.C.E. Monolatry means the exclusive worship of one god, without denying the existence of others. In this phase the people of Israel adopted as their national deity a god whose name was written "Yhwh" and was probably pronounced as if spelled "Yahweh," and they agreed to worship no other gods. Yahweh was conceived mainly in anthropomorphic terms. He possessed a physical body and was sometimes capricious or irascible, occasionally punishing someone who had sinned accidentally. For example, he struck someone dead merely for placing his hand on the Ark of the Covenant to steady it while it was being carried to Jerusalem (I Chronicles 13:9–10). Nor was Yahweh omnipotent, for his power was limited to the territory occupied by the Hebrews.

Transcendent theology

Despite these holdovers from more primitive religious systems, some of the Hebrews' most important contributions to subsequent Western thought emerged during this time. One was their unique *transcendent theology*. In their view God was not part of nature but entirely outside of it; thus he could become understood in purely intellectual or abstract terms. Complementing the principle of divine transcendence was the principle that humans were rulers of nature by divine mandate. This is stated explicitly in the famous line from Genesis in which God tells Adam and Eve, "be fruitful and multiply, and replenish the earth and subdue it, and have dominion over . . . every living thing." The quotation contrasts strikingly with parallel Babylonian creation accounts in which humans are created merely to serve the gods, "that they might be at ease." Finally, while not fully developed, ethical considerations are already present in this period. According to the Babylonian flood story a certain petulant god decides to destroy humanity on the grounds that their noise deprives him of sleep, whereas Yahweh in Genesis sends a flood because of human wickedness and saves only Noah and his family because "Noah was a just man."

Moral precepts, rituals, and tabus

The Hebrews honored Yahweh during the period of monolatry by subscribing to moral precepts, rituals, and tabus. Although it is uncertain whether the exact form of the Ten Commandments, as they became known from the seventh century B.C.E. onward (the form found in Exodus 20:3–17), existed before the Babylonian Captivity, the Hebrews cer-

Menorah Mosaic from a Synagogue Pavement. After the Romans destroyed the Second Temple the seven-branched candelabrum (*menorah*) became the identifying emblem for Judaism because the candelabrum formerly had been placed next to the "Ark of the Covenant" in the Temple and now stood for the missing Temple itself. In this mosaic from a synagogue of Jericho (twenty-five miles east of Jerusalem), done around 500 C.E., the menorah is complemented by a branch associated with the Harvest Festival and a ram's horn (shofar) sounded at the New Year. The inscription reads "Peace upon Israel."

tainly observed some set of commandments, including ethical ones such as injunctions against murder, adultery, bearing false witness, and "coveting anything that is thy neighbor's." In addition they observed ritualistic demands, such as celebrating feasts and offering sacrifices, and prohibitions, such as refraining from labor on the seventh day or boiling a kid in its mother's milk. Although moral standards may have been observed within the Hebrew community, they were not always considered applicable when dealing with outsiders. Thus even in regard to murder the Hebrews were no more averse to slaughtering civilians in warfare than were the Assyrians. When the Hebrews conquered territories in Canaan they took "all the spoil of the cities, and every man they smote with the sword . . . until they had destroyed them, neither left they any to breathe." Rather than having any doubts about such a brutal policy, they believed it had been ordered by their Lord himself—indeed that Yahweh had inspired the Canaanites to offer resistance so that there would be reason to slaughter them: "For it was of the Lord to harden their hearts, that they should come against Israel in battle, that He might destroy them utterly" (Joshua 11:20).

The prophetic revolution

In comparison to such dubious notions of divine justice, the ideas advanced during the third stage of Hebrew religious development can be deemed revolutionary; in fact the stage is customarily called that of the *prophetic revolution.* The "prophets" who effected this revolution in religious thought lived at the time of the threat to Hebrew nationhood coming from Assyria and Babylonia and during the period of the exile in Babylon, that is, from roughly 750 to roughly 550 B.C.E. Although the word "prophet" has come to mean someone who predicts the future, its original meaning is closer to "preacher"—more exactly someone who has an urgent message to proclaim, in the belief that his message derives from divine inspiration. The foremost Hebrew prophets were Amos and Hosea, who "prophesied" (i.e., preached and exhorted) in the Kingdom of Israel shortly before its fall in 722 B.C.E.; Isaiah and Jeremiah, who prophesied in Judah before its fall in 586 B.C.E.; and Ezekiel and the second Isaiah (the Book of Isaiah was written by three different authors), who prophesied "by the waters of Babylon." Initially warning of imminent disaster to Israelites who worshiped and behaved improperly, and then announcing the justice of God's retribution, these men's messages were sufficiently similar to each other to warrant treating them as if they formed a single coherent body of religious thought.

The prophets' teachings

Three doctrines made up the core of the prophets' teachings: (1) thoroughgoing monotheism—Yahweh is the ruler of the universe; He even makes use of nations other than the Hebrews to accomplish His purposes; the gods of others are false gods; (2) Yahweh is exclusively a god of righteousness; He wills only the good, and evil in the world comes from humanity, not from Him; (3) since Yahweh is righteous, He demands ethical behavior from His Hebrew children more than anything else; He cares less for ritual and sacrifice than that His followers should "seek justice, relieve the oppressed, protect the fatherless, and plead for the widow."

Merged with the Canaanites and practicing settled agriculture after the time of David, some Hebrews had reverted to offering sacrifices to Canaanite fertility gods in the hope that such sacrifices would ensure rich harvests, while others who remained loyal to Yahweh dedicated themselves ever more to ritualism as a demonstration of their loyalty. In fierce opposition to such practices, the prophet Amos summed up the prophetic revolution and marked one of the epoch-making moments in human cultural development when he expressed Yahweh's resounding warning:

> I hate, I despise your feasts,
> and I take no delight in your solemn assemblies.
> Even though you offer me your burnt offer-
> ings and cereal offerings,
> I will not accept them,
> and the peace offerings of your fatted beasts
> I will not look upon.
> Take away from me the noise of your songs;
> to the melody of your harps I will not listen.
> But let justice roll down like waters,
> and righteousness like an ever-flowing
> stream. —Amos 5:21–24

The postexilic stage

The last stage in the shaping of Judaism took place during the four centuries after the return of the Jews from Babylon; thus it is called the postexilic stage. The major contribution of postexilic religious thinkers was a set of eschatological doctrines, writings on "last things" or what will happen at the end of time. Under the indirect or direct sway of Persians and Greeks, and during the years of the Maccabean revolt, Jewish thinkers in Palestine began to wonder increasingly about what role their small and politically weak nation would play in the divine plan for the world, and hence began to fix upon messianic and millenarian expectations. In other words, they came to believe that God would soon send them a national savior or "messiah" (meaning "anointed one"), who would not only lift up the Jews to greatness but would spread the worship of Yahweh to the entire world during a millennium of peace and justice before the end of time. At first they assumed that the millennial kingdom of peace would be "this-worldly"—that humans would live to see and enjoy it, as in the words of the third Isaiah, "for as the earth bringeth forth her bud . . . so the Lord God will cause righteousness and praise to spring forth before nations" (Isaiah 61:11). But as time went on, the likelihood that the millennial kingdom would arise naturally "as the earth brings forth its bud" seemed for some ever more remote, with the alternative of otherworldly triumph seeming to them more inescapable. The fullest statement of otherworldly eschatology in the Old Testament appears in the Book of Daniel, written not by a Daniel who may have lived at the time of Nebuchadnezzar, but instead by someone who wrote under Daniel's name during the time of the revolt of the Maccabees. In the view of this seer, the messiah, called by him "the Son of Man," would come

Jewish Sarcophagus. A wealthy Jew commissioned this sarcophagus around 100 C.E. Today he would emblemize his religion with a Star of David, but then the standard emblem for Judaism was the menorah. Under the menorah are the three Hebrew children in the fiery furnace from the Book of Daniel, probably meant here to stand for the immortality of the soul and the patron's own hope for eternal life.

"with the clouds of heaven," and would have an "everlasting dominion, which shall not pass away" (Daniel 7:13–14). Integral to this otherworldly view was the belief that the messiah would preside over a "last judgment"; in other words, that by supernatural means all the human dead would be resurrected to stand at judgment before the messiah for the quality of their lives, evil men and women being condemned to eternal suffering, "saints" remaining to serve in the "greatness of the kingdom under the whole heaven" (Daniel 7:26–28).

Hopes for the coming of the messiah

The Jewish expectation of a messiah has obvious bearing on the career of Jesus, a Jew who was considered to be the messiah by Jewish and Gentile followers who thereafter became known as Christians. (Further treatment of the split of Christianity from Judaism will be found in Chapter 8.) The Jews who denied that Jesus was the messiah continued to expect that the messiah would come. Some thought of him as coming in the clouds, as in Daniel, but most expected him to be an earthly savior who would exalt the nation of Israel and rebuild the Temple. Either way the expectation of the miraculous coming of the messiah motivated the Jewish people to maintain all their other beliefs and practices steadfastly even when they were forced to live thousands of miles away from the Holy Land. To a large degree it accounts for the real Jewish miracle—the capacity of an otherwise insignificant nation to endure until the present despite appalling adversity, enriching the world by its accomplishments in myriad ways.

Hebrew Law and Literature

Hebrew culture: limitations and accomplishments

The ancient Hebrews were not great scientists, builders, or artists. So far as can be judged, even Solomon's Temple was not really a Hebrew building accomplishment, for it appears that Phoenician masons and artisans were called in to address the most challenging construction tasks involved in the project. Since the Hebrew religious code prohibited the making of any "graven image" or "likeness" of anything in heaven, earth, or water (Exodus 20:4), there was no sculpture and no painting. Instead it was in law and literature that ancient Hebrew culture found its most estimable expressions.

Hebrew law: the Deuteronomic Code

The major repository of Hebrew law is the Deuteronomic Code, which forms the core of the biblical Book of Deuteronomy. Although partly based on very ancient traditions that display kinship with the legal thought of the Old Babylonians, the Deuteronomic Code in its present form undoubtedly dates from the time of the prophetic revolution. In general its provisions are more altruistic and equitable than the laws found in the Old Babylonian Code of Hammurabi. It not only enjoins generosity to the poor and to the stranger, but it prescribes that the Hebrew slave who had served six years should be freed and given some provisions to start his own life. Fairness is found in principles dictating that children should not be held responsible for the guilt of their fathers and that judges under no circumstances should be allowed to accept gifts. Above all the Deuteronomic Code upholds the stringent ideal of what is "altogether just," for Yahweh demands no less.

Hebrew literature

Taken in total the literature of the Hebrews was the finest produced by any ancient civilization of western Asia. All of it that survives is found in the Old Testament and in the books of the Apocrypha (ancient Hebrew works not recognized as scriptural because of doubtful religious authority). Except for a few fragments like the Song of Deborah in Judges 5, the Old Testament is not really so old as is commonly supposed. Scholars now recognize that it was created from a series of collections and revisions in which old and new parts were merged and generally assigned to an ancient author such as Moses. The oldest of these revisions was not prepared any earlier than 850 B.C.E. and the majority of the books of the Old Testament were compiled still later.

Old Testament literary qualities

Granted that parts of the Old Testament consist of long lists of names or arcane ritual prohibitions, others, whether biographical or military narratives, thanksgiving prayers, battle hymns, prophetic exhortations, love lyrics, or dialogues, are rich in rhythm, evocative imagery, and emotional vigor. Few passages in any language can surpass the chaste beauty of the Twenty-third Psalm: "the Lord is my shepherd, I shall not want. He maketh me to lie down in green pastures, he leadeth me beside the still waters. He restoreth my soul . . ."; or the vision of peace in Isaiah: "and they shall beat their swords into plowshares, and their spears into pruninghooks; nation shall not lift up sword against nation, neither shall they learn war any more."

Song of Songs

Among the most beautiful of all the world's love lyrics is the biblical Song of Songs. Although generations of readers have sought to find figurative spiritual meaning in it (and some modern critics tell us we are free to

Hebrew Inscription from a Synagogue Pavement. The Hebrew people created no statuary because of the biblical injunction against "graven images," and the same injunction apparently prohibited all figural art until roughly the time of Christ. Here, in a mosaic pavement from Palestine dating from about 900 C.E., a dedication and prayer take the place of art. Note that Hebrew writing moves from right to left.

find any meaning in any text we choose), the Song of Songs surely originated around the fifth century B.C.E. as a collection of purely secular wedding poems. The bridegroom and bride rejoice together in the prospect of sharing caresses and a loving life together in the orchards and the vineyards: "Rise up, my love, my fair one, and come away. For lo, the winter is past, the rain is over and gone; the flowers appear on the earth . . . and the vines with the tender grape give a good smell. . . . Behold, thou art fair, my love . . . thou hast doves' eyes . . . thy teeth are like a flock of sheep that are even shorn." Particularly striking is the gender balance and the mutuality of sexual desire: "I am my beloved's, and my beloved is mine."

The Book of Job

An entirely different variety of Hebrew literary achievement is the Book of Job, written sometime between 500 and 300 B.C.E. In form the work is a drama of the tragic struggle between man and fate. Its central theme is the problem of evil: how it can be that the righteous suffer while the wicked prosper. The story was an old one, adapted very probably from an Old Babylonian writing of similar content. But the Hebrews introduced into it a much deeper realization of philosophical possibilities. The main character, Job, a man of virtue, is suddenly overtaken by a series of disasters: he is despoiled of his property, his children are killed, and his body is afflicted with disease. His attitude at first is one of stoic resignation; the evil must be accepted along with the good. But as his sufferings increase he is plunged into despair. He curses the day of his birth and praises death, where "the wicked cease from troubling and the weary be at rest."

The problem of evil in Job

Then follows a lengthy debate between Job and his friends over the meaning of evil. The latter take the view that all suffering is a punishment for sin, and that those who repent are forgiven and strengthened in character. But Job is not satisfied with any of their arguments. Torn between hope and despair, he strives to review the problem from every angle. He even considers the possibility that death may not be the end, that there may be some adjustment of the balance hereafter. But the mood of despair returns, and he decides that God is an omnipotent demon, destroying without mercy wherever His caprice or anger directs. Finally, in his anguish he appeals to the Almighty to reveal Himself and make known His ways to him. God answers him out of the whirlwind with a magnificent exposition of the tremendous works of nature. Convinced of his own insignificance and of the unutterable majesty of God, Job despises himself and repents in dust and ashes. In the end no solution for the problem of individual suffering is given. No promise is made of recompense in a life hereafter, nor does God make any effort to refute the hopeless pessimism of Job. Humans must take comfort in the philosophic reflection that the universe is greater than themselves, and that God in the pursuit of His sublime purposes cannot really be limited by human standards of equity and goodness.

Book of Ecclesiastes

As different as the lyric Song of Songs and the tragic Book of Job are from each other, the bleakly worldly-wise Book of Ecclesiastes is different from both. Unquestionably this book, attributed to Solomon but surely written no earlier than the third century B.C.E., contains some of the Bible's most pithy and forceful quotations. Yet its doctrine contradicts all the elevated presuppositions found in the rest of the Hebrew Bible, for the author of Ecclesiastes was a skeptic and a materialist. According to him humans die just like beasts, no afterlife being granted to either, and human history is no more than the successive passing away of generations. Everything is cyclical, and nothing adds up to lasting achievement, for "the sun also rises and the sun goeth down, and hasteth to the place where he arose . . . and there is nothing new under the sun." On top of all this purposeless repetition, in the realm of human affairs blind fate rather than merit predominates, for "the race is not to the swift, nor the battle to the strong . . . nor yet riches to men of understanding, nor yet favor to men of skill, but time and chance happen to them all." In light of these circumstances the author proposes taking life as it comes without excess: "be not righteous overmuch, neither make thyself over wise . . . be not over much wicked, neither be thou foolish: why shouldest thou die before thy time?" Surprisingly in view of his bleakness he also "commends mirth" on the grounds that "a man hath no better thing under the sun than to eat, and drink, and to be merry."

Old Testament ultimately affirmative

How it came about that a text which offers the maxim "be not righteous overmuch" crept into the Hebrew Bible remains uncertain, but it cannot be stressed overmuch that it is exceptional. Therefore, rather than ending this survey of Hebrew literature with Ecclesiastes, it is best to point out that the last prophetic book of the Hebrew Bible, Malachi, ends on a highly characteristic note, both in terms of its prophetic-eschatological message and its vigorously affirmative expression, when it has Yahweh state, "unto you that fear my name shall the Sun of righteousness arise with healing in his wings. . . . and ye shall tread down the wicked. . . . Behold, I will send you Elijah the prophet before the coming of the great and dreadful day of the Lord."

The Magnitude of the Hebrew Influence

The Hebrew legacy

The history of Western existence during the past two thousand years has been profoundly influenced by the Hebrew heritage, partly because of the activities of the Jews and partly because Judaism was the matrix from whence sprang Christianity. (As will be seen in Chapter 9, a third great world religion, Islam, grew from both Judaism and Christianity.) Virtually all religious believers in the West today are monotheists—descendants in belief, therefore, from the Hebrew prophets. In addition Hebrew transcendent theology has given westerners the sense of assurance that they are masters of nature and need not waver in cutting down trees or changing the courses of rivers for fear of angering forest or water deities. Whether in its religious version or its secular adaptations, this worldview has surely contributed enormously to Western technological initiative. The morality shaped by the great Hebrew prophets remains the morality most ethically sensitive people today cherish: "Love thy neighbor as thyself" (Leviticus 19:18) speaks better than any paraphrase. And the vision of a world united in peace, when "nation shall not lift up sword against nation" (Isaiah 2:4), is a vision that we all know must be implemented soon or else no tradition will mean anything to anyone.

The Minoan and Mycenaean Civilizations

Ancient Greek civilizations

Before 1870 no one guessed that great civilizations flourished in the Greek archipelago many hundreds of years before the rise of Athens. Students of the Greek epic Homer's *Iliad,* of course, knew that a mighty Greek king, Agamemnon, was supposed to have led all the Greeks to victory in the "Trojan War" long before the eighth century B.C.E., when the *Iliad* was first set down in writing. But it was simply assumed that Homer's entire plot was fictional. Today, however, scholars are certain that Greek history—and thus European history—began well over one thousand years before Socrates started discussing the nature of truth in the Athenian marketplace.

The discoveries of Schliemann

The breakthrough into certain knowledge of these ancient Greek civilizations came about as the result of the most famous "storybook triumph" in the annals of archeology. In the middle of the nineteenth century the German businessman Heinrich Schliemann, fascinated from youth by the narrative in the *Iliad,* determined to prove his hunch that there was substantial truth in it. Luckily Schliemann accumulated a fortune in his business ventures and thereupon retired to spend his time and his money in pursuit of Agamemnon. Although he had no archeological or scholarly training, in 1870 he began excavating in western Asia Minor at a site he felt confident was that of ancient Troy, and, amazingly enough, soon after he began digging he uncovered portions of nine different ancient cities, each built upon the ruins of its predecessor.

Schliemann identified the second of these cities as the Troy of the *Iliad,* but scholars now believe that Troy was the sixth or seventh city. Encouraged by his success, he started excavations in Greece in 1876, and lo and behold, he struck gold again—this time literally as well as figuratively because he hit upon a grave site containing gold in staggering quantities. Since Schliemann's dig of 1876 was located at a deserted Greek site called Mycenae (pronounced Myseénee), he felt vindicated because the *Iliad* stated that Mycenae was Agamemnon's place of residence and termed it "Mycenae rich in gold." It is sad to report that Schliemann's excavations were not unqualifiedly beneficial to the study of the distant past because in his zealous enthusiasm and disregard of scientific procedures he destroyed evidence as he dug and scorned meticulous record-keeping. Yet all told his discoveries were so exciting and momentous that they themselves almost merit being memorialized in an epic.

Arthur Evans discovers Knossos

Once Schliemann demonstrated that there was some truth in what formerly had been regarded as legend, others rushed to add to his discoveries. His most important successor in this regard was the Englishman Arthur Evans. In 1899 Evans began looking for "Minos" as Schliemann had been looking for Agamemnon—which meant that Evans began excavating on the Greek island of Crete because legend had identified the city

The Early Aegean World

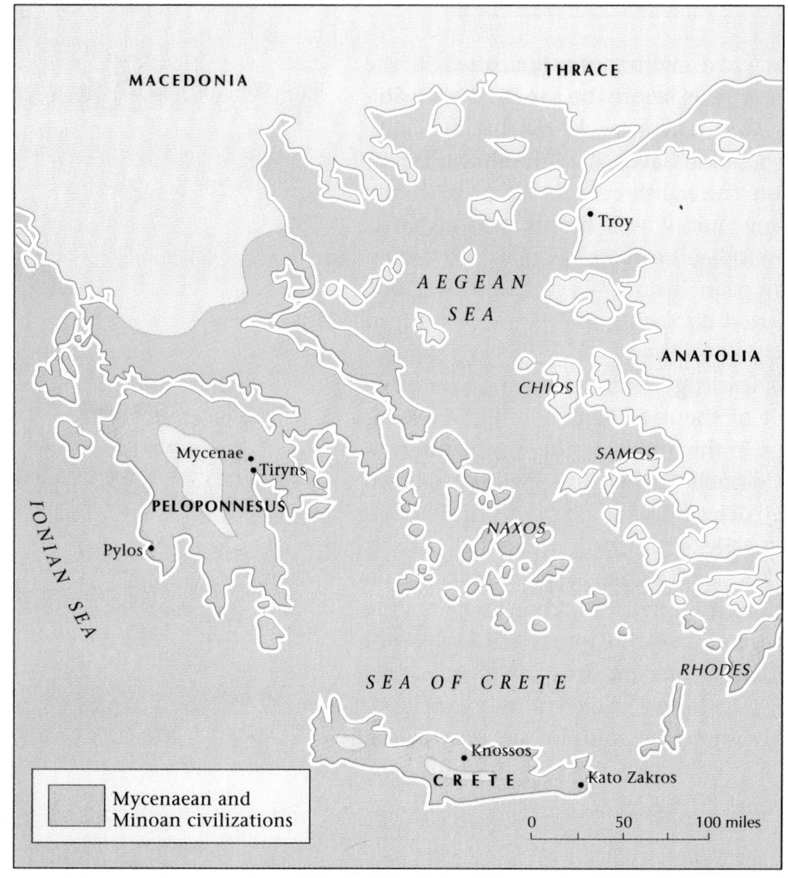

of Knossos on Crete as the capital of a mighty empire ruled over by a ruler named Minos. Again, legend proved to have some kernel of fact, for Evans soon found remains as rich (and indeed more beautiful) than anything dug up by Schliemann. Although Evans's work (which earned him a knighthood) followed after Schliemann's, the civilization he found at Knossos dates back earlier than the Greek civilization uncovered by Schliemann. Hence we should look at the "world of Minos" before we see how it became drawn into the "world of Agamemnon."

Cretan Labyrinth Coin. According to legend, King Minos of Crete built a labyrinth to pen in the Minotaur, part man, part bull. This coin from about 300 B.C.E. shows the labyrinth as the emblem of Knossos.

The earliest traces of the *Minoan civilization,* so called by modern scholars after the legendary Cretan ruler Minos, date from the period around 2000 B.C.E. Around that time the Minoans, whose origins before they inhabited Crete are unknown, had begun to build cities and to develop a unique form of writing. The half-millennium from about 2000 to 1500 B.C.E. saw Minoan civilization at its peak. Rather than being the center of an empire, Knossos was one of several thriving cities on Crete that coexisted so harmoniously that none of them found it necessary to build protective walls. Only earthquakes, which periodically shook the island, interrupted the Minoans' serene existence. These natural disasters caused much devastation, but after each the Minoans set about rebuilding their cities and usually managed to found more splendid ones than those that had just been destroyed. At Knossos Arthur Evans found not just beautiful stonework and paintings but humanity's first known flush-toilet. Later excavations at another Minoan site, Kato Zakros, unearthed a huge palace with 250 rooms, a swimming pool, and parquet floors.

Flowering of Minoan civilization

While the Minoan civilization was flourishing on Crete, potential rivals were gaining strength on the mainland of Greece. Around 2200 B.C.E. Indo-European peoples who spoke the earliest form of Greek invaded the Greek peninsula, and by 1600 B.C.E. they had begun to form small cities. Primarily owing to trading relations, these peoples gradually became influenced in their cultural development by Minoan Crete. The

Origins of the Mycenaean civilization

Central Staircase of the Palace at Knossos

A Linear B Tablet from Knossos

civilization that resulted from the fusion of Greek and Minoan elements is called Mycenaean after Mycenae, the leading city of Greece from about 1600 to 1200 B.C.E. It was this civilization that became dominant in the Aegean world (the Aegean Sea is that part of the Mediterranean lying between Greece and Asia Minor) after about 1500 B.C.E. and even gained predominance on Crete itself.

Linear B

One of the greatest scholarly accomplishments of the twentieth century radically altered our understanding of Cretan and Greek history in the century between 1500 and 1400 B.C.E. It was once thought that Greece throughout that time was still a semibarbarous economic colony of splendid Crete and that internal changes on Crete between 1500 and 1400 B.C.E. could be attributed to the rise of a "new dynasty." It was known that numerous specimens of the same linear script (called "Linear B") could be found on both Crete and the Greek mainland, but it was simply assumed that the script was Cretan in origin and spread from Crete to Greece. But in 1952 a brilliant young Englishman, Michael Ventris, who was then only thirty years old (and tragically died in an automobile accident four years later), succeeded in deciphering Linear B and demonstrating that it expressed an early form of Greek. Ventris's discovery revolutionized preclassical Greek studies by showing that the mainlanders dominated Crete in the late Minoan period and not vice versa.

Wall Painting from Thera. The volcanic eruption on the island of Thera preserved many splendid paintings. Here an elegant priestess is burning incense.

Scholars now agree that the Mycenaeans supplanted the Minoans as rulers of the Aegean world shortly after 1500 B.C.E., although they are uncertain exactly how that happened. In any event, during the following century and a half the Mycenaeans presided over an era of prosperity and artistic accomplishment on Crete. But around 1350 B.C.E. another wave of Mycenaeans crossed over to Crete, destroyed Knossos, and put a sudden end to advanced civilization on the island. Why this invasion was so destructive remains unknown, but it left mainland Greece unrivaled as the dominant power of the Aegean world for about another two hundred years. Around 1250 B.C.E., the Mycenaeans waged their successful war with the Trojans of western Asia Minor, but their own downfall was now on the horizon. In the course of the century between 1200 and 1100 B.C.E., the Mycenaeans succumbed to the Dorians—barbaric northern Greeks who had iron weapons. (Iron weapons may not at first have been much superior to the bronze ones used by the Mycenaeans, but since iron ore was found far more widely in western Asia and eastern Europe than the copper and tin needed for bronze, iron weapons were much cheaper, thereby allowing many more fighters to wield them.) Because the Dorians were primitive in all but their weaponry, their ascendancy constituted a dark age in Greek history that lasted until about 800 B.C.E.

Problems in interpreting Minoan civilization

As can be seen from the foregoing account, the Minoan and Mycenaean civilizations were closely interrelated; even the greatest experts have difficulty in determining exactly where one left off and the other began. The problem is complicated by the fact that two forms of writing that predate Linear B and have been found on Crete alone have not yet been deciphered. (Anyone who wishes to become as famous as Schliemann, Evans, or Ventris may take the decipherment of Minoan writing as his or her goal.) Accordingly, discussions of Minoan civilization before about 1500 B.C.E. rely exclusively on visual and archeological evidence, leaving much to the realm of speculation. Such evidence, however, does suggest that Minoan civilization was one of the most progressive in all of early history.

Minoan peace and plenty

Modern archeologists, convinced of "man's inhumanity to man," are constantly looking for evidence of hostile aggressiveness in the civilization of Minoan Crete but hitherto have had little success. The palaces lacked fortifications, the art lacked bristling warlords, and women's clothing, at least for the upper class, was so elegant that it would be eye-catching at a modern Milanese fashion show. Two circumstances help to account for what was so obviously a world of peace and prosperity. One was that, living on an island in an age unfamiliar with seaborne invasions, the Minoans must have felt insulated from foreign attack. The other was that a friendly climate and terrain suitable for pasturing and growing orchard crops (grapes, olives, nuts) freed the Minoans from heavy reliance on labor-intensive agriculture. This meant that not only did people have more leisure than their counterparts in agricultural societies, but produce was more diverse, providing a greater hedge against famine and allowing for long-distance trade in goods that were less easily produced elsewhere. To take but one example, the Minoans had plentiful wool and various kinds of natural dyes; since wool, unlike linen, is easily dyed, Minoans were exporting "exotic" multipatterned luxury cloths to Egypt as early as about 2000 B.C.E.

Minoan Textile Design. The elaborate patterning of Minoan cloth was recorded by an Egyptian artist around 1900 B.C.E.

At first, over a period of centuries, Crete seems to have had different regional rulers, each with a base in his own large palace. (The palaces were indeed so large and had so many rooms that one of them endured in later Greek legend as a "labyrinth.") In or near the palaces were workshops that manufactured fine pottery, textiles, and metal goods. The rulers seem to have lived in harmony with one another, although toward the end of the Minoan period (exactly when is uncertain) the ruler of Knossos managed to gain control over the entire island. The rulers governed by means of an administrative class: scribes who kept close accounts of all aspects of economic life. Farming and manufacturing were pursued either by the ruler's direct employees or by those who were subject to him; in either case their output was supervised for the purposes of taxation or exacting a part of it. Foreign trade seems to have been regulated in the same manner. Most likely the Minoan ships that landed in ports as far distant as Syria and Egypt were owned or at least heavily taxed by the ruler and carefully watched over by the bureaucratic administration.

Despite such close supervision, Minoans of all classes seem to have led reasonably prosperous lives. If slavery existed at all, it occupied an unimportant place. The dwellings apparently designed for laborers were well built and spacious, often with as many as six or eight rooms. (We do not know, however, how many families lived in them.) Women took part in public activities; in this regard they were the exception in the ancient world. Minoan Crete had female priests, female bullfighters, and even female boxers. Although the men wore simple loincloths, the women dressed gorgeously; flaring skirts and plunging necklines were characteristic. Cloths were woven out of brightly contrasting colors—red, blue, yellow, white—and dresses sometimes were decorated with flounces, tassels, and zigzag edgings. The modern historian of ancient cloth production, Elizabeth Wayland Barber, emphasizes that the women who designed such costumes must have been having fun.

The Minoans had sufficient leisure to engage in communal games and sports. Dancing, foot-racing, and boxing rivaled each other as the main attractions. Every palace yet excavated shows outdoor stone steps meant to serve like benches in a modern sports arena; surviving art shows that people sat on them to watch colorfully attired women dance. Archeological discoveries indicate that the Minoans were also gifted inventors and engineers. They built excellent stone roads about eleven feet wide. Many of the principles of modern sanitary engineering were known to the designers of the palace of Knossos, with the result that the royal family of Crete in the seventeenth century B.C.E. enjoyed comforts and conve-

Minoan Woman. This drawing is of a clay figurine dating from around 1900 B.C.E. The flaring skirt, plunging neckline, and "designer hat" show a delight in dressing that was intrinsic to upper-class Minoan culture.

Minoan Women Picking Saffron. This copy of a Minoan wall painting shows two young women, in characteristically elegant attire, gathering parts of flowers to be used in preparing a bright yellow dye.

niences, such as indoor running water, that were not available to the royalty of western Europe even in the seventeenth century C.E.

If any achievement of the Minoans best demonstrates the vitality of their civilization, it was their genius in painting. With the exception of the artistry that evolved a millennium later under the classical Greeks and Romans, no art of the ancient world was its equal. The distinguishing features of Minoan painting were delicacy and spontaneity. It served not to glorify the ambitions of an arrogant ruling class or to inculcate the doctrines of a religion, but to express the delight of the individual in the beauty of the Minoan world. Most of Minoan painting consisted of murals done in fresco, but painted reliefs were occasionally to be found. The murals in the palaces of Crete are surely the best that have survived from ancient times, revealing instincts for the dramatic and rhythmic and the capturing of nature in its changing moods. So sophisticated and elegant was Minoan art that a Frenchman who was unearthing the remains of a fresco at Knossos could not help exclaiming when he saw a painting of a striking woman portrayed with curls, vivid eyes, and sensuous lips: "Mais, c'est la Parisienne!" ("Why, she's just like a woman from Paris!").

"La Parisienne"

Sculpture and crafts

Not surprisingly for a people dedicated to elegance, artistic excellence among the Minoans extended from painting to sculpture and even to household objects of everyday use. Perhaps the most noteworthy fact about Minoan sculpture is that its scale is always reduced. One looks in vain among Minoan remains for equivalents of giant Mesopotamian kings smiting their puny enemies or colossal pharaohs of Egypt advancing toward the beholder like enormous zombies, for the ancient Minoans were averse to relying on size for creating stunning effects. Instead, Minoan statues of human figures are almost always smaller than life-size,

Scenes from the Bull Ring: Minoan Mural, c. 1500 B.C.E. Evident are the youth, skill, and agility of the Minoan athletes, the center one a male, the other two female. The body and horns of the bull are exaggerated, as are the slenderness of the athletes and their full-face eyes in profile heads. There is probably also some exaggeration in content: modern experts in bullfighting insist that it is impossible to somersault over the back of a charging bull.

and they rely on grace and delicacy to engage the imagination of the viewer. Similarly, carved gems, gold-work and bronze-work, and ceramics down to the humblest crockery utensils are invariably finely wrought and sometimes wryly humorous.

Minoan Snake Goddess. A statuette in ivory and gold discovered near the palace of Knossos and dating from about 1550 B.C.E.

Mycenaean civilization appears to have been more warlike and less refined than the Minoan, but recent scholarship warns us to beware of exaggerating these differences. Trade still flourished: Mycenaean artifacts have been found in areas as far distant as Britain and Egypt. As on Crete, so on mainland Greece, the palace was the center of civilization—the leading Mycenaean ones being located at Mycenae itself, Pylos, and Tiryns. Each palace and its surrounding area was ruled over by a king called a *wanax*. As on Crete, the Mycenaean state was a bureaucratic monarchy. We know about some of the workings of this monarchy because of the decipherment of numerous Linear B tablets, all of which are records of a highly regulatory government. Linear B tablets from Pylos report the minutest details of the economic lives of the king's subjects: the exact acreage of a given estate; the number of cooking utensils owned by so-and-so; the personal names given to somebody's two oxen ("Glossy" and "Blackie"). Such detailed inventories show us that the state was highly centralized and that it was supreme in its control over the economic activities of its citizens.

Although the bureaucratic monarchies of the Minoans and the Mycenaeans were similar, there were still at least a few notable differences between the two related civilizations. One was that the Mycenaeans definitely had a slave system. Mycenaean society was also geared much more toward warfare. Because Mycenaean cities frequently fought with one another they were built on hilltops and were heavily fortified. In keeping with a somewhat more rugged and barbaric style of life than that of Crete, Mycenaean kings built themselves ostentatious graves in which they buried their best inlaid bronze daggers and other signs of power and wealth.

Mycenaean art

It is also true that Mycenaean art is less elegant than Minoan art. Without question the Mycenaeans never equaled the artistic delicacy and grace of the Minoans. Nevertheless, Mycenaean artwork done in Knossos between 1500 and 1400 B.C.E., while stiffer and more symmetrical in composition than earlier Minoan work, is by no means wholly different in kind. Moreover, a female procession fresco from about 1300 B.C.E. found in Mycenaean Tiryns shows stylistic resemblance to the "Parisian woman" of Minoan Knossos. Nor should it be thought that all the best traits of Mycenaean art can be seen merely as debased borrowings from the Minoans: the superbly executed and exquisite Mycenaean inlaid daggers have no antecedents anywhere on Crete.

Influence of the Minoan and Mycenaean civilizations

The significance of the Minoan and the Mycenaean civilizations should not be estimated primarily in terms of subsequent influences. Minoan culture hardly influenced any peoples other than the Mycenaeans, and it was then destroyed more or less without a trace after about 1400

B.C.E. The Mycenaeans left behind a few more traces, but still not very many. Later Greeks retained some Mycenaean gods and goddesses such as Zeus, Hera, and Poseidon, but they completely altered their role in the religious pantheon. It may also be that the later Greeks gained from the Mycenaeans their devotion to athletics and their system of weights and measures, but these connections remain uncertain. Homer definitely remembered the successful Mycenaean siege of Troy, but it is just as important to realize how much Homer forgot: writing in the eighth century B.C.E. Homer (actually several different writers who have come down to us under that name) entirely forgot the whole pattern of Mycenaean bureaucracy that we know from the Linear B tablets. It may well be that the break between the Mycenaeans and the later Greeks was all for the good. Some historians maintain that the destruction of despotic Mycenae by the Dorians was a necessary prelude to the emergence of the freer and more enlightened later Greek outlook.

A Minoan Vase, c. 1400 B.C.E. Minoan potters glorified in creating a great variety of shapes.

Importance of the Minoan and Mycenaean civilizations

Although the Minoan and Mycenaean civilizations had little subsequent influence, they are still noteworthy for at least four reasons. First of all, they were the earliest civilizations of Europe. Before the Minoan accomplishments all civilizations had existed farther east, but afterward Europe was to witness the development of one impressive civilization after another. Second, in some respects the Minoans and the Mycenaeans seem to have looked forward to certain later European values and accomplishments even if they did not directly influence them. Minoan and Mycenaean political organization was similar to that of many Asian states, but Minoan art in particular seems very different and more characteristic of later European patterns. Third, the Minoan civilization, and to a lesser degree also the Mycenaean one, is significant for its worldly and progressive outlook. This is exemplified in the devotion of the Aegean peoples to comfort and opulence, in their love of amusement, zest for life, and courage for experimentation. And finally, whereas ancient Assyria, ancient Babylon, and even ancient Egypt all breathed their last as "corpses in armor," ancient Crete breathed its last amid joyous festivals celebrated in palaces without walls.

SUMMARY POINTS

- The Hebrews entered Canaan around 1200 B.C.E. and established a united kingdom to defend themselves against the Philistines. Their unity lasted only about a century, however, after which the Hebrews split into two weak kingdoms, Israel and Judah. Both of these were successively conquered, and the Hebrews were ruled in turn by the Assyrians and the Babylonians, then the Persians, the Greeks, and finally the Romans.

- Judaism evolved over a millennium into a monotheistic religion, characterized by a transcendent theology, ethical and moral precepts, and doctrines about what will happen at the end of time.
- Ancient Hebrew culture made its most impressive contributions in the realms of law and literature; much of the Hebrews' surviving work can be found in the Old Testament and the Apocrypha.
- The earliest civilizations of Europe, those of the Minoans and Mycenaeans, flourished on Crete and mainland Greece hundreds of years before classical Greek civilization arose. The peaceful and prosperous Minoans, noted for the grace and elegance of their surviving artwork, saw their peak between about 2000 and 1500 B.C.E. Both the Minoans and the more warlike Mycenaeans, who flourished between about 1500 and 1200 B.C.E., developed centralized administrative bureaucracies.

Selected Readings

HEBREWS

Anderson, Bernhard W., *Understanding the Old Testament,* 4th ed., Englewood Cliffs, N.J., 1986.

Baron, Salo W., *A Social and Religious History of the Jews,* rev. ed., 18 vols., New York, 1952–1980. A modern classic: much work on Jewish history takes Baron as a point of departure.

Hermann, Siegfried, *A History of Israel in Old Testament Times,* 2d ed., Philadelphia, 1981.

Meyers, Carol L., *Discovering Eve: Ancient Israelite Women in Context,* New York, 1988. Argues persuasively that women had a more active role in early Hebrew society than can be seen from most of the Hebrew Bible.

Moorey, P. R. S., *The Biblical Lands,* New York, 1991. A lavishly illustrated, well-written introduction that emphasizes recent archeological findings.

Shanks, Hershel, ed., *Ancient Israel: A Short History from Abraham to the Roman Destruction of the Temple,* Washington, D.C., 1988. A series of chapters meant for the beginner written by different experts.

MINOANS AND MYCENAEANS

Blegen, Carl W., *Troy and the Trojans,* New York, 1963. The most reliable archeological appraisal.

Chadwick, John, *The Mycenaean World,* New York, 1976. A lively account of Mycenaean society based on the evidence of the Linear B tablets.

Dickinson, Oliver, *The Aegean Bronze Age,* Cambridge, Eng., 1994. The most up-to-date survey, but difficult reading.

Higgins, Reynold, *Minoan and Mycenaean Art,* rev. ed., London, 1981.

McDonald, William A., and Carol G. Thomas, *Progress into the Past: The Rediscovery of Mycenaean Civilization,* 2d ed., Bloomington, Ind., 1990.

Vermeule, Emily, *Greece in the Bronze Age,* Chicago, 1972. The best book on the subject.

PART TWO

THE CLASSICAL CIVILIZATIONS OF GREECE AND ROME

AFTER ABOUT 600 B.C.E. the once mighty civilizations of Mesopotamia and Egypt became overshadowed and then dominated by the classical civilizations of Greece and Rome. The word *classical* comes from the Latin *classicus,* meaning "of the first class," and is customarily used to denote the civilization that flourished in Greece between about 600 B.C.E. and 300 B.C.E. and the one centered in Rome between about 300 B.C.E. and 300 C.E. Although the classical Roman civilization gradually began to take shape around the time when the classical Greek civilization was losing its independent identity, "Rome" did not directly supplant "Greece." Rather, transpiring chronologically between the heydays of the Greek and Roman civilizations was the time of the Hellenistic civilization, a hybrid composed of elements derived from Greece and western Asia. Based territorially on conquests of Alexander the Great completed in 323 B.C.E., the Hellenistic civilization extended over all of Greece, all of Egypt, and most of Asia up to the borders of India, and it maintained its separate identity from 323 B.C.E. until shortly before the birth of Christ. The outstanding characteristic that distinguishes the three civilizations in question from those that had gone before was their secularism. No longer did religion absorb the interests and expend the wealth of humans to the extent that it did in ancient Mesopotamia and Egypt. The state now became much more independent of the priesthood, and the life of the mind was freed from the dictates of organized belief systems. In addition, ideals of human freedom and an emphasis on the welfare of the individual superseded the despotism and collectivism that characterized the civilizations of the Tigris, Euphrates, and Nile. Only late in the development of Roman civilization did despotism begin to reassert itself. Around that time too, a new religion, Christianity, began to reshape the lives of those who lived in the Roman world.

Young Roman Woman with Pen. A wall painting from Pompeii.

THE CLASSICAL CIVILIZATIONS OF GREECE AND ROME

	Politics	Philosophy and Science	Economics	Religion	Arts and Letters
	Dark Ages of Greek history (1500–800)				
800 B.C.E.	Beginning of city-states in Greece (c. 800)				Greek alphabet (c. 800–c. 700)
	Rome founded (c. 753)		Concentration of landed wealth in Greece (c. 750–c. 600) Greek overseas expansion (c. 750–c. 600)		*Iliad* and *Odyssey* (c. 750)
700 B.C.E.					
	Shift from cavalry to infantry in Greece (c. 650)				Doric architectural style (c. 650–c. 500)
				Zoroaster formulates Zoroastrian religion in Persia (c. 625)	
600 B.C.E.		Thales of Miletus (c. 600)	Invention of coinage by Lydians (c. 600)		
	Reforms of Solon in Athens (594)				
					Sappho (c. 550)
		Pythagoras (c. 530)			
					Aeschylus (525–456)
	Reforms of Clisthenes in Athens (508)				
500 B.C.E.	Establishment of Roman Republic (c. 500)		Royal Road of Persians (c. 500)	Orphic and other mystery cults (c. 500–c. 100)	Phidias (c. 500–c. 432)
					Sophocles (496–406)
	Greco-Persian War (490–479) Perfection of Athenian democracy (487–429)	Protagoras (c. 490–c. 420)			
					Herodotus (c. 484–c. 420) Euripides (480–406) Thucydides (c. 471–c. 400)
		Socrates (469–399) Hippocrates (460–c. 377) Democritus (c. 460–c. 362)			
	Law of the Twelve Tables, Rome (c. 450)	The Sophists (c. 450–c. 400)			
					Aristophanes (c. 448–c. 380) The Parthenon (447–438)
	Peloponnesian War (431–404)				
		Plato (429–347)			
400 B.C.E.					

THE CLASSICAL CIVILIZATIONS OF GREECE AND ROME

Politics	Philosophy and Science	Economics	Religion	Arts and Letters	
	Aristotle (384–322)			Praxiteles (c. 370–c. 310)	
	Epicurus (342–270)				
Macedonian conquest of Greece (338)					
Conquests of Alexander the Great (334–323)					
Division of Alexander's empire (323)	Euclid (c. 323–285)				
	Zeno the Stoic (c. 320–c. 250)				
	Aristarchus (310–230)				
		Hellenistic international trade and growth of large cities (c. 300 B.C.E.–c. 100 C.E.)	Emergence of Mithraism (c. 300)		300 B.C.E.
	Archimedes (c. 287–212)				
	Eratosthenes (c. 276–c. 195)				
Punic Wars between Rome and Carthage (264–146)					
		Growth of slavery, decline of small farmer in Rome (c. 250–100)	Oriental mystery cults in Rome (c. 250–50)		
	Herophilus (c. 220–c. 150)				
	Polybius (c. 205–118)				
	The Skeptics (c. 200)				200 B.C.E.
Destruction of Carthage by Romans in Third Punic War (146 B.C.E.)					
	Introduction of Greek philosophy into Rome (c. 140–c. 60)				
Reforms of the Gracchi (133–121)					
	Cicero (106–43)				100 B.C.E.
	Lucretius (98–55)				
				Virgil (70–19)	
				Horace (65–8)	
				Livy (59 B.C.E.–17 C.E.)	
Dictatorship of Julius Caesar (46–44)					
				Ovid (c. 43 B.C.E.–17 C.E.)	
	Seneca (34 B.C.E.–65 C.E.)				
Principate of Augustus Caesar (27 B.C.E.–14 C.E.)			Spread of Mithraism in Rome (27 B.C.E.–270 C.E.)		

THE CLASSICAL CIVILIZATIONS OF GREECE AND ROME

	Politics	Philosophy and Science	Economics	Religion	Arts and Letters
				The Crucifixion (c. 30)	
					Tacitus (c. 55–c. 117)
				St. Paul's missionary work (c. 35–c. 67)	
					The Colosseum (c. 80)
100 C.E.	"Five good emperors" in Rome (96–180)				
		Marcus Aurelius (121–180) Galen (130–c. 200)	Decline of slavery in Rome (c. 120–c. 476)		The Pantheon (c. 120) Height of Roman portrait statuary (c. 120–c. 250)
200 C.E.	Completion of Roman jurisprudence by great jurists (c. 200)		Growth of serfdom in Rome (c. 200–500) Sharp economic contraction in Rome (c. 200–c. 300)		
		Plotinus (c. 204–270)			
	Civil war in Roman Empire (235–284)				
	Diocletian (284–305)				
300 C.E.	Constantine I (306–337)				
				Beginning of toleration of Christians in the Roman Empire (311) Conversion of Constantine (312) St. Augustine (354–430)	
	Theodosius I (379–395)			Christianity made Roman religion (392)	
400 C.E.	Visigoths sack Rome (410)				
	Deposition of last Western Roman emperor (476)				
		Boethius (c. 480–524)			
500 C.E.	Theodoric the Ostrogoth king of Italy (493–526)				
				Benedictine monastic rule (c. 520)	
	Justinian (527–565)				
	Corpus of Roman law (c. 550)				

CHAPTER 5

GREEK CIVILIZATION

We love beauty without extravagance, and wisdom without weakness of will. Wealth we regard not as a means for private display but rather for public service; and poverty we consider no disgrace, although we think it is a disgrace not to try to overcome it. We believe a man should be concerned about public as well as private affairs, for we regard the person who takes no part in politics not as merely uninterested but as useless.

—PERICLES, *Funeral Oration,* on the ideals of Athens

Now, what is characteristic of any nature is that which is best for it and gives most joy. Such to man is the life according to reason, since it is this that makes him man.

—ARISTOTLE, *Nicomachean Ethics*

AMONG ALL THE PEOPLES of the ancient world, the one whose culture most clearly exemplified the spirit of Western society was the Greek or Hellenic. No other Western people had so strong a devotion to freedom or so firm a belief in the nobility of human achievement. The Greeks glorified humanity as the most important creation in the universe and refused to submit to the dictates of priests or despots. The Greek view of the world was predominantly secular and rationalistic; it exalted the spirit of free inquiry and preferred knowledge to faith. With only a limited cultural inheritance from the past upon which to build, the Greeks produced intellectual and artistic monuments that have served ever since as standards of achievement. "Wonders are many on earth, and the greatest of these are humans," the Greek tragic poet Sophocles proposed, to which we might well respond, "wonders were many in the ancient West, and the greatest of these were the Greeks."

THE GREEK DARK AGES

The Dark Ages

The fall of the Mycenaean civilization resulted in catastrophic change for the Hellenic world (*Hellas* is the Greek for "Greece"). It ushered in a period usually called the Dark Ages, which lasted from about 1150 to 800 B.C.E. Written records disappeared, and culture reverted to simpler forms. Toward the end of the period some decorated pottery and skillfully crafted metal objects began to appear on the islands of the Aegean Sea, but basically the period was a long night. Given the lack of writing or physical remains, our knowledge of Greek society during the Dark Ages is scanty, almost all of it coming from inferences drawn from the *Iliad* and the *Odyssey*. Since these epic poems, mistakenly attributed by the Greeks of later centuries to a single blind genius named Homer, evolved from oral traditions during the Dark Ages, they tell us the most we can hope to know of how the Greeks then lived.

Political patterns

Political patterns were very simple. Village communities were autonomous. The ruler of each, called *basileus* (Greek for "king"), was little more than a tribal leader who commanded the local army. Whatever assemblies existed were gatherings of warriors, convened informally to decide where and how to fight the next battle. Occasionally when warriors came together at such times they conferred about other matters of common concern, and they did what they could to put their decisions into effect. Formal legal institutions were entirely lacking—murder was punished (if at all) when the family of the victim took its revenge. A good illustration of the indifference of Greeks during the Dark Ages to organized government comes from the *Odyssey:* when Ulysses, king of Ithaca, was absent for twenty years, no regent replaced him, no assemblies were convened, and no one seemed to think that the absence of government was a matter of importance.

Social and economic life

Forms of social and economic life toward the end of the Dark Ages were equally simple. Everyone lived on the land. The kings and warriors, who together owned most of the land, were steadily occupied in the daily administration of their estates. Otherwise agriculture and herding were the basic occupations of free men. Although slavery existed, male slaves were relatively few in number because the source of supply was war prisoners, and males were usually slaughtered rather than taken prisoner. Almost all women, including the rulers' wives, worked in the home: in the *Odyssey* Ulysses' wife, Penelope, occupies her time with weaving during her husband's absence. But women were not secluded; on the evidence of the *Iliad* and *Odyssey* they were free to receive male guests and could walk outdoors among men without causing comment. Every household raised its own food, manufactured its own clothing, and even produced most of its tools. Indeed, the Greeks of this time were so far from being a trading people that they had no word in their language for "merchant."

Poseidon. The naked god brandishing his trident, which raises storms. A coin of about 540 B.C.E. from the Greek city of Posidonia (southern Italy), named for Poseidon.

To the Greeks of the Dark Ages religion meant chiefly a polytheistic system for explaining the workings of the physical world and for obtaining such earthly benefits as health, offspring, and abundant harvests. The Greeks did not expect that their religion would endow them with virtue or grant them everlasting rewards. Since piety was only a matter of pleasing the numerous gods by means of gifts and sacrifices, and modes of worship varied greatly, Greek religion lacked commandments, dogmas, or sacraments. The multiplicity of gods and goddesses in early Greek religion arose from two circumstances. First, all the deities originally were associated with certain regions or cities. The goddess Pallas Athena, for example, was thought to take a special interest in the well-being of Athens.

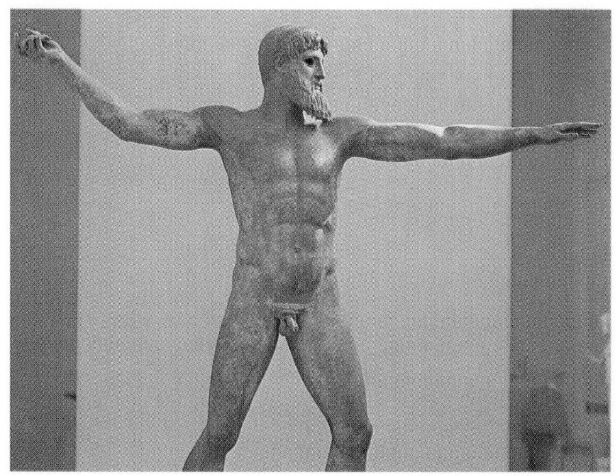

Left: **Zeus.** Right: **Aphrodite.** Both works of sculpture date from about 470 B.C.E. The male god communicates masculine majesty. Aphrodite (her Roman name was Venus) is shown rising from the sea in one of the earliest Greek works of art to exhibit naturalistic attention to the female body.

Second, the gods and goddesses, who continued to be worshipped as regional patrons, also became associated with specific blessings that all Greeks could obtain by appropriate invocations. Zeus, the mightiest of the gods, gathered the storms; if one wished to bring on or end rains, one gave gifts to him. Similarly, Poseidon might calm the waves; Aphrodite might bring success in love or marriage; Hermes might keep evil spirits away from doorways.

The gods of Hellas behaved much like humans. Thus individual believers could not rely on the gods' benevolence; rather they had to take divine jealousies and anger for granted. Truly chilling is the opening scene of the *Iliad,* wherein the god Apollo's implacable fury is vented on the whole Greek army because one of its leaders had offered a personal slight: "Phoebus Apollo came down from Olympus with a storm in his heart, descending black like the night. . . . With his arrows he shot at the pack-animals first, then at the dogs, then at the men, over and over again. Pyres burned for the dead day after day." With deities so terrible, individuals could only hope to ingratiate themselves with the gods by offering sacrifices and prayers as often and opportunely as possible. Despite this need for religious ceremonies, however, the Greeks perceived no need for a professional priesthood or houses of worship. Venerable members of a clan or community often presided over collective rites, but they did so only as a part-time duty; individuals could also sacrifice or pray alone. As for the well-known Greek temples, these were places where the gods were supposed to take up temporary residence rather than locations for human religious assemblage. Instead, rites were performed out of doors or at home.

Man Carrying a Calf for Sacrifice. A life-size Athenian sculpture from about 570 B.C.E.

Because the modern understanding of religion is so closely tied to hopes for the afterlife it may come as a surprise that the Greeks were largely indifferent to their fate after death. They did assume that shades or ghosts survived for a while after bodily death, yet all went to the same abode, a murky realm called Hades situated beneath the earth. This was neither a paradise nor a hell: no one was rewarded for good deeds, no one

The Early Greek Smile. Greek statues dating from the period when the city-states were taking shape already show a bemused view of human existence.

punished for sins. Since the shades in Hades gradually faded away, the only true immortality one might attain was earthly remembrance for one's earthly accomplishments.

Optimistic views of human life on earth

Indeed, the theme of human accomplishment bulks the largest in early Greek thought. The Greeks were convinced that life was worth living for its own sake and that glory resided not in self-abasement but in practicing human virtues such as bravery, wisdom (in the sense of cunning), and service to one's family and community. The Greeks also loved human beauty (according to the *Iliad,* the entire Trojan War was fought for the beautiful Helen) and sang songs in praise of great men and women. Whereas other neighboring early civilizations considered humanity contemptible in comparison to the omnipotent gods, the Greeks were well aware of forces beyond their control but did what they could to strike a balance between awe of their gods and pride in themselves. This confidence in human greatness was to characterize Hellenic civilization for centuries to come.

The Emergence of the City-States

The origin and nature of the city-states

About 800 B.C.E. the village communities, which rested mainly on tribal or clan organization, started growing into larger units centered on towns. Most often the towns were built on hills and were little more than fortifications with marketplaces. As time went on they gained more and more permanent residents and came to look more and more like cities. Thus emerged the *polis,* or city-state, consisting usually of a single city and all its surrounding territory. This was the unit that not only was to become the standard form of Hellenic political organization but created the modern notion of *political* life. (Our word "political" comes from polis.) In the years after 800 B.C.E., city-states emerged throughout the Greek world: Athens, Sparta, Thebes, and Corinth on the mainland; Miletus on the shore of Asia Minor; Naxos and Samos on the islands of the Aegean. The city-states varied greatly in area and population. Sparta with more than 3,000 square miles and Athens with 1,060 had the greatest territorial extent; the others averaged less than 100 square miles. Athens and Sparta, each with 300,000 to 350,000 inhabitants at the peak of their power, had approximately three times the populations of most of their neighbors.

The Greek alphabet

Behind the rise of the polis lay two interrelated developments: the revival of trade and the invention of the Greek alphabet. During the eighth century B.C.E., for reasons that remain unclear, the Greeks re-established trading links with western Asia, using new trading bases on Cyprus and the coast of Syria to gain access to commerce with wealthy Mesopotamia. As the Greeks' horizons broadened, they learned artisanal skills, especially of metalcraft. Most importantly, they also learned how to write—and now in a form entirely different from their writing of centuries earlier. Whereas the Bronze Age script assigned symbols for syllables, the Greeks now drew on the Phoenician system, which assigned symbols for individual sounds. But since the Phoenicians had no symbols for vowels, only consonants (this is still true of modern Arabic and Hebrew), the Greeks added letters to make up for that defect. The result was an alphabet consisting of separate signs for every consonant and vowel, a principle so familiar today it seems amazing it ever had to be invented.

Coin of the Gorgon Medusa. Viewing the face of Medusa supposedly turned men into stone. This Greek coin may have been meant to ward off evil spirits as well as to serve as an instrument of trade.

Because the Greek alphabet was so simple, literacy became widespread rather than being monopolized by a scribal caste. Consequently many Greeks learned how to keep records, sometimes for trading purposes, sometimes for estate management. This trend spurred the Greek economy ever more, producing greater wealth, as well as a growing population. The result was Greek expansion. At first, in the early eighth century B.C.E., this growth was of a purely commercial nature: warehouses and marketplaces would be established in overseas coastal settlements in order for small numbers of Greeks to carry on trade. But as the eighth century progressed and the Greek population at home began to outstrip its food supply, Greek settlers began to migrate abroad to establish new lives in farming rather than trade. This migration, which reached its peak during the period from about 735 until about 600 B.C.E., centered on southern Italy and Sicily, areas then thinly populated and agriculturally fertile. It resulted in the foundation of many autonomous city-states abroad, among them Croton and Posidonia (named for the god Poseidon) on the mainland, and Syracuse on Sicily. The modern Italian city of Naples takes its name from the Greek for "new city": *neapolis*. Greeks perched on the Mediterranean had become, as Plato later said, "like frogs around a pond."

Political consequences of new military techniques

As time went on the Greek city-states at home and abroad changed their forms of government, the general trend being toward a larger share in government for greater numbers of people. Expanding trade contributed to this trend, with newly rich elements in society seeking and gaining a greater share of the power. But a transformation in military techniques may have been even more influential. Around 650 B.C.E., Greek warfare gradually began to see a shift from the dominance of cavalry fighting from horse-drawn chariots to the dominance of infantry amassed on

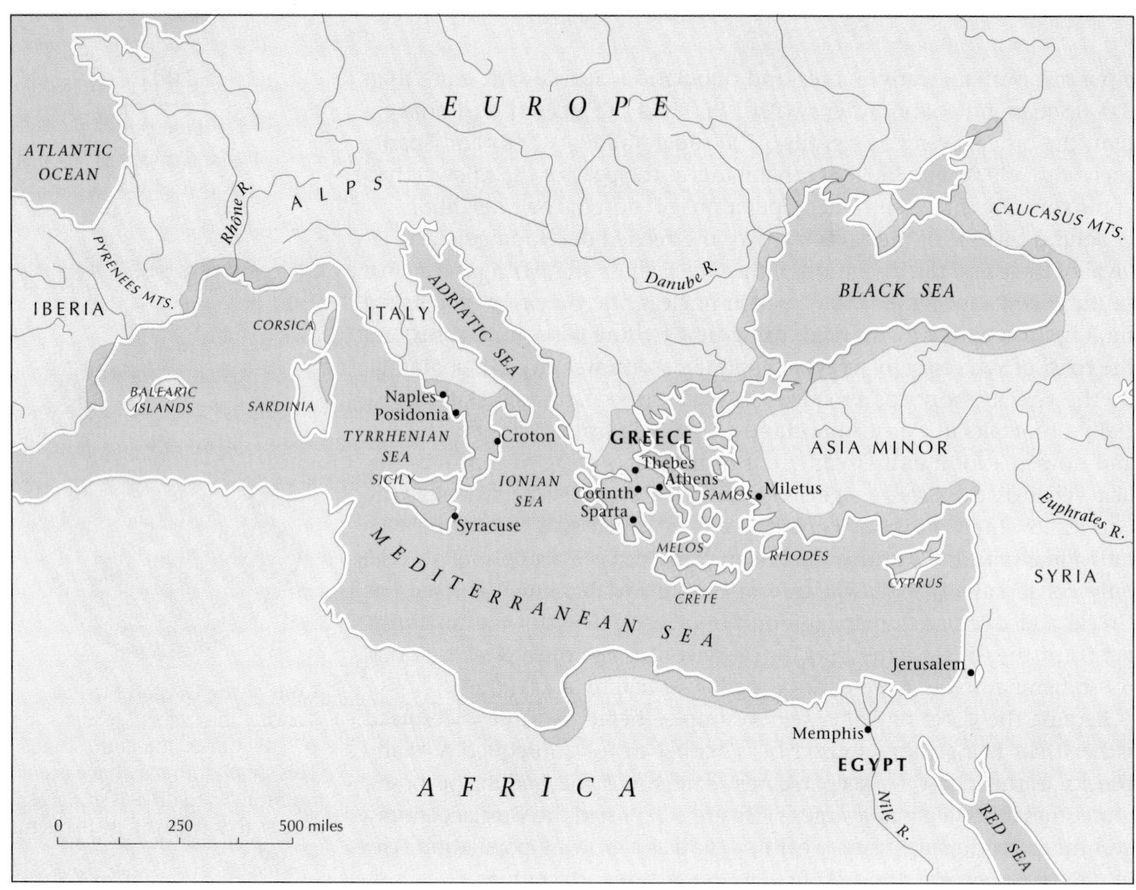

Greece and Its Settlements, 550 B.C.E.

Participatory government and exclusion of women

foot in tight formations known as *phalanxes.* Since the phalanxes were manned by comparatively large numbers of modest farmers, instead of the aristocrats who had fought in chariots (chariot warfare was inherently aristocratic since only the rich could afford horses), the shift gradually had profound political consequences. Simply stated, those who provided military service ultimately gained their say in Greek government.

Before looking more closely at the political and social structures of the two leading Greek city-states, Sparta and Athens, it is worth pointing out two differences between Greek city-state government and our own. In the first place, government in the city-states was participatory, with no difference existing whatsoever between the state and its citizens. In every polis all the citizens did all the governmental work; rather than employing people specifically as civil servants, judges, or professional soldiers, all citizens shared in collective decision-making, judiciary functions, and fighting. Thus one could never say "Sparta fought Athens," since no one conceived of such abstract political entities; instead one would say that "the Spartans fought the Athenians." Second, Greek political life was solely the preserve of males. As the Greeks saw things, biology made women weaker than men for the battlefield and relegated women to the home for

Greek Infantry Advancing into Combat. From a vase of about 650 B.C.E.

long periods of pregnancy, delivery, and child-rearing. It need not have been this way, but the Greeks never began to consider alternatives. Consequently women were never citizens and were not asked for their political opinions; worse, they often were denied legal rights such as being able to sue or to own property. If born to free parents they were technically free, but for practical purposes they were chained to the home.

The Armed Camp of Sparta

Origins of Spartan militarism

A story told by the later Greek writer Plutarch evokes the most famous quality of the Spartans, their tenacious militarism. According to Plutarch, when the Spartans met for public festivals the old men would sing, "We once were young, and brave, and strong"; then the young men would sing, "And we're so now"; and then the children would chime in, "But we'll be strongest soon enough." Sparta's governmental system and culture was heavily conditioned by the fact that the Spartans were originally Dorians who in the twelfth century B.C.E. had entered the Peloponnesian peninsula of southern Greece as an invading army. Instead of mingling with the local peoples in Laconia, the region they had conquered, the Spartans forced the natives to do all the farming while they remained full-time soldiers. Around 735 B.C.E., the Spartans' military superiority enabled them to annex neighboring Messenia and to force the Messenians into becoming subject agricultural laborers. About 650 B.C.E., the oppressed Messenians launched a revolt with the aid of the Peloponnesian city-state of Argos, and a bitter struggle ensued for several years before the Spartans achieved total victory. During this fighting and its aftermath the victors forged a repressive governmental and social system meant to ensure that no challenge to their power would occur again.

The Spartan government

Seen from the point of view of the Spartan rulers, their government was wonderfully equitable. The Spartan system of checks and balances was probably the first known to human history. The Spartans retained their ancient hereditary kingship as a concession to military necessity, for they thought that a supreme leader, well experienced in war, was necessary on the battlefield. But rather than having one king they had two, thereby balancing the influence of two great families. When wartime came, an assembly of all the Spartan citizens would decide which king would lead the army into battle, and he then would assume full military powers. Otherwise the government depended entirely on the combined workings of three bodies: a council of elders, the citizen assembly, and a panel of magistrates. The elders numbered thirty—the two kings and twenty-eight others chosen for life by the citizen assembly from a pool of Spartans over the age of sixty (throughout the ancient world the eldest people were presumed to be the wisest). The job of the elders was to propose motions to be voted upon by the assembly, which numbered about eight thousand and so was too large to formulate motions itself. The magistrates, who numbered five and were replaced annually by a vote in the assembly, were the executives who implemented the assembly's motions, performed all judicial business, and negotiated with outsiders.

Equality among the Spartan elite

With its large assembly and dual kingship, the Spartan political system emphasized equality; indeed the Spartan citizens actually called themselves "the equals." In fact, had there been no inhabitants in the territories of Laconia and Messenia other than the citizens, the Spartans might have been said to have had a perfect direct democracy. But the roughly 8,000 Spartan citizens were a mere handful in a total population of roughly 400,000, the vast majority of whom were the unfree farm laborers called *helots*. This circumstance helps account for the shared power among the Spartan elite, for they wished to make certain that no faction among them might feel a lack of power and seek alliance with elements of the oppressed. For the same motive the Spartans saw to it that most of their land was divided equally, and that the helots were attached to the land rather than owned individually. Helot families worked their own plots, from which they could never be moved, giving most of their produce to their masters and saving what was left to feed themselves.

Discipline for the benefit of the state

With a certain ironic justice the determination of the Spartan elite to keep the mass of the population in a state of subjugation led to a life bearing some resemblance to slavery even for themselves. Their culture prized toughness and iron discipline above all. Puny infants were immediately put to death, and Spartan boys from an early age were taught to endure pain. Once the boys reached the age of twelve they were taken from their families and forced to live together outdoors, covering themselves with the down of thistles in the winter, and sleeping on rushes (thick plant stems) that they broke off with their hands since knives would have made the job too easy. Later they moved to barracks where they lived collectively until age thirty. Since wives were selected for them and since they were allowed to visit their wives only at night for a single obvious purpose, it sometimes happened that men became fathers before they ever saw their wives' faces in daylight. Once they were age thirty they could finally live at home, but they were still obliged to eat together in military messes on rations of the coarsest food. (Supposedly a certain Greek king, having heard of the Spartans' famous black soup, asked a Spartan cook to make him some and found it truly awful; when the king complained, the cook replied, "Sir, the soup is delicious only if you've bathed in Spartan rivers.")

Spartan isolationism

Intent on never turning "soft," the Spartans not only shunned tasty food but any sort of outward show. This meant that they were indifferent to elegant crafts and had little need for imported goods. Sparta thus had relatively few artisans and very little foreign commerce. Although one effect was that the Spartan economy remained static, another was that the Spartans avoided overseas political entanglements. Indeed, militaristic Sparta generally managed better than most other Greek states to stay out of war. Contemptuous of foreign customs, and hoping to avoid any occasion upon which the helots might take advantage of their absence or weakness, the members of the Spartan elite struck defensive alliances that allowed them to remain behind their own frontiers. But when foreign war became inevitable—and this happened in the fifth century—they were well prepared, for, as the other Greeks said, the Spartans were "the only people to whom war might give repose."

THE ATHENIAN POLITICAL PARTNERSHIP

While Sparta was becoming a bastion of military repression, Athens was evolving in the direction of true democracy. The very word *democracy* is a Greek coinage, meaning "people power," and Athens was the city-state that cultivated democracy to the fullest. One explanation for the political differences between Sparta and Athens is that the district of Attica in which Athens is situated was never the scene of an armed invasion or conflict between opposing peoples. Consequently, no military caste imposed its rule upon a huge number of vanquished natives. In addition, Attica's natural resources were more varied, with mineral deposits and good harbors. This allowed Athens to develop a prosperous trade and a greater emphasis on urban life as the framework for democratic politics.

Athena. A relief dating from about 450 B.C.E., discovered in the ruins of ancient Athens. The mourning goddess is contemplating a list of citizens who had died fighting for her city.

Although little is known about the nature of government in Athens from about 750 until about 600 B.C.E., it seems clear that throughout this time Athens was ruled by a hereditary aristocracy. Economic trends that gained momentum toward the end of the period, together with the shift from cavalry to infantry, produced strains in that system. In 594 B.C.E. a grave economic crisis brought matters to a head. The growth of commerce had made the cultivation of grapes and olives more profitable than raising grain, a circumstance that led to the rise of new wealth and the impoverishment of farmers who had been unable to invest in vineyards or olive orchards. With the poor farmers apparently on the verge of revolt because they were being forced into semi-slavery for not paying their debts, the ruling aristocrats attempted to forestall class warfare by granting emergency powers to a merchant named Solon, who was renowned for his wisdom and fairness. Solon rescued the poor by cancelling all debts, and he mollified the rich by instituting a new governmental system that gave them the greatest political power. By this system wealth rather than hereditary status became the main qualification for ruling privileges: the richest Athenians carried the greatest weight, and they alone could hold office. But Solon also introduced a democratic principle for the first time into Athenian government by allowing even the poor (excluding women, resident foreigners, and slaves) to have some veto power in a general assembly of citizens.

Owl of Athens. In addition to the clear-sighted bird, sacred to Athena, coins of Athens bore olive leaves and the Greek letters ΑΘΕ for the name of the city.

Supposedly Solon, who lived on in legend as the Athenian George Washington, was later asked whether he had given the Athenians the best laws he could give them and replied "the best laws they could observe." In fact Solon's system by no means solved all the state's problems; elements among the old aristocracy were disgruntled about having lost their hereditary privileges, and the poor remained a volatile force. Quarrelling among Athens's ruling elite created such instability that finally, in 546 B.C.E., all factions seemed relieved when an Athenian strongman named Pisistratus seized dictatorial power. Ruling until 527, Pisistratus proved to be a benevolent tyrant. He aided poor farmers by granting them lands from confiscated estates and offering them advantageous loans. In addition, he patronized culture, bringing poets and sculptors to his court, and engaging—as dictators will—in ambitious building projects. His son Hippias, however, to whom he bequeathed his powers, was a ruthless oppressor who was overthrown in 510 B.C.E. by an Athenian faction that was aided by Sparta.

The reforms of Clisthenes

Renewed factional strife then briefly threatened to tear the Athenian state apart once more until a shrewd aristocrat, Clisthenes, enlisted enough support from the lower classes in 507 B.C.E. to eliminate his rivals from the scene and introduce lasting stability. Having promised concessions to the poorer elements in society as a reward for their help, Clisthenes, as the Greek historian Herodotus put it, "took the people into partnership." His main innovation was to introduce a system for electing

Detail of an Athenian Measurement Jug. The jug on which this owl appears, dating from about 500 B.C.E, was used to ensure standard measurement of liquids in the marketplace. The inscription indicates that it belonged to "the people," meaning that it was public property, and hence was one of the earliest examples in human history of "government by the people, for the people."

officeholders based on ten "tribes," each comprising a cross-section of the population, rather than on regions dominated by powerful families. Since every free man had a vote in one of the tribes and each of the tribes nominated an equal number of citizens to serve in Athenian governmental offices, every free man had a role in influencing Athenian affairs.

The assembly and the council

Clisthenes ruled for only one year, but the effects of his system were so profound that he properly counts as the father of Athenian democracy. After the system was perfected in 487 B.C.E. it worked as follows. Sovereign power resided in an assembly of all the male citizens: when matters of the greatest magnitude, such as going to war or raising emergency financial levies, had to be settled, the assembly would decide. Since the assembly was extraordinarily large (in the middle of the fifth century B.C.E. about 40,000 men were entitled to participate, and some 5,000 were likely to do so on any given occasion), measures were submitted to it by a council, which had supreme control over executive and administrative activities. Membership in the council was established annually by lot from nomination lists prepared in the tribal meetings instituted by Clisthenes, any male citizen over thirty being eligible for service. Since the council itself numbered five hundred men, and service was limited to a year, large numbers of Athenian men gained governmental experience.

Ostracism. The system took its name from the potsherds (in Greek, *ostraka*) on which the names of unpopular citizens were scratched. Many of the "ballots" have survived. Here we see "Aristeides," "Kimon," and "Themistokles."

The magistrates and the generals

Obviously even a body of five hundred people cannot make administrative decisions or exercise executive powers efficiently. Taking this into account, the Athenians gave special powers to a small number of magistrates, rotated in and out of office by lot for terms of one year. These magistrates had various duties, including the oversight of judicial panels mustered individually from lists of citizens for every different case. In all these matters the Athenians never supposed that any specialized training or particular gifts were prerequisites for holding office. But they did make an exception for military functions. Whereas magistrates were chosen by lot, generals were elected annually by the assembly from lists submitted by the tribes, and whereas magistrates could not serve for more than two nonconsecutive terms, generals could be re-elected as frequently as the assembly wished. When certain generals were re-elected frequently they became, for practical purposes, policymakers and leaders of the Athenian state. Nonetheless the citizens were always free to vote them out of office, and even to exercise the peculiar Athenian device of ostracism, whereby anyone considered a potential threat to the balanced workings of the constitution could be sent into honorable ten-year exile by vote of the citizen assembly.

Majority rule

In several ways Athenian democracy was quite different from democracies of today. The Athenian form was much more limited in one crucial respect, namely that all women, resident aliens, and slaves were excluded. These exclusions deprived roughly three-quarters of the adult population of Athens of any role in government. For the remainder, however, the system was as fully participatory as might be imagined. Everyone, rich or poor, had an opportunity to do everything, with the possible exception of becoming a general. So averse were the Athenians to being governed by a few men of wealth or reputation, so confident were they of the political capacities of all their citizens, and so determined were they to ensure equality of service, that they provided small payments when it became clear that poor people were declining office because they could not afford the unpaid time. More remarkably still, every important political decision was made by majority vote of all the citizens who decided to attend the general assembly. This uncompromising adherence to the principle of majority rule had advantages and disadvantages. The most obvious advantage was fairness and the most obvious disadvantage was the role that unreflective emotionalism might play in decision-making. The modern word *demagogue* comes from the Greek orator who was effective at swaying public opinion insincerely for his own gain; indeed, many Greek philosophers, including Plato and Aristotle, considered democracy no different from mob rule. Yet the system worked extremely well for about a century and brought Athens to its greatest triumphs in both foreign affairs and cultural achievements.

The Persian War and the Peloponnesian War

Greek Forces Defeat Persians. This piece from a fifth century B.C.E. Attic bowl depicts an Athenian soldier standing over a defeated Persian soldier from Xerxes's army.

While Sparta and Athens were developing their different forms of government they became engaged in life-or-death wars. In the first of these they were allies; in the second, the bitterest of enemies.

A Spartan-Athenian alliance gained a dramatic victory for all the Greek peoples in two campaigns known collectively as the Persian War. As we have seen in an earlier chapter, the Persians had replaced the Babylonians in 539 B.C.E. as the mightiest power in western Asia. One result was that the Persians came to rule all of Asia Minor, including formerly independent Greek city-states on the western coast. After turning their attentions to conquering Egypt, the Persians crossed over to Europe in 512 and occupied the northernmost Greek territory of Thrace. It is unclear whether they had designs on the rest of Greece, but many of the Greek city-states surely felt uncomfortable living under the Persian shadow. Moreover, the Greek-speaking cities in Asia Minor began to chafe under Persian rule and unsuccessfully tried to gain their independence in a revolt that lasted from 499 until 494 B.C.E. During this time Athens, for motives both economic and patriotic, dispatched a number of ships and troops to aid the rebels. (The Athenians shared with the Greeks of Asia Minor a common dialect, and thus a special sense of kinship.) Once the Persians had put down the revolt, they decided to teach the Athenians a lesson.

Campaigns of the Persian War

The two campaigns of the Persian War followed, one in 490 B.C.E., and the other extending from 480 to 479. In the first a Persian expeditionary force sent by sea to Attica was defeated by the Athenians in the battle of Marathon. Recognizing that a much greater military enterprise was necessary, the Persian ruler, Xerxes, sent an enormous army by the European land route to bring all Greece under his rule. At first his army was successful, conquering all of northern Greece down to Athens itself. The Athenians withdrew and watched from afar while their city was burned. But Sparta came to Athens's aid, and heroic resistance by the allies, first in the sea battle of Salamis (480) and then in the land battle of Platea (479) sent the Persians off and packing. The Greek exploits in these campaigns testified to their military resourcefulness and their heroism. Among the many stirring incidents is the retort of a Spartan general trying to hold off a huge Persian force at the pass at Thermopylae with just three hundred men: when a scout warned him that the Persians were so numerous that the mass of their arrows would darken the sun, he replied "so much the better, we will fight in the shade." He and the others then went down fighting to the last man.

Growth of Athenian hegemony

Without becoming misty-eyed it is possible to view the Persian War as one of the most significant in the history of the world, for it was a victory for Hellenic ideals of freedom against Persian autocracy, and it allowed the Greek city-states, above all Athens, to preserve these ideals for themselves and for posterity. And yet, for Athens the glorious war led relentlessly to an inglorious one, almost as if plotted by an Athenian tragic playwright. The first step was the creation by Athens in 478 B.C.E. of a naval confederacy meant to carry on the war against Persia and liberate the Greek cities of Asia Minor. Sparta, a land power, had no interest in joining, but Athens gained the support of many other Greek city-states, each of which was obliged to contribute annually a fixed number of ships or monetary payments. Since the expense was great, the island of Naxos sought to withdraw from the confederation in 467, but Athens refused to grant permission and made the point clear by taking punitive military action. By mid-century the league had lost its original purpose because the Asian Greek cities had all been freed. Just then Athens moved the league's treasury from the island of Delos to Athens itself, demonstrating that the confederation had been transformed into an empire shaped for Athenian financial and commercial interests. Meanwhile, the Spartans looked on and, not surprisingly, began strengthening a defensive alliance out of fear that Athenian hegemony might be extended over all of Greece.

Bust of Pericles. A Roman copy of a Greek work possibly done from life.

The immediate origins of the Peloponnesian War, fought between Athens and Sparta between 431 and 404 B.C.E., lay in a confrontation between the respective alliance systems. Athens needed to maintain ports on the Gulf of Corinth because that waterway led to Sicily, a source of imported grain for the Athenian populace and timber for its shipbuilding. This meant that Athens had to extend alliances to areas near the Peloponnesian peninsula, Sparta's bastion, bringing tensions to a peak. Each time a smaller city under the thumb of either Athens or Sparta tried to revolt, it gained help from the opposing power. Finally a relatively minor incident of this sort became the cause of all-out war. Athenian strategy, shaped by Pericles, the city's charismatic political and military leader of the time, was defensive. Pericles feared that the Athenian infantry could never match the well-drilled Spartan one, and thus he ordered that all

Athenians living in the country abandon their land to the invading Spartans and take refuge behind newly constructed Athenian walls. His hope was that the navy would ultimately win the day by coastal campaigns against Sparta. Unfortunately for Athens, however, not only did the Spartans lay waste to Attica, but crowding behind the walls led to an outbreak of plague in 430 B.C.E. that wiped out about a quarter of the population.

The defeat of Athens

One of the most famous scenes in Greek history, reported by the contemporary Athenian historian of the Peloponnesian War, Thucydides, was the Funeral Oration delivered by Pericles to commemorate the war dead after the first year of battle. In words of simple dignity (at least as Thucydides recorded them) Pericles proposed that the death of so many had not been in vain because they had fought for splendid ideals: democracy, an open society, and "beauty without extravagance." While this was surely true, Athens was also fighting to enforce its will on others, and as the war progressed Athens became ever more ruthless in its quest for total victory. Pericles, who himself succumbed to the plague in 429 B.C.E., was succeeded by leaders more unscrupulous than he; they began to balance the military score with Sparta but also embarked on overly ambitious

Greece at the End of the Age of Pericles

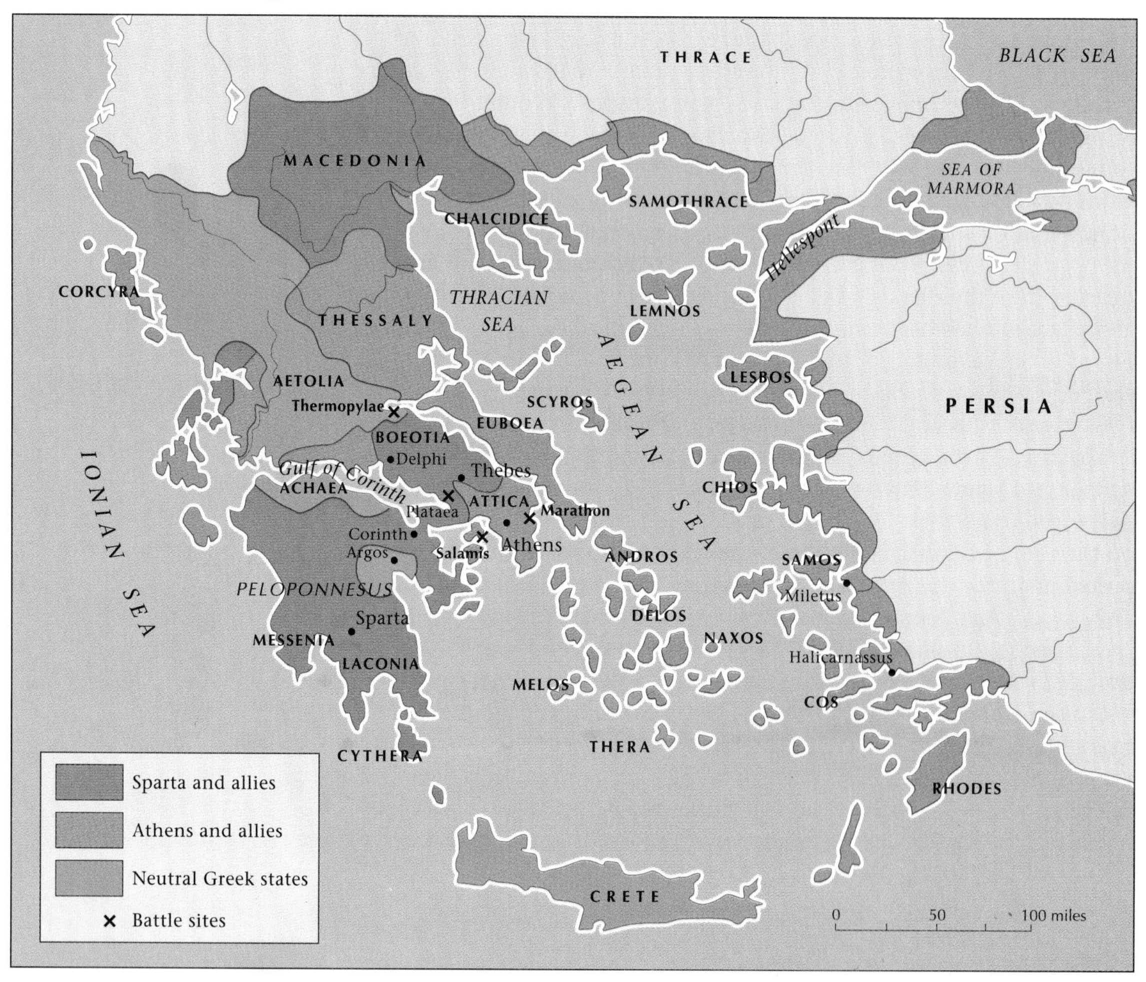

imperialistic ventures and a policy of forcing neutral states to join forces with Athens or face extermination. Having lost its own sense of mission and weakened by internal divisions, Athens was finally deserted by so many of its allies as the war dragged on that when it lost a naval battle to Sparta in 404 B.C.E. it had to surrender rather than starve. The terms then imposed by the victorious Spartans were harsh: Athens had to destroy all of its fortifications, surrender all of its foreign possessions, and submit to Sparta as a subject state.

Political weakness after the Peloponnesian War

The outcome of the Peloponnesian War led to political trials for all of Greece. At first Sparta assumed supremacy throughout the Greek world, installing dictatorships in cities formerly allied with Athens and governed by democracy. Yet it slowly became clear that Sparta lacked the will or the governmental strength to maintain hegemony beyond its earlier boundaries. The result was civil strife in several Greek cities, anti-Spartan democrats rising against Spartan-backed oligarchs, as well as attempts by Athens and Thebes—cities in which democrats had taken power—to wrest domination over Greece from Sparta. In 371 B.C.E. Thebes accomplished that goal by a victory over Spartan troops at the battle of Leuctra, but Thebes soon proved no more able to rule Greece firmly. Consequently from 371 until 338 B.C.E. shifting alliances between cities led to interminable warfare. Although the splendor of Greek culture had hardly dimmed (Plato and Aristotle, the greatest of Greek philosophers, flourished successively from about 390 to about 330 B.C.E.), all the leading cities of Greece had become militarily and politically exhausted.

Women and Men in the Daily Life of Ancient Athens

Toward the end of his stirring Funeral Oration, the Athenian leader Pericles briefly addressed the married women in his audience and urged them to remember three things: they should strive to rear more children for the sake of Athens; they should not show more weakness than is "natural to their sex"; and they should act in such a way as to avoid gossip, good or bad. Only recently have scholars become sensitive to such belittling remarks, recognizing that they cast a shadow on the glories of Athenian accomplishments.

Role of women in Dark Ages

Rather than leading to greater equality among the sexes, the growth of democracy throughout Greece had the opposite result. The Greeks of the Dark Ages had no difficulty in conceiving of awe-inspiring goddesses and heroic women. Part of the reason for this may be that female divinities often have a prominent role in societies where fertility is at a premium. Furthermore, in the primarily aristocratic society of the Dark Ages it was possible to conceive of a few select women as possessing extraordinary traits—of beauty, wisdom, or courage—that placed them above all others. Thus the Trojan War was allegedly fought over the beauteous Helen, and the wise Andromache offered her husband shrewd military advice. No

Women Bathing, c. 1440 B.C.E. A scene from daily life, including a woman "conditioning" her hair.

one would wish to idealize the situation of either character because Helen was merely an object of conquest and Andromache was immediately told by her husband to go back to her loom. Nonetheless, assuming that the epics represent some aspects of real life, such women did not exist entirely in the shadows.

Women relegated to domestic roles

But as aristocratic ideals gave way to more democratic ones throughout Greece, life in the shadows increasingly became women's lot. Limiting the present discussion to Athens, for which we have the most evidence, it seems that an emphasis on the infantry and its spirit of equality interrelated with an emphasis on men training together and developing close relationships, often of a homosexual nature. In addition, the ostentation of individual aristocratic women was frowned upon and the rearing of children to supply the infantry and serve the state was made almost a requirement. Finally, as town life became the norm, husbands thought it ever more urgent to keep their wives away from the desirous glances of male neighbors. Thus public spaces were located in towns for "male activities" such as athletics and political gatherings, and private spaces were delimited for female activities such as child-rearing and weaving.

Women treated like property

The result of these trends was that almost all Athenian women were kept in domestic seclusion. Married women were to bring into the world enough children to ensure the continued existence of the state. Thus girls would be married at age fourteen—as soon as they were biologically ready for childbearing—to husbands about twice their age (younger men were supposed to dedicate themselves more fully to war). A girl's father would arrange the marriage without caring about his daughter's preferences and provide her with a dowry that her husband was expected to use for her support without rapidly depleting the principal. In such ways the girl was treated rather like a piece of property. Shortly after she entered her new surroundings, a regular schedule of childbearing would begin. Typically the interval between births was about two years, meaning that the average young wife was either pregnant or nursing most of the time. The rigors of childbirth also affected the female death rate: scientists studying Greek skeletal remains estimate (not without controversy) that the average age of death for men was forty-five and for women thirty-six.

Male lack of respect for women

Women seldom went out of doors, partly because it was thought immodest to be seen frequently by other men, and partly because nursing and advanced stages of pregnancy made it difficult to attend public festivals. At home, women were expected to do "women's work"—mostly food preparation and cloth production. Since the ideology of democratic Athens opposed excessive displays of wealth or leisure, women were not supposed to sit around idly; but since "women's work" was basically menial, men looked down on women for engaging in it. In fact, male lack of respect for women was often blatant; a medical precept had it that "a pregnant woman has a good complexion if the child is male; a poor one if the child is female."

Little emotional attachment of husbands to wives

While we can never know how husbands and wives felt about each other from case to case, much evidence suggests that husbands customarily had little emotional attachment to their wives because they considered them their natural inferiors. In a revealing passage the historian Herodotus says of a certain king, "this Candaules fell in love with his own wife, a fancy that had strange consequences. . . ." Athenian men of the fifth and fourth centuries B.C.E. tended to idealize male homosexual rather than heterosexual relationships, assuming that since men were superior to women love between men was more exalted: when the sage Socrates was forced to take his own life, he sent his wife home because he wished to die solely among male companions. Athenian men did seek heterosexual physical pleasure, but for the purest sexual gratifications a man could always rely on household slaves or whores. Thus an Athenian orator once remarked, "prostitutes we have for pleasure, concubines for

Music and Poetry in Everyday Greek Life. The Greeks proudly used pottery design to depict their daily activities. Here a musician entertains a boy while a poet writes verses for another boy. The homoerotic implications of such scenes were intentional.

daily physical attendance, wives to bear us legitimate children and be our faithful housekeepers."

Increase in slavery

Another great shadow on Greek life in the fifth and fourth centuries was slavery. None of the extraordinary Greek accomplishments in politics, thought, or art would have been possible had slaves not been forced to do the heavy labor while free men debated policy in assemblies or discussed the true and beautiful while banqueting or strolling in the countryside. For modern lovers of democracy there is an awkward relationship between the rise of democratic government in Greece, especially in Athens, and the increase in slavery as compared with the Dark Ages. The Athenian ideal of division and rotation of governmental functions among all free men was founded on the assumption that slaves would be widely available to perform a variety of chores in the fields, in small businesses, and in the homes, while free men lavished time in political activities. In fact, the Athenian democratic system began to function fully only when the Athenians "struck it rich," coming upon a rich vein of silver in the Laurion mines of Attica just around the year 500 B.C.E. Whereas the supply of slaves had previously been limited to war captives, the newly found silver enabled the Athenians collectively to buy slaves in larger numbers from Eastern slave dealers or barbarian tribes.

Slaves distributed among Athenian families

Although widespread, Athenian slavery was small in scale. The only exception was in the state-owned silver mines, where large numbers of slaves toiled to produce enough wealth so that the Athenians could buy more slaves and thus keep the slave system solvent. Otherwise, slaves were distributed about equally in small numbers among Athenian families, rather than working in large teams on plantations or in industries. Typically every family would own a slave or two to perform its hardest and most menial work, tilling the soil or doing the laundry. In such circumstances slaves would seldom be treated cruelly, although their masters surely looked down on them as semi-human brutes or scoundrels and were free to punish them with blows. The very notion that slaves were not entirely human, perpetuated by such remarks as "the ox is the poor man's slave," made it easier for Athenian free men to assume that nature had chosen some for servile labor, and others, like themselves, for political life.

Social and economic equality of male citizens

If one puts aside the subjection of women and slaves—admittedly no small qualifications—daily life in ancient Athens had numerous attractive features. The male citizens enjoyed considerable social and economic equality. Small-scale farming and commerce were the norms, and what little industry existed—pottery and armaments manufacture—was also limited in scale, being carried on in shops owned by individual craftsmen who produced their own wares. Factories employing large numbers of workers were virtually unknown: one of the largest in fifth-century Athens, a shield factory, was staffed by only 120 workers and owned not by a citizen but by a resident alien. Some citizens were of course richer than others, but the richest were required to donate some of their wealth to support public festivals or equip the navy.

Simplicity of life

The social equality of citizens brought with it an extraordinary simplicity in their ways of life. In part, this simplicity owed much to the climate.

Men Weighing Goods on a Balance Scale.
From a pottery decoration of about 550 B.C.E.

Since the weather in Greece is predominantly warm and dry (300 days of sunshine) there was no need for elaborate housing or heavy overcoats. The democratic ideal and the absence of extremes in wealth reinforced this simplicity, which allowed the Athenians to make do with the barest essentials. Their beds had no springs, their houses had no drains, and their food consisted chiefly of cereals, handfuls of figs and olives, some goat cheese, and perhaps some dried fish, washed down with diluted wine. A rectangular piece of wool wrapped around the body and fastened with pins at the shoulders and with a rope around the waist served as the main garment. One could sleep in this, shake it out at dawn, and fasten it again for the day's wear, without a thought for changing fashions.

Leisure and sociability

All told, Athenian male citizens not only enjoyed a life full of simplicity, but also one in which the main qualities were leisure and sociability. Since Athenians demanded so little, they did not have to work very hard. This would have been true even if they did not have slaves (although of course to a lesser extent) since their main form of agriculture, raising olive trees and grapevines, called for a total of only about seventy days' work per year. Since they did not care about working hard for frills such as pajamas or pin-striped suits, when Athens was at peace they had plenty of time to spend in assemblies and festivals, as well as in games and athletics, or simply standing around chatting or arguing with each other. When Athens was at war—which it often was—its male citizens were obliged to fight, and then they might get killed, maimed, or taken into slavery. But in times of peace the average free Athenian male lived a fulfilling existence of work and play.

Greek Philosophy

Greeks pursue philosophical inquiry

The Greeks invented philosophy. The word itself comes from the Greek, meaning "love of wisdom." It is a mystery why the Greeks, beginning around the sixth century B.C.E., were the first to pursue sustained philosophical inquiry. But since they lacked palace bureaucracies or professional priests, no vested interests stood opposed to free speculation and observation. In addition, because literacy was widespread—owing to the simplified Greek alphabet—and because new military tactics and governmental institutions gradually strengthened their ideals of equality, the Greeks came to believe that they were different from others, especially their Persian neighbors, and began increasingly to speculate on the reasons for the differences. Finally, their relative indifference to material needs and the availability of leisure time offered the Greeks unprecedented opportunities for reflection.

The Pre-Socratics

From the sixth century until the fourth century B.C.E. Greek thinkers throughout the Hellenic world started addressing a wide range of questions about the nature of the universe and the meaning of life. The earliest Greek philosophers were the "Pre-Socratics" (so called because they preceded Socrates), all of whom lived during the sixth century in the city of Miletus on the coast of Asia Minor. Like their contemporaries, the New Babylonians, the Pre-Socratics studied the course of the stars as a way to observe the predictable regularities of nature. Thus the earliest of the Pre-Socratics, Thales (exact dates unknown), predicted a solar eclipse in 585 B.C.E. But whereas the New Babylonians interrelated their astronomy with supernatural doctrines about occult forces inherent in the stars, the Pre-Socratics excluded occult explanations for natural events and extended their strictly nonreligious inquiries into the workings of the entire physical universe. They believed that all things could be reduced to some primary substance and differed only about what it was. Thales, perceiving that all things contain moisture, believed that the basic substance was water, but one of his students insisted that it was primal, indestructible matter. Although the various conclusions of the Pre-Socratics would not stand up to later questioning and testing, their insistence on looking for natural laws and rational explanations was pathfinding and would remain characteristic of the Greeks.

The Pythagoreans

After the Persians conquered Asia Minor some of the Pre-Socratics became silent and others fled to distant Sicily in order to retain their personal independence. Philosophical speculation thus continued in the Greek "Far West," but it was now tinged with a pessimism and religious coloration that reflected Greek distress at seeing their freedoms crushed and a diminished trust in the strength of human rationality. Typifying this reaction was the system of Pythagoras, a thinker who migrated around 530 B.C.E. from the island of Samos near Asia Minor to southern Italy, where he founded a sect—half philosophical, half mystical—in the city of Croton. Pythagoras and his followers held the speculative life to be the highest good, but they believed that in order to pursue it, the individual must be purified of evil fleshly desires. They also believed that the essence of things is not a material but an abstract principle, number. Accordingly they concentrated on the study of mathematics, dividing numbers up into various categories such as odd and even, and devising the famous "Pythagorean theorem"—that the square of the hypotenuse of any right-angled triangle is equal to the sum of the squares of the other two sides. Thus even though the Pythagoreans turned away from the material world, they still exhibited the characteristic Greek quest for regularities and predictabilities in the abstract world.

The Sophists

Victory in the Persian War enabled the Greeks to overcome the failure of nerve exemplified by the Pythagoreans. Above all in Athens, a state that became exuberantly optimistic after the victory over the Persians and the creation of a Greek naval empire, the increasing power of the individual citizen motivated inquiry into how the individual might best act in the here and now. Roughly around 450 B.C.E., to fulfill the demand to cultivate such worldly wisdom, teachers emerged who were called *Sophists,* a term simply meaning "those who are wise," or perhaps "those who know things." Unlike the Pre-Socratics or the Pythagoreans, the Sophists were professional teachers, the first in the history of the West who made a living from selling their knowledge. Because they were later opposed bitterly by Socrates and Plato, the term "Sophist" became one of abuse, meaning someone who deviously employs false reasoning, and their entire movement acquired a poor reputation. But modern research has shown that the Sophists were often impressive thinkers and educators.

Protagoras

The Sophists did not comprise a coherent philosophical school; indeed some were paid teachers of such practical matters as public speaking who were not engaged at all in philosophy as commonly understood. But their work displayed certain common threads, as shown by that of Protagoras, who was active in Athens from about 445 until about 420 B.C.E. and was the most prototypic of the intellectually ambitious Sophists. His famous dictum, "man is the measure of all things," meant that goodness, truth, and justice are relative to the needs and interests of man. (Protagoras and all other thinkers in the male-dominated world of ancient Greece had males in mind when they said "man," unless they specified the contrary.) In religious matters Protagoras was agnostic; in a second famous remark he said that he did not know whether or not the gods existed or what they did—"for there are many hindrances to such knowledge—the obscurity of the subject and the brevity of life." Since he knew nothing of the gods, he found that there were no absolute truths or eternal standards of right. Sense perception being the only source of knowledge, there can be only particular truths valid for the individual knower.

Relativism of Sophists

Such teachings could be progressive and liberating or corrosive of social cohesion, depending on who phrased them and the circumstances in which they were phrased. Sophists such as Protagoras were courageous in calling into doubt outmoded traditions and encouraging Athenians to examine each situation afresh to see what might work best in each case. With their urgings and precepts everyday life became for the first time the subject of systematic discussion. Yet it is also true that the relativism of Sophists like Protagoras could easily degenerate into the doctrine that the wise man is the one who knows best how to manipulate others and gratify his own desires. Since the Sophists competed with each other for students and fees, some taught no more than debating skills as a way of getting ahead in the shifting sands of Athenian politics.

Opposition to Sophists

Inevitably the relativism and occasional opportunism of the Sophists aroused strenuous opposition. In the judgment of conservative critics the Sophists were pointing the way straight to atheism and anarchy. If there is no final truth, and if goodness and justice are merely relative to the whims of the individual, then religion, morality, the state, and society itself cannot long be maintained. This conviction led to the growth of a new philosophic movement grounded upon the theory that truth is real and that absolute standards do exist. The leaders of this movement were perhaps the three most famous individuals in the history of Western thought—Socrates, Plato, and Aristotle.

Socrates

Socrates was born in Athens in 469 B.C.E. and drew on sufficient income so that he never had to teach for a living. Having twice fought as part of the Athenian infantry, he was an ardent patriot who believed Athens was being corrupted by what he considered the shameful doctrines of the Sophists. Yet far from being an unthinking patriot who cherished slogans, he wished to submit every slogan to rigorous questioning in order to build the life of the Athenian state on the firm basis of ethical certainties. It is bitterly ironic that such a dedicated idealist was put to death by his own countrymen. Shortly after the end of the Peloponnesian War, in 399 B.C.E., while Athens was recovering from the shock of defeat and from violent internal upheavals, a democratic faction determined that Socrates was a threat to the state, and condemned him to death on a charge of "corrupting the youth and introducing new gods." Although his friends made arrangements for him to flee, Socrates decided to accept the popular judgment and died by calmly taking a cup of poison.

Socrates. According to Plato, Socrates looked like a goatman but spoke like a god.

Teaching of Socrates

Because Socrates wrote nothing himself, it is difficult to determine exactly what he taught. Contemporary reports, however, especially by his student Plato, make a few points clear. First, Socrates wished to subject all inherited assumptions to reexamination. In his view the complacent people who went around thinking they knew everything really knew nothing. Acting as a gadfly, he continually engaged such people in conversation and managed to show them by "Socratic" questioning that all their supposed certainties were nothing more than unthinking prejudices resting on false assumptions. According to Plato, an oracle once said that Socrates was the wisest person in the world and Socrates agreed: everyone else thought he knew something, but he was wiser because he knew he knew nothing. Secondly, he wished to build an edifice of the firmest truth by means of utilizing sound definitions. Others went around mouthing such words as justice, love, or piety without quite knowing what they meant by them; one had to establish clear and mutually agreed-upon meaning to such words or else they could not be used to build any system at all. Thirdly, he wished to advance to a new system of truth by examining ethics rather than by studying the physical world. He shunned discussions of why things exist, why they grow, and why they perish, urging people instead to reflect on principles of conduct both for their own sake and for that of society. One should think of the meaning of one's life and actions at all times, for according to one of his most memorable sayings, "the unexamined life is not worth living."

Absolute standards

So far, Socrates might seem rather like a Sophist; indeed, some archconservatives in his own day thought he was just that. Together with the Sophists, he was a "philosopher of the marketplace" who held tradition

Socrates Gaining Wisdom from the Wise Woman Diotima. In Plato's *Symposium* Socrates learns the philosophical meaning of love from Diotima, an ethereal female being, wiser than he. In this sculptural representation of the scene the winged figure between Diotima and Socrates is probably a personification of love itself.

and cliché up to doubt, and like them he treated daily affairs in order to help people improve their lives. But the overwhelming differences between Socrates and the Sophists lay in his belief in certainties—even if he avoided saying what they were—and in the standard of absolute good rather than expediency. To defeat the Sophists, however, it was necessary to go further and construct a system that offered a positive framework of truth and reality. This was the task accomplished by Socrates' most brilliant student, Plato.

The Platonic dialogues

Born in Athens around 429 B.C.E., Plato joined Socrates' circle as a young man and soon saw his mentor condemned to death. This experience made such an indelible impression on Plato that from then until his own death around 349 B.C.E. he sought to vindicate Socrates by constructing a philosophical system based on Socratic precepts. Plato set forth this system by teaching in Athens in an informal school (no buildings, tuition, or set curriculum) called the Academy, and also by writing a series of dialogues (treatises expressed in dramatic form) in which Socrates was the main speaker. The Platonic dialogues, among which some of the most important are the *Phaedo,* the *Symposium,* and the *Republic,* are enduringly great works of literature as well as the earliest surviving complete works of philosophy.

Plato's doctrine of Ideas

Plato understood that in order to combat skepticism and refute the Sophists he needed to provide a secure foundation for ethics. This he did by means of his doctrine of Ideas. He granted that relativity and change are characteristics of the world we perceive with our senses, but he denied that this world is the entire universe. A higher, spiritual realm exists, composed of eternal forms or Ideas that only the mind can grasp. The

Plato

Ideas are not mere abstractions but have a real existence. Each is the pattern of some class of objects or relation between objects on earth. Thus there are Ideas of chair, tree, shape, color, proportion, beauty, and justice. Highest is the Idea of the Good, the cause and guiding purpose of the universe. The things we perceive through our senses are merely imperfect copies of the supreme realities, the Ideas, and relate to them as shadows relate to material objects.

Plato's moral philosophy was founded on his doctrine of Ideas. Since earthly life is delusive and corruptible, as opposed to the realm of Ideas, which is true and eternal, the goal of human existence must be to enter as fully as possible into the realm of Ideas. And since that realm is spiritual, one can attain it only by subduing the material side of one's earthly existence and cultivating the intellectual or spiritual side. Plato's thought regarding the body seems to have undergone some evolution, for at first he granted that physical sensations might legitimately serve as a basis for ascending to spiritual heights, but he later taught a more ascetic doctrine associating the flesh and its appetites with evil. At all times, however, he taught the superiority of soul to body, and insisted that the virtuous life on earth would prepare the soul for rising to the heights of eternal truth and beauty. Those who live rightly might possibly gain some glimpse of the Idea of the Good in the here and now; even if not, such a life will prepare the soul for union with the Idea of the Good in the afterlife. As may be gathered, Plato's "Good" resembled the Judeo-Christian conception of an omnipotent God; in fact, some Christians wondered later whether Plato had not somehow been instructed by the Jewish prophets. (Of course he never was.) On the other hand, Plato neither portrayed his "Good" as an interventionist force in human affairs nor proposed any system of worship.

Plato's political philosophy

Understanding that the virtuous life would be difficult to attain in a society full of turbulence, Plato addressed himself to politics in his most famous dialogue, the *Republic,* the earliest systematic treatment of political philosophy ever written. Since Plato sought social harmony and efficiency rather than liberty or equality, he argued for an elitist state in which most of the people—the farmers, artisans, and traders—would be governed by intellectually superior "guardians." The guardian class itself would be divided. All guardians would serve first as soldiers, living together without private property, but then those found to be the wisest would receive more education and ultimately become Plato's famous "philosopher-kings." In Plato's view neither wealth nor hereditary title equipped one properly to rule but only the greatest intelligence, enhanced by the best possible education. Once philosophers were in power they would always choose the wisest to succeed them and see to it that everyone in the state was subordinated to the Idea of the Good. Later commentators have usually found this ideal of rule by the wisest to be seductive, but they ask of Plato, "who will guard the guardians?" In other words, Plato's elitist system seems to founder not only on the controversial assumption that people are born with unequal intelligence but also on the assumption that just because some rulers may be very wise they will never be corrupted by the lures of wealth or family ties.

Aristotle

Such practical considerations were typical of the thought of Plato's student Aristotle (384–322 B.C.E.), a philosopher who sought never to have his "head in the clouds." Aristotle was the son of a physician and apparently learned from his father the importance of careful observation of natural phenomena. He accepted Plato's assumption that there are some things that only the mind can grasp, but he constructed his own philosophical system based on his confidence in human abilities to understand the universe by the rational ordering of sense experience. As opposed to Plato, who taught that everything we see and touch is but an untrustworthy reflection of some intangible truth, Aristotle believed in the objective reality of material objects and taught that systematic investigation of tangible things, combined with rational inquiry into how they function, could yield full comprehension of nature and nature's plan.

Aristotle's logic and metaphysics

Aristotle surveyed a wide variety of subjects in numerous separate but interrelated treatises. Among the most insightful and influential were those devoted to logic, metaphysics, ethics, and politics. Aristotle was the earliest formal logician known to human history, and probably the greatest. He established rules for the *syllogism,* a form of reasoning in which certain premises inevitably lead to a valid conclusion, and he established precise categories for underpinning all philosophical and scientific analysis, such as substance, quantity, relation, and place. Using his own logical methods he then constructed a rigorously ordered system of metaphysics. (The word *metaphysics,* meaning "next to physics," was invented by Aristotle and means the study of the nature and causes of things, free from appeals to divine intervention or the supernatural.) Aristotle's central metaphysical belief was that all things in the universe consist of the imprint of *form* upon matter. This was a compromise between Platonism, which tended to ignore matter, and the purest materialism, which saw no patterns in the universe other than the accidents of matter impinging on matter. Forms are the purposeful forces that shape the world of matter; thus the presence of the form of humanity molds and directs the human embryo until it ultimately becomes a human being. Since everything has a purposeful form, the universe for Aristotle is *teleological,* that is, every item and every class of items is inherently aiming toward an end.

Aristotle's moral philosophy

Aristotle's moral philosophy, expressed in his *Nicomachean Ethics* (often known simply as *Ethics*), was concerned with life in this world rather than as a path to otherworldly salvation. Aristotle taught that the highest good consists in human self-realization, the harmonious functioning of mind and body. Humans differ from the animals by means of their rational capacities and find happiness by means of exercising these appropriately. For most this means exercising reason in practical affairs. Good conduct is virtuous conduct, and virtue resides in aiming for the *golden mean:* for example, courage rather than rashness or cowardice, temperance rather than excessive indulgence or ascetic denial. Better even than the practical life, however, is the contemplative life, for such a life allows men (Aristotle meant males alone) the possibility of exercising their rational capacities to the utmost. Aristotle thus believed that philosophers were the happiest of men, but he understood that even they could not engage in contemplation without interruption. As a practical person, moreover, he deemed it necessary for them to intersperse their speculative activities with practical life in the real world.

Aristotle's political philosophy

Whereas Plato conceived of politics as a means to an end, the orderly pursuit of the supernatural Good, Aristotle thought of politics as an end in itself, the collective exercise of the good life. An enormous qualification is that Aristotle, like Plato, was an elitist; he took it for granted that some people—"barbarians"—were not quite human and were meant by nature to be slaves. Similarly, he assumed that women were outside politics and should dedicate themselves to raising children and managing domestic concerns for the family. By implication Aristotle believed that women could not be happy to the same degree as men since they could not share in the life of the state in which human rational faculties enjoyed their fullest exercise. All male citizens, on the other hand, were indeed meant to share in it, for, as Aristotle proposed, "man is by nature a political animal." This view by no means implied that the best form of government was democracy, for Aristotle saw that as a "debased" form of government. What he preferred was the *polity,* the well-functioning *polis* in which monarchical, aristocratic, and democratic elements are combined by means of checks and balances. Such a government would allow all free men to realize their rational potential, showing themselves to be located in nature's hierarchy right above the animals and right below the gods.

Medicine

Strange though it may seem, two subjects that today are hardly thought of as "philosophical" were closely interrelated with the earliest developments of philosophy in Greece. One was medicine. We have seen that Aristotle's father was a physician and that this may have influenced Aristotle to emphasize observation based on sense experience. Greek medicine itself was inseparable from the emergence of orderly philosophy, for it rested on the unprecedented assumption that regularities divorced from supernatural causes existed in human health and illness. By general consent the father of scientific medicine was the Greek physician Hippocrates (c. 460–377 B.C.E.), who dinned into the ears of his pupils the precept that "every disease has a natural cause, and without natural causes, nothing ever happens." Using methods of careful study and comparison of symptoms he laid the foundations for clinical diagnosis and also discovered the phenomenon of crisis in disease. Unfortunately, however, he thought his examinations proved that the body consists of four "humors"—yellow bile, black bile, blood, and phlegm—and that illness occurs from excess amounts of any of these. The practice of bleeding the patient, most damaging to women, was the sad consequence of this theory.

History-writing

The other subject that was closely related to philosophy was the writing of history. Like so many other words we take for granted, *history* is a Greek coinage meaning nothing more than "inquiry" or "research." As this fact suggests, Greek history-writing was an original form of gathering knowledge that began by asking questions about human affairs, rather than just reporting data such as lists of kings or outcomes of battles. As an "inquirer" or "researcher," moreover, the historian looked for evidence rather than making things up himself or reporting legends. Another original feature of Greek history was that it was humanistic: the characters were always humans, never gods, and explanations were usually found in the realm of human decision-making.

Herodotus writes about the Persian War

As Hippocrates was the father of medicine, so Herodotus (c. 484–c. 420 B.C.E.) was the "father of history." Indeed, Herodotus was the first who employed the word "history" in its current sense. The questions he asked were about the Persian War: Why did the Greeks and Persians fight each other? Why did the outcome fall out as it did? To gain answers Herodotus traveled all over the Mediterranean world collecting evidence by interviews. Since these netted him a wealth of wonderful stories, he could not resist repeating them, even if they were often digressive and sometimes obviously legendary. (Some propose that his fascination with the legendary traditions of foreign peoples allows Herodotus to rank as the father of anthropology as well as the father of history.) Yet in its main lines his narrative adheres to the theme of the great war between the Greeks and the Persians seen as an epic struggle for liberty against despotism. In his conception, liberty inspires valor and ultimately triumphs.

Thucydides writes about the Peloponnesian War

In contrast to Herodotus his younger contemporary Thucydides (c. 460–c. 400 B.C.E.), who wrote a history of the Peloponnesian War, wished to reconstruct events as scientifically as possible by rejecting legends and untrustworthy hearsay in favor of only the most reliable evidence. Much like a physician of the body politic, Thucydides sought to diagnose the causes of human social diseases, such as war and civil strife, by dispassionate observation and comparison of symptoms. By presenting an accurate record of the greatest war of his own day he believed he could be useful to statesmen and generals of all time. Although his dispassionate tone and single-minded emphasis on war and politics often make him difficult to read, Thucydides' feat in presenting a coherent and accurate analysis of a highly complex event is beyond comparison in the writing of history until modern times. Individual passages of his history are so keenly insightful that they rank among the classics not just of history but of social science.

Literature and Art

Simultaneous achievements in literature and art

Just as it is extremely difficult to account for the sudden emergence of philosophy among the Greeks, so is it difficult to account for the emergence among them of the most profoundly beautiful and awe-inspiring works of literature and art. Doubtless the economic and political factors adduced to explain the appearance of philosophy help to explain the Greek accomplishments in the literary and artistic realms too. But when all is said and done the simultaneous achievements of the Greeks in the

Greek Woman Playing a Lyre, c. 1440 B.C.E. The representation depicts a woman who is no longer alive; she is making sweet music in "Helikon," the realm of the muses.

activities of mind and imagination can only be thought of as the "Greek miracle."

The Homeric epics

Any consideration of the Greek triumphs in literature must begin with the Homeric epics, the *Iliad* and the *Odyssey,* set down in writing around 750 B.C.E. The first deals with the Trojan War, concentrating on the exploits of the Greek hero Achilles; the second describes the adventurous homeward journey after the Trojan War of the Greek hero Odysseus (also known as Ulysses). Both epics emphasize memorable deeds: in the case of the *Iliad,* of military prowess; in the case of the *Odyssey,* of a wily protagonist cleverly coping with adversities by stratagem. In both epics the characters are seldom reflective; they are intent on avoiding shame and live entirely for their public reputation, showing no notion of conscience, self-discovery, or psychological growth. On the other hand, the Homeric epics excel in their exuberant descriptions of battles, personal confrontations, and a full range of fierce passions. Written in verse, they also are studded with interludes of quiet beauty: a ship skimming the seas, water being heated for a bath, preparations for bedtime, the washing of clothing in a stream. Declaimed publicly on ceremonial occasions for decade after decade, century after century, the Homeric epics exerted an enormous influence upon subsequent Greek thought and expression, continually reinforcing a faith in human greatness and a delight in the beautiful.

Lyric poetry

Both traits found a new and different mode of expression in the Greek lyric poetry of the sixth century B.C.E. Lyric poetry, so named because it was sung to the music of the lyre rather than being declaimed to large groups, was more gentle and personal than epic poetry, musing over disappointments and disillusionments, singing of love or of wine or the starlit summer night. One of the most gifted of the Greek lyric poets of this period was a woman named Sappho, who lived on the island of Lesbos, off the shore of Asia Minor. Most surviving fragments of her poetry address themselves to other women, with loving and probably erotic intent. Thus she writes to a beloved, "some say the thing most lovely is a host of horsemen, and others, infantry or a host of ships, but I say the most beautiful sight on earth is that which one loves." Although it is impossible to be certain about Sappho's amorous practices, later Greeks had no doubt that she and her circle on the isle of Lesbos engaged in female homosexuality. Hence the origin of the modern word "lesbian."

Tragic drama

Stirring as was the epic, and lovely as was the lyric, the supreme literary achievement of the Greeks was the tragic drama. This form of poetic expression, invented by the Athenians, took shape around 500 B.C.E. as part of the outdoor public festivals that played a central role in the life of the state. Although Greek tragedy was the ancestor of modern theater, it differed from most plays we know today in many respects. All the characters wore masks, men played the roles of women, and several actors played the "chorus," chanting poetic lines in unison as a way of commenting on the action and driving home certain conclusions. Initially there was only a chorus and a single actor; later a few more actors were added. Plot was always central and straightforward, without subplots or subsidiary incidents. The reason for this was that tragedy was meant to inspire the audience with "pity or fear," and this could only be done—especially in outdoor theaters that might hold 17,000 people—by concentrating relentlessly on a single highly dramatic line of action. The ideal tragic plot inspired pity or fear by depicting a terrible change in the central character's fortunes, thereby leading the audience to feel a "catharsis" or cleansing.

Greek Theater in Epidauros. Greek dramas were invariably presented in the open air. The construction of this theater, to take advantage of the slope of the hill, and the arrangement of the stage are of particular interest. The plan for the theater is shown below.

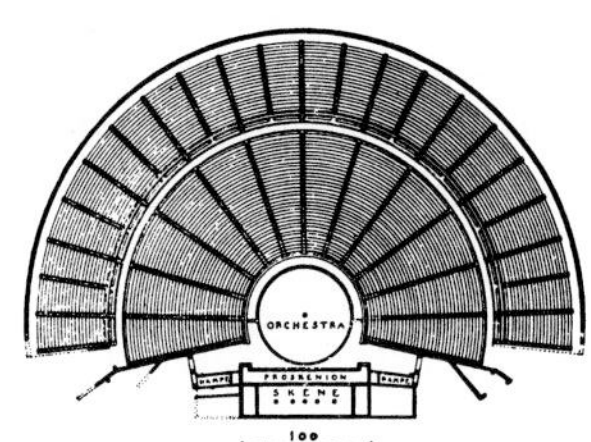

Aeschylus

Although Greek tragedy focused on plot, it was not indifferent to ideas or character. Those two elements were always present, with greater emphasis on ideas at the beginning of the fifth century and on character by the end of the century. The first of the great Greek tragedians, Aeschylus (525–456 B.C.E.), used the simplest dramatic means for primarily patriotic purposes. His tragedies were poetic dialogues between a chorus and no more than two characters on the stage at a single time. Having fought in the Persian War, Aeschylus was an ardent Athenian patriot who aimed to express high-minded, uplifting ideas. Although he managed surprisingly well in plot, given his limited means, he was less concerned about inspiring pity or fear than in arousing enthusiasm for sentiments of societal harmony. Aeschylus's *The Persians* is the only surviving Greek tragedy about contemporary events and celebrates the victory of freedom; his *Agamemnon* is a stripped-down narrative of the penalties for crime and the inevitable triumph of justice.

Sophocles

With Sophocles (496–406 B.C.E.) comes the perfection of the most "classic" traits of Greek tragedy. In his plays in particular we witness the fullest exemplification of the dramatic plot creating pity or fear and leading the audience to catharsis. Sophocles was able to accomplish this partly because his plots had more complexity than those of Aeschylus. Mostly, however, Sophocles heightened the sense of tragedy in his plays by paying more attention to character. For example, whereas the central character of *The Persians* was the ranting "barbarian" Xerxes, with whom no Athenian could ever have felt real sympathy, the titular hero of Sophocles' *Oedipus the King* was a fairly decent human being with no exceptional virtues or vices. Thus the audience was able to identify with Oedipus and feel deep pity when, by a twist in plot, he is stripped of power and blinded. Sophocles, of course, was still interested in driving home ideas: *Oedipus* teaches humans to avoid the complacency that comes with transitory material success and to recognize an order in the universe higher than any individual. This interest in ideas, moreover, leads Sophocles to emphasize universal qualities of human nature rather than nuanced particular ones.

Euripides

A shift to the particular was one of the accomplishments of Euripides (480–406 B.C.E.), the third of the great Athenian tragedians. Unlike his predecessors, Euripides was a strong critic of established ways, and this led him to theatrical innovation. He was the first to introduce elements of satiric wit into tragic writing, and the first to present sympathetic lower-class characters who used lower-class speech instead of the customary elevated poetic diction. Most notably, Euripides displayed a sense of sympathy for women. He made women his central characters in such plays as *Alcestis, Medea, Electra,* and *Helen;* in *Medea* he proposed that "esteem shall come to women," and that if the gods had allowed them to play the lyre, women would have "sung an answer to the male sex." Euripides' critical intellect led him to look for nuance in character more than universal qualities; thus he seems the most psychological and in this sense the most "modern" of the three great tragedians.

Greek comedy

No discussion of the great literary achievements of classical Greece can end without mention of comedy, brought to its perfection by the Athenian playwright Aristophanes (c. 448–c. 380 B.C.E.). Greek comedy lacked all "politeness" and subtlety, for it was performed in the open air before large crowds by actors in masks who shouted to be heard. Instead it was very broad—full of slapstick, absurdity, and vulgarity. Aristophanes delighted in ridiculing "newfangled" trends: the philosophy of Socrates, the tragedy of Euripides, the imperialistic warmongering of contemporary politicians. His jokes sometimes were simply crude, as when he had Socrates explain thunder as "farting of the clouds." Some of his humor is now hard to follow because of its topicality, but some is timeless, as in his masterwork, *Lysistrata,* in which women of enemy cities bring an end to a stupid war by refusing to have sex with their husbands until a peace agreement is signed. The idea has yet to be tried.

Greek Sculptor at Work. The Greeks were not prudish.

The same Greeks who were so innovative and accomplished in both comedy and tragedy showed a similar range of genius in the visual arts. Their comic gift—exuberance, cheerful sensuality, and often coarse wit—can be seen especially in their pottery. In "black figure" vases and jugs done throughout the Greek world in the sixth and fifth centuries B.C.E., the characters often look like glinting rascals up to some sort of mischief, usually sexual. More dignified and uplifting were the marble statuary and sculptured reliefs the Greeks made for temples and public places. Here Athens once more took the lead in a series of extraordinary artistic accomplishments. Athenian sculptors took human greatness as their main theme, depicting even gods or goddesses as humans. Their statuary shows that the Athenians could conceive of nothing more beautiful or awe-inspiring than the human form.

Flute Player. An Athenian marble relief dating from about 470 B.C.E. The relaxed pose (reclining position, crossed legs) and naturalistic representation of the naked female form were unprecendented in human art before the classical age of the Greeks.

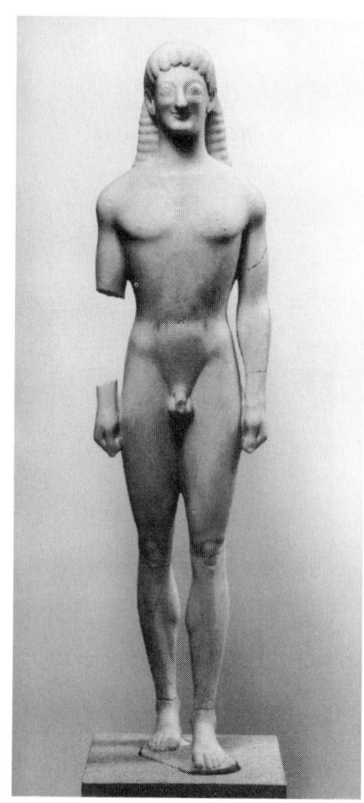

Apollo of Tenea; Apollo of Piombino; "The Critian Boy." These three statues, dating from about 560, 500, and 480 B.C.E. respectively, display the progressive "unfreezing" of Greek statuary art. The first stiff and symmetrical statue is imitative of Egyptian sculpture (see statue of the Pharaoh Menkaure, p. 53). Roughly half a century later it is succeeded by a figure that begins to display motion, as if awakening from a sleep of centuries in a fairy tale. The last figure introduces genuine naturalism in its delicate twists and depiction of the subject's weight resting on one leg.

Naturalistic statues of human figure

Perhaps the most miraculous aspect of the Greek "miracle" is the nearly sudden appearance of the well-proportioned, naturalistic statue of the naked human figure. This happened in Athens in the years around 490 to 480 B.C.E., perhaps not coincidentally the time of the Greek victory over Persia. Until then Greek statuary had been dominated by Egyptian influence; rigid figures with square shoulders met the viewer frontally, one foot slightly advanced. Then there suddenly appeared well-proportioned, well-modeled figures, resting their weight gracefully and naturally. Nothing like this had ever been seen in the human record, and it is hard to avoid the conclusion that the triumph of Greek ideals of human dignity in the Persian War had something to do with it. Convinced that all Persians bowed down to their rulers like slaves, while they themselves enjoyed political and social equality, the Greeks expressed their idea of human greatness by commemorating the dignity of the naked human form.

Universalized qualities in statues

The sudden appearance of naturalistic statuary in Athens coincided not only with the victory over Persia but also with the earliest tragedies of Aeschylus. On that basis it is tempting to draw specific analogies between the development of Athenian tragic theater and Athenian sculpture. To a certain extent these analogies are valid since the most "classic" of the Athenian sculptors whose names survive, Phidias and Myron, were contemporaries of the most "classic" tragedian, Sophocles (that is, they all flourished in the middle of the fifth century B.C.E.), and achieved similar qualities of universality. They all sought to portray humans who were deeply and recognizably human, and yet not so unique in physical features as to be identifiable as any particular human. On the other hand, Phidias and Myron differed from Sophocles in their idealizing: if showing an athlete or a poet they depicted the perfect athletic body or the most poetic-looking face rather than specimens that were less than perfect for their type. In addition, since their aesthetic values were always those of balance and restraint, the notion of instilling "pity or fear" as did the tragedians was foreign to them. Finally, although some Greek sculptors were the rough equivalents of Euripides in emphasizing particularity

Left: **The Discobolus, or Discus Thrower**, by Myron. The statue reflects the glorification of the human body characteristic of Athens in the Golden Age. Now in the Vatican Museum. Right: **Hermes with the Infant Dionysus**, by Praxiteles, fourth century B.C.E. Original in the Olympia Museum, Greece.

The Parthenon. The largest and most famous of Athenian temples, the Parthenon is considered the classic example of Doric architecture. Its columns were made more graceful by tapering them in a slight curve toward the top. Its friezes and pediments were decorated with lifelike sculptures of prancing horses, fighting giants, and confident deities.

rather than universality, they came much later than he did. It is certain, for example, that no portrait statuary of specific people was done from life in the entire Greek world before the middle of the fourth century B.C.E. And not until Lysippus, who worked at the very end of the century, can we find a truly great master of the realistic portrait.

Greek temples

Almost as if all the citizens of Athens met together on some bright morning in the fifth century B.C.E. and agreed to excel in as many forms of artistic expression as possible, the Athenians made exceptionally fine contributions to architecture as well as to literature and representational art. Actually the "classic" Greek temple was not an Athenian invention; it emerged gradually throughout the entire Greek world in the period from about 550 to 500 B.C.E. Nonetheless, of all the Greek temples ever built, the Parthenon of Athens, constructed between 447 and 438 B.C.E., while Sophocles was writing his plays, and with statuary and reliefs by Phidias, is generally considered the finest. Greek temple architecture was dramatically different from the massive temples that aimed for the skies of western Asia or Egypt. Stressing the horizontal rather than the vertical, the Greeks sought to create an impression of harmony and repose. The most characteristic feature of the Greek temple was the imposing yet graceful fluted column, surmounted by a plain capital in the so-called *Doric order,* and by a scroll-shaped one in the *Ionic order.* When the Athenians built the Parthenon, a temple dedicated to their patron goddess Athena and intended as the most prominent visual expression of their civic accomplishments, they chose for it the more restrained Doric order as if to demonstrate to all the world that "less is more."

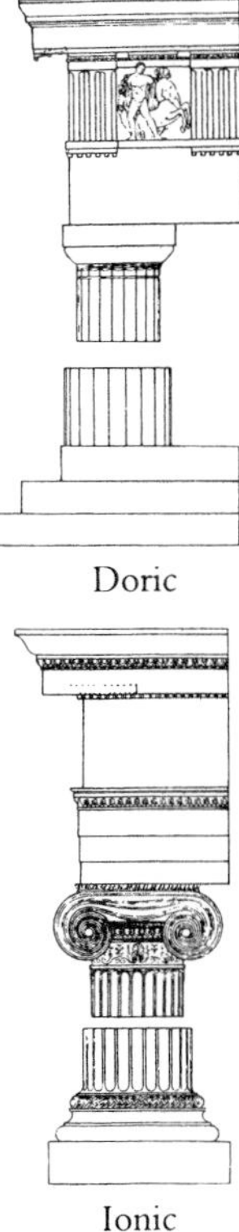

Details of the Doric and Ionic Orders

THE GREEK ACHIEVEMENT

It is necessary to be on guard against uncritical admiration of the ancient Greeks. The Spartans kept the mass of their population in serf-like subjugation, and the Athenians took slavery for granted, subjecting slaves who toiled in the mines to the most brutal treatment. Women throughout the Greek world were exploited by what today would be called a "patriarchy"—a repressive system managed by fathers and husbands. Greek statecraft was not sufficiently enlightened to avoid imperialism and aggressive war, and the Greeks made no great advances in economic enterprise. Finally, not even the Athenians were unfailingly tolerant: Socrates was put to death for nothing more than expressing his opinions.

Contrast of Greek and Near Eastern ideals

And yet, where would we be without the ancient Greeks? The profound significance of the Greek adventure for the history of the Western world can be seen with particular clarity by a comparison of Greek cultural traits with those of Mesopotamia and Egypt. The Mesopotamian and Egyptian civilizations were dominated by autocracy, supernaturalism, and the subjection of the individual to the group. The Greek word for freedom—*eleutheria*—cannot be translated into any ancient Near Eastern language, not even Hebrew. The typical political regime of western Asia was that of an absolute monarch supported by a powerful priesthood. Culture served mainly as an instrument to enhance the prestige of rulers and priests. In contrast, the civilization of Greece, notably in its Athenian form, was founded upon ideals of freedom, optimism, secularism, rationalism, measured beauty, the glorification of body and mind, and a high regard for the dignity and worth of the individual. The culture of the Greeks was the first in the West to be based upon the primacy of intellect; there was no subject they feared to investigate. As Herodotus has a Greek (in this case a Spartan) say to a Persian, "You understand how to be a slave, but you know nothing of freedom. . . . if you had but tasted it you would counsel us to fight for it not only with spears but with axes."

Uniqueness of Greek civilization

Another way of appreciating the uniqueness of Greek civilization and its enduring importance is to recall some of the words that come to us from this civilization: politics, democracy, philosophy, metaphysics, history, tragedy. These are all ways of thinking and acting that have helped enrich human life immeasurably and that had hardly been known before the Greeks invented them. To a startling degree the Western concept of "humanity" itself—the exalted role within nature of the human race in general and the individual human in particular—comes to us from the Greeks. For them the aim of existence was the fullest development of one's human potential: the work of becoming a person, called in Greek *paideia,* meant that everyone was supposed to be the sculptor of his or her own statue. When the Roman civilization later took up this ideal from the Greeks, the Romans called it *humanitas,* from which we gain our word "humanity." The Romans admitted the fact when they said that "Greece was where humanity was invented," and it is hard to doubt that they were right.

SUMMARY POINTS

- The civilization of Greece was founded upon ideals of freedom, optimism, secularism, rationalism, measured beauty, the glorification of body and mind, and a high regard for the dignity and worth of the individual.
- Greek politics centered around the city-state, a participatory government that controlled a city and its surrounding territory. The two most prominent city-states, Athens and Sparta, cooperated in the Persian War (490–479 B.C.E.) but then fought each other in the Peloponnesian War (431–404 B.C.E.).
- The Athenian ideals of democracy and equality were not upheld in daily life; women and slaves in both Athens and Sparta were subjugated to "free men" at all levels of society.
- Out of the sustained Greek philosophical inquiry emerged several schools of thought. The philosophy of Plato taught that the world is a shadow of a higher, spiritual realm; the philosophy of Aristotle emphasized the trustworthiness of sense experience.
- The Greeks made notable contributions to literature, including the Homeric epics, lyric poetry, and dramatic tragedy and comedy; brought realism into sculpture and other representational arts; and created a lasting legacy with the harmony and grace of their architecture.

Andrewes, Antony, *Greek Society,* Harmondsworth, Eng., 1975. The best single-author general introduction to ancient Greek history.

Austin, M., and P. Vidal-Naquet, *The Economic and Social History of Ancient Greece,* Berkeley, 1977.

Boardman, John, *Greek Art,* 4th ed., New York, 1996.

———, *The Greeks Overseas,* rev. ed., London, 1982. The standard treatment of Greek colonization.

Burkert, Walter, *Greek Religion,* Cambridge, Mass., 1985. Up-to-date and encyclopedic. Best used as a reference work.

Burn, A. R., *The Lyric Age of Greece,* New York, 1961. A lively introduction to the seventh and sixth centuries B.C.E.

Davies, J. K., *Democracy and Classical Greece,* 2d ed., Cambridge, Mass., 1993. Lucid and authoritative.

Dover, K. J., *Greek Homosexuality,* Cambridge, Mass., 1989. The standard treatment of a basic aspect of classical Greek life.

Finley, M. I., *The Ancient Greeks: An Introduction to Their Life and Thought,* New York, 1963. An expert, brief introduction to the Greeks.

———, *The World of Odysseus,* 2d ed., New York, 1978. Attempts to use the Homeric poems as a guide to Dark-Age Greece.

Grant, Michael, *The Rise of the Greeks,* New York, 1988. A clear account of the early period until c. 500 B.C.E. Goes beyond the traditional emphasis on Athens.

Kagan, Donald, *Pericles of Athens and the Birth of Democracy,* New York, 1991.

Kitto, H. D. F., *The Greeks,* Baltimore, 1957. A delightfully written, highly personal interpretation.

Lloyd, G. E. R., *Early Greek Science: Thales to Aristotle,* New York, 1974.

Marrou, H. I., *A History of Education in Antiquity,* Madison, Wis. 1982. A modern classic that covers the entire ancient world.

Meiggs, Russell, *The Athenian Empire,* Oxford, 1979. The major study of fifth-century Athenian imperialism; a monumental work.

Pollitt, J. J., *Art and Experience in Classical Greece,* Cambridge, Eng., 1972. The best introduction to the social and intellectual forces behind Greek art.

Pomeroy, Sarah B., *Families in Classical and Hellenistic Greece,* New York, 1996.

———, *Goddesses, Whores, Wives, and Slaves: Women in Classical Antiquity,* New York, 1995. The best treatment of the role of women in Greece and Rome. Relies on a variety of source material and covers women of all classes.

Sinclair, R. K., *Democracy and Participation in Athens,* New York, 1988. A keen-sighted and clearly written account of one of Athens's greatest experiments.

Snell, Bruno, *The Discovery of the Mind: The Greek Origins of European Thought,* Cambridge, Mass., 1953. Stimulating essays.

Starr, Chester G., *The Economic and Social Growth of Early Greece, 800–500 B.C.,* New York, 1977. An excellent study of this difficult but important topic.

Stockton, D. L., *The Classical Athenian Democracy,* Oxford, 1990. A nontechnical, clearly written summary of recent research; highly recommended.

Source Materials

Most Greek authors have been translated in the appropriate volumes of the Loeb Classical Library, Harvard University Press.

In addition the following may be helpful:

Barnstone, Willis, tr., *Greek Lyric Poetry,* New York, 1962.

Kagan, Donald, *Sources in Greek Political Thought,* Glencoe, Ill., 1965.

Lattimore, R., tr., *Greek Lyrics,* Chicago, 1960.

———, tr., *The Iliad,* Chicago, 1961.

———, tr., *The Odyssey,* New York, 1968.

CHAPTER 6

HELLENISTIC CIVILIZATION

> Alexander wept when he heard from Anaxarchus that there was an infinite number of worlds. When his friends asked if any accident had befallen him, he answered: "Do you not think it a matter worthy of lamentation that when there is such a vast multitude of them, we have not yet conquered one?"
>
> —PLUTARCH, *On the Tranquillity of the Mind*

The exploits of Alexander the Great

THE SUPREME TRAGEDY OF THE GREEKS was their failure to solve the problem of political conflict. Gravely weakened by the wars between cities that transpired from 431 B.C.E. until 338 B.C.E. Greek civilization was simultaneously rescued and transformed by one of the most remarkable characters who ever trod the world's stage, a young man later known as Alexander the Great. In 338 B.C.E. Alexander's father, Philip of Macedon, a semibarbarian chieftain from the rocky wildernesses north of Greece, took over all of Greece by decisively defeating a combined Athenian-Theban force in pitched battle. Two years later Philip was killed in a family feud, and his dashingly handsome and energetic son Alexander succeeded him at the age of twenty. Swiftly consolidating his rule throughout Greece by putting to death all possible rivals, in 334 B.C.E. Alexander felt secure enough to leave behind a deputy and cross into Asia with an army of 48,000 troops to carve out some additional territory. The Persians may first have looked askance at this brash twenty-two-year-old advancing in their direction, but within four years, as the victor of three brilliantly fought battles—the Granicus (334), Issus (333), and Gaugamela (331)—Alexander had conquered the entire Persian Empire. During this campaign Alexander's troops performed some of the most stunning feats in the annals of military history. In the midst of hot and arid Persian terrain, for example, they marched with heavy packs on their backs from sundown until noon in sixteen-hour stretches, averaging a march rate of 33 miles per day. Rather than returning home or residing peacefully in the Persian capital of Persepolis after this whirlwind campaign, Alexander then marched farther east to conquer Bactria (modern Afghanistan) and cross the Indus River into India, spending two years (327–326 B.C.E.) in an attempt to destroy Hindu armies equipped with war elephants. When his troops finally refused to fight any more in such distant lands, he took them back to the Persian heartland and died in Babylon of an infectious disease in 323 B.C.E. while preparing for another aggressive campaign—this time to Arabia. Although Alexander supposedly wept because he had not conquered the globe, he still had traversed some 20,000 miles, fighting as he went, to become in his twenties the ruler of the largest empire the world had ever seen.

A hybrid civilization

Alexander the Great's conquests laid the foundations for the *Hellenistic civilization,* a civilization that endured from his own time until roughly the beginning of the Christian era in all the lands of the eastern Mediterranean and western Asia. The term *Hellenistic* means "Greek-like," and stands in contrast to *Hellenic,* or purely Greek. Hellenistic civilization was "Greek-like" because it was a hybrid, composed of Greek and Asian elements. Alexander himself spoke Greek and had been educated by none other than the great Greek philosopher Aristotle, yet he ignored the Greek precepts of modesty and living according to the "golden mean." Similarly, during the Hellenistic era Greek became the language of government in Mesopotamia, Syria, and Egypt, and Greek philosophy and literature were cultivated throughout western Asia, yet Greek-speaking rulers insisted upon being adored as divinities. We will presently see that Hellenistic culture was not just a hodgepodge but had its own distinctive traits. But before we examine the fascinating Hellenistic civilization itself, it is necessary to take account of its Persian background because, just as the Hellenistic world could not have existed without Alexander the Great and the Greeks, so it could not have existed without the prior accomplishments of Cyrus the Great and the Persians.

Marble Head of Alexander. Alexander the Great was reputed to have been very handsome, but all surviving representations doubtless make him more handsome still. This one dates from about 180 B.C.E. and is typical in showing Alexander with "lion's-mane hair."

THE PERSIAN EMPIRE

The rise of Cyrus

Almost nothing is known of the Persians before the middle of the sixth century B.C.E., other than that they lived on the eastern shore of the Persian Gulf, spoke an Indo-European language, and were subject to the Medes, a kindred people who inhabited territories east and north of the River Tigris. Out of this obscurity the Persians emerged suddenly into the spotlight of history owing to the extraordinary exploits of a prince named Cyrus, who succeeded to the rule of a southern Persian tribe in 559 B.C.E. Swiftly thereafter Cyrus made himself ruler of all the Persians, and around 549 B.C.E. he threw off the lordship of the Medes, taking over their domination of lands that stretched from the Persian Gulf to the Halys River in Asia Minor.

The annexation of Lydia

By occupying part of Asia Minor, Cyrus became a neighbor of the kingdom of Lydia, which then comprised the western half of Asia Minor up to the Halys. The Indo-European Lydians had created one of the successor states of the Hittites and had attained great prosperity as a result of gold-prospecting and acting as intermediaries for overland commerce between Mesopotamia and the Aegean Sea. In connection with their commercial enterprises the Lydians invented the use of metallic coinage as a medium of exchange for goods and services. When Cyrus reached their border, the

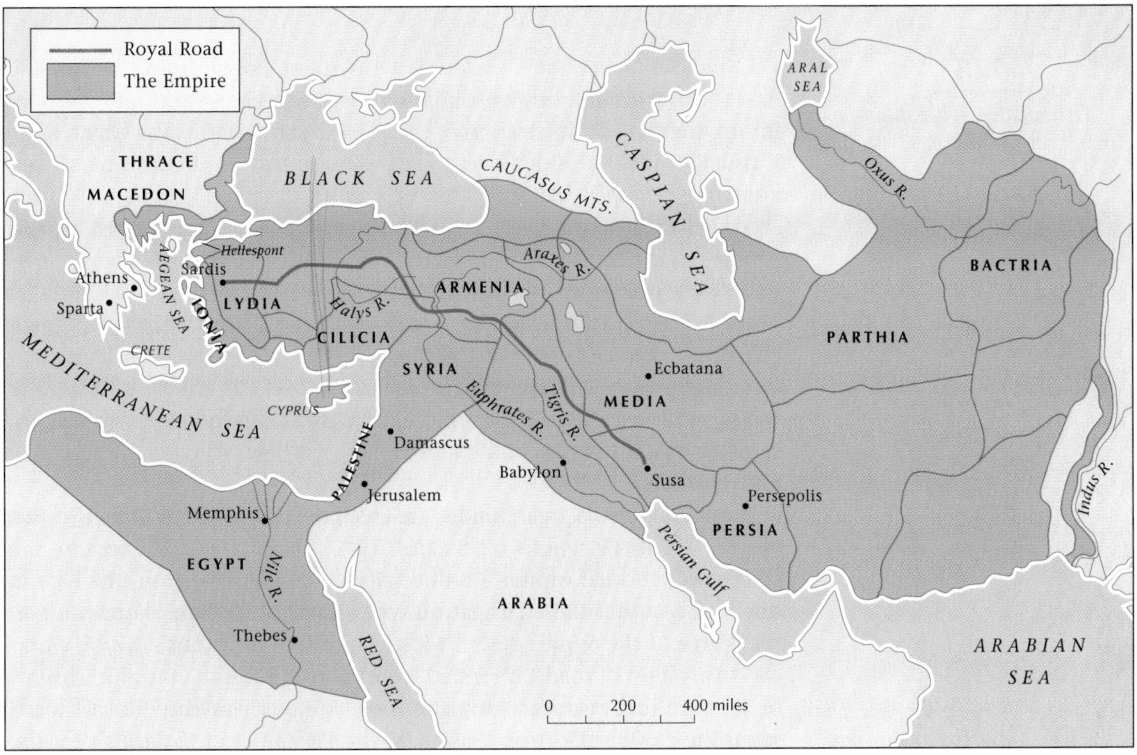

The Persian Empire under Darius I, 521–486 B.C.E.

reigning king of the Lydians was Croesus (pronounced Creesus), so rich that the simile "rich as Croesus" remains embedded in our language. Distrusting the newcomer, Croesus decided in 546 B.C.E. to wage a preventive war in order to preserve his kingdom from conquest. According to the Greek historian Herodotus, Croesus consulted the oracle at Delphi as to the advisability of an immediate attack and gained the reply that if he would cross the Halys he would destroy a great nation. He did, but the nation he destroyed was his own. His forces were overwhelmed, and his prosperous realm was annexed as a province of the Persian state.

An Early Lydian Coin. Probably struck during the reign of Croesus.

Cyrus invaded Mesopotamia in 539 B.C.E. and struck so quickly that he was able to take Babylon without a fight. Once in Babylon the entire Babylonian Empire was his. We have seen earlier that Cyrus allowed the Jews who had been held captive in Babylon to return to Palestine and set up a semi-independent vassal state; here it can be added that Cyrus allowed other conquered peoples considerable self-determination as well. Dying in 529 of wounds incurred in a minor skirmish with barbarian tribes to the north of his realms near the Aral Sea, Cyrus left behind him an empire vaster than any that had previously existed. Yet shortly afterward, in 525, the Persian Empire became vaster still when Cyrus's son Cambyses conquered all of Egypt.

Consolidation of the Persian Empire under Darius the Great

Cambyses's successor, Darius I, who ruled Persia from 521 to 486 B.C.E., concentrated on consolidating his predecessors' military gains by improving the administration of the Persian state. Darius the Great, as he is usually called, presided over the division of the empire into provinces, known as *satrapies,* administered by governors called *satraps,* who were accorded extensive powers but who were obliged to send fixed annual tributes to the central government. (Vassal states such as the Jewish kingdom were obliged to send the Persian government annual tributes as well.) Adhering to the tolerant policy of Cyrus, Darius allowed the various non-Persian peoples of the Persian Empire to retain most of their local institutions while enforcing a standardized currency and system of weights and measures. For example, Darius's satrap in Egypt restored ancient Egyptian temples and codified Egyptian laws in consultation with native priests.

Darius as a builder

Darius was also a great builder. He erected a new royal residence, called by the Greeks Persepolis ("Persian City"), which thereafter became the Persian ceremonial capital. Additionally he dug a canal from the Nile to the Red Sea and installed irrigation systems on the Persian plateau and on the fringe of the Syrian desert. Most impressive of Darius's public works was his system of roads, intended to enhance trade and communications in his far-flung realms. Justly the most famous was the "Royal Road" spanning 1,600 miles from Susa near the Persian Gulf to Sardis near the Aegean. Government couriers along this road were the first "postal system" because they passed messages and goods in relay stages from one "post" to another, with each post measured by the distance traversable in

The Great Palace of Darius and Xerxes at Persepolis. Persian architecture made use of fluted columns, copied from the Greeks, and reliefs resembling those of the Assyrians.

a day's horseback ride: a fresh horse and rider would be ready at each post to carry what had been brought by the "postman" before him. Few people today realize that the motto of the U.S. Postal Service is borrowed from Herodotus's praise for the Persian messengers on the Royal Road: "neither snow nor rain nor heat nor gloom of night stays these couriers from the swift completion of their appointed rounds."

Greek resistance to Persian overlordship

Extraordinarily gifted as an administrator, Darius the Great made one enormous mistake in geopolitical strategy: his attempt to extend Persian hegemony into Greece. After Cyrus's conquest of Lydia had made Persia the ruler of Greek-speaking cities on the western coast of Asia Minor, no matter how tolerant Persia's rule was, these cities continued to yearn for the freedom of all other Greek city-states. Consequently, between 499 and 494 B.C.E. the Greeks on the Asian mainland waged a war for independence and briefly gained the support of troops from Athens, who joined the Asian Greeks in burning Sardis, the Persian regional administrative center. After Darius had quelled the uprising he decided to be certain that his Greek subjects would never again receive foreign aid: he sent a force across the Aegean in 490 to punish Athens and let all European Greeks know that henceforth he intended to be their overlord. At the battle of Marathon in 490, the Athenians dealt Darius the only major setback he ever experienced. Although in 480 his son and successor, Xerxes, attempted to avenge the humiliation by crushing all Greece with a tremendous army, heroic resistance by Athens and Sparta forced him to retreat and abandon his plans a year later. At that point the Persians must have realized that the limits of their expansionism had been reached, and that they now had to beware of the European Greeks as their implacable enemies.

Persian Gold Drinking Cup. Persian fondness for lions probably derived from the art of the Assyrians.

In fact from 479 B.C.E. until Alexander the Great's invasion of Asia Minor in 334 B.C.E. the Greeks were usually too embroiled by internal rivalries to pose any challenge to Persia. From the Persian perspective that was extremely fortunate, for during the period in question the Persian Empire was beset by governmental instability caused by intrigues for the throne and rebellions in various provinces. By the time of Alexander, although the empire had survived intact, it had become extremely rickety. Nonetheless, when Alexander gained the expanses won by Cyrus he also gained two intangible legacies—one religious, the other broadly cultural.

The founding of Zoroastrianism

Persia's religious legacy was Zoroastrianism, which along with Buddhism and Judaism, was one of the three major *universal* and *personal* religions known to the world before Christianity and Islam. Although distant origins of Zoroastrianism can be traced back as far as the sixteenth century B.C.E., the religion's real founder, and the one who gave it its name, was Zoroaster (the Greek form of the Persian name Zarathustra), a Persian who seems to have lived shortly before 600 B.C.E. (There is scholarly disagreement on when Zoroaster lived, with some authorities arguing for a date many centuries earlier.) Zoroaster was probably the first real theologian in history, the first known person to devise a fully developed system of religious belief. He seems to have conceived it as his mission to purify the traditional customs of the Persian tribes—to eradicate polytheism, animal sacrifice, and magic—and to establish their worship on a more coherent and ethical plane.

A universal religion characterized by dualism

Zoroastrianism was a universal religion inasmuch as Zoroaster taught that there was one supreme god in the universe, whom he called Ahura-Mazda, meaning "the wise lord." Ahura-Mazda embodied the principles of light, truth, and righteousness; there was nothing wrathful or evil about him, and his light shone everywhere, not just upon one tribe. Because sin or sorrow in the world could not be explained by reference to Ahura-Mazda, Zoroaster posited the existence of a counter-deity, Ahriman, treacherous and malignant, who presided over the forces of darkness and evil. Apparently in Zoroaster's own view Ahura-Mazda was vastly stronger than Ahriman, whom Ahura-Mazda allowed to exist almost by absentmindedness, but the priests of Zoroastrianism, known as *magi,* gradually came to emphasize the dualistic aspect of the founder's thought by insisting that Ahura-Mazda and Ahriman were about evenly matched and were engaged in a desperate struggle for supremacy. According to them, only on the last great day would "light" decisively triumph over "darkness," when Ahura-Mazda would overpower Ahriman and cast him into the abyss.

A personal religion

Zoroastrianism was a personal religion, making private rather than public demands. Ahura-Mazda patronized neither tribes nor states but only individuals who served his cause of truth and justice. Humans possessed free will and were free to sin or not to sin. Of course Zoroastrianism urged them not to sin but to be truthful, to love and help one another to the best of their powers, to aid the poor, and to practice generous hospitality. Those who did so would be rewarded in an afterlife, for the religion posited the resurrection of the dead on "judgment day" and their consignment to a realm either of bliss or of flames. In the scriptures of the Zoroastrian faith known as the *Avesta* (a work compiled by accretion over the course of many centuries) the rewards for righteousness are explicit: "Whosoever shall give meat to one of the faithful . . . shall go to Paradise."

Zoroastrianism's similarities to Judaism and Christianity

The brief recital of Zoroastrianism's tenets makes clear that the religion bore numerous similarities to Judaism and Christianity. Zoroastrianism's ethical content resembles the teachings of the Jewish prophets, its eschatology resembles aspects of postexilic Judaism, and its heaven and hell resemble aspects of the afterlife teaching of Christianity. Even the existence of authoritative scriptures is reminiscent of the weight accorded by Jews to the Old Testament and by Christians to the Old and New Testaments. Unfortunately it is not possible to determine with any precision in what direction influences may have flown because of nearly insuperable chronological complexities. Yet it is surely not coincidental that central aspects of Jewish religious thought took shape in an Asian world dominated by Cyrus and Darius—both convinced Zoroastrians—or that later Jewish beliefs about a judgment day, which themselves influenced Christianity, evolved in a Hellenistic world in which Zoroastrianism continued to exert influence. Furthermore, entirely aside from likely Zoroastrian influence on Judaism, the Persian faith exerted some influence on western Asia's Greek conquerors in encouraging them to think of religion in ever more universalistic and personal terms.

Persian universalism

Universalism is also the expression that best characterizes Persia's cultural contribution to the Hellenistic synthesis. Unlike the Assyrians, the Babylonians, and the Egyptians, all of whom tried to impose their own customs on conquered peoples (when they did not simply enslave them), the Persians adopted a tolerant "one world" policy, by which they conceived themselves to be the guiding force over an assemblage of united nations. Whereas Mesopotamian potentates characteristically called themselves "true king," the rulers of the Persian Empire took the title "king of kings," thereby implying that they recognized the continued existence of various peoples with various rulers under the canopy of their rule. Moreover, the greatest Persian monarchs, Cyrus and Darius, continually sought to learn whatever they could from the customs and the science of the peoples they conquered. For example, they adopted the Lydian invention of metallic coinage and learned to chart the night skies from Babylonian astronomers.

The eclectic character of Persian architecture

The Persian habit of borrowing ideas from others, known as *eclecticism*, can be observed most clearly in their architecture. The Persians copied the terraced building style that had been standard in Babylonia, and they also imitated the winged bulls, the brilliantly colored glazed bricks, and other decorative motifs of Mesopotamian architecture. Yet in place of the Mesopotamian arch and vault they adopted the column and the colonnade from Egypt. In addition, interior arrangement and the use of palm and lotus designs at the base of columns also derived from Egyptian influence. Finally, the fluting of the columns and the scrolls beneath the capitals were not Egyptian, but Greek, adopted from the Greek cities of Asia Minor. With Alexander's arrival the Persians would become directly subject to the mainland Greeks, but the Greeks would immediately begin borrowing from the Persians.

Two Reliefs from the Staircase of the Great Palace at Persepolis

Philip of Macedon and Alexander the Great

Political division in Greece

Throughout the first two-thirds of the fourth century B.C.E. many Greeks took to heart a verse from Euripides's play *Andromache*—"In Greece, alas! how ill things ordered are!"—but none seemed able to do much about it. Greece's "ill order" was its political division: city fought city and faction fought faction. As Thebes warred with Sparta and Athens warred with Thebes, ever more Greeks began to long for a national "strongman" to quell all strife, however much imperialism and tyranny were at variance with pristine Greek ideals. Finally a strongman appeared in the person of Philip of Macedon.

Macedon transformed under Philip

Had Philip's fame not been overshadowed by that of his son Alexander, he surely would have been known as Philip the Great. Before he assumed rule in Macedon in 359 B.C.E. the Greek-speaking territory north of Greece had no cities, little agriculture, and no political stability, being little more than a warring ground for rival clans. Yet by sheer force of will Philip transformed Macedon into a major power within two decades. First he eliminated all his rivals, then he introduced autocratic institutions of government, and then he began to expand his frontiers by a combination of military skill and "divide and conquer" diplomacy. Philip's fighting style led to a revolution in the art of warfare. Hitherto the Greeks had formed their armies almost exclusively from citizen-volunteers and conscripts, all of whom could fight for only part of the year because they could not abandon their crops during farming seasons. With limited periods of training, almost all soldiers in such armies fought the same way, as massed infantry with heavy arms. In contrast, drawing partly on mercenaries and partly on loyal Macedonians who had no farming commitments, Philip built a professional army.

The Macedonian professional army

The advantages of the Macedonian professional army, which later served Alexander the Great as well as Philip, were manifold. For one, the commander of such a force could count on a wide range of "specialists." Philip's army had an effective mobile cavalry and it had *skirmishers*—fighters whose goal was to demoralize and confuse the enemy at the onset of battle by distracting them with a rain of projectiles coming from the wrong part of the field. Not least among Philip's specialists were well-

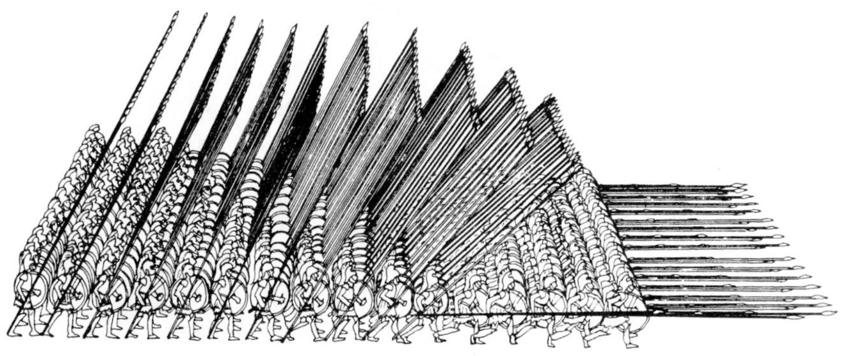

Macedonian Phalanx. Philip of Macedon's infantry—and Alexander the Great's thereafter—was armed with two-handed pikes and massed in squares sixteen rows deep and wide. Members of the phalanx were trained to wheel in step in any direction or to double their front by filing off in rows of eight.

trained spies and counterspies, adept at the art of spreading "disinformation." Another advantage of professionalism was that it brought the strictest discipline. Free Greeks who volunteered for service might, from idealism, have imposed some discipline on themselves, yet it would have been difficult for a commander to address them peremptorily, and their idealism would have tended to diminish in inverse proportion to the length of campaigns. Philip's army, on the other hand, took orders without flinching, having no doubts about the consequences of insubordination: supposedly Philip once murdered a sleeping sentry on the spot, stating coolly as he walked off, "I left him as I found him." Finally, professionalism allowed Philip to eliminate large numbers of noncombatant servants who carried provisions. Earlier Greek forces moved slowly from site to site and were hampered by logistical problems because they were swelled with men who carried food and arms for other men, but Philip forced his fighters to carry their necessities for themselves as much as strength allowed. All of Philip's innovations were considered uncouth by the "gentlemanly" Greeks of the city-states, but his indifference to military "good manners" allowed him to engage in lightning strikes and ensured his victory in 338 B.C.E. over combined Athenian and Theban forces at the battle of Chaeronea.

Despotism and conquest

That victory ended Greek city-state freedom because after Chaeronea Philip installed his despotic rule throughout Greece, and his son Alexander thereafter maintained that despotism as the springboard for the conquest of half of Asia. Much irony resides in the fact that Alexander's tutor during his early teenage years had been Aristotle, the very Greek philosopher who insisted that humans are so designed by nature for life in city-states that "he who can live without one must be either a beast or a god," for Alexander proved indifferent to this teaching and proceeded to act as if his tutor had been not a Greek but a Persian. Some historians used to think that Alexander's amazing march through Asia Minor, Egypt, Mesopotamia, Persia, and Afghanistan to the borders of India was motivated by an urgent sense of mission to bring Greek enlightenment to purportedly benighted Asians, but it is now widely agreed upon that Alexander was driven forward solely by a quest for power and glory that verged on megalomania. (He named several cities "Alexandria" after himself.) In his own day the story was told that a sea pirate taken captive by the mighty conqueror told him that the only difference between them was one of scale. If we put aside motives, however, it was Alexander's conquests, and not the pirate's, that provided the foundations for the Hellenistic civilization.

Intermarriage encouraged

Alexander's pattern of rule itself was Hellenistic in mixing Greek and Asiatic traits. For propaganda purposes the young Macedonian claimed to be punishing Persia for insults inflicted earlier on Greeks, and in fact he not only customarily replaced Persian governors with Greek-speaking ones but imported Greek settlers to inhabit newly founded cities as a means of keeping conquered populations in a state of subordination. Yet

Alexander in Battle. A scene from a sarcophagus of about 300 B.C.E. Alexander is shown on horseback at the left.

Alexander also recognized that he and his Greeks could never hope to rule a gigantic Asian empire as hated foreigners, and hence encouraged intermarriage. In keeping with this policy Alexander himself married a Bactrian princess (although his ultimate preferences were homosexual), and divided a loaf of bread with his bride at the wedding as a gesture of deference to local custom.

Alexander's Asian trappings

What inspired Alexander most about the ways of Asia were not princesses or loaves of bread, but any Asian customs that might enhance his autocracy and his glamour. The traditions of Greece, of course, were at odds with flattery and ostentation. Well known is the story that when Alexander first assumed rule in Greece he met the philosopher Diogenes sitting in a wooden tub that served as his home and asked the sage if he would like a favor. "Yes," said Diogenes, "move out of my sun." Determined not to be spoken to this way if he could possibly help it, Alexander adopted lavish Persian dress as he moved through Asia and commanded subjects to approach him, depending on their rank, on bended knee or fully prostrate. Groveling before the ruler was thus not just a figure of speech. Most extreme was Alexander's decision to proclaim himself a god. Although he did this only in Egypt, where the pharaohs had long been worshiped as offspring of the sun-god Amon, claiming divinity was an extraordinary measure for a Greek who was expected to move out of the sun at the behest of an unkempt philosopher.

The Hellenistic states

When Alexander died in 323 B.C.E., he left no legitimate heir to succeed him save a feeble-minded half brother. Tradition relates that when his friends requested him on his deathbed to designate a successor, he replied "to the strongest." After his death his highest-ranking generals proceeded to divide the empire among themselves. Some of the younger commanders contested this arrangement, and a series of wars followed culminating in the decisive battle of Ipsus in 301 B.C.E. The result was a new division among the victors. Seleucus took possession of Persia, Mesopotamia, and Syria; Lysimachus assumed control over Asia Minor and Thrace; Cassander established himself in Macedonia; and Ptolemy added Phoenicia and Palestine to his original domain of Egypt. Twenty years later these four states were reduced to three when Seleucus defeated and killed Lysimachus in battle and appropriated his territory in Asia Minor. In the meantime most of the Greek cities had revolted against Macedonian rule. By banding together in defensive leagues, several of them succeeded in maintaining some independence in federalist form for nearly a century. Finally, between 146 and 30 B.C.E. nearly all of the Hellenistic territory passed under Roman rule, except the easternmost part, which reverted to rule under native Persians.

Despotism of semi-divine rulers beyond Greece

The dominant form of government in the Hellenistic age throughout all the lands once conquered by Alexander, except for mainland Greece,

Alexander the Great and the Hellenistic World

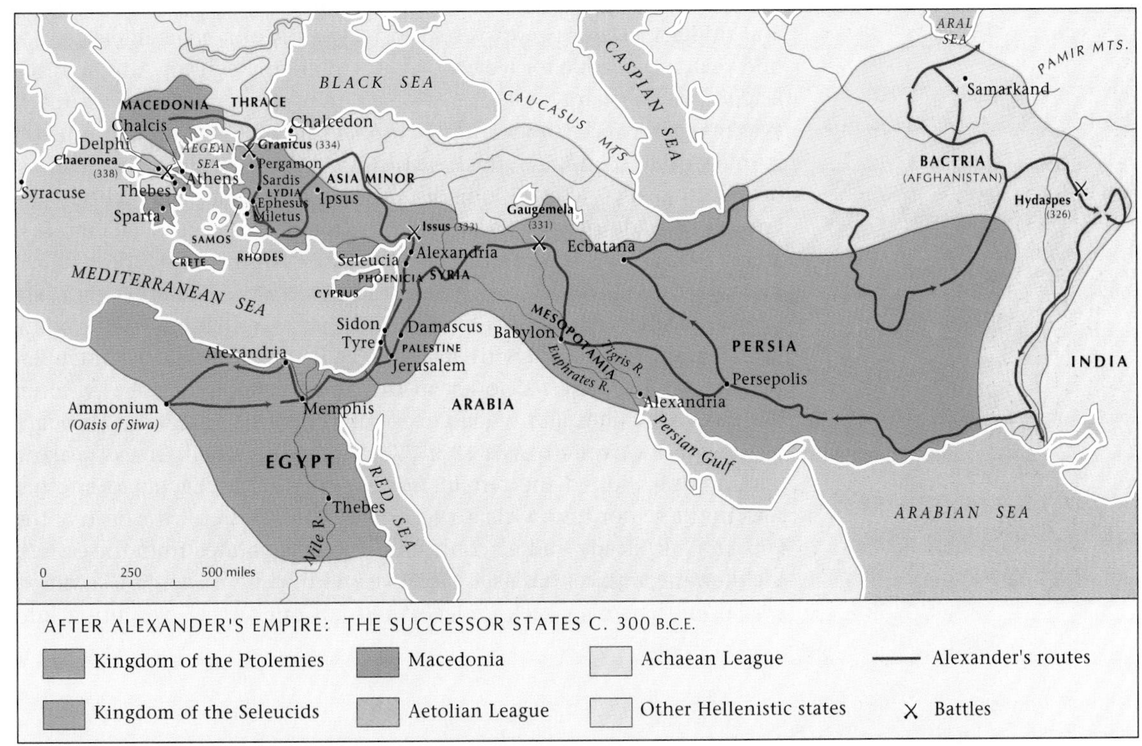

was the despotism of rulers who represented themselves as at least semi-divine. Alexander's most powerful successors, the Seleucid kings in western Asia and the Ptolemies in Egypt, made systematic attempts to deify themselves. A Seleucid monarch, Antiochus IV, adopted the title "Epiphanes," or "God manifest." The later members of the dynasty of the Ptolemies signed their decrees "Theos" (God) and revived the practice of sister marriage that had been followed by the pharaohs as a means of preserving the divine blood of the royal family from contamination. Rulers such as these brooked no formal opposition, yet the inevitable consequence of untrammeled autocracy was frequent palace intrigue, leading to stabbings, poisonings, conspirings with foreign rivals, invasions, and wars. Following a policy of kill or be killed, Ptolemy IV of Egypt (221–204 B.C.E.) put to death his mother, his uncle, and his brother. Generations later his descendant, the beauteous Cleopatra (69–30 B.C.E.), intrigued with Romans in a vain attempt to maintain some semblance of Hellenistic Egyptian independence. (It is often forgotten that this most famous of Egyptians was purely Greek by her ancestry.)

Alexander the Great. Hellenistic rulers depicted Alexander on their coins in order to stress their connection with the revered hero. This dramatic profile was struck by Lysimachus of Thrace around 300 B.C.E.

Greek city leagues

The only viable alternative to despotism during the Hellenistic era was the city-state federalism developed in mainland Greece. After having gained independence from the Hellenistic state of Macedon, several Greek cities formed defensive alliances that rapidly evolved into two confederations: the Aetolian League and the Achaean League. These leagues dominated all of Greece until 146 B.C.E., when they were supplanted by Roman rule. The organization of both leagues was basically the same. Each had a federal council that was composed of representatives of the member cities and that had power to enact laws on subjects of general concern. An assembly that all of the citizens of the member cities could attend decided questions of war and peace and elected officials. Executive and military authority was vested in the hands of a general, elected for one year and eligible for reelection only in alternate years. Although the leagues were certainly not unified states, they were the nearest approach ever made in Greece to voluntary national union before modern times.

Dynamic aspects of Hellenistic economy: the growth of trade

In regard to economics, the Hellenistic world was generally prosperous, owing to the growth of long-distance trade, finance, and cities. The growth of trade may be explained by reference to several factors, first among which was the opening up of a vast trading area as the result of Alexander's conquests. Long before the time of Alexander, Greeks had been energetic long-distance traders, but they were hampered in trading with Persian realms and with areas east of Persia because Persian emperors and satraps preferred to act in their own economic interests rather than in Greek ones. But when Greek rulers became ensconced throughout Egypt and western Asia after 323 B.C.E., and when Greek-speaking communities dotted the terrain from Alexandria in Egypt, to another Alexandria in northern Syria, to yet another Alexandria at the head of the Persian Gulf, steady trading connections were facilitated from the eastern Mediterranean to central Asia. Moreover, with bases in Egypt, Asia Minor, Persia, and Bactria, Greek traders could fan out farther, venturing into sub-Saharan Africa, Russia, and India. Second, Alexander unwittingly stimulated a growth of intensive investment when he placed in circulation hoards of Persian gold and silver in the form of coins, jewelry, and luxury utensils. And third, manufacturing industries aimed at providing items for trade were now more consciously promoted by autocratic rulers as a means of increasing their revenues.

New trading facilities and merchandise

New trading ventures were particularly vigorous and lucrative in Ptolemaic Egypt and the area of western Asia ruled over by the Seleucid monarchs, the heartland of which was Syria. Every facility was provided by the Ptolemies and the Seleucids for the encouragement of trade. Harbors were improved, warships were sent out to police the seas, and roads and canals were built. Moreover, the Ptolemies employed geographers to discover new routes to distant lands and thereby open up valuable markets. As a result of such methods Egypt developed a flourishing commerce in the widest variety of products. Into the port of Alexandria came spices from Arabia, gold from Ethiopia and India, tin from Britain, elephants and ivory from Nubia, silver from Spain, fine carpets from Asia Minor, and even silk from China. Profits for the government and for some of the merchants were often as high as 20 or 30 percent.

The growth of cities

Cities grew enormously during the Hellenistic Age, for a combination of reasons. Entirely aside from economic motives, Greek rulers imported Greek officials and especially Greek soldiers to maintain their control over non-Greek populations. Often this policy resulted in the creation of urban settlements from nothing. Alexander the Great himself had founded some seventy cities as outposts of Greek domination, and in the next two centuries his successors founded about two hundred more. Yet urbanization also increased because of the expansion of commerce and industry and the proliferation of governmental bureaus responsible for economic oversight. Hence the growth of populations in some urban centers was explosive. The population of Antioch in Syria quadrupled during a single century. Seleucia on the Tigris grew from nothing to a metropolis of several hundred thousand in less than two centuries. The largest and most famous of all the Hellenistic cities was Alexandria in Egypt, with about 500,000 inhabitants. No other city in ancient times before imperial Rome surpassed it in size or in magnificence. Its streets were well paved and laid out in regular order. It had splendid public buildings and parks, a museum, and a library of half a million scrolls. The masses of its people, however, had no share in the brilliant and luxurious life around them, although it was paid for in part out of the fruits of their labor.

Antiochus I, "Soter." A Hellenistic ruler of Syria (281–261 B.C.E.), whose chosen title of *soter* meant "savior." The faraway stare connotes supernatural inspiration.

The predominance of agriculture and the advance of manual industry

While the Hellenistic economy was basically a dynamic one, throughout the Hellenistic period agriculture remained the major occupation and the primary source of wealth. (Only within the last century did trade and industry replace agriculture as the major source of wealth in western Europe and North America.) Furthermore, although industry advanced in Hellenistic Egypt and parts of western Asia, nowhere did a true "industrial revolution" based on any technological breakthrough occur. Rather, all industry was based on manual labor rather than being power driven.

The Marble Streets of Ephesus. Taken from the Persians by Alexander in 334 B.C.E., this cosmopolitan city on the west coast of Asia Minor was noted for its splendor.

The uneven impact of prosperity

Despite the overall growth and prosperity of the Hellenistic economy, prosperity was by no means enjoyed by everyone. Quite to the contrary, for some people sudden wealth was followed by sudden penury, and for others poverty was a constant. Individual merchants and speculators were those most subject to drastic fluctuations in their fortunes, owing to the natural precariousness of mercantile endeavors. A trader who did very well selling a luxury cloth might have decided to invest heavily in it, only to find that tastes had changed, or that a ship he had dispatched to convey his wares had sunk. Merchants were also particularly exposed to what economists now recognize as the "boom and bust" syndrome. A merchant, thinking he would make a fortune during an upward price spiral, might go into debt in order to take advantage of the upward trend, only to find that supply in the commodity he traded suddenly exceeded demand, leaving him nothing with which to pay back his creditors. Among those whose poverty remained unchanged were small-scale farmers who grew crops for sale in regional markets. (In Greece they may have become poorer because Greece suffered during the Hellenistic era from a negative balance of payments, having little to offer for long-distance trade except objects of art.) Those who immigrated to cities in most cases probably did not improve their economic status, and many of them became subject to badly overcrowded living conditions. All told, therefore, it seems clear that the economic landscape of the Hellenistic world was one of contrasting extremes, an image worth remembering in moving to a consideration of Hellenistic thought and culture.

Hellenistic Culture: Philosophy and Religion

Trends in philosophy and religion

Hellenistic philosophy exhibited two trends that ran almost parallel throughout the civilization. The major trend, exemplified by Epicureanism and Stoicism, showed a fundamental regard for reason as the key to the solution of human problems. This trend was a manifestation of

Greek influence, though philosophy and science, as combined in Aristotle, had now come to a parting of the ways. The minor trend, exemplified by the Skeptics and various Asian cults, tended to reject reason, to deny the possibility of attaining truth, and in some cases to turn toward mysticism and reliance upon faith. Despite the differences in their teachings, the philosophers and religious enthusiasts of the Hellenistic Age generally agreed upon one thing: the necessity of finding some release from the trials of human existence, for with the decline of free civic life as a means for the expression of human idealism, alternatives needed to be found to make life seem meaningful, or at least endurable.

Epicureanism and Stoicism

Epicureanism and Stoicism both originated about 300 B.C.E. The founders were, respectively, Epicurus (c. 342–270) and Zeno (fl. after 300), both residents of Athens. The two philosophies had several features in common. Both were individualistic, concerned not with the welfare of society but with the good of the individual. Both were materialistic, denying the existence of any spiritual substances; even divine beings and the soul were declared to be formed of matter. Moreover, Stoicism and Epicureanism alike contained elements of universalism since both taught that people are the same the world over and recognized no distinctions between Greeks and non-Greeks.

The Stoics' pursuit of tranquillity of mind through fatalism

But in most ways the two systems were quite different. The Stoics believed that the cosmos is an ordered whole in which all contradictions are resolved for ultimate good. Evil is, therefore, relative; the particular misfortunes that befall human beings are but necessary incidents to the final perfection of the universe. Everything that happens is rigidly determined in accordance with rational purpose. No individual is master of his fate; human destiny is a link in an unbroken chain. People are free only in the sense that they can accept their fate or rebel against it. But whether they accept or rebel, they cannot overcome it. Their supreme duty is to submit to the order of the universe in the knowledge that this order is good. Through such an act of resignation the highest happiness will be attained, which consists of tranquillity of mind. Those who are most truly happy are thus the ones who by the assertion of their rational natures have accomplished a perfect adjustment of their lives to the cosmic purpose and purged their souls of all bitterness and whining protest against evil turns of fortune.

The ethical and social teachings of the Stoics

The Stoics' ethical and social theory grew from their general philosophy. Believing that the highest good is serenity of mind, they emphasized duty and self-discipline as cardinal virtues. Recognizing the prevalence of particular evils, they taught tolerance for and forgiveness of one another. They also urged participation in public affairs as a duty for those of rational mind. They condemned slavery and war, although they took no real actions against these evils since they believed that the results that might arise from violent measures of social change would be worse than the diseases they were meant to cure. With appropriate qualifications, then, the Stoic philosophy was one of the noblest products of the Hellenistic Age in teaching egalitarianism, pacifism, and humanitarianism.

Epicureans and pleasure

The Epicureans based their philosophy on the materialistic "atomism" of an earlier Greek thinker named Democritus, who lived in the latter part of the fifth century B.C.E. According to this theory the ultimate constituents of the universe are atoms, infinite in number, indestructible, and indivisible. Every individual object or organism in the universe is the product of a fortuitous concourse of atoms. Taking this as given, Epicurus and his followers proposed that since there is no ultimate purpose in the universe, the highest good is pleasure—the moderate satisfaction of bodily appetites, the mental pleasure of contemplating excellence and satisfactions previously enjoyed, and above all, serenity of soul. The last end can be best achieved through the elimination of fear, especially fear of the supernatural, since that is the greatest source of mental pain. The individual must understand that the soul is material and therefore cannot survive the body, that the universe operates of itself, and that no gods intervene in human affairs. The Epicureans thus came by a different route to the same general conclusion as the Stoics—there is nothing better than tranquillity of mind.

Woman Playing a Lyre. A marble relief from mainland Greece, first century B.C.E.

The practical moral teachings and the politics of the Epicureans rested upon utilitarianism. In contrast to the Stoics, they did not insist upon virtue as an end in itself but taught that the only reason why one should be good is to increase one's own happiness. In like manner, they denied that there is any such thing as absolute justice: laws and institutions are just only insofar as they contribute to the welfare of the individual. Certain rules have been found necessary in every society for the maintenance of order. These rules should be obeyed solely because it is to each individual's advantage to do so. Epicurus considered the state as a mere convenience and taught that the wise man should take no active part in politics. He did not propose that civilization should be abandoned; yet his conception of the happiest life was essentially passive and defeatist. Epicurus taught that the thinking person will recognize that evils in the world cannot be eradicated by human effort; the individual will therefore withdraw to study philosophy and enjoy the fellowship of a few congenial friends.

The defeatist philosophy of the Skeptics

A more radically defeatist philosophy was that propounded by the Skeptics. Skepticism reached the zenith of its popularity about 200 B.C.E. under the influence of Carneades. The chief source of its inspiration was the teaching that all knowledge is derived from sense perception and therefore must be limited and relative. From this the Skeptics deduced that we cannot prove anything. Since the impressions of our senses deceive us, no truth can be certain. All we can say is that things *appear* to be such and such; we do not know what they really *are*. We have no definite knowledge of the supernatural, of the meaning of life, or even of right and wrong. It follows that the sensible course to pursue is suspension of judgment; this alone can lead to happiness. If we will abandon the fruitless quest for absolute truth and cease worrying about good and evil, we will attain peace of mind, which is the highest satisfaction that life affords. The Skeptics were even less concerned than the Epicureans with political and social problems. Their ideal was one of escape from a world neither reformable nor understandable.

Hellenistic religion similarly tended to offer vehicles of escape from collective political commitments. Although Greek religion in the age of the city-states had emphasized the worship of gods associated with given cities to advance the fortunes of those cities, such civic-oriented worship now lost its vitality. Its place was taken for many of society's leaders by the philosophies of Stoicism, Epicureanism, and Skepticism. Most ordinary people, on the other hand, tended to embrace emotional personal religions offering elaborate ritual in this world and salvation in the next. In Greek-speaking communities cults that stressed extreme ascetic atonement for sin, ecstatic mystical union with divinity, and otherworldly salvation attracted ever more followers. Among these *mystery cults,* so called because their membership was secret and their rites held in private, one of the most popular was the Orphic cult, based on the myth of the death and resurrection of the god Dionysius. Even today the word *Dionysian* connotes dedication to ecstatic religious practices bordering on the orgiastic. In Persian communities Zoroastrianism became ever more extreme in its dualism, with Zoroastrian magi insisting that everything material was evil and demanding that believers practice austerities in order to ready their immaterial souls for ethereal joy in the afterlife. Finally, among Greeks and non-Greeks alike, an offshoot of Zoroastrianism known as Mithraism gained ever more popularity.

The appeal of emotional personal religions

Exactly when Mithraism became an independent religion is unknown, but it was certainly not later than the fourth century B.C.E. The cult gained its name from Mithras, at first a minor deity in Zoroastrianism. Mithras gradually became recognized by many as the god most deserving of worship, probably because of his emotional appeal. He was believed to have lived an earthly existence involving great suffering and sacrifice. He performed miracles giving bread and wine to humanity and ending a drought and also a disastrous flood. He proclaimed Sunday as the most sacred day of the week since the sun was the giver of light. He declared the twenty-fifth of December as the most sacred day of the year because, as the approximate date of the winter solstice, it was the "birthday" of the sun, when its life-giving powers began to increase for the benefit of humankind. Drawing its converts mostly from the lower classes of Hellenistic society, Mithraism offered them an elaborate ritual, contempt for life in this world, and a clearly defined doctrine of redemption through Mithras, a personal savior. Not surprisingly it outlasted the Hellenistic period, becoming after about 100 C.E. one of the most popular religions in the Roman Empire and exerting some influence on Christianity.

The spread and influence of Mithraism

Hellenistic Culture: Literature and Art

Both the literature and the art of the Hellenistic Age were characterized by a tendency to take aspects of earlier Greek accomplishments to extremes. It is hard to be sure of the reasons for this, but apparently writers and artists wished to demonstrate their purely formal skills in order to please their autocratic patrons. Furthermore, the greater uncertainties of existence in Hellenistic times may have led consumers of art to seek gratification from more dramatic and less subtle forms of artistic expression. Whatever the case, rather than being an integral expression of civic activities, art definitely became more of a commodity, which meant that much of it was ephemeral or even trash: we know the names of at least 1,100 Hellenistic authors, yet hardly more than a handful of these possessed any true literary distinction. Nonetheless, rising above the numerous mediocre works of literature and art dating from the Hellenistic period, a few stand out as enduring masterpieces.

The pastoral

The most prominent Hellenistic verse form was the pastoral, a new genre depicting a make-believe world of shepherds, nymphs, and pipes of Pan. The inventor of the genre was a Greek named Theocritus, who lived and wrote around 270 B.C.E. in the big-city environment of Alexandria. Theocritus was a merchant of escapism. In the midst of urban bustle, faced with despotic rulers, and within sight of overcrowded, slum-like conditions, he celebrated the charms of hazy country values and idealized the "simple pleasures" of rustic folk. One of his pastorals might start like this: "Begin my country song, sweet muses, begin, I am Thrysis from Etna, this is Thrysis's lovely voice." To many the falseness of such verse is alienating; how could shepherds talk this way? But other readers enjoy the poetic lushness. Surely in creating the pastoral Theocritus founded an enduring tradition that outlasted the Hellenistic world to be taken up by such masters as Virgil and Milton and that provided a wealth of themes for the visual arts. Even composers of modern concert music, such as Claude Debussy in his *Afternoon of a Faun,* bear a debt to the escapist poet from Alexandria.

Cupid and Psyche. Hellenistic tastes often inclined toward "dainty" representations of eroticism. Cupid's right hand conveys a studied sensuality held in check only by his fig leaf.

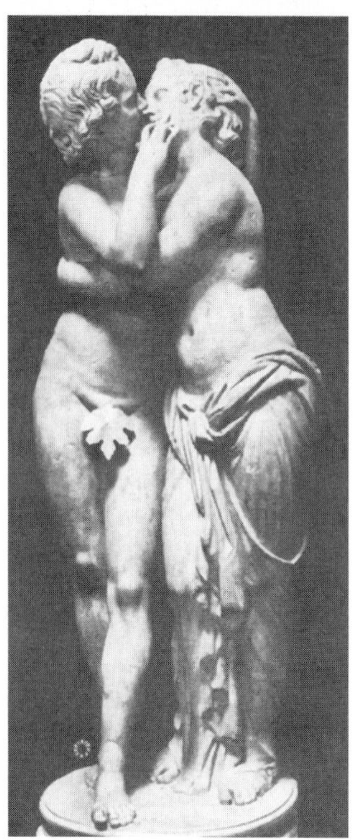

The field of Hellenistic prose literature was dominated by historians and biographers. By far the most profound of the writers of history was the mainland Greek Polybius who lived during the second century B.C.E. According to Polybius, historical development proceeds in cycles, nations passing so inevitably through stages of growth and decay that it is possible to predict exactly where a nation is heading if one knows what has happened to it in the past. From the standpoint of his scientific approach, Polybius deserves to be ranked second only to Thucydides among all the historians of ancient times, and he even surpassed Thucydides in his grasp of the importance of social and economic forces. Although most biographies of the time were light and gossipy, their popularity bears eloquent testimony to the literary tastes of the Hellenistic period.

Consonant with the despotic style of rule, the main traits of Hellenistic architecture were grandeur and ornamentation. In place of the balance and restraint that had distinguished Greek architecture of the fifth and early fourth centuries B.C.E., Hellenistic public building drew on Greek elements but moved toward standards set by Persian monarchs and Egyptian pharaohs. Two examples (both of which unfortunately no longer survive) are the great lighthouse of Alexandria, which rose to a height of nearly four hundred feet and had three diminishing stories and eight

Old Market Woman, second century B.C.E. Sculptures of this period often showed ordinary people engaged in ordinary activities. This realistic marble sculpture is of an old, tired woman who is carrying a basket of fruits and vegetables and chickens to market.

columns to support the light at the top, and the citadel of Alexandria, which was dedicated to the god Serapis, built of stone covered with blue-tinted plaster, and said by a contemporary to have "risen into mid-air." In Pergamon in Asia Minor an enormous altar to Zeus (transported in modern times to Berlin) and an enormous open-air theater looked out over a high hill. In Ephesus, not far away, the streets were paved with marble. The "signature" of Hellenistic architecture of whatever dimension was the Corinthian column, a form of column more ornate than the simple and dignified Doric and Ionic alternatives that had predominated in earlier Greek building.

The Corinthian Order of Architecture. Note how much more ornate this Hellenistic style is in comparison to the earlier Doric and Ionic orders depicted on p. 121.

Hellenistic sculpture

In the final analysis, probably the most influential of all products of Hellenistic culture, and almost certainly the most congenial to modern tastes, were works of sculpture. Whereas earlier Greek sculpture had sought to idealize humanity and to express Greek ideals of modesty by understated restraint, Hellenistic sculpture emphasized extreme naturalism and unashamed extravagance. In practice this meant that sculptors went to great lengths to recreate facial furrows, muscular distensions, and complex folds of drapery. Awkward human postures were considered to offer the greatest challenges to the artist in stone, to the degree that sculptors might prefer to show people stretching themselves or balancing themselves on one leg in ways that hardly ever occur in real life. Since most Hellenistic sculpture was executed for wealthy private patrons, it is clear that the goal was to create something unique in terms of its conception and craftsmanship—something a collector could show off as the only one of its type. Not surprisingly, therefore, complexity came to be admired for its own sake, and extreme naturalism sometimes teetered on the brink of distorted stylization. Yet when moderns see such works they frequently experience a shock of recognition, for the bizarre and exaggerated postures of Hellenistic sculptures later exerted an enormous influence on Michelangelo and his followers, and later inspired some of the most "modern" sculptors of the nineteenth and twentieth centuries. Three of the most famous examples of Hellenistic sculpture, which reveal different aspects of Hellenistic aesthetic ideals, may be cited here: the *Dying Gaul,* done in Pergamon around 220 B.C.E., shows consummate skill in portraying a distended human body; the *Winged Victory of Samothrace,* of about 200 B.C.E., displays flowing drapery as if it were not stone but real cloth; and the *Laocoön* group, of the first century B.C.E., offers one of the most intensely emotional as well as complex compositions known in the entire history of sculptural art.

Dying Gaul Seen from Front and Back. A famous example of Hellenistic realism and pathos, this statue was executed around 220 B.C.E. in the court of Pergamon in Asia Minor. (The original is lost; shown here is a faithful Roman copy.) The sculptor clearly wished to exhibit skill in depicting an unusual human posture and succeeded remarkably in evoking the thin line that separates human dignity from unappeasable loneliness and physical suffering.

The Winged Victory of Samothrace. In this figure, done around 200 B.C.E., a Hellenistic sculptor preserved some of the calmness and devotion to grace and proportion characteristic of Hellenic art in the Golden Age.

Laocoön. In sharp contrast to the serenity of the Winged Victory is this famous sculpture group from the first century B.C.E., depicting the death of Laocoön. According to legend, Laocoön warned the Trojans not to touch the wooden horse sent by the Greeks and was punished by Poseidon, who sent two serpents to kill him and his sons. The intense emotionalism of this work later had a great influence on western European art from Michelangelo onward. See, for example, the painting by El Greco on page 536.

Top: **Hellenistic Aphrodite.** This figure, dating from the fourth century B.C.E., displays the Hellenistic fascination with ungainly, "unnatural" postures. Bottom: **French Bather.** This statuette done by Edgar Degas around 1890 shows some evident continuities between Hellenistic and modern art.

The First Great Age of Science

The most brilliant age in the history of science prior to the seventeenth century C.E. was the period of the Hellenistic civilization. There are two major reasons for the impressive development of science in the centuries after Alexander's conquest of the Persian Empire. One was the enormous stimulus given to intellectual inquiry by the fusion of Mesopotamian and Egyptian science with the learning and the curiosity of the Greeks. The other was that many Hellenistic rulers were generous patrons of scientific research, subsidizing scientists who belonged to their retinues just as they subsidized sculptors. It was once thought that the motive for such patronage was purely practical—that rulers believed the progress of science would enhance the growth of industry in their territories and would also improve their own material comforts. Yet students of Hellenistic civilization now doubt that any ruler was hoping for an "industrial revolution" in the sense of applying technology to save human labor, for labor was cheap and autocratic princes were completely indifferent to the pains and sufferings of the laboring classes. As for the supposed connection between science and the enhancement of material comfort, Hellenistic rulers in fact hardly thought along those lines because they had adequate numbers of slaves to fan them and were not inclined to introduce mechanical devices that would have lessened the public grandeur of being fanned by deferential subordinates. To be sure, practical aims motivated the patronage of science in some areas, above all in medicine and anything that might relate to military technology. Yet it has become clear that the autocrats who financed the scientific endeavors did so primarily for motives of prestige: sometimes a scientist might fashion a splendid gadget for a ruler that he could show off to visitors as he would show off his sculptures; and even if not, purely theoretical achievements were so much admired among the Greek-speaking leisured classes that a Hellenistic prince who subsidized a theoretical breakthrough would share the prestige for it in the way the mayor of an American city might bask in prestige today if his city's football team were to win the Superbowl.

Astronomy

The major Hellenistic sciences were astronomy, mathematics, geography, medicine, and physics. The most renowned of the earlier Hellenistic astronomers was Aristarchus of Samos (310–230 B.C.E.), sometimes called the "Hellenistic Copernicus." His primary accomplishment was his deduction that the earth and the other planets revolve around the sun. This view was not accepted by his successors because it conflicted with the teachings of Aristotle and with the conviction of the Greeks that humanity, and therefore the earth, must be at the center of the universe. Later the fame of Aristarchus was overshadowed by that of Ptolemy of Alexandria (second century C.E.). Although Ptolemy made few original discoveries, he systematized the work of others. His principal writing, the *Almagest,* based upon the geocentric theory (the view that all heavenly bodies revolve around the earth), was handed down to medieval Europe as the classic summary of ancient astronomy.

Closely allied with astronomy were mathematics and geography. The most influential Hellenistic mathematician was Euclid, the master of geometry. Until the middle of the nineteenth century his *Elements of Geometry* (written around 300 B.C.E. as a synthesis of the work of others) remained the accepted basis for the study of that branch of mathematics. The most original of the Hellenistic mathematicians were probably Hipparchus (second century B.C.E.), who laid the foundations of both plane and spherical trigonometry. Hellenistic geography owed most of its development to Eratosthenes (c. 276–c. 196 B.C.E.), astronomer and librarian of Alexandria. By means of sundials placed some hundreds of miles apart, he calculated the circumference of the earth with an error of less than 200 miles. Eratosthenes was also the first to suggest the possibility of reaching eastern Asia by sailing west. One of his successors divided the earth into the five climatic zones that are still recognized, and explained the ebb and flow of the tides as due to the influence of the moon.

Mathematics and geography

Other Hellenistic advances in science were in the field of medicine. Especially significant was the work of Herophilus of Chalcedon (c. 335–c. 280 B.C.E.), who conducted his research in Alexandria at about the beginning of the third century B.C.E. Herophilus was the greatest anatomist of antiquity and probably the first to practice human dissection. Among his achievements were a detailed description of the brain, with an insistence (against Aristotle) that the brain is the seat of human intelligence; the discovery of the significance of the pulse, and its use in diagnosing illness; and the discovery that the arteries contain blood alone (not a mixture of blood and air as Aristotle had taught), and that their function is to carry blood from the heart to all parts of the body. About the middle of the third century, Erasistratus of Alexandria gained much of his knowledge of bodily functions from vivisection. He discovered the valves of the heart and distinguished between motor and sensory nerves. In addition, he rejected Hippocrates's theory that the body consists of four "humors" and consequently criticized excessive bloodletting as a method of cure. Unfortunately the humoral theory and an emphasis on bloodletting were revived by Galen, the great encyclopedist of medicine who lived in the Roman Empire in the second century C.E.

Anatomy and physiology

Prior to the third century B.C.E. physics had been a branch of philosophy. It was made a separate experimental science by Archimedes of Syracuse (c. 287–212 B.C.E.), who discovered the law of floating bodies, or specific gravity, and formulated with scientific exactness the principles of the lever, the pulley, and the screw. Among his memorable inventions were the compound pulley and the screw propeller for ships. Although he has been considered the greatest technical genius of antiquity, in fact he placed no emphasis on his mechanical contraptions and preferred to devote his time instead to pure scientific research. Tradition relates that he discovered "Archimedes's principle" (specific gravity) while pondering possible theories in his bath: when he reached his stunning insight he dashed out naked into the street crying "Eureka" ("I have found it").

Archimedes and physics

THE BALANCE SHEET

The Hellenistic contribution

Judged from the vantage of classical Greece, Hellenistic civilization may at first seem no more than a degenerate phase of Greek civilization. Doubtless the autocratic governments of the Hellenistic Age appear debased and repugnant in contrast to Athenian democracy, and the Hellenistic penchant for extravagance appears debased in contrast to the earlier Greek taste for chaste beauty. It must also be admitted that the best Hellenistic literary works lack the inspired majesty of the great Greek tragedies and that none of the Hellenistic philosophers matched the profundity of Plato and Aristotle. Yet the Hellenistic civilization had its own accomplishments to offer. For example, most Hellenistic cities offered a greater range of public facilities, such as museums and libraries, than earlier Greek cities did, and we have seen that numerous Hellenistic thinkers, writers, and artists left to posterity important new ideas, impressive new genres, and imaginative new styles. Above all, the fact that Hellenistic science was the most advanced in the Western world until the seventeenth century demonstrates that the Hellenistic civilization was by no means retrograde on all fronts.

Intermediary between Greece and Rome

Probably the most important contribution of the Hellenistic era to subsequent historical development was the role it played as intermediary between Greece and Rome. In some cases the Hellenistic contribution was simply that of preservation. For example, most of the familiarity the ancient Romans had with classical Greek thought came to them by way of copies of Greek philosophical and literary texts preserved in Hellenistic libraries. In other areas, however, transfer involved transmutation. A case in point is architecture and art: as we have seen, Hellenistic art evolved from earlier Greek art into something related but quite different, and it was this "Greek-like" art that exerted the greatest influence on the tastes and artistic accomplishments of the Romans.

Young Athlete. Hellenistic sculptors felt challenged to take "snapshots" of fleeting moments from real life.

In conclusion, two particularly remarkable aspects of Hellenistic culture deserve special comment—Hellenistic cosmopolitanism and Hellenistic "modernity." Not only does the word "cosmopolitan" itself come from Greek *cosmopolis,* meaning "universal city," but it was the Greeks of the Hellenistic period who came the closest among westerners to turning this ideal of cosmopolitanism into reality. Specifically, around 250 B.C.E. a leisure-class Greek could have traveled from Sicily to the borders of India, always meeting people who "spoke his language," both literally and in terms of shared ideals. Moreover, this same Greek would not have been a nationalist in the sense of professing any deep loyalty to a city-state or kingdom. Rather, he would have considered himself a "citizen of the world." Hellenistic cosmopolitanism was partly a product of the cosmopolitanism of Persia, and it helped in turn to create the cosmopolitanism of Rome, but in contrast to both it was not imperial—that is, it was entirely divorced from constraints imposed by a supranational state—although unfortunately it was achieved by means of Greek exploitation of subject peoples. Finally, although cosmopolitanism is surely not an obvious condition of the present, other aspects of Hellenistic civilization must seem very familiar to observers today. Authoritarian governments, ruler worship, economic instability, extreme skepticism existing side by side with intense religiosity, rational science existing side by side with irrational superstition, flamboyant art and ostentatious art collecting: all these traits might make the thoughtful student of history wonder whether the Hellenistic Age is not one of the most relevant in the entire human record for comparison with our own.

SUMMARY POINTS

- The Hellenistic world blended aspects of Greek civilization with those of Asia, in particular the former Persian Empire. The vast span of the Hellenistic world arose from the conquests of the Greek Philip of Macedon and his son Alexander the Great.
- Despotism prevailed over much of the Hellenistic world after the death of Alexander and the division of his empire, except in Greece, where city-states once again prevailed. During this time trade and manufacturing flourished.
- Hellenistic culture embraced a variety of philosophies and religions. Stoic philosophers taught humanitarianism and self-discipline; Epicureans sought individual pleasure and serenity; while the Skeptics, like the Sophists of classical Greece, denied the existence of any universal truths.
- The greatest achievements of Hellenistic culture were in sculpture and the sciences: Hellenistic sculpture is noted for its detailed naturalism, complexity, and extravagance; and Hellenistic scientists made fundamental discoveries and advances in mathematics, astronomy, geography, medicine, and physics.

SELECTED READINGS

Boyce, Mary, *A History of Zoroastrianism,* Leiden, 1975.

Cambridge History of Iran, vol. II, Cambridge, 1985. The most up-to-date large-scale treatment of affairs relating to the Persian Empire during the centuries covered by this chapter.

Clagett, Marshall, *Greek Science in Antiquity,* rev. ed., New York, 1971. A dependable introduction.

Engels, Donald W., *Alexander the Great and the Logistics of the Macedonian Army,* Berkeley, 1978. Treats Alexander's amazing campaigns.

Ferguson, John, *The Heritage of Hellenism: The Greek World from 323 to 31 B.C.,* New York, 1973. An engagingly written and lavishly illustrated exposition of typical characteristics of Hellenistic culture.

Finley, M. I., *The Ancient Economy,* 2d ed., Berkeley, 1985. A fundamental topical treatment by a brilliant scholar. Seeks to emphasize what was truly ancient about the ancient economy.

Grant, F. C., *Hellenistic Religions,* New York, 1953. A standard work.

Grant, Michael, *From Alexander to Cleopatra: The Hellenistic World,* New York, 1982. A useful elementary introduction.

Green, Peter, *Alexander to Actium: The Historical Evolution of the Hellenistic Age,* Berkeley, 1990. A rich, panoramic account.

———, *Alexander of Macedon,* Berkeley, 1991. The best concise biography.

Lane Fox, Robin, *Alexander the Great,* London, 1973. Very long, very interpretative, very good.

Lewis, Naphtali, *Greeks in Ptolemaic Egypt,* New York, 1986. Studies Greek colonists as a ruling class.

Source Materials

Austin, M. M., *The Hellenistic World from Alexander to the Roman Conquest: A Selection of Ancient Sources in Translation,* Cambridge, 1981.

Bagnall, R. S., and P. Derow, *Greek Historical Documents: The Hellenistic Period,* Chico, Calif., 1981.

Boyce, Mary, *Textual Sources for the Study of Zoroastrianism,* Totowa, N.J., 1984.

CHAPTER 7

ROMAN CIVILIZATION

My city and country, so far as I am Antoninus, is Rome, but so far as I am a man, it is the world.

—MARCUS AURELIUS ANTONINUS, *Meditations*

For the categories into which you divide the world are not Hellenes and Barbarians. . . . The division which you substituted is one into Romans and non-Romans. To such a degree have you expanded the name of your city.

—AELIUS ARISTIDES, *Oration to Rome*

WELL BEFORE THE GLORY that was Greece had begun to fade, another civilization, ultimately much influenced by Greek culture, had started its growth in the West on the banks of the Tiber. Around the time of Alexander's conquests the emerging power of Rome was already a dominant force on the Italian peninsula. For five centuries thereafter Rome's power increased. By the end of the first century B.C.E. it had imposed its rule over most of the Hellenistic world and over most of western Europe. By conquering Hellenistic territory and destroying the North African civilization of Carthage, Rome was able to make the Mediterranean a "Roman lake." In so doing it brought Greek institutions and ideas to the western half of the Mediterranean world. And by pushing northward to the Rhine and Danube Rivers it brought Mediterranean urban culture to lands still sunk in the Iron Age. Rome, then, was the builder of a great historical bridge between East and West.

The Roman synthesis

Of course Rome would not have been able to play this role had it not followed its own peculiar course of development. This was marked by the tension between two different cultural outlooks. On the one hand, Romans throughout most of their history tended to be conservative: they revered their old agricultural traditions, household gods, and ruggedly warlike ways. But they also strove to be builders and could not resist the attractions of Greek culture. For a few centuries their greatness was based on a synthesis of these different traits: respect for tradition, order, and military prowess, together with Greek urbanization and cultivation of the mind. The synthesis could not last forever, but as long as it did the glory that was Greece was replaced by the grandeur that was Rome.

Early Italy and the Roman Monarchy

The impact of geography on Roman history

The geographical character of the Italian peninsula contributed significantly to the course of Roman history. Except for some excellent marble and small quantities of tin, copper, iron, and gold, Italy has no mineral resources. The extensive coastline is broken by few good harbors. On the other hand, the amount of fertile land in Italy is greater than that in Greece. As a result, the Romans remained a predominantly agrarian people through the greater part of their history. They seldom enjoyed the intellectual stimulus that comes from extensive trading with other areas. In addition, the Italian peninsula was more open to invasion than was Greece. The Alps posed no effective barrier to the influx of peoples from central Europe, and the low-lying coast in many places invited conquest by sea. Domination of the territory by force was therefore more common than peaceful intermingling of immigrants with original settlers. The Romans became absorbed in military pursuits almost from the moment of their settlement on Italian soil, for they were forced to defend their own conquests against other invaders.

The Etruscans

Among the many peoples who inhabited Italy before the establishment of Roman hegemony, the most dominant were the Etruscans, the Greeks, and gradually the Romans themselves. In all probability the Etruscans were natives of the Italian peninsula: certainly they were not members of the Indo-European language group. Whatever their origins, by the sixth century B.C.E. they had established a confederation of cities that stretched over most of northern and central Italy. Although their writing has never been completely deciphered, enough materials survive to indicate the nature of their culture. They had an alphabet based upon the Greek, much skill in metalwork, a flourishing trade with the East, and a religion based

Left: **An Etruscan Musician.** Right: **Etruscan Winged Horses.** Both the well-coordinated flutist dating from about 480 B.C.E. and the proud horses (carved from terracotta) dating from about 300 B.C.E. reflect the Etruscans' delight in fluid movement.

Etruscan Pottery Duck

upon the worship of gods in human form. Etruscan art was extremely vibrant. As the novelist D. H. Lawrence remarked, "This sense of vigorous, strongbodied liveliness is characteristic of the Etruscans and is somehow beyond art. You cannot think of art, but only of life itself." The Etruscans bequeathed to the Romans a knowledge of the arch and the vault, the cruel amusement of gladiatorial combats, and the practice of foretelling the future by supernatural means such as studying the entrails of animals or the flight of birds. One of the most distinctive Etruscan traits was the comparatively great respect they showed for women. Etruscan women, some of whom knew how to read, participated in public life, attending dramatic performances and dancing in ways that shocked the Greeks and Romans. Etruscan wives, unlike those in other contemporary societies, ate with their husbands, reclining together with them on the banqueting couch, and some Etruscan families listed descent through the maternal line.

The Greeks in Italy

The Greeks in Italy were immigrants who began to arrive in the eighth century B.C.E. and who settled mainly in the south, as well as on the island of Sicily. Greek civilization in Italy and Sicily, based on independent

Etruscan Sarcophagus. This highly naturalistic statuary depicting a gravely pensive husband and wife dates from roughly 300 B.C.E. The use of terra-cotta (clay) instead of stone allowed easier modeling and enabled the Etruscans to achieve startling visual effects.

Coins from Greek Colonies in Italy. Above is a coin from Syracuse depicting the nymph Arethusa surrounded by dolphins. Below, a bull from Sybaris, a Greek colony so famous for its easy living that "sybaritic" remains a word in the English language.

Greek city-states, was as advanced as in Greece itself. Such famous Greeks as Pythagoras, Archimedes, and even Plato for a time, lived in the "Italian West." From the Greeks the Romans derived their alphabet, some of their religious concepts, and much of their art and mythology.

As for the Romans themselves, they descended from a cluster of peoples of the Indo-European language group who entered Italy by way of the Alps between 2000 and 1000 B.C.E. Recent archeological research places the founding of the city of Rome by Latin-speaking people, thereafter known as Romans, quite near the traditional date of 753 B.C.E. Partly because of their strategic location on the Tiber River, the Romans soon began to exercise hegemony over several neighboring cities. One conquest followed another until, by the sixth century B.C.E., Rome came to dominate most of the surrounding area.

Initially Roman government was monarchical—aimed at establishing stability and military efficiency. The earliest Roman political system was an application of the idea of the patriarchal family to the whole community, with the king exercising a jurisdiction over his subjects comparable to that of the head of the family over the members of his household. A *Senate,* or council of elders (*senex* is Latin for "old man"), was composed of the heads of the various clans that formed the community. So far as we know (and we know extremely little about Roman government in this period), the Senate could exercise veto power over royal actions when it seemed absolutely necessary, also providing some government when the royal office became vacant.

Legend has it that in 534 B.C.E. an Etruscan tyrant, Tarquin the Proud, managed to gain control of the kingship in Rome. Supposedly Tarquin lorded it over the Romans with extreme cruelty, the final indignity occurring in 510 B.C.E. when his son raped a virtuous Roman wife, Lucretia. When Lucretia committed suicide rather than living on "in dishonor," the Romans rose up in revolt, overthrowing not only the Etruscan tyranny but the monarchical form of government itself. Almost all of this is patriotic myth, but it is possible that the Etruscans had gained some

The Diver. A painted tomb-covering from about 480 B.C.E., unearthed near Paestum, a Greek settlement in southern Italy.

temporary dominion over Rome around the time indicated, and it is all but certain that there was a change in government in Rome around 500 B.C.E. (whether gradual or sudden is unknown) that ended the kingship and replaced it with a republic. It is also evident that Etruscan power throughout Italy began to decline after 500 and that the Romans gradually cultivated a conviction that kingship was dangerous.

THE EARLY REPUBLIC

Early Roman expansion

The history of the Roman Republic for more than two centuries after its establishment was one of practically annual warfare. At first the Romans were on the defensive because rival cities took advantage of the confusion accompanying the change of regime by invading Roman territory. After Rome managed to ward off these attacks the city began to shift to the offensive; as time went on the Romans steadily conquered all the Etruscan territories and then took over all the Greek cities in the south on the Italian mainland. Not only did the latter conquests add to the Roman domain, they also brought the Romans into fruitful contact with Greek culture. As the Romans conquered new areas they were confronted with revolts of the newly subjected populations; the suppression of these revolts whetted the appetite of the victors for further triumphs. Thus new wars followed each other in relentless succession, until by 265 B.C.E. Rome had conquered almost the entire Italian peninsula.

Effects of the early military conflicts

This long series of conflicts reinforced both the agrarian and military character of the Roman nation. The acquisition of new lands enabled needy Romans to engage in agricultural pursuits in the Roman colonies. As a consequence Romans saw no need for the development of industry and commerce. In addition, the continual warfare served to confirm among the Romans a steely military ideal. Many of the most familiar Roman legends of martial heroism date from this period. The brave Horatio, for example, supposedly held off an entire army with only two friends in front of a bridge; the retired soldier Cincinnatus supposedly left his farm at a moment's notice for the battlefield.

King replaced by two consuls

During this same period of the early Republic, Rome underwent some glacial political evolution. The replacement of the monarchy was about as conservative a political change as it is possible for any political change to be. Its chief effect was to substitute two elected officials called *consuls* for the king and to exalt the position of the aristocratic Senate by granting it control over the public funds. Although the consuls were chosen by a citizen assembly, it differed greatly from the citizen assembly of ancient Athens because it met in groups. Each group in the Roman assembly had a vote, and since groups consisting of the wealthiest citizens voted first, a majority could be reached even before the votes of the poorer groups were cast. Consequently the consuls, who served annually, were usually senators who acted as the agents of aristocratic interests. Each consul was supposed to possess the full executive and judicial authority that had

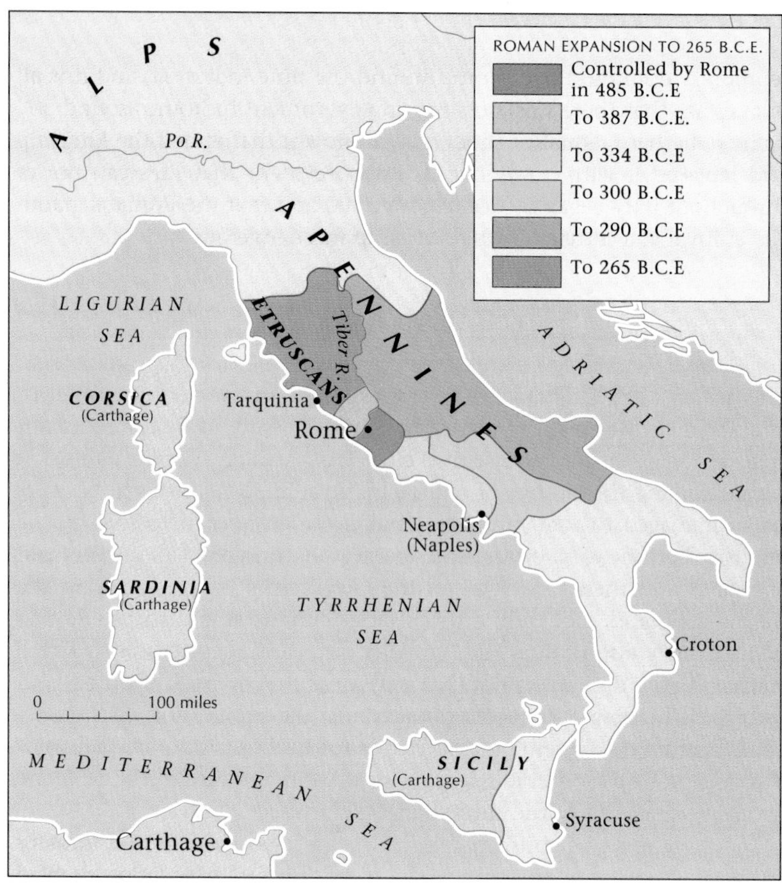

Roman Expansion in Italy, 485–265 B.C.E.

previously been wielded by the king, limited by the right each possessed to veto the action of the other. If a conflict arose between them, the Senate might be called upon to decide; or in time of grave emergency a dictator might be appointed for a term of not greater than six months.

The struggle between patricians and plebeians

After the establishment of the Republic the political dominance of the aristocracy, known in the Rome of this period as the *patricians,* began to be challenged by the *plebeians.* The latter were mostly small farmers, and occasionally tradesmen, although plebeian ranks also included some wealthy families who were barred from the patriciate because of recent foreign origin. The grievances of the plebeians were numerous. Forced to serve in the army in time of war, they were nevertheless excluded from office-holding. Moreover, they felt themselves the victims of discriminatory decisions in judicial trials. They did not even know what legal rights they were supposed to enjoy, for the laws were unwritten, and the patricians alone had the power to interpret them. Worst was the oppression that could stem from debt because a debtor could be sold into slavery outside Rome by the creditor.

The victories of the plebeians

To obtain a redress of these grievances the plebeians rebelled soon after the beginning of the fifth century B.C.E. At that time they forced the patricians to agree to the election of a number of officers known as *tribunes* with power to protect the plebeians by means of a veto over unlawful patrician acts. This victory was followed by a successful demand for codification of the laws about 450 B.C.E. The result was the issuance of the famous Law of the Twelve Tables, so called because it was written on tablets ("tables") of wood. Although this came to be revered by the Romans of later times as a kind of charter of the people's liberties, it was really nothing of the sort, for it mostly perpetuated ancient custom without even abolishing enslavement for debt. Nevertheless at least there was now a clear definition of law. Roughly a generation later the plebeians won eligibility to positions as lesser magistrates, and about 367 B.C.E. the first plebeian consul was elected. Since ancient custom provided that, upon completing their terms of office, consuls should automatically enter the Senate, the patrician monopoly of seats in that body was broken. The final plebeian victory came in 287 with the passage of a law stipulating that measures enacted by the citizen assembly (now balanced in its composition between patricians and plebeians) should become binding upon the Roman government whether the Senate approved them or not.

Rome, an oligarchic republic with balance of powers

All told, the significance of these changes was not great, for the fact remained that Rome was the model of an *oligarchic republic* and by no means a democracy. As the historian Theodor Mommsen once put it, the Romans "never really abandoned the principle that the people were not to govern but to be governed." A republic differs from a monarchy insofar as supreme power resides in a body of citizens and is exercised by officers in some way responsible to the citizens. But a republic need not be *democratic* in granting supreme power to the mass of the people in the state, for it can devise systems for reserving power to an oligarchy or privileged group. The Roman constitution became best known for ensuring the rule of its oligarchy by means of a balance of governmental institutions: the assembly, the Senate, and office-holders such as consuls, tribunes, and various judges and administrators. By this system no single individual or family clique could become overwhelmingly strong, nor could direct expressions of the popular will unduly influence Roman policy.

Roman society and culture still rather primitive

As political changes in Rome moved glacially, so did intellectual and cultural ones. Though writing had been adopted as early as the sixth century B.C.E., little use was made of it except for the copying of laws, treaties, and funerary inscriptions. Inasmuch as education was limited to instruction imparted by fathers to sons in manly sports, practical arts, and soldierly virtues, the great majority of the people remained illiterate. War and agriculture continued to be the chief occupations for the bulk of the population. A few craftsmen were found in the cities, and a minor development of trade had occurred. But the fact that the Republic had no standard system of coinage until 269 B.C.E. reflects the comparative insignificance of Roman commerce at this time.

Roman religion compared with that of the Greeks

During the period of the early Republic, religion assumed the character it retained through the greater part of Roman history. In several ways this religion resembled that of the Greeks—not surprising since it was directly

Diana. A Roman republican coin showing Diana, the goddess of the hunt.

influenced by Roman knowledge of Greek beliefs. Thus major Roman deities performed the same functions as their Greek equivalents: Jupiter corresponded to Zeus as god of the skies, Neptune to Poseidon as god of the waves, Venus to Aphrodite as goddess of love. Like the Greeks the Romans had no dogmas or sacraments, nor did they place great emphasis on rewards and punishments after death. But there were also significant differences between the two religions. One was that Romans literally revered their ancestors; their "household gods" included deceased members of a lineage who were worshiped in order to ensure a family's continued prosperity. Another difference was that Roman religion was decidedly more political. Since the Romans believed that their state could flourish only with divine support, they appointed committees of priests, virtually as branches of government, to tend to the cult of various gods, preside over public rites, and serve as guardians of sacred traditions. These priests were not full-time professionals, but rather prominent oligarchs who were rotated in and out of priestly offices in addition to serving otherwise as leaders of state. This system made religion even more an integral part of the fabric of public life.

Stern morality

The morality of the Romans in this as in later periods had almost no connection with religion. The Romans did not ask their gods to reward them for virtue, but to bestow upon the community and their families material blessings. Morality lay in patriotism and respect for authority and tradition. The chief virtues were bravery, honor, self-discipline, and loyalty to country and family. Loyalty to Rome took precedence over everything else. For the good of the Republic, citizens had to be ready to sacrifice not only their own lives but, if necessary, those of their family and friends. The cold-bloodedness of certain consuls who put their sons to death for breaches of military discipline was a matter of deep admiration.

THE FATEFUL WARS WITH CARTHAGE

The beginning of overseas expansion

By 265 B.C.E. the Romans had reduced the last vestiges of Etruscan resistance and thereby controlled three-quarters of the Italian peninsula. Unprecedentedly in the history of Mediterranean city-states they gained the loyalty of the vanquished by generously granting them Roman citizenship. This meant that male residents of most Italian cities who were not slaves were immune from arbitrary enactments by Roman governors and had the vote if they moved to Rome. In return they were liable for military service. Confident of their strength over Italy, the Romans were now free to engage in overseas ventures. Scholars disagree as to whether the Romans continually extended their rule as a matter of unspoken but consistent rapacious policy, or more accidentally by a series of reactions to changes in the status quo that could be interpreted as a threat to Rome's security. Probably the truth lies between these extremes. Whatever the case, beginning in 264, a year after the final mastery over the Etruscans, Rome became embroiled in a series of wars with overseas nations that decidedly altered the course of its history.

Carthage

By far the most crucial was the struggle with Carthage, a great maritime empire that stretched along the northern coast of Africa from modern-day Tunisia to the Straits of Gibraltar. Carthage had been founded about 800 B.C.E. as a Phoenician colony. In the sixth century it developed into a rich and powerful independent state. The prosperity of its upper classes was founded upon commerce and the exploitation of North African natural resources. Carthaginian government was oligarchic. The real rulers were thirty merchant princes who constituted an inner council of the Senate. Despite a cruel religion that demanded blood sacrifices, Carthage during the third century B.C.E. had a civilization superior in luxury to that of Rome.

Causes of the First Punic War

The protracted struggles between Rome and Carthage are known collectively as the Punic Wars since the Romans called the Carthaginians *Poeni,* that is, "Phoenicians." The First Punic War began in 264 B.C.E., apparently because of Rome's genuine fear of potential Carthaginian expansion. Carthage already controlled most of Sicily and now was threatening to gain control of Messina, directly across from the Italian mainland. Unwilling to allow Carthage to become a menacing next-door neighbor, a Roman consul brought an army over the straits to defend Messina. Carthage took massive measures to counterattack and twenty-three years of bitter fighting ensued. Finally, by a peace agreement of 241, Carthage was forced to cede all of Sicily to Rome, as well as to pay a large indemnity. As a result Sicily became Rome's first overseas province.

The Second Punic War

Because the Romans had fought so hard to defeat Carthage, they became determined not to let their enemy become dominant in other Mediterranean areas. Accordingly, in 218 the Romans interpreted Carthage's attempt to expand its rule in Spain as a threat to Roman interests and responded with a declaration of war. The renewed struggle, known as the Second Punic War, raged for sixteen years. At first Rome was entirely thrown off guard by the brilliant exploits of the famous Carthaginian commander Hannibal. Already commanding an army in Spain, Hannibal in a truly remarkable military feat brought this force, including war elephants, through southern France and then over the Alps into Italy. (Scholars are uncertain through which Alpine pass Hannibal brought his troops and elephants but continue to investigate this urgent subject on many a happy vacation in the French mountains.) With Carthaginian troops on Italian soil, Rome escaped defeat by the narrowest of margins. Only "delaying tactics" ultimately saved the day, for time was on the side of those who could keep an invader short of supplies and worn down by harrassment. Such tactics called for iron discipline, but this was Rome's greatest strength. As pursued by the Roman general Fabius, known as "Fabius the Delayer" (whence the modern term "Fabianism," meaning gradualism), delaying tactics robbed Hannibal of his advantage until a more aggressive Roman general, Scipio Africanus, finally defeated Hannibal in pitched battle at Zama in 202 B.C.E.

Hannibal. A coin from Carthage representing Hannibal as a victorious general, with an elephant on the reverse.

With Scipio's victory, the Second Punic War came to an end. Carthage was now more completely humbled than before, being compelled to abandon all its possessions except the city of Carthage itself and its

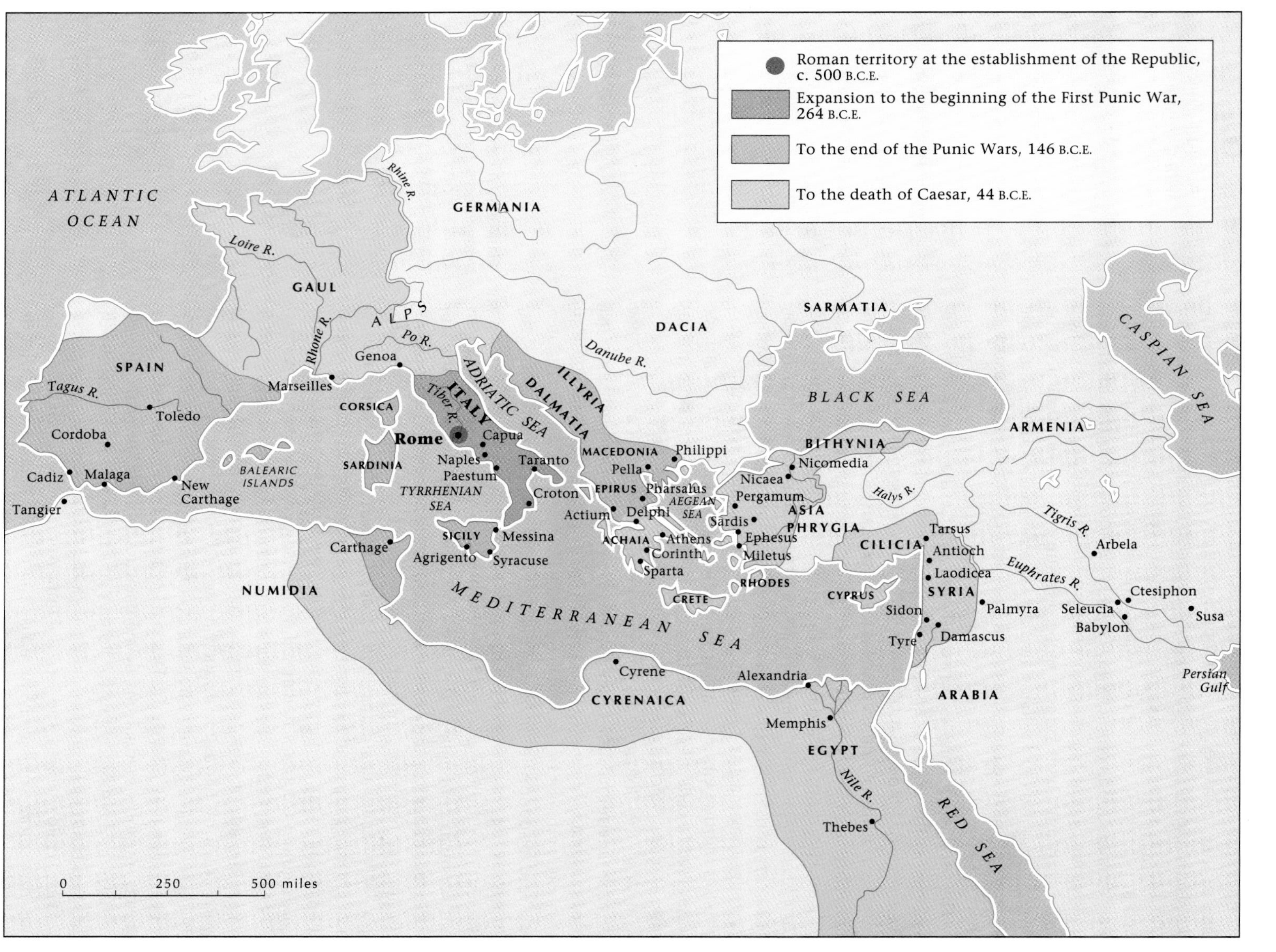

The Expansion of Rome under the Republic

surrounding territory in Africa, and to pay an indemnity three times greater than that paid at the end of the First Punic War. Yet Roman suspicion of Carthage remained obsessive. About the middle of the second century B.C.E. Carthage had recovered some of its former prosperity—and this was enough to provoke the displeasure of the Romans. Nothing now would satisfy the most influential Roman senators but the total demolition of the Carthaginian state. In 150 B.C.E. the Roman warhawk Cato the Censor ended every speech he made in the Senate with the same words: "Carthage must be destroyed." Not surprisingly, in the following year the Senate seized on a minor pretext to demand that the Carthaginians abandon their city and settle at least ten miles from the coast. Since this demand amounted to a death sentence for a nation dependent upon commerce, it was refused—as the Romans probably realized it would be. The result was the Third Punic War, a conflict fought between 149 and 146 B.C.E. The final Roman assault was carried into the city of Carthage, and a frightful butchery took place. When the victorious Roman general saw Carthage going up in flames he said, "It is a glorious moment, but I have a strange feeling that some day the same fate will befall my own homeland." With the might of the Carthaginians completely broken, the 55,000 that remained alive were sold into slavery, their once magnificent city was razed, and the ground was plowed over with salt.

The Third Punic War and the destruction of Carthage

The wars with Carthage had momentous effects on Rome's development. Most obvious was an enormous increase in Roman territory. The Roman victories over Carthage led to the creation of overseas provinces in Sicily, North Africa, and Spain. This not only brought Rome great new wealth—above all from Sicilian and African grain, and Spanish silver—but in the case of Spain was the beginning of a policy of westward expansion that proved to be one of the great formative influences on the history of Europe. Then too the wars brought Rome into conflict with eastern Mediterranean powers and thereby paved the way for still greater dominion. During the Second Punic War, Philip V of Macedon had entered into an alliance with Carthage and was said to have had designs on Egypt. Declaring a disinterested intention to forestall Philip's moves, Rome sent an army to the east; the extension of Roman rule was evidently the real item on the Roman agenda. The result was the conquest of Greece and Asia Minor and the reduction of Egypt into a Roman sphere of influence. Thus before the end of the second century B.C.E. virtually the entire Mediterranean world had been brought under Roman control.

Results of the wars with Carthage: (1) conquest of Spain and the Hellenistic East

As Roman tentacles stretched out over the Mediterranean, a host of fundamental economic and social changes ensued. One was a huge increase in slavery due to the capture and sale of prisoners of war. We have seen that 55,000 Carthaginians were enslaved in 146 B.C.E.; not long before, 150,000 Greeks had met the same fate. By the end of the second century about a million slaves toiled in Italy, mainly in the fields, making Rome one of the most slave-based economies known to history. Concomitant with this development was the decline of the small farmer as a result of the establishment of the plantation system based on slave labor

(2) A social and economic revolution

and the influx of cheap grain from the provinces. Small farmers, in turn, took refuge in the cities, above all the city of Rome itself, creating a large new urban element. Inevitably this trend, along with the incorporation of overseas areas long oriented to trade, and the need for an administrative apparatus, led to the appearance of a middle class comprising merchants, moneylenders, and men who held government contracts to operate mines, build roads, or collect taxes. Yet the cities were also full of impoverished drifters because Rome never made a transition to industrialism; with slaves to do all the hard work, a great disincentive existed for the technological initiative that might have led to industrialism, and without large-scale manufacture the urban population remained underemployed. Thus a traveler to Italy around 150 B.C.E. would have found a countryside full of slaves and cities full of disgruntled ex-farmers, living from hand to mouth.

Free marriage and divorce

Yet another change that accompanied the acquisition of new territories was a change in the nature of family life and the status of women. In earlier times the Roman family was based on the husband's legal and financial authority, which gave him nearly absolute powers. The wife was subordinated and served as custodian of the home while the husband managed outside affairs and expected to be treated with reverence. In the second century B.C.E., however, two legal innovations greatly altered this pattern. One was the introduction of "free marriage," whereby the wife's share of her father's property remained her own instead of passing to her husband and reverted to her father or her father's heirs upon her death. Together with that came new rules for divorce, whereby either side, instead of just the man, could initiate proceedings. Apparently the motive of both legal novelties was to prevent the transfer of property from one family to another, which would diminish the size of the large estates created with the influx of slaves. Yet both changes obviously resulted in giving the wife greater legal independence. In addition, the slave system itself gave wealthier women greater practical independence, for slaves could now take over tasks of child-rearing and household maintenance. Upper-class Roman women accordingly spent more time away from the home and began to engage in a range of social, intellectual, and artistic activities.

Introduction of Greek ideas and customs

Cultivated upper-class life for both men and women had been made possible by a final change attendant on Roman expansion, the introduction of Greek ideas and customs. These flowed more easily to Rome with the conquest of the Hellenistic East and were adopted once upper-class Romans began to become really wealthy as a result of their conquests. In particular, children were given much more education, theater and literature became ever more the mode, and the creature comforts that Hellenistic Greeks had begun to prize in Syria and Egypt became equally prized in turn by the Roman conquerors of the Mediterranean world. Some conservative Roman males viewed such changes with repugnance. For them the "good old Roman ways" with emphasis on family life based on fatherly authority and sober military discipline were giving way to the collapse of the family and the debilitating lures of soft living. But whether they liked it or not, Rome had now become irreversibly transformed from a republic of farmers into a complex society with vast gaps between rich and poor and new habits, at least among the well-to-do, of greater personal autonomy.

THE SOCIAL STRUGGLES OF THE LATE REPUBLIC

The new period of turbulence

The period from the end of the Third Punic War in 146 to about 30 B.C.E. was one of enormous turbulence. Social conflicts, assassinations, struggles between rival dictators, wars, and insurrections were the common occurrences of the time. Slave uprisings were also part of the general disorder. Some 70,000 slaves defeated a Roman army in Sicily in 134 B.C.E. before this revolt was put down by further Roman reinforcements, with slaves again ravaging Sicily in 104. But the most threatening slave revolt of all was one led by a slave named Spartacus from 73 to 71. Spartacus, who was being trained to become a gladiator (which meant certain death in the arena), escaped with a band of fugitives to Mount Vesuvius near Naples, there attracting a huge host of other fugitive slaves. For two years the escapees under his leadership held off Roman armies and overran much of southern Italy until they were finally defeated and Spartacus was slain in battle. Six thousand of those captured were left crucified along the length of a road from Capua to Rome (about 150 miles) to provide a terrible warning.

The land program of Tiberius Gracchus

Meanwhile an extended conflict between elements of the Roman governing class began in 133 B.C.E. with the attempts at social and economic reform instituted by the two Gracchus brothers. Though of aristocratic lineage themselves, they proposed to alleviate social and economic stress by granting government lands to the landless. In 133 Tiberius Gracchus, as tribune, proposed a law that restricted the current renters or holders of state lands to a maximum of 300 acres per citizen plus 150 acres for each child in the family. The excess was to be given to the poor in small plots. Conservative aristocrats bitterly opposed this proposal and engineered its veto by Octavius, Tiberius's fellow tribune. Tiberius removed Octavius from office, and when his own term expired attempted to stand for reelection. Both of these moves seemed to threaten a dictatorship and offered the conservative senators an excuse for resistance. Armed with clubs, they went on a rampage during the elections and murdered Tiberius and many of his followers.

Gaius Gracchus and the renewed fight for reform

Nine years later Tiberius's younger brother, Gaius Gracchus, renewed the struggle. Though Tiberius's land law had finally been enacted by the Senate, Gaius believed that the campaign had to go further. Elected tribune in 123 B.C.E., and reelected in 122, he enacted several laws for the benefit of the less privileged. One provided for stabilizing the price of grain in Rome. For this purpose public granaries were built along the Tiber. Another exercised controls on governors suspected of exploiting the provinces for their own advantage. These and similar measures provoked so much anger among the vested interests that they resolved to eliminate their enemy. The Roman Senate proclaimed Gaius Gracchus an outlaw and authorized the consuls to take all necessary steps for the defense of the Republic. In the ensuing conflict Gaius was killed, and about 3,000 of his followers lost their lives in vengeful purges.

Pompey

After the downfall of the Gracchi, two military leaders who had won fame in foreign wars successively made themselves rulers of the state. The first was Marius, who was elevated to the consulship by the plebeian party in 107 B.C.E. and reelected six times. Unfortunately, Marius was no statesman and accomplished nothing for his followers beyond demonstrating the ease with which a general with an army behind him could override opposition. Following his death in 86 B.C.E. the aristocrats took a turn at government by force. Their champion was Sulla, another victorious commander. Appointed dictator in 82 B.C.E. for an unlimited term, Sulla ruthlessly proceeded to exterminate his opponents, extend the powers of the aristocratic Senate, and curtail the authority of the tribunes. After three years of rule Sulla decided his job was done and retired to a life of luxury on his country estate.

Pompey and Caesar

The actions of Sulla did not stand unchallenged after he relinquished his office, for the effect of his decrees was to give control to a selfish aristocracy. Several new leaders now emerged to espouse the cause of the people. The most prominent were Pompey (106–48 B.C.E.) and Julius Caesar (100–44 B.C.E.). For a time they cooperated in a plot to gain control of the government, but later they became rivals and sought to outdo each other in bids for popular support. Pompey won fame as the conqueror of Syria and Palestine, while Caesar devoted his energies to a series of brilliant forays against the Gauls, adding to the Roman state the territory of modern Belgium, Germany west of the Rhine, and France. In 52 B.C.E., after protracted mob disorders in Rome, the Senate turned to Pompey and engineered his election as sole consul. Caesar, stationed in Gaul, was branded an enemy of the state, and Pompey conspired with the senatorial faction to deprive him of political power. The result was a deadly war between the two men. In 49 B.C.E. Caesar crossed the Rubicon River into Italy (ever since then an image for a fateful decision) and marched on Rome. Pompey fled to the east in the hope of gathering an army large enough to regain control of Italy. In 48 B.C.E. the forces of the rivals met at Pharsalus in Greece. Pompey was defeated and soon afterward murdered by schemers in favor of Caesar.

Julius Caesar

Caesar then intervened in Egyptian politics at the court of Cleopatra (whom he left pregnant). Then he conducted another military campaign in Asia Minor in which victory was so swift that he could report "I came, I saw, I conquered" *(Veni, vidi, vici)*. After that Caesar returned to Rome. No one now dared challenge his power. With the aid of his veterans he cowed the Senate into granting his every desire. In 46 B.C.E. he became dictator for ten years, and two years later for life. In addition, he assumed nearly every other title that could augment his power. He obtained from the Senate full authority to make war and peace and to control the revenues of the state. For all practical purposes he was above the law, and rumors spread that he intended to make himself king. Such fears led to his assassination on the Ides of March in 44 B.C.E. by a group of conspirators, under the leadership of Brutus and Cassius, who hoped to return Rome to republican government.

Ides of March Coin. This coin was struck by Brutus to commemorate the assassination of Julius Caesar. Brutus is depicted on the obverse; on the reverse is a liberty cap between two daggers and the Latin abbreviation for the Ides of March.

Caesar's accomplishments

Although Caesar was once revered by historians as a superhuman hero, he is now often dismissed as insignificant. Both extremes of interpretation should be avoided. Certainly he did not "save Rome" and was not the greatest statesman of all time, for he treated the Republic with contempt and made the problem of governing more difficult for those who came after him. Yet some of the measures he took as dictator did have lasting effects. With the aid of a Greek astronomer he revised the calendar so as to make a year last for 365 days (with an extra day added every fourth year). This "Julian" calendar—subject to adjustments made by Pope Gregory XIII in 1582—is still with us. It is thus only proper that the seventh month is named after Julius as "July." By conferring citizenship upon thousands of Spaniards and Gauls, Caesar took an important step toward eliminating the distinction between Italians and provincials. He also helped relieve economic inequities by settling many of his veterans and some of the urban poor on unused lands. Vastly more important than these reforms, however, was Caesar's farsighted resolve, made before he seized power, to invest his efforts in the West. While Pompey, and before him Alexander, went to the East to gain fame and fortune, Caesar was the first great leader to recognize the potential significance of northwestern Europe. By incorporating Gaul into the Roman world he brought Rome great agricultural wealth and helped bring urban life and culture to what was then the wild West. Western European civilization, later to be anchored in just those regions that Caesar conquered, might not have been the same without him.

Rome Becomes Sophisticated

Epicureanism

The culture that Rome brought to Gaul was itself taken from the Greek East, for during the time between the end of the Punic Wars and the death of Julius Caesar Rome came ever more under the influence of Hellenistic civilization. One result was the adoption of Hellenistic schools of thought, especially Epicureanism and Stoicism, by the upper classes, and another was the flowering of intellectual activity. The most renowned of the Roman exponents of Epicureanism was Lucretius (98–55 B.C.E.), author of a book-length philosophical poem, *On the Nature of Things.* In writing this work Lucretius wished to explain the universe in such a way as to remove fear of the supernatural, which he regarded as the chief obstacle to peace of mind. Worlds and all things in them, he taught, are the result of fortuitous combinations of atoms. Though he admitted the existence of the gods, he conceived of them as living in eternal peace, neither creating nor governing the universe. Everything is a product of mechanical evolution, including human beings and their habits and beliefs. Since mind is indissolubly linked with matter, death means utter extinction; consequently, no part of the human personality can survive to be rewarded or punished in an afterlife. Lucretius's conception of the good life was simple: what one needs, he asserted, is not enjoyment but "peace and a pure heart." Whether one agrees with Lucretius's philosophy or not, there is no doubt that he was an extraordinarily fine poet. In fact his musical cadences, sustained majesty of expression, and infectious enthusiasm earn him a rank among the greatest poets who ever lived.

The Stoic philosophy of Cicero

Stoicism was introduced into Rome about 140 B.C.E. and soon came to include among its converts numerous influential leaders of public life. The greatest of these was Cicero (106–43 B.C.E.), the "father of Roman eloquence." Although Cicero adopted doctrines from a number of philosophers, including both Plato and Aristotle, he derived more of his ideas from the Stoics than from any other source. Cicero's ethical philosophy was based on the Stoic premises that virtue is sufficient for happiness and that tranquillity of mind is the highest good. He conceived of the ideal human being as one who has been guided by reason to an indifference toward sorrow and pain. Cicero diverged from the Greek Stoics in his greater approval of the active, political life. To this degree he still spoke for the older Roman tradition of service to the state. Cicero never claimed to be an original philosopher but rather conceived his goal to be that of bringing the best of Greek philosophy to the West. In this he was remarkably successful, for he wrote in a rich and elegant Latin prose style that has never been surpassed. Cicero's prose immediately became a standard for composition and has remained so until the present century. Thus even though not a truly great thinker Cicero was the most influential Latin transmitter of ancient thought to the medieval and modern western European worlds.

Works of Plautus, Catullus, and Julius Caesar

Lucretius and Cicero were the two leading exponents of Greek thought but not the only fine writers of the later Roman Republic. It now became the fashion among the upper classes to learn Greek and to strive to reproduce in Latin some of the more popular forms of Greek literature. Some results of enduring literary merit were the ribald comedies of Plautus (257?–184 B.C.E.), the passionate love poems of Catullus (84?–54? B.C.E.), and the crisp military memoirs of Julius Caesar.

Social conditions in the late Republic

In addition to its intellectual effects, Roman interaction with the Hellenistic world accelerated the process of social change, foremost of which was the cleavage between classes. The Italian people, numbering about eight million on the death of Caesar, had come to be divided into four main social orders: the senatorial aristocracy, the equestrians, the common citizens, and the slaves. The senatorial aristocrats numbered 300 citizens and their families. Most of the aristocrats gained their living as office-holders and as owners of great landed estates. The equestrian order was made up of propertied aristocrats who were not in the Senate. Originally this class had been composed of those citizens with incomes sufficient to enable them to serve in the cavalry at their own expense, but the term *equestrian* came to be applied to all outside of the senatorial class who possessed substantial property. The equestrians were the chief offenders in the exploitation of the poor. As moneylenders they often charged exorbitant interest rates. By far the largest number of the citizens were mere commoners. Most of these were independent farmers, a few were industrial workers, and some were indigent city dwellers who lived by intermittent employment and public relief. When Julius Caesar became dictator, 320,000 citizens were receiving free grain from the state.

The status of slaves

The Roman slaves were scarcely considered people at all but instruments of production like cattle. Notwithstanding the fact that some of them were cultivated foreigners taken as prisoners of war, the standard policy of their owners was to get as much work out of them as possible during their prime until they died of exhaustion or were released to fend for themselves. Although domestic slaves might from time to time have been treated decently, and some slave artisans in the city of Rome were relatively free to run their own businesses, the general lot of the slave was horrendous. Moreover, it is a sad commentary on Roman civilization that most of its productive labor was done by slaves. They produced much of the food supply, for the amount contributed by the few surviving independent farmers was quite insignificant, and they did much of the work in the urban shops as well. In addition, slaves were employed in numerous nonproductive activities. A lucrative form of investment for the business classes was ownership of slaves trained as gladiators, who could be slaughtered by wild animals for amusement. The growth of luxury also required the employment of thousands of slaves in domestic service. The man of great wealth insisted on having his doorkeepers, his litter-bearers, his couriers, his valets, and his tutors for his children. In some great households there were special servants with no other duties than to rub the master down after his bath or to care for his sandals.

Changes in religion

The religious beliefs of the Romans were altered in various ways in the last two centuries of the Republic—again mainly because of Rome's interaction with the Hellenistic world. Most pronounced was the spread of Eastern mystery cults, which satisfied the craving for a more emotional religion than traditional Roman worship and offered the reward of immortality to the wretched of the earth. From Egypt came the cult of Osiris (or Serapis, as the god was now more commonly called), while from Asia Minor was introduced the worship of the Great Mother, with her eunuch priests and ritualistic orgies. Most popular of all at the end of the period was the Persian cult of Mithraism, which offered awe-inspiring underground rites and a doctrine of the afterlife of the soul.

Roman Mystery Rites. The "Villa of the Mysteries" in Pompeii preserves an astonishing cycle of wall paintings done around 50 B.C.E. The exact meaning is debatable, but the most persuasive interpretation is that it shows a succession of cult rites. Here a young woman is being whipped, probably an initiation ceremony, while a cult member performs a solemn dance in the nude.

The Principate or Early Empire (27 B.C.E.–180 C.E.)

An alliance to avenge Caesar's death

Shortly before his death in 44 B.C.E., Julius Caesar had adopted as his sole heir his grandnephew Octavian (63 B.C.E.–14 C.E.), then a young man of eighteen acting in his uncle's service in Illyria across the Adriatic Sea. Upon learning of Caesar's death, Octavian hastened to Rome to see if he could claim his inheritance. He soon found that he had to join forces with two of Caesar's powerful friends, Mark Antony and Lepidus. The following year the three formed an alliance to crush the power of the aristocratic group responsible for Caesar's murder. The methods employed were not to the new leaders' credit. Prominent members of the aristocracy were hunted down and slain and their property confiscated. The most noted of the victims was Cicero, brutally slain by Mark Antony's thugs though he had taken no part in the conspiracy against Caesar's life.

Caesar's real murderers, Brutus and Cassius, escaped and organized an army, but they were defeated by Octavian and his colleagues near Philippi in 42 B.C.E.

Thereafter a quarrel developed between the members of the alliance, inspired primarily by Antony's jealousy of Octavian. The subsequent struggle became a contest between East and West. Antony went to the East and made an alliance with Cleopatra that was dedicated to introducing principles of despotism into Roman rule. Octavian consolidated the forces of the West and came forward as the champion of Greek cultural traditions. As in the earlier contest between Caesar and Pompey the victory again went to the West. In the naval battle of Actium (31 B.C.E.) Octavian's forces defeated those of Antony and Cleopatra, both of whom soon afterward committed suicide. It was now clear that Rome would not be swallowed up by the East. Octavian's victory guaranteed that there would be several more centuries for the consolidation of Greek ideals and urban life, a development important above all for the future of western Europe.

Octavian. When Octavian gained sole rule he became known as Augustus. Many statues of him survive, all of them idealized.

Octavian creates the Empire

The victory at Actium ushered in a new period in Roman history, the most glorious and the most prosperous that Rome ever experienced. When Octavian returned to Rome he announced the restoration of complete peace. First he ruled for four years as consul, but in 27 B.C.E. he accepted from the Senate the honorific titles of "emperor" and "augustus," a step that historians count as the beginning of the Roman Empire. This periodization is somewhat arbitrary because Octavian was as strong before his title change as after; moreover, "emperor" at the time meant only "victorious general." But gradually, after his successors took the title of emperor as well, it became the primary designation for the ruler of the Roman state. Actually the title by which Octavian preferred to have his authority designated was the more modest *princeps,* or "first citizen." For this reason the period of his rule and that of his successors is properly called the Principate (or, alternatively, the early Empire), to distinguish it from the periods of the Republic (sixth century to 27 B.C.E.), the time of upheavals (180 C.E. to 284 C.E.), and the later Empire (284 to 610 C.E.).

Reforms of Augustus

Octavian, or Augustus as he was now more commonly called, was determined not to seem a dictator. In theory the Senate and the citizens were the supreme sovereigns, as they had always been. Hence most of the republican institutions were left in place even though their functioning had clearly become a charade. Augustus himself, in practical control of the army, freely determined all governmental policy. Fortunately he was a very gifted statesman. Among the measures he instituted were the establishment of a new coinage system for use throughout the Roman Empire; the introduction within Rome itself of a range of public services, including police and fire fighting; and more self-government for cities and provinces than they had enjoyed before. He also abolished the old system of farming out the collection of financial dues. Whereas previously tax collectors were remunerated solely by being allowed to keep a percentage

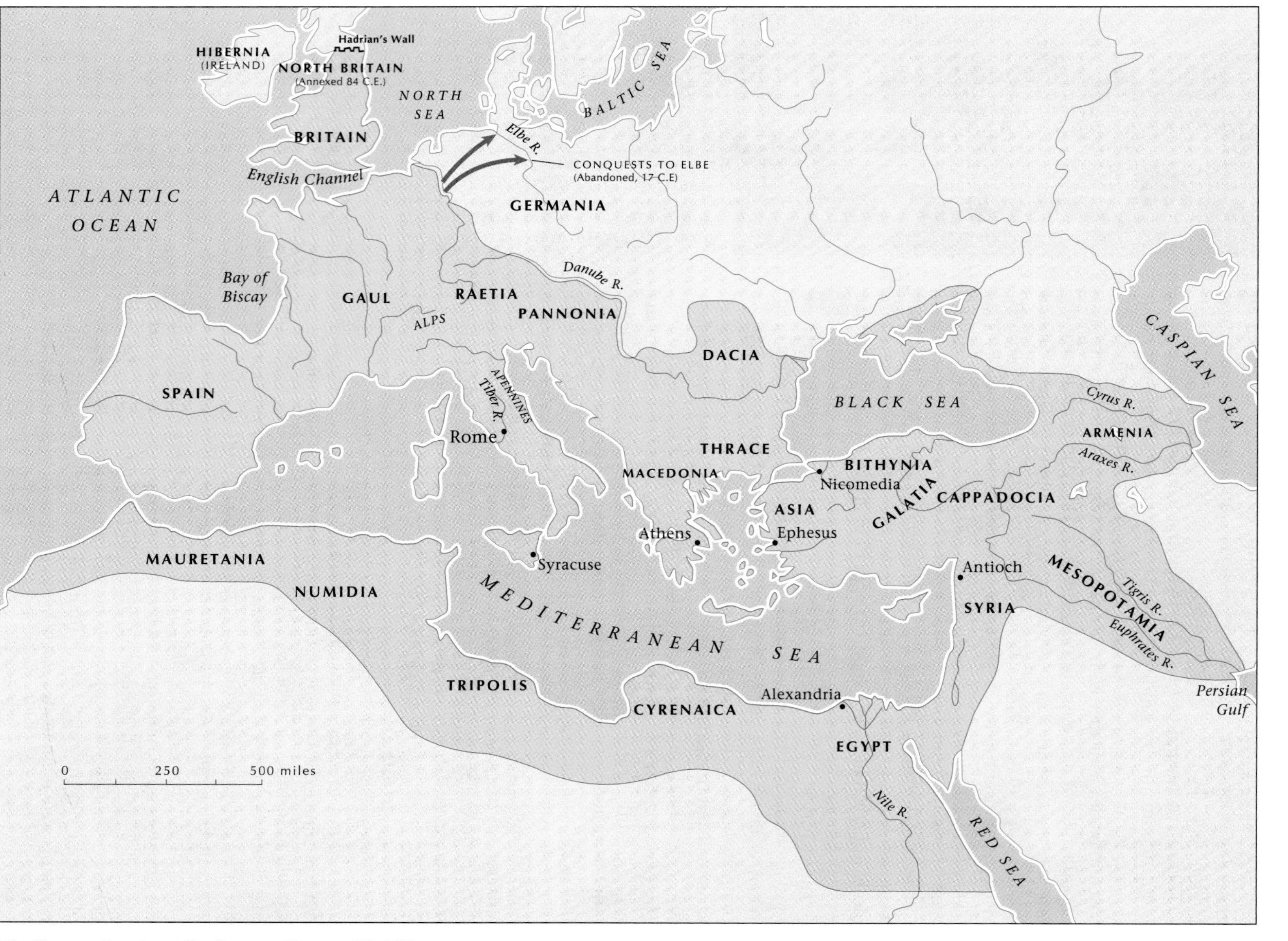

The Roman Empire at Its Greatest Extent, 97–117 C.E.

of their intake, a system that led inevitably to graft and extortion, Augustus now appointed his own representatives as tax collectors, paid them regular salaries, and kept them under strict supervision. Above all, Augustus instituted a program of incentives for colonization of the provinces in order to shift the excess free population out of Italy and thereby remove a major source of social tensions and political upheaval. All told, such measures did enhance local peace.

After the death of Augustus in 14 C.E. until almost the end of the first century, Rome had no really capable rulers, with the single exception of Claudius (41–54). Several of Augustus's successors, most infamously Caligula (37–41) and Nero (54–68), were brutal tyrants who squandered the resources of the state and kept the city of Rome in an uproar by their deeds of bloody violence. But starting in 96 C.E., a period of strong and stable government returned with the advent of "five good emperors": Nerva (96–98), Trajan (98–117), Hadrian (117–138), Antoninus Pius (138–161), and Marcus Aurelius (161–180). Each of them was a gifted administrator, and each in turn was able to bequeath a well-ordered and united realm to his designated successor.

Trajan

New conquests

From the time of Augustus until that of Trajan, the Roman Empire continued to expand. Augustus gained more land for Rome than did any other Roman ruler. His generals advanced into central Europe, conquering the territories known today as Switzerland, Austria, and Bulgaria. Only in what is today central Germany did Roman troops meet defeat, a setback that convinced Augustus to hold the Roman borders at the Rhine and Danube. Subsequently, in 43 C.E., the Emperor Claudius began the conquest of Britain, and at the beginning of the next century Trajan pushed beyond the Danube to add Dacia (now Romania) to the Empire's realms. Trajan also conquered territories in Mesopotamia but thereby incurred the enmity of the Persians, causing his successor Hadrian to embark on a defensive policy. The Roman Empire had now reached its territorial limits; in the third century these limits would begin to recede.

Hadrian

The *Pax Romana*

Rome's peaceful sway over a vast empire for about two centuries, from the time of Augustus to that of Marcus Aurelius, was certainly one of its most impressive accomplishments. As the historian Gibbon said, "the Empire of Rome comprehended the fairest part of the earth and the most civilized portion of mankind." The celebrated *Pax Romana,* or Roman peace, was unprecedented. The Mediterranean was now under the control of one power (as it has never been before or since) and experienced the passage of centuries without a single naval battle. On land Roman officials ruled from the borders of Scotland to those of Persia. A contemporary orator justly boasted that "the whole civilized world lays down the arms which were its ancient load, as if on holiday . . . all places are full of gymnasia, fountains, monumental approaches, temples, workshops, schools; one can say that the civilized world, which had been sick from the beginning . . . , has been brought by the right knowledge to a state of health." But much of this health, as we will see, proved illusory.

Marcus Aurelius. This equestrian statue is one of the few surviving from the ancient world: the Christians destroyed most Roman equestrian statues because they found them idolatrous, but they spared this one because they mistakenly believed that it represented Constantine, the first Christian Roman emperor. The statue stood outdoors in Rome from the second century until 1980, when it was taken into storage to protect it from air pollution.

Culture and Life in the Period of the Principate

Roman Stoics: Seneca, Epictetus, and Marcus Aurelius

The intellectual and artistic achievements of the Principate outshone those of all other ages in the history of Rome. Three eminent exponents of Stoicism lived in Rome in the two centuries that followed the rule of Augustus: Seneca (4 B.C.E.–65 C.E.), wealthy adviser for a time to Nero; the slave Epictetus (60?–120 C.E.); and the Emperor Marcus Aurelius (121–180 C.E.). All of them agreed that inner serenity is the ultimate human goal, that true happiness can be found only in surrender to the benevolent order of the universe. They preached the ideal of virtue for virtue's sake, deplored the sinfulness of human nature, and urged obedience to conscience. Seneca and Epictetus both expressed deep mystical yearnings as part of their philosophy, making it almost a religion. They worshiped the cosmos as divine, governed by an all-powerful Providence that ordained all that happened for ultimate good. The last of the Roman Stoics, Marcus Aurelius, was more fatalistic and less hopeful. Although he did not reject the conception of an ordered and rational universe, he did not believe that immortality would balance suffering on earth and was inclined to think of humans as creatures buffeted by evil fortune for which no distant perfection of the whole could fully compensate. He urged, nevertheless, that people should continue to live nobly, that they should abandon themselves to neither gross indulgence nor angry protest, but that they should derive what contentment they could from dignified resignation to suffering and tranquil submission to death.

Roman literature of the Principate is conventionally divided into two periods: works of the *golden age,* written during the reign of Augustus, and works of the *silver age,* written during the first century C.E. Most of the literature of the golden age was vigorous, affirmative, and uplifting. The poetry of the greatest of all Roman poets, Virgil (70–19 B.C.E.), was prototypic. In a set of pastoral poems, the *Eclogues,* Virgil expressed an idealized vision of human life led in harmony with nature. The *Eclogues* also implicitly extolled Augustus as the bringer of peace and abundance. Virgil's masterpiece, the *Aeneid,* is an epic poem about a Trojan hero, Aeneas, understood to have been the distant ancestor of the Roman people and the model of Roman greatness. Written in elevated, yet sinewy and stirring metrical verse ("Arms and the man, I sing . . ."), the *Aeneid* tells of the founding of a great state by means of warfare and toil and foretells Rome's glorious future.

Virgil. The earliest surviving painted representation, dating from about 600 C.E.

Other major golden-age writers were Horace (65–8 B.C.E.), Livy (59 B.C.E.–17 C.E.), and Ovid (43 B.C.E.–17 C.E.). Of these, Horace was the most philosophical. His *Odes* drew from the practical teachings of both Epicureans and Stoics, combining the Epicurean justification of pleasure with the Stoic passivity in the face of trouble. The chief claim to fame of Livy, a narrative historian, rests on his skill as a prose stylist. His *History of Rome,* starting "from the founding of the city," is factually unreliable but replete with dramatic and picturesque narrative designed to appeal to patriotic emotions. Ovid was the least typical of the Latin golden-age writers insofar as his outlook tended to be more satiric than heroically affirmative. His main poetic accomplishment was a highly sophisticated retelling of Greek myths in a long poem of fifteen books, the *Metamorphoses,* full of wit and eroticism. Whereas the Emperor Augustus delighted in the *Aeneid,* he found the mocking and dissolute tone of Ovid's verses to be so repellant that he banished Ovid from his court.

Silver-age literature

The literature of the silver age was typically less calm and balanced than that of the golden age. Its effects derived more often from self-conscious artifice. The tales of Petronius and Apuleius describe the more exotic and sometimes sordid aspects of Roman life. The aim of the authors is less to instruct or uplift than to tell an entertaining story or turn a witty phrase. An entirely different viewpoint is presented in the works of the other most important writers of this age: Juvenal, the satirist (60?–140 C.E.), and Tacitus, the historian (55?–117? C.E.). Juvenal wrote with savage indignation about what he took to be the moral degeneracy of his contemporaries. His taste for bitingly compressed rhetorical phrases has made him a favorite source for quotation. A similar attitude toward Roman society characterized the writing of his younger contemporary Tacitus, who described the events of his age not with a view to dispassionate analysis but largely for the purpose of moral indictment. His description of the customs of the ancient Germans in his *Germania* served to heighten the contrast between the manly virtues of an unspoiled race and the effeminate vices of the

Diana. A Roman painting depicting the goddess of the hunt. Roman art was often gentle and impressionistic, far from the military grandeur most often associated today with the Romans.

decadent Romans. Whatever his failings as a historian, he was a master of ironic wit and brilliant aphorism. Referring to Roman conquests, he makes a barbarian chieftain say, "They create a wilderness and call it peace."

Achievements in art

Roman art first assumed its distinctive character during the period of the Principate. Before this time what passed for an art of Rome was really an importation from the Hellenistic East. Conquering armies brought back to Italy wagonloads of statues, reliefs, and marble columns as part of the plunder from Greece and Asia Minor. These became the property of the wealthy and were used to embellish their sumptuous mansions. As the demand increased, hundreds of copies were made, with the result that by the end of the Republic Rome came to have a profusion of objects of art that had no more roots in the culture than the Picassos hanging on the walls of modern corporate offices.

Architecture and sculpture

The aura of national glory that surrounded the Principate, however, stimulated the growth of an art that was more indigenous. This art was more varied than is often assumed, running from the grandest public architecture to the most delicate wall paintings. In architecture Romans experimented with the dome and pioneered in the building of amphitheaters, public baths, and race courses. Public buildings were customarily of massive proportions and solid construction. Among the largest and most noted were the Pantheon, with its dome having a diameter of 142 feet, and the Colosseum, which could accommodate 50,000 spectators at gladiatorial combats. Roman sculpture stayed close to the Greek, preferring ideals that were ever more naturalistic. This was particularly apparent on coins since new coins with images of the current emperor were issued every year. Rather than being prettified, the rulers were usually depicted just as they looked: often one can trace on an annual basis a ruler's receding hairline or advancing double chin. But painting

Mosaic. From the first century C.E. A floor design composed of small pieces of colored marble fitted together to form a picture.

was the Romans' most original art. Wealthy Romans loved intense colors and surrounded themselves with wall paintings and mosaics—pictures produced by fitting together small pieces of colored glass or stone. These created a gamut of effects from fantastic seascapes to dreamy landscapes to introspective portraiture.

Engineering and public services

Closely related to their achievements in architecture were Roman triumphs in engineering (although they accomplished little in science). The imperial Romans built marvelous roads and bridges, many of which still survive. In the time of Trajan eleven aqueducts brought water into Rome from the nearby hills and provided the city with 300 million gallons daily for drinking and bathing as well as for flushing a well-designed sewage system. Water was cleverly funneled into the homes of the rich for their private gardens, fountains, and pools. The Emperor Nero, something of a megalomaniac, built a famous "Golden House" in the center of Rome with pipes fitted for sprinkling his guests with perfume, baths supplied with medicinal waters, and a pond "like a sea." In addition, a spherical ceiling in the banquet hall revolved day and night like the heavens. (Supposedly when Nero moved in he was heard to say, "At last I can live like a human being.")

Upper-class Roman women

One of the more impressive aspects of Roman society under the Principate was the role played by upper-class women. We have seen that under the Republic wealthier women were less confined to domesticity and obscurity than their counterparts in Athens, and this trait became even

Roman Aqueduct at Segovia, Spain. Aqueducts conveyed water from mountains to the larger cities.

more pronounced in the early Empire. It is true that Roman women were assigned the names of their fathers with feminine endings—for example, Julia from Julius, Claudia from Claudius, Marcia from Marcus. Yet unlike women in most modern societies they did not change their names when they were married. This was a reflection of the fact that wealthier Roman women had a status quite independent from that of their husbands. With numerous slaves to take care of their households and wealth of their own to draw on, upper-class Roman women customarily were educated in the liberal arts and were free to engage in intellectual and artistic pursuits. Some wrote poetry, others studied philosophy, and others presided over literary salons. Aristocratic Roman women often had their portraits painted or chiseled in stone, revealing their cultivation of physical elegance. The busts of several emperors' wives or daughters even appeared on the Roman coinage, partly because the emperors wished to proclaim the greatness of their families, and partly because some of these women really did play an influential role (albeit an informal one) in affairs of state. Of course, women wielded none of the power of men, yet by the standards of the ancient world they were relatively liberated.

Coin Depicting Emperor's Wife. This Roman coin, dating from about 200 C.E., bears the image of Julia Domna, wife of the Emperor Septimius Severus.

Gladiatorial combats

For most modern sensibilities, the most repellant aspect of Roman culture during the period of the Principate was cruelty. Whereas the Greeks entertained themselves with theater, the Romans more and more preferred "circuses," which were really exhibitions of human slaughter. During the Principate the spectacles became bloodier than ever. The Romans could no longer obtain a sufficient thrill from mere exhibitions of athletic prowess: pugilists were now required to have their hands wrapped with thongs of leather loaded with iron or lead. The most popular amusement of all was watching the gladiatorial combats in amphitheaters built for thousands of spectators. Fights between gladiators were nothing new, but they were now presented on a much more elaborate scale. Not only common people attended them, but also wealthy aristocrats, and frequently the head of the government himself. The gladiators fought to the accompaniment of savage cries and curses from the audience. When one went down with a disabling wound, the crowd was asked to decide whether his life should be spared or whether the weapon of his opponent should be plunged into his heart. One contest after another, often featuring the sacrifice of men to wild animals, was staged in the course of a single exhibition. Should the arena become too sodden with blood, it was covered over with a fresh layer of sand, and the revolting performance went on. Most of the gladiators were condemned criminals or slaves, but some were volunteers even from the respectable classes. Commodus, the worthless son of Marcus Aurelius, entered the arena several times for the sake of the plaudits of the mob; this was his idea of a Roman holiday.

Portrait Bust of a Roman Lady. The ostentatiousness of upper-class culture during the period of the Principate is well displayed by this sculpture, done around 90 C.E.

Notwithstanding its low moral tone, the age of the Principate was characterized by an even deeper interest in salvationist religions than that which had prevailed under the Republic. Mithraism now gained adherents by the thousands, absorbing many of the followers of the cults of the Great Mother and of Serapis. About 40 C.E. the first Christians appeared

The Colosseum. Built by the Roman emperors between 75 and 80 C.E. as a place of entertainment, it was the scene of gladiatorial combats. The most common form of Greek secular architecture was the theater (see p. 115), but the most common Roman form was the amphitheater.

in Rome. The new sect grew steadily and eventually succeeded in displacing Mithraism as the most popular of the salvationist faiths.

The spread of Mithraism and Christianity

The establishment of stable government by Augustus ushered in a period of prosperity for Italy that lasted for more than two centuries. Trade was now extended to all parts of the known world, even to Arabia, India, and China. Manufacturing increased somewhat, especially in the production of pottery, textiles, and articles of metal and glass. In spite of all this, the economic order was far from healthy. Prosperity was not evenly distributed but was confined primarily to the upper classes. Since the stigma attached to manual labor persisted as strongly as ever, production was bound to decline as the supply of slaves diminished. Perhaps worse was the fact that Italy had a decidedly unfavorable balance of trade. The meager industrial development was by no means sufficient to provide enough articles of export to meet the demand for luxuries imported from the provinces and from the outside world. As a consequence, Italy was gradually drained of its supply of precious metals. By the third century the Western Roman economy began to collapse.

ROMAN LAW

There is general agreement that one of the most important legacies that the Romans left to succeeding cultures was their system of law. This resulted from a gradual evolution that began roughly with the publication of the Twelve Tables about 450 B.C.E. In the later centuries of the Republic the Law of the Twelve Tables was transformed by the growth of new precedents and principles. These emanated from different sources: from changes in custom, from the teachings of the Stoics, from the decisions of judges, but especially from the edicts of the *praetors,* magistrates who had authority to define and interpret the law in a particular suit and issue instructions to judges.

The early development of Roman law

Roman law attained its highest stage of development under the Principate. This resulted in part from the extension of the law over a wider field of jurisdiction, over the lives and properties of aliens in strange environments as well as over the citizens of Italy. But the major reason was the fact that Augustus and his successors gave to certain eminent jurists the right to deliver opinions on the legal issues of cases under trial in the courts. The most prominent of the men thus designated from time to time were Gaius, Ulpian, Papinian, and Paulus. Although most of them held high judicial office, they had gained their reputations primarily as lawyers and writers on legal subjects. The responses of these jurists came to embody a science and philosophy of law and were accepted as the basis of Roman jurisprudence.

Roman law under the Principate; the great jurists

The Roman law as it was developed under the influence of the jurists comprised three great branches or divisions: the civil law, the law of peoples, and the natural law. The civil law was the law of Rome and its citizens. As such it existed in both written and unwritten forms. It included the statutes of the Senate, the decrees of the emperor, the edicts of magistrates, and also certain ancient customs operating with the force of law. The law of peoples was the law held to be common to all people regardless of nationality. This law authorized slavery and private ownership of property and defined the principles of purchase and sale, partnership, and contract. It was not superior to the civil law but supplemented it as especially applicable to the alien inhabitants of the Empire.

The three divisions of Roman law

The most interesting and in many ways the most important branch of Roman law was the natural law, a product not of judicial practice, but of philosophy. The Stoics had developed the idea of a rational order of nature that is the embodiment of justice and right. They had affirmed that all men are by nature equal, and that they are entitled to certain basic rights that governments have no authority to transgress. The father of the law of nature as a legal principle, however, was not one of the Hellenistic Stoics, but Cicero. "True law," he declared, "is right reason consonant with nature, diffused among all men, constant, eternal. To make enactments infringing this law, religion forbids, neither may it be repealed even in part, nor have we power through Senate or people to

The natural law

free ourselves from it." This law was prior to the state itself, and any ruler who defied it automatically became a tyrant. Most of the great jurists subscribed to conceptions of the law of nature very similar to those of the philosophers. Although the jurists did not regard this law as an automatic limitation upon the civil law, they thought of it as an ideal to which the statutes and decrees of men ought to conform. This development of the concept of abstract justice as a legal principle was one of the noblest achievements of the Roman civilization.

Commodus. The self-deluded ruler encouraged artists to portray him as the equal of the superhuman Hercules.

The Crisis of the Third Century (180–284 C.E.)

With the death of Marcus Aurelius in 180 C.E. the period of beneficent imperial rule came to an end. One reason for the success of the "five good emperors" was that the first four designated particularly promising young men, rather than sons or close relatives, for the succession. But Marcus Aurelius broke this pattern with unfortunate results. Although he was one of the most philosophic and thoughtful rulers who ever reigned, he was not wise enough to recognize that his son Commodus was a vicious incompetent. Made emperor by his father's wishes, Commodus indulged his taste for perversities, showed open contempt for the Senate, and ruled so brutally that a palace clique finally had him murdered by strangling in 192. Matters thereafter became worse. With the lack of an obvious successor to Commodus, the armies of the provinces raised their own candidates and civil war ensued. Although a provincial general, Septimius Severus (193–211), emerged victorious, it now became clear that provincial armies could interfere in imperial politics at will. Severus and some of his successors aggravated the problem by eliminating even the theoretical rights of the Senate and ruling as military dictators. Once the role of brute force was openly revealed any aspiring general could try his luck at seizing power. Hence civil war became endemic. From 235 to 284 there were no less than twenty-six "barracks emperors," of whom only one managed to escape a violent death.

End of political stability

The half-century between 235 and 284 was certainly the worst for Rome since its rise to world power. In addition to political chaos, a number of other factors combined to bring the Empire to the brink of ruin. One was that civil war had disastrous economic effects. Not only did constant warfare interfere with agriculture and trade, but the rivalry of aspirants to rule led them to drain the wealth of their territories in order to gain favor with their armies. Following the maxim of "enriching the soldiers and scorning the rest," they could raise funds only by debasing the coinage and by nearly confiscatory taxation of civilians. Landlords, small tenants, and manufacturers thus had little motive to produce at a time when production was most necessary. In human terms the poorest, as is usual in times of economic contraction, suffered the most. Often they were driven to the most abject destitution. In the wake of war and hunger, disease became

The Emperor Decius. The extreme naturalism and furrowed brow are typical of portraits of this period.

rampant. Already in the reign of Marcus Aurelius a terrible plague had swept through the Empire, decimating the army and the population at large. In the middle of the third century pestilence returned and struck at the population with its fearful scythe for fifteen years.

The resulting strain on human resources came at a time when Rome could least afford it, for still another threat to the Empire in the middle of the third century was the advance of Rome's external enemies. With Roman ranks thinned by disease and Roman armies fighting each other, Germans in the West and Persians in the East broke through the old Roman defense lines. In 251 the Goths defeated and slew the Emperor Decius, crossed the Danube, and marauded at will in the Balkans. A more humiliating disaster came in 260 when the Emperor Valerian was captured in battle by the Persians and made to kneel as a footstool for their ruler. When he died his body was stuffed and hung on exhibition. Clearly the days of Augustus were very far off.

Persian Coin. This stylized representation of a monarch dates from about 220 C.E.

Neoplatonism

Understandably enough the culture of the third century was marked by pervasive anxiety. One can even see expressions of worry in the surviving statuary, as in the bust of the Emperor Philip (244–249), who appears almost to realize that he will soon be killed in battle. Suiting the spirit of the age, the Neoplatonic philosophy of withdrawal from the world came to the fore. *Neoplatonism* (meaning "New Platonism") drew the spiritualist tendency of Plato's thought to extremes. The first of its basic teachings was emanationism: everything that exists proceeds from the divine in a continuing stream of emanations. The initial stage in the process is the emanation of the world-soul. From this come the divine Ideas or spiritual patterns, and then the souls of particular things. The final emanation is matter. But matter has no form or quality of its own; it is simply the privation of spirit, the residue that is left after the spiritual rays from the divine have burned themselves out. It follows that matter is to be despised as the symbol of evil and darkness. The second major doctrine was mysticism. The human soul was originally a part of God, but it has become separated from its divine source through its union with matter. The highest goal of life should be mystic reunion with the divine, which can be accomplished through contemplation and through emancipation of the soul from bondage to matter. Human beings should be ashamed of the fact that they possess a physical body and should seek to subjugate it in every way possible. Asceticism was therefore the third main teaching of this philosophy.

The Emperor Philip the Arab. An artistic legacy of the Roman "age of anxiety."

Plotinus

The real founder of Neoplatonism was Plotinus, who was born in Egypt about 204 C.E. In the later years of his life he taught in Rome and won many followers among the upper classes before he died in 270. His principal successors diluted the philosophy with more and more bizarre superstitions. In spite of its antirational viewpoint and its utter indifference to the state, Neoplatonism became so popular in Rome in the third and fourth centuries C.E. that it almost completely supplanted Stoicism. No fact could have expressed more eloquently the turn of Rome away from the realities of the here and now.

Causes of Rome's Decline

Turning point in 284

As Rome was not built in a day, so it was not lost in one. As we will see in the next chapter, strong rule returned in 284. Thereafter the Roman Empire endured in the West for two hundred years more and in the East for a millennium. But the restored Roman state differed greatly from the old one—so much so that it is proper to end the story of characteristically Roman civilization here and review the reasons for Rome's decline.

Theories of decline

More has been written on the fall of Rome than on the death of any other civilization. The theories offered to account for the decline have been many and varied. A popular recent one is that Rome fell from the effects of lead ingested from cooking utensils, but if this were true one would have to ask why Rome did so well for so long. Moralists have found the explanation for Rome's fall in the descriptions of lechery and gluttony presented in the writings of such authors as Juvenal and Petronius. Such an approach, however, overlooks the facts that much of this evidence is patently overdrawn, and that nearly all of it comes from the period of the early Principate: in the later centuries, when the Empire was more obviously collapsing, morality became more austere through the influence of ascetic religions. One of the simplest explanations is that Rome fell only because of the severity of German attacks. But barbarians had always stood ready to attack Rome throughout its long history: German pressures indeed mounted at certain times but German invasions would never have succeeded had they not come at moments when Rome was already weakened internally.

Internal causes of decline

It is best then to concentrate on Rome's most serious internal problems. Some of these were political. The most obvious political failing of the Roman constitution under the Principate was the lack of a clear law of succession. Especially when a ruler died suddenly, there was no certainty about who was to follow him. In modern America the deaths of a Lincoln or Kennedy might shock the nation, but people at least knew what would happen next; in imperial Rome no one knew and civil war was generally the result. From 235 to 284 such warfare fed upon itself. Civil war was also nurtured by the lack of constitutional means for reform. If regimes became unpopular, as most did after 180, the only means to alter them was to overthrow them. But the resort to violence always bred more violence. In addition to those problems, imperial Rome's greatest political weakness may ultimately have been that it did not involve enough people in the work of government. The vast majority of the Empire's inhabitants were subjects who did not participate in the government in any way. Hence they looked on the Empire at best with indifference and often with hostility, especially when tax collectors appeared. Loyalty to Rome was needed to keep the Empire going, but when the tests came such loyalty was lacking.

Economic causes of decline

Even without political problems the Roman Empire would probably have been fated to extinction for economic reasons. Rome's worst economic problems derived from its slave system and from manpower shortages. Roman civilization was based on cities, and Roman cities existed largely by virtue of an agricultural surplus produced by slaves. Slaves were worked so hard that they did not normally reproduce to fill their own ranks. Until the time of Trajan, Roman victories in war and fresh conquests provided fresh supplies of slaves to keep the system going, but thereafter the economy began to run out of human fuel. Landlords could no longer be so profligate of human life, barracks slavery came to an end, and the countryside produced less of a surplus to feed the towns. The fact that no technological advance took up the slack may also be attributed to slavery. Later in Western history agricultural surpluses were produced by technological revolutions, but Roman landlords were indifferent to technology because interest in it was thought to be demeaning. As long as slaves were present to do the work there was no interest in labor-saving devices, and attention to any sort of machinery was deemed a sign of slavishness. Landlords proved their nobility by their interest in "higher things," but while they were contemplating these heights their agricultural surpluses gradually became depleted.

Inadequate manpower

Manpower shortages greatly aggravated Rome's economic problems. With the end of foreign conquests and the decline of slavery there was a pressing need for people to stay on the farm, but because of constant barbarian pressures there was also a steady need for men to serve in the army. The plagues of the second and third centuries sharply reduced the population just at the worst time. It has been estimated that between the reign of Marcus Aurelius and the restoration of strong rule in 284 the population of the Roman Empire was reduced by one-third. (Demoralization seems also to have lowered the birthrate.) The result was that there were neither sufficient forces to work the land nor enough men to fight Rome's enemies. No wonder Rome began to lose battles as it had seldom lost them before.

Lack of civic ideals

Enormous dedication and exertion on the part of large numbers might just possibly have saved Rome, but few were willing to work hard for the public good. For this, cultural explanations may be posited. Simply stated, the Roman Empire of the third century could not draw upon commonly shared civic ideals. By then the old republican and senatorial traditions had been rendered manifestly obsolete. Worse, provincials could hardly be expected to fight or work hard for Roman ideals of any sort, especially when the Roman state no longer stood for beneficent peace but brought only recurrent war and oppressive taxation. Regional differences, the lack of public education, and social stratification were further barriers to the development of any unifying public spirit. As the Empire foundered new ideals indeed emerged, but these were religious, otherworldly ones. Ultimately, then, the decline of Rome was accompanied by disinterest, and the Roman world slowly came to an end not so much with a bang as with a whimper.

The Pantheon in Rome. Built by the Emperor Hadrian it boasted the largest dome without interior supports of the ancient world. The dome forms a perfect sphere, exactly as high as it is wide.

The Roman Heritage

Comparison of Rome with the modern world

It is tempting to believe that we today have many similarities to the Romans: first of all, because Rome is nearer to us in time than any of the other civilizations of antiquity; and second, because Rome seems to bear such a close kinship to the modern temper. The resemblances between Roman history and the history of Great Britain or the United States in the nineteenth and twentieth centuries have often been noted. The Roman economic evolution progressed all the way from a simple agrarianism to a complex urban system with problems of unemployment, gross disparities of wealth, and financial crises. The Roman Empire, in common with the British, was founded upon conquest. It must not be forgotten, however, that the heritage of Rome was an ancient heritage and that consequently the similarities between the Roman and modern civilizations are not so important as they seem. As noted already, the Romans disdained industrial activities. Neither did they have any idea of the modern national state; the provinces beyond Italy were really colonies, not integral parts of a body politic. The Romans also never developed an adequate system of representative government. Finally, the Roman conception of religion was vastly different from our own. Their system of worship was external and mechanical, designed to reap rewards for the family or the state rather than to bring individuals closer to gods and godliness.

The influence of Roman civilization

Nevertheless, the civilization of Rome exerted a great influence upon later cultures. The form of Roman architecture was preserved in the ecclesiastical architecture of the Middle Ages and survives to this day in the design of many of our government buildings. Although subjected to new interpretations, the law of the great jurists became an important part of the Code of Justinian and was thus handed down to the Middle Ages and modern times. American judges frequently cite maxims coined by Gaius or Ulpian. Further, the legal systems of nearly all continental European countries today incorporate much of the Roman law. This law was one of the grandest of the Romans' achievements and reflected their genius for governing a vast and diverse empire. It should not be forgotten either that Roman literary achievements set the standards for prose composition in Europe and America until the nineteenth century. Perhaps not so well known is the fact that the organization of the Catholic Church was adapted from the structure of the Roman state and the complex of the Roman religion. For example, the pope still bears the title of supreme pontiff *(pontifex maximus),* which was used to designate the authority of the emperor as head of the civic religion.

The Forum. The civic center of imperial Rome consisted of avenues, public squares, triumphal arches, temples, and government buildings. The arch of Titus, erected to celebrate Rome's final victory over Hebrew rebels, is in the background at the far right. Roman streets and buildings were arranged in rectilinear patterns to emphasize a sense of order and to facilitate triumphal processions.

Rome's role as conveyor of Greek civilization

Most important of all Rome's contributions to the future was the transmission of Greek civilization to the European West. The development in Italy of a culture that was highly suffused by Greek ideals from the second century B.C.E. onward was in itself an important counterweight to the earlier predominance of Greek-oriented civilization in the East. Then, following the path of Julius Caesar, this culture advanced still farther west. Before the coming of Rome the culture of northwestern Europe (modern France, the Benelux countries, western and southern Germany, and England) was tribal. Rome brought cities and Greek ideas, and above all conceptions of human freedom and individual autonomy that went along with the development of highly differentiated urban life. It is true that ideals of freedom were often ignored in practice—they did not temper Roman dependence on slavery, or prevent Roman rule in conquered territories from being exploitative and sometimes oppressive. Nonetheless, Roman history is the real beginning of Western history as we now know it. Greek civilization brought to the East by Alexander was not enduring, but the same civilization brought west by the work of such men as Caesar, Cicero, and Augustus was the starting point for many of the subsequent accomplishments of western Europe. As we will see, the development was not continuous, and there were many other ingredients to later European success, but the influence of Rome was still profound.

SUMMARY POINTS

- The Roman Republic (c. 500 B.C.E.–c. 27 B.C.E.) was primarily an agrarian and militaristic society that initially was led by aristocrats, called *patricians*. Gradually Roman commoners, called *plebeians,* succeeded in establishing a system of shared power, which was nonetheless still an oligarchy.
- By fighting the three Punic Wars (264 B.C.E.–146 B.C.E.) against Carthage, the Romans expanded their territory to include modern-day Spain, Sicily, North Africa, Greece, and Asia Minor. These conquests also resulted in urbanization, a marked increase in slavery, and the introduction of Greek and Hellenistic ideas and customs into Roman culture.
- Some of ancient Rome's most famous rulers came to power during the political struggles of the late Republic (146 B.C.E.–30 B.C.E.), including Tiberius and Gaius Gracchus, Sulla, Pompey, and Julius Caesar. While political intrigue surrounding these leaders occupied generals and politicans, Roman culture began to flourish but societal stratification increased.
- With the rise of Octavian (Augustus) the period of the Principate (27 B.C.E.–180 C.E.) began. Augustus and his successors expanded the Roman empire to its greatest extent and brought about the *Pax*

Romana, during which Roman culture reached peaks of accomplishment in literature, art, architecture, and engineering, as well as in the liberation of women, but sank to depths of cruelty with the practices of slavery and gladiatorial combat. The development of Roman law was one of the Principate's most important legacies.

- Following the Principate, Rome entered a long era of periodic crisis and gradual decline. Internal problems, such as succession contests, unpopular governments, decreasing supplies of slaves, and a general demoralization and lack of unity contributed significantly to the process of decline.

SELECTED READINGS

POLITICAL HISTORY

Chambers, Mortimer, ed., *The Fall of Rome,* 2d ed., New York, 1970. A collection of readings on this perennially fascinating subject.

Crawford, Michael H., *The Roman Republic,* 2d ed., Cambridge, Mass., 1993.

Crook, J. A., *Law and Life of Rome, 90 B.C.–A.D. 212,* Ithaca, N.Y., 1977.

Gruen, Erich S., *The Last Generation of the Roman Republic,* Berkeley, 1964.

Harris, William V., *War and Imperialism in Republican Rome,* Oxford, 1979. A searching and original examination of why the Romans became expansionists.

Millar, Fergus, *The Emperor in the Roman World: 31 B.C.–A.D. 337,* Ithaca, N.Y., 1977.

Mommsen, Theodor, *The History of Rome,* Chicago, 1957. An abridged reissue of one of the greatest historical works of the nineteenth century. Emphasizes personalities, especially that of Julius Caesar.

Ogilvie, R. M., *Early Rome and the Etruscans,* Atlantic Heights, N.J., 1976. The best specialized review of the earliest period.

Pallottino, Massimo, *The Etruscans,* rev. ed., Baltimore, 1978. The standard introduction.

Scullard, H. H., *From the Gracchi to Nero,* 5th ed., London, 1988. Good survey of events in this central period.

Syme, Ronald, *The Roman Revolution,* New York, 1939. A pathfinding work on the late Republic and early Empire that stresses power politics and the role of factions rather than the clash of institutional principles. Also extremely well written.

Taylor, Lily Ross, *Party Politics in the Age of Caesar,* Berkeley, 1949. Still the best introduction to society and politics in the late republican period.

ECONOMIC, SOCIAL, AND CULTURAL HISTORY

Africa, Thomas W., *Rome of the Caesars,* New York, 1965. An entertaining approach to the history of imperial Rome by means of short biographies.

Balsdon, J. P. V. D., *Life and Leisure in Ancient Rome,* New York, 1969.

Bradley, Keith R., *Slavery and Rebellion in the Roman World, 140 B.C.–70 B.C.,* Bloomington, Ind., 1989. A masterful treatment of the conditions of slavery and the three great slave wars of the later republican period.

Brunt, P. A., *Social Conflicts in the Roman Republic,* London, 1971.

Duff, J. Wight, *A Literary History of Rome in the Golden Age,* New York, 1964.

———, *A Literary History of Rome in the Silver Age,* New York, 1960.

Earl, Donald, *The Moral and Political Tradition of Rome,* Ithaca, N.Y., 1967.

Garnsey, Peter, and Richard Saller, *The Roman Empire: Economy, Society, and Culture,* Berkeley, 1987. A straightforward short survey.

Hopkins, Keith, *Conquerors and Slaves,* Cambridge, 1978. Interconnected essays that approach the world of the Roman Empire from an innovative sociological perspective.

Laistner, M. L. W., *The Greater Roman Historians,* Berkeley, 1947.

MacMullen, Ramsey, *Enemies of the Roman Order,* Cambridge, Mass., 1966.

———, *Paganism in the Roman Empire,* New Haven, 1981.

———, *Roman Social Relations: 50 B.C. to A.D. 284,* New Haven, 1974.

Pomeroy, Sarah B., *Goddesses, Whores, Wives, and Slaves: Women in Classical Antiquity,* New York, 1995. A superb review of the lives and status of women in the Roman world.

Rostovtzeff, Mikhail I., *Social and Economic History of the Roman Empire,* 2d ed., 2 vols., New York, 1957. By one of the greatest historians of the early twentieth century. Important both for its interpretations and the wealth of information it contains.

Sandbach, F. H., *The Stoics,* London, 1975.

Starr, Chester G., *Civilization and the Caesars,* Ithaca, N.Y., 1954. Surveys Roman intellectual developments in the four centuries after Cicero.

Thompson, Lloyd A., *Romans and Blacks,* Norman, Okla., 1989. A fascinating, broad-gauged study, based on a wide variety of evidence.

Wallace-Hadrill, Andrew, *Houses and Society in Pompeii and Herculaneum,* Princeton, 1994. A wonderful reconstruction of urban life in the early Empire based on the archeological record.

Westermann, W. L., *The Slave Systems of Greek and Roman Antiquity,* Philadelphia, 1955. A still-useful overview.

Wheeler, Mortimer, *The Art of Rome,* New York, 1964.

Source Materials

Translations of Roman authors are available in the appropriate volumes of the Loeb Classical Library, Harvard University Press.

See also:

Gruen, E. S., *The Image of Rome,* Englewood Cliffs, N.J., 1969.

Lewis, Naphtali, and M. Reinhold, *Roman Civilization,* 2 vols., New York, 1955.

CHAPTER 8

CHRISTIANITY AND THE TRANSFORMATION OF THE ROMAN WORLD

> Who will hereafter credit the fact . . . that Rome has to fight within her own borders not for glory but for bare life? . . . The poet Lucan describing the power of the city in a glowing passage says: "If Rome be weak, where shall we look for strength?" We may vary his words and say: "If Rome be lost, where shall we look for help?"
>
> For mortals this life is a race: we run it on earth that we may receive our crown elsewhere. No one can walk secure amid serpents and scorpions.
>
> —ST. JEROME, *Letters*

The protracted decline of the Roman Empire

THE ROMAN EMPIRE DECLINED AFTER 180 C.E., but it did not collapse. In 284 the vigorous soldier-emperor Diocletian began a reorganization of the Empire that gave it a new lease on life. Throughout the fourth century the Roman state continued to surround the Mediterranean. In the fifth century the western half of the Empire did fall to invading Germans, but even then Roman institutions were not entirely destroyed, and in the sixth century the Empire managed to reconquer a good part of the western Mediterranean shoreline. Only in the seventh century did it become fully evident that the Roman Empire could hope to survive only by turning away from the West and consolidating its strength in the East. When that happened antiquity clearly came to an end.

The age of late antiquity (284–610)

Historians used to underestimate the longevity of Roman institutions and begin their discussions of medieval history in the third, fourth, or fifth century. Since historical periodization is always approximate and depends largely on which aspects of development a historian wishes to emphasize, this approach cannot be dismissed. Certainly the transition from the ancient to the medieval world was gradual and many "medieval" ways were slowly emerging in the West as early as the third century. But it is now more customary to conceive of ancient history as continuing after 284 and lasting until the Roman Empire lost control over the Mediterranean in the seventh century. The period from 284 to about 610, although transitional (as, of course, all ages are), has certain themes of its own and is perhaps best described as neither Roman nor medieval but as the age of late antiquity.

The rise of Christianity and decline of urban life

The major cultural trend of late-antique history was the spread and triumph of Christianity throughout the Roman world. At first Christianity was just one of several varieties of otherworldlyism that appealed to increasing numbers of people during the later Empire. But in the fourth century it was adopted as the Roman state religion and thereafter became one of the greatest shaping forces in the development of the West. While Christianity was spreading, the Roman Empire was indubitably declining. Central to this decline was a contraction of the urban life on which the Empire had been based. As the Empire began to experience severe pressures, urban contraction was most pronounced in the European northwest because city civilization there was least deeply rooted and most distant from the Empire's major trade and communications lifelines on the Mediterranean. Contraction was also felt in parts of the West that were closer to the Mediterranean because Western cities depended far more on declining agricultural production than did Eastern cities, which relied more on trade in luxury goods and industry. Consequently the entire period saw a steady shift in the weight of civilization and imperial government from West to East. The most visible manifestations of this shift were the German successes of the fifth century. These surely helped open a new chapter in Western political history, but their immediate impact should not be exaggerated. Even with the influx of Germans, Roman institutions continued to decline gradually. Particularly in areas that were on or close to the Mediterranean, Roman city life persisted, albeit with steadily declining vigor, until the Mediterranean was no longer a Roman lake.

The Reorganized Empire

The reforms of Diocletian

Before we examine the emergence and triumph of Christianity, it is best to survey the nature of the government and society in which the new religion became a dominant force. The fifty years of chaos that threatened to destroy Rome in the third century were ended by the energetic work of a remarkable soldier named Diocletian, who ruled as emperor from 284 to 305. Conscious of some of the more obvious problems that had undone his predecessors, Diocletian embarked on a number of fundamental political and economic reforms. Recognizing that the dominance of the army in the life of the state had hitherto been too great, he introduced measures to separate military from civilian administrative chains of command. Aware that new pressures, both external and internal, had made it nearly impossible for one man to govern the entire Roman Empire, he divided his realm in half, granting the western part to a trusted colleague, Maximian, who recognized Diocletian as the senior ruler. The two then chose lieutenants, called *caesars,* to govern large subsections of their territories. This system was also meant to provide for an orderly succession, for the caesars were supposed to inherit the major rule of either East or West and then appoint new caesars in their stead. In the economic sphere Diocletian stabilized the badly debased currency, introduced a new system of taxation, and issued legislation designed to keep agricultural workers and town-dwellers at their jobs so that the basic work necessary to support the Empire would continue to be done.

Although Diocletian's program of reorganization was remarkably successful in restoring an empire that had been on the verge of expiring, it also transformed the Empire by "orientalizing" it in three primary and lasting ways. Most literally, Diocletian began a geographical orientalization of the Empire by shifting its administrative weight toward the East. Since he was a "Roman" emperor we might assume that he ruled from Rome, but in fact between 284 and 303 he was never there, ruling instead from Nicomedia, a city in modern-day Turkey. This he did in tacit recognition of the fact that the wealthier and more vital part of the Empire was clearly in the East. Second, as befitting one who turned his back on Rome, Diocletian adopted the titles and ceremonies of an Oriental potentate. Probably he did this less because he had Eastern tastes than because he wished to avoid the fate of his predecessors who were insufficiently respected. Most likely he thought that if he were feared and worshiped he would stand a greater chance of dying in bed. Accordingly, Diocletian completely abandoned Augustus's policy of appearing to be a constitutional ruler and came forward as an undisguised autocrat. He took the title not of *princeps,* or "first citizen," but of *dominus,* or "lord," and he introduced Oriental ceremony into his court. He wore a diadem and a purple gown of silk interwoven with gold. Those who gained an audience had to prostrate themselves before him; a privileged few were allowed to kiss his robe.

Diocletian. His short hair is in the Roman military style.

The growth of imperial bureaucracy

The third aspect of orientalization in Diocletian's policy was his growing reliance on an imperial bureaucracy. By separating civilian from military commands and legislating on a wide variety of economic and social matters, Diocletian created the need for many new officials. Not surprisingly, by the end of his reign subjects were complaining that "there were more tax-collectors than taxpayers." The officials did keep the Empire going, but the new bureaucracy was prone to graft and corruption; worse, the growth of officialdom called for reservoirs of manpower and wealth at a time when the Roman Empire no longer had large supplies of either. Taken together, the various aspects of Diocletian's easternizing made him seem more like a pharaoh than a Roman ruler: it was almost as if the defeat of Antony and Cleopatra at Actium was now being avenged.

Regularization in architecture

The new coercive regime of Diocletian left no room for the cultivation of individual spontaneity or freedom. The results can be seen most clearly in the architecture and art of the age. Diocletian himself preferred a colossal, bombastic style of building that was meant to emphasize his own power. The baths he had constructed in Rome, when he finally arrived there in 303, were the largest yet known, encompassing about thirty acres. When he retired in 305 Diocletian built a palace for himself in what is now Split (Croatia) that was laid out along a rectilinear grid like an army camp. A plan of this palace shows clearly how Diocletian favored regimentation in everything.

Impassive statuary

Also in the age of Diocletian, Roman portrait statuary, which had hitherto featured striking naturalism and individuality, became impersonal.

Diocletian's Palace in Split. An artistic reconstruction.

Human faces became impassive and symmetrical rather than reflecting a free play of emotions. Porphyry, a particularly hard and dark stone that had to be imported from Egypt—another sign of easternization—often replaced marble for imperial busts. Sculpted in porphyry, groups of statues of Diocletian, Maximian, and their two caesars show the new hardness and symmetry at their fullest, for the figures were made to look so similar that they are indistinguishable from each other.

In 305 Diocletian decided to abdicate to raise cabbages—an unprecedented achievement for a late-Roman ruler. At the same time he obliged his colleague Maximian to retire as well, and their two caesars moved peacefully up the ladders of succession. Such concord, however, could not last. Soon civil war broke out among Diocletian's successors and continued until Constantine, the son of one of the original caesars, emerged victorious. From 312 until 324 Constantine ruled only in the West, but from the latter year until his death in 337 he did away with power sharing and ruled over a reunited Empire. Except for the fact that he favored Christianity, an epoch-making decision to be examined in the next section, Constantine otherwise continued to govern along the lines laid down by Diocletian. Bureaucracy proliferated and the state became so vigilant in keeping town-dwellers and agricultural laborers at their posts that society began to harden into a caste system. Although Constantine was a Christian, he never thought for a moment of acting with any Christlike humility: on the contrary, he made court ceremonial more elaborate and generally behaved as if he were a god. In keeping with this he built a new capital in 330 and named it Constantinople, after himself. Although he declared that he moved his government from Rome to Constantinople in order to demonstrate his abandonment of paganism, self-esteem was no doubt a major factor, and the shift was the most visible manifestation of the continued move of Roman civilization to the East. Situated on the border of Europe and Asia, Constantinople had commanding advantages as a center

The Emperor Honorius. An example of the impassive portrait sculpture brought in by the age of Diocletian. Compare the lack of individuality of this bust to the portraits of Decius and Philip the Arab, pp. 180 and 181.

for Eastern-oriented communications, trade, and defense. Surrounded on three sides by water and protected on land by walls, it was to prove nearly impregnable and would remain the center of "Roman" government for as long as the Roman Empire was to endure.

Wars of the fourth century

Constantine also made the succession hereditary. By so doing he brought Rome back to the principle of dynastic monarchy that it had thrown off about eight hundred years earlier. But Constantine, who treated the Empire as if it were his private property, did not pass on united rule to one son. Instead he divided his realm among three of them. Not surprisingly his three sons started fighting each other upon their father's death, a conflict exacerbated by religious differences. The warfare and succeeding dynastic squabbles that continued on and off for most of the fourth century need not detain us here. Suffice it to say that they were not as serious as the civil wars of the third century, and that from time to time one or another contestant was able to reunite the Empire for a period of years. The last to do so was Theodosius I (379–395), who butchered thousands of innocent citizens of Thessalonica in retribution for the death of one of his officers, but whose energies in preserving the Empire by holding off Germanic barbarians still gave him some claim to his surname "the Great."

Regionalism and poverty

The period between Constantine and Theodosius saw the hardening of earlier tendencies. With Constantinople now the leading city of the Empire, the center of commerce and administration was located clearly in the East. Regionalism too grew more pronounced: the Latin-speaking West was losing a sense of rapport and contact with the Greek-speaking East, and in both West and East local differences were becoming accentuated. In economic life the hallmark of the age was the growing gap between rich and poor. In the West large landowners were able to consolidate their holdings, and in the East some individuals became prosperous by rising through the bureaucracy and enriching themselves with graft, or

Left: **Porphyry Sculptures of Diocletian and His Colleagues in Rule.** Every effort is made to make the two senior rulers and their two junior colleagues look identical by means of stylization. Note also the emphasis on military strength. Right: **Colossal Head of Constantine.** In this head of Constantine the eyes are enlarged as if to emphasize the ruler's spiritual vision. The head is approximately seven times larger than life and weighs about nine tons.

by trading in luxury goods. But the taxation system initiated by Diocletian and maintained throughout the fourth century weighed down heavily on the poor, forcing them to carry the burden of supporting the bureaucracy, the army, and the lavish imperial court or courts. The poor, moreover, had no chance to escape their poverty, for legislation demanded that they and their heirs stay at their unrewarding and heavily taxed jobs. Since most people in the fourth century were poor, most lived in desperate and unrelenting poverty against a backdrop of ostentatious wealth. The Roman Empire may have been restored in the years from 284 to 395, but it was nonetheless a fertile breeding ground for a new religion of otherwordly salvation.

The Emergence and Triumph of Christianity

Christian beginnings of course go back several centuries before Constantine to the time of Jesus. Christianity was formed primarily by Jesus and St. Paul and gained converts steadily thereafter. But the new religion became widespread only during the chaos of the third century and triumphed in the Roman Empire only during the demoralization of the fourth century. At the time of its humble beginnings nobody could have known that Christianity would be decreed the sole religion of the Roman Empire by the year 392.

Jesus of Nazareth; his milieu

Jesus of Nazareth was born in Judea sometime near the beginning of the Christian era (but not exactly in the "year one"—we owe this mistake in our dating system to a sixth-century monk). While Jesus was growing up, Judea was under Roman overlordship. The atmosphere of the region was charged with religious emotionalism and political discontent. Some of the people, notably the *Pharisees,* concentrated on preserving the Jewish law and looked forward to the coming of a political messiah who would rescue the Jews from Rome. Most extreme of those who sought hope in politics were the *Zealots,* who wished to overthrow the Romans by means of armed force. Some groups, on the other hand, were not interested in politics at all. Typical of these were the *Essenes,* who hoped for spiritual deliverance through asceticism, repentance, and mystical union with God. The ministry of Jesus was clearly more allied to this pacific orientation.

Sources for the life of Jesus

In considering the story of Jesus' career as a historical event, it is important to recognize that virtually the only sources of information are the first four books of the New Testament, the Gospels, the earliest of which (the Gospel of Mark) was written some thirty years after Jesus' death. Inevitably these sources are full of inaccuracies, in part because they were not eyewitness accounts, and even more because they were never meant to be strictly factual reports but were intended as proclamations of supernatural faith. Bearing in mind that more or less anything in the Gospel record may not be true in the historical sense, so far as we know, when Jesus was about thirty years old he was acclaimed by a preacher of moral reform, John the Baptist, as one "mightier than I, whose shoes I am not worthy to stoop down and unloose." For about three years thereafter Jesus' career was a continuous course of preaching, healing the sick, "casting out devils," and teaching humility by precepts, parables, and by his own example.

Jesus. Conception from a sixth-century mosaic in Ravenna.

Believing he had a mission to save humanity from sin, Jesus denounced greed and licentiousness and urged love of God and neighbor. Additionally, it seems reasonably clear that he taught the following: (1) the fatherhood of God and the brotherhood of humanity; (2) the Golden Rule ("do unto others as you would have others do unto you"); (3) forgiveness and love of one's enemies; (4) repayment of evil with good; (5) shunning of hypocrisy; (6) opposition to religious ceremonialism; (7) the imminent approach of the kingdom of God; (8) the resurrection of the dead and the establishment of the kingdom of heaven.

The Gospel record is particularly controversial when it reaches the story of Jesus' death because aspects of it, which may or may not be true, fueled Christian persecutions of Jews in subsequent eras. Purportedly when Jesus began to preach in Jerusalem, Judea's major city and religious center, the city's religious leaders quickly became antagonistic to him because of his contempt for form and ceremony. Moving swiftly to silence the troublemaker, they arrested him, tried him in their highest court for blasphemy, condemned him, and handed him over to Pontius Pilate, the Roman governor, for sentencing and execution of the sentence. Some scholars hold that this version of Jesus' last days is a fabrication, designed to shift blame for his death from the Romans, who were really responsible, to the Jews, who were not. Others believe that it is substantially correct. All that can be said here is that whoever arrested, tried, condemned, and executed Jesus, he did indeed die in agony by crucifixion.

The crucifixion of Jesus and belief in the Resurrection

The crucifixion of Jesus certainly marked a decisive moment in Christian history. At first Jesus' death was viewed by his followers as the end of their hopes. Yet after a few days their despair began to dissipate, for rumors began to spread that the Master was alive and had been seen by some of his faithful disciples. In short order Jesus' followers became convinced that not only had Jesus risen from the dead but that he had walked on earth thereafter for forty days and hence that he truly was a divine being. With their courage restored, they fanned out to preach the good news of Jesus' divinity and to testify in the name of their martyred leader. Soon belief in Jesus' godliness and resurrection became articles of faith for thousands: Jesus was the "Christ" (Greek for "the anointed one"), the divine Son of God who was sent to earth to suffer and die for the sins of humanity, and who, after three days in the tomb, had risen from the dead and ascended into heaven, whence he would come again to judge the world at the end of time.

The Apostle Paul and Christianity as universal

Christianity was broadened and invested with a more elaborate theology by some of the successors of Jesus, above all the Apostle Paul, originally known as Saul of Tarsus (c. 10–c. 67 C.E.). Paul was not a native of Palestine but a Jew born in the city of Tarsus in southeastern Asia Minor. Originally a persecutor of Christians, he later converted to Christianity and devoted his limitless energy to propagating that faith throughout the

St. Paul. From a Ravenna mosaic.

Near East. It would be almost impossible to overestimate the significance of his work. Denying that Jesus was sent merely as the redeemer of the Jews, Paul proclaimed Christianity to be a universal religion. Furthermore, he placed major emphasis on the idea of Jesus as the Christ, as the anointed God-man whose death on the cross was an atonement for the sins of humanity. Not only did he reject the works of the Law (i.e., Jewish ritualism) as of primary importance in religion, but he declared them to be utterly worthless in procuring salvation. Sinners by nature, human beings can be saved only by faith and by the grace of God "through the redemption that is in Christ Jesus." It follows, according to Paul, that human fate in the life to come is almost entirely dependent upon the will of God, for "hath not the potter power over the clay, of the same lump to make one vessel unto honor, and another unto dishonor?" (Romans 9:21). God has mercy "on whom He will have mercy, and whom He will He hardeneth" (Romans 9:18).

Although it may be something of a simplification, it seems basically true to say that whereas Jesus proclaimed the imminent coming of the kingdom of God, Paul laid the basis for a religion of personal salvation through Christ and the ministry of the Church. Therefore, after Paul, Christianity developed both ceremonies, or sacraments, to bring the believer closer to Christ and an organization of priests to administer those sacraments. In teaching that priests who administered sacraments were endowed with supernatural powers, Christianity gradually posited a distinction between clergy and laity much sharper than that which had existed in most earlier religions. This would become the basis of subsequent Western controversies and divisions between "church" and "state." In the meantime, Christianity's emphasis on otherworldly salvation ministered by a priestly organization helped it greatly to grow.

The appeal of religion in an "age of anxiety"

Christianity began to gain substantial numbers only in the third century after Christ. To understand this we must recall that in Roman history the third century was an "age of anxiety." During a time of extreme political turbulence and economic hardship people began to treat life on earth as an illusion and place their hopes in the beyond. The human body and the material world were more and more regarded as either evil or basically unreal. As the philosopher Plotinus wrote, "when I come to myself, I wonder how it is that I have a body . . . by what deterioration did this happen?" Plotinus devised a philosophical system to answer this question, but this was far too abstruse to have much meaning for large numbers of people. Instead, several religions that emphasized the dominance of spiritual forces in this world and the absolute preeminence of otherworldly salvation gained hold as never before.

Reasons for Christianity's success

At first Christianity was just another of these religions; Mithraism and the cult of Serapis were others. It is natural to ask, therefore, why Christianity gained converts in the third century at the expense of its rivals. A number of answers may be posited. One of the simplest, but not the least important, is that even though Christianity borrowed elements from older religions—above all, Judaism—it was new and hence possessed a sense of dynamism lacking among the salvationist religions, which had existed for centuries. Christianity's dynamism was also enhanced by its rigorous exclusiveness. Hitherto people had adopted religions as people today take on insurance policies, piling one on another in order to feel more secure. The fact that Christianity prohibited this, demanding that the Christian God be worshiped alone, made the new religion most appealing at a time when people were searching desperately for absolutes. Similarly, Christianity alone among its rivals had an all-embracing theory to explain evil on earth, namely as the work of demons governed by the devil. When Christian missionaries sought converts they successfully emphasized the new faith's ability to combat these demons by reputed miracles.

Christianity's doctrine of afterlife, social structure, and organization

Although Christianity's novelty, exclusiveness, and theory of evil help greatly to explain its success, probably the greatest attractions of the religion had to do with three other traits: its view of salvation, its social dimensions, and its organizational structure. Exorcism of demons might help to make life more tolerable on earth, but ultimately people in the later Roman Empire were most concerned with otherworldly salvation. Rival religions also promised an afterlife, but Christianity's doctrine on this subject was the most far-reaching. Christian preachers who warned that nonbelievers would "liquefy in fierce fires" for eternity and that believers would enjoy eternal blessedness understandably made many converts in an age of fears. They made converts too among all classes because Christianity had from its origins been a religion of the humble—carpenters, fishermen, and tentmakers—that promised the exaltation of the lowly. As the religion grew it gained a few wealthy patrons, but it continued to find its greatest strength among the lower and middle classes who comprised the greatest numbers in the Roman Empire. Moreover, while Christianity forbade women to become priests or discuss the faith and, as we will see, adopted many attitudes hostile to women, it at least accorded women some rights of participation in worship and equal hope for salvation. This fact gave it an advantage over Mithraism, which excluded women from its cult entirely. In addition to all these considerations, a final reason for Christianity's success lay in its organization. Unlike the rival mystery religions, by the third century it had developed an organized hierarchy of priests to direct the life of the faith. More than that, Christian congregations were tightly knit communities that provided services to their members—such as nursing, support of the unprotected, and burial—that went beyond strictly religious concerns. Those who became Christians found human contacts and a sense of mission while the rest of the world seemed to be collapsing about them.

Altar of Mithras. Dating from the third century C.E., this altar used for Mithraic services in an underground chamber in the heart of Rome depicts Mithras slaying a bull. A century later, when Christianity triumphed in the Roman Empire, a Christian church was built over the Mithraic sanctuary.

Christians were never as brutally persecuted by the Roman state as used to be thought. In fact the attitude of Rome was usually one of indifference: Christians were customarily tolerated unless certain magistrates decided to prosecute them for refusing to worship the official state gods. From time to time there were more concerted persecutions, but these were too intermittent and short-lived to do irreparable damage; on the

An Early Christian Woman. A wall painting from the catacomb of Priscilla, Rome, third century C.E.

contrary, they served to give Christianity some helpful publicity. To this degree the blood of martyrs really was the seed of the Church, but only because the blood did not flow too freely. One last great persecution took place toward the end of the reign of Diocletian and was continued by one of his immediate successors, a particularly bitter enemy of Christianity named Galerius. But by then the religion had gained too many converts to be wiped out by persecution, a fact that Galerius finally recognized by issuing an edict of toleration just before his death in 311.

Despite all that has been said, the triumph of Christianity in the Roman Empire was by no means inevitable. Although exact statistics are impossible to come by, estimates of the number of Christians in the Empire around 300 range from 1 percent to 5 percent of the total population. Thus it was only the conversion of the Emperor Constantine in 312 that ensured the success of the new faith. Exactly why Constantine became a Christian will never be known; most likely he thought he saw a cross in the sky while preparing for battle and then switched allegiance to the new faith, hoping that it would yield him victory in a contest for political supremacy. Certainly, as Constantine did in fact gain military victories and ultimately rose to become sole emperor, his commitment to Christianity became ever more pronounced. By the time of his death in 337 he had showered favors on the Christian clergy and patronized the building of churches throughout the Empire. This was the turning point, for although Constantine did not yet prohibit paganism, his sons and emperors after them were raised as Christians and were ever less inclined to tol-

Jonah under the Gourd. A Christian marble statue done around the time of Constantine's conversion. Jonah resting after leaving the whale's belly was a symbol for the risen Christ.

erate competing faiths. A brief exception was the reign from 360 to 363 of Julian, "the Apostate," an emperor who attempted to launch a pagan revival. But after Julian was killed in battle with the Persians, his pro-pagan edicts were revoked, and by the end of the century Theodosius the Great had completed Constantine's work by prohibiting pagan worship of any sort, public or private. Meanwhile most citizens of the Roman Empire had converted to Christianity because of the environment of official support.

THE NEW CONTOURS OF CHRISTIANITY

Once the new faith became dominant within the Roman Empire it underwent some major changes in forms of thought, organization, and conduct. These changes all bore relationships to earlier tendencies, but the triumph of the faith greatly accelerated certain trends and altered the course of others. The result was that in many respects the Christianity of the late fourth century was a very different religion from the one persecuted by Diocletian and Galerius.

Controversy over doctrinal matters

One consequence of Christianity's triumph was the flaring up of bitter doctrinal disputes. These brought great turmoil to the Church but resulted in the hammering out of dogma and discipline. Before the conversion of Constantine there had of course been disagreements among Christians about doctrinal matters, but as long as Christianity was a minority religion it managed to control its internal divisions in order to present a united front against hostile outsiders. As soon as the new faith emerged victorious, however, sharp splits developed within its own ranks. These were due partly to the fact that there had always been a tension between the intellectual and emotional tendencies within the religion that could now come more fully into the open, and partly to the fact that different regions of the Empire tried to preserve a sense of their separate identities by preferring different theological formulas.

Division between Arians and Athanasians

The first of the bitter disputes was between the Arians and Athanasians over the nature of the Trinity. The Arians—not to be confused with Aryans (a racial term)—were followers of a priest named Arius and were the more intellectual group. Under the influence of Greek philosophy they rejected the idea that Christ could be equal with God. Instead they maintained that the Son was created by the Father and therefore was not co-eternal with Him or formed of the same substance. The followers of St. Athanasius, indifferent to apparent logic, held that even though Christ was the Son he was fully God: that Father, Son, and Holy Ghost were all absolutely equal and composed of an identical substance. After protracted struggles Athanasius's side won out and the Athanasian doctrine became the Christian dogma of the Trinity, as it remains today.

Consequences of successive doctrinal disputes

The struggle between the Arians and Athanasians was followed by numerous other doctrinal quarrels during the next few centuries. The issues at stake were generally too abstruse to warrant explaining here, but the results were momentous. One was that the dogmas of the Catholic faith gradually became fixed. Granted, this was a slow development and many basic tenets of Catholicism were defined much later (for example, the theory of the Mass was not formally promulgated until 1215; the doctrine of the Immaculate Conception of the Virgin Mary until 1854; and that of the Bodily Assumption of the Virgin until 1950). Nonetheless, the faith was beginning to take on a sharply defined form unprecedented in the history of earlier religions. Above all, this meant that anyone who differed from a certain formulation would be excluded from the community and often persecuted as a heretic. In the subsequent history of Christianity this concern for doctrinal uniformity was to result in both strengths and weaknesses for the Church.

Regionalism

A second result of the doctrinal quarrels was that they aggravated regional hostilities. In the fourth century differences among Christians increased alienation between West and East and also aggravated hostilities among regions within the East. Although the Roman Empire was evolving toward regionalism for many different reasons, including economic and administrative ones, and although regionalism was partly a cause of religious differences, the sharper and more frequent doctrinal quarrels became, the more they served to intensify regional hostilities.

Imperial involvement in religious conflicts

Finally, the doctrinal quarrels provoked the interference of the Roman state in the governance of the Church. Because Constantine had hoped that Christianity would be a unifying rather than a divisive force in the Empire, he was horrified by the Arian conflict and intervened in it by calling the Council of Nicea (325), which condemned Arius. It is noteworthy that this council—the first general council of the Church—was convened by a Roman emperor and that Constantine served during its meetings as a presiding officer. Thereafter secular interference in Church matters continued, above all in the East. There were two major reasons for this. First, religious disputes were more prevalent in the East than the West and quarreling parties often appealed to the emperor for support. Second, the weight of imperial government was generally heavier in the East, and after 476 there were no Roman emperors in the West at all. When Eastern emperors were not appealed to by quarreling parties they interfered in religious disputes themselves, as Constantine had done be-

Christ Separating the Sheep from the Goats as an Image for the Last Judgment. This early Christian sarcophagus (fourth century C.E.) illustrates a verse from the New Testament: "And before Him shall be gathered all nations: and He shall separate them one from another, as a shepherd divideth his sheep from his goats" (Matthew 25:31). The theme was obviously appropriate for a burial repository.

fore them, in order to preserve unity. The result was that in the East the emperor assumed great religious authority and control, while in the West the future of relations between the state and the Church was more open.

The organization of the clergy

Even while emperors were interfering in religious matters, however, the Church's own internal organization was becoming more complex and articulated. We have seen that a clear distinction between clergy and laity was already a hallmark of the early Christian religion after the time of St. Paul. The next step was the development of a hierarchical organization within the ranks of the clergy. The superiority of bishops over priests was recognized before Christianity's triumph. Christian organization was centered in cities, and one bishop in each important city became the authority to which all the clergy in the surrounding vicinity answered. This organization was sufficient for a minority religion, but as the number of congregations multiplied and as the influence of the Church increased due to the adoption of Christianity as the official religion of Rome, distinctions of rank among the bishops themselves began to appear. Those who had their headquarters in the larger cities came to be called *metropolitans* (today known in the West as *archbishops*), with authority over the clergy of an entire province. In the fourth century the still higher rank of *patriarch* was established to designate those bishops who ruled over the oldest and largest of Christian communities—such cities as Rome, Jerusalem, Constantinople, Antioch, and Alexandria, and their surrounding districts. Thus the Christian clergy by 400 C.E. had come to embrace a definite hierarchy of patriarchs, metropolitans, bishops, and priests.

The rise of the papacy

The climax of all this development would be the growth of the primacy of the bishop of Rome, or the rise of the papacy. For several reasons the bishop of Rome enjoyed a preeminence over the other patriarchs of the Church. The city in which he ruled was venerated by the faithful as a scene of the missionary activities of the Apostles Peter and Paul. The tradition was widely accepted that Peter had founded the bishopric of Rome and that therefore all of his successors were heirs of his authority and prestige. This tradition was supplemented by the theory that Peter had been commissioned by Christ as his vicar on earth and had been given the keys of the kingdom of heaven with power to punish people for their sins and even to absolve them from guilt (Matthew 16:18–19). This theory, known as the doctrine of the Petrine Succession, has been used by popes ever since as a basis for their claims to authority over the Church. The bishops of Rome had an advantage also in the fact that after the transfer of the imperial capital to Constantinople there was seldom any emperor with effective sovereignty in the West. Finally, in 445 the Emperor Valentinian III issued a decree commanding all Western bishops to submit to the jurisdiction of the pope. It must not be supposed, however, that the Church was by any means yet under a monarchical form of government. The patriarchs in the East regarded the extreme assertions of papal claims as brazen effrontery, and even many bishops in the West continued to ignore them for some time. The clearest example of the papacy's early weakness is the fact that the popes did not even attend the first eight general councils of the Church (from 325 to 869), although later they were to convene and preside over all the others.

Effects of the rationalization of ecclesiastical administration

The growth of ecclesiastical organization helped the Church to conquer the Roman world in the fourth century and to minister to the needs of the faithful thereafter. The existence of an episcopal administrative structure was particularly influential in the West as the Roman Empire decayed and finally collapsed in the fifth century. Since every city had a bishop trained to some degree in the arts of administration, the Church in the West took over many of the functions of government and helped to preserve order amid the deepening chaos. But the new emphasis on administration also had its inevitably detrimental effects: as the Church developed its own rationalized administrative structure it inevitably became more worldly and distant in spirit from the simple faith of Jesus and the Apostles.

The rise of monasticism

The clearest reaction to this trend was expressed in the spread of monasticism. Today we are accustomed to thinking of monks as groups of priests who live communally in order to dedicate themselves primarily to lives of contemplation and prayer. In their origins, however, monks were not priests but laymen who almost always lived alone and who sought extremes of self-torture rather than ordered lives of spirituality. Monasticism began to emerge in the third century as a response to the anxieties of that age, but it became a dominant movement within Christianity only in the fourth century. Two obvious reasons for this fact stand out. First of all, the choice of extreme hermitlike asceticism was a substitute for martyrdom. With the conversion of Constantine and the abandonment of persecution, most chances of winning a crown of glory in heaven by undergoing death for the faith were eliminated. But the desire to prove one's religious ardor by self-abasement and suffering was still present. Second, as the fourth century progressed the priesthood became more and more immersed in worldly concerns. Those who wished to avoid secular temptations fled to the deserts and woods to practice an asceticism that priests and bishops were forgetting. (Monks customarily be-

A Monastery near Assisi, in Italy. One can see well how some monks succeeded in being as isolated as possible.

came priests only later, during the Middle Ages.) In this way even while Christianity was accommodating itself to practical needs, monasticism satisfied the inclinations of ascetic extremists.

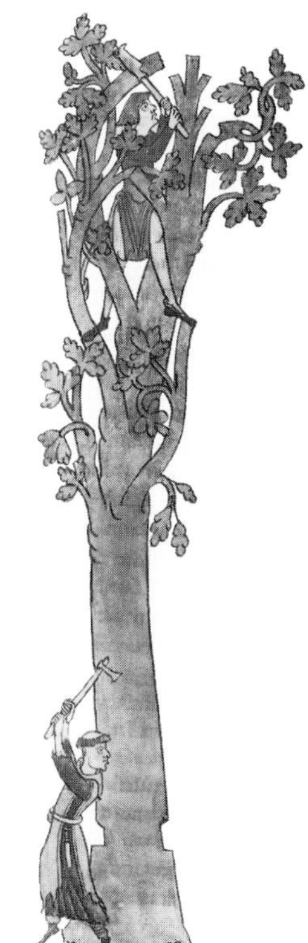

Above: **Monks Chopping Down Trees** and below: **Harvesting Grain.** From a twelfth-century French manuscript.

Monasticism first emerged in the East, where for about one hundred years after Constantine's conversion it spread like a mania. Hermit monks of Egypt and Syria vied with each other in their pursuit of the most inhuman and humiliating excesses. Some grazed in the fields after the manner of cows, others penned themselves into small cages, and others hung heavy weights around their necks. A monk named Cyriacus stood for hours on one leg like a crane until he could bear it no more. The most extravagant of these monastic ascetics was St. Simeon Stylites, who performed self-punishing exercises—such as touching his feet with his head 1,244 times in succession—on top of a high pillar for thirty-seven years, while crowds gathered below to worship "the worms that dropped from his body."

In time such ascetic hysteria subsided, and it became recognized that monasticism would be more enduring if monks lived in a community and did not concentrate on self-torture. The most successful architect of communal monasticism in the East was St. Basil (c. 330–379), who started his monastic career as a hermit and ascetic extremist but came to prefer communal and more moderate forms of life. Basil expressed this preference in writings for monks that laid down the basic guidelines for Eastern monasticism down to the present. Rather than encouraging extremes of self-torture, Basil encouraged monks to discipline themselves by useful labor. Although his teachings were still extremely severe by modern standards, he prohibited monks from engaging in prolonged fasts or lacerating their flesh. Instead he urged them to submit to obligations of poverty and humility, and to spend many hours of the day in silent religious meditation. With the triumph of St. Basil's ideas, Eastern monasticism became more organized and subdued, but even so Basilian monks preferred to live as far away from the "world" as they could and never had the same civilizing influence on external society as did their brothers in western Europe.

The Benedictine rule

Monasticism did not at first spread quickly in the West because the appeal of asceticism was much weaker there. This situation changed only in the sixth century when St. Benedict (c. 480–c. 547) drafted his famous Latin rule, which ultimately became the guide for nearly all Western monks. Modern scholarship has shown that Benedict copied much of his rule from an earlier Latin text known as the "Rule of the Master," but he still produced a document notable for its brevity, flexibility, and moderation. The Benedictine rule imposed obligations similar to those laid down by St. Basil: poverty, obedience, labor, and religious devotion. Yet Benedict prescribed less austerity than Basil did: the monks were granted a sufficiency of simple food, clothing, and enough sleep; they were even allowed to drink a small amount of wine, although meat was granted only to the sick. The abbot's authority was absolute, and the abbot was allowed to flog monks for disobedience, yet Benedict urged him to try "to be

St. Benedict Offering His Rule to Grateful Monks. A late-medieval conception from an Austrian manuscript of about 1355.

loved rather than feared," and ordained that the abbot gather advice before making decisions "because the Lord often reveals to a younger member what is best." For such reasons the Benedictine monastery became a home of religious enrichment rather than a school for punishment.

The significance of Benedictine monasticism: (1) missionary activities; (2) attitude toward manual labor

We will have occasion for continuing the story of Benedictine monasticism later on, but here we may point in advance to some of its greatest contributions to the development of Western civilization. One was that Benedictine monks were committed from an early date to missionary work: they were primarily responsible for the conversion of England and later most of Germany. Such activities not only helped to spread the faith but also served to create a sense of cultural unity for western Europe. Another positive contribution lay in the attitude of the Benedictines toward work. Whereas the highest goal for ancient philosophers and aristocrats was to have enough leisure time for unimpeded contemplation, St. Benedict wanted his monks always to keep busy, for he believed that "idleness is an enemy of the soul." Therefore he prescribed that they should be occupied at certain times in manual labor, a prescription that would have horrified most thinkers of earlier times. Accordingly, early Benedictines worked hard themselves and spread the idea of the dignity of labor to others. With Benedictine support, this idea would become one of the most distinctive traits of Western culture. We read of Benedictines who gladly milked cows, threshed, plowed, and hammered: in so doing they increased the prosperity of their own monasteries and provided good examples for others. Benedictine monasteries became particularly successful in farming and later in estate-managing. Thus they often helped to advance the level of the western European economy and sometimes even to provide wealth that could be drawn upon by emerging western European states.

The fact that Benedictine monasteries were often islands of culture when literacy and learning were all but forgotten in the secular world is better known. St. Benedict himself was no admirer of classical culture. Quite to the contrary, he wanted his monks to serve only Christ—not literature or philosophy. But he did assume that monks would have to read well enough to say their prayers. That meant that some teaching in the monasteries was necessary because it was seldom available outside and because boys were often given over from birth to the monastic profession. Once there was teaching there would obviously be at least a few writing implements and books. This explains why Benedictines always maintained some literacy but not why some of them became devoted to perpetuating classical culture. The impetus behind the latter development was the work of a monastic thinker named Cassiodorus (c. 477–c. 570). Inspired by St. Augustine, whom we will treat in more detail later, Cassiodorus believed that some basic classical learning was necessary for the proper understanding of the Bible; this justified the study of the classics by monks. Furthermore, Cassiodorus recognized that copying manuscripts was in itself "manual labor" (literally work with the hands) and might be even more appropriate for monks than hard work in the fields. As Benedictines began to subscribe to these ideas, Benedictine monasteries became centers for learning and transcribing that were without rival for centuries. No work of classical Latin literature, including such "licentious" writings as the poems of Catullus and Ovid, would survive today had they not been copied and preserved during the early Middle Ages by Benedictine monks.

(3) The preservation of classical culture; Cassiodorus

Cassiodorus. This frontispiece of a Bible executed around 700 C.E. in an English Benedictine monastery depicts Cassiodorus as a copyist and preserver of books. (Since books were exceedingly rare until the invention of printing in the fifteenth century, they customarily were stored in cupboards, lying flat.)

Returning to our original subject—the changes that took place in Christian institutions and attitudes during the fourth century—a final fateful trend was the development of a negative attitude toward women. Compared to most other religions, Christianity was favorable to women. Female souls were regarded as equal to male souls in the eyes of God, and human nature was deemed to be complete only in both sexes. St. Paul even went so far as to say that after baptism "there is neither male nor female" (Galatians 3:28), a spiritual egalitarianism which meant that women could be saved as fully as men. But Christians from earliest times shared the view of their contemporaries that in everyday life and in marriage women were to be strictly subject to men. Not only did early Christians believe, with all male supremacists of the ancient world, that women should be excluded from positions of leadership or decision-making, meaning that they should be "silent in Church" (I Corinthians 14:34–35) and could never be priests, but they added to this the view that women were more "fleshly" than men and therefore should be subjected to men as the flesh is subjected to the spirit (Ephesians 5:21–33).

Christianity's negative attitude toward women

With the growth of the ascetic movement in the third and fourth centuries, the denigration of women as dangerously "fleshly" creatures became more and more pronounced. Since sexual abstinence lay at the heart of asceticism, the most perfect men were expected to shun women. Monks, of course, shunned women the most. This was a primary reason why they fled to deserts and forests. One Eastern ascetic was struck by the

Sexual abstinence

need for virginity in the midst of his marriage ceremony, ran off to a hermit's cell, and blocked the entrance; another monk who was forced to carry his aged mother across a stream swaddled her up as thoroughly as he could so that he would not catch any "fire" and no thoughts of other women would attack him. With monks taking such an uncompromising attitude, the call for continence was extended to the priesthood. Originally priests could be married; it seems that even some of the Apostles had wives (I Corinthians 9:5). But in the course of the fourth century the doctrine spread that priests could not be married after ordination, and that those already married were obliged to live continently with their wives afterward.

Attitudes toward marriage

Once virginity was accepted as the highest standard, marriage was taken to be only second best. St. Jerome expressed this view most earthily when he said that virginity was wheat, marriage barley, and fornication cow-dung: since people should not eat cow-dung he would permit them barley. The major purposes of marriage were to keep men from "burning" and to propagate the species. (Jerome went so far as to praise marriage above all because it brought more virgins into the world!) Thus Christianity reinforced the ancient view that woman's major earthly purpose was to serve as mother. Men and women were warned not to take pleasure even in marital intercourse but to indulge in it only for the purpose of procreation. Women were to be "saved in childbearing" (I Timothy 2:15). Since they could not become priests and only a very few could become nuns (female monasticism was regarded as a very expensive luxury in the premodern world), almost all women were expected to become submissive wives and mothers. As wives they were not expected to have their own careers and were not meant to be educated or even literate. Hence even though they had full hopes for salvation, they were treated as inferiors in the everyday affairs of the world, a treatment that would endure until modern times.

The Germanic Invasions and the Fall of the Roman Empire in the West

The victories of the Germanic tribes

While Christianity was conquering the Roman Empire from within, another force, that of the Germanic barbarians, was threatening it from without. The Germans, who had already almost brought Rome to its knees in the third century, were held off from the time of Diocletian until shortly before the reign of Theodosius the Great. But thereafter they demolished Western Roman resistance and, by the end of the fifth century, succeeded in conquering all of the Roman West. Germanic kingdoms then became the new form of government in territories once ruled over by Caesar and Augustus.

Character of the Germans

It was once customary to think that the Germans were fierce and thoroughly uncouth savages who wantonly destroyed the Western Roman Empire out of sheer hatred for civilization. But that is a misunderstanding. The Germans were barbarians in Roman eyes because they did not live in cities and were illiterate, but they were not therefore savages. On the contrary, they often practiced settled agriculture—although they preferred hunting and grazing—and were adept in making iron tools and weapons as well as lavish jewelry. Physically they looked enough like Romans to intermarry without causing much comment, and their Indo-European language was related to Latin and Greek. Prolonged interaction with the Romans had a decisive civilizing influence on the Germans before they started their final conquests. Germans and Romans who shared common borders along the Rhine and Danube had steady trading relations with each other. Even during times of war Romans were often allied with some German tribes while they fought others. By the fourth century, moreover, German tribes often served as auxiliaries of depleted Roman armies and were sometimes allowed to settle on borderlands of the Empire where Roman farmers had given up trying to cultivate the land. Finally, many German tribes had been converted to Christianity in the fourth century, although the Christianity they accepted was of the heretical Arian version. All these interactions made the "barbarians" very familiar with Roman civilization and substantially favorable to it.

The Visigoths and the Vandals

The Germans began their final push not to destroy Rome but to find more and better land. The first breakthrough occurred in 378 when one tribe, the Visigoths, which had recently settled on some Roman lands in the Danube region, revolted against mistreatment by Roman officials and then decisively defeated a punitive Roman army in the Battle of Adrianople. The Visigoths did not immediately follow up this victory because they were cleverly bought off and made allies of the Empire by Theodosius the Great. But when Theodosius died in 395 he divided his realm between his two sons, neither of whom was as competent as he, and both halves of the Empire were weakened by political intrigues. The Visigoths under their leader Alaric took advantage of this situation to wander through Roman realms almost at will, looking for the best land and provisions. In 410 they sacked Rome itself—a great shock to some contemporaries—and in the following years marched into southern Gaul. Meanwhile, in December of 406, a group of allied Germanic tribes led by the Vandals crossed the frozen Rhine and capitalized on Roman preoccupation with the Visigoths by streaming through Gaul into Spain. Later they were able to cross the straits of Gibraltar into northwest Africa, then one of the richest agricultural regions of the Empire. From Africa they took control of the central Mediterranean, even sacking Rome from the sea in 455. By 476 the entirely ineffectual Western Roman emperor, a mere boy derisively nicknamed Augustulus ("little Augustus"), was easily deposed by a leader of a mixed band of Germans who then assumed the title of king of Rome. Accordingly, 476 is conventionally given as the date for the end of the Western Roman Empire. But it must be remembered that a Roman emperor, who maintained some claims to authority in the West, continued to rule in Constantinople.

Reasons for the German success

Two questions that historians of the German invasions customarily ask are: How did the Germans manage to triumph so easily? and Why was it that they were particularly successful in the West rather than the East?

The ease of the German victories appears particularly striking when it is recognized that the German armies were remarkably small: the Visigoths who won at Adrianople numbered no more than 10,000 men, and the total number of the Vandal "hordes" (including women and children) was about 80,000—a population about the same as that of an average-sized American suburb. But the Roman armies themselves were depleted because of declining population and the need for manpower in other occupations, above all in the new bureaucracies. More than that, German armies often won by default (Adrianople was one of the few pitched battles in the history of their advance) because the Romans were no longer zealous about defending themselves. Germans were seldom regarded with horror—many German soldiers had even risen to positions of leadership within Roman ranks—and the coercive regime begun by Diocletian was not deemed worth fighting for.

A Roman Empress of the Mid-Fifth Century. The long headdress is possibly a sign of Germanic influence.

The reasons why the Germans fared best in the West are complex—some having to do with personalities and mistakes of the moment, and others with geographical considerations. But the primary explanation why the Eastern Roman Empire survived while the Western did not is that the East was simply richer. By the fifth century most Western Roman cities had shrunk in terms of both population and space to a small fraction of their earlier size, and they were often little more than empty administrative shells or fortifications. The economy of the West was becoming more and more strictly agricultural, and agricultural produce served only to feed farm laborers and keep rich landlords in luxuries. In the East, on the other hand, cities like Constantinople, Antioch, and Alexandria remained teeming metropolises because of their trade and industry. Because the Eastern state had greater reserves of wealth to tax, it was more vigorous. It could also afford to buy off the barbarians with tribute money, which it did with increasing regularity. So Constantinople was able to stay afloat while Rome floundered and then sank.

Consequences of the Germanic invasions

The effects of the Germanic conquests in the West were not cataclysmic. The greatest difference between the Germans and the Romans had been that the former did not live in cities, but since the Western Roman cities were already in a state of decline, the invasions only served at most to accelerate the progress of urban decay. On the land Germans replaced Roman landlords without interrupting basic Roman agricultural patterns. Moreover, since the Germans never comprised very large numbers, they usually never took over more than a part of Roman lands. Germans also tried to avail themselves of Roman administrative apparatuses, but these tended to diminish gradually because of the diminishing of wealth and literacy. Thus the only major German innovation was to create separate tribal kingdoms in the West in place of a united empire.

Political divisions of western Europe

The map of western Europe around the year 500 reveals the following major political divisions. Germanic tribes of Anglo-Saxons, who had crossed the English Channel in the middle of the fifth century, were extending their rule on the island of Britain. In the northern part of Gaul, around Paris and east to the Rhine, the growing kingdom of the Franks

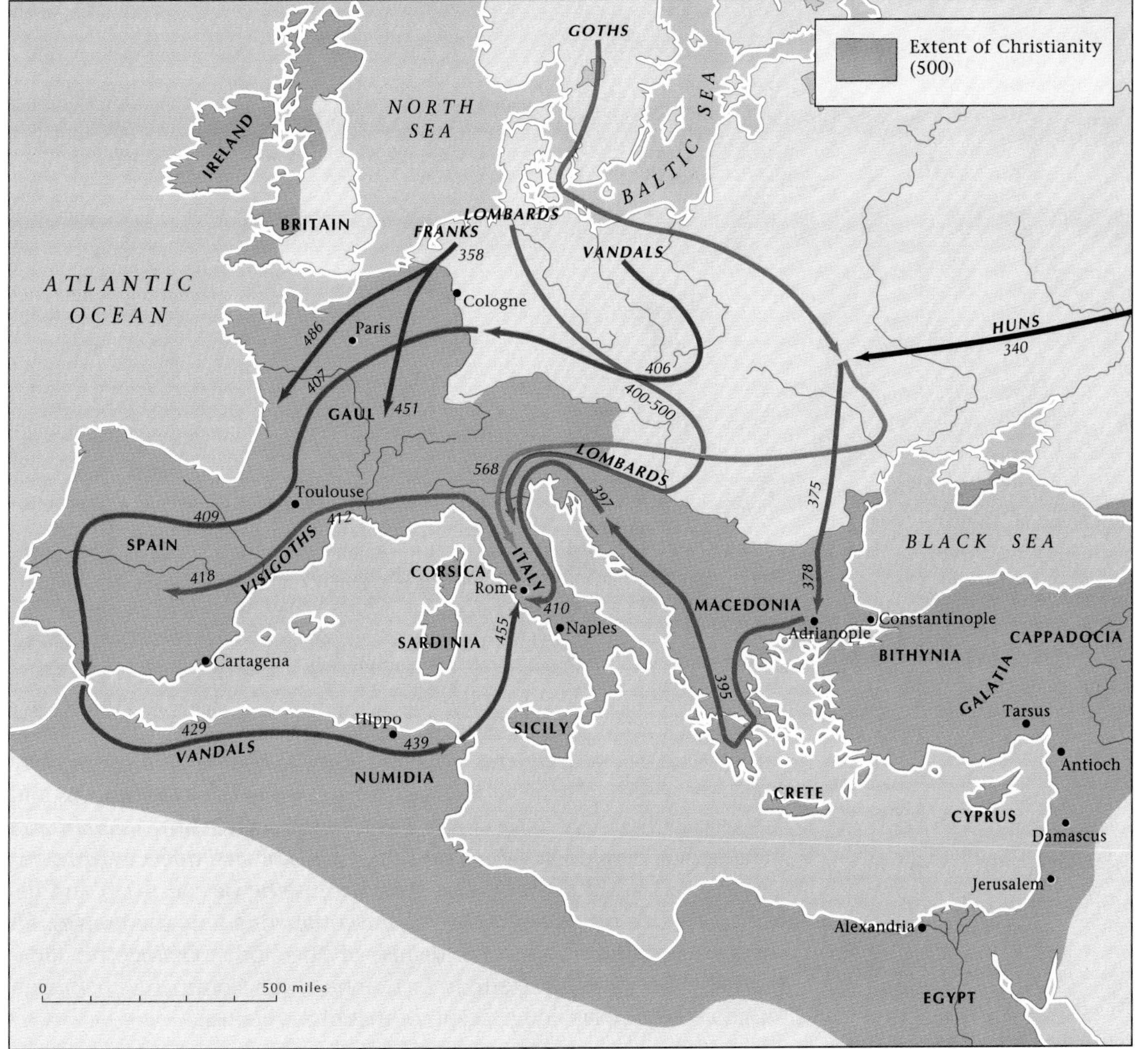

The Barbarian Invasion of the Fifth and Sixth Centuries

was ruled by a crafty warrior named Clovis. South of the Franks stood the Visigoths, who ruled the southern half of Gaul and most of Spain. South of them were the Vandals, who ruled throughout previously Roman Northwest Africa. In all of Italy the Ostrogoths, Eastern relatives of the Visigoths, held sway under their impressive King Theodoric. Of these kingdoms that of the Franks would be the most promising for the future (for that reason it will be taken up in the next chapter), and the seemingly strongest for the present was that of the Ostrogoths.

Theodoric

Theodoric the Ostrogoth, who ruled in Italy from 493 to 526, was a great admirer of Roman civilization; thus he tried to preserve it as best he could. He fostered agriculture and commerce, repaired public buildings and roads, patronized learning, and maintained a policy of religious toleration. In short he gave Italy a more enlightened rule than it had known

Mosaic of Theodoric's Palace at Ravenna. At the right is a stylized conception of the ruler's palace, with the Latin inscription PALA TIVM ("royal residence"); to the left of it is a row of saints, who would be indistinguishable were it not for the initials on their clothing: for early Christian artists, supernatural merits rather than individual personality traits were of the essence.

under most of its earlier emperors. But since Theodoric and his sparsely numbered Ostrogoths were Arian Christians while the local bishops and native population were Catholics, his rule, no matter how tolerant and benign, was viewed with some hostility. The "Roman" rulers in Constantinople were also hostile to Theodoric because he was an Arian and because they had not given up hopes of reconquering Italy themselves. All these circumstances led to the demise of Theodoric's Ostrogothic kingdom not long after his death. In fact, none of the Continental barbarian kingdoms would last long except for that of the Franks.

Theodoric the Ostrogoth. The barbarian ruler is shown here in Roman dress, with an ornate Roman hairstyle and a Roman symbol of victory in his hand. The inscription reads REX THEODERICVS PIVS PRINCIS, Latin for "King Theodoric, pious prince."

The Shaping of Western Christian Thought

The period of the decline and fall of the Roman Empire in the West was also the time when a few Western Christian thinkers formulated an approach to the world and to God that was to guide the thought of the West for roughly the next 800 years. This concurrence of political decline and theological advance was not coincidental. With the Empire falling and being replaced by barbarian kingdoms, it seemed clearer than ever to thinking Christians both that the classical inheritance had to be reexamined and that God had not intended the world to be anything more than a transitory testing place. The consequences of these assumptions accordingly became urgent questions. Between about 380 and 525, answers were worked out by Western Christian thinkers whose accomplishments were intimately interrelated. The towering figure among them was St. Augustine, but some others had great influence as well.

St. Jerome

Three contemporaries who knew and influenced each other—St. Jerome (c. 340–420), St. Ambrose (c. 340–397), and St. Augustine (354–430)—count as three of the four greatest "fathers" of the Western, Latin Church. (The fourth, St. Gregory the Great, came later and will be discussed in the next chapter.) St. Jerome's greatest single contribution was his translation of the Bible from Hebrew and Greek into Latin. His version, known as the *Vulgate* (or "common" version), became the standard Latin Bible used throughout the Middle Ages; with minor variations it continued to be used long afterward by the Roman Catholic Church. Fortunately Jerome was one of the best writers of his day, and he endowed his translation with vigorous, often colloquial prose and, occasionally, fine poetry. Since the Vulgate was the most widely read work in Latin for centuries, Jerome's writing had as much influence on Latin style and thought as the King James Bible has had on English literature. Jerome, who was the least original thinker of the great Latin fathers, also influenced Western Christian thought by his contentious but eloquent formulations of contemporary views. Among the most important of these were the beliefs that much of the Bible was to be understood allegorically rather than literally, that classical learning could be valid for Christians if it was thoroughly subordinated to Christian aims, and that the most perfect Christians were rigorous ascetics. In keeping with the last position Jerome avidly supported monasticism. He also taught that women should not take baths so that they would not see their own bodies naked.

St. Ambrose

Unlike Jerome, who was primarily a scholar, St. Ambrose was most active in the concerns of the world. As archbishop of Milan, Ambrose was the most influential Church official in the West—more so even than the pope. Guided by practical concerns, he wrote an ethical work, *On the Duties of Ministers,* which followed closely upon Cicero's *On Duties* in title and form, and also drew heavily on Cicero's Stoic ethics. But Ambrose differed from Cicero and most of traditional classical thought on two major points. One was that the beginning and end of human conduct should be reverence for God rather than any self-concern or interest in social adjustment. The other—Ambrose's most original contribution—was that God helps some Christians but not others in this pursuit by the gift of grace, a point that was to be greatly refined and amplified by St. Augustine. Ambrose put his concern for proper conduct into action by his most famous act, his confrontation with the Emperor Theodosius the Great over the massacring of innocent civilians. Ambrose argued that by violating divine commandments Theodosius had made himself subject to Church discipline. Remarkably the archbishop succeeded in forcing the sovereign emperor to do penance. This was the first time that a churchman had subordinated the Roman secular power in matters of morality. Consequently it symbolized the Church's claim to preeminence in this sphere, and particularly the Western Church's developing sense of autonomy and moral superiority that would subsequently make it so much more independent and influential on the secular world than the Eastern Church.

St. Augustine

St. Ambrose's disciple, St. Augustine, was the greatest of all the Latin fathers; indeed he was one of the most powerful Christian intellects of all time. Augustine's influence on subsequent medieval thought was incalculable. Even after the Middle Ages his theology had a profound influence on the development of Protestantism; in the twentieth century many leading Christian thinkers have called themselves neo-Augustinians. Augustine's Christianity may have been so searching because he began his career by searching for it. Nominally a Christian from birth, he hesitated until the age of thirty-three to be baptized, passing from one system of thought to another without being able to find intellectual or spiritual satisfaction in any. Only increasing doubts about all other alternatives, the appeals of St. Ambrose's teachings, and a mystical experience movingly described in his *Confessions* led Augustine to embrace the faith wholeheartedly in 387. Thereafter he advanced rapidly in ecclesiastical positions, becoming bishop of the North African city of Hippo in 395. Although he led a most active life in this office, he still found time to write a large number of profound, complex, and powerful treatises in which he set forth his convictions concerning the most fundamental problems of Christian thought and action.

Augustine's theology

St. Augustine's theology revolved around the principles of the profound sinfulness of humanity and divine omnipotence. Ever since Adam and Eve turned away from God in the Garden of Eden humans have remained basically sinful. One of Augustine's most vivid illustrations of human depravity appears in the *Confessions,* where he tells how he and some other boys once were driven to steal pears from a neighbor's garden, not because they were hungry or because the pears were beautiful, but for the sake of the evil itself. God would be purely just if He condemned all human beings to hell, but since He is also merciful He has elected to save a few. Ultimately human will has nothing to do with this choice: although one has the power to choose between good and evil, one does not have the power to decide whether he will be saved. God alone, from eternity, predestined a portion of the human race to be saved and sentenced the rest to be damned. In other words, God fixed for all time the number of human inhabitants of heaven. If any mere mortals were to respond that this seems unfair, the answer is first that strict "fairness" would confine all to perdition, and second that the basis for God's choice is a mystery shrouded in His omnipotence—far beyond the realm of human comprehension.

The doctrine of predestination

Even though it might seem to us that the practical consequences of this rigorous doctrine of predestination would be lethargy and fatalism, Augustine and subsequent medieval Christians did not see it that way at all. Humans themselves must do good, and if they are "chosen" they usually will do good; since no one knows who is chosen and who is not, all should try to do good in the hope that they are among the chosen. For

Augustine the central guide to doing good was the doctrine of "charity," which meant leading a life devoted to loving God and loving one's neighbor for the sake of God, rather than a life of "cupidity," of loving earthly things for their own sake. Put in other terms, Augustine taught that humans should behave on earth as if they were travelers or "pilgrims," keeping their eyes at all times on their heavenly home and avoiding all materialistic concerns.

On the City of God

Augustine built an interpretation of history on this view in one of his major works, *On the City of God*. In this, he argued that the entire human race from the Creation until the Last Judgment was and will be composed of two warring societies, those who "live according to man" and love themselves, and those who "live according to God." The former belong to the "City of Earth" and will be damned, while the blessed few who compose the "City of God" will on Judgment Day put on the garment of immortality. As for the time when the Last Judgment would come, Augustine argued vehemently that no human could know its exact date; nonetheless since the Judgment might come at any time, and since no other world-historical events were in store for humans that mattered, all mortals should devote their utmost efforts to preparing for it by leading lives of righteousness.

Augustine's view of classical learning

Although St. Augustine formulated major new aspects of Christian theology, he believed that he was doing no more than drawing out truths found in the Bible. Indeed, he was convinced that the Bible alone contained all the wisdom worth knowing. But he also believed that much of the Bible was expressed obscurely, and that it was therefore necessary to have a certain amount of education in order to understand it thoroughly. This conviction led him to a modified acceptance of classical learning.

"The City of the Earth." A medieval illustration for Augustine's *On the City of God* showing Cain slaying Abel and Romulus slaying Remus. Its message is that all human society on earth is a product of sin.

The ancient world had already worked out an educational system based on the "liberal arts," or those subjects necessary for the worldly success and intellectual growth of free men. Augustine argued that privileged Christians could learn the fundamentals of these subjects, but only in a limited way and for a completely different end—study of the Bible. Since nonreligious schools existed in his day which taught these subjects, he permitted a Christian elite to attend them; later, when such schools died out, their place was taken by schools in monasteries and cathedrals. Thus Augustine's teaching laid the groundwork for some continuity of educational practice as well as for the theory behind the preservation of some classical treatises. But we must qualify this by remarking that Augustine intended liberal education only for an elite; all others were simply to be catechized, or drilled, in the faith. He also thought it far worse that anyone should become engaged in classical thought for its own sake than that someone might not know any classical thought at all. The true wisdom of mortals, he insisted, was piety.

Boethius

Augustine had many followers, of whom the most interesting and influential was Boethius, a Roman aristocrat who lived from about 480 to 524. Until recently, it was not customary to say that Boethius was a follower of St. Augustine because some of Boethius's works do not make explicit mention of Christianity. Indeed, since Boethius was indisputably interested in ancient philosophy, wrote in a polished, almost Ciceronian style, and came from a noble Roman family, it has been customary to view him as the "last of the Romans." But in fact he intended the classics to serve Christian purposes, just as Augustine had prescribed, and his own teachings were basically Augustinian.

Because Boethius lived a century after Augustine he could see far more clearly that the ancient world was coming to an end. Therefore he made it his first goal to preserve as much of the best ancient learning as possible by a series of handbooks, translations, and commentaries. Accepting a contemporary division of the liberal arts into seven subjects—grammar, rhetoric, logic, arithmetic, geometry, astronomy, and music—he wrote handbooks on two: arithmetic and music. These summaries were meant to convey all the basic aspects of the subject matter that a Christian might need to know. Had Boethius lived longer he probably would have written similar treatments of the other liberal arts, but as it was he concentrated his efforts on his favorite subject: logic. In order to preserve the best of classical logic, he translated from Greek into Latin some of Aristotle's logical treatises as well as an introductory work on logic by Porphyry (another ancient philosopher). He also wrote his own explanatory commentaries on these works in order to help beginners. Since Latin writers had never been interested in logic, even in the most flourishing periods of Roman culture, Boethius's translations and commentaries became a crucial link between the thought of the Greeks and that of the Middle Ages. Boethius helped endow the Latin language with a logical vocabulary, and when interest in logic was revived in the twelfth-century West it rested first on a Boethian basis.

Boethius. A twelfth-century artist's conception of Boethius as a musician, a reputation he earned because of his treatise on music.

The Consolation of Philosophy

Although Boethius was an exponent of Aristotle's logic, his worldview was not Aristotelian but Augustinian. This can be seen both in his several orthodox treatises on Christian theology and above all in his masterpiece, *The Consolation of Philosophy.* Boethius wrote the *Consolation* at the end of his life, after he had been condemned to death for treason by Theodoric the Ostrogoth, whom he had served as an official. (Historians are unsure about the justice of the charges.) In it Boethius asks the age-old question of what is human happiness and concludes that it is not found in earthly rewards such as riches or fame but only in the "highest good," which is God. Human life, then, should be spent in pursuit of God. Since Boethius speaks in the *Consolation* as a philosopher rather than a theologian, he does not refer to Christian revelation or to the role of divine grace in salvation. But his basically Augustinian message is unmistakable. *The Consolation of Philosophy* became one of the most popular books of the Middle Ages because it was extremely well written, because it showed how classical expression and some classical ideas could be appropriated and subordinated into a clearly Christian framework, and most of all, because it seemed to offer a real meaning to life. In times when all earthly things really did seem crude or fleeting it was genuinely consoling to be told eloquently and "philosophically" that life has purpose if led for the sake of God.

The myth of Orpheus as a symbol for Christian truths

At a climactic moment in the *Consolation* Boethius retold in verse the myth of Orpheus in a way that might stand for the common position of the four writers just discussed: i.e., how Christian thinkers were willing to accept and maintain some continuity with the classical tradition. But

Orpheus and Eurydice. This manuscript illustration from the fifteenth century probably intends to deliver the message that he who turns to look on the joys of earthly life is inviting eternal damnation. (A devil on the far right is standing before the gate of hell.)

Boethius also made new sense of the story. According to Boethius Orpheus's wife, Eurydice, symbolized hell; since Orpheus could not refrain from looking at her he was forced to die and was condemned to hell himself. In other words, Orpheus was too worldly and material; he should not have loved a woman but should have sought God. True Christians, on the other hand, know that "happy is he who can look into the shining spring of good [i.e., the divine vision]; happy is he who can break the heavy chains of earth."

Boethius and "Lady Philosophy." A late-medieval depiction of the opening scene from *The Consolation of Philosophy.*

Eastern Rome and the West

Boethius's execution by Theodoric the Ostrogoth in 524 was in many ways an important historical turning point. For one, Boethius was both the last noteworthy philosopher and last writer of cultivated Latin prose the West was to have for many hundreds of years. Then too Boethius was a layman, and for hundreds of years afterward almost all western European writers would be priests or monks. In the political sphere Boethius's execution was symptomatic as well because it was the harbinger of the collapse of the Ostrogothic kingdom in Italy. Whether or not he was justly condemned, Boethius's execution showed that the Arian Ostrogoths could not live in perfect harmony with Catholic Christians. Soon afterward, therefore, the Ostrogoths were overthrown by the Eastern Roman Empire. That event in turn was to be a major factor in the ultimate divorce between East and West and the consequent final disintegration of the old Roman world.

The Emperor Justinian

The conquest of the Ostrogoths was part of a larger plan for Roman revival conceived and directed by the Eastern Roman emperor Justinian (527–565). Eastern Rome, with its capital at Constantinople, had faced many external pressures from barbarians and internal religious dissensions since the time of Theodosius. But throughout the fifth century it had managed to weather these, and by the time of Justinian's accession had regained much of its strength. Although the Eastern Roman Empire—which then encompassed the modern-day territories of Greece, Turkey, most of the Middle East, and Egypt—was largely Greek- and Syriac-speaking, Justinian himself came from a western province (modern-day Serbia) and spoke Latin. Not surprisingly, therefore, he concentrated his interests on the West. He saw himself as the heir of imperial Rome, whose ancient power and western territory he was resolved to restore. Aided by his astute and determined wife Theodora, who, unlike earlier imperial Roman consorts, played an influential role in his reign, Justinian took great strides toward this goal. But ultimately his policy of recovering the West proved unrealistic.

Codification and revision of Roman law; the *Corpus Juris Civilis*

One of Justinian's most impressive and lasting accomplishments was his codification of Roman law. This project was part of his attempt to emphasize continuities with earlier imperial Rome and was also meant to enhance his own prestige and absolute power. Codification of the law was necessary because between the third and sixth centuries the volume of statutes had continued to grow, with the result that the vast body of enactments contained many contradictory or obsolete elements. Moreover, conditions had changed so radically that many of the old legal principles could no longer be applied, due to the establishment of an Oriental despotism and the adoption of Christianity as the official religion. When Justinian came to the throne in 527, he immediately decided upon a revision and codification of the existing law to bring it into harmony with the new conditions and to establish it as an authoritative basis of his rule. To carry out the actual work he appointed a commission of lawyers under the supervision of his minister, Tribonian. Within two years the commission published the first result of its labors. This was the *Code,* a systematic revision of all of the statutory laws that had been issued from the reign of Hadrian to the reign of Justinian. The *Code* was later supplemented by the *Novels,* which contained the legislation of Justinian and his immediate successors. By 532 the commission had completed the *Digest,* a summary of all of the writings of the great jurists. The final product of the work of revision was the *Institutes,* a textbook of the legal principles reflected in both the *Digest* and the *Code.* All four volumes together constitute the *Corpus Juris Civilis,* or the "body of civil law."

General significance of Justinian's *Corpus*

Justinian's *Corpus* was a brilliant achievement in its own terms: the *Digest* alone has been justly called "the most remarkable and important law-book that the world has ever seen." In addition, the *Corpus* had an extraordinarily great influence on subsequent legal and governmental history. Revived and restudied in western Europe from the eleventh century on, Justinian's *Corpus* became the basis of all the law and jurisprudence of European states, exclusive of England (which followed its own "common law"). The nineteenth-century Napoleonic Code, which provided the basis for the laws of modern European countries and also of Latin America, is fundamentally the *Institutes* of Justinian in modern dress.

Other influences of the *Corpus*

Only a few of the more specific influences of Justinian's legal work can be enumerated here. One is that in its basic governmental theory it was a bastion of absolutism. Starting from the maxim that "what pleases the prince has the force of law," it granted untrammeled powers to the imperial sovereign and therefore was adopted with alacrity by later European monarchs and autocrats. But the *Corpus* also provided some theoretical support for constitutionalism because it maintained that the sovereign originally obtained his powers from the people rather than from God. Since government came from the people it could in theory be given back to them. Perhaps most important and influential was the *Corpus's* view of the state as an abstract public and secular entity. In the Middle Ages rival views of the state as the private property of the ruler or as a supernatural creation meant to control sin often predominated. The modern conception of the state as a public entity concerned not with the future life but with everyday affairs gained strength toward the end of the Middle Ages largely because of the revival of assumptions found in Justinian's legal compilations.

Justinian and Theodora. Sixth-century mosaics from the Church of San Vitale, Ravenna. The emperor and empress are conceived here to have supernatural, almost priestly powers: they are advancing toward the altar, bringing the communion dish and chalice respectively. Both rulers are set off from their retinues by

Justinian's policy of reconquest in the West

Justinian aimed to be a full Roman emperor in geographical practice as well as in legal theory. To this end he sent out armies to reconquer the West. At first they were quickly successful. In 533 Justinian's brilliant general Belisarius conquered the Vandal kingdom in Northwest Africa, and in 536 Belisarius seemed to have won all of Italy, where he was welcomed by the Catholic subjects of the Ostrogoths. But the first victories of the Italian campaign were illusory. After their initial defeats the Ostrogoths put up stubborn resistance and the war dragged on for decades until the exhausted Eastern Romans finally reduced the last Gothic outposts in 563. Shortly before he died Justinian became master of all Italy as well as Northwest Africa and coastal parts of Spain that his troops had also managed to recapture. The Mediterranean was once more briefly a "Roman" lake. But the cost of the endeavor was soon going to call the very existence of the Eastern Roman Empire into question.

The Western campaigns unwise

There were two major reasons why Justinian's Western campaigns were ill-advised. One was that his realm really could not afford them. Belisarius seldom had enough troops to do his job properly: he began his Italian campaign with only 8,000 men. Later, when Justinian did grant his generals enough troops, it was only at the cost of oppressive taxation. But additional troops would probably have been insufficient to hold the

their haloes. The observant viewer is also meant to note the representation of the "three wise kings from the East" at the hem of Theodora's gown: just as the "three magi" once had supernatural knowledge of Christ, so now do their counterparts, Justinian and Theodora.

new lines in the West because the Empire had greater interests, as well as enemies, to the East. While the Eastern Roman Empire was exhausting itself in Italy the Persians were gathering strength. Justinian's successors had to pull away from the West in order to meet the threat of a revived Persia, but even so, by the beginning of the seventh century, it seemed as if the Persians would be able to march all the way to the waters that faced Constantinople. Only a heroic reorganization of the Empire after 610 avoided that fate, but it was one that helped withdraw Eastern Rome from the West and helped the West begin to lead a life of its own.

The end of Roman unity

In the meantime Justinian's wars had left most of Italy in a shambles. In the course of the protracted fighting much devastation had been wrought. Around Rome aqueducts were cut and parts of the countryside returned to marshes not drained until the twentieth century. In 568, only three years after Justinian's death, another Germanic tribe, the Lombards, invaded the country and took much of it away from the Eastern Romans. They met little resistance because the latter were now paying more attention to the East, but the Lombards were still too weak to conquer the whole Italian peninsula. Instead, Italy became divided between Lombard, Eastern Roman, and papal territories. At the same time Slavs took advantage of Eastern Roman weakness to sweep into the Balkans. Farther west

Hen and Chicks. North Italian small figures from the sixth century made from silver overlaid with gold. The purpose of this luxurious and seemingly humorous work dating from a time of economic decline and grave political crisis is unknown; there are as many theories offered for it as there are chicks.

Iron Crown. This splendidly bejewelled iron chaplet may have been used to crown the Lombard kings of Italy.

the Franks in Gaul were fighting among themselves, and it would be only a matter of time before northwest Africa and most of Spain would fall to Arabs. So the Roman unity had finally come to an end. The future in this decentralized world may have looked bleak, but new forces in the separate areas would soon be gathering strength.

SUMMARY POINTS

- Between 284 and 395, the focus of the Roman Empire began to shift fundamentally from West to East. From the Easternizing of imperial rule under Diocletian (284–305) to the removal of the Empire's capital from Rome to Constantinople (330), the divide between East and West became ever more pronounced.
- The major cultural trend of late-antique history was the rise and spread of Christianity. This trend can be attributed to several factors, including the desire of many for a philosophy of salvation and absolutes during a time of heightened anxiety, the social services provided by Christian groups, and the general religious tolerance of the Empire. The conversion of Constantine in 312 and the subsequent official support for Christianity ensured its success.
- As soon as Christianity emerged victorious, sharp doctrinal and practical disputes arose within its ranks. These disputes led to the development of a uniform religious doctrine and the involvement of the imperial government in Church matters.
- The weakness of the Roman Empire and its focus on the East provided the opportunity for Germanic invaders to seize the western portion of the Empire (410–476).
- Several significant intellectual developments also took place during late antiquity: the spread of the practice of monasticism led to the founding of Benedictine monasteries, which would become the focus of learning and transcribing; St. Augustine developed his highly influential Christian theology; and the Emperor Justinian directed the codification of Roman laws in the *Corpus Juris Civilis,* which became the basis of nearly all modern Western law.

SELECTED READINGS

Anderson, Hugh, comp., *Jesus,* Englewood Cliffs, N.J., 1967. An excellent collection of readings displaying many different scholarly points of view.

Bonner, Gerald, *St. Augustine of Hippo,* London, 1963. The best biography for beginners.

Brown, Peter, *Augustine of Hippo,* Berkeley, 1967. An extremely subtle study.

———, *The Body and Society: Men, Women and Sexual Renunciation in Early Christianity,* New York, 1988. Exquisitely written and sensitive treatment of sexual asceticism.

———, *Power and Persuasion in Late Antiquity: Towards a Christian Empire,* Madison, Wis., 1992. Treats the nature of Roman imperial government and implicit strategies for reducing its severity.

———, *The World of Late Antiquity,* New York, 1971. A survey that approaches the period in its own terms rather than as a prelude to the Middle Ages.

Bury, J. B., *The Invasion of Europe by the Barbarians,* New York, 1963. A straightforward narrative.

Chadwick, Henry, *The Early Church,* Baltimore, 1967.

Daniélou, Jean, and Henri I. Marrou, *The Christian Centuries; Vol. I: The First Six Hundred Years,* New York, 1964. A survey from the Roman Catholic perspective.

Dodds, E. R., *Pagan and Christian in an Age of Anxiety,* Cambridge, 1990. A short but brilliant study of what pagans and Christians had in common as well as what made Christianity ultimately successful.

Fredriksen, Paula, *From Jesus to Christ: The Origins of the New Testament Images of Jesus,* New Haven, 1988. Analyzes the different conceptions of Jesus found in Christian scripture. A stimulating work, presented with clarity.

Knowles, David, *Christian Monasticism,* New York, 1969.

Lane Fox, Robin, *Pagans and Christians,* New York, 1987. A highly acclaimed major study of religion in the Late Roman world.

L'Orange, H. P., *Art Forms and Civic Life in the Late Roman Empire,* Princeton, 1965. An imaginative and stimulating essay displaying how developments in art reflected developments in political and social life.

MacMullen, Ramsay, *Constantine,* New York, 1987. A good popular biography.

Markus, R. A., *The End of Ancient Christianity,* New York, 1990. An expert synthetic study of Christianity in the Western Roman Empire between 350 and 600 C.E.

Metzger, Bruce, *The Canon of the New Testament,* New York, 1987. A careful survey of the process of composition of the New Testament.

Moorhead, John, *Justinian,* New York, 1994. A first-rate review of the career of the emperor and the times in which he lived.

Pelikan, Jaroslav, *The Christian Tradition; Vol. I: The Emergence of the Catholic Tradition,* Chicago, 1971. An advanced survey of doctrine.

Rand, E. K., *Founders of the Middle Ages,* Cambridge, Mass., 1928. A thoroughly engaging account of the early Christian reactions to the classics.

Riché, Pierre, *Education and Culture in the Barbarian West,* Columbia, S.C., 1976. A magisterial survey of learning in the Christian West from the fall of Rome to about 800.

Thompson, E. A., *Romans and Barbarians: The Decline of the Western Empire,* Madison, Wis., 1982. A collection of essays, organized geographically. For advanced readers.

White, Lynn T., Jr., *The Transformation of the Roman World,* Berkeley, 1966. Stimulating essays.

Williams, Stephen, *Diocletian and the Roman Recovery,* New York, 1997. A well-informed "life and times."

Workman, Herbert B., *The Evolution of the Monastic Ideal,* Boston, 1962. Highly interpretative but still one of the best works on the subject.

SOURCE MATERIALS

St. Augustine, *City of God,* tr. H. Bettenson, Baltimore, 1972.

———, *Confessions,* tr. R. S. Pine-Coffin, Baltimore, 1961.

———, *The Enchiridion on Faith, Hope and Love,* ed. H. Paolucci, Chicago, 1961.

———, *On Christian Doctrine,* tr. D. W. Robertson, Jr., New York, 1958.

Boethius, *The Consolation of Philosophy,* tr. R. Green, Indianapolis, 1962.

Cassiodorus, *An Introduction to Divine and Human Readings,* tr. L. W. Jones, New York, 1946.

Early Christian Writings: The Apostolic Fathers, tr. M. Staniforth, Baltimore, 1968.

Eusebius, *The History of the Church,* tr. G. A. Williamson, Baltimore, 1965.

Procopius, *The Secret History,* tr. G. A. Williamson, Baltimore, 1966.

PART THREE

THE MIDDLE AGES

THE TERM "Middle Ages" was coined by Europeans in the seventeenth century to express their view that a long and dismal period of interruption extended between the glorious accomplishments of classical Greece and Rome and their own "modern age." Because the term became so widespread, it is now an ineradicable part of our historical vocabulary; but no serious scholar uses it with the sense of contempt it once invoked. Between about 600 and 1500—the rough opening and closing dates of the Middle Ages—too many different things happened to be characterized in any single way. In the eastern parts of the old Roman Empire two new civilizations emerged, the Byzantine and the Islamic, which rank among the most impressive civilizations of all time. Although the Byzantine civilization came to an end in 1453, the Islamic one has continued to exist without major interruption right up to the present. Seen from an Islamic perspective, therefore, the "Middle Ages" was not a middle period at all but a marvelous time of birth and vigorous early youth. The history of western Europe in the Middle Ages is conventionally divided into three parts: the Early Middle Ages, the High Middle Ages, and the Later Middle Ages. Throughout these periods the Christian religion played an extraordinarily important role in human life, but otherwise there are few common denominators. The Early Middle Ages, from about 600 to about 1050, came closest to seeming to be an interval of darkness, for the level of material and intellectual accomplishment was, in fact, very low. Nonetheless, even during the Early Middle Ages important foundations were being laid for the future: above all, western Europe was beginning to develop its own distinct sense of cultural identity. The High Middle Ages, from about

Ekkehard and Uta. Aristocratic figures from the Cathedral of Naumberg, Germany, dating from c. 1260.

1050 to 1300, was one of the most creative epochs in the history of human endeavor. Europeans greatly improved their standard of living, established enduring national states, developed new institutions of learning and modes of thought, and created magnificent works of literature and art. During the Later Middle Ages, from about 1300 to 1500, the survival of many high-medieval accomplishments was threatened by numerous disasters, particularly profound economic depression and lethal plague. But people in the Later Middle Ages rose above adversity, tenaciously held on to what was most valuable in their inheritance, and, where necessary, created new institutions and thought patterns to fit their altered circumstances. The Middle Ages thus were really many hundred years of enormous diversity. They may be studied profitably both for their own intrinsic interest and for the fundamental contributions they made to the development of the modern world.

THE MIDDLE AGES

Politics	Philosophy and Science	Economics	Religion	Arts and Letters	
		Decline of towns and trade in the West (c. 500–c. 700)	Muhammad (c. 570–632) Pope Gregory I (590–604)	Byzantine church of Santa Sophia (532–537)	500
Byzantine emperor Heraclius (610–641) Muhammad enters Mecca in triumph (630) Arab Muslims conquer Syria, Persia, and Egypt (636–651) Umayyad dynasty in Islam (661–750)			Muhammad's *Hijrah* (622) Split in Islam between Shiites and Sunnites (c. 656)		600
Muslims conquer Spain (711) Muslim attack on Constantinople repulsed (717) Charles Martel defeats Muslims at Tours (732) Abbasid dynasty in Islam (750–1258) Pepin the Short anointed king of the Franks (751) Charlemagne (768–814)		Height of Islamic commerce and industry (c. 700–c. 1300) Predominantly agrarian economy in the West (c. 700–c. 1050)	Missionary work of St. Boniface in Germany (c. 715–754) Iconoclasm in Byzantine Empire (726–843)	The Venerable Bede (d. 735) *Beowulf* (c. 750) Irish *Book of Kells* (c. 750)	700
Charlemagne crowned emperor (800) Carolingian Empire disintegrates (c. 850–911) Alfred the Great of England (871–899) High point of Viking raids in Europe (c. 880–911)	Height of Islamic philosophy (c. 850–1200)	Height of Byzantine commerce and industry (c. 800–c. 1000)		Carolingian Renaissance (c. 800–c. 850)	800
Otto the Great of Germany (936–973) Foundation of Kievan state (c. 950)	Al-Farabi (d. 950)		Foundation of Cluny (910) Byzantine conversion of Russia (c. 988)		900

THE MIDDLE AGES

	Politics	Philosophy and Science	Economics	Religion	Arts and Letters
1000			Destruction of Byzantine free peasantry (c. 1025–c. 1100)		Romanesque style in architecture and art (c. 1000–c. 1200)
		Avicenna (d. 1037)			
				Beginning of reform papacy (1046)	
			Agricultural advance, revival of towns and trade in the West (c. 1050–c. 1300)	Schism between Roman and Eastern Orthodox Churches (1054)	
				"College of Cardinals" assumes sole power to choose new popes (1059)	
	Norman Conquest of England (1066)				
	Seljuk Turks defeat Byzantines at Manzikert (1071)				
	Penance of Henry IV of Germany at Canossa (1077)			Pope Gregory VII (1073–1085)	
		Peter Abelard (1079–1142)		St. Bernard of Clairvaux (1090–1153)	
				First Crusade (1095–1099)	*Song of Roland* (c. 1095)
				Hildegard of Bingen (1098–1179)	
1100	Henry I of England (1100–1135)	Origins of universities in the West (c. 1100–c. 1300)			Troubadour poetry (c. 1100–c. 1220)
	Louis VI of France (1108–1137)				
				Height of Cistercian monasticism (c. 1115–c. 1153)	*Rubaiyat* of Umar Khayyam (c. 1120)
				Concordat of Worms ends investiture struggle (1122)	
		Translation of Aristotle's works into Latin (c. 1140–c. 1260)			
					Gothic style in architecture and art (c. 1150–c.1500)
	Frederick I (Barbarossa) of Germany (1152–1190)				
	Henry II of England (1154–1189)	Peter Lombard's *Sentences* (c. 1155–1157)			Poetry of Chrétien de Troyes (c. 1165–c. 1190)
		Robert Grosseteste (c. 1168–1253)			
		Windmill invented (c. 1170)			
	Philip Augustus of France (1180–1223)				

THE MIDDLE AGES

Politics	Philosophy and Science	Economics	Religion	Arts and Letters	
			Crusaders lose Jerusalem to Saladin (1187)		
	Averroës (d. 1198)		Pope Innocent III (1198–1216)		
		Decline of serfdom (c. 1200–1300)		Wolfram von Eschenbach (c. 1200)	1200
Constantinople taken in Fourth Crusade (1204)	Maimonides (d. 1204)	Venetian and Genoan trading outposts in Byzantine territories (c. 1204–)			
			Albigensian Crusade (1208–1213)		
			Founding of Franciscan Order (1210)	Gottfried von Strassburg (c. 1210)	
Spanish victory over Muslims at Las Navas de Tolosa (1212) Frederick II of Germany and Sicily (1212–1250)					
	Roger Bacon (c. 1214–1294)				
Magna Carta (1215)			Fourth Lateran Council (1215)		
			Founding of Dominican Order (1216)		
Louis IX (St. Louis) of France (1226–1270)	St. Thomas Aquinas (1225–1274)				
	Height of Scholasticism (c. 1250–c. 1277)			Persian poetry of Sadi (c. 1250) *Romance of the Rose* (c. 1270)	
Edward I of England (1272–1307)					
Philip IV (the Fair) of France (1285–1314)	William of Ockham (c. 1285–1349) Mechanical clock invented (c. 1290)				
			Fall of last Christian outposts in Holy Land (1291) Pope Boniface VIII (1294–1303)		
	Master Eckhart (active c. 1300–c. 1327) Magnetic compass invented (c. 1300)	European economic depression (c. 1300–c. 1450)	Babylonian Captivity of papacy (1305–1378)	Paintings of Giotto (c. 1305–1337) Dante's *Divine Comedy* (c. 1310)	1300
		Floods through western Europe (1315)			

THE MIDDLE AGES

	Politics	Philosophy and Science	Economics	Religion	Arts and Letters
	Hundred Years' War (1337–1453)	Height of nominalism (c. 1320–c. 1500)	Black Death (1347–1350)	John Wyclif (c. 1330–1384)	
	Political chaos in Germany (c. 1350–c. 1450)		Height of Hanseatic League (c. 1350–c. 1450)		Boccaccio's *Decameron* (c. 1350)
					Persian poetry of Hafiz (c. 1370)
				Great Schism of papacy (1378–1417)	
			English Peasants' Revolt (1381)		
					Chaucer's *Canterbury Tales* (c. 1390)
			Medici Bank (1397–1494)		
1400					Paintings of Jan van Eyck (c. 1400–c. 1441)
				John Hus preaches in Bohemia (c. 1408–1415) Council of Constance (1414–1417) Hussite Revolt (1420–1434) *Imitation of Christ* (c. 1427)	
	Activity of Joan of Arc (1429–1431)			Council of Basel, defeat of conciliarism (1431–1449)	
	Rise of princes in Germany (c. 1450–c. 1500) Capture of Constantinople by Ottoman Turks (1453) Reassertion of royal power in France (c. 1453–c. 1513) Peace among northern Italian states (1454–1485) Wars of the Roses in England (1455–1485) Ivan III lays groundwork for Russian Empire (1462–1505) Marriage of Ferdinand and Isabella (1469) Strong Tudor dynasty in England (1485–1603)	Printing with movable type (c. 1450) Heavy artillery helps Turks capture Constantinople and French end Hundred Years' War (1453)			

CHAPTER 9

ROME'S THREE HEIRS: THE BYZANTINE, ISLAMIC, AND EARLY-MEDIEVAL WESTERN WORLDS

> Constantinople is a bustling city, and merchants come to it from all over, by sea or land, and there is none like it in the world except Baghdad, the great city of Islam. In Constantinople is the church of Santa Sophia, and the seat of the Pope of the Greeks, since the Greeks do not obey the Pope of Rome. There are also as many churches as there are days of the year. A quantity of wealth is brought to them from the islands, and the like of this wealth is not to be found in any other church in the world.
>
> —BENJAMIN OF TUDELA, *Travels*

> You have become the best community ever raised up for mankind, enjoining the right and forbidding the wrong, and having faith in God.
>
> —The Koran, III, 110

> He who ordains the fate of kingdoms and the march of events, the almighty Disposer, having destroyed one extraordinary image, that of the Romans, which had feet of iron, or even feet of clay, then raised up among the Franks the golden head of a second image, just as remarkable, in the person of the glorious Charlemagne.
>
> —A Monk of St. Gall

The successors of Rome

A NEW PERIOD in the history of Western civilizations began in the seventh century, when it became clear that there would no longer be a single empire ruling over all the territories bordering the Mediterranean. By about 700 C.E., in place of a united Rome, there were three successor civilizations that stood as rivals on different Mediterranean shores: the Byzantine, the Islamic, and the Western Christian. Each of these had its own language and distinctive forms of life. The Byzantine civilization, which descended directly from the Eastern Roman Empire, was Greek-speaking and dedicated to combining Roman governmental traditions with intense pursuit of the Christian faith. The Islamic civilization was Arabic-speaking and inspired in government as well as culture by the idealism of a dynamic new religion. Western Christian civilization in comparison to the others was a laggard. It was the least economically advanced and faced organizational weaknesses in both government and religion. But it did have some base of unity in Christianity and the Latin language, and would soon begin to find greater political and religious cohesiveness.

Reappraisal of the Byzantine and Islamic civilizations

Because the Western Christian civilization ultimately outstripped its rivals, Western writers until recently have tended to denigrate the Byzantine and Islamic civilizations as backward and even irrational. Of the three, however, the Western Christian was certainly the most backward from about the seventh to the eleventh centuries. For some four or five hundred years the West lived in the shadow of Constantinople and Mecca. Scholars are only now beginning to recognize the full measure of Byzantine and Islamic accomplishments. These greatly merit our attention both for their own sakes and because they influenced western European development in many direct and indirect ways.

The Byzantine Empire and Its Culture

The Byzantine achievement impressive despite weaknesses

Once dismissed by the historian Gibbon as "a tedious and uniform tale of weakness and misery," the story of Byzantine civilization is today recognized as a most interesting and impressive one. It is true that the Byzantine Empire was in many respects not very innovative; it was also continually beset by grave external threats and internal weaknesses. Nonetheless it managed to survive for a millennium. In fact the empire did not just survive, it frequently prospered and greatly influenced the world around it. Among many other achievements, it helped preserve ancient Greek thought, created magnificent works of art, and brought Christian culture to pagan peoples, above all the Slavs. Simply stated it was one of the most enduring and influential empires the world has ever known.

Problems of periodization in Byzantine history

It is impossible to date the beginning of Byzantine history with any precision because the Byzantine Empire was the uninterrupted successor of the Roman state. For this reason different historians prefer different beginnings. Some argue that "Byzantine" characteristics had already emerged in Roman history as a result of the easternizing policy of Diocletian; others assert that Byzantine history began when Constantine moved his capital from Rome to Constantinople, the city that subsequently became the center of the Byzantine world. (The old name for the site on which Constantinople was built was "Byzantium," from which we get the adjective "Byzantine"; it would be more accurate but cumbersome to say Constantinopolitine.) Diocletian and Constantine, however, continued to rule a united Roman Empire. As we have seen, as late as the sixth century, after the western part of the empire had fallen to the Germans, the Eastern Roman emperor Justinian thought of himself as an heir to Augustus and fought hard to win back the West. Justinian's reign was clearly an important turning point in the direction of Byzantine civilization because it saw the crystallization of new forms of thought and art

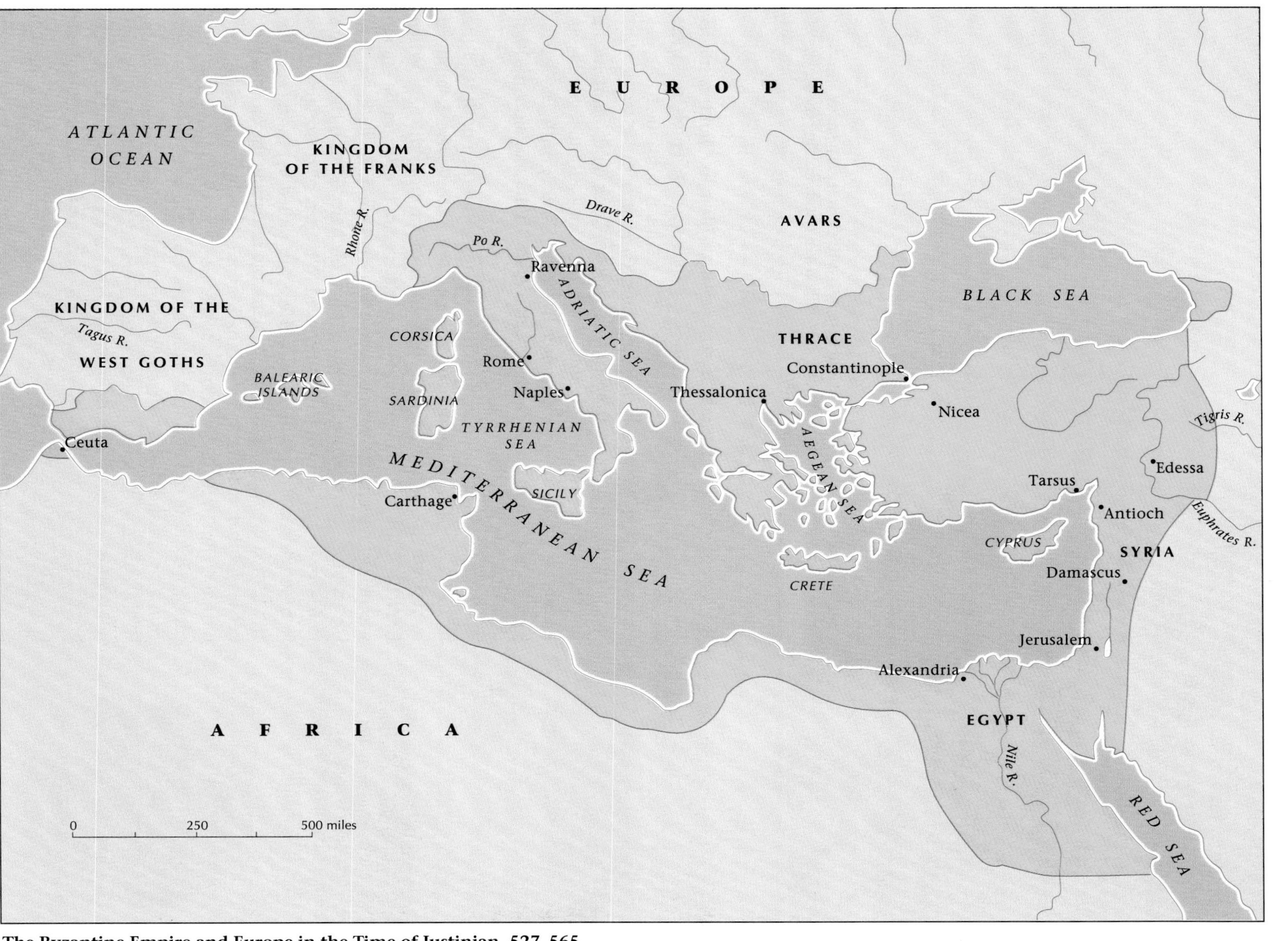

The Byzantine Empire and Europe in the Time of Justinian, 527–565

Byzantine Gold Cup, 6th–9th Century. The relief shows Constantinople personified as a queen holding the sceptre of imperial rule.

that can be considered more "Byzantine" than "Roman." But this still remains a matter of subjective emphasis: some scholars emphasize these newer forms, while others respond that Justinian continued to speak Latin and dreamed of restoring old Rome. Only after 610 did a new dynasty emerge that came from the East, spoke Greek, and maintained a fully Eastern or properly "Byzantine" policy. Hence although good arguments can be made for beginning Byzantine history with Diocletian, Constantine, or Justinian, we will begin here with the accession in 610 of the Emperor Heraclius.

It is also convenient to begin in 610 because from then until 1071 the main lines of Byzantine military and political history were determined by resistance against successive waves of invasion from the East. When Heraclius came to the throne the very existence of the Byzantine Empire was being challenged by the Persians, who had conquered almost all of the empire's Asian territories. As a symbol of their triumph the Persians in 614 even carried off the relic believed to be part of the original cross from Jerusalem. By enormous effort Heraclius rallied Byzantine strength and turned the tide, routing the Persians and retrieving the cross in 627. Persia was then reduced to subordination and Heraclius reigned in glory until 641. But in his last years new armies began to invade Byzantine territory, swarming out of hitherto placid Arabia. Inspired by the new religion of Islam and profiting from Byzantine exhaustion after the struggle with Persia, the Arabs made astonishingly rapid gains. By 650 they had taken most of the Byzantine territories that the Persians had occupied briefly in the early seventh century, had conquered all of Persia itself, and were making their way westward across North Africa. Having be-

The Byzantine Emperor Heraclius and His Son. Comparison to the coin of Trajan (p. 171) shows that a new style of civilization had emerged with much less attachment to naturalistic portraiture.

come a Mediterranean power, the Arabs also took to the sea. In 677 they tried to conquer Constantinople with a fleet. Failing that, they attempted to take the city again in 717 by means of a concerted land and sea operation.

Byzantine revival prior to the Battle of Manzikert

The Arab threat to Constantinople in 717 marked a new low in Byzantine fortunes, but the threat was countered by the Emperor Leo the Isaurian (717–741) with as much resolution as Heraclius had met the Persian threat with a century before. With the help of a secret incendiary device known as "Greek fire" (a mixture of sulphur, naphtha, and quicklime aimed at the enemy from the prows of ships) and great military ability, Leo was able to defeat the Arab forces on sea and land. Leo's relief of Constantinople in 717 was one of the most significant battles in European history, not just because it allowed the Byzantine Empire to endure for centuries more, but also because it helped to save the West: had the Islamic armies taken Constantinople there would have been little to stop them from sweeping through the rest of Europe. Over the next few decades the Byzantines were able to reconquer most of Asia Minor. This territory, together with Greece, became the heartland of their empire for the next three hundred years. A stalemate with the Islamic forces prevailed until the Byzantines were able to take the offensive against a decaying Islamic power in the second half of the tenth century. In that period—the greatest in Byzantine history—Byzantine troops reconquered most of Syria. But in the eleventh century a different Islamic people, the Seljuk Turks, cancelled out all the prior Byzantine gains. In 1071 the Seljuks annihilated a Byzantine army at Manzikert in Asia Minor, a stunning victory

Greek Fire

that allowed them to overrun the remaining Byzantine eastern provinces. Constantinople was now thrown back upon itself more or less as it had been in the days of Heraclius and Leo.

The Emperor John I (969–976) Being Crowned by Christ. Byzantine rulers characteristically used coins as objects of propaganda designed to show that their powers came to them supernaturally.

After Manzikert the Byzantine Empire managed to survive, but it never regained its earlier vigor. One major reason for this was the fact that, from 1071 until the final destruction of the empire in 1453, Byzantine fortunes were greatly complicated by the rise of western Europe. Hitherto the West had been far too weak to present any major challenge to Byzantium, but that situation changed entirely in the course of the eleventh century. In 1071, the same year that saw the victory of the Seljuks over the Byzantines in Asia Minor, westerners known as the Normans expelled the Byzantines from their last holdings in southern Italy. Despite this clear sign of Western enmity, in 1095 a Byzantine emperor named Alexius Comnenus issued a call for Western help against the Turks. He could hardly have made a worse mistake: his call helped inspire the Crusades, and the Crusades became a major cause for the fall of the Byzantine state. Westerners on the First Crusade did help the Byzantines win back Asia Minor, but they also carved out territories for themselves in Syria, which the Byzantines considered to be their own. As time went on frictions mounted and the westerners, now militarily superior, looked more and more upon Constantinople as a fruit ripe for the picking. In 1204 they finally picked it: Crusaders who should have been intent on conquering Jerusalem conquered Constantinople instead and sacked the city with ruthless ferocity. A greatly reduced Byzantine government was able to survive nearby and return to Constantinople in 1261, but thereafter the Byzantine state was an "empire" in name and recollection of past glories only. After 1261 it eked out a reduced existence in parts of Greece until 1453, when powerful Turkish successors to the Seljuks, the Ottomans, completed the Crusaders' work of destruction by conquering the last vestiges of the empire and taking Constantinople. Turks rule in Constantinople—now called Istanbul—even today.

Factors contributing to the stability of the Byzantine Empire: (1) occasional able rulers

That Constantinople was finally taken was no surprise. What is a cause for wonder is that the Byzantine state survived for so many centuries in the face of so many different hostile forces. This wonder becomes all the greater when it is recognized that the internal political history of the empire was exceedingly tumultuous. Because Byzantine rulers followed their late-Roman predecessors in claiming the powers of divinely appointed absolute monarchs, there was no way of opposing them other than by intrigue and violence. Hence Byzantine history was marked by repeated palace revolts; mutilations, murders, and blindings were almost commonplace. Byzantine politics became so famous for their behind-the-scenes complexity that we still use the word "Byzantine" to refer to highly complex and devious backstage machinations. Fortunately for the empire, some very able rulers did emerge from time to time to wield their untrammeled powers with efficiency, and, even more fortunately, a bureaucratic machinery continued to function during times of palace upheaval.

(2) Efficient bureaucratic administration

Efficient bureaucratic government indeed was one of the major elements of Byzantine success and longevity. The Byzantines could count on having an adequate supply of manpower for their bureaucracy because Byzantine civilization preserved and encouraged the practice of education for the laity. This was one of the major differences between the Byzantine East and the early Latin West: from about 600 to about 1200 there was practically no literate laity in Western Christendom, while lay literacy in the Byzantine East was the basis of governmental accomplishment. Byzantine officialdom regulated many aspects of life, far more than we would think proper today. Bureaucrats helped supervise education and religion and presided over all forms of economic endeavor. Urban officials in Constantinople, for example, regulated prices and wages, maintained systems of licensing, controlled exports, and enforced the observance of the Sabbath. What is more, they usually did this with comparative efficiency and did not stifle business initiative. Bureaucratic methods also helped regulate the army and navy, the courts, and the diplomatic service, endowing them with organizational strengths incomparable for their age.

(3) Firm economic base

Another explanation for Byzantine endurance was the comparatively sound economic base of the state until the eleventh century. As the historian Sir Steven Runciman has said, "if Byzantium owed her strength and security to the efficiency of her Services, it was her trade that enabled her to pay for them." While long-distance trade and urban life all but disappeared in the West for hundreds of years, commerce and cities continued to flourish in the Byzantine East. Above all, in the ninth and tenth centuries Constantinople was a vital trade emporium for Far Eastern luxury goods and Western raw materials. The empire also nurtured and protected its own industries, most notably that of silk-making, and it was renowned until the eleventh century for its stable gold and silver coinage. Among its great urban centers was not only Constantinople, which at times may have had a population of close to a million, but also in certain periods Antioch, and up until the end of Byzantine history the bustling cities of Thessalonica and Trebizond.

The significance of Byzantine agricultural history

Historians emphasize Byzantine trade and industry because these were so advanced for the time and provided most of the surplus wealth that supported the state. But agriculture was really at the heart of the Byzantine economy as it was of all premodern ones. The story of Byzantine agricultural history is mainly one of a struggle of small peasants to stay free of the encroachments of large estates owned by wealthy aristocrats and monasteries. Until the eleventh century the free peasantry just managed to maintain its existence with the help of state legislation, but after 1025 the aristocracy gained power in the government and began to transform the peasants into impoverished tenants. This had many unfortunate results, not the least of which was that the peasants became less interested in resisting the enemy. The defeat at Manzikert was the inevitable result. The destruction of the free peasantry was accompanied and followed in the last centuries of Byzantine history by foreign domination of

Byzantine trade. Primarily the Italian cities of Venice and Genoa established trading outposts and privileges within Byzantine realms after 1204, channeling off much of the wealth on which the state had previously relied. In this way the empire was defeated by the Venetians from within before it was destroyed by the Turks from without.

Preoccupation with religion

So far we have spoken about military campaigns, government, and economics as if they were at the center of Byzantine survival. Seen from hindsight they were, but what the Byzantines themselves cared about most was usually religion. Remarkable as it might seem, Byzantines fought over abstruse religious questions as vehemently as we today might argue about politics and sports—indeed more vehemently because the Byzantines were often willing to fight and even die over words in a religious creed. The intense preoccupation with questions of doctrine is well illustrated by the report of an early Byzantine writer who said that when he asked a baker for the price of bread, the answer came back, "the Father is greater than the Son," and when he asked whether his bath was ready, was told that "the Son proceeds from nothing." Understandably such zealousness could harm the state greatly during times of religious dissension, but it could also endow it with a powerful sense of confidence and mission during times of religious concord.

Imperial participation in religious controversies

Byzantine religious dissensions were greatly complicated by the fact that the emperors took an active role in them. Because the emperors carried great power in the life of the Church—emperors were sometimes deemed by churchmen to be "similar to God"—they exerted great influence in religious debates. Nonetheless, especially in the face of provincial separatism, rulers could never force all their subjects to believe what they did. Only after the loss of many eastern provinces and the refinement of doctrinal formulae did religious peace seem near in the eighth century. But then it was shattered for still another century by what is known as the *Iconoclastic Controversy.*

The religious rationale for Iconoclasm

The Iconoclasts were those who wished to prohibit the worship of icons—that is, images of Christ and the saints. Since the Iconoclastic movement was initiated by the Emperor Leo the Isaurian, and subsequently directed with even greater energy by his son Constantine V (740–775), historians have discerned in it different motives. One was certainly theological. The worship of images seemed to the Iconoclasts to smack of paganism. They believed that nothing made by human beings should be worshiped by them, that Christ was so divine that he could not be conceived of in terms of human art, and that the prohibition of worshiping "graven images" in the Ten Commandments (Exodus 20:4) placed the matter beyond dispute.

Political and financial motives

In addition to these theological points, there were probably other considerations. Since Leo the Isaurian was the emperor who saved Constantinople from the onslaught of Islam, and since Muslims zealously shunned images on the grounds that they were "the work of Satan" (Koran, V. 92), it has been argued that Leo's Iconoclastic policy was an attempt to answer one of Islam's greatest criticisms of Christianity and

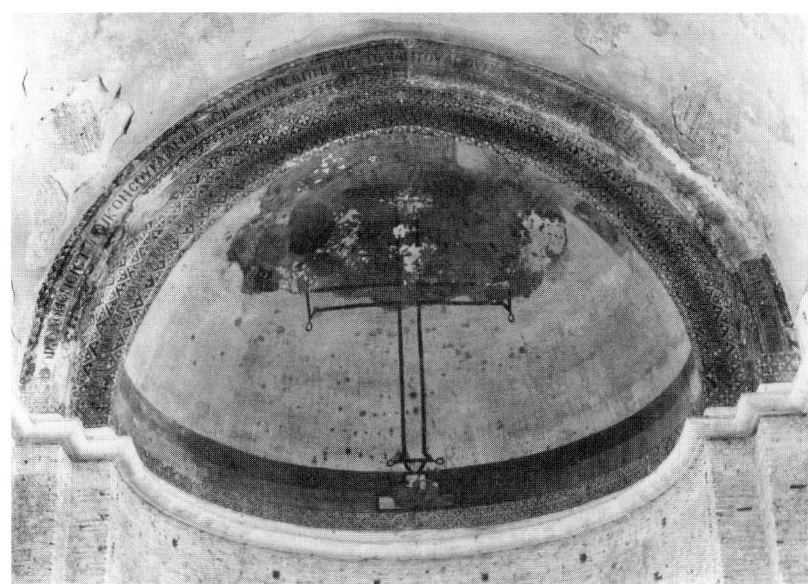

Iconoclasts' Cross. The Iconoclasts covered over beautiful apse mosaics with unadorned crosses. This example survives in St. Irene's Church, Istanbul, Turkey.

thereby deprive Islam of some of its appeal. There may also have been certain internal political and financial motives. By proclaiming a radical new religious movement the emperors may have wished to reassert their control over the Church and combat the growing strength of monasteries. As events turned out, the monasteries did rally behind the cause of images, and as a result, they were bitterly persecuted by Constantine V, who took the opportunity to appropriate much monastic wealth.

Significance of the Iconoclastic Controversy

The Iconoclastic Controversy was resolved in the ninth century by a return to the status quo, namely the worship of images, but the century of turmoil over the issue had some profound results. One was the destruction by imperial order of a large amount of religious art. Pre-eighth-century Byzantine religious art that survives today comes mostly from places like Italy or Palestine, which were beyond the easy reach of the Iconoclastic emperors. When we see how great this art is we can only lament the destruction of the rest. A second consequence of the controversy was the opening of a serious religious breach between East and West. The pope, who until the eighth century had usually been a close ally of the Byzantines, could not accept Iconoclasm for many reasons. The most important of these was that extreme Iconoclasm tended to question the cult of saints, and the claims of papal primacy were based on an assumed descent from St. Peter. Accordingly, the eighth-century popes combated Byzantine Iconoclasm and turned to the Frankish kings for support. This "about-face of the papacy" was both a major step in the worsening of East-West relations and a landmark in the history of western Europe.

Other results: (1) reaffirmation of tradition

In contrast to the above consequences of Iconoclasm's temporary victory, a major consequence of its defeat was the reassertion of some major traits of Byzantine religiosity, which from the ninth century until the end

Christ as Ruler of the Universe. A twelfth-century Byzantine mosaic from the Cathedral of Cefalù in Sicily. Although the Byzantines did not rule in Sicily in the twelfth century, the Norman rulers employed Byzantine workmen. Note the use of Greek—the Byzantine language—on the left-hand Bible page and Latin—the Norman language—on the right.

of Byzantine history remained predominant. One of these was the reemphasis of a faith in traditionalism. Even when Byzantines were experimenting in religious matters they consistently stated that they were only restating or developing the implications of tradition. Now, after centuries of turmoil, they abandoned experiment almost entirely and reaffirmed tradition more than ever. As one opponent of Iconoclasm said, "If an angel or an emperor announces to you a gospel other than the one you have received, close your ears." This view gave strength to Byzantine religion internally by ending controversy and heresy, and it helped it gain new adherents in the ninth and tenth centuries. But it also inhibited free speculation not just in religion but also in related intellectual matters.

(2) The triumph of Byzantine contemplative piety

Allied to this development was the triumph of Byzantine contemplative piety. Supporters defended the use of icons not on the grounds that they were meant to be worshiped for themselves but because they helped lead the mind from the material to the immaterial. The emphasis on contemplation as a road to religious enlightenment thereafter became the hallmark of Byzantine spirituality. While westerners did not by any means reject such a path, the typical Western saint was an activist who saw sin as a vice and sought salvation through good works. Byzantine theologians on the other hand saw sin more as ignorance and believed that salvation was to be found in illumination. This led to a certain religious passivity and mysticism in Eastern Christianity, which makes it seem different from Western varieties up to the present time.

Byzantine classicism

Since religion was so dominant in Byzantine life, certain secular aspects of Byzantine civilization often go unnoticed, but there are good reasons why some of these should not be forgotten. One is Byzantine cultivation of the classics. Commitment to Christianity by no means inhibited the

Byzantines from revering their ancient Greek heritage. Byzantine schools based their instruction on classical Greek literature to the degree that educated people could quote Homer more extensively than we today can quote Shakespeare. Byzantine scholars studied and commented on the philosophy of Plato and Aristotle, and Byzantine writers imitated the prose of Thucydides. Such dedicated classicism both enriched Byzantine intellectual and literary life, which is too often dismissed entirely by moderns because it generally lacked originality, and it helped preserve the Greek classics for later ages. The bulk of classical Greek literature that we have today survives only because it was copied by Byzantine scribes.

The education of women

Byzantine classicism was a product of an educational system for the laity that extended to the education of women as well as men. Given attitudes and practices in the contemporary Christian West and in Islam, Byzantine commitment to female education was truly unusual. Girls from aristocratic or prosperous families did not go to schools but were relatively well educated at home by private tutors. We are told, for example, of one Byzantine woman who could discourse like Plato or Pythagoras. The most famous Byzantine female intellectual was the Princess Anna Comnena, who described the deeds of her father Alexius in an urbane biography in which she copiously cited Homer and Euripides. In addition to such literary figures there were female doctors in the Byzantine Empire, a fact of note given their scarcity in Western society until recent times.

Byzantine architecture: the Church of Santa Sophia

Byzantine achievements in the realms of architecture and art are more familiar. The finest example of Byzantine architecture was the Church of Santa Sophia (Holy Wisdom), built at enormous cost in the sixth century. Although built before the date taken here as the beginning of Byzantine history, it was typically Byzantine in both its style and subsequent influence. Though designed by architects of Hellenic descent, it was vastly different from any Greek temple. Its purpose was not to express human pride in the power of the individual, but to symbolize the inward and spiritual character of the Christian religion. For this reason the architects gave little attention to the external appearance of the building. Nothing but plain brick covered with plaster was used for the exterior walls; there were no marble facings, graceful columns, or sculptured entablatures. The interior, however, was decorated with richly colored mosaics, gold leaf, colored marble columns, and bits of tinted glass set on edge to refract the rays of sunlight after the fashion of sparkling gems. To emphasize a sense of the miraculous, the building was constructed in such a way that light appeared not to come from the outside at all, but to be manufactured within.

Novel structural design

The structural design of Santa Sophia was something altogether new in the history of architecture. Its central feature was the application of the principle of the dome to a building of square shape. The church was designed in the form of a cross that would have a magnificent dome over its central square. The main problem was how to fit the round circumference of the dome to the square area it was supposed to cover. The solution was to have four great arches spring from pillars at the four corners of the square. The rim of the dome was then made to rest on the keystones of the

Santa Sophia. The greatest monument of Byzantine architecture. The four minarets were added after the fall of the Byzantine Empire, when the Turks turned the church into a mosque.

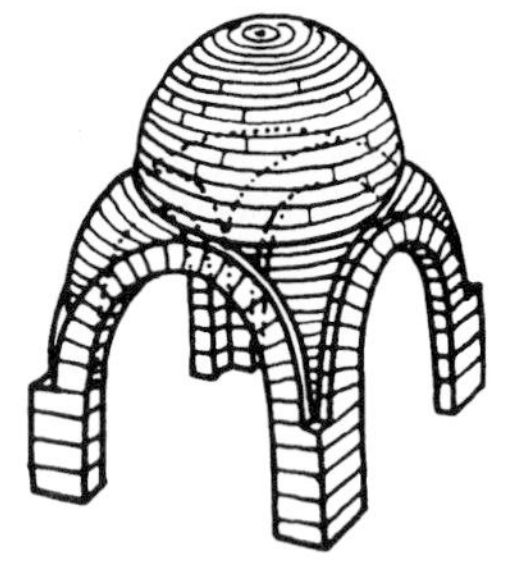

Diagram of Santa Sophia Dome

arches, with the curved triangular spaces between the arches filled in with masonry. The result was an architectural framework of marvelous strength, which at the same time made possible a style of imposing grandeur and even some delicacy of treatment. The great dome of Santa Sophia has a diameter of 107 feet and rises to a height of nearly 180 feet from the floor. So many windows are placed around its rim that the dome appears to have no support at all but to be suspended in midair.

Byzantine art

As in architecture, so in art the Byzantines profoundly altered the earlier Greek classical style. Byzantines excelled in ivory-carving, manuscript illumination, jewelry-making, and, above all, the creation of mosaics—that is, designs of pictures produced by fitting together small pieces of colored glass or stone. Human figures in these mosaics were usually distorted and elongated in a very unclassical fashion to create the impression of intense piety or extreme majesty. Most Byzantine art is marked by highly abstract, formal, and jewel-like qualities. For this reason many consider Byzantine artistic culture to be a model of timeless perfection. The modern poet W. B. Yeats expressed this point of view most eloquently when he wrote in his "Sailing to Byzantium" of artificial birds made by Byzantine goldsmiths ". . . to sing/To lords and ladies of Byzantium/Of what is past, or passing, or to come."

Conversion of Slavic peoples

Probably the single greatest testimony to the vitality of Byzantine civilization at its height was the conversion of many Slavic peoples, especially those of Russia. According to legend, which has a basic kernel of fact, an east-Slavic prince named Vladimir who ruled most of Russia and the Ukraine decided around 988 to abandon the paganism of his ancestors. Accordingly, he sent emissaries to report on the religious practices of Islam, Roman Catholicism, and Byzantine Christianity. When they returned to tell him that only among the Byzantines did God seem to "dwell among men," he promptly agreed to be baptized by a Byzantine missionary. The event was momentous because Russia thereupon became a cultural province of Byzantium. From then until the twentieth century Russia remained a bastion of the Eastern Orthodox religion.

Russian Icon. This painting from the early seventeenth century depicts an angel in a distinctly Byzantine style.

After Constantinople fell in 1453 Russians began to feel that they were chosen to carry on both the faith and the imperial mission of the fallen Byzantine Empire. Thus their ruler took the title of *tsar*—which simply means "caesar"—and Russians asserted that Moscow was "the third Rome": "Two Romes have fallen," said a Russian spokesman, "the third is still standing, and a fourth there shall not be." Such ideology helps explain in part the later growth of Russian imperialism. Byzantine traditions also may help explain the dominance of the ruler in the Russian state. Without question Byzantine stylistic principles influenced Russian religious art, and Byzantine ideas influenced the thought of modern Russia's greatest writers, Dostoevsky and Tolstoy.

Tense relations between Eastern and Western Christians

Unfortunately, just at the time when relations between Constantinople and Russia were solidifying, relations with the West were deteriorating to a point of no return. After the skirmishes of the Iconoclastic period relations between Eastern and Western Christians remained tense, partly because Constantinople resented Western claims (initiated by Charlemagne in 800) of creating a rival empire, but most of all because cultural and religious differences between the two were growing. From the Byzantine point of view westerners were uncouth and ignorant, while to western European eyes Byzantines were effeminate and prone to heresy. Once the West started to revive, it began to take the offensive against a weakened East in theory and practice. In 1054 extreme papal claims of primacy over the Eastern Church provoked a religious schism that has never been healed. Thereafter the Crusades drove home the dividing wedge.

Turks benefit from hostility between East and West

After the sack of Constantinople in 1204 Byzantine hatred of westerners became understandably intense. "Between us and them," one Byzantine wrote, "there is now a deep chasm: we do not have a single thought in common." Westerners called easterners "the dregs of the dregs . . . unworthy of the sun's light," while easterners called westerners the children of darkness, alluding to the fact that the sun sets in the West. The beneficiaries of this hatred were the Turks, who not only conquered Constantinople in 1453, but soon after conquered most of southeastern Europe up to Vienna.

The Byzantine contribution to Western civilization

In view of this sad history of hostility it is best to end our treatment of Byzantine civilization by recalling how much we owe to it. In simple physical terms the Byzantine Empire acted as a bulwark against Islam

St. Mark's Basilica, Venice. The most splendid example of Byzantine architecture in Italy.

from the seventh to the eleventh centuries, thus helping to preserve an independent West. If the Byzantines had not prospered and defended Europe, Western Christian civilization might well have been snuffed out. Then too we owe an enormous amount in cultural terms to Byzantine scholars who helped preserve classical Greek learning. The most famous moment of communication between Byzantine and western European scholars came during the Italian Renaissance, when Byzantines helped introduce Italian humanists to the works of Plato. But westerners had been learning from Byzantines even before then, and they continued to gain riches from Byzantine manuscripts until the sixteenth century. Similarly, Byzantine art exerted a great influence on the art of western Europe over a long period of time. To take only some of the most famous examples, St. Mark's Basilica in Venice was built in close imitation of the Byzantine style, and the art of such great Western painters as Giotto and El Greco owes much in different ways to Byzantine influences. Nor should we stop at listing influences because the great surviving monuments of Byzantine culture retain their imposing appeal in and of themselves. Travelers who view Byzantine mosaics in such cities as Ravenna and Palermo are continually awestruck; others who make their way to Istanbul still find Santa Sophia to be a marvel. In such jeweled beauty, then, the light from the Byzantine East, which once glowed so brightly, continues to shimmer.

The Flowering of Islam

The phenomenon of Islam

In contrast to Byzantine history, which has no clearly datable beginning but a definite end in 1453, the history of Islamic civilization has a clear point of origin, beginning with the career of Muhammad in the seventh century, but no end since Islam, Muhammad's religion, is still a major force in the modern world. Believers in Islam, known as Muslims, currently comprise about one-seventh of the global population: in their greatest concentrations they extend from Africa through the Middle East and the states of the former Soviet Union to South Asia and Indonesia. All these Muslims subscribe both to a common religion and a common way of life, for Islam has always demanded from its followers not just adherence to certain forms of worship but also adherence to set social and cultural norms. Indeed, more than Judaism or Christianity, Islam has been a great experiment in trying to build a worldwide society based on the fullest harmony between religious requirements and precepts for everyday existence. In practice, of course, that experiment has differed in its success and quality according to time and place, but it is still being tested, and it accounts for the fact that there remains an extraordinary sense of community between all Muslims regardless of race, language, and geographical distribution. In this section we will trace the early history of the Islamic experiment, with primary emphasis on its orientation toward the West. Nonetheless it must be remembered that Islam expanded in many directions and that it ultimately had as much influence on the history of Africa and South Asia as it did on that of Europe or western Asia.

Conditions in Arabia before the rise of Islam

Although Islam spread to many lands it was born in Arabia, so the story of its history must begin there. Arabia, a peninsula of deserts, had been so backward before the founding of Islam that the two dominant neighboring empires, the Roman and the Persian, had not deemed it worthwhile to extend their rule over Arabian territories. Most Arabs were Bedouins, wandering camel herders who lived off the milk of their animals and the produce, such as dates, that was grown in desert oases. In the second half of the sixth century there was a quickening of economic life owing to a shift in long-distance trade routes. The protracted wars between the Byzantine and Persian empires made Arabia a safer transit route for caravans going between Africa and Asia than were other alternatives, and some towns grew to direct and take advantage of this growth of trade. The most prominent of these was Mecca, which not only lay on the junction of major trade routes, but also had long been a local religious center. In Mecca was located the *Kabah,* a pilgrimage shrine that served as a central place of worship for many different Arabian clans and tribes. (Within the Kabah was the Black Stone, a meteorite worshiped as a miraculous relic by adherents of many different divinities.) The men who controlled this shrine and also directed the economic life of the Meccan area belonged to the tribe of Quraish, an aristocracy of traders and entrepreneurs who provided the area with whatever little government it knew.

The Kabah. It contains the black stone which was supposed to have been miraculously sent down from heaven, and rests in the courtyard of the great mosque in Mecca.

Muhammad proclaims a new faith

Muhammad, the founder of Islam, was born in Mecca to a family of Quraish about 570. Orphaned early in life, he entered the service of a rich widow whom he later married, thereby attaining financial security. Until middle age he lived as a prosperous trader, behaving little differently from his fellow townsmen, but around 610 he underwent a religious experience that changed the course of his life and ultimately that of a good part of the world. Although most Arabs until then had been polytheists who recognized at most the vague superiority of a more powerful god they called Allah, Muhammad in 610 believed he heard a voice from heaven tell him that there was no god but Allah alone. In other words, as the result of a conversion experience he became an uncompromising monotheist. Thereafter he received further messages that served as the basis for a new religion and that commanded him to accept the calling of "Prophet" to proclaim the monotheistic faith to the Quraish. At first he was not very successful in gaining converts beyond a limited circle, perhaps because the leading Quraish tribesmen believed that establishment of a new religion would deprive the Kabah, and therewith Mecca, of its central place in local worship. The town of Yathrib to the north, however, had no such concerns, and its representatives invited Muhammad to emigrate there so that he could serve as a neutral arbiter of local rivalries. In 622 Muhammad and his followers accepted the invitation. Because their migration—called in Arabic the *Hijrah* (or *Hegira*)—saw the beginning of an advance in Muhammad's fortunes, it is considered by Muslims to mark the beginning of their era: as Christians begin their era with the birth of Christ so Muslims begin their dating system with the Hijrah of 622.

The consolidation of Muhammad's religion

Muhammad changed the name of Yathrib to Medina (the "city of the Prophet") and quickly succeeded in establishing himself as ruler of the town. In the course of doing this he consciously began to organize his converts into a political as well as religious community. But he still needed to find some means of support for his original Meccan followers, and he also desired to wreak vengeance on the Quraish for not heeding his calls for conversion. Accordingly, he started leading his followers in raids on Quraish caravans traveling beyond Mecca. The Quraish endeavored to defend themselves, but after a few years Muhammad's band, fired by religious enthusiasm, succeeded in defeating them. In 630, after several desert battles, Muhammad entered Mecca in triumph. The Quraish thereupon submitted to the new faith and the Kabah was not only preserved but made the main shrine of Islam, as it remains today. With the taking of Mecca other tribes throughout Arabia in turn accepted the new faith. Thus, although Muhammad died in 632, he lived long enough to see the religion he had founded become a success.

The doctrines of Islam

The doctrines of Islam are straightforward. The word *islam* itself means "submission," and the faith of Islam called for absolute submission to God. Although the Arabic name for the one God is Allah, it is mistaken to believe that Muslims worship a god like Zeus or Jupiter who is merely the first among many: Allah for Muslims means the Creator God Almighty—the same omnipotent deity worshiped by Christians and Jews. Instead of saying, then, that Muslims believe "there is no god but Allah," it is more correct to say they believe that "there is no divinity but God." In keeping with this, Muslims believe that Muhammad himself was God's last and greatest prophet, but not that he was God himself. In addition to strict monotheism Muhammad taught above all that men and women must surrender themselves entirely to God because divine judgment was imminent. Mortals must make a fundamental choice about whether to begin a new life of divine service: if they decide in favor of this, God will guide them to blessedness, but if they do not, God will turn away from them and they will become irredeemably wicked. On judgment day the pious will be granted eternal life in a fleshly paradise of delights, but the damned will be sent to a realm of eternal fire and torture. The practical steps the believer can take are found in the Koran, the compilation of the revelations purportedly sent by God to Muhammad, and hence the definitive Islamic scripture. These steps include thorough dedication to moral rectitude and compassion, and fidelity to set religious observances—i.e., a regimen of prayers and fasts, pilgrimage to Mecca, and frequent recitation of parts of the Koran.

Judeo-Christian influence on Islam

The fact that much in the religion of Islam resembles Judaism and Christianity is not just coincidental; Muhammad was definitely influenced by the two earlier religions. (There were many Jews in Mecca and Medina; Christian thought was also known to Muhammad, although more indirectly.) Islam most resembles the two earlier religions in its strict

The Archangel Gabriel Brings Revelation to Muhammad. A much later Persian conception.

monotheism, its stress on personal morality and compassion, and its reliance on written, revealed scripture. Muhammad proclaimed the Koran as the ultimate source of religious authority but accepted both the Old and New Testaments as divinely inspired. From Christianity Muhammad seems to have derived his doctrines of the last judgment and the resurrection of the body with subsequent rewards and punishments, and his belief in angels (he thought that God's first message to him had been sent by the angel Gabriel). But although Muhammad accepted Jesus Christ as one of the greatest of a long line of prophets, he did not believe in Christ's divinity and laid claim to no miracles himself other than the writing of the Koran. He also preached a religion without sacraments or priests. For Muslims every believer has direct responsibility for living the life of the faith without intermediaries; instead of priests there are only religious scholars who may comment on problems of Islamic faith and law. Muslims are expected to pray together in mosques, but there is no such thing as a Muslim mass. The absence of clergy makes Islam more like Judaism, a similarity that is enhanced by Islamic stress on the inextricable connection between the religious and sociopolitical life of the divinely inspired community. But, unlike Judaism, Islam laid claim to a unique role in uniting the world as it started to spread far beyond the confines of Arabia.

The unification of Arabia after Muhammad: the caliphs

This move toward world influence began immediately upon Muhammad's death. Since he had made no provision for the future, and since the Arabs had no clear concept of political succession, it was unclear whether Muhammad's community would survive at all. But his closest followers, led by his father-in-law, Abu-Bakr, and a zealous early convert named Umar, quickly took the initiative by naming Abu-Bakr *caliph,* meaning "deputy of the Prophet." Thereafter, for about three hundred years, the caliph was to serve as the supreme religious and political leader of all

Muslims. Immediately after becoming caliph Abu-Bakr began a military campaign to subdue various Arabian tribes that had followed Muhammad but were not willing to accept his successor's authority. In the course of this thoroughly successful military action Abu-Bakr's forces began to spill northward over the borders of Arabia. Probably to their surprise they found that they met minimal resistance from Byzantine and Persian forces.

Arab expansion and conquests

Abu-Bakr died two years after his accession but was succeeded as caliph by Umar, who continued to direct the Arabian invasions of the neighboring empires. In the following years triumph was virtually uninterrupted. In 636 the Arabs routed a Byzantine army in Syria and then quickly swept over the entire area, occupying the leading cities of Antioch, Damascus, and Jerusalem; in 637 they destroyed the main army of the Persians and marched into the Persian capital of Ctesiphon. Once the Persian administrative center was taken, the Persian Empire offered little resistance: by 651 the Arabian conquest of the entire Persian realm was complete. Since Byzantium was centered around distant Constantinople, the Arabs were not similarly able to stop its imperial heart from beating, but they did quickly manage to deprive the Byzantine Empire of Egypt by 646 and then swept west across North Africa. In 711 they crossed from there into Spain and quickly took almost all of that area too. Thus within less than a century Islam had conquered all of ancient Persia and much of the old Roman world.

Reasons for the spread of Islam

How can we explain this prodigious expansion? The best approach is to see first what impelled the conquerors and then to see what circumstances

Exterior and Interior of the Dome of the Rock, Jerusalem. According to Muslim tradition, Muhammad made a miraculous journey to Jerusalem before his death and left a footprint in a rock. The mosque that was erected over the site in the seventh century is, after the Kabah, Islam's second-holiest shrine.

helped to ease their way. Contrary to widespread belief the early spread of Islam was not achieved through a religious crusade. At first the Arabs were not at all interested in converting other peoples: instead, they hoped that conquered populations would not convert so that they could maintain their own identity as a community of rulers and tax-gatherers. But although their motives for expansion were not religious, religious enthusiasm played a crucial role in making the hitherto unruly Arabs take orders from the caliph and in instilling a sense that they were carrying out the will of God. What really moved the Arabs out of the desert was the search for richer territory and booty, and what kept them moving ever farther was the ease of acquiring new wealth as they progressed.

Weakness of enemies

Fortunately for the Arabs their inspiration by Islam came just at the right time in terms of the weakness of their enemies. The Byzantines and Persians had become so exhausted by their long wars that they could hardly rally for a new effort. Moreover, Persian and Byzantine local populations were hostile to the financial demands made by their bureaucratic empires; also, in the Byzantine lands of Syria and Egypt "heretical" Christians were at odds with the persecuting orthodoxy of Constantinople. Because the Arabs did not demand conversion and exacted fewer taxes than the Byzantines and Persians, they were often welcomed as preferable to the old rulers. One Christian writer in Syria went so far as to say, "the God of vengeance delivered us out of the hands of the Romans [i.e., the Byzantine Empire] by means of the Arabs." For all these reasons Islam quickly spread over the territory between Egypt and Iran, and has been rooted there ever since.

Division between Shiites and Sunnites

While the Arabs were extending their conquests they ran into their first serious political divisions. In 644 the Caliph Umar died; he was replaced by one Uthman, a weak ruler who had the added drawback for many of belonging to the Umayyad family, a wealthy clan from Mecca that had not at first accepted Muhammad's call. Those dissatisfied with Uthman rallied around the Prophet's cousin and son-in-law Ali, whose blood, background, and warrior spirit made him seem a more appropriate leader of the cause. When Uthman was murdered in 656 by mutineers, Ali's partisans raised him up as caliph. But Uthman's powerful family and supporters were unwilling to accept Ali. In subsequent disturbances Ali was murdered and Uthman's party emerged triumphant. In 661 a member of the Umayyad family took over as caliph and that house ruled Islam until 750. Even then, however, Ali's followers did not accept defeat. As time went on they hardened into a minority religious party known as *Shiites* (*Shi'a* is Arabic for "party," or "faction"); this group insisted that only descendants of Ali could be caliphs or have any authority over the Muslim community. Those who stood instead for the actual historical development of the caliphate and became committed to its customs were called *Sunnites* (*Sunna* is Arabic for "religious custom"). The cleft between the two parties has been a lasting one in Islamic history. Often persecuted, Shiites developed great militancy and a deep sense of being the only true preservers of the faith. From time to time they were able to seize power in one or

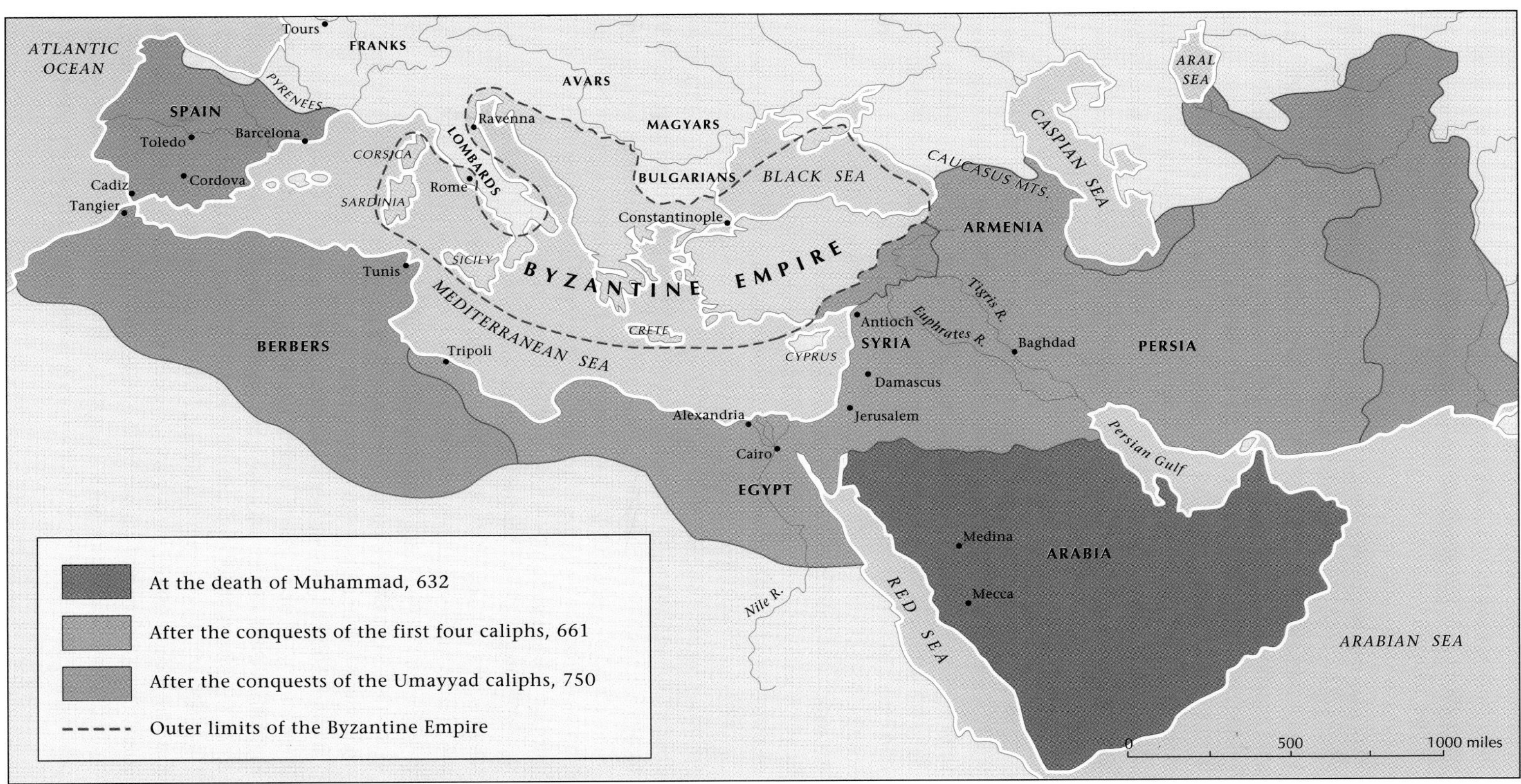

The Expansion of Islam

another area, but they never succeeded in converting the majority of Muslims. Today they rule in Iran and are very numerous in Iraq but comprise only about one-tenth of the worldwide population of Islam.

The Umayyads

The triumph of the Umayyads in 661 began a more settled period in the history of the caliphate, lasting until 945. During that time there were two major governing orientations: that represented by the rule of the Umayyads, and that represented by their successors, the Abbasids. The Umayyads centered their strength in the old Byzantine territories in Syria and continued to use local officials who were not Muslims for their administration. For these reasons the Umayyad caliphate appears to some extent like a Byzantine successor state. With their more Western orientation the Umayyads concentrated their energies on dominating the Mediterranean and conquering Constantinople. When their most massive attack on the Byzantine capital failed in 717, Umayyad strength was seriously weakened; it was only a matter of time before a new orientation would develop.

The Abbasids

This new perspective was represented by the takeover by a new family, the Abbasids, in 750. Their rule may be said to have stressed Persian more than Byzantine elements. Characteristic of this change was a shift in capitals, for the second Abbasid caliph built his new capital of Baghdad in Iraq, near the ruins of the old Persian capital, and even appropriated stones from the ruins. The Abbasids developed their own Muslim administration and imitated Persian absolutism. Abbasid caliphs ruthlessly cut down their enemies, surrounded themselves with elaborate court ceremonies, and lavishly patronized sophisticated literature. This is the world described in the *Arabian Nights,* a collection of stories of dazzling Oriental splendor written in Baghdad under the Abbasids. The dominating presence in those stories, Harun al-Rashid, actually reigned as caliph from 786 to 809 and behaved as extravagantly as he was described, tossing coins in the streets, passing out sumptuous gifts to his favorites and severe punishments to his enemies. From a Western point of view the Abbasid caliphate was of significance not just in creating legends and literature but also because its Eastern orientation took much pressure off the Mediterranean. The Byzantine state, accordingly, was able to revive, and the Franks in the West began to develop some strength of their own. (The greatest Frankish ruler, Charlemagne, maintained diplomatic relations with the caliphate of Harun al-Rashid, who patronizingly sent the much poorer westerner a gift of an elephant.)

Islamic political history after the fall of the Abbasid Empire

When Abbasid power began to decline in the tenth century there followed an extended period of decentralization. The major cause for growing Abbasid weakness was the gradual impoverishment of their primary economic base, the agricultural wealth of the Tigris-Euphrates basin. Their decline was further accelerated by the later Abbasids' practice of surrounding themselves with Turkish soldiers, who soon realized that they could take over actual power in the state. In 945 the Abbasid Empire fell apart when a Shiite tribe seized Baghdad. Thereafter the Abbasids became powerless figureheads until their caliphate was completely destroyed with the destruction of Baghdad by the Mongols in 1258. From 945 until the sixteenth century Islamic political life was marked by localism, with different petty rulers, most often Turkish, taking command in different areas. It was once thought that this decentralization also meant decay, but in fact Islamic civilization greatly prospered in the "middle period," above all from about 900 to about 1250, a time also when Islamic rule expanded into modern-day Turkey and India. Later, new Islamic empires developed, the leading one in the West being that of the Ottoman Turks, who controlled much of eastern Europe and western Asia from the fifteenth century until 1918. It is therefore entirely false to believe that Islamic history descended upon an ever-downward course sometime shortly after the reign of Harun al-Rashid.

The character of Islamic culture and society

For those who approach Islamic civilization with modern preconceptions, the greatest surprise is to realize that from the time of Muhammad until at least about 1500 Islamic culture and society was extraordinarily cosmopolitan and dynamic. Muhammad himself was not a desert Arab but a town-dweller and trader imbued with advanced ideals. Subsequently, Muslim culture became highly cosmopolitan for several reasons: it inherited the sophistication of Byzantium and Persia; it remained centered at the crossroads of long-distance trade between the Far East and West; and the prosperous town life in most Muslim territories counterbalanced agriculture. Because of the importance of trade there was much geographical mobility. Muhammad's teachings furthermore encouraged social mobility because the Koran stressed the equality of all Muslims. The result was that at the court of Baghdad, and later at those of the decentralized Muslim states, careers were open to those with talent. Since literacy was remarkably widespread—a rough estimate for around the year 1000 is 20 percent of all Muslim males—many could rise through education. Offices were seldom regarded as being hereditary and "new men" could arrive at the top by enterprise and skill. Muslims were also remarkably tolerant of other religions. As stated above, they rarely sought forced conversions, and they generally allowed a place within their own states for Jews and Christians, whom they accepted as "people of the book" because the Bible was seen as a precursor of the Koran. In keeping with this attitude of toleration an early caliph employed a Christian as his chief secretary, the Umayyads patronized a Christian who wrote poetry in Arabic, and Muslim Spain saw the greatest flowering of Jewish culture between ancient and modern times. The greatest fruit of this Jewish flowering was the work of Moses Maimonides (1135–1204), a profound religious thinker sometimes called "the second Moses," who wrote in both Hebrew and Arabic.

Women in Islam

There was one major exception to this rule of Muslim egalitarianism and tolerance: the treatment of women. Perhaps because social status was so fluid, successful men were extremely anxious to preserve and enhance their positions and their "honor." They could accomplish this by maintaining or expanding their worldly possessions, which included women. For a man's females to be most "valuable" to his status, their inviolability had to be assured. The Koran allowed a man to marry four wives, so women were at a premium, and married ones were segregated from other males. A prominent man would also have a number of female servants and concubines, and he kept all these women in a part of his residence called the harem, where they were guarded by eunuchs, i.e., castrated men. Within these enclaves women vied with each other for preeminence and engaged in intrigues to advance the fortunes of their children. Although large harems could be kept only by the wealthy, the system was imitated as far as possible by all classes. Based on the principle that women were chattel, these practices did much to debase women and to emphasize attitudes of domination in sexual life. Male homosexual relations were tolerated in upper-class society, yet they too were based on patterns of domination, usually that of a powerful adult over an adolescent.

Islamic religious life: the *ulama* and the *sufis*

There were two major Islamic avenues for devotion to the particularly religious life. One was that of the *ulama,* learned men who came closest to being like priests. Their job was to study and offer advice on all aspects of religion and religious law. Not surprisingly they usually stood for tradition and rigorous maintenance of the faith; most often they exerted great influence on the conduct of public life. But complementary to them were the *sufis,* religious mystics who might be equated with Christian monks were it not for the fact that they were not committed to celibacy and seldom withdrew from the life of the community. Sufis stressed contemplation and ecstasy as the ulama stressed religious law; they had no common program and in practice behaved very differently. Some sufis were "whirling dervishes," so known in the West because of their dances; others were *faqirs,* associated in the West with snake-charming in marketplaces; and others were quiet, meditative men who practiced no exotic rites. Sufis were usually organized into "brotherhoods," which did much to convert outlying areas such as Africa and India. Throughout the Islamic world sufism provided a channel for the most intense religious impulses. The ability of the ulama and sufis to coexist is in itself a remarkable index of Islamic cultural pluralism.

Islamic philosophy

More remarkable still is the fact that these two groups often coexisted with representatives of yet another worldview, students and practitioners of philosophy and science. Islamic philosophers were actually called *faylasufs* in Arabic because they were dedicated to the cultivation of what the Greeks had called *philosophia.* Islamic philosophy was based on the study of earlier Greek thought, above all the Aristotelian and Neoplatonic strains. Around the time when the philosophical schools were closed in Athens by order of the Emperor Justinian, Greek philosophers migrated east, and the works of Aristotle and others were translated into Syriac, a Semitic dialect. From that point of transmission Greek philosophy gradually entered the life of Islam and became cultivated by the class of *faylasufs,* who believed that the universe is rational and that a philosophical approach to life was the highest God-given calling. The *faylasufs'* profound knowledge of Aristotle can be seen, for example, in the fact that Avicenna (d. 1037), one of the greatest *faylasufs,* read practically all of

Aristotle's works in the Far Eastern town of Bukhara before he reached the age of eighteen.

The problem of reconciling Greek ideas with Islamic religion

The most serious problem faced by the *faylasufs* was that of reconciling Greek philosophy with Islamic religion because they followed their Greek sources in believing—in opposition to Islamic doctrine—that the world is eternal and that there is no immortality for the individual soul. Different *faylasufs* reacted to this problem in different ways. Of the three greatest, Al-Farabi (d. 950), who lived mainly in Baghdad, was least concerned by it; he taught that an enlightened elite could philosophize without being distracted by the binding common beliefs of the masses. Even so, he never attacked these beliefs, considering them necessary to hold society together.

Avicenna and Averroës

Unlike Al-Farabi, Avicenna, who was active farther east, taught a less rationalistic philosophy that came close in many points to sufi mysticism. (A later story held that Avicenna said of a sufi, "all I know, he sees," while the sufi replied, "all I see, he knows.") Finally, Averroës (1126–1198) of Cordova, in Spain, was a thoroughgoing Aristotelian who led two lives, one in private as an extreme rationalist and the other in public as a believer in the official faith, indeed even as an official censor. Averroës was the last really important Islamic philosopher: after him rationalism either blended into sufism, the direction pointed to by Avicenna, or became too constrained by religious orthodoxy to lead an independent existence. But in its heyday between about 850 and 1200 Islamic philosophy was far more advanced and sophisticated than anything found in either the Byzantine or Western Christian realms.

Islamic science; the practice of astrology

Before their decline Islamic *faylasufs* were as distinguished in studying natural science as they were in philosophical speculation. Usually the same men were both philosophers and scientists because they could not make a living by commenting on Aristotle (there were no universities in which to teach) but could rise to positions of wealth and power by practicing astrology and medicine. Astrology sounds to us today less like science than superstition, but among the Muslims it was more of an "applied science" intimately related to accurate astronomical observation. After an Islamic astrologer carefully studied and foretold the courses of the heavenly bodies, he would endeavor to apply his knowledge to the course of human events, particularly the fortunes of wealthy patrons. In order to account most simply for heavenly motions, some Muslims considered the possibilities that the earth rotates on its axis and revolves around the sun, but these theories were not accepted because they did not fit in with ancient preconceptions such as the assumption of circular planetary orbits. It was therefore not in these suggestions that Muslim astrologers later influenced the West, but rather in their extremely advanced observations and predictive tables that often went beyond the most careful work of the Greeks.

Islamic contributions to medicine

Islamic accomplishments in medicine were equally remarkable. *Faylasufs* serving as physicians appropriated the knowledge contained in the medical writings of the Hellenistic Age but were rarely content with that.

The Planetary Constellation of Andromeda as Visualized by the Muslims. This manuscript illumination executed in western Iran in 1009 retells the classical Greek myth by adding a traditional Bedouin Arabic symbol: two fish.

Avicenna discovered the contagious nature of tuberculosis, described pleurisy and several varieties of nervous ailments, and pointed out that disease can be spread through contamination of water and soil. His chief medical writing, the *Canon of Medicine,* was accepted in Europe as authoritative until late in the seventeenth century. Avicenna's older contemporary, Rhazes (865–925), was the greatest clinical physician of the medieval world. His major achievement was the discovery of the difference between measles and smallpox. Other Islamic physicians discovered the value of cauterization and of styptic agents, diagnosed cancer of the stomach, prescribed antidotes for cases of poisoning, and made notable progress in treating diseases of the eyes. In addition, they recognized the infectious character of bubonic plague, pointing out that it could be transmitted by clothes. Finally, the Muslims excelled over all other medieval peoples in the organization of hospitals and in the control of medical practice. There were at least thirty-four great hospitals located in the principal cities of Persia, Syria, and Egypt, which appear to have been organized in a strikingly modern fashion. Each had wards for particular cases, a dispensary, and a library. The chief physicians and surgeons lectured to the students and graduates, examined them, and issued licenses to practice. Even the owners of leeches, who in most cases were also barbers, had to submit them for inspection at regular intervals.

Optics, chemistry, and mathematics

Other great Islamic scientific achievements were in optics, chemistry, and mathematics. Islamic physicists founded the science of optics and drew a number of significant conclusions regarding the theory of magnifying lenses and the velocity, transmission, and refraction of light. Islamic chemistry was an outgrowth of alchemy, an invention of the Hellenistic Greeks, the system of belief that was based upon the principle that all metals were the same in essence, and that baser metals could therefore be transmuted into gold if only the right instrument, the philosopher's stone, could be found. But the efforts of scientists in this field were by no means confined to this fruitless quest; some even denied the whole theory of transmutation of metals. As a result of experiments by Muslim scientists, various new substances and compounds were discovered, among them carbonate of soda, alum, borax, nitrate of silver, saltpeter, and nitric and sulphuric acids. In addition, Islamic scientists were the first to describe the chemical processes of distillation, filtration, and sublimation. In mathematics Islam's greatest accomplishment was to unite the geometry of the Greeks with the number science of the Hindus. Borrowing what westerners know as "Arabic numerals," including the zero, from the Hindus, Islamic mathematicians were able to develop an arithmetic based on the decimal system and also make advances in algebra (itself an Arabic word). Building upon Greek geometry with reference to heavenly motions, they made great progress in spherical trigonometry. Thus they brought together and advanced all the areas of mathematical knowledge that would later be further developed in the Christian West.

Islamic poets

In addition to its philosophers and scientists Islam had its poets too. The primitive Arabs themselves had excelled in writing poetry, and literary accomplishment became recognized as a way to distinguish oneself at court. Probably the greatest of Islamic poets were the Persians (who wrote in their own language), of whom the best known in the West is Umar Khayyam (d. 1123) because his *Rubaiyat* was turned into a popular English poem by the Victorian Edward Fitzgerald. Although Fitzgerald's translation distorts much, Umar's hedonism ("a jug of wine, a loaf of bread—and thou") shows us that by no means were all Muslims dour puritans. Actually Umar's poetry was excelled by the works of Sadi (1193–1292) and Hafiz (d. 1389). And far from Persia lush poetry was cultivated as well in the courts of Muslim Spain. This poetry too was by no means inhibited, as can be seen from lines like "such was my kissing, such my sucking of his mouth/that he was almost made toothless."

The eclectic art of the Muslims

In their artistic endeavors Muslims were highly eclectic. Their main source of inspiration came from the art of Byzantium and Persia. The former contributed many of the structural features of Islamic architecture, especially the dome, the column, and the arch. Persian influence was probably responsible for the intricate, nonnaturalistic designs that were used as decorative motifs in practically all of the arts. From both Persia

The Court of the Lions in the Alhambra, Granada, Spain. The palace-fortress of the Alhambra is one of the finest monuments of the Islamic architectural style. Notable are the graceful columns, the horseshoe arches, and the delicate tracery in stone that surmounts the arches.

and Byzantium came the tendency to subordinate form to rich and sensuous color. Architecture was the most important of the Islamic arts; the development of both painting and sculpture was inhibited by religious prejudice against representation of the human form. By no means were all of the examples of this architecture mosques; many were palaces, schools, libraries, private dwellings, and hospitals. Indeed, Islamic architecture had a much more secular character than any in medieval Europe. Among its principal elements were bulbous domes, minarets, horseshoe arches, and twisted columns, together with the use of tracery in stone, alternating stripes of black and white, mosaics, and Arabic script as decorative devices. As in the Byzantine style, comparatively little attention was given to exterior ornamentation. The so-called minor arts of the Muslims included the weaving of gorgeous pile carpets and rugs, magnificent leather tooling, and the making of brocaded silks and tapestries, inlaid metalwork, enameled glassware, and painted pottery. Most of the products of these arts were embellished with complicated patterns of interlacing geometric designs, plants and fruits and flowers, Arabic script, and fantastic animal figures. In general, art laid particular emphasis on pure visual design. Separated from any role in religious teaching, it became highly abstract and nonrepresentational. For these reasons Islamic art often seems more secular and "modern" than any other art of premodern times.

The economic development of the Islamic world: (1) commerce

The economic life of the Islamic world varied greatly according to time and place, but underdevelopment was certainly not one of its primary characteristics. On the contrary, in the central areas of Islamic civilization from the first Arab conquests until about the fourteenth century mercan-

Interior of the Great Mosque at Cordova, Spain. This splendid specimen of Moorish architecture gives an excellent view of the cusped arches and alternating stripes of black and white so commonly used by Islamic architects.

tile life was extraordinarily advanced. The principal reason for this was that the Arabs inherited in Syria and Persia an area that was already marked by an enterprising urban culture and that was at the crossroads of the world, lying on the major trade routes between Africa, Europe, India, and China. Islamic traders and entrepreneurs built venturesomely on these earlier foundations. Muslim merchants penetrated into southern Russia and even into the equatorial regions of Africa, while caravans of thousands of camels traveled to the gates of India and China. (The Muslims used camels as pack animals instead of building roads and drawing wheeled carts.) Ships from Islam established new routes across the Indian Ocean, the Persian Gulf, and the Caspian Sea. For periods of time Islamic ships also dominated parts of the Mediterranean. Indeed, one reason for subsequent Islamic decline was that the Western Christians took hold of the Mediterranean in the eleventh and twelfth centuries and wrested control of the Indian Ocean in the sixteenth century.

(2) Industry

The great Islamic expansion of commerce would scarcely have been possible without a corresponding development of industry. It was the ability of the people of one region to turn their natural resources into finished products for sale to other regions that provided a basis for a large part of the trade. Nearly every one of the great cities specialized in some particular variety of manufacture. Mosul, in Syria, was a center of the manufacture of cotton cloth; Baghdad specialized in glassware, jewelry, pottery, and silks; Damascus was famous for its fine steel and for its "damask" or woven-figured silk; Morocco was noted for the manufacture of leather; and Toledo, in Spain, for its excellent swords. The products of these cities did not exhaust the list of manufactures. Drugs, perfumes, carpets, tapestries, brocades, woolens, satins, metal items, and a host of other products were turned out by the craftsmen of many cities. From the Chinese the Muslims learned the art of papermaking, and the products of that industry were in great demand, not only within the empire itself but in Europe as well.

Islamic economic influence on the West

In all the areas we have reviewed Islamic civilization so overshadowed that of the Christian West until about the twelfth century that there can be no comparison. When the West did move forward it was able to do so partly because of what it learned from Islam. In the economic sphere westerners absorbed many accomplishments of Islamic technology, such as irrigation techniques, the raising of new crops, papermaking, and the distillation of alcohol. The extent of our debt to Islamic economic influence is well mirrored in the large number of common English words that were originally of Arabic or Persian origin. Among these are traffic, tariff, magazine, alcohol, muslin, orange, lemon, alfalfa, saffron, sugar, syrup, and musk. (Our word "admiral" also comes from the Arabic—in this case deriving from the title of *emir.*)

Intellectual and scientific contributions

The West was as much indebted to Islam in intellectual and scientific as in economic life. In those areas, too, borrowed words tell some of the story: algebra, cipher, zero, nadir, amalgam, alembic, alchemy, alkali, soda, almanac, and names of many stars such as Aldebaran and Betelgeuse. Islamic civilization both preserved and expanded Greek philosophical and scientific knowledge when such knowledge was almost entirely forgotten in the West. All the important Greek scientific works surviving from ancient times were translated into Arabic, and most of these in turn were translated in the medieval West from Arabic into Latin. Above all, the preservation and interpretation of the works of Aristotle was one of Islam's most enduring accomplishments. Not only was Aristotle first reacquired in the West by means of the Arabic translations, but Aristotle was interpreted with Islamic help, above all that of Averroës, whose prestige was so great that he was simply called "the Commentator" by medieval Western writers. Of course Arabic numerals, too, rank as a tremendously important intellectual legacy, as anyone will discover by trying to balance a checkbook with Roman ones.

The shaping of a cultural unity in the early-medieval West

Aside from all these specific contributions, the civilization of Islam probably had its greatest influence on the West merely by standing as a powerful rival and spur to the imagination. Byzantine civilization was at once too closely related to the Christian West and too weak to serve this function. Westerners usually, for right or wrong, looked down on the Byzantine Greeks, but they more often respected and feared the Muslims. And right they were as well, for Islamic civilization at its zenith (to use another Arabic word) was surely one of the world's greatest. Though loosely organized, it united peoples as diverse as Arabs, Persians, Turks, various African tribes, and Hindus by means of a great religion and common institutions. Unity within multiplicity was an Islamic hallmark, which created both a splendid, diverse society and a splendid legacy of original discoveries and achievements.

Christ and the Apostles. A German manuscript illumination from the tenth century showing Christ appointing the apostles to become "princes over all the earth." The leader of the apostles is Peter, as shown by the letters "PETRVS" on the staff.

Western Christian Civilization in the Early Middle Ages

Western Europeans in the Early Middle Ages (the period between about 600 and 1050) were so backward in comparison to their Byzantine and Islamic neighbors that a tenth-century Arabic geographer could write of them that "they have large bodies, gross natures, harsh manners, and dull intellects . . . those who live farthest north are particularly stupid, gross, and brutish." Material conditions throughout this period were so primitive that one can almost speak of five centuries of camping out. Yet new and promising patterns were definitely taking shape. Above all, a new center of civilization was emerging in the North Atlantic region. Around 800 the Frankish monarchy, based in agriculturally rich northwestern Europe, managed to create a western European empire in alliance with the Western Christian Church. Although this empire did not last long, it still managed to hew out a new Western cultural unity that was to be an important building block for the future.

Decorative Cross. Lombard work from the seventh century.

The kingdom of the Franks: the Merovingian period

Once the Eastern Romans under Justinian had destroyed the Ostrogothic and Vandal kingdoms in Italy and Africa, and the Arabs had eliminated the Visigothic kingdom in Spain, the Frankish rulers in Gaul remained as the major surviving barbarian power in western Europe. But it took about two centuries before they began to exercise their full hegemony. The founder of the Frankish state was the brutal and wily chieftain Clovis, who conquered most of modern-day France and Belgium around 500 and cleverly converted to Western Catholic Christianity, the religion of the local bishops and indigenous population. Clovis founded the Merovingian dynasty (so called from Merovech, the founder of the family to which he belonged). He did not, however, pass on a united realm but followed the typical barbarian custom of dividing up his kingdom among his sons. More or less without interruption for the next two hundred years sons fought sons for a larger share of the Merovingian inheritance. Toward the end of that period the line also began to degenerate, and numerous so-called do-nothing kings left their government and fighting to their chief ministers, known as "mayors of the palace." Throughout this era, one of the darkest in the recorded history of Europe, trade contracted, towns declined, literacy was almost forgotten, and violence was endemic. Minimal agricultural self-sufficiency coexisted with the rule of the battle-ax.

Largely unnoticed, however, some hope for the future was coalescing around the institutions of the Roman papacy and Benedictine monasticism. The architect of a new western European religious policy that was based on an alliance between these two institutions was Pope Gregory I (590–604),* known as St. Gregory the Great. Until his time the Roman popes were generally subordinate to the emperors in Constantinople and to the greater religious prestige of the Christian East, but Gregory sought to counteract this situation by creating a more autonomous, Western-oriented Latin Church. This he tried to do in many ways. As a theologian—the fourth great "Latin father" of the Church—he built upon the work of his three predecessors, Jerome, Ambrose, and especially Augustine, in articulating a theology that had its own distinct characteristics. Among these were emphasis on the idea of penance and the concept of purgatory as a place for purification before admission into heaven. (Western belief in purgatory was thereafter to become one of the major differences in the dogmas of the Eastern and Western Churches.) In addition to his theological work, Gregory pioneered in the writing of a simplified unadorned Latin prose that corresponded to the actual spoken language of his contemporaries, and presided over the creation of a powerful Latin liturgy. If Gregory did not actually invent the "Gregorian chant," it was under his impetus that this new plainsong—later a central part of the Roman Catholic ritual—developed. All of these innovations helped to make the Christian West religiously and culturally more independent of the Greek-speaking East than it had ever been before.

Pope Gregory the Great. In this tenth-century German ivory panel the pope is receiving inspiration from the Holy Spirit in the form of a dove.

Pope Gregory's religious policies

Gregory the Great was as much a statesman as he was a theologian and shaper of Latin. Within Italy he assured the physical survival of the papacy in the face of the barbarian Lombard threat of his day by clever diplomacy and expert management of papal landed estates. He also began to reemphasize earlier claims of papal primacy, especially over Western bishops, that were in danger of being forgotten. Above all, he patronized the order of Benedictine monks and used them to help evangelize new Western territories. Gregory himself had been a Benedictine—perhaps the first Benedictine monk to become pope—and he wrote the standard life of St. Benedict. Because the Benedictine order was still very young and the times were turbulent, Gregory's patronage helped the order to survive and later to become for centuries the only monastic order in the West. In return the pope could profit from using the Benedictines to carry out special projects. The most significant of these was the conversion of Anglo-Saxon England to Christianity. This was a long-term project that took about a century to complete, but its great result was that it left a Christian outpost to the far northwest that was thoroughly loyal to the papacy and that would soon help to bring together the papacy and the Frankish state. Gregory the Great himself did not live to see that union, but it was his policy of invigorating the Western Church that most helped to bring it about.

* Here, and throughout, the dates following a pope's name refer to the dates of his pontificate.

Book Cover. The cover of a gospel book encrusted with jewels and ivory cameos presented by Pope Gregory the Great to a Lombard queen around the year 600.

Factors in the increasing stability of Frankish Gaul

Around 700, when the Benedictines were completing their conversion of England, the outlook for Frankish Gaul was becoming somewhat brighter. The most profound reason for this was that the long, troubled period of transition between the ancient and medieval worlds was finally coming to an end. The ancient Roman civilization of cities and Mediterranean trade was in its last gasps in Gaul in the time after Clovis. Then, when the Arabs conquered the southern Mediterranean shore and took to the sea in the seventh century, northwestern Europe was finally thrown back upon itself and forced to look away from the Mediterranean. In fact the lands of the north—modern-day northern France, the Low Countries, Germany, and England—were extremely fertile; with adequate farming implements they could yield great natural wealth. Given the proper circumstances, a new power could emerge in the north to make the most of a new pattern of life based predominantly on agrarianism instead of urban commerce and Mediterranean trade. Around 700 that is exactly what happened in Merovingian Gaul.

Charles Martel's alliance with the Church

The proper circumstances were the triumph of a succession of able rulers and their alliance with the Church. In 687 an energetic Merovingian mayor of the palace, Pepin of Heristal, managed to unite all the Frankish lands under his rule and build a new power base for his own family in the region of Belgium and the Rhine. He was succeeded by his aggressive son, Charles Martel ("the Hammer"), who is sometimes considered a second founder of the Frankish state. Charles's claim to this title is twofold. First, in 732 he turned back a Muslim force from Spain at the Battle of Tours, some 150 miles from Paris. Although the Muslim contingent was not a real army but merely a marauding band, the incursion was the high-water mark of their progress toward the northwest, and Charles's victory won him great prestige. Equally important, around the end of his reign Charles began to develop an alliance with the Church, particularly with the Benedictines of England. Having finished most of the conversion work on their island, the Benedictines, under their idealistic leader St. Boniface, were moving across the English Channel in an attempt to convert central Germany. Charles Martel realized that he and they had common interests, for after he had guarded his southern flank against the Muslims he was seeking to direct Frankish expansion eastward in the direction of Germany. Missionary work and Frankish expansion could go hand in hand, so Charles offered St. Boniface and his Benedictines material aid in return for their support of his territorial aims.

Pepin the Short takes the royal title

Once allied with the Franks, St. Boniface provided further service in the next reign in contributing to one of the most momentous events in Western history. Charles Martel had never assumed the royal title, but his son, Pepin the Short, wished to take it. Even though Pepin and not the reigning "do-nothing king" was the real power, Pepin needed the prestige of the Church for supporting a change in dynasties. Fortunately for him the times were highly propitious for obtaining Church support. St. Boniface supported Pepin because the young ruler continued his father's policy of collaborating with the Benedictines in Germany. And Boniface had great influence in Rome because the Anglo-Saxon Benedictines had remained in close touch with the papacy since the time of Gregory the Great.

The "about-face" of the papacy

The papacy was now fully prepared to cast its own lots with a strong Frankish ruler because it was in the midst of a bitter fight with the Byzantine emperors over Iconoclasm. The Byzantines until then had offered papal territories in Italy some protection against the Lombards, but the increasingly powerful Franks were now fully able to take over that role. The papacy accordingly made an epochal about-face, turning once and for all to the West. In 750 the pope encouraged Pepin to depose the Merovingian figurehead, and in 751 St. Boniface, acting as papal emissary, anointed Pepin as a divinely sanctioned king. Thus the Frankish monarchy attained a spiritual mandate and was fully integrated into the papal-Benedictine orbit. Shortly afterward Pepin paid his debt to the pope by conquering the Lombards in Italy. The West was now achieving its own unity based on the Frankish state and the Latin Church, not coincidentally just at the time when the Abbasid caliphate was being founded in the East and the Byzantines were going their own fully Greek way.

Charlemagne and territorial expansion

The ultimate consolidation of the new pattern took place in the reign of Pepin's son, Carolus Magnus or Charlemagne (768–814), from whom the new dynasty takes its name of "Carolingian." Without question

Charlemagne ranks as one of the most important rulers of the whole medieval period. Had it been possible to ask him what his greatest accomplishment was, he almost certainly would have replied that it lay in greatly increasing the Frankish realm. Except for the English, there was scarcely a people of western Europe against whom he did not fight. Most of his campaigns were successful; he annexed the greater part of central Europe and northern and central Italy to the Frankish domain. To rule this vast area he bestowed all the powers of local government upon his own appointees, called counts, and tried to remain in control of them by sending representatives of the court to observe them. Among the counts' many duties were the administration of justice and the raising of armies. Although Charlemagne's system in practice was far from perfect, it led to the best government that Europe had seen since the Romans. Because of the military triumphs and internal peace of his reign, Charlemagne was long remembered and revered as a western European folk hero.

Charlemagne. A silver penny struck between 804 and 814 in Mainz (as indicated by the letter M at the bottom) showing Charlemagne in a highly stylized fashion as emperor with Roman military cloak and laurel. The inscription reads KAROLVS IMP AVG (Charles, Emperor, Augustus). See p. 171 for the variety of late-Roman coin portraiture that must have served as the Carolingian minter's model.

Primarily to aid his territorial expansion and help administer his realm Charlemagne presided over a revival of learning known as the "Carolingian Renaissance." Charlemagne extended his rule into Germany in the name of Christianity, but in order to proselytize he needed educated monks and priests. More than that, in order to administer his far-flung territories he needed at least a few people who could read and write. Amazing as it may seem to us, at first hardly any people in his entire realm were literate, so thoroughly had the rudiments of learning been forgotten since the decay of Roman city life. Only in Anglo-Saxon England had literacy been cultivated by the Benedictine monks. The reason for this was that the Anglo-Saxons spoke a form of German but the monks needed to learn Latin in order to say their offices and study the Bible. Since they knew no Latin to begin with they had to go about learning it by a very self-conscious program of studies. The greatest Anglo-Saxon Benedictine scholar before Charlemagne's time was the Venerable Bede (d. 735), whose *History of the English Church and People,* written in Latin, was one of the best historical writings of the early-medieval period and can still be read with pleasure. When Charlemagne came to the throne he invited the Anglo-Saxon Benedictine Alcuin—a student of one of Bede's students—to direct a revival of studies on the Continent. With Charlemagne's active support Alcuin helped establish new schools to teach reading, directed the copying and correcting of important Latin works, including many Roman classics, and inspired the formulation of a new clear handwriting that is the ancestor of our modern "Roman" print. These were the greatest achievements of the Carolingian Renaissance, which stressed practicality rather than original literary or intellectual endeavors. Thoroughly unpretentious as they were, they established a bridgehead for literacy on the Continent which thereafter would never be completely lost. They also helped to preserve Latin literature, and they made the Latin language the language of state and diplomacy for all of western Europe, as it remained until comparatively recent times.

The Carolingian Renaissance

The climax of Charlemagne's career came in 800 when he was crowned emperor on Christmas Day in Rome by the pope. Historians continue to

Carolingian Handwriting. Even the untrained reader has little difficulty in reading this excerpt from a Carolingian manuscript. For example, the first two words in the heading read "Incipit Liber," and the two words below them "Haec Hannibal."

debate whether this was Charlemagne's or the pope's idea, but there is no doubt that the pope did not gain any immediate power from it. Once the Franks ruled Italy they came to dominate the papacy, and indeed the whole Church, to such a degree that by 800 the pope was very close to being Charlemagne's puppet. Charlemagne did not gain any actual new power by taking the imperial title either, but the significance of the event is nonetheless great. Up until 800 the only emperor ruled in Constantinople and could lay claim to being the direct heir of Augustus. Although the Byzantines had lost most of their interest in the West, they still continued to regard it vaguely as an outlying province and were actively opposed to any westerner calling himself emperor. Charlemagne's assumption of the title was virtually a declaration of Western self-confidence and independence. Since Charlemagne's vast realm was fully as large as that of the Byzantines, had great reserves of agricultural wealth, and was defining its own culture based on Western Christianity and the Latin linguistic tradition, the claim to empire was largely justified. More than that, it was never forgotten. Both for its symbolism and for its contribution toward giving westerners a sense of unity and purpose it was a major landmark on the road to the making of a great western Europe.

Charlemagne's coronation as emperor

Although the claim to empire was bold and memorable, Charlemagne's actual empire disintegrated quickly after his death for many reasons. The simplest was that hardly any of his successors were as competent and decisive as he was. In order to rule an empire in those still

The collapse of the Carolingian Empire

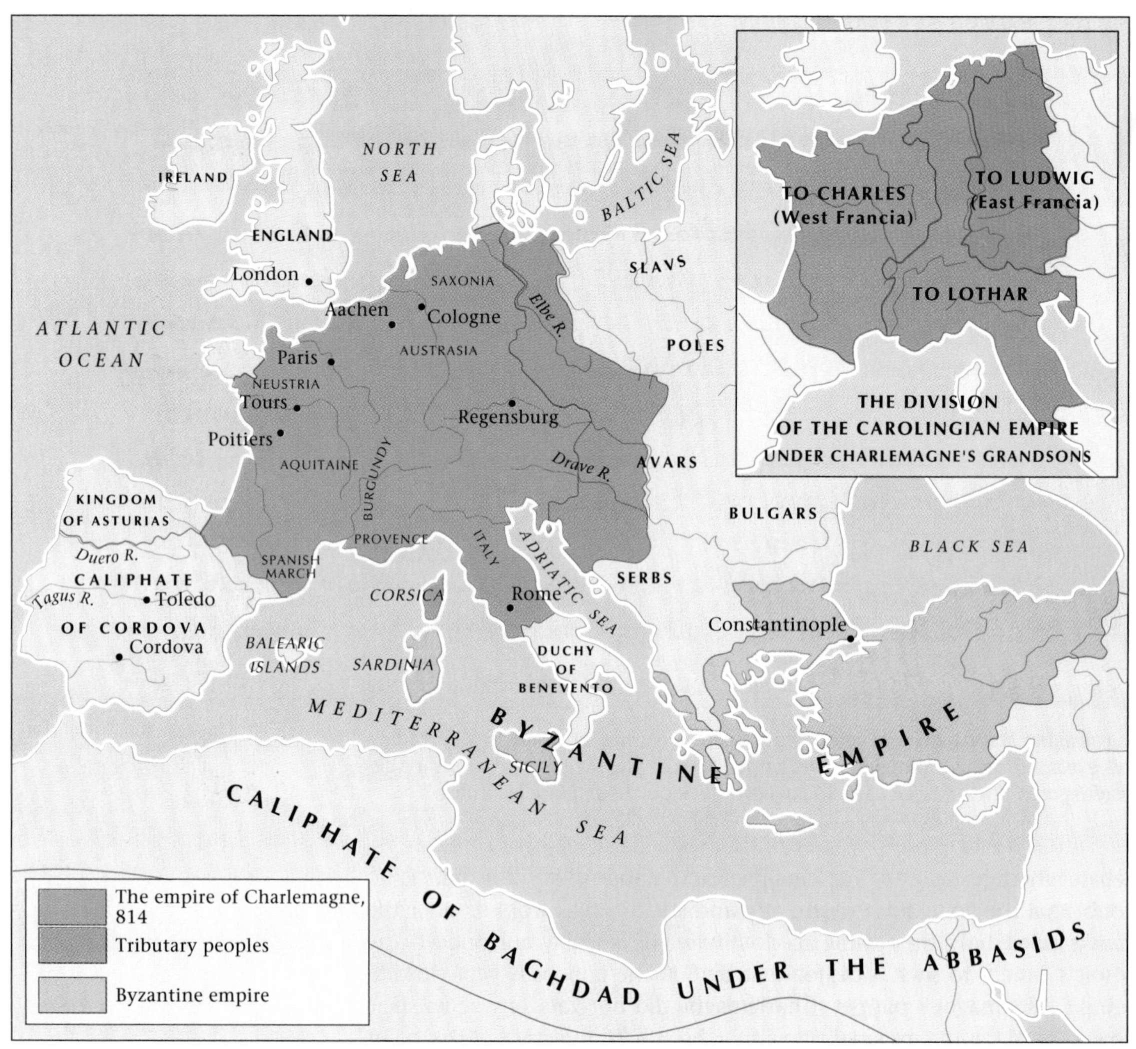

The Empire of Charlemagne, 814

extremely primitive times, one had to have enormous reserves of strength and energy—one had to travel on horseback over enormous distances, fight and win battles at the head of unruly armies, and know how to delegate power to others yet guard against its abuse. Unfortunately for western Europe few of Charlemagne's heirs had such combinations of energy and talent. To make matters worse, Charlemagne's sole surviving son, Louis the Pious, who inherited the Frankish realm intact, divided his inheritance among his own three sons, thereby bringing civil war back to Frankish Europe. And to make matters worst of all, new waves of invasions began just as Charlemagne's grandsons and great-grandsons started fighting each other: from the north came the Scandinavian Vikings; from the east came the Asiatic Magyars (or Hungarians); and from the south came new assaults by marauding Muslims, attacking now from the sea. Under these pressures the Carolingian Empire completely fell apart and a new political map of Europe was drawn in the tenth century.

As the Carolingian period was crucial for marking the beginnings of a common North Atlantic, western European civilization, so the tenth century was crucial for marking the beginnings of the major modern European political entities. England, which never had been part of Charlemagne's empire, and which hitherto had been divided among smaller warring Anglo-Saxon states, became unified in the late ninth and the tenth century owing to the work of King Alfred the Great (871–899) and his direct successors. Alfred and his heirs reorganized the army, infused new vigor into local government, and codified the English laws. In addition, Alfred founded schools and fostered an interest in Anglo-Saxon writing and other elements of a national culture.

Viking Dragon Head. Wooden carvings like these on the stemposts of Viking ships were calculated to inspire terror.

Across the Channel, France (now the name for the main part of Roman Gaul because it was the original seat of the Frankish monarchy) was devastated by the invasions of Vikings, who had sailed up the French rivers. For that reason France broke up into small principalities rather than developing a strong national monarchy on the pattern of England. Nonetheless there was a king in France, who, however weak, was recognized as the ruler of the western part of Charlemagne's former territories. Directly to the east, the kings of Germany were the strongest Continental monarchs of the tenth century, ruling over an essentially united realm. In addition to Germany, their lands encompassed most of the Low Countries and a good part of modern eastern France.

The most important German ruler of the period was Otto the Great. He became king in 936, resoundingly defeated the Hungarians in 955—thereby relieving Germany of its greatest foreign threat—and took the title of emperor in Rome in 962. By this last act Otto strengthened his claim to being the greatest Continental monarch since Charlemagne. Otto and his successors, who continued to call themselves emperors, tried to rule over Italy but barely succeeded in doing so. Instead, Italy in the tenth century saw the greatest western European development of urban life, a pattern on which the Italians would subsequently build.

The economy of western Europe in the Early Middle Ages

Although Italy did develop some city life in the tenth century, this was by no means typical of the early-medieval period in western Europe as a whole. Quite to the contrary, from the eighth to the eleventh century the European economy was based almost entirely on agriculture and very limited local trade. Roads deteriorated and barter widely replaced the use of money. Whatever cities survived from Roman days were usually empty shells that served at most as administrative centers for bishops and fortified places in case of common danger. The main economic unit throughout the period was the self-supporting, large landed estate, usually owned by a king, a warrior aristocrat, or a large monastery. Although the northern European soil was rich, farming tools in most places were still too primitive to bring in an adequate return on the enormous investment of effort expended by the laboring masses. Agricultural yields in all but the most fertile Carolingian lands (and often even in them) were pitifully low, and Europeans, except the rulers and the higher clergy, lived on the edge of subsistence. It is true that some increase in agricultural income had underpinned the Carolingian successes, and some progress in farming might have continued had the peace of Charlemagne's reign endured. But the subsequent invasions of the ninth and tenth centuries set agricultural life back and new beginnings would have to be made in the years thereafter.

The low level of intellectual life

Given the low level of early-medieval economic life, it is not surprising that the age was not a prosperous time for learning or the arts: with scarcely enough wealth to keep most people alive, there was not much to support schools or major artistic projects. Throughout the period, even in the best of years, learning was a privilege for the few: the masses received no formal education, and even most members of the secular aristocracy were illiterate. Learning also consisted mostly of memorization, without regard for criticism or refutation. We have seen that there was some revival of learning under Charlemagne that may be called a "renaissance" but that it did not issue into any real intellectual creativity. Its major accomplishment was the founding of enough schools to educate the clergy in the rudiments of reading and the training of enough monastic scribes to recopy and preserve some major works of Roman literature. Even this accomplishment was jeopardized in the period of invasions that accompanied the fall of the Carolingian Empire. Fortunately just enough schools and manuscripts survived to become the basis for another—far greater—revival of learning that began in the eleventh and twelfth centuries.

Carolingian Art. The fountain of life: an illuminated manuscript page from Gottschalk's Evangeliary (book with four gospels), dating from 781.

In the realm of literature the early Middle Ages had an extremely meager production. This was because few Christians could write and those who could were usually monks and priests, who were not supposed to engage in purely literary endeavors. There was some impressive writing of history in Latin, most notably that of Bede and Charlemagne's eloquent biographer, Einhard, but otherwise Latin composition was little cultivated. Toward the close of the period, however, the vernacular languages, which were either Germanic or based on different regional dialects of Latin (the "Romance" languages, so called because they were based on "Roman" speech), began to be employed for crude poetic expression, usually first by oral transmission.

Beowulf

The best-known example of this literature in the vernacular is the Anglo-Saxon epic poem *Beowulf.* First put into written form about the eighth century, this poem incorporates ancient legends of the Germanic peoples of northwestern Europe. It is a story of fighting and seafaring and of heroic adventure against deadly dragons and the forces of nature. The background of the epic is pre-Christian, but the author of the work introduced into it some qualities of Christian idealism. *Beowulf* is important not only as one of the earliest specimens of Anglo-Saxon or Old English poetry but also for the picture it gives of the society of the English and their ancestors in the Early Middle Ages.

The *Book of Kells*

The artistic history of the Early Middle Ages was a story of isolated and interrupted accomplishments because artistic life relied most of all on brief moments of local peace or royal patronage. The earliest enduring monuments of early-medieval art were those created by monks in Ireland—which had its own unique culture—between the sixth and the eighth centuries. Above all in manuscript illumination (i.e., painted illustrations) the Irish monks developed a thoroughly anticlassical and almost surrealistic style, whose origins are most difficult to account for. The greatest surviving product from this school is the stunning *Book of Kells,* an illuminated Gospel book that has been called "the most sophisticated work of decorative art in the history of painting." The Irish school declined without subsequent influence and was followed by artistic products of the Carolingian Renaissance.

Irish Art. The opening of a gospel page that shows the Irish style at its most surrealistic.

For much of its inspiration, the art of Charlemagne's period returned to classical models, yet it also retained some of the spontaneous vitality of barbarian decoration. When Charlemagne's empire declined and disintegrated there was a corresponding decline and then interruption in the history of Western art. In the tenth century, however, new regional schools emerged. The greatest of these were the English, which emphasized restless fluency in manuscript illumination; the German, which was more grave but still managed to communicate extreme religious ecstasy; and the northern Spanish, which, though Christian, created a rather strange and independent style mostly influenced by the decorative style of Islamic art.

A distinct western European civilization evident in 1050

Undoubtedly there is no single, obvious terminal date for early-medieval history as a whole. The date 1000 is sometimes given because it is a convenient round number, but even as late as 1050 Europe had not changed on the surface very much from the way it had been since the end of the Carolingian period. Indeed, looking at Europe as late as 1050 it would at first seem that not much progress had been made over the entire

Left: **Utrecht Psalter.** This Carolingian manuscript of the Psalms from about 820 later provided the basis for the "nervous expressiveness" of the tenth-century English regional school. Right: **Bamberg Apocalypse.** In this manuscript illumination from about 1000 the fall of Babylon in the Book of Revelation (18:1–20) is displayed by depicting the city upside down. This is an example of the grave regional German style.

course of the early-medieval centuries. Except for Germany, there was hardly any centralized government, for by 1050 the Anglo-Saxon English state created by King Alfred and his successors was falling apart. Throughout Europe, all but the most privileged individuals continued to live on the brink of starvation, and cultural attainments were minimal and sparse. But actually much had been accomplished. By shifting its main weight to the Atlantic northwest, European civilization became centered in lands that would soon harvest great agricultural wealth. By preserving some of the traditions developed by Gregory the Great, St. Boniface, Pepin, and Charlemagne, European civilization had also developed an enduring sense of cultural unity based on Western Christianity and the Latin inheritance. And in the tenth century the beginnings of the future European kingdoms and city-states started to coalesce. Western European civilization was thus for the first time becoming autonomous and distinctive. From then on it would be a leading force in the history of the world.

SUMMARY POINTS

- The Byzantine Empire (c. 610–1453) was one of the most impressive and influential empires in the world. It held off hostile invaders for centuries while building a religious tradition that endures to the present. The Iconoclastic Controversy of the eighth and ninth centuries created tensions between Constantinople and Rome. Worsening relations led to a schism between the Eastern Orthodox and Roman Catholic Churches in 1054.
- Islam was founded by Muhammad in Arabia around 622; within less than a century Islamic caliphs had conquered North Africa, most of Spain, the Middle East, and the entire former Persian Empire. Around 656 a disagreement over Islamic leadership caused a split between followers of Muhammad's son-in-law Ali, who came to be called Shiites, and their rivals, the Islamic majority, who came to be called Sunnites.
- Islamic civilization developed distinguished schools of philosophy, the sciences, and medicine. Islamic merchants expanded the foundations of trade and industry that had been established by their Persian and Byzantine predecessors.
- In northwestern Europe a succession of able Frankish rulers began to create a strong power base during the eighth century. In the middle of the century they struck an alliance with the Roman papacy that helped to create a Western-oriented Catholic Church.
- The Carolingian Empire reached its peak during the reign of Charlemagne (768–814), but after his death the empire broke up, laying the ground for the emergence of the modern European political entities of France and Germany.

BYZANTINE CIVILIZATION

Angold, Michael, *The Byzantine Empire: 1025–1204,* 2d ed., New York, 1997. Concentrates on political topics.

Beckwith, John, *The Art of Constantinople,* 2d ed., London, 1968. A standard account.

Hussey, Joan M., *The Byzantine World,* 3d ed., London, 1967. Half-narrative, half-topical; a useful short introduction.

Kazhdan, Alexander P., and Giles Constable, *People and Power in Byzantium: An Introduction to Modern Byzantine Studies,* Washington, D.C., 1982. The best introduction to Byzantine society and culture.

Kazhdan, Alexander P., and Ann Wharton Epstein, *Change in Byzantine Culture in the Eleventh and Twelfth Centuries,* Berkeley, 1985. Complements Angold in treating the social and cultural history of the "middle Byzantine period."

Krautheimer, Richard, *Early Christian and Byzantine Architecture,* 4th ed., New York, 1986.

Magoulias, Harry J., *Byzantine Christianity: Emperor, Church and the West,* Detroit, 1982. Limited to the three themes mentioned in the title.

Ostrogorsky, George, *History of the Byzantine State,* rev. ed., New Brunswick, N.J., 1969. The most authoritative longer account of political developments.

Pelikan, Jaroslav, *The Christian Tradition; Vol. II: The Spirit of Eastern Christendom,* Chicago, 1974. An advanced treatment of religious doctrines.

Vasiliev, A. A., *History of the Byzantine Empire,* 2 vols., Madison, Wisc., 1928. Supplements Ostrogorsky; valuable for its detail on social and intellectual as well as political history.

Vryonis, Speros, *Byzantium and Europe,* New York, 1967. Noteworthy for its illustrations.

ISLAMIC CIVILIZATION

Gibb, H. A. R., *Arabic Literature: An Introduction,* 2d rev. ed., Oxford, 1974. An excellent survey.

———, *Mohammedanism: An Historical Survey,* 2d rev. ed., Oxford, 1969. The best brief interpretation of Islamic religion.

Goitein, S. D., *Jews and Arabs: Their Contacts through the Ages,* 3d rev. ed., New York, 1974.

Hodgson, Marshall, *The Venture of Islam,* 3 vols., Chicago, 1974. A masterwork. One of the greatest works of history written by a modern American. Advanced and sometimes difficult, but always rewarding.

Kennedy, Hugh, *The Early Abbasid Caliphate: A Political History,* Totowa, N.J., 1981.

———, *The Prophet and the Age of the Caliphates,* London, 1986. A lucid introduction to the political history of Islam from the sixth through the eleventh centuries.

Lewis, Bernard, *The Arabs in History,* 6th ed., New York, 1993. The best short survey of the conquests and political fortunes of the Arabs.

Lombard, Maurice, *The Golden Age of Islam,* New York, 1975.

Peters, F. E., *Muhammad and the Origins of Islam,* Albany, N.Y., 1994.

———, *Aristotle and the Arabs,* New York, 1968. Well-written and engaging.

Watt, W. Montgomery, *Islamic Philosophy and Theology,* 2d ed., Edinburgh, 1985.

———, *Muhammad: Prophet and Statesman,* Oxford, 1961. A good short biography.

Watt, W. Montgomery, and Pierre Cachia, *A History of Islamic Spain,* Edinburgh, 1965. Briefly covers an undeservedly neglected subject.

Barraclough, Geoffrey, *The Crucible of Europe: The Ninth and Tenth Centuries in European History,* Berkeley, 1976. A controversial, but clear and stimulating interpretation of political developments.

Brown, Peter, *The Rise of Western Christendom: Triumph and Diversity, AD 200–1000,* Cambridge, Mass., 1996. A subtle, lushly written interpretation of how Christianity fit into different early-medieval environments.

Dawson, Christopher, *The Making of Europe,* New York, 1956. An impassioned study of the cultural origins of western European uniqueness by one of this century's most eminent Catholic historians.

Duby, Georges, *The Early Growth of the European Economy,* Ithaca, N.Y., 1974. Emphasizes role of lords and peasants; very sophisticated economic history.

Fichtenau, Heinrich, *The Carolingian Empire,* Toronto, 1978. A highly interpretative account that aims to whittle its subject down to size.

Kitzinger, Ernst, *Early Medieval Art,* 2d ed., Bloomington, Ind., 1983. A very short but masterful introduction.

McKitterick, Rosamond, *The Frankish Kingdoms under the Carolingians, 751–987,* New York, 1983.

———, ed., *The Uses of Literacy in Early Mediaeval Europe,* New York, 1990. A collection of essays that are representative of new trends in scholarship and that treat a broad variety of early-medieval societies.

Mayr-Harting, Henry, *The Coming of Christianity to Anglo-Saxon England,* 3d ed., University Park, Pa., 1991. Probably the best introduction to the history of Anglo-Saxon England up through the end of the eighth century.

Pirenne, Henri, *Mohammed and Charlemagne,* New York, 1968. A bold interpretation, now no longer widely accepted but still thought-provoking.

Stenton, Frank, *Anglo-Saxon England,* 3d ed., Oxford, 1990. A standard work.

Wemple, Suzanne F., *Women in Frankish Society: Marriage and the Cloister, 500–900,* Philadelphia, 1981. Describes changing attitudes toward marriage among the early Franks.

Wolff, Philippe, *The Awakening of Europe,* Baltimore, 1968. Emphasizes the material context of intellectual developments. Masterfully written and organized.

Wood, Ian, *The Merovingian Kingdoms, 450–751,* New York, 1994. Up to date, but difficult reading because of its encyclopedic detail.

SOURCE MATERIALS

Arberry, Arthur John, *The Koran Interpreted,* 2 vols., London, 1955.

Bede, *A History of the English Church and People,* tr. L. Sherley-Price, Baltimore, 1955.

Brand, Charles M., ed., *Icon and Minaret: Sources of Byzantine and Islamic Civilization,* Englewood Cliffs, N.J., 1969.

Brentano, Robert, ed., *The Early Middle Ages: 500–1000,* New York, 1964. The best shorter anthology of the Western Christian sources, enlivened by the editor's subjective commentary.

Einhard and Notker the Stammerer, *Two Lives of Charlemagne,* tr. L. Thorpe, Baltimore, 1969.

Gregory, Bishop of Tours, *History of the Franks,* tr. E. Brehaut, New York, 1969.

McNamara, Jo Ann, and John E. Halborg, eds., *Sainted Women of the Dark Ages,* Durham, N.C., 1992.

CHAPTER 10

THE HIGH MIDDLE AGES (1050–1300): ECONOMIC, SOCIAL, AND POLITICAL INSTITUTIONS

> I judge those who write at this time to be in a certain measure happy. For, after the turbulence of the past, an unprecedented brightness of peace has dawned again.
>
> —The historian OTTO OF FREISING, writing around 1158

Western Europe emerges from backwardness

THE PERIOD BETWEEN about 1050 and 1300, termed by historians the High Middle Ages, was the time when western Europe first clearly emerged from backwardness to become one of the greatest powers on the globe. Around 1050 the West was still less developed in most respects than the Byzantine Empire or the Islamic world, but by 1300 it had forged ahead of these two rivals. From a global perspective, only China was its equal in economic, political, and cultural prosperity. Given the sorry state of western Europe around 1050, this startling leap forward was certainly one of the most impressive achievements of human history. Those who think that the entire Middle Ages were times of stagnation could not be more wrong.

Reasons for the "great leap forward"

The reasons for Europe's enormous progress in the High Middle Ages are predictably complex, yet medieval historians agree upon certain broad lines of interpretation. One is that Europe between 900 and 1050 was already poised for growth and could finally begin to live up to its potential once the devastating invasions of Vikings, Hungarians, and Muslims had ceased. Most of these invasions had tapered off by around 1000, but in the eleventh century England was still troubled by the Danes: the year 1066, more famous as the year of the Norman Conquest, was also the year of the last Viking invasion of England. Once foreign invasions were no longer imminent, western Europeans could concentrate on developing their economic life with much less fear of interruption than before. Because of the relative continuity allowed by this change, extraordinarily important technological breakthroughs were made, above all those that contributed to the first great western European "agricultural revolution." The revolution in agriculture made food more bountiful and provided a solid basis for economic development and diversification in other spheres. Population grew rapidly, and towns and cities grew to such a degree that we can speak also of an "urban revolution," even though western Europe remained predominantly agrarian. At the same time political life in the West became more stable. In the course of the High Middle Ages strong new secular governments began to provide more and more internal peace for their subjects and became the foundations of our modern nation-states. In addition to all these advances, there were also striking new religious and intellectual developments, to be treated in the next chapter, which helped give the West a new sense of mission and self-confidence. Although in this chapter we will treat only the economic, social, and political accomplishments of the High Middle Ages, it is well to bear in mind that religion played a pervasive role in all of medieval life, and that all aspects of the high-medieval "great leap forward" were inextricably interrelated.

The First Agricultural Revolution

The state of agriculture before 1050

The agricultural worker, the "Man with the Hoe," supported European civilization materially by his labors more than anyone else until the industrialization of modern times. Yet, amazing as it seems, until about 1050 he had hardly so much as a hoe. Inventories of farm implements from the Carolingian period reveal that metal tools on the wealthiest rural estates were extremely rare, and even wooden implements were so few in number that many laborers must have had to grapple with nature quite literally with only their bare hands. Between about 1050 and 1250 all that changed. In roughly those two centuries an agricultural revolution took place that entirely altered the nature and vastly increased the output of western European farming.

Prerequisites for the medieval agricultural revolution: (1) shift in area of cultivation

Many of the prerequisites for the medieval agricultural revolution had been present before the middle of the eleventh century. The most important was the shift in the weight of European civilization from the Mediterranean to the North Atlantic regions. Most of northern Europe from southern England to the Urals is a vast, wet, and highly fertile alluvial plain. The Romans had hardly begun to cultivate this area because they ruled only part of it, because it lay too far away from the center of their civilization, and because they did not have the proper tools and systems to work the soil. Starting around the time of the Carolingians much more attention was paid to colonizing and cultivating the great alluvial plain. The Carolingians opened up all of western and central Germany to agricultural settlement and started experimenting with new tools and methods that would be most appropriate for cultivating the newly settled lands. The results helped support other Carolingian achievements, but the Carolingian peace, as we have seen, was too brief to allow for any cumulative development. After the invasions of the tenth century, it was necessary to start again in a systematic attempt to exploit the potential wealth of the north. As long as Western civilization was centered in England, northern France, the Low Countries, and Germany, however, the rich lands remained available for cultivation.

(2) Improved climate

Another prerequisite for agricultural development was improved climate. We know far less about European climatic patterns in past centuries than we would like to, but historians of climate are reasonably certain that there was an "optimum," or period of improved climate, for western Europe lasting from about 700 to 1200. This meant not only that during those centuries the temperature on the average was somewhat warmer than it had been before (at most a rise of only about 1° Centigrade), but also that the weather was somewhat drier. Dryness was of primary advantage to northern Europe, where lands were, if anything, usually too wet for good farming, whereas it was disadvantageous to the Mediterranean south, which was already dry enough. Among other things, the occurrence of this optimum helps explain why there was more agricultural cultivation in northern climes such as Iceland than there has been since then. (Also, with fewer icebergs in the northern seas, Norsemen were able to reach Greenland and Newfoundland, and Greenland then was probably indeed more green than white.) Although the optimum began around 700 and continued through the ninth and tenth centuries, it could not by itself counteract the deleterious effects of the tenth-century invasions. Fortunately the weather stayed propitious when Europeans again were able to take advantage of it.

(3) Technology in conjunction with favorable circumstances

Similar remarks apply to the fact that the Carolingians knew about many of the technological devices to be discussed presently that later helped western Europeans accomplish their first agricultural revolution. Although the most basic new devices were known before 1050, all came into widespread use and were brought to greatest perfection between then and about 1200 because only then was there a conjunction of the most favorable circumstances. Not only did the invasions end and good climate continue, but better government gradually provided the more lasting peace necessary for agricultural expansion. Landlords too became more interested in profit-making than mere consumption. Above all, from about 1050 to 1200 there was a greater consolidation of wealth for further investment as one advance helped support another; quite simply, technological devices could now be afforded.

Technological innovations: (1) the heavy plow

One of the first and most important breakthroughs in agriculture was the use of the heavy plow. The plow itself, of course, is an ancient tool, but the Romans knew only a light "scratch plow" that broke up the surface of the ground without fully turning it over. This implement was sufficient for the light soil of the Mediterranean regions but was virtually useless with the much heavier, wetter soil of the European north. During the course of the Early Middle Ages a much heavier and more efficient plow was developed that could cultivate the northern lands. Not only could this heavier plow deal with heavier soils, but it was fitted with new parts that enabled it to turn over furrows and fully aerate the ground. The benefits were immeasurable. In addition to the fact that the plow allowed for the cultivation of hitherto unworkable lands, the furrows it made

Light Plow and Heavy Plow. Note that the peasant using the light plow (left) had to press his foot on it to give it added weight. The major innovation of the heavy plow (often wheeled, as shown at right) was the long moldboard, which

provided excellent drainage systems for water-logged territories. It also saved labor: whereas the Roman scratch plow had to be dragged over the fields twice in two different directions, the heavy plow did more thorough work in one operation. In short, the opening up of northern Europe for intensive agriculture and everything that followed would have been inconceivable without the heavy plow.

(2) The three-field system of crop rotation

Closely allied to the use of the heavy plow was the introduction of the three-field system of crop rotation. Before modern times, farmers always let a large part of their arable land lie fallow for a year to avoid exhaustion of the soil because there was not enough fertilizer to support more intensive agriculture, and nitrogen-fixing crops such as clover and alfalfa were almost unknown. But the Romans were especially unproductive due to their inability to cultivate any more than half of their arable land in any year. The medieval innovation was to reduce the fallow to one-third by introducing a three-field system. In a given year one-third of the land would lie fallow, one-third would be given to cereal that was sown in the fall and harvested in early summer, and one-third to a new crop—oats, barley, or legumes—that would be planted in the late spring and harvested in August or September. The fields were then rotated over a three-year cycle. The major innovation was the planting of the new crop that grew over the summer. The Romans could not have supported this system because their lands were poorer and especially because the Mediterranean area is too dry to support much summer growth at all. In this respect the wetter north obviously had a great advantage. The benefits of the new crop were that it did not deplete the soil as much as cereal like wheat and rye (in fact, it restored nitrogen taken from the soil by these

turned over the ground after the plowshare cut into it. The picture on the right depicts a second crucial medieval invention as well—the padded horse collar, which allowed horses to throw their full weight into pulling.

crops); that it provided some insurance against loss from natural disasters by diversifying the growth of the fields; and that it produced new types of food. If the third field were planted with oats, the crop could be consumed by both humans and horses; if planted with legumes, it helped to balance the human diet by providing a source of protein to balance the major intake of cereal carbohydrates. Since the new system also helped to diversify labor over the course of the year and raised production from one-half to two-thirds, it was nothing short of an agricultural miracle.

(3) Use of mills

A third major innovation was the use of mills. The Romans had known about water mills but hardly used them, partly because they had enough slaves to be indifferent to labor-saving devices and partly because most Roman territories were not richly endowed with swiftly flowing streams. Starting around 1050, however, there was a veritable craze in northern Europe for building increasingly efficient water mills. One French area saw a growth from 14 water mills in the eleventh century to 60 in the twelfth; in another part of France about 40 mills were built between 850 and 1080, 40 more between 1080 and 1125, and 245 between 1125 and 1175. Once Europeans had mastered the complex technology of building water mills, they turned their attention to harnessing the power of wind: around 1170 they constructed the first European windmills. Thereafter, in flat lands like Holland that had no swiftly flowing streams, windmills proliferated as rapidly as water-powered ones had spread elsewhere. Although the major use of mills was to grind grain, they were soon adapted for a variety of other important functions: for example, they were employed to drive saws, process cloth, press oil, brew beer, provide power for iron forges, and crush pulp for manufacturing paper. Paper had been made in China and the Islamic world before this but never with the aid of paper mills, which is evidence of the technological sophistication the West was achieving in comparison to other advanced civilizations.

Other important technological breakthroughs that gathered force around 1050 should be mentioned. Several related to providing the means for using horses as farm animals. Around 800 a padded collar was first introduced into Europe; this allowed the horse to put his full weight into pulling without choking himself. Roughly a century later iron horseshoes were first used to protect hooves, and perhaps around 1050 tandem harnessing was developed to allow horses to pull behind each other. With these advances and the greater abundance of oats due to the three-field system, horses replaced oxen as farm animals in some parts of Europe and brought with them the advantages of working more quickly and for longer hours. Further inventions were the wheelbarrow and the harrow, a tool drawn over the field after the plow to level the earth and mix in the seed. Important for most of these inventions was the greater use of iron in the High Middle Ages to reinforce all sorts of agricultural implements, most crucially the parts of the heavy plow that came into contact with the soil.

A Hammer Mill. One of the many uses of water power.

Extension and intense cultivation of arable land

So far we have been speaking of technological developments as if they alone account for the high-medieval agricultural revolution. But that is by no means the case. Along with improved technology came a great extension in the amount of land made arable and more intensive cultivation of the land already cleared. Although the Carolingians had begun to open the rich plain of northwestern Europe to tillage, they had chosen to clear only the most easily workable patches: a map of Carolingian agricultural settlements would show numerous tiny islands of cultivated lands surrounded by vast stretches of forests, swamps, and wastes. Starting around 1050, and greatly accelerating in the twelfth century, movements of land-clearing entirely changed the topography of northern Europe. First, greater peace and stability allowed farm workers in northern France and western Germany to begin pushing beyond the islands of settlement, clearing little bits of land at a time. At first they did this surreptitiously because they were poaching on territories that were actually owned by aristocratic lords. In time the aristocratic landowners gave their

Medieval Windmill. The peasant on the left is bringing his grain in a sack to be ground into flour. Note that the mill is built on a pivot so that it can rotate in the direction of any prevailing wind.

support to the clearing activities because they demanded their own profits from them. When that happened the work of clearing forests and draining swamps was carried on more swiftly. Thus, as the twelfth century progressed the isolated arable islands of Carolingian times expanded to meet each other. While this was going on, and continuing somewhat later, entirely new areas were colonized and opened to cultivation, for example, in northern England, Holland, and above all the eastern parts of Germany. Finally, in the twelfth and thirteenth centuries, peasants began working all the lands they had cleared more efficiently and intensively in order to gain more income for themselves. They harrowed after plowing, hoed frequently to keep down weeds, and added extra plowings to their yearly cycle, thereby greatly helping to renew the fertility of the soil.

"Dawn." A medieval peasant, up with the roosters, returns from outdoors after attending to some early-morning business. The woman overhead is "dawn" herself.

The result of all these changes was an enormous increase in agricultural production. With more land opened for cultivation obviously more crops were raised, but the increase was magnified by the introduction of more efficient farming methods. Thus, average yields from grains of seed sown increased from at best twofold in Carolingian times to three- or fourfold by around 1300. And all the additional grain could be ground far more rapidly than before because a mill could grind grain in the same time that it would have taken forty men or women to do the same job. Europeans, therefore, could for the first time begin to rely on a regular and stable food supply.

Consequences of the agricultural revolution

That fact in turn had the profoundest consequences for the further development of European history. To begin with, it meant that more land could be given over to uses other than raising grain. Accordingly, as the High Middle Ages progressed, there was greater agricultural diversification and specialization. Large areas were turned over to sheep-raising, others to viniculture, and others to raising cotton and dyestuffs. Many of the products of these new enterprises were consumed locally, but many were also traded over long distances or used to provide the raw materials for new industries—above all those of cloth-making. The growth of this trade and manufacturing helped initiate and support the growth of towns, as we will see. The agricultural boom also helped sustain the growth of towns in another way: by supporting a great spurt in population. With more food and a better diet (above all the increase in proteins) life expectancy increased from perhaps as low as an average of thirty years for the poor of Carolingian Europe to between forty and fifty years in the High Middle Ages. Healthier people also increased their birthrate. For these reasons the population of the West grew about threefold between about 1050 and 1300. More people and more labor-saving devices meant that not everybody had to stay on the farm: some could migrate to new towns and cities where they found a new way of life.

Higher incomes

Still other results of the agricultural revolution were that it raised the incomes of lords, thereby underpinning a great increase in the sophistication of aristocratic life, and raised the incomes of monarchs, underpinning the growth of states. European-wide prosperity also helped support the growth of the Church and paid the way for the burgeoning of schools and intellectual enterprises. One final, more intangible result was that Europeans apparently became more optimistic, more energetic, and more willing to experiment and take risks than any of their rivals on the world scene.

Lord and Serf: Social Conditions and Quality of Life in the Manorial Regime

The meaning of the term "manorialism"

While agriculture was being transformed, social and economic conditions began to change for both landowners and agricultural laborers. Since for much of the High Middle Ages, however, rural life revolved around the institution of the manor owned by lords and worked by serfs, it is best to describe this manorial regime in its most typical form before describing basic changes. In reading the following it should be understood that the term "manorialism" is not synonymous with feudalism: *manorialism* was an economic system in which large agricultural estates were worked by serfs, whereas *feudalism,* in the sense the word is used by most medieval historians, was a political system in which government was greatly decentralized (see the fourth section of this chapter). It should also be borne in mind that when scholars talk about manorialism based on a "typical manor" they are resorting to a historical approximation: no two manors were ever exactly alike; indeed many differed enormously in size and basic characteristics. Moreover, in those parts of Europe farthest away from the original centers of Carolingian settlement between the Seine and the Rhine, there were few, if any, manors at all. In Italy there was still much agriculture based on slavery, and in central and eastern Germany there were many smaller farms worked by free peasants.

Manor worked by serfs

The manor first clearly emerged in Carolingian times and continued to be the dominant form of agrarian social and economic organization in most of northwestern Europe until about the thirteenth century. It descended from the large Roman landed estate, but, unlike the Roman estate, the manor was worked by *serfs* (sometimes called villeins) and not slaves. Serfs were definitely not free in the modern sense: above all, they could not leave their lands, were forced to work for their lords regularly without pay, and were subject to numerous humiliating dues and to the jurisdiction of the lord's court. But they were much better off than slaves insofar as they were allocated land that they cultivated to support themselves and that normally could not be taken away from them. Thus, when agricultural improvements took place the serfs themselves could hope to profit at least a little from them. More than that, although the lord theoretically had the right to levy dues at will, in practice obligations tended to remain fixed. Although the lot of the serfs was surely terribly hard, they were seldom entirely at their lord's whim.

Open-field system

The lands of the manor, which might run from several hundred to several thousand acres, were divided into those that belonged to the lord and those that were allocated to the serfs. The former, called the lord's

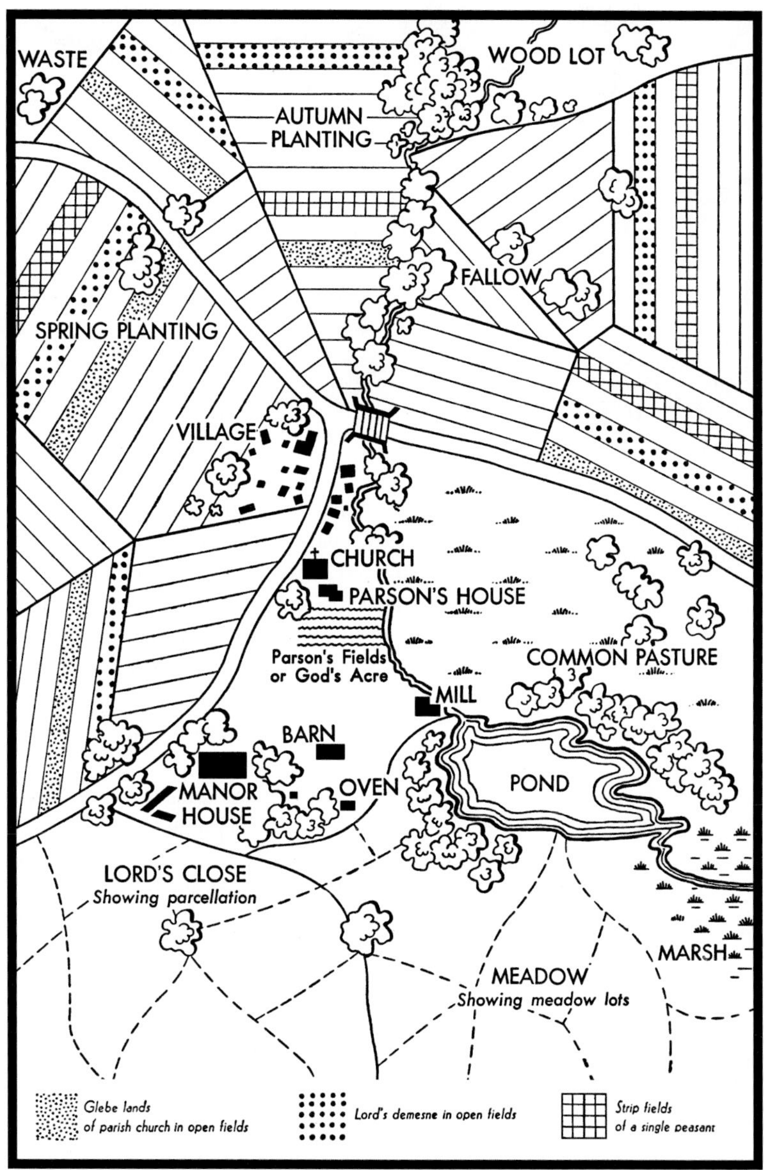

Diagram of a Manor

demesne (pronounced demean), usually comprised between a third and a half of the arable land. It was worked by the serfs on certain days, perhaps three days a week. The demesne did not consist of big parcels but was made up of narrow strips alternating with strips belonging to different peasants (and sometimes also strips set aside for the Church). All these strips were long and narrow because a heavy plow drawn by a yoke of horses or oxen could not be turned around easily. Because all the strips were generally separated only by a narrow band of unplowed turf, the whole regime is sometimes called the *open-field system*. Even when the serfs tilled their own lands they almost always worked together because

Sowing Seed. When the peasant sows his seed broadcast, the crows are not far off to help themselves. Here, one is bold enough to peck at the sack while another is momentarily chased off by a dog.

they usually owned farm animals and implements in common. For the same reason, grazing lands were called *commons* because the commonly owned herds grazed there together. In addition to cultivated fields and pastures, the serfs usually had their own small gardens. Most manors also had forests set aside primarily for the lord's hunting which were also useful for the foraging of pigs and the gathering of firewood. Insofar as serfs were allowed to take advantage of such opportunities they did that too in common: indeed, the entire manorial system emphasized communal enterprise and solidarity.

Living conditions of serfs

Communalism must have helped make a barely endurable life seem slightly more bearable. Even though the lot of the medieval serf was surely far superior to that of the Roman slave, and even though it improved from around 1050 to 1300, it was still primitive and pitiful beyond modern comprehension. Dwellings were usually miserable hovels constructed of wattle—braided twigs—smeared over with mud. As late as the thirteenth century an English peasant was convicted of destroying his neighbor's house simply by sawing apart one central beam. The floors of most huts were usually no more than the bare earth, often cold or damp. For beds there was seldom more than bracken—large, coarse ferns—and beyond that there was hardly any furniture. Not entirely jokingly it may be said that a good meal often consisted of two courses: one a porridge very much like gruel and the other a gruel very much like porridge. Fruit was almost unheard of, and meager vegetables were limited to such fare as onions, leeks, turnips, and cabbages—all boiled to make a thin soup. Meat came at most a few times a year, either on holidays or deep in winter, when all the fodder for a scrawny ox or pig had run out. Cooking utensils were never cleaned, so as to make sure that there was never any waste. In addition, there was always the possibility of crop failures, which affected the serfs far more than their lords since the lords demanded the same income as always. At such times the serfs were forced to surrender whatever grain they had and watch their children die slowly of starvation. It is particularly heart-rending to realize that children might be dying while there was still a bit of grain in the granaries: but that grain

Medieval Peasants Threshing Wheat

could not be touched because it was set aside as next year's seed, and without that there would be no future at all.

Improvements in the condition of serfs

To counterbalance this grim picture we may now turn to patterns of change and improvement. One, as we have already seen, was dietary. In the High Middle Ages famines were actually far rarer than before, and people grew stronger because some protein, mostly in the form of legumes, was added to their fare. There was also a widespread enfranchisement (i.e., freeing) of serfs for many reasons. Once landlords started opening up new lands, they could attract laborers only by guaranteeing their freedom. Such areas of free labor usually attracted runaway serfs and became models of a new system whereby landlords asked for fixed rents rather than demanding services. Then, even on the old manors, lords began to realize that they might be able to raise profits by demanding rents instead of duties. Alternatively, by selling their excess produce at free markets serfs might become sufficiently rich to buy their freedom.

The decline of serfdom

In these different ways serfdom gradually came to an end throughout most of Europe in the course of the thirteenth century. The process, however, moved more or less swiftly in different areas—it was somewhat delayed in England and was seldom so complete that former serfs did not owe some remnant of labor service and dues to powerful local lords. In France some of these obligations continued to exist as nagging indignities right down to the French Revolution in 1789. Serfs who became enfranchised often continued to work communally, but they were now free peasants who produced more for the open market than for their own subsistence.

Benefits of the agricultural revolution for lords

The lords profited even more than their serfs from the agricultural revolution for several reasons. One was that whenever lords enfranchised serfs they obtained large sums of cash, usually about all the wealth that

Medieval Peasants Slaughtering a Pig. Deep in winter, probably around Christmas, it is finally time to slaughter the household pig. But nothing can be wasted, so even the blood is caught in a pan to make blood pudding.

the serfs had hitherto amassed. Afterward the lords lived mainly on their rents. Since some of these were levied on lands that the lords had once owned but had never cultivated, noble income rose greatly. Even more than that, once the lords began to prefer rents to services, they found that rents were easier to increase. In their capacity as rent-collectors the lords did not personally supervise their lands as much as before but traveled more freely, sometimes going off crusading and sometimes living at royal courts. Consequently, added wealth allowed them to live better, and greater mobility gave them new ideas for improving their style of life.

The rise of chivalry

Increased sophistication of the nobility was much enhanced by the fact that in the High Middle Ages there was less tumultuous local warfare than before. Until around 1100 the typical European noble was a crude and brutal warrior who spent most of his time engaging in combat with his neighbors and pillaging the defenseless. Much of this violence decreased in the twelfth century because of ecclesiastical constraints, because emerging states were more effectively enforcing local peace, and because the nobles themselves were beginning to enjoy a more settled existence. Nobles continued to go on crusades and to fight in national wars, but they engaged in petty quarrels with each other less frequently. Apparently as an unconscious surrogate for the old fighting spirit the code of *chivalry* was developed. This channeled martial conduct into relatively benign activities. Chivalry literally means "horsemanship," and the chivalrous noble was expected to be thoroughly adept at the equestrian arts. Chivalry also imposed the obligation of fighting in defense of honorable causes; if none was to be found there were opportunities for combat in tournaments, mock battles that at first were quite savage but later became elaborate ceremonial affairs. Above all, the chivalric lord—typically a "knight" who owned less land than the upper aristocracy—

Jousting in a Tournament

Aristocratic Table Manners. There are knives but no forks or napkins on the table. The large stars mark these nobles as members of a chivalric order.

was expected to be not only brave and loyal but generous, truthful, reverent, and disdainful of unfair advantage or sordid gain.

Improvements in the quality of noble life

By-products of the increase in noble wealth and the rise of chivalry were improvements in the quality of living conditions and the treatment of women. Until around 1100 most noble dwellings were made of wood and burned down frequently because of primitive heating and cooking methods. With increasing wealth and more advanced technology, castles after 1100 were usually built of stone and were thus far less flammable. Moreover, they were now equipped with chimneys and mantled fireplaces, both medieval inventions, which meant that instead of having one large fire in a central great hall, individual rooms could be heated and individuals gained some privacy. Nobles customarily ate fewer vegetables than peasants, but their diet was laden with meat; increased luxury trade also brought costly exotic spices like pepper and saffron to their tables. Although table manners were still atrocious—all used only knives and spoons but no forks and blew their noses on their sleeves—nobles tried to show their superiority to others by dressing elegantly, indeed ostentatiously. During this period snug-fitting clothing also became available because both knitting and the button and buttonhole had just been invented.

Changes in noble attitudes toward women

The history of noble attitudes toward women in the High Middle Ages is somewhat controversial for two reasons. One is that most of our evidence comes from literature, and historians differ as to what degree literature actually reflects life. The other is that according to some scholars women were at best put on a pedestal, itself a position of constraint. Nonetheless, there can be no question that as the material quality of noble life improved it did so for women as well as men. More than that, there definitely was a revolution in some verbalized attitudes toward the female sex. Until the twelfth century, aside from a few female saints, women were virtually ignored in literature: the typical French epic told of bloody warlike deeds that either made no mention of women or portrayed them only in passing as being totally subservient. But within a few

An Aristocratic Family of the Twelfth Century. Warm family feelings existed among medieval people as they did at any other time. Here a mother is telling her two boys to bid good-bye to their father, who is about to depart on the Third Crusade.

decades after 1100, noblewomen were suddenly turned into objects of veneration by lyric poets and writers of romances (see the next chapter). A typical troubadour poet could write of his lady that "all I do that is fitting I infer from her beautiful body," and that "she is the tree and the branch where joy's fruit ripens."

Changes in the status of noblewomen

Although the new "courtly" literature was extremely idealistic and somewhat artificial, it surely expressed the values of a gentler culture wherein upper-class women were in practice more respected than before. Moreover, there is no question that certain royal women in the twelfth and thirteenth centuries actually did rule their states on various occasions when their husbands or sons were dead or unable to do so. The indomitable Eleanor of Aquitaine, wife of Henry II, for example, helped rule England even though she was over seventy years old when her son Richard I went on a crusade from 1190 to 1194, and the strong-willed Blanche of Castile ruled France extremely well twice in the thirteenth century, once during the minority of her son Louis IX and again when he was off crusading. No doubt from a modern perspective high-medieval women were still very constrained, but from the point of view of the past the High Middle Ages was a time of progress for the women of the upper classes. The most striking symbol comes from the history of the game of chess: before the twelfth century chess was played in Eastern countries, but there the equivalent of the queen was a male figure, the king's chief minister, who could move only diagonally one square at a time; in twelfth-century western Europe, however, this piece was turned into a queen, and sometime before the end of the Middle Ages she began to move all over the board.

The Revival of Trade and the Urban Revolution

Patterns of trade

Inseparable from the agricultural revolution, the freeing of serfs, and the growing sophistication of noble life was the revival of trade and the burgeoning of towns. Reviving trade was of many different sorts. Most fundamental was the mundane trade at local markets, where serfs or free peasants sold their excess grain or perhaps a few dozen eggs. But with growing specialization, produce like wine or cotton might be shipped over longer distances. River and sea routes were used wherever possible, but land transport was also necessary, and this was aided by improvements in road-building, the introduction of packhorses and mules, and the building of bridges. Whereas the Romans were really only interested in land *communications,* medieval people, starting in the eleventh century, concentrated on land *transport* to the degree that they were much better able to maintain a vigorous land-based trade. And that is not to say that they ignored Mediterranean transport either. On the contrary,

Medieval Trade Routes

Venetian Coin. The patron saint of Venice, Saint Mark, grants a banner symbolizing worldly rule to the Venetian doge. The Venetians consciously imitated Byzantine coinage (see p. 236) as part of a successful effort to replace the Byzantine Empire as the dominant trading power in the Mediterranean basin.

starting again in the eleventh century they began to make the former Roman "lake" the intermediary for an extensive seaborne trade that stretched over shorter and longer distances. Between 1050 and 1300 the Italian city-states of Genoa, Pisa, and Venice freed much of the Mediterranean from Muslim control, started monopolizing trade on formerly Byzantine waters, and began to establish in eastern Mediterranean outposts a flourishing commerce with the Orient. As a result, luxury goods such as spices, gems, perfumes, and fine cloths began to appear in Western markets and stimulated economic life by inspiring nobles to accelerate the agricultural revolution in order to pay for them.

This revival of trade called for new patterns of payment and the development of new commercial techniques. Most significantly, western Europe returned to a money economy after about four centuries when coined money was hardly used as a medium of exchange. The traditional manor had been almost self-sufficient and the few external items needed could be bartered for. But with the growth of markets coins became indispensable. At first these were coins of only the smallest denominations, but as luxury trade grew in the West the denominations increased apace; by the thirteenth century gold coins were minted by Italian states such as Florence and Venice.

Trade fairs

In a similar pattern of development, long-distance trade at first consisted of little more than peddlers crisscrossing over dusty roads with pack-laden mules. But during the course of the twelfth century such peddlers evolved into more prosperous merchants who managed to decrease their year-round traveling and to offer their wares instead at international trade fairs. The most prominent of these fairs, reaching the pinnacle of their prosperity in the thirteenth century, were held in the French region of Champagne, a meeting place between north and south, where Flemish merchants sold cloth to Italians, and Italian merchants sold Eastern spices to Flemings. By such means a unified European economy came into being. Thereafter even the trade fairs became outmoded because around 1300, Italian merchants succeeded in replacing costly overland transport over the Alps by means of dispatching shipping fleets via the Straits of Gibraltar and the Atlantic directly to the ports of northern Europe. Now staying at home entirely themselves, such large-scale trading entrepreneurs perfected modern techniques of business partnerships, accounting, and letters of credit. Because they invested in trade intentionally for profit and devised and used sophisticated credit mechanisms, most modern historians agree in calling them the first Western commercial capitalists.

Medieval Tollbooth. Whoever made use of a medieval road for transporting merchandise had to pay tolls to pay for its upkeep.

In addition to the expansion of money and credit, trade was vastly facilitated by the rapid growth of towns. If we could imagine an aerial view of twelfth-century Europe, the mushrooming of towns would be the most strikingly visible phenomenon after the clearing of forests and wastes. Some historians misleadingly include under the heading of towns the numerous new agricultural village communities of peasants that were established in clearings. These, however, were not really urban in any sense.

View of Paris. The city looked this way at the end of the Middle Ages, around 1480. Note the prominence of the Cathedral of Notre Dame in the center and the large number of other church spires; note, too, how closely all the buildings are packed behind the walls.

Putting them aside, many urban agglomerations were built from the ground up in the High Middle Ages, and existing towns that had barely survived from the Roman period grew enormously in size. To take some examples, in central and eastern Germany, which had not been part of the old Roman area of settlement, new towns such as Freiburg, Lübeck, Munich, and Berlin were founded in the twelfth century. Farther west, where old Roman towns had become little more than episcopal residences or stockades, formerly small towns like Paris, London, and Cologne roughly doubled in size between 1100 and 1200 and doubled again in the next century. Urban life was above all concentrated in Italy, which encompassed most of Europe's largest cities: Venice, Genoa, Milan, Bologna, Palermo, Florence, and Naples. In the thirteenth century the populations of the largest of these—Venice, Genoa, and Milan—were in the range of 100,000 each. We lack accurate statistics for most Italian cities, but it seems likely that many at least trebled in population between about 1150 and 1300, because we do know that the smaller Italian town of Imola, near Bologna, grew from some 4,200 in 1210 to 11,500 in 1312. Considering that town life had come very close to disappearing in most of Europe between 750 and 1050, it is warranted to speak of a high-medieval urban revolution. Moreover, from the High Middle Ages until now a vigorous urban life has been a major characteristic of western European and subsequently modern world civilization.

Growth of towns

It was once thought that the primary cause of the medieval urban revolution was the revival of long-distance trade. Theoretically, itinerant peddlers, who had no secure place in the dominantly agrarian society of Europe, gradually settled together in towns in order to offer each other much-needed protection and establish markets to sell their wares. In fact, the picture is far more complicated than that. While some towns did receive great stimulus from long-distance trade, and the growth of a major

Causes of the urban revolution

Old Houses in Strassburg. In the Middle Ages food was stored in attics, with special openings for ventilation, as insurance against famine. Of course there was still much spoilage.

city such as Venice would have been unthinkable without it, most towns relied for their origin and early economic vitality far more on the wealth of their surrounding areas. These brought them surplus agricultural goods, raw materials for manufacture, and an influx of population. In other words, the quickening of economic life in general was the major cause of urban growth: towns existed in a symbiotic relationship with the countryside by providing markets and also wares made by artisans, while they lived off the rural food surplus and grew with the migration of surplus serfs or peasants who were seeking a better life. (Escaped serfs were guaranteed their freedom if they stayed in a town a year and a day.) Once towns started to flourish, many of them began to specialize in certain enterprises. Paris and Bologna gained considerable wealth by becoming the homes of leading universities; Venice, Genoa, Cologne, and London became centers of long-distance trade; and Milan, Ghent, and Bruges specialized in manufactures. The most important urban industries were those devoted to cloth-making. Cloth manufacturers sometimes developed techniques of large-scale production and investment that are ancestors of the modern factory system and industrial capitalism. Nonetheless large industrial enterprises were atypical of medieval economic life as a whole.

Distinctive features of medieval towns

Medieval cities and towns were not smaller-scale facsimiles of modern ones; to our own eyes they would still have seemed half-rural and uncivilized. Streets were often unpaved, houses had gardens for raising vegetables, and cows and pigs were kept in stables and pigsties. Passing along the streets of a major metropolis one might be stopped by a flock of bleating sheep or a crowd of honking geese. Sanitary conditions were often

A City on Fire. Once a fire began to spread in a medieval city, women, children, and priests were swiftly evacuated and servants of the rich would start carrying out their masters' possessions. Here the Swiss city of Bern is shown in flames: although a "bucket-brigade" tried desperately to extinguish the fire with water taken from the town moat, chronicles report that the city was leveled by flames in less than half an hour.

very poor and the air must often have reeked of excrement—both animal and human. Town-dwellers were cursed by frequent fires that swept quickly through closely settled wooden or straw quarters and went unstopped for lack of fire stations. People were also highly susceptible to contagious diseases bred by unsanitary conditions and crowding. Still another problem was that economic tensions and family rivalries could lead to bloody riots. Yet for all this, urban folk took great pride in their new cities and ways of life. A famous paean to London, for example, written by a twelfth-century denizen of that city, boasted of its prosperity, piety, and perfect climate (!), and claimed that except for frequent fires, London's only nuisance was "the immoderate drinking of fools."

The guild as representative of special interests

The most distinctive form of economic and social organization in the medieval towns was the *guild*. This was, roughly speaking, a professional association organized to protect and promote special interests. The main types were merchant guilds and craft guilds. The primary functions of the merchant guild were to maintain a monopoly of the local market for its members and to preserve a stable economic system. To accomplish these ends the merchant guild severely restricted trading by foreigners in the city, guaranteed to its members the right to participate in sales offered by other members, enforced uniform pricing, and did everything possible to ensure that no individual would corner the market for goods produced by its members.

Craft guilds limit competition

Craft guilds similarly regulated the affairs of artisans. Usually their only full-fledged voting members were so-called master craftsmen, who were experts at their trades and ran their own shops. Hence if these guilds were anything like modern trade unions, they were unions of bosses. Second-class members of craft guilds were journeymen, who had learned their trades but still worked for the masters (*journeyman* is from the French *journée*, meaning "day," or by extension "day's work"), and apprentices. Terms of apprenticeship were carefully regulated: if an apprentice wished to become a master he often had to produce a "masterpiece" for judging by the masters of the guild. Craft guilds, like merchant guilds, sought to preserve monopolies and to limit competition. Thus they established uniformity of prices and wages, prohibited working after hours, and formulated detailed regulations governing methods of production and quality of materials. In addition to all their economic functions, both kinds of guild served important social ones. Often they acted in the capacity of religious associations, benevolent societies, and social clubs. Wherever possible guilds tried to minister to the human needs of their members. Thus in some cities they came close to becoming miniature governments.

The Seal of a Leprosarium. Lepers with their crutches were common sights in medieval cities. This seal of a French leper house dates from 1208.

Town merchants and artisans were particularly concerned with protecting themselves because they had no accepted role in the older medieval scheme of things. Usually merchants were disdained by the landed aristocracy because they could claim no ancient lineages and were not versed in the ways of chivalry. Worst of all, they were too obviously concerned with pecuniary gain. Although nobles too were gradually becoming interested in making profits, they displayed this less openly: they paid little attention in their daily lives to accounts and made much of their free-spending largesse. Still another reason why medieval merchants were on the defensive was that the Church, opposed to illicit gain, taught a doctrine of the "just price" that was often at variance with what the merchants thought they deserved. Clergymen too condemned usury—i.e., the lending of money for interest—even though it was often essential for doing business. A decree of the Second Lateran Council of 1139, to take one example, excoriated the "detestable, shameful, and insatiable rapacity of moneylenders." As time went on, however, attitudes slowly changed. In Italy it often became hard to tell merchants from aristocrats because the latter customarily lived in towns and often engaged in trade themselves. In the rest of Europe, the most prosperous town-dwellers, called patricians, developed their own sense of pride verging on that of the nobility. The medieval Church never abandoned its prohibition of usury, but it did come to approve making profits on commercial risks, which was often close to the same thing. Moreover, starting around the thirteenth century leading churchmen came to speak more favorably of merchants. St. Bonaventure, a leading thirteenth-century churchman, argued that God showed special favors to shepherds like David in the time of the Old Testament, to fishers like Peter in the time of the New, and to merchants like St. Francis in the thirteenth century.

Significance of the urban revolution: (1) development of the economy and government

All in all, the importance of the high-medieval urban revolution can scarcely be overestimated. The fact that the new towns were the vital pumps of the high-medieval economy has already been sufficiently emphasized: in providing markets and producing wares they kept the entire economic system thriving. In addition, cities and towns made important contributions to the development of government because in many areas they gained their own independence and ruled themselves as city-states. Primarily in Italy, where urban life was by far the most advanced, city governments experimented with new systems of tax-collecting, record-

Medieval Walled City of Carcassonne, France. These walls date from 1240 to 1285.

keeping, and public participation in decision-making. Italian city-states were particularly advanced in their administrative techniques and thereby helped influence a general European-wide growth in governmental sophistication.

(2) Towns as a foundation for intellectual life

Finally, the rise of towns contributed greatly to the quickening of intellectual life in the West. New schools were invariably located in towns because towns afforded domiciles and legal protection for scholars. At first, students and teachers were always clerics, but by the thirteenth century the needs of merchants to be trained in reading and accounting led to the foundation of numerous lay primary schools. Equally momentous for the future was the fact that the stimulating urban environment helped make advanced schools more open to intellectual experimentation than any in the West since those of the Greeks. Not coincidentally, Greek intellectual life too was based on thriving cities. Thus it seems that without commerce in goods there can be little exciting commerce in ideas.

Feudalism and the Rise of the National Monarchies

If any western European city of around 1200 epitomized Europe's greatest new accomplishments it was Paris: that city was not only a bustling commercial center and an important center of learning, it was also the capital of what was becoming Europe's most powerful government. France, like England and the new Christian kingdoms of the Iberian peninsula, was taking shape in the twelfth and thirteenth centuries as a *national monarchy,* a new form of government that was to dominate Europe's political future. Because the developing national monarchies were the most successful and promising European governments we will concentrate on them. But before we do it is well to see what was happening from the political point of view in Germany and Italy.

The political decline of medieval Germany an intriguing historical problem

Around 1050 Germany was unquestionably the most centralized and best-ruled territory in Europe, but by 1300 it had turned into a snake pit of warring petty states. Since most other areas of Europe were gaining stronger rule in the very same period, the political decline of Germany is an intriguing historical problem. It is also a problem of fundamental importance because from a political point of view Germany only caught up with the rest of Europe in the nineteenth century, and its belated efforts to gain its full place in the European political system created difficulties that have just come to be resolved in our own age.

The German monarchy in the tenth and eleventh centuries

The major sources of Germany's strength from the reign of Otto the Great in the middle of the tenth century until the latter part of the eleventh century were its succession of strong rulers, its resistance to political fragmentation, and the close alliance of its crown with the Church. By resoundingly defeating the Hungarians and taking the title of emperor, Otto kept the country from falling prey to further invasions and won great prestige for the monarchy. For over a century afterward there was a nearly uninterrupted succession of rulers as able and vigorous as Otto. Their nearest political rivals were the dukes, military leaders of five large German territories (Lorraine, Saxony, Franconia, Swabia, and Bavaria), but throughout most of this period the dukes were overawed by the emperors' greater power. In order to rule their wide territories—which included Switzerland, eastern France, and most of the Low Countries, as well as claims to northern Italy—the emperors relied heavily on cooperation with the Church. The leading royal administrators were archbishops and bishops whom the emperors appointed without interference from the pope and who often came from their own families. The German emperors were so strong that, when they chose to do so, they could march down to Italy and name their own popes. The archbishops and bishops ran the German government fairly well for the times without any elaborate administrative machinery, and they counterbalanced the strength of the dukes. In the course of the eleventh century the emperors were starting tentatively to develop their own secular administration. Had they been allowed to continue this policy, it might have provided a really solid governmental foundation for the future. But just then the whole system shaped by Otto the Great and his successors was dramatically challenged by a revolution within the Church.

The struggle between Henry IV and Gregory VII

The challenge to the German government came in the reign of Henry IV (1056–1106) and was directed by Pope Gregory VII (1073–1085). For reasons that will be discussed in the next chapter, Gregory wished to free the Church from secular control and launched a struggle to achieve this aim against Henry IV. Gregory immediately placed Henry on the defensive by forging an alliance with the dukes and other German princes, who only needed a sufficient pretext to rise up against their ruler. When the princes threatened to depose Henry because of his disobedience to the pope, the hitherto mighty ruler was forced to seek absolution from Gregory VII in one of the most melodramatic scenes of the Middle Ages. In the depths of winter in 1077 Henry hurried over the Alps to abase himself before the pope in the north Italian castle of Canossa. As Gregory described the scene in a letter to the princes, "There on three successive days, standing before the castle gate, laying aside all royal insignia, barefooted and in coarse attire, Henry ceased not with many tears to beseech the apostolic help and comfort." No German ruler had ever been so humiliated. Although the events at Canossa forestalled Henry's deposition, they robbed him of his great prestige. By the time his struggle with the papacy, continued by his son, was over, the princes had won far more practical independence from the crown than they had ever had. More than that, in 1125 they made good their claims to be able to elect a new ruler regardless of hereditary succession—a principle that would thereafter often lead them to choose the weakest successors or to embroil the country in civil war. Meanwhile, the crown had lost much of its control of the Church and thus in effect had its administrative rug pulled out from under it. While France and England were gradually consolidating their centralized governmental apparatuses, Germany was losing its own.

A major attempt to stem the tide running against the German monarchy was made in the twelfth century by Frederick I (1152–1190), who came from the family of Hohenstaufen. Frederick, called "Barbarossa" (meaning "red beard"), tried to reassert his imperial dignity by calling his realm the "Holy Roman Empire," on the theory that it was a universal empire descending from Rome and blessed by God. Laying claim to Roman descent, he promulgated old Roman imperial laws—preserved in the Code of Justinian—that gave him much theoretical power. But he could not hope to enforce such laws unless he had his own material base of support. Therefore the major policy of his reign was to balance the power of the princes by carving out his own geographical domain from which he might draw wealth and strength.

Frederick Barbarossa. A stylized contemporary representation.

Unfortunately for Frederick, his ancestral lands were located in Swabia, a poorer part of Germany that even today still consists of relatively unproductive hill country and the Black Forest. So Frederick decided to make northern Italy his power base in addition to Swabia. In this he could hardly have made a worse decision. Northern Italy was certainly wealthy, but it was also fiercely independent. Its rich towns and cities, led by Milan, offered stiff resistance. The papacy, which had no wish to see a strong German emperor ruling powerfully in Italy, further lent them helpful moral support. Frederick came very close to overpowering the urban-papal alliance but ultimately the Alps proved to be too great a barrier to allow him to enforce his will in Italy and hope to rule in Germany as well. Whenever he subdued the towns he would shortly afterward have to leave for home, and the towns, with papal encouragement, would then rise up again. Finally, in 1176, insufficient German imperial forces were resoundingly defeated by the troops of a north Italian urban coalition—the Lombard League—at Legnano, and Barbarossa was forced to concede the area's de facto independence. In the meantime, the princes in Germany were continuing to gather strength, especially by colonizing the rich agricultural lands east of the Elbe where Frederick really should have busied himself, and the emperor's struggle with the popes further alienated elements within the German church. Because Barbarossa was a dashing figure he was well remembered by Germans, but his reign virtually made it certain that the German empire would not rise again during the medieval period.

The failure of Frederick's policy

The reign of Barbarossa's equally famous grandson, Frederick II (1212–1250), was merely a playing out of Germany's fate. In terms of his personality Frederick was probably the most fascinating of all medieval rulers. Because his father, Henry VI, had inherited through marriage the kingdom of southern Italy and Sicily (later called the Kingdom of the Two Sicilies), Frederick grew up in Palermo, where he absorbed elements of Islamic culture. (Arabs had ruled in Sicily for two and a half centuries, from 831 to 1071.) Frederick II spoke five or six languages, was a patron of learning, and wrote his own book on falconry, which takes an honored place in the early history of Western observational science. He also performed bizarre and brutal "experiments," such as disemboweling men to

The Emperor Frederick II. He is shown holding a *fleur de lis,* as a symbol of rule, with a falcon, his favorite bird, at his side.

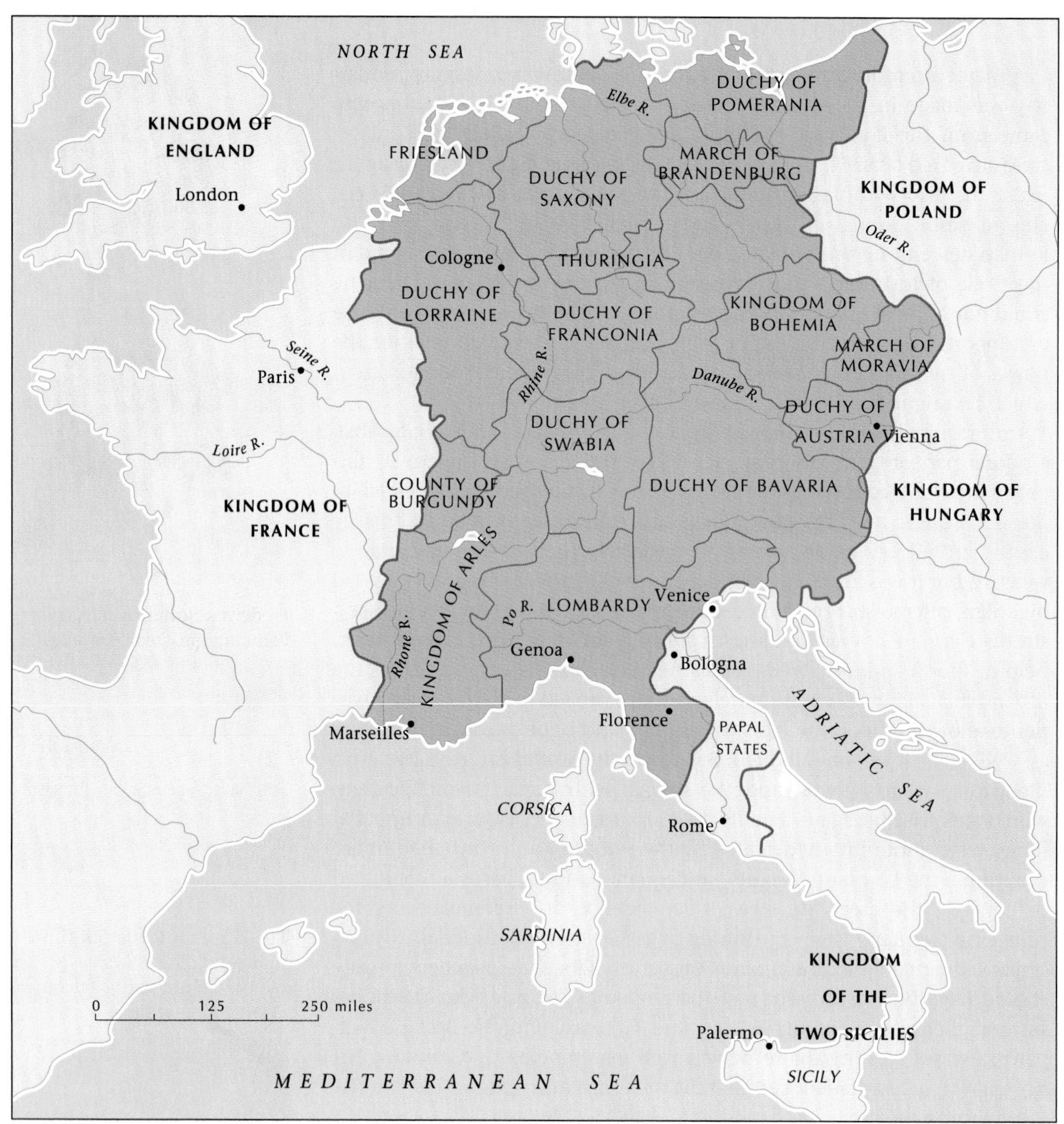

The German Empire, c. 1200

Frederick II

observe the comparative effects of rest and exercise upon digestion. Such practices corresponded to Frederick's overall policy of trying to rule like an Oriental despot. In his autonomous kingdom of southern Italy he introduced Eastern forms of absolutist and bureaucratic government. He established a professional army, levied direct taxation, and promulgated uniform Roman law. Typically, Frederick tried to create a ruler cult and decreed it an act of sacrilege even to discuss his statutes or judgments. For a while these policies seemed successful in ruling southern Italy, but Frederick's power base in Italy led to renewed conflicts with the papacy and the northern Italian cities. These dragged on indecisively until his death, but thereafter the papacy was resolved to see no further Hohenstaufens ruling in Italy and proceeded to eliminate the remaining contenders from the line by calling crusades against them. Overtaxed by Frederick's ruthlessness and subsequent wars, southern Italy gradually sank into the backwardness from which it is only barely emerging today. And Frederick's reign was damaging to Germany as well. Bent on pursuing his Italian policies without hindrance, Frederick formally wrote Germany off to the princes by granting them large areas of sovereignty. Although titular "emperors" afterward continued to be elected, the princes were the real rulers of the country. Yet they fought with each other so much that peace was rare, and they subdivided their lands among their heirs to such an extent that the map of Germany began to look like a jigsaw puzzle. As the French writer Voltaire later said, the German "Holy Roman Empire" had become neither holy, nor Roman, nor an empire.

The political situation in high-medieval Italy

The story of high-medieval Italian politics may be told more quickly. Southern Italy and Sicily had been welded together into a strong monarchical state in the twelfth century by Norman-French descendants of the Vikings. But then, as we have seen, the area went to the Hohenstaufens and was subsequently brought to ruin. Central Italy was largely ruled by the papacy in the High Middle Ages, but the popes were seldom strong enough to create a really well-governed state, partly because they were at constant loggerheads with the German emperors. Farthest north were the rich commercial and manufacturing cities that had successfully fought off Barbarossa. These were usually organized politically in the form of republics or "communes." They offered much participation in governmental life to their more prosperous inhabitants. But because of diverse economic interests and family antagonisms, the Italian cities were usually riven with internal strife. Moreover, although they could unite in leagues against foreign threats such as those represented by Barbarossa or Frederick II, the cities often fought each other when foreign threats were absent. The result was that although economic and cultural life was very far advanced in the Italian cities, and although the cities made important experiments in administrative techniques, political stability was widely lacking in northern Italy throughout most of the high-medieval period.

Feudalism defined

If one looks for the centers of growing political stability in Europe, then one has to seek them in high-medieval France and England. Ironically, some of the most basic foundations for future political achievement in France were established without any planning just when that area was most politically unstable. These foundations were aspects of a level of political decentralization often referred to by historians as the system of *feudalism.* The use of this word is controversial because, ever since Marx, some historians have preferred to use it as a term to describe an agrarian economic and social system wherein large estates are worked by a dependent peasantry. The difficulty with this usage is that it is too imprecise, for such large estates existed in many times and places beyond the

European Middle Ages and the medieval agrarian system can best be called manorialism. Some historians on the other extreme argue that even if the word "feudalism" is used to describe a medieval political system, medieval realities were so diverse that no one definition of feudalism can accurately or even usefully be extended to cover more than a single case. Nonetheless, for convenience we can retain the use of the word here and apply it to a specific point in medieval political development so long as we bear in mind that, like manorialism, it is only meant to serve as an approximation and that other historians may use it as a term for economic or sociological analysis.

Political feudalism

Political feudalism was essentially a system of extreme political decentralization wherein what we today would call public power was widely vested in private hands. From a historical perspective it was most fully experienced in France during the tenth century when the Carolingian Empire had disintegrated and the area was being buffeted by devastating Viking invasions. The Carolingians had maintained a modicum of public authority, but they proved to be no help whatsoever in warding off the invasions. So local landlords had to fend for themselves. In the end, the landlords turned out to offer the best defense against the Vikings and accordingly were able to acquire practically all the old governmental powers. They raised their own small armies, dispensed their own crude justice, and occasionally issued their own primitive coins. Despite such decentralization, however, it was never forgotten that there once had been higher and larger units of government. Above all, no matter how weak the king was (and he was indeed usually very weak), there always remained a king in France who descended directly or indirectly from the western branch of the Carolingians. There also were scattered remaining dukes or counts, who in theory were supposed to have more power and authority than petty landlords or knights. So, by a complicated and hard-to-trace process of rationalization, a vague theory was worked out in the course of the tenth and eleventh centuries that tried to establish some order within feudalism. According to this, minor feudal lords did not hold their powers outright but held them only as so-called *fiefs* (rhymes with "reefs"), which could be revoked upon noncompliance with certain obligations. In theory—and much of this theory was ignored in practice for long periods of time—the king or higher lords granted fiefs, that is, governmental rights over various lands, to lesser lords in return for a stipulated amount of military service. In turn, the lesser lords could grant some of those fiefs to still lesser lords for military services until the chain stopped at the lowest level of knights. The holder of a fief was called a *vassal* of the granter, but this term had none of the demeaning connotations that it has gained today. Vassalage—much unlike serfdom—was a purely honorable status and all fief-holders were "noble."

Feudalism a force for political progress

Since feudalism was originally a form of decentralization, it once was considered by historians to have been a corrosive or divisive historical force; in common speech today many use the word "feudal" as a synonym for backward. But scholars more recently have come to the conclusion that feudalism was a force for progress and a fundamental point of departure for the growth of the modern state. They note that in areas such as Germany and Italy, where there was hardly any feudalism, political stabilization and unification came only in later times, whereas in the areas of France and England, which saw full feudalization, stabilization and governmental centralization came rapidly afterward. Scholars now posit several reasons for this. Because feudalism was originally spontaneous and makeshift, it was highly flexible. Local lords, instead of being bound by anachronistic, procrustean principles, could rule as seemed best at the moment, or could bend to the dictates of particular local customs. Thus their governments, however crude, worked the best for their times and could be used for building an even stronger government as time went on. A second reason for the effectiveness of feudalism was that it drew more people into direct contact with the actual workings of political life than had the old Roman or Carolingian systems. Government on the most local level could most easily be seen or experienced; as it became tangible people began to appreciate and identify with it far more than they had identified with empires. The result was that feudalism inculcated growing governmental loyalty, and once that loyalty was developed it could be drawn upon by still larger units. Third, feudalism helped lead to certain more modern institutions by its emphasis on courts. As the feudal system became more regularized, it became customary for vassals to appear at the court of their overlords at least once a year. There they were expected to "pay court," i.e., show certain ceremonial signs of loyalty, and also to serve on "courts" in the sense of participating in trials and offering counsel. Thus they became more and more accustomed to performing governmental business and began to behave more like courtiers or politicians. As the monarchical states of France and England themselves developed, kings saw how useful the feudal court was and made it the administrative kernel of their expanding governmental systems. A final reason why feudalism led to political progress is not really intrinsic to the system itself. Because the theory of larger units was never forgotten, it could be drawn upon by greater lords and kings when the right time came to reacquire their rights.

The Norman Conquest

The greatest possibilities for the use of feudalism were first demonstrated in England after the Norman Conquest of 1066. We have seen that England became unified and enjoyed strong kingship under the Saxon Alfred and his successors in the late ninth and tenth centuries. But then the Saxon kingship began to weaken, primarily as the result of renewed Viking invasions and poor leadership. In 1066 William, the duke of Normandy (in northwestern France), laid claim to the English crown and crossed the Channel to conquer what he had claimed. Fortunately for him the newly installed English king, Harold, had just warded off a Viking attack in the north and thus could not offer resistance at full strength. At the Battle of Hastings Harold and his Saxon troops fought bravely, but ultimately could not withstand the onslaught of the fresher Norman troops. As the day waned Harold fell, mortally wounded by a

The Bayeux Tapestry. Embroidered shortly after the Battle of Hastings, the Bayeux Tapestry is a 231-foot document of the battle and the events leading up to it. Here the Saxons have sighted a shooting star (Halley's comet, actually) and, taking it for an omen, report it to King Harold.

random arrow, his forces dispersed, and the Normans took the field and with it, England. Duke William now became King William, the Conqueror, and proceeded to rule his new prize as he wished.

The feudal system under William the Conqueror

With hindsight we can say that the Norman Conquest came at just the right time to preserve and enhance political stability. Before 1066 England was threatened with disintegration under warrior aristocrats called earls, but William destroyed their power entirely. In its place he substituted the feudal system, whereby all the land in England was newly granted in the form of fiefs held directly or indirectly from the king. Fief-holders had most of the governmental rights they had obtained less formally on the Continent, but William retained the prerogatives of coining money, collecting a land tax, and supervising justice in major criminal cases. He also retained the Anglo-Saxon officer of local government, known as the *sheriff,* to help him administer and enforce these rights. In order to make sure that none of his barons (the English term for major fief-holders) became too powerful, William was careful to scatter the fiefs granted to them throughout various parts of the country. In these ways William used feudal practices to help govern England when there were not yet enough trained administrators to allow any real governmental professionalization. But he also retained much royal power and kept the country thoroughly unified under the crown.

The growth of national monarchy in England; the reign of Henry I

The history of English government in the two centuries after William is primarily a story of kings tightening up the feudal system to their advantage until they superseded it and created a strong national monarchy. The first to take steps in this direction was the Conqueror's energetic son Henry I (1100–1135). One of his most important accomplishments was to start a process of specialization at the royal court whereby certain officials began to take full professional responsibility for supervising financial accounts; these officials became known as clerks of the *Exchequer.* Another accomplishment was to institute a system of traveling circuit-judges to administer justice as direct royal representatives in various parts of the realm.

After an intervening period of civil war Henry I was succeeded by his grandson Henry II (1154–1189), who was very much in his grandfather's activist mold. Henry II's reign was certainly one of the most momentous in all of English history. One reason for this was that it saw a great struggle between the king and the flamboyant archbishop of Canterbury, Thomas Becket, over the status of Church courts and Church law. In Henry's time priests and other clerics were tried for any crimes in Church courts under the rules of canon law. Punishment in these courts was notoriously lax. Even murderers were seldom sentenced to more than penance and loss of their clerical status. Also, decisions handed down in English Church courts could be appealed to the papal *curia* in Rome. Henry, who wished to have royal law prevail as far as possible and maintain judicial standards for all subjects in his realm, tried to limit these practices by the Constitutions of Clarendon of 1164. On the matter of clerics accused of crime he was willing to compromise by allowing them to be judged in Church courts

The struggle between Henry II and Thomas Becket

Martyrdom of Thomas Becket. From a thirteenth-century English psalter. One of the knights has struck Becket so mightily that he has broken his sword.

but then have them sentenced in royal courts. Becket, however, resisted all attempts at change with great determination. The quarrel between king and archbishop was made more bitter by the fact that the two had earlier been close friends. It reached a tragic climax when Becket was murdered in Canterbury Cathedral by four of Henry's knights, after the king, in an outburst of anger, had rebuked them for doing nothing to rid him of his antagonist. The crime so shocked the English public that Becket was quickly revered as a martyr and became the most famous English saint. More important for the history of government, Henry had to abandon most of his program of bringing the Church courts under royal control, and his aims were fulfilled only in the sixteenth century with the coming of the English Reformation.

The judicial reforms of Henry II

Despite this major setback, Henry II made enormous governmental gains in other areas, so much so that some historians maintain that he was the greatest king that England has ever known. His most important contributions were judicial. He greatly expanded the use of the itinerant judges instituted by Henry I and began the practice of commanding sheriffs to bring before these judges groups of men who were familiar with local conditions. These men were required to report under oath every case of murder, arson, robbery, or other major crimes known to them to have occurred since the judges' last visit. This was the origin of the grand jury. Henry also for the first time allowed parties in civil disputes to obtain royal justice. In the most prevalent type of case, someone who claimed to have been recently dispossessed of his land could obtain a writ from the crown, which would order the sheriff to bring twelve men who were assumed to know the facts before a judge. The twelve were then asked under oath if the plaintiff's claim was true, and the judge rendered his decision in accordance with their answers. Out of such practices grew the institution of the trial jury, although the trial jury was not used in criminal cases until the thirteenth century.

Medieval Justice. Medieval sentencing was usually harsh. Here a convicted offender pays for his crime with the loss of his right hand.

Henry II's legal innovations benefited both the crown and the country in several ways. Most obviously, they made justice more uniform and equitable throughout the realm. They also thereby made royal justice sought after and popular. Particularly in disputes over land—the most important and frequent disputes of the day—the weaker party was no longer at the mercy of a strong-arming neighbor. Usually the weaker parties were knights, with whom the crown before then had not been in close touch. In helping defend their rights Henry gained valuable allies in his policy of keeping the stronger barons in tow. Finally, the widespread use of juries in Henry's reign brought more and more people into actual participation in royal government. In so doing it got them more interested in government and more loyal to government. Since these people served without pay, Henry brilliantly managed to expand the competence and popularity of his government at very little cost.

Efficient governmental administration during Richard's absence

The most concrete proof of Henry II's success is that after his death his government worked so well that it more or less ran on its own. Henry's son, the swashbuckling Richard I, the "Lionhearted," ruled for ten years, from 1189 to 1199, but in that time he stayed in England for only six months because he was otherwise engaged in crusading or defending his possessions on the Continent. Throughout the time of Richard's absence governmental administration actually became more efficient, owing to the work of capable ministers. The country also raised two huge sums for Richard by taxation: one to pay for his crusade to the Holy Land and the other to buy his ransom when he was captured by an enemy on his return. But later when a new king needed still more money, most Englishmen were disinclined to pay it.

King John and Magna Carta

The new king was Richard's brother, John (1199–1216), who has the reputation of being a villain but was more a victim of circumstances. Ever since the time of William the Conqueror, English kings had continued to rule in large portions of modern-day France, but by John's reign the kings of France were becoming strong enough to take back much of these territories. John had the great misfortune of facing the able French king Philip Augustus, who won back Normandy and neighboring lands by force of arms in 1204 and reinsured this victory by military successes in 1214. John needed money both to govern England and to fight in France, but his defeats made his subjects disinclined to give it to him. The barons particularly resented John's financial exigencies and in 1215 they made him renounce these in the subsequently famous Magna Carta (Great Charter), a document that was also designed to redress all the other abuses the barons could think of. Most common conceptions of Magna Carta are erroneous. It was not intended to be a bill of rights or a charter of liberties for the common people. On the contrary, it was basically a feudal document in which the king as overlord pledged to respect the traditional rights of his vassals. Nonetheless, it did enunciate in writing the important principles that large sums of money could not be raised by the crown without consent given by the barons in a common council, and that no free man could be punished by the crown without judgment by his equals and by the law of the land. Above all, Magna Carta was important as an expression of the principle of limited government and of the idea that the king is bound by the law.

Edward I. A contemporary representation forming part of the initial "E" in a document that regranted Magna Carta.

The progress of centralized government in the reign of Henry III

As the contemporary American medievalist J. R. Strayer has said, "Magna Carta made arbitrary government difficult, but it did not make centralized government impossible." In the century following its issuance, the progress of centralized government continued apace. In the reign of John's son, Henry III (1216–1272), the barons vied with the weak king for control of the government but did so on the assumption that centralized government itself was a good thing. Throughout that period administrators continued to perfect more efficient legal and administrative institutions. Whereas in the reign of Henry I financial administration began to become a specialized bureau of the royal court, in the reign of Henry III this became true of legal administration (the creation of permanent High Courts) and administration of foreign correspondence (the so-called Chancery). English central government was now fully developing a trained officialdom.

The origins of Parliament

The last and most famous branch of the medieval English governmental system was Parliament. This gradually emerged as a separate branch of government in the decades before and after 1300, above all owing to the wishes of Henry III's son, Edward I (1272–1307). Although Parliament later became a check against royal absolutism, nothing could be further from the truth than to think that its first meetings were "demanded by the people." In its origins Parliament actually had little to do with popular representation, but was rather the king's feudal court in its largest gathering. Edward I was a strong king who called Parliaments frequently to raise money as quickly and efficiently as possible in order to help finance his foreign wars. Those present at Parliaments were not only expected to give their consent to taxation—in fact, it was virtually inconceivable for them to refuse—but while they were there they were told why taxes were necessary so that they would pay them less grudgingly. They could also agree upon details of collection and payment. At the same meetings Edward could take advice about pressing concerns, have justice done for exceptional cases, review local administration, and promulgate new laws. Probably the most unusual trait of Edward's Parliaments in comparison to similar assemblies on the Continent was that they began to include representatives from the counties and towns in addition to the higher nobility. These representatives, however, scarcely spoke for "the people" because most of the people of England were unenfranchised serfs and peasants—not to mention women—who were never consulted in any way. Most likely, Edward had predominantly financial motives for calling representatives from the "commons." He probably also realized the propaganda value of overawing local representatives with royal grandeur at impressive parliamentary meetings so that they would then spread a favorable impression of the monarchy back home. As time went on, commoners were called to Parliament so often that they became a recognized part of its organization: by the middle of the fourteenth century they sat regularly in their own "house." But they still represented only the prosperous people of countryside and towns and were usually manipulated by the crown or the nobles.

The English monarchy under Edward I

Edward I's reign also saw the culmination of the development of a strong national monarchy in other aspects. By force of arms Edward nearly unified the entire island of Britain, conquering Wales and almost subduing Scotland (which, however, was to rise up again soon after his death). Edward began the practice of regularly issuing statute law, that is, original public legislation designed to apply indefinitely to the entire realm. Because of his role as a lawgiver, Edward is sometimes referred to as the "English Justinian." Most important, Edward also curtailed the feudal powers of his barons by limiting their rights to hold private courts and to grant their own lands as fiefs. Thus, by the end of his reign much of the independent power once consciously vested with the barons by William the Conqueror was being taken away from them. The explanation for this is that in the intervening high-medieval centuries the king was developing his own royal institutions of government to the degree that old-fashioned feudalism was now no longer of any real service. Because Edward pressed his strong government and financial demands somewhat excessively for the spirit of the age, there was an antimonarchical reaction after his death. But it is striking that after Edward's time whenever there were baronial rebellions they were always made on the assumption that England would remain a unified country, governed by the basic high-medieval monarchical institutions. England was unified around the crown in the High Middle Ages and would remain a basically well-governed and unified country right up to modern times.

The process of political centralization in France

While the process of governmental centralization was making impressive strides in England, it developed more slowly in France. But by around 1300 it had come close to reaching the same point of completion. French governmental unification proceeded more slowly because France in the eleventh century was more decentralized than England and faced greater problems. The last of the weak Carolingian monarchs was replaced in 987 by Hugh Capet, the count of Paris, but the new Capetian dynasty—which was to rule without interruption until 1328—was at first no stronger than the old Carolingian one. Even through most of the twelfth century the kings of France ruled directly only in a small area around Paris known as the Île-de-France, roughly the size of Vermont. Beyond that territory the kings had shadowy claims to being the feudal overlords of numerous counts and dukes throughout much of the area of modern France, but for practical purposes those counts and dukes were almost entirely independent. It was said that when the king of France demanded homage from the first duke of Normandy, the duke had one of his warriors pretend to kiss the king's foot but then seize the royal leg and pull the king over backwards, to the mockery of all those present. While the French kingship was so weak, the various parts of France were developing their own distinct local traditions and dialects. Thus, whereas William the Conqueror inherited in England a country that had already been unified and was just on the verge of falling apart, the French kings of the High Middle Ages had to unify their country from scratch, with only a vague reminiscence of Carolingian unity to build upon.

Factors facilitating the growth of the French monarchy

In many respects, however, luck was on their side. First of all, they were fortunate for hundreds of years in having direct male heirs to succeed them. Consequently, there were no deadly quarrels over the right of succession. In the second place, most of the French kings lived to an advanced age, the average period of rule being about thirty years. That meant that sons were already mature men when they came to the throne and there were few regencies to squander the royal power during the minority of a prince. More than that, the kings of France were always highly visible, if sometimes not very imposing, when there were power struggles elsewhere, so people in neighboring areas became accustomed to thinking of the kingship as a force for stability in an unstable world. A third favorable circumstance for the French kings was the growth of agricultural prosperity and trade in their home region; this provided them with important sources of revenue. A fourth fortuitous development was that the kings were able to gain the support of the popes because the latter usually

France, c. 1000

needed allies in their incessant struggles with the German emperors. The popes lent the French kings prestige, as they earlier had done for the Carolingians, and they also allowed them much direct power over the local Church, thereby bringing the kings further income and influence from patronage. A fifth factor in the French kings' favor was the growth in the twelfth and thirteenth centuries of the University of Paris as the leading European center of studies. As foreigners came flocking to the university, they learned of the French kings' growing authority and spread their impressions when they returned home. Finally, and by no means least of all, great credit must be given to the shrewdness and vigor of several of the French kings themselves.

The first noteworthy Capetian king was Louis VI, "the Fat" (1108–1137). While accomplishing nothing startling, Louis at least managed to pacify his home base, the Île-de-France, by driving out or subduing its turbulent "robber barons." Once this was accomplished, agriculture and trade could prosper and the intellectual life of Paris could start to flourish. Thereafter, the French kings had a geographical source of power of exactly the kind that the German ruler Barbarossa sought but never found. The really startling additions to the realm were made by Louis's grandson, Philip Augustus (1180–1223). Philip was wily enough to know how to take advantage of certain feudal rights in order to win large amounts of western French territory from King John of England. He was also decisive enough to know how to defend his gains in battle. Most impressive of all, Philip worked out an excellent formula for governing his new acquisitions. Since these increased his original lands close to fourfold, and since each new area had its own highly distinct local customs, it would have been hopeless to try to enforce strict governmental standardization by means of what was then a very rudimentary administrative system. Instead, Philip allowed his new provinces to maintain most of their indigenous governmental practices but superimposed on them new royal officials known as *baillis.* These officials were entirely loyal to Philip because they never came from the regions in which they served and were paid impressive salaries for the day. They had full judicial, administrative, and military authority in their bailiwicks: on royal orders they tolerated regional diversities but guided them to the king's advantage. Thus there were no revolts in the conquered territories and royal power was enhanced. This pattern of local diversity balanced against bureaucratic centralization was to remain the basic pattern of French government. Thus Philip Augustus can be seen as an important founder of the modern French state.

A Seal Depicting King Philip Augustus

Foundations of the French monarchy; Louis VI and Philip Augustus

In the brief reign of Philip's son, Louis VIII (1223–1226), almost all of southern France was added to the crown in the name of intervention against religious heresy. Once incorporated, this territory was governed largely on the same principles laid down by Philip. The next king, Louis IX (1226–1270), was so pious that he was later canonized by the Church and is commonly referred to as St. Louis. He ruled strongly and justly (except for great intolerance of Jews and heretics), decreed a standardized coinage for the country, perfected the judicial system, and brought France a long, golden period of internal peace. Because he was so well-loved, the monarchy lived off his prestige for many years afterward.

King Philip the Fair of France. An author is presenting a copy of his book to the mighty king, enthroned on a pedestal.

That prestige, however, came close to being squandered by St. Louis's more ruthless grandson, Philip IV, "the Fair" (1285–1314). Philip fought many battles at once, seeking to round out French territories in the northeast and southwest and to gain full control over the French Church instead of sharing it with the pope in Rome. All these activities forced him to accelerate the process of governmental centralization, especially with the aim of trying to raise money. Thus his reign saw the quick formulation of many administrative institutions that came close to completing the development of medieval French government, as the contemporary reign of Edward I did in England. Philip's reign also saw the calling of assemblies that were roughly equivalent to the English Parliaments, but these—later called "Estates-General"—never played a central role in the French governmental system. Philip the Fair was successful in most of his ventures; above all, as we will later see, in reducing the pope to the level of a virtual French figurehead. After his death there would be an antimonarchical reaction, as there was at the same time in England, but by his reign France was unquestionably the strongest power in Europe. With only a sixteenth-century interruption, it would remain so until the nineteenth century.

Comparison of England and France

While England and France followed certain similar processes of monarchical centralization and nation-building, they were also marked by basic differences that are worth describing because they were to typify differences in development for centuries after. England, a far smaller country than France, was much better unified. Aside from Wales and Scotland, there were no regions in Britain that had such different languages or traditions that they thought of themselves as separate territories. Correspondingly, there were no aristocrats who could move toward separatism by drawing on regional resentments. This meant that England never really had to face the threat of internal division and could develop strong institutions of united national government such as Parliament. It also meant that the English kings, starting primarily with Henry II, could rely on numerous local dignitaries, above all, the knights, to do much work of local government without pay. The obvious advantage was that local government was cheap, but the hidden implication of the system was that government also had to be popular, or else much of the voluntary work would grind to a halt. This doubtless was the main reason why English kings went out of their way to seek formal consent for their actions. When they did not they could barely rule, so wise kings learned the lesson and as time went on England became most clearly a limited monarchy. The French kings, much to the contrary, ruled a richer and larger country, which gave them—at least in times of peace—sufficient wealth to pay for a more bureaucratic, salaried administration at both the central and local levels. French kings therefore could rule more absolutely. But they were continually faced with serious threats of regional separatism. Different regions continued to cherish their own traditions and often veered toward separatism in league with the upper aristocracy. So French kings often had to struggle with attempts at regional breakaways and take various measures to subdue their aristocrats. Up to around 1700 the monarchy had to fight a steady battle against regionalism, but it had the resources to win consistently and thereby managed to grow from strength to strength.

Medieval Spain

The only continental state that would rival France until the rise of Germany in the nineteenth century was Spain. The foundations of Spain's greatness were also laid in the High Middle Ages on the principle of national monarchy, but in the Middle Ages there was not yet one monarchy that ruled through most of the Iberian peninsula. After the Christians

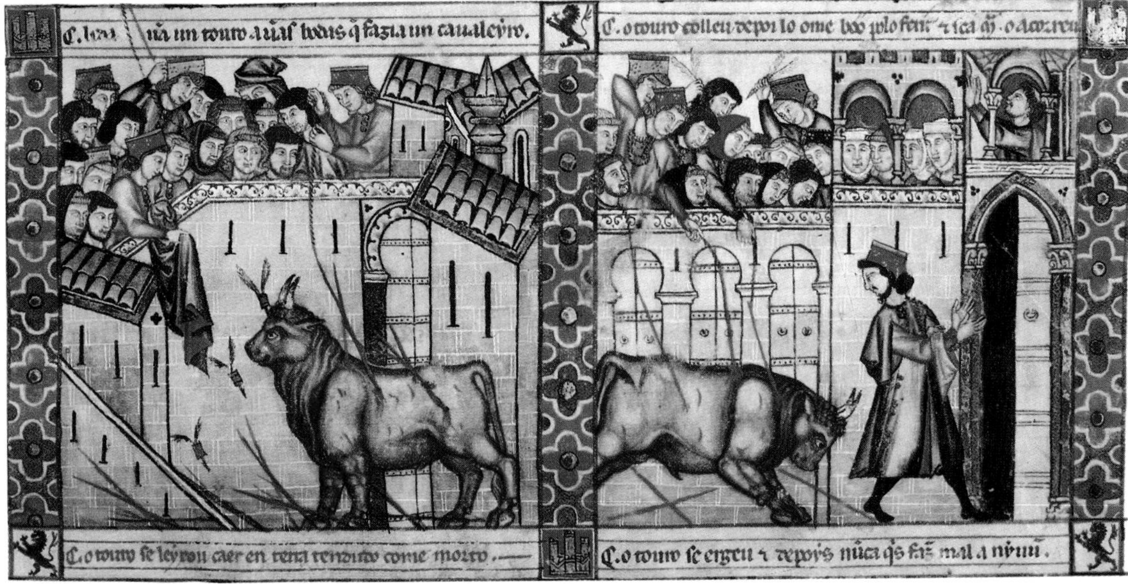

Bullfighting in a Thirteenth-Century Spanish Arena. Times do not seem to have changed much, although here the spectators are taking a rather unsporting part in the action.

started pushing back the forces of Islam around 1100 there were four Spanish Christian kingdoms: the tiny northern mountain state of Navarre, which would always remain comparatively insignificant; Portugal in the west; Aragon in the northeast; and Castile in the center. The main Spanish occupation in the High Middle Ages was the *Reconquista,* i.e., the reconquest of the peninsula for Christianity. This reached its culmination in the year 1212 in a major victory of a combined Aragonese-Castilian army over the Muslims at Las Navas de Tolosa. The rest was mostly mopping up. By the end of the thirteenth century all that remained of earlier Muslim domination was the small state of Granada in the extreme south, and Granada existed mostly because it was willing to pay tribute to the Christians. Because Castile had the largest open frontier, it became by far the largest Spanish kingdom, but it was balanced in wealth by the more urban and trade-oriented Aragon. Both kingdoms developed institutions in the thirteenth century that roughly paralleled those of France. But until the union of Aragon and Castile under King Ferdinand and Queen Isabella in the fifteenth century, the Iberian states individually could not hope to be as strong as the much richer and more populous France.

Historical role of the national monarchies

Before concluding this chapter it is best to assess the general significance of the rise of the national monarchies in high-medieval western Europe. Until their emergence there had been two basic patterns of government in Europe: city-states and empires. City-states had the advantage of drawing heavily upon citizen participation and loyalty and thus were able to make highly efficient use of their human potential. But they were often divided by economic rivalries, and they were not sufficiently large or militarily strong to defend themselves against imperial forces. The empires, on the other hand, could win battles and often had the resources to support an efficient bureaucratic administrative apparatus, but they drew on little voluntary participation and were too far-flung or rapacious to inspire any deep loyalties. The new national monarchies were to prove the "golden mean" between these extremes. They were large enough to have adequate military strength, and they developed administrative techniques that would rival and eventually surpass those of the Roman or Byzantine empires. More than that, building at first upon the bases of feudalism, they drew upon sufficient citizen participation and loyalty to help support them in times of stress when empires would have foundered. By about 1300 the monarchies of England, France, and the Iberian peninsula had gained the primary loyalties of their subjects, superseding loyalties to communities, regions, or to the government of the Church. For all these reasons they brought much internal peace and stability to large parts of Europe where there had been little stability before. Thus they contributed greatly to making life fruitful. The medieval national monarchies were also the ancestors of the modern nation-states—the most effective and equitable governments of our day (the former Soviet Union was more like an empire). In short, they were one of the Middle Ages' most beneficial bequests to modern times.

SUMMARY POINTS

- Between about 1050 and 1250 an agricultural revolution in western Europe vastly increased the output of farming. This revolution was driven by greater peace and stability, increased cultivation of land in northern Europe, and new technology such as the heavy plow, three-field crop rotation, and mills.
- The economic system of the High Middle Ages was based on manorialism, in which large estates owned by lords were farmed by serfs. Serfdom gradually declined during the thirteenth century and the quality of life for both serfs and lords improved.
- Both long-distance trade and cities grew rapidly during the High Middle Ages.
- Feudalism was a highly flexible system of government at the lowest regional level. Monarchs in England and France gradually were able to use it to their own advantage.
- During the High Middle Ages strong national monarchies developed in England, France, and modern-day Spain. In Germany and Italy, however, regional and local political interests and German power struggles with the papacy prevented the development of strong national institutions.

Selected Readings

GENERAL STUDIES

Bartlett, Robert, *The Making of Europe: Conquest, Colonization and Cultural Change, 950–1350,* Princeton, 1993. An original approach to identifying essential qualities of medieval western European civilization by studying the expansion of Latin Christendom on four frontiers.

Bloch, Marc, *Feudal Society,* Chicago, 1961. A modern classic, first published in France in 1940. Full of valuable insights but outdated in some respects.

Southern, R. W., *The Making of the Middle Ages,* New Haven, 1992. A subtle and brilliant reading of eleventh- and twelfth-century developments. Difficult but most rewarding.

Strayer, J. R., *Western Europe in the Middle Ages,* 3d ed., Glenview, Ill., 1982. In a class by itself as the best short introduction to medieval political and cultural history.

ECONOMIC AND SOCIAL CONDITIONS

Duby, Georges, *Rural Economy and Country Life in the Medieval West,* London, 1968. The best work on agrarian history. Highly recommended as an example of French historiography at its highest level.

Ennen, Edith, *The Medieval Town,* New York, 1979. Complements Duby on urban development.

Gies, Frances, and Joseph Gies, *Marriage and the Family in the Middle Ages,* New York, 1987. The Gieses have a knack for communicating the best scholarship to a nonspecialist audience.

———, *Women in the Middle Ages,* New York, 1978. An engaging account of women's lives in many different walks of life.

Gies, Joseph, and Frances Gies, *Life in a Medieval City,* New York, 1973. An engaging popular account concentrating on life in thirteenth-century Troyes.

Herlihy, David, *Medieval Households,* Cambridge, Mass., 1985. Covers family history from late antiquity until the end of the Middle Ages.

Keen, Maurice, *Chivalry,* New Haven, 1984.

Labarge, Margaret W., *A Small Sound of the Trumpet: Women in Medieval Life,* London, 1986. A lively survey.

Leyser, Henrietta, *Medieval Women: A Social History of Women in England, 440–1500,* New York, 1995. Although limited to one country, this is perhaps the best of the many recent surveys treating medieval women.

Lopez, Robert S., *The Commercial Revolution of the Middle Ages, 950–1350,* Englewood Cliffs, N.J., 1971.

Postan, M. M., *The Medieval Economy and Society: An Economic History of Britain in the Middle Ages,* London, 1993.

White, Lynn, Jr., *Medieval Technology and Social Change,* Oxford, 1962. Controversial but excellently written and thought-provoking.

POLITICAL DEVELOPMENTS

Baldwin, John W., *The Government of Philip Augustus,* Berkeley, 1986. A landmark of scholarship.

Barraclough, Geoffrey, *The Origins of Modern Germany,* New York, 1984. Highly interpretative.

Davies, R. G., and J. H. Denton, eds., *The English Parliament in the Middle Ages,* Manchester, England, 1981. Essays communicating scholarly findings about the history of Parliament.

Douglas, David, *The Norman Achievement, 1050–1100,* Berkeley, 1969. An insightful comparative study of Norman conquests in England and southern Italy.

———, *The Norman Fate, 1100–1154,* Berkeley, 1976. A comparison of government in Norman England and Norman Sicily.

Fuhrmann, Horst, *Germany in the High Middle Ages,* Cambridge, 1986. The best short introduction to the "hinge" period of medieval German history.

Hallam, Elizabeth M., *Capetian France, 987–1328,* New York, 1980. The best survey of the consolidation of royal power in medieval France.

Hyde, J. K., *Society and Politics in Medieval Italy,* New York, 1973. An excellent survey that integrates political and social history.

Loyn, H. R., *The Norman Conquest,* 3d ed., London, 1982.

Matthew, Donald, *The Norman Kingdom of Sicily,* New York, 1992. An introductory account of the Sicilian kingdom in the twelfth and thirteenth centuries.

Mortimer, Richard, *Angevin England, 1154–1258,* Cambridge, Mass., 1994. An expert treatment of politics and society that proceeds by topics.

Poole, Austin L., *From Domesday Book to Magna Carta, 1087–1216,* Oxford, 1993. Very detailed yet clear.

Richard, Jean, *Saint Louis: Crusader King of France,* Cambridge, Eng., 1992. A brisk and lively biography by a master medievalist of one of the Middle Ages' most successful kings.

Reilly, Bernard F., *The Medieval Spains,* New York, 1993. A succinct account of the broad sweep of events on the Iberian peninsula throughout the entire medieval period from about 500 to 1500.

Sayles, G. O., *The Medieval Foundations of England,* London, 1952. Probably still the best one-volume interpretation of medieval English political developments through the end of the thirteenth century.

Stow, Kenneth R., *Alienated Minority: The Jews of Medieval Latin Europe,* Cambridge, Mass., 1992. An excellent survey of all aspects of Jewish life in medieval western Europe.

Strayer, J. R., *On the Medieval Origins of the Modern State,* Princeton, 1970. A distillation of the ideas of one of America's greatest medievalists.

Warren, W. L., *The Governance of Norman and Angevin England, 1086–1272,* Stanford, 1987. Controversial in its view that royal government succeeded less well in sustained centralization than is often assumed.

Source Materials

Andrea, Alfred J., *The Medieval Record: Sources of Medieval History,* Boston, 1997.

Herlihy, David, ed., *The History of Feudalism,* New York, 1970.

Lopez, Robert S., and Irving W. Raymond, eds., *Medieval Trade in the Mediterranean World,* New York, 1990.

Otto, Bishop of Freising, *The Deeds of Frederick Barbarossa,* tr. C. C. Mierow, New York, 1953. A contemporary chronicle that is interesting enough to read from start to finish.

Suger, Abbot of Saint Denis, *The Deeds of Louis the Fat,* tr. R. Cusimano and J. Moorhead, Washington, D.C., 1992. Communicates well the challenges that faced King Louis VI of France.

CHAPTER 11

THE HIGH MIDDLE AGES (1050–1300): RELIGIOUS AND INTELLECTUAL DEVELOPMENTS

> You would see men and women dragging carts through marshes . . . everywhere miracles daily occurring, jubilant songs rendered to God. . . . You would say that the prophecy was fulfilled, "The Spirit of Life was in the wheels."
>
> —ABBOT ROBERT OF TORIGNI, on the building of the Cathedral of Chartres, 1145

Religious changes

THE RELIGIOUS and intellectual changes that transpired in the West between 1050 and 1300 were as important as the economic, social, and political ones. In the sphere of religion, the most fundamental organizational development was the triumph of the *papal monarchy.* Before the middle of the eleventh century certain popes had laid claim to primacy within the Church, but very few were able to come close to making good on such claims. Indeed, most popes before about 1050 were hardly able to rule effectively as bishops of Rome. But then, most dramatically, the popes emerged as the supreme religious leaders of Western Christendom. They centralized the government of the Church, challenged the sway of emperors and kings, and called forth the crusading movement. By 1300 the temporal success of the papacy had proven to be its own nemesis, but the popes still ruled the Church internally, as they continue to rule the Roman Catholic Church today.

Intellectual changes

While the papacy was assuming power, a new vitality infused the Christian religion itself, enabling Christianity to capture the human imagination as never before. At the same time too there was a remarkable revival of intellectual and cultural life. In education, thought, and the arts, as in economics and politics, the West before 1050 had been a backwater. Thereafter it emerged swiftly from backwardness to become an intellectual and artistic leader of the globe. Westerners boasted that learning and the arts had moved northwest to them from Egypt, Greece, and Rome—a boast that was largely true. In the High Middle Ages Europeans first started building on ancient intellectual foundations and also contributed major intellectual and artistic innovations of their own.

The Consolidation of the Papal Monarchy

The sorry state of religious life in the tenth and early eleventh centuries

To understand the origins and appreciate the significance of the western European religious revival of the High Middle Ages it is necessary to have some idea of the level to which religion had sunk in the tenth and early eleventh centuries. Around 800 the Emperor Charlemagne had made some valiant attempts to enhance the religious authority of bishops, introduce the parish system into rural regions where there had hardly been any priests before, and provide for the literacy of the clergy. But with the collapse of the Carolingian Empire, religious decentralization and ensuing corruption prevailed throughout most of Europe. Most churches and monasteries became the private property of strong local lords. The latter disposed of Church offices under their control as they wished, often by selling them or by granting them to close relatives. Obviously this was not the best way to find the most worthy candidates, and many priests were quite unqualified for their jobs. They were almost always illiterate, and often they lived openly with concubines. When archbishops or bishops were able to control appointments the results were not much better because such officials were usually close relatives of secular lords who followed their practices of financial or family aggrandizement. As for the popes, they were usually incompetent or corrupt, the sons or tools of powerful families who lived in or around the city of Rome. Some were astonishingly debauched. John XII may have been the worst of them. He was made pope at the age of eighteen in 955 because of the strength of his family. It is certain that he ruled for nine years as a thorough profligate, but there is some uncertainty about the cause of his death: either he was caught in *flagrante delicto* by a jealous husband and murdered on the spot, or else he died in the midst of a carnal act from sheer amorous exertion.

Religious revival: (1) Cluny and monastic reform

Once Europe began to catch its breath from the wave of external invasions that peaked in the tenth century, the wide extent of religious corruption or indifference was bound to call forth some reaction. Bishops could do little to effect change because the work of a bishop was limited to what he could do in his lifetime, and even more because most archbishops and bishops were unable to disentangle themselves from the political affairs of their day. The first successful measures of reform were taken in the monasteries because monasteries could be somewhat more independent and could count more on the support of their reforms by lay lords, insofar as lords feared for the health of their souls if monks did not serve their proper function in saying offices (i.e., prayers). The movement for monastic reform began with the foundation of the monastery of Cluny in Burgundy in 910 by a pious nobleman. Cluny was a Benedictine house but it introduced two constitutional innovations. One was that, in order to remain free from domination by either local secular or ecclesiastical powers, it was made directly subject to the pope. The other was that it undertook the reform or foundation of numerous "daughter monasteries": whereas formerly all Benedictine houses had been independent and equal, Cluny founded a monastic "family," whose members were subordinate to it. Owing to the succession of a few extremely pious, active, and long-lived abbots, the congregation of Cluniac houses grew so rapidly that there were sixty-seven by 1049. In all of them dedicated priors were chosen who followed the dictates of the abbot of Cluny rather than being responsible to local potentates. Cluniac monks accordingly became famous for their industry in the saying of offices. And Cluny was only the most famous of the new congregations. Other similar ones spread just as rapidly in the years around 1000 and succeeded in making the reformed monasteries vital centers of religious life and prayer.

(2) Reform of the clerical hierarchy

Around the middle of the eleventh century, after so many monasteries had been taken out of the control of secular authorities, the leaders of the monastic reform movement started to lobby for the reform of the clerical hierarchy as well. They centered their attacks upon *simony*—i.e., the buying and selling of positions in the Church—and they also demanded celibacy for all levels of clergy. Their entire program was directed toward depriving secular powers of their ability to dictate appointments of bishops, abbots, and priests, and toward making the clerical estate as "pure" and as distinct from the secular one as possible. Once this reform program was appropriated by the papacy, it would begin to change the face of the entire Church.

Emperor Henry III and reform of the papacy

Considering that the reformers were greatly opposed to lay interference, it is ironic that the first reformer was installed in the papacy by a German emperor, namely Henry III. In 1046 this ruler came to Italy, deposed three rival Italian claimants to the papal title, and named as pope a German reformer from his own retinue. Henry III's act brought in a series of reforming popes, who started to promulgate decrees against simony, clerical marriage, and immorality of all sorts throughout the Church. These popes also insisted upon their own role as primates and universal spiritual leaders in order to give strength to their actions. One of the most important steps they took was the issuance in 1059 of a decree on papal elections. This vested the right of naming a new pope solely with the cardinals, thereby depriving the Roman aristocracy or the German emperor of the chance to interfere in the matter. The decree preserved the independence of papal elections thereafter. In granting the right of election to cardinals the decree also became a milestone in the evolution of a special body within the Church. Ever since the tenth century a number of bishops and clerics, known as cardinals, from churches in and near Rome had taken on an important role as advisers and administrative assistants of the popes, but the election decree of 1059 first gave them their clearest powers. Thereafter the "college of cardinals" took on more and more administrative duties and helped create continuity in papal policy, especially when there was a quick succession of pontiffs. The cardinals still elect the pope today.

The ideals of Pope Gregory VII

A new and most momentous phase in the history of the reform movement was initiated during the pontificate of Gregory VII (1073–1085). Scholars disagree about how much Gregory was indebted to the ideas and policies of his predecessors in the reform movement and how much he departed from them. The answer seems to be that Gregory supported reform as much as others; indeed he explicitly renewed his predecessors' decrees against simony and clerical marriage. Yet he was not only more zealous in trying to enforce these decrees—a contemporary even called him a "Holy Satan"—but he brought with him a basically new conception of the role of the Church in human life. Whereas the older Christian ideal had been that of withdrawal, and the perfect "athlete of Christ" had been a passive contemplative, or ascetic monk, Gregory VII conceived of Christianity as being much more activist and believed that the Church was responsible for creating "right order in the world." To this end he demanded absolute obedience and strenuous chastity from his clergy: some of his clerical opponents complained that he wanted clerics to live like angels. Equally important, he thought of kings and emperors as his inferiors, who would carry out his commands obediently and help him reform and evangelize the world. Gregory allowed that secular princes would continue to rule directly and make their own decisions in purely secular matters, but he expected them to accept ultimate papal overlordship. Put in other terms, in contrast to his predecessors who had sought merely a duality of ecclesiastical and secular authority, Gregory VII wanted to create a papal monarchy over both. When told that his ideas were novel, he and his immediate followers replied, "The Lord did not say 'I am custom'; the Lord said 'I am truth.' " Since no pope had spoken like this before, it is proper to accept the judgment of a modern historian who called Gregory "the great innovator, who stood quite alone."

The investiture struggle

Gregory's actual conduct as pope was nothing short of revolutionary. From the start he was determined to enforce a decree against "lay investiture," the practice whereby secular rulers ceremonially granted clerics the symbols of their office. The German emperor Henry IV was bound to resist this because the ceremony was a manifestation of his long-accepted rights to appoint and control churchmen: without these his own authority would be greatly weakened. The ensuing fight is often called "the investiture struggle" because the problem of investitures was a central one, but the struggle was really about the relative obedience and strength of pope and emperor. The larger issue was immediately joined when Henry IV flouted Gregory's injunctions against appointing prelates. Whereas earlier popes might have tried to deal with such insubordination diplomatically, Gregory rapidly took the entirely unprecedented step of excommunicating the emperor and suspending him from all his powers as an earthly ruler. This bold act amazed all who learned of it. Between 955 and 1057 German emperors had deposed five and named twelve out of twenty-five popes; now a pope dared to dismiss an emperor! We have seen in the preceding chapter that in 1077 Henry IV abased himself before the pope in order to forestall a formal deposition: that act amazed contemporaries even more. Thereafter Henry was able to rally some support and sympathy for himself and a terrible war of words ensued, while on the actual battlefield the emperor was able to place troops supporting the pope on the defensive. In 1085 Gregory died, seemingly defeated. But Gregory's successors continued the struggle with Henry IV and later with his son, Henry V.

Concordat of Worms resolves conflict

The long and bitter contest on investiture came to an end only with the Concordat of Worms (a city in Germany) of 1122. Under this compromise the German emperor was forbidden to invest prelates with the religious symbols of their office but was allowed to invest them with the symbols of their rights as temporal rulers because the emperor was recognized as their temporal overlord. That settlement was ultimately less significant than the fact that the struggle had lastingly impaired the prestige of the emperors and raised that of the popes. In addition, the dramatic struggle helped rally the Western clergy behind the pope and galvanized the attentions of all onlookers. As one contemporary reported, nothing else was talked about "even in the women's spinning-rooms and the artisans' workshops." This meant that people who had earlier been largely indifferent to or excluded from religious issues became much more absorbed by them.

Growth of canon law

Gregory VII's successors and most of the popes of the twelfth century were fully committed to the goal of papal monarchy. But they were far less impetuous than Gregory had been and were more interested in the everyday administration of the Church. They apparently recognized that there was no point in claiming to rule as papal monarchs unless they could avail themselves of a governmental apparatus to support their claims. To this end they presided over an impressive growth of law and administration. Under papal guidance the twelfth century saw the basic formulation of the *canon law* of the Church. Canon law claimed ecclesiastical jurisdiction for all sorts of cases pertaining not only to the clergy but also to problems of marriage, inheritance, and rights of widows and orphans. Most of these cases were supposed to originate in the courts of bishops, but the popes insisted that they alone could issue dispensations from the strict letter of the law and that the papal *consistory*—the pope and cardinals—should serve as a final court of appeals. As the power of the papacy and the prestige of the Church mounted, cases in canon law courts and appeals to Rome rapidly increased; after the middle of the twelfth century legal expertise became so important for exercising the papal office that most popes were trained canon lawyers, whereas previously they had usually been monks. Concurrent with this growth of legalism was the growth of an administrative apparatus to keep records and collect income. As the century wore on, the papacy developed a bureaucratic government that was far in advance of most of the secular governments of the day. This allowed it to become richer, more efficient, and ever stronger. Finally, the popes asserted their powers within the Church by gaining greater control over the election of bishops and by calling general councils in Rome to promulgate laws and demonstrate their leadership.

Innocent III aims to unify Christendom

By common consent the most capable and successful of all high-medieval popes was Innocent III (1198–1216). Innocent, who was elected at the age of thirty-seven, was one of the youngest and most vigorous individuals ever to be raised to the papacy; more than that, he was expertly trained in theology and had also studied canon law. His major goal was to unify all Christendom under papal hegemony and to bring in the "right order in the world" so fervently desired by Gregory VII. He never questioned the right of kings and princes to rule directly in the secular sphere but believed that he could step in and discipline kings whenever they "sinned," a wide opening for interference. Beyond that, he saw himself as the ultimate overlord of all. In his own words he said that "as every knee is bowed to Jesus . . . so all men should obey His Vicar [i.e., the pope]."

Innocent's policies in action

Innocent sought to implement his goals in many different ways. In order to give the papacy a solid territorial base of support, like the one drawn upon by the French kings, he tried to initiate strong rule in the papal territories around Rome by consolidating them where possible and providing for efficient and vigilant administration. For this reason Innocent is often considered to be the real founder of the Papal States. But because some urban communities tenaciously sought to maintain their independence, he never came close to dominating the papal lands in Italy so completely as the French kings controlled the Île-de-France. In other projects he was more completely successful. He intervened in German politics assertively enough to engineer the triumph of his own candidate for the imperial office, the Hohenstaufen Frederick II. He disciplined the French King Philip Augustus for his marital misconduct and forced John of England to accept an unwanted candidate as archbishop of Canterbury. To demonstrate his superiority and also gain income, Innocent forced John to grant England to the papacy as a fief, and he similarly gained the feudal overlordship of Aragon, Sicily, and Hungary. When southern France was threatened by the spread of the Albigensian heresy (to be discussed later) the pope effectively called a crusade that would extinguish it by force. He also levied the first income tax on the clergy to support a crusade to the Holy Land. The crown of Innocent's religious achievement was the calling of the Fourth Lateran Council in Rome in 1215. This defined central dogmas of the faith and made the leadership of the papacy within Christendom more apparent than ever. The pope was now clearly both disciplining kings and ruling over the Church without hindrance.

Pope Innocent III. A mosaic dating from the thirteenth century.

Problems for Innocent's successors

Innocent's reign was certainly the zenith of the papal monarchy, but it also sowed some of the seeds of future ruin. Innocent himself could administer the Papal States and seek new sources of income without seeming to compromise the spiritual dignity of his office. But future popes who followed his policies had less of his stature and thus began to appear more like ordinary acquisitive rulers. Moreover, because the Papal States bordered on the Kingdom of Sicily, Innocent's successors quickly came into conflict with the neighboring ruler, who was none other than Innocent's protégé Frederick II. Although Innocent had raised up Frederick, he did not suppose that Frederick would later become an inveterate opponent of papal power in Italy.

Popes become involved in political struggles

At first these and other problems were not fully apparent. The popes of the thirteenth century continued to enhance their powers and centralize the government of the Church. They gradually asserted the right to name candidates for ecclesiastical positions, both high and low, and they asserted control over the curriculum and doctrine taught at the University of Paris. But they also became involved in a protracted political struggle that led to their own demise as temporal powers. This struggle began with the attempt of the popes to destroy Frederick II. To some degree they were acting in self-defense because Frederick threatened their own rule in central Italy. But in combating him they overemployed their spiritual weapons. Instead of merely excommunicating and deposing Frederick, they also called a crusade against him—the first time a crusade was called on a large scale for blatantly political purposes.

After Frederick's death in 1250 a succession of popes made a still worse mistake by renewing and maintaining their crusade against all of the emperor's heirs, whom they called the "viper brood." In order to implement this crusade they became preoccupied with raising funds, and they sought and won as their military champion a younger son from the French royal house, Charles of Anjou. But the latter helped the popes only for the purely political motive of winning the Kingdom of Sicily for himself. Charles in fact won Sicily in 1268 by defeating the last of Frederick II's male heirs. But he then taxed the realm so excessively that the Sicilians revolted in the "Sicilian Vespers" of 1282 and offered their crown to the king of Aragon, who had married Frederick II's granddaughter. The king of Aragon accordingly entered the Italian arena and came close to winning Frederick's former kingdom for himself. To prevent this Charles of Anjou and the reigning pope prevailed upon the king of France—then Philip III (1270–1285)—to embark on a crusade against Aragon. This crusade was a terrible failure and Philip III died on it. In the wake of these events Philip's son, Philip IV, resolved to alter the traditional French pro-papal policy. By that time France had become so strong that such a decision was fateful. More than that, by misusing the institution of the crusade and trying to raise increasingly large sums of money to support it, the popes had lost much of their prestige. The denouement would be played out at the very beginning of the next century.

Charles of Anjou. One of the earliest known medieval statues that may have been done from life.

Boniface VIII

The temporal might of the papacy was toppled almost melodramatically in the reign of Boniface VIII (1294–1303). Many of Boniface's troubles were not of his own making. His greatest obstacle was that the national monarchies had gained more of their subjects' loyalties than the papacy could draw upon because of the steady growth of royal power and erosion of papal prestige. Boniface also had the misfortune to succeed a particularly pious, although inept, pope who resigned his office within a year. Since Boniface was entirely lacking in conventional piety or humility, the contrast turned many Christian observers against him. Some even maintained—incorrectly—that Boniface had convinced his predecessor to resign and had murdered him shortly afterward. Boniface ruled assertively and presided over the first papal "jubilee" in Rome in 1300. This was an apparent, but, as events would show, hollow demonstration of papal might.

The contest over clerical taxation

Two disputes with the kings of England and France proved to be Boniface's undoing. The first concerned the clerical taxation that had been initiated by Innocent III. Although Innocent had levied this tax to support a crusade and had collected it himself, in the course of the thirteenth century the kings of England and France had begun to levy and collect clerical taxes on the pretext that they would use them to help the popes on future crusades to the Holy Land or aid in papal crusades against the Hohenstaufens. Then, at the end of the century, the kings started to levy their own war taxes on the clergy without any pretexts at all. Boniface understandably tried to prohibit this step, but quickly found that he had lost the support of the English and French clergy. Thus when the kings offered resistance he had to back down.

Pope Boniface VIII's defeat

Boniface's second dispute was with the king of France alone. Specifically it concerned Philip IV's determination to try a French bishop for treason. As in the earlier struggle between Gregory VII and Henry IV of Germany, the real issue was the comparative strength of papal and secular power, but this time the papacy was decisively defeated. As before, there was a bitter propaganda war, but now hardly anyone listened to the pope. The king instead pressed absurd charges of heresy against Boniface and sent his minions to arrest the pope to stand trial. At the papal residence of Anagni in 1303 Boniface, who was in his seventies, was captured and mistreated before he was released by the local citizens. These events exhausted the old man's strength and he died a month later. Immediately thereupon it was said that he had entered the papacy like a fox, reigned like a lion, but died like a dog.

Pope Boniface VIII. Boniface was so lacking in humility that he had a statue of himself erected during his lifetime on the side of the cathedral of Anagni, overlooking the town square.

After Boniface VIII's death the papacy became virtually a pawn of French temporal authority for most of the fourteenth century. But the emergence and success of the papal monarchy in the High Middle Ages had several beneficial effects during the course of that period. One was that the international rule of the papacy over the Church enhanced international communications and uniformity of religious practices. Another was that the papal cultivation of canon law led to a growing respect for law of all sorts and often helped protect the causes of otherwise defenseless subjects, like widows and orphans. The popes also managed to achieve some success in their campaigns to eliminate the sale of Church offices and to raise the morals of the clergy. By centralizing appointments they made it easier for worthy candidates who had no locally influential relatives to gain advancement. There was of course corruption in the papal government too, but in an age of entrenched localism the triumph of an international force was mainly beneficial. Finally, as we will see later, the growth of the papal monarchy helped bring vitality to popular religion and helped support the revival of learning.

The Crusades

Crusading movement affects authority of pope

The rise and fall of the crusading movement was closely related to the fortunes of the high-medieval papal monarchy. The First Crusade was initiated by the papacy, and its success was a great early victory for the papal monarchy. But the later decline of the crusading movement helped undermine the pope's temporal authority. Thus the Crusades can be seen as part of a chapter in papal and religious history. In addition, the Crusades opened the first chapter in the history of Western colonialism.

The direct cause of the First Crusade

The immediate cause of the First Crusade was an appeal for aid in 1095 by the Byzantine emperor Alexius Comnenus. Alexius hoped to reconquer territory in Asia Minor that had recently been lost to the Turks. Since he had already become accustomed to using Western mercenaries as auxiliary troops, he asked the pope to help rally some Western military support. But the emperor soon found, no doubt to his great surprise, that he was receiving not just simple aid but a *crusade.* In other words, instead of a band of mercenaries to fight in Asia Minor, the West sent forth an enormous army of volunteers whose goal was to wrest Jerusalem away from Islam. Since the decision to turn Alexius's call for aid into a crusade was made by the pope, it is well to examine the latter's motives.

The Gregorian theory of Christian warfare

The reigning pope in 1095 was Urban II, an extremely competent disciple of Gregory VII. Without question, Urban called the First Crusade to help further the policies of the Gregorian papacy. Urban's very patronage of Christian warfare was Gregorian. Early Christianity had been pacifistic: St. Martin, for example, a revered Christian saint of the fourth century, gave up his career as a soldier when he converted with the statement "I am Christ's soldier; I cannot fight." The Latin fathers St. Augustine and St. Gregory worked out theories to justify Christian warfare, but only in the eleventh century, with the triumph of the Gregorian movement, were these put into practice. Gregory VII engineered papal support for the Norman Conquest even before he became pope, and he, or popes under his influence, blessed Christian campaigns against Muslims in Spain, Greeks in Italy, and Slavs in the German east. All these campaigns were considered by Gregory VII and his followers to be steps toward gaining "right order in the world."

Urban II's motives

Following in Gregory VII's footsteps, Urban II probably conceived of a great crusade to the Holy Land as a means for achieving at least four ends. One was to bring the Eastern Orthodox Church back into the fold. By sending a mighty volunteer army to the East, Urban might overawe the Byzantines with Western strength and convince them to reaccept Roman primacy. If he was successful in that, he would gain a great victory for the Gregorian program of papal monarchy. A second motive was to embarrass the pope's greatest enemy, the German emperor. In 1095 Henry IV had become so militarily strong that Urban had been forced to flee Italy for France. By calling a mighty crusade, Urban might hope to show up the emperor as a narrow-minded, un-Christian persecutor, and demonstrate his own ability to be the spiritual leader of the West. Third, by sending off a large contingent of fighters Urban might help to achieve peace at home. Earlier, the French Church had supported a "peace movement" that prohibited attacks on noncombatants (the "Peace of God") and then prohibited fighting on certain holy days (the "Truce of God"). Right before he called the First Crusade Urban promulgated the first full papal

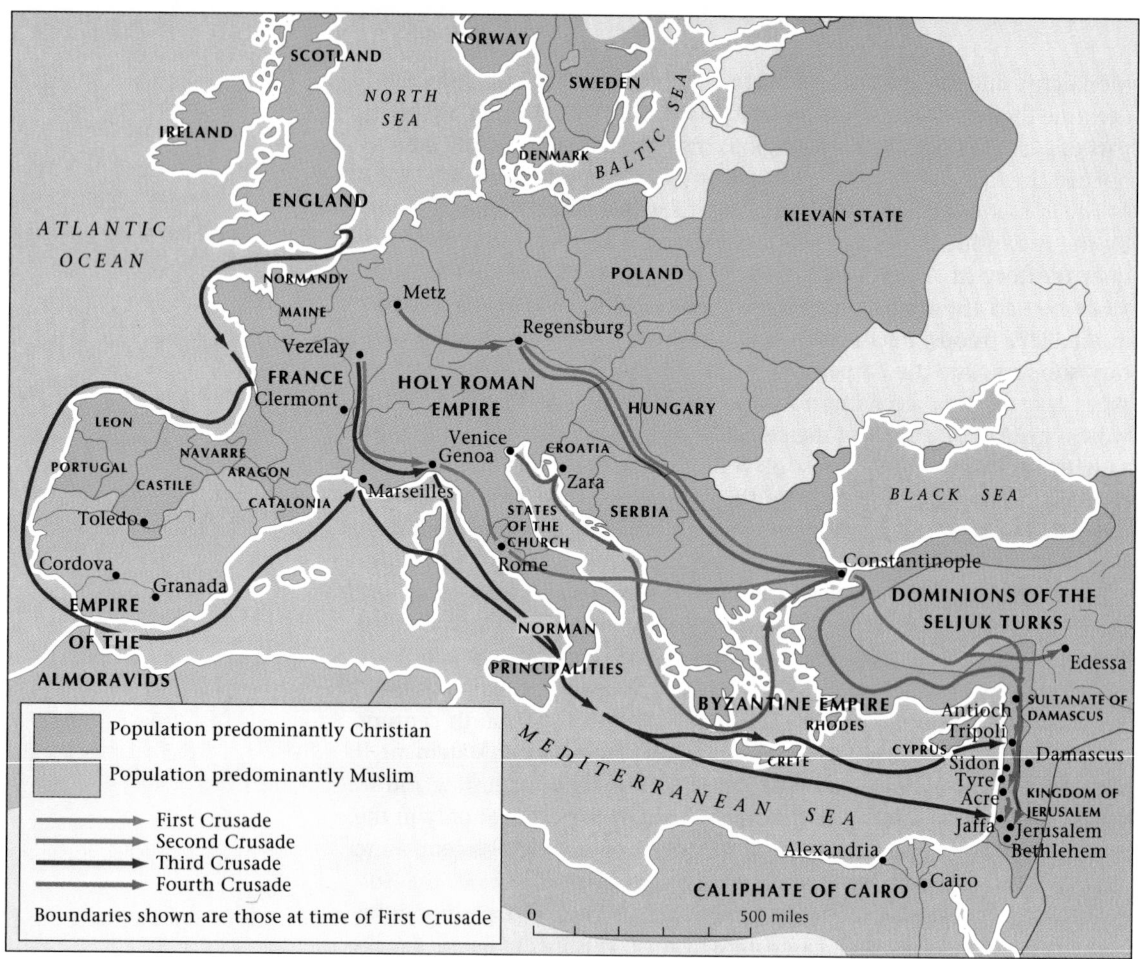

The Major Crusades

approval and extension of this peace movement. Clearly the crusade was linked to the call for peace: in effect, Urban told unruly warriors that if they really wished to fight they could do so justly for a Christian cause overseas. Finally, the goal of Jerusalem itself must have genuinely inspired Urban. Jerusalem was thought to be the center of the earth and was the most sacred shrine of the Christian religion. It must have seemed only proper that pilgrimages to Jerusalem should not be impeded and that Christians should rule the city directly. "Right order in the world" could scarcely mean less.

Economic and political causes of the First Crusade

When Urban called his crusade at a Church council in the French town of Clermont in 1095, the response was more enthusiastic than he could possibly have expected. Many in the crowd interrupted the pope's speech with spontaneous cries of "God wills it," and many impetuously rushed off to the East shortly thereafter. All told, there were probably about a hundred thousand men in the main crusading army, an enormous number for the day. Accordingly, the question arises as to why Urban's appeal was so remarkably successful. Certainly there were economic and political reasons. Many of the poorer people who went crusading came from areas that by 1095 were already becoming overpopulated: these Crusaders may have hoped to do better for themselves in the East than they could on their crowded lands. Similarly, some lords were feeling the pressures of growing political stability and a growing acceptance of *primogeniture* (inheritance limited to the eldest male heir). Hitherto younger sons might have hoped to make their own fortune in endemic warfare, or at least inherit a small piece of territory for themselves, but now there were more and longer-lived siblings, warfare was becoming limited, and only the eldest son inherited his father's lands. Clearly, leaving for the East was an attractive alternative to chafing at home.

Religion the dominant motive; crusades as armed pilgrimages

But the dominant motive for going on the First Crusade was definitely religious. Nobody could have gone crusading out of purely calculating motives because nobody could have predicted for certain that new lands would be won. Indeed, any rational calculation would have predicted at best an unremunerative return trip, or, more likely, death at the hands of the Muslims. But the journey offered great solace for the Christian soul. For centuries pilgrimages had been the most popular type of Christian penance, and the pilgrimage to Jerusalem was considered to be the most sacred and efficacious one of all. Obviously the greatest of all spiritual rewards would come from going on an armed pilgrimage to Jerusalem in order to win back the holiest of sacred places for Christianity. To make this point explicit, Urban II at Clermont promised that Crusaders would be freed from all other penances imposed by the Church. Immediately afterward some Crusade preachers went even further by promising, without Urban's authorization, what became known as a *plenary indulgence*. This was the promise that all Crusaders would be entirely freed from otherworldly punishments in purgatory and that their souls would go straight to heaven if they died on the Crusade. The plenary indulgence was a truly extraordinary offer and crowds streamed in to take advantage of it. As they flocked together they were further whipped up by preachers into a religious frenzy that approached mass hysteria. They were convinced that they had been chosen to cleanse the world of unbelievers. One terrible consequence was that even before they had fully set out for the East they started slaughtering European Jews in the first really virulent outbreak of Western anti-Semitism.

The brutal conduct of the Crusaders

Against great odds the First Crusade was a thorough success. In 1098 the Crusaders captured Antioch and with it most of Syria; in 1099 they took Jerusalem. Their success came mainly from the facts that their Muslim opponents just at that time were internally divided and that the appearance of the strange, uncouth, and terribly savage Westerners took the Muslims by surprise. From the start the Crusaders in the Holy Land acted like imperialists. As soon as they conquered new territories they claimed them as property for themselves, carving out their acquisitions into four different principalities. They also exulted in their own ferocity. When they captured Antioch, instead of taking prisoners they killed all the

Burning of Jews. From a late-medieval German manuscript. After the persecutions of the First Crusade, treatment of Jews in Western Europe became worse and worse. These Jews were set upon by the populace because they were suspected of poisoning wells.

Turks they laid their hands on. Similarly, when they conquered Jerusalem they ignored Christ's own pacifistic precepts, mercilessly slaughtering all the Muslim inhabitants of the city. Some Crusaders actually boasted in a joint letter home that "in Solomon's Porch and in his temple our men rode in the blood of the Saracens up to the knees of their horses." Those Crusaders who stayed on in the Holy Land gradually became more civilized and tolerant, but new waves of armed pilgrims from the West continued to act brutally. Moreover, even the settled Crusaders never became fully integrated with the local population but remained a separate, exploiting foreign element in the heart of the Islamic world.

Failure of subsequent crusades; the triumph of Frederick II's diplomacy

Given the fact that the Christian states comprised only an underpopulated, narrow strip of colonies along the coastline of Syria and Palestine, it was only a matter of time before they would be won back for Islam. By 1144 the northernmost principality fell. When Christian warriors led by the king of France and emperor of Germany came east in the Second Crusade to recoup the losses, they were too internally divided to win any victories. Not long afterward the Islamic lands of the region were united from the base of Egypt by the Sultan Saladin, who recaptured Jerusalem in 1187. Again a force from the West tried to repair the damages: this was the Third Crusade, led by the German emperor Frederick Barbarossa, the French king Philip Augustus, and the English king Richard the Lion-hearted. Even this glorious host, however, could not triumph, above all because rival leaders again quarreled among themselves. When Innocent III became pope his main ambition was to win back Jerusalem. He called the Fourth Crusade to that end, but that crusade was an unprecedented disaster from the point of view of a united Christendom. The pope could not control its direction and the Crusaders in 1204 wound up seizing Orthodox Christian Constantinople instead of marching on the Holy Land. As we have seen, the ultimate result of this act was to help destroy the Byzantine Empire and open up eastern Europe to the Ottoman Turks. Innocent convened the Fourth Lateran Council in 1215 partially to prepare for yet another crusade that would be more directly under papal guidance. That crusade, the fifth, was launched from the sea against Egypt in order to penetrate Muslim power at its base, but after a promising start it too was a failure. Only the Sixth Crusade, led from 1228 to 1229 by the Emperor Frederick II, was a success; this, however, was not for any military reasons. Frederick, who knew Arabic and could communicate easily with the Egyptian sultan, did not fight but skillfully negotiated a treaty whereby Jerusalem and a narrow access route were restored to the Christians. Thus diplomacy triumphed where warfare had failed. But the Christians could not hold on to their gains and Jerusalem fell again in 1244, never to be recaptured by the West until 1917. The Christian "states" were now only a small enclave around the Palestinian city of Acre.

The papacy's sacrifice of the crusading ideal to political interests

While Frederick II was negotiating for Jerusalem, he was under excommunication by the pope; therefore, when he entered the city, he had to crown himself king of Jerusalem in the Church of the Holy Sepulcher with his own hands. This was indicative of the fact that by then the papacy was becoming more intent on advancing European political aims than on reconquering the Holy Land. The victory of the First Crusade had greatly enhanced the prestige and strength of the papal monarchy, but the subsequent failures were increasingly calling into question the papal ability to unite the West for a great enterprise. The Albigensian

King Louis VII of France and His Queen, Eleanor of Aquitaine, Embarking for the Second Crusade. This late-medieval conception is idealized inasmuch as Louis did not travel to the Holy Land by sea but took a land route.

Crusade, called by Innocent III against French heretics in 1208 (see pp. 333–334), established the crucial precedent that a believer could receive the same spiritual rewards by crusading within Europe as by going on a much longer and more risky crusade to the East. The Albigensian Crusade did not damage the papacy's religious image, however, because the Albigensian heretics (whose beliefs will be discussed later) were a clear religious threat to the Church. Once the papacy launched its crusade against Frederick II and his heirs, however, it fully sacrificed the crusading ideal to political interests.

The decline of the crusading movement and the decline of the papacy interrelated

It was then that the decline of the crusading movement and the decline of the papacy became most closely interrelated. In the crusades against Frederick and his successors, and later against the king of Aragon, the popes offered the same plenary indulgence that was by then officially offered to all Crusaders against Islam. Worse, they granted the same indulgence to anyone who simply contributed enough money to arm a Crusader for the enterprise. This created a great inflation in indulgences. By 1291 the last Christian outposts in the Holy Land had fallen without any Western help while the papacy was still trying to salvage its losing crusade against Aragon. Boniface VIII's papal jubilee of 1300, which offered a plenary indulgence to all those who made a pilgrimage to Rome, was a tacit recognition that the Eternal City and not the Holy Land would henceforth have to be the central goal of Christian pilgrimage. Boniface fell from power three years later for many reasons, but one was certainly that the prestige of the papacy had become irreparably damaged by the misuses and failure of crusading.

Positive effects of the Crusades

So, while the crusading idea helped build up the papal monarchy, it also helped destroy it. Other than that, what practical significance did the Crusades have? On the credit side, the almost incredible success of the First Crusade greatly helped raise the self-confidence of the medieval West. For centuries western Europe had been on the defensive against Islam; now a Western army could march into a center of Islamic power and take a coveted prize seemingly at will. This dramatic victory contributed to making the twelfth century an age of extraordinary buoyancy and optimism. To Western Christians it must have seemed as if God was on their side and that they could accomplish almost anything they wished. The Crusades also helped broaden Western horizons. Few westerners in the Holy Land ever bothered to learn Arabic or profit from specific Islamic institutions or ideas—the most profitable cultural communications between Christians and Muslims took place in Spain and Sicily—but Crusaders who traveled long distances through foreign lands were bound to become somewhat more sophisticated. The Crusades certainly stimulated interest in hitherto unknown luxury goods and presented a wealth of subjects for literature and fable.

Commerce and taxation

From an economic point of view, the success of the First Crusade helped open up the eastern Mediterranean to Western commerce. The Italian cities of Venice and Genoa particularly began to dominate trade in that area, thereby helping to enhance Western prosperity as a whole. The

Krak des Chevaliers. This Crusader castle in northern Syria is one of the best preserved fortresses of the Middle Ages. The word *krak* comes from the Arabic *karak,* meaning "strong fort."

need to transfer money over long distances also stimulated early experiments in banking techniques. Politically, the precedent of taxing the clergy for financing the crusades was not only quickly turned to the advantage of the Western monarchies, it also stimulated the development of various forms of national taxation. More than that, the very act of organizing a country to help support a royal crusade by raising funds and provisions was an important stimulus to the development of efficient administrative institutions in the emerging nation-states.

Negative consequences

But there was a debit as well as a credit side to the crusading balance sheet. There is no excusing the Crusaders' savage butchery—of Jews at home and of Muslims abroad. As we have seen too in Chapter 9, the Crusades greatly accelerated the deterioration of Western relations with the Byzantine Empire and contributed fundamentally to the destruction of that realm, with all the disastrous consequences that followed. And Western colonialism in the Holy Land was only the beginning of a long history of colonialism that has continued until modern times.

The Outburst of Religious Vitality

The awakening of religious interest

The First Crusade would never have succeeded if westerners had not become enthusiastic about religion. The growth of that enthusiasm itself was a most remarkable development. Had the First Crusade been called about fifty years earlier it is doubtful that many people would have joined it. But the eleventh-century reform movement and the pontificate of Gregory VII awakened interest in religion in all quarters. Thereafter the entire high-medieval period was to be marked by extraordinary religious vitality.

The impact of the Gregorian reform movement on religious revival

The reformers and Gregory VII stimulated a European religious revival for two reasons. One was that the campaign to cleanse the Church actually achieved a large measure of success: the laity could now respect the clergy more and increasingly large numbers of people were inspired to join the clergy themselves. According to a reliable estimate, the number of people who joined monastic orders in England increased tenfold between 1066 and 1200, a statistic that does not include the increase in priests. The other reason why the work of Gregory VII in particular helped inspire a revival was that Gregory explicitly called upon the laity to help discipline their priests. In letters of great propagandistic power he denounced the sins of "fornicating priests" (by which he really meant just married ones) and urged the laity to drive them from their pulpits or boycott their services. Not surprisingly, this touched off something close to a vigilante movement in many parts of Europe. This excitement, taken together with the fact that the papal struggle with Henry IV was really the first European event of universal interest, increased religious commitment immensely. Until about 1050 most western Europeans were Christians in name, but religious commitment seems to have been lukewarm and attendance at church services quite rare; after the Gregorian period Christianity was becoming an ideal and practice that really began to direct human lives.

The new piety: the Carthusian and Cistercian orders; St. Bernard of Clairvaux

One of the most visible manifestations of the new piety was the spread of the Cistercian movement in the twelfth century. By around 1100 no form of Benedictine monasticism seemed fully satisfactory to aspirants to holiness who sought great asceticism and, above all, intense "interiority"—unrelenting self-examination and meditative striving toward knowledge of God. The result was the founding of new orders to provide for the fullest expression of monastic idealism. One was the Carthusian order, whose monks were required to live in separate cells, abstain from meat, and fast three days each week on bread, water, and salt. The Carthusians never sought to attract great numbers and therefore remained a small group. But the same was by no means true of the Cistercians. The latter were monks who were first organized around 1100 and who sought to follow the Benedictine Rule in the purest and most austere way possible. In order to avoid the worldly temptations to which the Cluniacs had succumbed, they founded new monasteries in forests and wastelands as far away from civilization as possible. They shunned all unnecessary church decoration and ostentatious utensils, abandoned the Cluniac stress on an elaborate liturgy in favor of more contemplation and private prayer, and seriously committed themselves to hard manual labor. Under the charismatic leadership of St. Bernard of Clairvaux (1090–1153), a spellbinding preacher, brilliant writer, and the most influential European religious personality of his age, the Cistercian order grew exponentially. There were only 5 houses in 1115 but no less than 343 at the time of St. Bernard's death in 1153. This growth not only meant that many more men were becoming monks—the older houses did not disappear—but that many pious laymen were donating funds and lands to support the new monasteries.

St. Bernard of Clairvaux. From a wall painting in a church in Italy.

New forms of religious belief and practice

As more people were entering or patronizing new monasteries, the very nature of religious belief and devotion was changing. One of many examples was a shift away from the cult of saints to emphasis on the worship of Jesus and veneration of the Virgin Mary. Older Benedictine monasteries encouraged the veneration of the relics of local saints that they housed in order to attract pilgrims and donations. But the Cluniac and Cistercian orders were both centralized congregations that allowed only one saintly patron for all their houses: respectively, St. Peter (to honor the founder of the papacy) and the Virgin. Since these monasteries contained few relics (the Virgin was thought to have been taken bodily into heaven, so there were no corporeal relics for her at all) they deemphasized their cult. The veneration of relics was replaced by a concentration on the Eucharist, or the sacrament of the Lord's Supper. Of course celebration of the Eucharist had always been an important part of the Christian faith, but only in the twelfth century was it made really central, for only then did theologians fully work out the doctrine of *transubstantiation.* According to this the priest during mass cooperates with God in the performance of a miracle whereby the bread and wine on the altar are changed or "transubstantiated" into the body and blood of Christ. Popular reverence for the Eucharist became so great in the twelfth century that for the first time the practice of elevating the consecrated bread, or host, was initiated so that the whole congregation could see it. The new theology of the Eucharist greatly enhanced the dignity of the priest and also encouraged the faithful to meditate on the sufferings of Christ. As a result many developed an intense sense of identification with Christ and tried to imitate his life in different ways.

Mary and Eve. The "correct" medieval theological view of women. On the left (Latin: *sinister*) side of the naked Adam the naked Eve takes the apple of sin from the serpent and feeds it to erring mortals while a skeleton waits to carry them to hell. On Adam's right Mary counteracts Eve by feeding a different "fruit"—the eucharistic wafer—to the devout.

The cult of the Virgin Mary

Coming a very close second to the renewed worship of Christ in the twelfth century was veneration of the Virgin Mary. This development was more unprecedented because until then the Virgin had been only negligibly honored in the Western Church. Exactly why veneration of the Virgin became so pronounced in the twelfth century is not fully clear, but whatever the explanation, there is no doubt that in the twelfth century the cult of Mary blossomed throughout all of western Europe. The Cistercians made her their patron saint, St. Bernard constantly taught about her life and virtues, and practically all the magnificent new cathedrals of the age were dedicated to her: there was Notre Dame ("Our Lady") of Paris, and also a "Notre Dame" of Chartres, Rheims, Amiens, Rouen, Laon, and many other places. Theologically, Mary's role was that of intercessor with her son for the salvation of human souls. It was held that Mary was the mother of all, an infinite repository of mercy who urged the salvation even of sinners so long as they were loving and ultimately contrite. Numerous stories circulated about seeming reprobates who were saved because they venerated Mary and because she then spoke for them at the hour of death.

The significance of the cult

The significance of the new cult was manifold. For the first time a woman was given a central and honored place in the Christian religion. Theologians still taught that sin had entered the world through the woman, but they now counterbalanced this by explaining how the tri-

Mary and Christ. The sculpture over the main entrance to the Cathedral of Senlis (northern France), dating from about 1180, shows perhaps for the first time in Western history a woman represented in a position equal in dignity with a man.

umph over sin transpired with the help of Mary. Another result was that artists and writers who portrayed Mary were able to concentrate on femininity and scenes of human tenderness and family life. This contributed greatly to a general softening of artistic and literary style. But perhaps most important of all, the rise of the cult of Mary was closely associated with a general rise of hopefulness and optimism in the twelfth-century West.

Hildegard of Bingen

Not only did a woman, Mary, gain a particularly prominent role in the religious cult of the twelfth century, but a few living women gained great religious authority. By far the most famous and influential was the German nun and visionary Hildegard of Bingen (1098–1179). Hildegard's descriptions of her religious visions, dictated in freshly original Latin prose, were so compelling that contemporaries had no difficulty in believing that she was directly inspired by God. Consequently when the pope visited Germany he gave her his blessings, and religious and secular leaders sought her advice. Hildegard wrote on a variety of other subjects such as pharmacology and women's medicine. Not least she composed religious songs whose beauty has been rediscovered in recent times. Visionary though she was, she probably would be surprised to see people today looking for her works in racks of compact disks, where she is often alphabetized as "Bingen" between Beethoven and Brahms.

The Virgin in Majesty. A representation from a stained-glass window in the Cathedral of Chartres.

Sometimes the great religious enthusiasm of the twelfth century went beyond the bounds approved by the Church. After Gregory VII had called upon the laity to help discipline their clergy it was difficult to control lay enthusiasm. As the twelfth century progressed and the papal monarchy concentrated on strengthening its legal and financial administration, some people began to wonder whether the Church, which had once been so inspiring, had not begun to lose sight of its idealistic goals. Another difficulty was that the growing emphasis on the miraculous powers of priests tended to inhibit the religious role of the laity and place it in a distinct position of spiritual inferiority. The result was that in the second half of the twelfth century large-scale movements of popular heresy swept over western Europe for the first time in its history. The two major twelfth-century heresies were Albigensianism and Waldensianism. The former, which had its greatest strength in Italy and southern France, was a recrudescence of Eastern dualism. The Albigensians believed that all matter was created by an evil principle and that therefore the flesh should be thoroughly mortified. This teaching was completely at variance with Christianity, but it seems that most Albigensians believed themselves to be Christians and subscribed to the heresy mainly because it challenged the authority of insufficiently zealous Catholic priests and provided an outlet for intense lay spirituality. More typical of twelfth-century religious dissent was Waldensianism, a movement that originated in the French city of Lyons and spread to much of southern France, northern Italy, and Germany. Waldensians were layfolk who wished to imitate the life of Christ and the Apostles to the fullest. They therefore translated and studied the Gospels and dedicated themselves to lives of poverty and preaching. Since the earliest Waldensians did not attack any Catholic doctrines, the Church hierarchy did not at first interfere with them. But it was soon recognized that they were becoming too independent and that their voluntary poverty was proving an embarrassing contrast to the luxurious lives of worldly prelates. So the papacy forbade them to preach without authorization and condemned them for heresy when they refused to obey. At that point they became more radical and started to create an alternative church, which they maintained offered the only route to salvation.

Innocent III's response to heresy

When Innocent III became pope in 1198 he was faced with a very serious challenge from growing heresies. His response was characteristically decisive and fateful for the future of the Church. Simply stated it was two-pronged. On the one hand, Innocent resolved to crush all disobedience to papal authority, but on the other, he decided to patronize whatever idealistic religious groups he could find that were willing to acknowledge obedience. Papal monarchy could thus be protected without frustrating all dynamic spirituality within the Church. Innocent not only launched a full-scale crusade against the Albigensians, he also encouraged the use against heresy of judicial procedures that included ruthless techniques of religious "inquisition." In 1252 the papacy first approved the use of torture in inquisitorial trials, and burning at the stake became the prevalent punishment for religious disobedience. Neither the crusade nor the inquisitorial procedures were fully successful in uprooting the Albigensian heresy in Innocent's own lifetime, but the extension of such measures did result in destroying the heresy by fire and sword after about the middle of the thirteenth century. Waldensians, like Albigensians, were hunted down by inquisitors and their numbers reduced, but scattered Waldensian groups did manage to survive until modern times.

Innocent III's emphasis on the sacraments

Another aspect of Innocent's program was to pronounce formally the new religious doctrines that enhanced the special status of priests and the ecclesiastical hierarchy. Thus at the Fourth Lateran Council of 1215 he reaffirmed the doctrine that the sacraments administered by the Church were the indispensable means of procuring God's grace, and that no one could be saved without them. The decrees of the Lateran Council emphasized two sacraments: the Eucharist and penance. The doctrine of transubstantiation was formally defined and it was made a requirement—as it remains today—that all Catholics confess their sins to a priest and then take Communion at least once a year. The council also promulgated other doctrinal definitions and disciplinary measures that served both to oppose heresy and to assert the unique dignity of the clergy.

The new orders of friars

As stated above, the other side of Innocent's policy was to support obedient idealistic movements within the Church. The most important of these were the new orders of *friars*—the Dominicans and the Franciscans. Friars resembled monks in vowing to follow a rule, but they differed greatly from monks in their actual conduct. Above all, they did not retreat from society into monasteries. Assuming that the way of life originally followed by Christ and the Apostles was the most holy, they wandered through the countryside and especially the towns, preaching and offering spiritual guidance. They also accepted voluntary poverty and begged for their subsistence. In these respects they resembled the

Waldensian heretics, but they professed unquestioning obedience to the pope and sought to fight heresy themselves.

The Dominican order, founded by the Spaniard St. Dominic and approved by Innocent III in 1216, was particularly dedicated to the fight against heresy and also to the conversion of Jews and Muslims. At first the Dominicans hoped to achieve these ends by preaching and public debate. Hence they became intellectually oriented. Many members of the order gained teaching positions in the infant European universities and contributed much to the development of philosophy and theology. The most influential thinker of the thirteenth century, St. Thomas Aquinas, was a Dominican who addressed one of his major theological works to converting the "gentiles" (i.e., all non-Christians). The Dominicans always retained their reputation for learning, but they also came to believe that stubborn heretics were best controlled by legal procedures. Accordingly, they became the leading medieval administrators of inquisitorial trials.

The Earliest Known Portrait of St. Francis. Dating from the year 1228, this fresco shows the saint without the "stigmata," the wounds of Christ's crucifixion he was believed to have received miraculously toward the end of his life.

In its origins the Franciscan order was quite different from the Dominican, being characterized less by a commitment to doctrine and discipline and more by a sense of emotional fervor. Whereas St. Dominic and his earliest followers had been ordained priests who were licensed to preach by their office, the founder of the Franciscans, the Italian St. Francis of Assisi (1182–1226), was a layman who behaved at first remarkably like a social rebel and a heretic. The son of a rich merchant, he became dissatisfied with the materialistic values of his father and determined to become a servant of the poor. Giving away all his property, he threw off his clothes in public, put on the tattered garb of a beggar, and began without official approval to preach salvation in town squares and minister to outcasts in the darkest corners of Italian cities. He rigorously imitated the life of Christ and displayed indifference to doctrine, form, and ceremony, except for reverencing the sacrament of the Eucharist. But he did wish to gain the support of the pope. One day in 1210 he appeared in Rome with a small ragged band to request that Innocent III approve a primitive "rule" that was little more than a collection of Gospel precepts. Some other pope might have rejected the layman Francis as a hopelessly unworldly religious anarchist. But Francis was thoroughly willing to profess obedience, and Innocent had the genius to approve Francis's rule and grant him permission to preach. With papal support, the Franciscan order spread, and though it gradually became more "civilized," conceding the importance of administrative stability and doctrinal training for all its members, it continued to specialize in revivalistic outdoor preaching and in offering a model for "apostolic living" within an orthodox framework. Thus Innocent managed to harness a vital new force that would help maintain a sense of religious enthusiasm within the Church.

The alliance between the friars and the papacy

Until the end of the thirteenth century both the Franciscans and Dominicans worked closely together with the papal monarchy in a mutually supportive relationship. The popes helped the friars establish themselves throughout Europe and often allowed them to infringe on the duties of parish priests. On their side, the friars combatted heresy, helped preach papal crusades, were active in missionary work, and otherwise undertook special missions for the popes. Above all, by the power of their examples and by their vigorous preaching, the friars helped maintain religious intensity throughout the thirteenth century.

The entire period from 1050 to 1300 was hence unquestionably a great "age of faith." The products of this faith were both tangible and intangible. We will examine the tangible products—works of theology, literature, art, and architecture—presently. Great as these were, the intangible products were equally important. Until the Christian religion became deeply felt in the High Middle Ages hardly any common ideals inspired average men and women. Life in the Middle Ages was extraordinarily hard, and until about 1050 there was not much to give it meaning. Then, when people began to take Christianity more seriously, an impetus was provided for performing hard work of all sorts. As we have seen in the preceding chapter, Europeans after 1050 literally had better food than before, and now we have seen that they were better fed figuratively as well. With more spiritual as well as material nourishment they accomplished great feats in all forms of human endeavor.

A Portrait of St. Francis by the Florentine Painter Cimabue. Although this conception, dating from about 1285, may have been modeled on the one shown on the preceding page, it clearly depicts the stigmata: notice the nail wound in the saint's hand and the lance wound in his side.

The Medieval Intellectual Revival

The major intellectual accomplishments of the High Middle Ages were of four related but different sorts: the spread of primary education and literacy; the origin and spread of universities; the acquisition of classical and Islamic knowledge; and the actual progress in thought made by westerners. Any one of these accomplishments would have earned the High Middle Ages a signal place in the history of Western learning; taken together they began the era of Western intellectual predominance that became a hallmark of modern times.

The spread of primary education

Around 800 Charlemagne ordered that primary schools be established in every bishopric and monastery in his realm. Although it is doubtful that this command was carried out to the letter, many schools were certainly founded during the Carolingian period. But their continued existence was later endangered by the Viking invasions. Primary education in some monasteries and cathedral towns managed to survive, but until around 1050 the extent and quality of basic education in the European West were meager. Thereafter, however, there was a blossoming that paralleled the efflorescence we have seen in other human activities. Even contemporaries were struck by the rapidity with which schools sprang up all over Europe. One French monk writing in 1115 stated that when he was growing up around 1075 there was "such a scarcity of teachers that there were almost none in the villages and hardly any in the cities," but that by his maturity there was "a great number of schools," and the study of grammar was "flourishing far and wide." Similarly, a Flemish chronicle referred to an extraordinary new passion for the study and practice of rhetoric around 1120. Clearly, the economic revival, the growth of towns, and the emergence of strong government allowed Europeans to dedicate themselves to basic education as never before.

Changes in medieval education: (1) the development of cathedral schools

The high-medieval educational boom was more than merely a growth of schools, for the nature of the schools changed, and as time went on so did the curriculum and the clientele. The first basic mutation was that monasteries in the twelfth century abandoned their practice of educating outsiders. Earlier, monasteries had taught a few privileged nonmonastic students how to read because there were no other schools for such pupils. But by the twelfth century sufficient alternatives existed. The main centers of European education became the cathedral schools located in the growing towns. The papal monarchy energetically supported this development by ordering in 1179 that all cathedrals should set aside income for one schoolteacher, who could then instruct all who wished, rich or poor, without fee. The papacy believed correctly that this measure would enlarge the number of well-trained clerics and potential administrators.

(2) Revived interest in ancient texts

At first the cathedral schools existed almost exclusively for the basic training of priests, with a curriculum designed to teach only such literacy necessary for reading the Church offices. But soon after 1100 the curriculum was broadened, for the growth of both ecclesiastical and secular

Two Medieval Conceptions of Elementary Education. On the left, an illumination from a fourteenth-century manuscript depicts a master of grammar who simultaneously points to the day's lesson and keeps order with a cudgel. Grammar-school education is portrayed more gently on the right, a late-medieval scene in which a woman personifying the alphabet leads a willing boy into a tower of learning wherein the stories ascend from grammar through logic and rhetoric to the heights of theology.

governments created a growing demand for trained officials who had to know more than how to read a few prayers. The revived reliance on law especially made it imperative to improve the quality of primary education in order to train future lawyers. Above all, a thorough knowledge of Latin grammar and composition began to be inculcated, often by studying some of the Roman classics such as the works of Cicero and Virgil. The revived interest in these texts, and attempts to imitate them, have led scholars to refer to a "renaissance of the twelfth century."

(3) The growth of lay education

Until about 1200 the students in the urban schools remained predominantly clerical. Even those who hoped to become lawyers or administrators rather than mere priests usually found it advantageous to take Church orders. But afterward more pupils entering schools were not in the clergy and never intended to be. Some were children of the upper classes who began to regard literacy as a badge of status. Others were future notaries (i.e., men who drew up official documents) or merchants who needed some literacy and/or computational skills to advance their own careers. Customarily, the latter groups would not go to cathedral schools but to alternate ones that were more practically oriented. Such schools grew rapidly in the course of the thirteenth century and became completely independent of ecclesiastical control. Not only were their students recruited from the laity, their teachers were usually laymen as well. As time went on instruction ceased being in Latin, as had hitherto been the case, and was offered in the European vernacular languages instead.

Significance of the rise of lay education

The rise of lay education was an enormously important development in western European history for two related reasons. The first was that the Church lost its monopoly over education for the first time in almost a millennium. Learning and resultant attitudes could now become more secular, and they did just that increasingly over the course of time. Laymen could not only evaluate and criticize the ideas of priests, they could also pursue entirely secular lines of inquiry. Western culture therefore ultimately became more independent of religion, and much of the traditionalism associated with religion, than any other culture in the world. Second, the growth of lay schools, taken together with the growth of church schools that trained the laity, led to an enormous growth of lay literacy: by 1340 roughly 40 percent of the Florentine population could read; by the later fifteenth century about 40 percent of the total population of England was literate as well. (These figures include women, who were usually taught to read by paid tutors or male family members at home rather than in schools.) When one considers that literacy around 1050 was almost entirely limited to the clergy and that the literate comprised less than 1 percent of the population of western Europe, it can be appreciated that an astonishing revolution had taken place. Without it, many of Europe's other accomplishments would have been inconceivable.

The origins of universities

The emergence of universities was part of the same high-medieval educational boom. Originally, universities were institutions that offered instruction in advanced studies that could not be pursued in average cathedral schools: advanced liberal arts and the professional studies of law, medicine, and theology. The earliest Italian university was that of

Bologna, an institution that took shape during the course of the twelfth century. Although liberal arts were taught at Bologna, the institution gained its greatest prominence from the time of its twelfth-century origins until the end of the Middle Ages as Europe's leading center for the study of law. North of the Alps, the earliest and most prominent university was that of Paris. The University of Paris started out as a cathedral school like many others, but in the twelfth century it began to become a recognized center of northern intellectual life. One reason for this was that scholars there found necessary conditions of peace and stability provided by the increasingly strong French kingship; another was that food was plentiful because the area was rich in agricultural produce; and another was that the cathedral school of Paris in the first half of the twelfth century boasted the most charismatic and controversial teacher of the day, Peter Abelard (1079–1142). Abelard, whose intellectual accomplishments we will discuss later, attracted students from all over Europe in droves. According to an apocryphal story that was told at the time, he was such an exciting teacher that when he was forbidden to teach in French lands because of his controversial views, he climbed a tree and students flocked under it to hear him lecture; when he was then forbidden to teach from the air he started lecturing from a boat and students massed to hear him from the banks. As a result of his reputation many other teachers settled in Paris and began to offer much more varied and advanced instruction than anything offered in other French cathedral schools. By 1200 Paris was evolving into a university that specialized in liberal arts and theology. Around then Innocent III, who had studied in Paris himself, called the school "the oven that bakes the bread for the entire world."

Illuminated Manuscript Initial. The joy taken by medieval monks in splendid ornamentation is nowhere more apparent than in this letter B, opening a book of psalms. From a French manuscript of the later twelfth century.

The emergence of universities

It should be emphasized that the institution of the university was really a medieval invention. Of course advanced schools existed in the ancient world, but they did not have fixed curricula or organized faculties, and they did not award degrees. At first, medieval universities themselves were not so much places as groups of scholars. The term "university" originally meant a corporation or guild. In fact, all of the medieval universities were corporations, either of teachers or students, organized like other guilds to protect their interests and rights. But gradually the word "university" came to mean an educational institution with a school of liberal arts and one or more faculties in the professional subjects of law, medicine, and theology. After about 1200 Bologna and Paris were regarded as the prototypic universities. During the thirteenth century such famous institutions as Oxford, Cambridge, Montpellier, Salamanca, and Naples were founded or granted formal recognition. In Germany there were no universities until the fourteenth century—a reflection of the disorganized condition of that area—but in 1385 Heidelberg, the first university on German soil, was founded and many others quickly followed.

Organization of universities

Every university in medieval Europe was patterned after one or the other of two different models. Throughout Italy, Spain, and southern France the standard was generally the University of Bologna, in which the students themselves constituted the corporation. They hired the

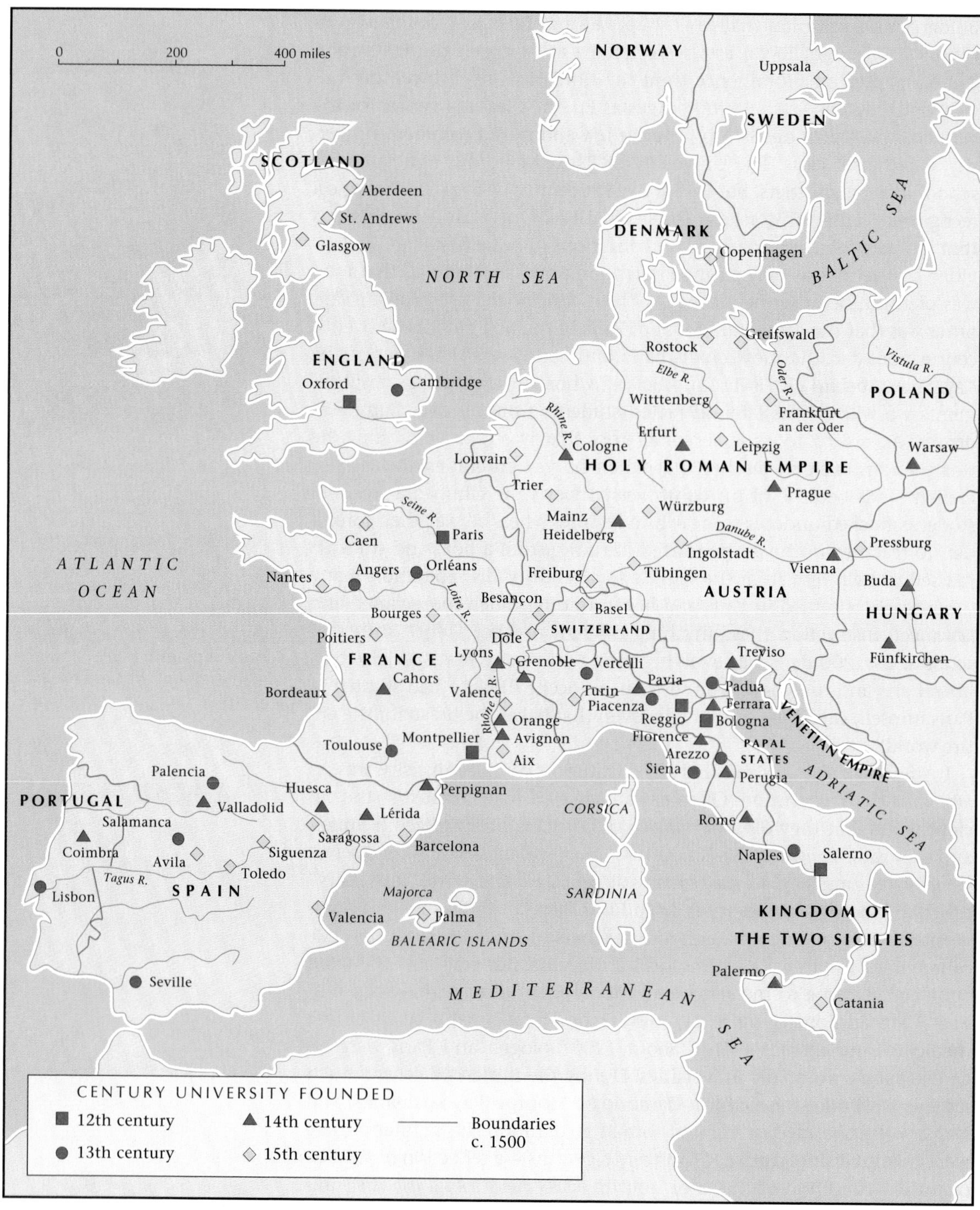

The Rise of the Medieval University

teachers, paid their salaries, and fined or discharged them for neglect of duty or inefficient instruction. The universities of northern Europe were modeled after Paris, which was a guild not of students but of teachers. It included four faculties—arts, theology, law, and medicine—each headed by a dean. In the great majority of the northern universities arts and theology were the leading branches of study. Before the end of the thirteenth century separate colleges came to be established within the University of Paris. The original college was nothing more than an endowed home for poor students, but eventually the colleges became centers of instruction as well as residences. While most of these colleges have disappeared from the Continent, the universities of Oxford and Cambridge still retain the pattern of federal organization copied from Paris. The colleges of which they are composed are semi-independent educational units.

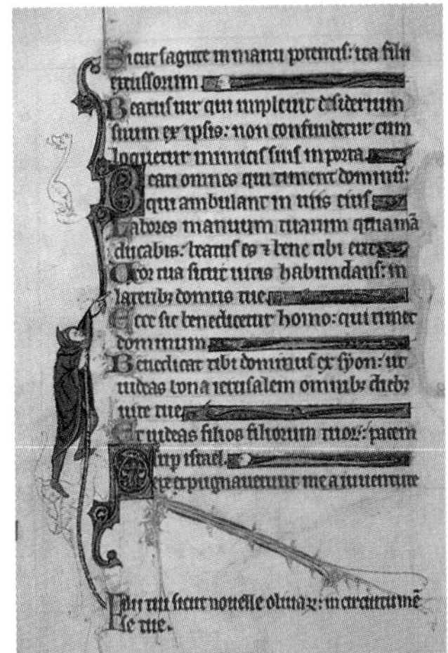

A Scribe with a Sense of Humor. An English scribe of around 1300, having noticed that he left out a whole line in a luxurious prayerbook, devised this ingenious way to rectify the error.

The courses of study

Most of our modern degrees as well as our modern university organization derive from the medieval system, but actual courses of study have been greatly altered. No curriculum in the Middle Ages included history or anything like the modern social sciences. The medieval student was assumed to know Latin grammar thoroughly before entrance into a university—this he learned in the primary, or "grammar," schools. Upon admission, limited to males, he was required to spend about four years studying the basic liberal arts, which meant doing advanced work in Latin grammar and rhetoric and mastering the rules of logic. If he passed his examinations he received the preliminary degree of bachelor of arts (the prototype of our B.A.), which conferred no unusual distinction. To assure himself a place in professional life he then usually had to devote additional years to the pursuit of an advanced degree, such as master of arts (M.A.), or doctor of laws, medicine, or theology. For the M.A. degree three or four years had to be given to the study of mathematics, natural science, and philosophy. This was accomplished by reading and commenting on standard ancient works, such as those of Euclid and especially Aristotle. Abstract analysis was emphasized and there was no such thing as laboratory science. The requirements for the doctor's degrees included more specialized training. Those for the doctorate in theology were particularly arduous: by the end of the Middle Ages the course for the doctorate in theology at the University of Paris had been extended to twelve or thirteen years after the roughly eight years taken for the M.A.! Continuous residence was not required, and it was accordingly rare to become a doctor of theology before the age of forty; statutes in fact forbade awarding the degree to anyone under thirty-five. Strictly speaking, doctor's degrees, including even the one in medicine, conferred only the right to teach. But in practice university degrees of all grades were recognized as standards of attainment and became pathways to nonacademic careers.

Student life in medieval universities

Student life in medieval universities was often rowdy. Many students were very immature because it was customary to begin university studies between the ages of twelve and fifteen. Moreover, all university students believed that they comprised an independent and privileged community, set aside from that of the local townspeople. Since the latter tried to reap

A Lecture Class in a Medieval University. Some interesting similarities and contrasts may be observed between this scene and a modern classroom.

financial profits from the students and the students were naturally boisterous, there were frequent riots and sometimes pitched battles between "town" and "gown." But actual study was very intense. Because the greatest emphasis was placed on the value of authority and also because books were prohibitively expensive (they were handwritten and made from rare parchment), there was an enormous amount of rote memorization. As students advanced in their disciplines they were also expected to develop their own skills in formal, public disputations. Advanced disputations could become extremely complex and abstract; sometimes they might last for days. The most important fact pertaining to medieval university students was that, after about 1250, there were so many of them. The University of Paris in the thirteenth century numbered about seven thousand students, and Oxford somewhere around two thousand in any given year. This means that a relatively appreciable proportion of male Europeans who were more than peasants or artisans were gaining at least some education at the higher levels.

Acquisition of Greek and Arabic scientific knowledge

As the numbers of those educated at all levels vastly increased during the High Middle Ages, so did the quality of learning. This was owing first and foremost to the reacquisition of Greek knowledge and to the absorption of intellectual advances made by the Muslims. Since practically no western Europeans knew Greek or Arabic, works in those languages had to be transmitted by means of Latin translations. But there were very few of these before about 1140: of all the many works of Aristotle only a few logical treatises were available in Latin translations before the middle of the twelfth century. But then, suddenly, an enormous burst of translating activity made almost all of ancient Greek and Arabic scientific knowledge accessible to western Europeans. This activity transpired in Spain and Sicily because Christians there lived in close proximity with Arabic speakers, or Jews who knew Latin and Arabic, either of whom could aid them in their tasks. Greek works were first translated into Latin from earlier Arabic translations; then many were retranslated directly from the Greek by a few westerners who had managed to learn that language, usually by traveling in Greek-speaking territories. The result was that by about 1260 almost the entire Aristotelian corpus that is known today was made available in Latin. So also were basic works of such important Greek scientific thinkers as Euclid, Galen, and Ptolemy. Only the milestones of Greek literature and the works of Plato were not yet translated because they had not been made available to the Arabs; they existed only in inaccessible Byzantine manuscripts. But in addition to the thought of the Greeks, Western scholars became familiar with the accomplishments of all the major Islamic philosophers and scientists such as Avicenna and Averroës.

Medicine as Monkey Business. Even after a medieval physician had studied Galen, he was equipped with only two fairly reliable diagnostic methods: taking the pulse and examining urine. A visual parody from a French manuscript of 1316 makes this observation dryly.

Having acquired the best of Greek and Arabic scientific and speculative thought, the West was able to build on it and make its own advances. This progress transpired in different ways. When it came to natural science, westerners were able to start building on the acquired learning without much difficulty because it seldom conflicted with the principles of Christianity. But when it came to philosophy, the basic question arose as to how thoroughly Greek and Arabic thought was compatible with the Christian faith. One of the most advanced thirteenth-century scientists was the Englishman Robert Grosseteste (c. 1168–1253), who was not only a great thinker but was also very active in public life as bishop of Lincoln. Grosseteste became so proficient at Greek that he translated all of Aristotle's *Ethics*. More important, he made very significant theoretical advances in mathematics, astronomy, and optics. He formulated a sophisticated scientific explanation of the rainbow, and he posited the use of lenses for magnification. Grosseteste's leading disciple was Roger Bacon (c. 1214–1294), who is today more famous than his teacher because he seems to have predicted automobiles and flying machines. Bacon in fact had no real interest in machinery, but he did follow up on Grosseteste's work in optics, discussing, for example, further properties of lenses, the rapid speed of light, and the nature of human vision. Grosseteste, Bacon, and some of their followers at the University of Oxford argued that natural knowledge was more certain when it was based on sensory evidence than when it rested on abstract reason. To this degree they can be seen as early forerunners of modern science. But the important qualification remains that they did not perform any real laboratory experiments.

Medieval Dentistry. The only remedy for a decayed tooth was extraction without benefit of anesthesia.

The meaning of Scholasticism

The story of the high-medieval encounter between Greek and Arabic philosophy and Christian faith is basically the story of the emergence of *Scholasticism*. This word can be, and has been, defined in many ways. In its root meaning Scholasticism was simply the method of teaching and learning followed in the medieval schools. That meant that it was highly systematic and also that it was highly respectful of authority. Yet Scholasticism was not only a method of study: it was a worldview. As such, it taught that there was a fundamental compatibility between the knowledge humans can obtain naturally, i.e., by experience or reason, and the teachings imparted by divine revelation. Since medieval scholars believed

The Creator as Architect. An underlying assumption of thirteenth-century philosophy and theology was that God created the universe according to scientific principles. This scene from a late-thirteenth-century French Bible shows God working on Creation with a draftsman's compass.

that the Greeks were the masters of natural knowledge and that all revelation was in the Bible, Scholasticism consequently was the theory and practice of reconciling classical philosophy with Christian faith.

Peter Abelard

One of the most important thinkers who paved the way for Scholasticism without yet being fully a Scholastic himself was the stormy Peter Abelard, who was active in and around Paris in the first half of the twelfth century. Probably the first western European who consciously sought to forge a career as an intellectual (rather than being merely a cleric who taught on the side or a schoolteacher who had no goal of adding to knowledge), Abelard was so adept at logic and theology that even as a student he easily outshone the experts of his day who had the misfortune to be his teachers. Others might have been tactful about such superiority, but Abelard gloried in openly humiliating his elders in public debate, thereby making himself many enemies. To complicate matters, in 1118 he seduced a brilliant seventeen-year-old girl, Heloise, who had been taking private lessons with him. When a child was the issue, Abelard married Heloise, but the two decided to keep the marriage secret for the sake of his career. This, however, enraged Heloise's uncle because he thought that Abelard was planning to abandon Heloise; therefore he took revenge for his family's honor by having Abelard castrated. Seeking refuge as a monk, Abelard soon witnessed his enemies engineer his first conviction for heresy. Still restless and cantankerous, he found no spiritual solace in monasticism and after quarreling and breaking with the monks of two different monastic communities he returned to life in the world by setting himself up as a teacher in Paris from about 1132 to 1141. This was the peak of his career. But in 1141 he again was charged with heresy, now by the highly influential St. Bernard, and condemned by a Church council. Not long afterward the persecuted thinker abjured, and in 1142 he died in retirement.

The Story of My Calamities

Abelard told of many of these trials in a letter called *The Story of My Calamities,* one of the first autobiographical accounts written in the West since St. Augustine's *Confessions*. On first reading, this work appears atypically modern because the author seems to defy the medieval Christian virtue of humility by constantly boasting about himself. But actually Abelard did not write about his calamities in order to boast. Rather, his main intention was to moralize about how he had been justly punished for his "lechery" by the loss of those parts which had "offended" and for his intellectual pride by the burning of his writings after his first condemnation. Since Abelard urged intense self-examination and analysis of human motives in an ethical treatise programmatically entitled *Know Thyself,* it seems wisest to conclude that he never intended to recommend egotism but rather was one of several prominent twelfth-century thinkers (ironically including his mortal enemy St. Bernard) who sought to take stock of the human personality by means of personal introspection.

Sic et Non and the Scholastic method

Abelard's greatest contributions to the development of Scholasticism were made in his *Sic et Non* (Yes and No) and in a number of original theological works. In the *Sic et Non* Abelard prepared the way for the Scholastic method by gathering a collection of statements from the Church fathers that spoke for both sides of 150 theological questions. It was once thought that the brash Abelard did this in order to embarrass authority, but the contrary is true. What Abelard really hoped to do was begin a process of careful study whereby it could be shown that the Bible was infallible and that other authorities, despite any appearances to the contrary, really agreed with each other. Later Scholastics would follow his method of studying theology by raising fundamental questions and arraying the answers that had been put forth in authoritative texts. Abelard did not propose any solutions of his own in the *Sic et Non,* but he did start to do this in his original theological writings. In these he proposed to treat theology like a science, by studying it as comprehensively as possible and by applying to it the tools of logic, of which he was a master. He did not even shrink from applying logic to the mystery of the Trinity, one of the excesses for which he was condemned. Thus he was one of the first to try to harmonize religion with rationalism and was in this capacity a herald of the Scholastic outlook.

Abelard. A late-medieval conception.

Immediately after Abelard's death two further steps were taken to prepare for mature Scholasticism. One was the writing of the *Book of Sentences* between 1155 and 1157 by Abelard's student Peter Lombard. This raised all the most fundamental theological questions in rigorously consequential order, adduced answers from the Bible and Christian authorities on both sides of each question, and then proposed judgments on every case. By the thirteenth century Peter Lombard's work became a standard text. Once formal schools of theology were established in the universities, all aspirants to the doctorate were required to study and comment upon it; not surprisingly, theologians also followed its organizational procedures in their own writings. Thus the full Scholastic method was born.

The other basic step in the development of Scholasticism was the reacquisition of classical philosophy that occurred after about 1140. Abelard would probably have been glad to have drawn upon the thought of the Greeks, but he could not because few Greek works were yet available in translation. Later theologians, however, could avail themselves fully of the Greeks' knowledge, above all, the works of Aristotle and his Arabic

Peter Lombard

St. Thomas Aquinas. A fifteenth-century painting by Justus of Ghent, after an earlier copy.

commentators. By around 1250 Aristotle's authority in purely philosophical matters became so great that he was referred to as "the Philosopher" pure and simple. Scholastics of the mid-thirteenth century accordingly adhered to Peter Lombard's organizational method, but added the consideration of Greek and Arabic philosophical authorities to that of purely Christian theological ones. In doing this they tried to construct systems of understanding the entire universe that most fully harmonized the earlier separate realms of faith and natural knowledge.

By far the greatest accomplishments in this endeavor were made by St. Thomas Aquinas (1225–1274), the leading Scholastic theologian of the University of Paris. As a member of the Dominican order, St. Thomas was committed to the principle that faith could be defended by reason. More important, he believed that natural knowledge and the study of the created universe were legitimate ways of approaching theological wisdom because "nature" complements "grace." By this he meant to say that because God created the natural world He can be approached through its terms even though ultimate certainty about the highest truths can only be obtained through the supernatural revelation of the Bible. Imbued with a deep confidence in the value of human reason and human experience, as well as in his own ability to harmonize Greek philosophy with Christian theology, Thomas was the most serene of saints. In a long career of teaching at the University of Paris and elsewhere he indulged in few controversies and worked quietly on his two great Summaries of theology: the *Summa contra Gentiles* and the much larger *Summa Theologica*. In these he hoped to set down all that could be said about the faith on the firmest of foundations.

St. Thomas's Summaries

Most experts think that St. Thomas came extremely close to fulfilling this extraordinarily ambitious goal. His vast Summaries are awesome for their rigorous orderliness and intellectual penetration. He admits in them that there are certain "mysteries of the faith," such as the doctrines of the Trinity and the Incarnation, that cannot be approached by the unaided human intellect; otherwise, he subjects all theological questions to philosophical inquiry. In this, St. Thomas relied heavily on the work of Aristotle, but he was by no means merely "Aristotle baptized." Instead, he fully subordinated Aristotelianism to basic Christian principles and thereby created his own original philosophical and theological system. Scholars disagree about how far this system diverges from the earlier Christian thought of St. Augustine, but there seems little doubt that Aquinas placed a higher value on human reason, on human life in this world, and on the abilities of humans to participate in their own salvation. Not long after his death St. Thomas was canonized, for his intellectual accomplishments seemed like miracles. His influence lives on today insofar as he helped to revive confidence in rationalism and human experience. More directly, philosophy in the modern Roman Catholic Church is supposed to be taught according to the Thomistic method, doctrine, and principles.

Western medieval thought reaches its pinnacle

With the achievements of St. Thomas Aquinas in the middle of the thirteenth century, Western medieval thought reached its pinnacle. Not coincidentally, other aspects of medieval civilization were reaching their pinnacles at the same time. France was enjoying its ripest period of peace and prosperity under the rule of St. Louis, the University of Paris was defining its basic organizational forms, and the greatest French Gothic cathedrals were being built. Some ardent admirers of medieval culture have fixed on these accomplishments to call the thirteenth the "greatest of centuries." Such a judgment, of course, is a matter of taste, and many might respond that life was still too harsh and requirements for religious orthodoxy too great to justify this extreme celebration of the lost past. Whatever our individual judgments, it seems wise to end this section by correcting some false impressions about medieval intellectual life.

False impressions concerning Scholastic thinkers

It is often thought that medieval thinkers were excessively conservative, but in fact the greatest thinkers of the High Middle Ages were astonishingly receptive to new ideas. As committed Christians they could not allow doubts to be cast upon the principles of their faith, but otherwise they were glad to accept whatever they could from the Greeks and Arabs. Considering that Aristotelian thought differed radically from anything accepted earlier in its emphasis on rationalism and the fundamental goodness and purposefulness of nature, its rapid acceptance by the Scholastics was a philosophical revolution. Another false impression is that Scholastic thinkers were greatly constrained by authority. Certainly they revered authority more than we do today, but Scholastics like St. Thomas did not regard the mere citation of texts—except biblical revelation concerning the mysteries of the faith—as being sufficient to clinch an argument. Rather, the authorities were brought forth to outline the possibilities, but reason and experience then demonstrated the truth. Finally, it is often believed that Scholastic thinkers were "antihumanistic," but modern scholars are coming to the opposite conclusion. Scholastics unquestionably gave primacy to the soul over the body and to otherworldly salvation over life in the here and now. But they also exalted the dignity of human nature because they viewed it as a glorious divine creation, and they believed in the possibility of a working alliance between themselves and God. Moreover, they had extraordinary faith in the powers of human reason—probably more than we do today.

THE BLOSSOMING OF LITERATURE, ART, AND MUSIC

Medieval Latin literature; the poetry of the Goliards

The literature of the High Middle Ages was as varied, lively, and impressive as that produced in any other period in Western history. The revival of grammatical studies in the cathedral schools and universities led to the production of some excellent Latin poetry. The best examples were secular lyrics, especially those written in the twelfth century by a group of poets known as the *Goliards*. How these poets got their name is uncertain, but it possibly meant followers of the devil. That would have been appropriate because the Goliards were riotous poets who wrote parodies of the liturgy and burlesques of the Gospels. Their lyrics celebrated the beauties of the changing seasons, the carefree life of the open road, the pleasures of drinking and sporting, and especially the joys of love. The authors of these rollicking and satirical songs were mainly wandering students, although some were men in more advanced years. The names of most are unknown. Their poetry is particularly significant both for its robust vitality and for being the first clear counterstatement to the ascetic ideal of Christianity.

The growth of vernacular literature; the epic

In addition to the use of Latin, the vernacular languages of French, German, Spanish, and Italian became increasingly popular as media of literary expression. At first, most of the literature in the vernacular languages was written in the form of the heroic epic. Among the leading examples were the French *Song of Roland,* the Norse eddas and sagas, the German *Song of the Nibelungs,* and the Spanish *Poem of the Cid.* Practically all of these works were originally composed between 1050 and 1150, although some were first set down in writing afterward. These epics portrayed a virile but unpolished warrior society. Blood flowed freely, skulls were cleaved by battle-axes, and heroic warfare, honor, and loyalty were the major themes. If women were mentioned at all, they were subordinate to men. Brides were expected to die for their beloveds, but husbands were free to beat their wives. In one French epic a queen who tried to influence her husband met with a blow to the nose; even though blood flowed she replied, "Many thanks, when it pleases you, you may do it again." Despite the repugnance we find in such passages, the best of the vernacular epics have much unpretentious literary power. Above all, the *Song of Roland,* though crude, is like an uncut gem.

The love songs of the troubadours

In comparison to the epics, an enormous change in both subject matter and style was introduced in twelfth-century France by the troubadour poets and the writers of courtly romances. The dramatic nature of this change represents further proof that high-medieval culture was not at all conservative. The troubadours were courtier poets who came from southern France and wrote in a language related to French known as Provençal. The origin of their inspiration is debated, but there can be no doubt that they initiated a movement of profound importance for all subsequent Western literature. Their style was far more finely wrought and sophisticated than that of the epic poets, and the most eloquent of their lyrics, which were meant to be sung to music, originated the theme of romantic love. The troubadours idealized women as marvelous beings who could grant intense spiritual and sensual gratification. Whatever greatness the poets found in themselves they usually attributed to the inspiration they found in love. But they also assumed that their love would lose its magic if it were too easily or frequently gratified. Therefore, they wrote more often of longing than of romantic fulfillment.

Other troubadour poems

In addition to their love lyrics, the troubadours wrote several other kinds of short poems. Some were simply bawdy. In these, love is not mentioned at all, but the poet revels in thoughts of carnality, comparing, for example, the riding of his horse to the "riding" of his mistress. Other troubadour poems treat feats of arms, others comment on contemporary

Charlemagne Weeping for His Knights. A scene from the *Song of Roland.*

political events, and a few even meditate on matters of religion. But whatever the subject matter, the best troubadour poems were always cleverly and innovatively expressed. The literary tradition originated by the southern French troubadours was continued by the *trouvères* in northern France and by the *minnesingers* in Germany. Thereafter many of their innovations were developed by later lyric poets in all Western languages. Some of their poetic devices were consciously revived in the twentieth century by such "modernists" as Ezra Pound.

The Arthurian romances; Chrétien de Troyes

An equally important twelfth-century French innovation was the composition of longer narrative poems known as *romances.* These were the first clear ancestors of the modern novel: they told engaging stories, they often excelled in portraying character, and their subject matter was usually love and adventure. Some romances elaborated on classical Greek themes, but the most famous and best were "Arthurian." These took their material from the legendary exploits of the Celtic hero King Arthur and his many chivalrous knights. The first great writer of Arthurian romances was the northern Frenchman Chrétien de Troyes, who was active between about 1165 and 1190. Chrétien did much to help create and shape the new form, and he also introduced innovations in subject matter and attitudes. Whereas the troubadours exalted unrequited, extramarital love, Chrétien was the first to hold forth the ideal of romantic love within marriage. He also described not only the deeds but the thoughts and emotions of his characters.

German literature: *Parzival* and *Tristan*

A generation later, Chrétien's work was continued by the great German poets Wolfram von Eschenbach and Gottfried von Strassburg, who are recognized as the greatest writers in the German language before the eighteenth century. Wolfram's *Parzival,* a story of love and the search for the Holy Grail, is more subtle, complex, and greater in scope than any other

Courtly Love. From a manuscript of the romance *Willehalm,* by Wolfram von Eschenbach. Although authors of medieval romances did not themselves use the term "courtly love," they did propagate the ideal of intense romantic feeling between a knightly lover and his faraway beloved.

high-medieval literary work except Dante's *Divine Comedy.* Like Chrétien, Wolfram believed that true love could be fulfilled only in marriage, and in *Parzival,* for the first time in Western literature since the Greeks, one can see a full psychological development of the hero. Gottfried von Strassburg's *Tristan* is a more somber work, which tells of the hopeless adulterous love of Tristan and Isolde. Indeed, it might almost be regarded as the prototype of modern tragic romanticism. Gottfried was one of the first to develop fully the idea of individual suffering as a literary theme and to point out the indistinct line that separates pleasure from pain. For him, to love is to yearn, and suffering and unfulfilled gratification are integral chapters of the book of life. Unlike the troubadours, he could see complete fulfillment of love only in death. *Parzival* and *Tristan* have become most famous today in the form of their operatic reconceptions by the nineteenth-century German composer Richard Wagner.

Not all high-medieval narratives were so elevated as the romances in either form or substance. A very different new narrative form was the *fabliau,* or verse fable. Although *fabliaux* derived from the moral animal tales of Aesop, they quickly evolved into short stories that were written less to edify or instruct than to amuse. Often they were very coarse, and sometimes they dealt with sexual relations in a broadly humorous and thoroughly unromantic manner. Many were also strongly anticlerical, making monks and priests the butts of their jokes. Because the *fabliaux* are so "uncourtly" it was once thought that they were written solely for the new urban classes. But there is now little doubt that they were addressed at least equally to the "refined" aristocracy who liked to have their laughs too. They are significant as expressions of growing worldliness and as the first manifestations of the robust realism that was later to be perfected by Boccaccio and Chaucer.

Romance of the Rose

Completely different in form but similar as an illustration of growing worldliness was the sprawling *Romance of the Rose.* As its title indicates, this was begun as a romance, specifically around 1230 by the courtly Frenchman William of Lorris. But William left his rather flowery, romantic work unfinished, and it was completed around 1270 by another Frenchman, John of Meun. The latter changed its nature greatly. He inserted long, biting digressions in which he skewered religious hypocrisy, and made his major theme the need for procreation. Not love, but the service of "Dame Nature" in sexual fecundity is urged in numerous witty but extremely earthy images and metaphors. At the climax the originally dreamy hero seizes his mistress, who is allegorically depicted as a rose, and rapes her. Since the work became enormously popular, it seems fair to conclude that tastes, then as now, were very diverse.

Nature Perpetuates the Species. A miniature from a manuscript of the *Romance of the Rose.*

In a class by itself as the greatest work of medieval literature is Dante's *Divine Comedy.* Not much is known about the life of Dante Alighieri (1265–1321), except that he was active during the early part of his career in the political affairs of his native city of Florence. Despite his engagement in politics and the fact that he was a layman, he managed to acquire an awesome mastery of the religious, philosophic, and literary

"Monkey in the Middle." A lively portrayal of a children's game from a medieval songbook of roughly 1280.

Rabbit on the Hunt. Marginal illustrations in medieval manuscripts (this one dates from about 1340) often exhibit ironic humor.

The Poet Dante Driven into Exile. On the left Dante is expelled from Florence; on the right he begins work on his great poem, the *Divine Comedy.* From a mid-fifteenth-century Florentine manuscript. (The nearly completed dome of Florence's cathedral can be seen at the far left.)

Dante

knowledge of his time. He not only knew the Bible and the Church fathers, but—most unusual for a layman—he also absorbed the most recent Scholastic theology. In addition, he was thoroughly familiar with Virgil, Cicero, Boethius, and numerous other classical writers, and was fully conversant with the poems of the troubadours and the Italian poetry of his own day. In 1302 he was expelled from Florence after a political upheaval and was forced to live the rest of his life in exile. The *Divine Comedy,* his major work, was written during this final period.

The *Divine Comedy*

Dante's *Divine Comedy* is a monumental narrative in powerful rhyming Italian verse, which describes the poet's journey through hell, purgatory, and paradise. At the start Dante tells of how he once found himself in a

A Romanesque Vision of Original Sin. One of the masterpieces of Romanesque style, this sculptural relief, dating from about 1100, appears on a bronze door of the cathedral of Hildesheim (Germany) and depicts the moment of punishment in the Garden of Eden. Anatomical distortion and spare abstraction create a haunting effect of tremulous human vulnerability. Caught in the profoundest act of disobedience the first humans hope to shift the blame for their own actions.

Romanesque Annunciation. An angel arrives to tell the Virgin Mary, shown here spinning, that she will bear the Christ child. In between is a dove representing the Holy Spirit. This twelfth-century manuscript illumination bears many typically nonnaturalistic features of Romanesque art such as Mary's contorted position (meant to show that she is being taken by surprise), her awkward seating on her three-legged throne, and the spilling of the angel's wings over the border.

"dark wood," his metaphor for a deep personal midlife crisis. He is led out of this forest of despair by the Roman Virgil, who stands for the heights of classical reason and philosophy. Virgil guides Dante on a trip through hell and purgatory, and afterward Dante's deceased beloved, Beatrice, who stands for Christian wisdom and blessedness, takes over and guides him through paradise. In the course of this progress Dante meets both historical beings and the poet's contemporaries, all of whom have already been assigned places in the afterlife, and he is instructed by them and his guides as to why they met their several fates. As the poem progresses the poet himself leaves the condition of despair to grow in wisdom and ultimately to reach assurance of his own salvation.

Qualities of Dante's work

Every reader finds a different combination of wonder and satisfaction in Dante's magnificent work. Some—especially those who know Italian—marvel at the vigor and inventiveness of Dante's language and images. Others are awed by his subtle complexity and poetic symmetry; others by his array of learning; others by the vitality of his characters and individual stories; and still others by his soaring imagination. The historian finds it particularly remarkable that Dante could sum up the best of medieval learning in such an artistically satisfying manner. Dante stressed the precedence of salvation, but he viewed the earth as existing for human benefit. He allowed humans free will to choose good and avoid evil, and accepted Greek philosophy as authoritative in its own sphere; for example, he called Aristotle "the master of them that know." Above all, his sense of

Romanesque and Gothic. Left: West front of the Church of Notre Dame la Grande, Poitiers. Constructed between 1135 and 1145, this typical example of Romanesque architecture emphasizes the repetition of rounded arches and horizontal lines. Right: Rheims Cathedral. Built between 1220 and 1299, this High Gothic cathedral places great stress on vertical elements. The gabled portals, pointed arches, and multitude of pinnacles all accentuate the height of this structure.

hope and his ultimate faith in humanity—remarkable for a defeated exile—most powerfully expresses the dominant mood of the High Middle Ages and makes Dante one of the two or three most stirringly affirmative writers who ever lived.

Medieval architecture: (1) the Romanesque style

The closest architectural equivalents of the *Divine Comedy* are the great high-medieval Gothic cathedrals, for they too have qualities of vast scope, balance of intricate detail with careful symmetry, soaring height, and affirmative religious grandeur. But before we approach the Gothic style, it is best to introduce it by means of its high-medieval predecessor, the style of architecture and art known as the *Romanesque*. This style had its origins in the tenth century, but became fully formed in the eleventh and first half of the twelfth centuries, when the religious reform movement led to the building of many new monasteries and large churches. The Romanesque was primarily a building style: it aimed to manifest the glory of God in ecclesiastical construction by rigorously subordinating all architectural details to a uniform system. In this it was very severe: we may think of it as the architectural analogue of the unadorned hymn. Aside from its primary stress on systematic construction, the essential features of the Romanesque style were the rounded arch, massive stone

The Upper Chapel of the Sainte-Chapelle, Paris. High Gothic is here carried to its extreme. Slender columns, tracery, and stained-glass windows take the place of walls.

walls, enormous piers, small windows, and the predominance of horizontal lines. The plainness of interiors was sometimes relieved by mosaics or frescoes in bright colors and, a very important innovation for Christian art, the introduction of sculptural decoration, both within and without. For the first time, full-length human figures appeared on facades. These are usually grave and elongated far beyond natural dimensions, but they have much evocative power and represent the first manifestations of a revived interest in sculpting the human form.

(2) The development of the Gothic style

In the course of the twelfth and thirteenth centuries the Romanesque style was supplanted throughout most of Europe by the *Gothic*. Although trained art historians can see how certain traits of the one style led to the development of the other, the actual appearance of the two styles is enormously different. In fact, the two seem as different as the epic is different from the romance, an appropriate analogy because the Gothic style emerged in France in the mid-twelfth century exactly when the romance did, and because it was far more sophisticated, graceful, and elegant than its predecessor, in the same way that the romance compared with the epic. The rapid development and acceptance of the Gothic shows for a last time—if any more proof be needed—that the twelfth century was

Gothic Sculpture. The three kings bearing gifts, from the thirteenth-century cathedral of Amiens. Note the greater naturalism in comparison to the Romanesque sculptural scenes shown on pages 352 and 357.

experimental and dynamic, at least as much as the twentieth. When the abbey church of St. Denis, venerated as the shrine of the French patron saint and burial place of French kings, was torn down in 1144 in order to make room for a much larger one in the strikingly new Gothic style, it was as if the president of the United States were to tear down the White House and replace it with a Mies van der Rohe or Helmut Jahn edifice. Such an act today would be highly improbable, or at least would create an enormous uproar. But in the twelfth century the equivalent actually happened and was taken in stride.

Elements of the Gothic style

Gothic architecture was one of the most intricate of building styles. Its basic elements were the pointed arch, groined and ribbed vaulting, and the flying buttress. These devices made possible a much lighter and loftier construction than could ever have been achieved with the round arch and the engaged pier of the Romanesque. In fact, the Gothic cathedral could be described as a skeletal framework of stone enclosed by enormous windows. Other features included lofty spires, rose windows, delicate tracery in stone, elaborately sculptured facades, multiple columns, and the use of gargoyles, or representations of mythical monsters, as decorative devices. Ornamentation in the best of the cathedrals was generally concentrated on the exterior. Except for the stained-glass windows and the intricate carving on woodwork and altars, interiors were kept rather simple and occasionally almost severe. But the inside of the Gothic cathedral was never somber or gloomy. The stained-glass windows served not to exclude the light but to glorify it, to catch the rays of sunlight and suffuse them with a richness and warmth of color that nature itself could hardly duplicate even in its happiest moods.

Many people still think of the Gothic cathedral as the expression of purely ascetic otherworldliness, but this estimation is highly inaccurate. Certainly all churches are dedicated to the glory of God and hope for life everlasting, but Gothic ones sometimes included stained-glass scenes of daily life that had no overt religious significance at all. More important, Gothic sculpture of religious figures such as Jesus, the Virgin, and the saints was becoming far more naturalistic than anything hitherto created in the medieval West. So also was the sculptural representation of plant and animal life, for interest in the human person and in the world of natural beauty was no longer considered sinful. Moreover, Gothic architecture was also an expression of the medieval intellectual genius. Each cathedral, with its mass of symbolic figures, was a kind of encyclopedia of medieval knowledge carved in stone for those who could not read. Finally, Gothic cathedrals were manifestations of urban pride. Always located in the growing medieval cities, they were meant to be both centers of community life and expressions of a town's greatness. When a new cathedral went up the people of the entire community participated in erecting it, and rightfully regarded it as almost their own property. Many of the Gothic cathedrals were the products of urban rivalries. Each city or town sought to overawe its neighbor with ever bigger or taller buildings, to the degree that ambitions sometimes got out of bounds and many of the cathedrals were left unfinished. But most of the finished ones are still vast enough. Built to last into eternity, they provide the most striking visual manifestation of the soaring exuberance of their age.

A Romanesque Vision of the Last Judgment. A detail from the reliefs made for the Cathedral of Autun (central France) around 1135 shows an angel sounding his trumpet while one of the human elect ascends to heaven. Extreme vertical elongation here creates a sense of dramatic intensity.

The revival of drama

Surveys of high-medieval accomplishments often omit drama and music, but such oversights are unfortunate. Our own modern drama descends at least as much from the medieval form as from the classical one. Throughout the medieval period some Latin classical plays were known in manuscript but were never performed. Instead drama was born all over again within the Church. In the early Middle Ages certain passages in the liturgy began to be acted out. Then, in the twelfth century, primarily in Paris, these were superseded by short religious plays in Latin, performed inside a church. Rapidly thereafter, and still in twelfth-century Paris, the Latin plays were supplemented or supplanted by ones in the vernacular so that the whole congregation could understand them. Then, around 1200, these started to be performed outside, in front of the church, so that they would not take time away from the services. As soon as that happened, drama entered the everyday world: nonreligious stories were introduced, character portrayal was expanded, and the way was fully prepared for the Elizabethans and Shakespeare.

Medieval music: polyphony

As the drama grew out of developments within the liturgy and then moved far beyond them, so did characteristically Western music. Until the High Middle Ages Western music was *homophonic,* as is most non-Western music even today. That is, it developed only one melody at a time without any harmonic background. The great high-medieval invention was *polyphony,* or the playing of two or more harmonious melodies together. Some experiments along these lines may have been made in the West as early as the tenth century, but the most fundamental breakthrough was achieved in the Cathedral of Paris around 1170, when the Mass was first sung by two voices weaving together two different melodies in "counterpoint." Roughly concurrently, systems of musical notation were invented and perfected so that performance no longer had to rely on memory and could become more complex. All the greatness of Western music followed from these first steps.

The enduring achievements of the High Middle Ages

It may have been noticed that many of the same people who made such important contributions to learning, thought, literature, architecture, drama, and music, must have intermingled with each other in the Paris of the High Middle Ages. Some of them no doubt prayed together in the Cathedral of Notre Dame. The names of the leading scholars are remembered, but the names of most of the others are forgotten. Yet taken together they did as much for civilization and created as many enduring monuments as their counterparts in ancient Athens. If their names are forgotten, their achievements in many different ways live on still.

SUMMARY POINTS

- Pope Gregory VII (1073–1085) inaugurated two hundred years of papal activism, during which the popes claimed political supremacy over European monarchs. The reforms of this period cleansed much of the Church of corrupt local influence.
- Although the First Crusade (1095–1099) was called to liberate the Holy Land from Muslim control, later crusades were increasingly called for political, not religious, reasons. Thus although the Crusades initially bolstered the prestige of the papal monarchy, they later contributed to its downfall.
- The period from 1050 to 1300 saw a dramatic increase in religious fervor, punctuated by the foundation of the Dominican and Franciscan Orders and the rise and defeat of the Albigensian and Waldensian heresies.
- A remarkable growth of education and thought took place during the High Middle Ages: universities were founded through much of western Europe; the works of Greek and Arabic philosophers and scientists were translated into Latin; and Scholastic theologians sought to reconcile faith and natural knowledge.
- Art and literature in the High Middle Ages became much more attuned to natural life: vernacular languages and romantic topics were more prevalent, and both literature and architecture were marked by vast scope and intricate detail.

RELIGION AND THE CRUSADES

Barraclough, Geoffrey, *The Medieval Papacy,* New York, 1968. A forcefully argued analytical treatment. Noteworthy too for its illustrations.

Blumenthal, Uta-Renate, *The Investiture Controversy,* Philadelphia, 1988. A clear review of a complicated subject.

Erdmann, Carl, *The Origin of the Idea of Crusade,* Princeton, 1977. A brilliant advanced work on the background to the First Crusade.

Grundmann, Herbert, *Religious Movements in the Middle Ages,* Notre Dame, Ind., 1995. A classic work, recently translated into English, that shows how much of high-medieval religious vitality, orthodox and heretical, originated from the search for the "apostolic life."

Lambert, Malcolm, *Medieval Heresy,* 2d ed., London, 1992. The standard synthesis.

Lawrence, C. H., *The Friars: The Impact of the Early Mendicant Movement on Western Society,* London, 1994. The best introduction to the early history of Franciscans and Dominicans.

Leclercq, Jean, *Bernard of Clairvaux and the Cistercian Spirit,* Kalamazoo, Mich., 1976.

Mayer, Hans Eberhard, *The Crusades,* 2d ed., New York, 1988. The best one-volume survey.

Morris, Colin, *The Papal Monarchy: The Western Church from 1050 to 1250,* Oxford, 1989. An encyclopedic survey.

Runciman, Steven, *A History of the Crusades,* 3 vols., Cambridge, 1951–1954. Colorful and engrossing.

Sayers, Jane, *Innocent III: Leader of Europe, 1198–1216,* New York, 1994. An efficient survey of this central papal regime.

Southern, R. W., *Western Society and the Church in the Middle Ages,* Baltimore, 1970. An extremely insightful and well-written interpretation of the interplay between society and religion.

Tellenbach, Gerd, *Church, State and Christian Society at the Time of the Investiture Contest,* Toronto, 1991. Stresses revolutionary aspects of Gregory VII's thought and career.

THOUGHT, LETTERS, AND THE ARTS

Baldwin, John W., *The Scholastic Culture of the Middle Ages,* Lexington, Mass., 1971. A fine introduction.

Cobban, Alan B., *The Medieval Universities,* London, 1975. The best shorter treatment in English.

______, *The Medieval English Universities: Oxford and Cambridge to c. 1500,* Berkeley, 1988.

Curtius, E. R., *European Literature and the Latin Middle* Ages, Princeton, 1967. An exhaustive treatment of medieval Latin literature in terms of its classical background and influence on later times.

Dronke, Peter, *Women Writers of the Middle Ages,* New York, 1984. A rich literary study, with a strong treatment of Hildegard of Bingen, among others.

Fox, John Howard, *A Literary History of France, I: The Middle Ages,* London, 1974. The best general history.

Gilson, Etienne, *Reason and Revelation in the Middle Ages,* New York, 1938. A brief but illuminating treatment by the greatest modern student of Scholasticism.

Henderson, George, *Gothic,* Baltimore, 1967.

Hoppin, Richard H., *Medieval Music,* New York, 1978.

Jacoff, Rachel, ed., *The Cambridge Companion to Dante,* New York, 1993. A collection of essays that constitutes the best recent introduction to this greatest of medieval imaginative writers.

Knowles, David, *The Evolution of Medieval Thought,* 2d ed., London, 1988. An authoritative survey, thoroughly revised in the second edition.

Leclercq, Jean, *The Love of Learning and the Desire for God,* 3d ed. New York, 1982. About monastic culture, with special reference to St. Bernard.

Lewis, C. S., *The Discarded Image: An Introduction to Medieval and Renaissance Literature,* Cambridge, 1964.

Lindberg, David C., ed., *Science in the Middle Ages,* Chicago, 1978. A collection of introductory essays by leading authorities in their respective fields.

Mâle, Emile, *The Gothic Image: Religious Art in France in the Thirteenth Century,* New York, 1958.

Morris, Colin, *The Discovery of the Individual, 1050–1200,* Toronto, 1987. A provocative interpretation that sees "individualism" as a twelfth-century discovery.

Radding, Charles M., and William W. Clark, *Medieval Architecture, Medieval Learning,* New Haven, 1992. Treats parallel trends in French architecture and Scholastic learning as the result of growing specialization among builders and schoolmasters.

Smalley, Beryl, *The Study of the Bible in the Middle Ages,* 3d ed., Oxford, 1983. A standard work that is also gracefully written and original in its argumentation.

Southern, R. W., *Scholastic Humanism and the Unification of Europe,* Vol. 1: *Foundations,* Cambridge, Mass., 1995. The first volume of a planned three-volume major interpretation by the foremost English-speaking medieval historian of the twentieth century.

Ullmann, Walter, *Medieval Political Thought,* rev. ed., Baltimore, 1976.

Van Steenberghen, Fernand, *Aristotle in the West,* 2d ed., New York, 1970. A short account of the recovery of Aristotelian thought in the High Middle Ages.

Weisheipl, James A., *Friar Thomas d'Aquino: His Life, Thought, and Works,* 2d ed., Washington, D.C., 1983.

Source Materials

An Aquinas Reader, ed. Mary T. Clark, New York, 1972.

Chrétien de Troyes, *Arthurian Romances,* tr. W. W. Kibler, New York, 1991.

Dante, *The Divine Comedy,* tr. M. Musa, 3 vols., Baltimore, 1984–86.

Goldin, F., ed., *Lyrics of the Troubadours and Trouvères,* Garden City, N.Y., 1973.

Gottfried von Strassburg, *Tristan,* tr. A. T. Hatto, Baltimore, 1960.

Joinville and Villehardouin, *Chronicles of the Crusades,* tr. M. R. B. Shaw, Baltimore, 1963.

The Letters of Abelard and Heloise (includes Abelard's *Story of My Calamities*), tr. B. Radice, Baltimore, 1974.

Peters, Edward, ed., *The First Crusade: The Chronicle of Fulcher of Chartres and Other Source Materials,* Philadelphia, 1971.

The Romance of the Rose, tr. Harry W. Robbins, New York, 1962.

The Song of Roland, tr. F. Goldin, New York, 1978.

Thorndike, Lynn, ed., *University Records and Life in the Middle Ages,* New York, 1944.

Tierney, Brian, ed., *The Crisis of Church and State, 1050–1300,* Englewood Cliffs, N.J., 1964. An excellent anthology of readings with masterful commentary.

Wolfram von Eschenbach, *Parzival,* tr. H. M. Mustard and C. E. Passage, New York, 1961.

CHAPTER 12

THE LATER MIDDLE AGES (1300–1500)

My lot has been to live amidst a storm
Of varying disturbing circumstances.
For you . . . a better age awaits.
Our descendants—the darkness once dispersed—
Can come again to the old radiance.

—The poet PETRARCH,
writing in the 1340s

The Later Middle Ages: catastrophe and adaptation

IF THE HIGH MIDDLE AGES were "times of feasts," then the late Middle Ages were "times of famine." From about 1300 until the middle or latter part of the fifteenth century calamities struck throughout western Europe with appalling severity and dismaying persistence. Famine first prevailed because agriculture was impeded by soil exhaustion, colder weather, and torrential rainfalls. Then, on top of those "acts of God," came the most terrible natural disaster of all: the dreadful plague known as the "Black Death," which cut broad swaths of mortality throughout western Europe. As if all that were not enough, incessant warfare continually brought hardship and desolation. Common people suffered most because they were most exposed to raping, stabbing, looting, and burning by soldiers and organized bands of freebooters. After an army passed through a region one might see miles of smoldering ruins littered with putrefying corpses; in many places the desolation was so great that wolves roamed the countryside and even entered the outskirts of the cities. In short, if the serene Virgin symbolized the High Middle Ages, the grinning death's-head symbolized the succeeding period. For these reasons we should not look to the Later Middle Ages for the dramatic progress we saw transpiring earlier, but this is not to say that there was no progress at all. In the last two centuries of the Middle Ages Europeans displayed a tenacious perseverance in the face of adversity. Instead of abandoning themselves to apathy, they resolutely sought to adjust themselves to changed circumstances. Thus there was no collapse of civilization as there was with the fall of the Roman Empire, but rather a period of transition that resulted in preserving and building upon what was most solid in Europe's earlier legacy.

Economic Depression and the Emergence of a New Equilibrium

Economic crisis

By around 1300 the agricultural expansion of the High Middle Ages had reached its limits. Thereafter yields and areas under cultivation began to decline, causing a decline in the whole European economy that was accelerated by the disruptive effects of war. Accordingly, the first half of the fourteenth century was a time of growing economic depression. The coming of the Black Death in 1347 made this depression particularly acute because it completely disrupted the affairs of daily life. Recurrences of the plague and protracted warfare continued to depress most of the European economy until deep into the fifteenth century. But between roughly 1350 and 1450 Europeans learned how to adjust to the new economic circumstances and succeeded in placing their economy on a sounder basis. This became most evident after around 1450, when the tapering off of disease and warfare permitted a slow but steady economic recovery. All told, therefore, despite a prolonged depression of roughly 150 years, Europe emerged in the later fifteenth century with a healthier economy than it had known earlier.

Agricultural adversity

The limits to agricultural expansion reached around 1300 were natural ones. There was a limit to the amount of land that could be cleared and a limit to the amount of crops that could be raised without the introduction of scientific farming. In fact, Europeans had gone further in clearing and cultivating than they should have: in the enthusiasm of the high-medieval colonization movement, marginal lands had been cleared that

Death at the Baptism. In the Later Middle Ages recurrent outbreaks of plague, coupled with other natural and man-made disasters, led to an obsession with the omnipresence of death. This chilling illumination from a fifteenth-century German manuscript shows a friar baptizing a newborn child while death stands ready to "dry him off," implying that death stands waiting for all of us, even from the first minute of life.

were not rich enough to sustain intense cultivation. In addition, even the best plots were becoming overworked. To make matters worse, after around 1300 the weather deteriorated. Whereas western Europe had been favored with a drying and warming trend in the eleventh and twelfth centuries, in the fourteenth century the climate became colder and wetter. Although the average decline in temperature over the course of the century was only at most 1° Centigrade, this was sufficient to curtail viticulture in many northern areas such as England. Cereal farming too became increasingly impractical in far northern regions because the growing season became too short: in Greenland and parts of Scandinavia agricultural settlements were abandoned entirely. Increased rainfall also took its toll. Terrible floods that deluged all of northwestern Europe in 1315 ruined crops and caused a prolonged, deadly famine. For three years peasants were so driven by hunger that they ate their seed grain, ruining their chances for a full recovery in the following season. In desperation they also ate cats, dogs, and rats. Many peasants were so exposed to unsanitary conditions and weakened by malnutrition that they became highly susceptible to disease. Thus there was an appalling death rate. In one Flemish city a tenth of the population was buried within a six-month period of 1316 alone. Relatively settled farming conditions returned after 1318, but in many parts of Europe heavy rains or other climatic disasters came again. In Italy floods swept away Florentine bridges in 1333 and a tidal wave destroyed the port of Amalfi in 1343. With nature so recurrently capricious economic life could only suffer.

Bubonic Plague. This representation from a late-fifteenth-century French painting shows a man in the throes of death from the plague. The swelling on his neck is a "bubo," a form of lymphatic swelling that gave the bubonic plague its name.

The pressure of population

Although ruinous wars combined with famine to kill off many, Europe remained overpopulated until the middle of the fourteenth century. The reason for this was that population growth was still outstripping food supply. Since people continued to multiply while cereal production declined, there was just not enough food to go around. Accordingly, grain prices soared and the poor throughout Europe paid the penalty in hunger. And then a disaster struck that was so appalling that it seemed to many to presage the end of the world.

Black Death decimates population

This was the Black Death, a combined onslaught of bubonic and pneumonic plague that first swept through Europe from 1347 to 1350, and returned at periodic intervals for roughly the next hundred years. This calamity was fully comparable—in terms of the death, dislocation, and horror it wrought—to the two world wars of the twentieth century. The clinical effects of the plague were hideous. Once infected with bubonic plague by a flea bite, the diseased person would develop enormous swellings in the groin or armpits; black spots might appear on the arms and legs, diarrhea would ensue, and the victim would die between the third and fifth day. If the infection came in the pneumonic form, i.e., caused by inhalation, there would be coughing of blood instead of swellings, and death would follow within three days. Some people went to bed healthy and were dead the next morning after a night of agony; ships with dead crews floated aimlessly on the seas. Although the successive epidemics left a few localities unscathed, the overall demographic effects of the plague were devastating. To take just a few examples: the population of Toulouse declined from roughly 30,000 in 1335, to 26,000 in 1385, to 8,000 in 1430; the total population of eastern Normandy fell by 30 percent between 1347 and 1357, and again by 30 percent before 1380; in the rural area around Pistoia a population depletion of about 60 percent occurred between 1340 and 1404. Altogether, the combined effects of famine, war, and, above all, plague reduced the total population of western Europe by at least one-half and probably more like two-thirds between 1300 and 1450.

Initial response to the Black Death

At first, the Black Death caused great hardships for most of the survivors. Since panic-stricken people wished to avoid contagion, many fled from their jobs to seek isolation. Town-dwellers fled to the country and country-dwellers fled from each other. Even the pope retreated to the interior of his palace and allowed no one entrance. With large numbers dead and others away from their posts, harvests were left rotting, manufacturing was disrupted, and conveyance systems were abandoned. Hence basic commodities became scarcer and prices rose. For these reasons the onslaught of the plague greatly intensified Europe's economic crisis.

Economic consequences of the Black Death: (1) agricultural specialization

But after around 1400 the new demographic realities began to turn prices around and alter basic economic patterns. In particular, the prices of staple foodstuffs began to decline because production gradually returned to normal and there were fewer mouths to feed. Recurrent appearances of the plague or natural disasters sometimes caused prices to fluctuate greatly in certain years, but overall prices of basic commodities throughout most of the fifteenth century went down or remained stable. This trend led to new agricultural specialization. Since cereals were cheaper, people could afford to spend a greater percentage of their income on comparative luxuries such as dairy products, meat, and wine. Hitherto farmers all over Europe had concentrated on cereals because bread was

A Late-Medieval Funeral Scene

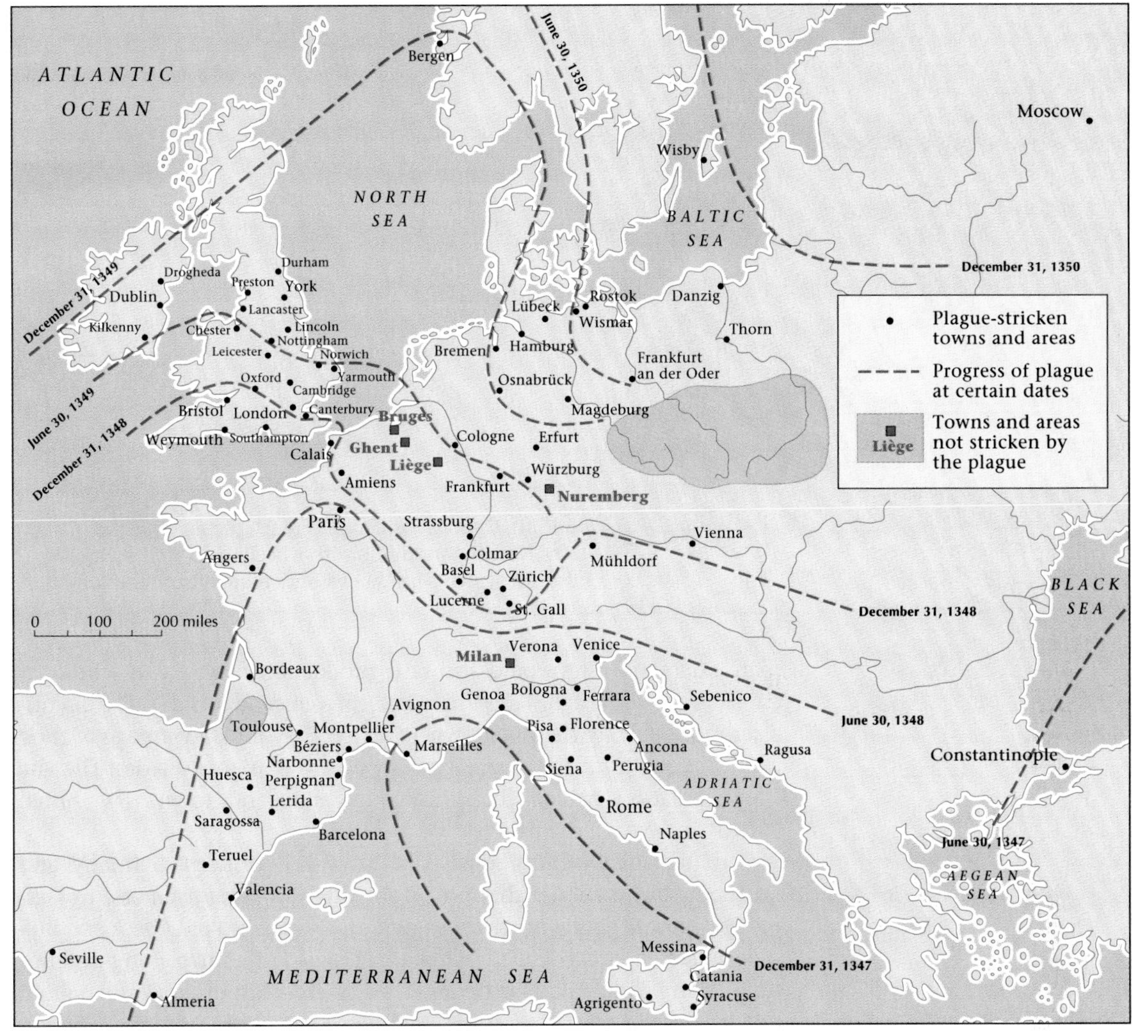

Progress of the Black Death, Fourteenth Century

the staff of life, but now it was wisest, particularly in areas of poorer soil or unpropitious climate, to shift to specialized production. Depending upon whatever seemed most feasible, land might be used for the raising of livestock for milk, grapes for wine, or malt for beer. Specialized regional economies resulted: parts of England were given over to sheep-raising or beer production, parts of France concentrated on wine, and Sweden traded butter for cheap German grain. Most areas of Europe turned to what they could do best, and reciprocal trade of basic commodities over long distances created a sound new commercial equilibrium.

(2) Growth in importance of urban centers

Another economic result of the Black Death was an increase in the relative importance of towns and cities. Urban manufacturers usually could respond more flexibly than landlords to drastically changed economic conditions because their production capabilities were more elastic. When markets shrank, manufacturers could cut back supply more easily to

Building Operations. From a French picture Bible, c. 1300. Note the treadmill, with wheel, ropes, and pulley, by means of which a basket of stones is brought to the construction level.

match demand; they could also raise production more easily when circumstances warranted. Thus urban entrepreneurs bounced back from disaster more quickly than landowners. Often they took advantage of their greater strength to attract rural labor by means of higher salaries. Thereby the population balance between countryside and town was shifted slightly in favor of the latter.

(3) Growth in trade

Certain urban centers, especially those in northern Germany and northern Italy, profited the most from the new circumstances. In Germany a group of cities and towns under the leadership of Lübeck and Bremen allied in the so-called Hanseatic League to control long-distance trade in the Baltic and North Seas. Their fleets transported German grain to Scandinavia and brought back dairy products, fish, and furs. The enhanced European per capita ability to buy luxury goods brought new wealth to the northern Italian trading cities of Genoa and, especially, Venice because these cities controlled the importation of spices from the East. Greater expenditures on luxury also aided the economies of Florence, Venice, Milan, and other neighboring cities because those cities concentrated on the manufacture of silks and linens, light woolens, and other fine cloths. Milan, in addition, prospered from its armaments industry, which kept the warring European states supplied with armor and weapons. Because of varying local conditions, some cities and towns, above all those of Flanders, became economically depressed, but altogether European urban centers profited remarkably well from the new economic circumstances and emphasis on specialization.

An Artisan Making Chain Mail. One can easily see why late-medieval knightly armor was terribly expensive.

The changed circumstances also helped stimulate the development of sophisticated business, accounting, and banking techniques. Because sharp fluctuations in prices made investments precarious, new forms of partnerships were created to minimize risks. Insurance contracts were also invented to take some of the risk out of shipping. Europe's most useful accounting invention, double-entry bookkeeping, was first put into use in Italy in the mid-fourteenth century and spread rapidly thereafter north of the Alps. This allowed for quick discovery of computational errors and easy overview of profits and losses, credits and debits. Large-scale banking had already become common after the middle of the thirteenth century, but the economic crises of the Later Middle Ages encouraged banks to alter some of their ways of doing business. Most important was the development of prudent branch-banking techniques, especially by the Florentine house of the Medici. Earlier banks had built branches, but the Medici bank, which flourished from 1397 to 1494, organized theirs along the lines of a modern holding company. The Medici branches, located in London, Bruges, and Avignon, as well as several Italian cities, were dominated by senior partners from the Medici family who followed common policies. Formally, however, each branch was a separate partnership which did not carry any other branch down with it if it collapsed. Other Italian banks experimented with advanced credit techniques. Some even allowed their clients to transfer funds between each other without any real money changing hands. Such "book transfers" were at first executed only by oral command, but around 1400 they started to be carried out by written orders. These were the earliest ancestors of the modern check.

The growth of advanced business and financial techniques

In surveying the two centuries of late-medieval economic history, both the role of nature and that of human beings must be emphasized. The premodern history of all parts of the globe tends to show that whenever population becomes excessive natural controls manage to reduce it. Bad weather and disease may come at any time, but when humans are already suffering from hunger and conditions of overcrowding, the results of natural disasters will be particularly devastating. That certainly is what happened in the fourteenth century. Nature intervened cruelly in human affairs, but no matter how cruel the immediate effects, the results were ultimately beneficial. By 1450 a far smaller population had a higher average standard of living than the population of 1300. In this result humans too played their part. Because people were determined to make the best of the new circumstances and avoid a recurrence of economic depression, they managed to reorganize their economic life and place it on a sounder footing. The gross European product of about 1450 was probably lower than it was in 1300, but this is not surprising given the much smaller population. In fact, per capita output had risen with per capita income, and the European economy was ready to move on to new conquests.

The interaction of man and nature in late-medieval economic history

Social and Emotional Dislocation

Before the healthy new equilibrium was reached, the economic crises of the Later Middle Ages contributed from about 1300 to 1450 to provoking a rash of lower-class rural and urban insurrections more numerous than Europe had ever known before or has ever known since. It was once

Economic crises lead to lower-class revolts

thought that these were all caused by extreme deprivation, but as we will see, that was often not the case.

Rural insurrections: the Jacquerie

The one large-scale rural uprising that was most clearly caused by economic hardship was the northern French "Jacquerie" of 1358. This took its name from the prototypical French peasant, "Jacques Bonhomme," who had suffered more than he could endure. In 1348 and 1349 the Black Death had brought its terror and wreaked havoc with the economy. Then a flare-up of war between England and France had spread great desolation over the countryside. The peasants, as usual in late-medieval warfare, suffered most from the pillaging and burning carried out by the rapacious soldiers. To make matters even less endurable, after the English decisively defeated the French in 1356 at the Battle of Poitiers the French king, John II, and numerous aristocrats had to be ransomed. As always in such cases, the peasants were asked to bear the heaviest share of the burden, but by 1358 they had had enough and rose up with astounding ferocity. Without any clear program they burned down castles, murdered their lords, and raped their lords' wives. Undoubtedly their intense economic resentments were the major cause for the uprising, but two qualifications remain in order. The first is that the peasants who participated in the Jacquerie were, comparatively speaking, among the richest in France: apparently those who suffered most abjectly were entirely unable to organize themselves for revolt. The other qualification is that political factors surely help account for the Jacquerie as well as economic ones. While the king was in captivity in England, groups of townsmen were trying to reform the governmental system by limiting monarchical powers, and aristocratic factions were plotting to seize power. Since nobody quite knew which element was going to rule where, the peasants seem to have sensed an opportunity to take advantage of France's political confusion. But in fact the opportunity was not as great as they may have thought: within a month the privileged powers closed ranks, massacred the rebels, and quickly restored order.

Background of the English Peasants' Revolt

The English Peasants' Revolt of 1381—the most serious lower-class rebellion in English history—is frequently bracketed with the Jacquerie, but its causes were very different. Instead of being a revolt of desperation, it was one of frustrated rising expectations. By 1381 the effects of the Black Death should have been working in favor of the peasants. Above all, a shortage of labor should have placed their services in demand. In fact, the incidence of the plague did help to increase manumissions (i.e., freeings) of serfs and raise salaries or lower rents of free farm laborers. But aristocratic landlords fought back to preserve their own incomes. They succeeded in passing legislation that aimed to keep wages at pre-plague levels and force landless laborers to work at the lower rates. Aristocrats furthermore often tried to exact all their old dues and unpaid services. Because the peasants were unwilling to be pushed down into their previous poverty and subservience, a collision was inevitable.

The course of the revolt

The spark that ignited the great revolt of 1381 was an attempt to collect a national tax levied equally on every head instead of being made proportional to wealth. This was an unprecedented development in English tax-collecting that the peasants understandably found unfair. Two head-taxes were levied without resistance in 1377 and 1379, but when agents tried to collect a third in 1381 the peasantry rose up to resist and seek redress of all their grievances. First they burned local records and sacked the dwellings of those they considered their exploiters; then they marched on London, where they executed the lord chancellor and treasurer of England. Recognizing the gravity of the situation, the fifteen-year-old king, Richard II, went out to meet the peasants and won their confidence by promising to abolish serfdom and keep rents low; meanwhile, during negotiations the peasant leader, Wat Tyler, was murdered in a squabble with the king's escort. Lacking leadership, the peasants, who mistakenly thought they had achieved their aims, rapidly dispersed. But once the boy-king was no longer in danger of his life he kept none of his promises. Instead, the scattered peasant forces were quickly hunted down and a few alleged trouble-makers were executed without any mass reprisals. The revolt itself therefore accomplished nothing, but within a few decades the natural play of economic forces caused serfdom to disappear and considerably improved the lot of the rural wage laborer.

Tombstone of a Leader of a Fourteenth-Century German Peasant Uprising. In 1336 a petty knight from Franconia (central Germany) marched at the head of impoverished peasants who vented their resentments by robbing and murdering all the Jews they could find in the nearby towns. After several months of leading this rampage the knight was finally apprehended and executed by governing authorities. His tombstone shows him with bound hands at the moment of his beheading, but the inscription calls him "blessed," a sign that some wished to view him as a martyred saint.

Other rural revolts took place in other parts of Europe, but we may now look at some urban ones. Conventionally, the urban revolts of the Later Middle Ages are viewed as uprisings of exploited proletarians who were more oppressed than ever because of the effects of economic depression. But this is probably too great a simplification because each case differed and complex forces were always at work. For example, an uprising in the north German town of Brunswick in 1374 was much less a movement of the poor against the rich than a political upheaval in which one political alliance replaced another. A different north German uprising, in Lübeck in 1408, has been aptly described as a "taxpayer's" revolt. This again was less a confrontation of the poor versus the rich than an attempt of a faction that was out of power to initiate less costly government.

The uprising of the Ciompi

The nearest thing to a real proletarian revolt was the uprising in 1378 of the Florentine *Ciompi* (pronounced "cheeompi"). The Ciompi were woolcombers who had the misfortune to be engaged in an industry that had become particularly depressed. Some of them had lost their jobs and others were frequently cheated or underpaid by the masters of the woolen industry. The latter wielded great political power in Florence, and thus could pass economic legislation in their own favor. This fact in itself meant that if there were to be economic reforms, they would have to go together with political changes. As events transpired it was a political crisis that called the Ciompi into direct action. In 1378 Florence had become exhausted by three years of war with the papacy. Certain patrician leaders overthrew the old regime to alter the war policy and gain their own political advantage. Circumstances led them to seek the support of the lower classes and, once stirred up, the Ciompi became emboldened after a few months to launch their own far more radical rebellion. This was inspired primarily by economic hardship and grievances, but personal hatreds also played a role. The Ciompi gained power for six weeks, during which they tried to institute tax relief, fuller employment, and representation of themselves and other proletarian groups in the Florentine government. But they could not maintain their hold on power and a new oligarchical government revoked all their reforms.

General observations on the nature of popular uprisings

If we try to draw any general conclusions about these various uprisings, we can certainly say that few if any of them would have occurred had there not been an economic crisis. But political considerations always had some influence, and the rebels in some uprisings were more prosperous than in others. It is noteworthy that all the genuinely lower-class uprisings of economically desperate groups quickly failed. This was certainly because the upper classes were more accustomed to wielding power and giving orders; even more important, they had access to the money and troops necessary to quell revolts. Sometimes elements within the lower classes might fight among themselves, whereas the privileged always managed to rally into a united front when faced by a lower-class threat to their domination. In addition, lower-class rebels were usually more intent on redressing immediate grievances than on developing fully coherent long-term governmental programs; inspiring ideals for cohesive action were generally lacking. The case of the Hussite Revolution in Bohemia—to be treated later—shows that religion in the Later Middle Ages was a more effective rallying ground for large numbers of people than political, economic, and social demands.

The crisis of the late-medieval aristocracy

Although the upper classes succeeded in overcoming popular uprisings, they perceived the economic and emotional insecurities of the Later Middle Ages and the possibility of revolt as a constant threat, and became

A Party of Late-Medieval Aristocrats. Notice the pointed shoes and the women's pointed hats, twice as high as their heads.

obsessed with maintaining their privileged social status. Late-medieval aristocrats were in a precarious economic position because they gained most of their income from land. In times when grain prices and rents were falling and wages rising, landowners were obviously in economic trouble. Some aristocrats probably also felt threatened by the rapid rise of merchants and financiers who could make quick killings because of sharp market fluctuations. In practice, really wealthy merchants bought land and were absorbed into the aristocracy. Moreover, most landowning aristocrats were able to stave off economic threats by expert estate management; in fact, many of them actually became richer than ever. But most still felt more exposed to social and economic insecurities than before. The result was that they tried to set up artificial barriers with which they separated themselves from other classes.

The aristocratic emphasis on luxury

Two of the most striking examples of this separation were the aristocratic emphasis on luxury and the formation of exclusive chivalric orders. The Later Middle Ages was the period par excellence of aristocratic ostentation. While famine or disease raged, aristocrats regaled themselves with lavish banquets and magnificent pageants. At one feast in Flanders in 1468 a table decoration was forty-six feet high. Aristocratic clothing too was extremely ostentatious: men wore long, pointed shoes, and women ornately festooned headdresses. Throughout history rich people have always enjoyed dressing up, but the aristocrats of the Later Middle Ages seem to have done so obsessively to comfort themselves and convey the message that they were entirely different from others. The insistence on maintaining a sharply defined social hierarchy also accounts for the late-medieval proliferation of chivalric orders, such as those of the Knights of the Garter or the Golden Fleece. By joining together in exclusive orders that prescribed special conduct and boasted special insignia of membership, aristocrats who felt threatened by social pressures again tried to set themselves off from others, in effect, by putting up a sign that read "for members only."

Duke Philip the Good of Burgundy. The duke proudly wears the emblem of the Order of the Golden Fleece around his neck.

Another explanation for the exorbitant stress on luxury is that it was a form of escapism. Aristocrats who were continually exposed to the sight and smell of death must have found it emotionally comforting to retreat into a dream-world of elegant manners, splendid feasts, and multicolored clothes. In a parallel fashion, nonaristocrats who could not afford such luxuries often sought relief from the vision of death in crude public entertainments: for example, crowds would watch blind beggars try to catch a squealing pig but beat each other with clubs instead, or they would cheer on boys to clamber up greasy poles in order to win prizes of geese.

It must not be thought, however, that late-medieval Europeans gave themselves over to riotous living without interruption. In fact, the same people who sought elegant or boisterous diversions just as often went to the other emotional extreme when faced by the psychic stress caused by the troubles of the age, and abandoned themselves to sorrow. Throughout the period grown men and women shed tears in abundance. The queen mother of France wept in public when she first

A Late-Medieval Crucifixion Scene. The Virgin has to be held up to keep from swooning, and the angels are weeping.

viewed her grandson; the great preacher Vincent Ferrer had to interrupt his sermons on Christ's Passion and the Last Judgment because he and his audience were sobbing too convulsively; and the English king, Edward II, supposedly wept so much when imprisoned that he gushed forth enough hot water for his own shave. The last story taxes the imagination, but it does illustrate well what contemporaries thought was possible. We know for certain that the Church encouraged crying because of the survival of moving statuettes of weeping St. Johns, which were obviously designed to call forth tears from their viewers.

People also were encouraged by preachers to brood on the Passion of Christ and on their own mortality. Fearsome crucifixes abounded, and the figure of the Virgin Mary was less a smiling madonna than a sorrowing mother: now she was most frequently depicted slumping with grief at the foot of the cross, or holding the dead Christ in her lap. The late-medieval obsession with mortality can also still be seen in sculptures, frescoes, and book illustrations that reminded viewers of the brevity of life and the torments of hell. The characteristic tombs of the High Middle Ages were mounted with sculptures that either showed the deceased in some action that had been typical of his or her accomplishments in life,

Left: **A Dead Man Before His Judge.** A late-medieval reminder of human mortality. Right: **Tomb of François de la Sarra.** This late-fourteenth-century Swiss nobleman is shown with snakes around his arms and toads littering his face.

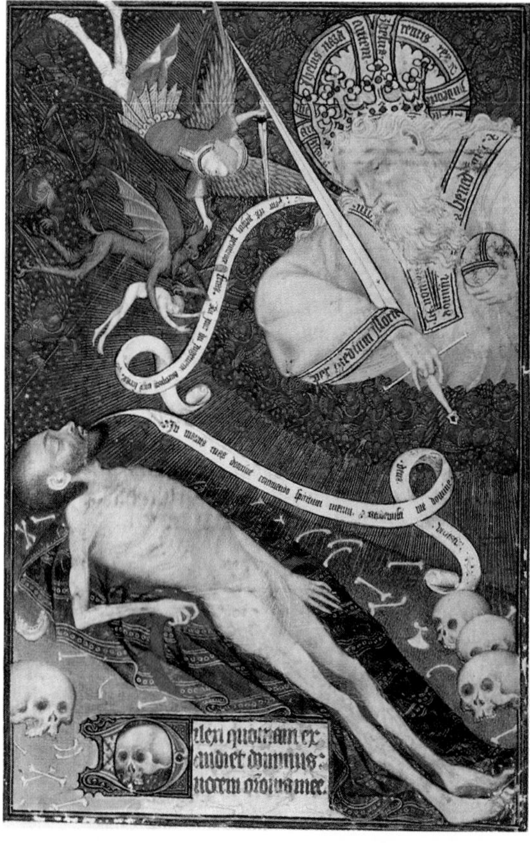

or else in a state of repose that showed death to be nothing more than peaceful sleep. But in the late fourteenth century, tombs appeared that displayed the physical ravages of death in the most gruesome ways imaginable: emaciated corpses were displayed with protruding intestines or covered with snakes or toads. Some tombs bore inscriptions stating that the viewer would soon be "a fetid cadaver, food for worms"; some warned chillingly, "What you are, I was; what I am, you will be." Omnipresent illustrations displayed figures of grinning Death, with his scythe, carrying off elegant and healthy men and women, or sadistic devils roasting pain-wracked humans in hell. Because people who painted or brooded on such pictures might the next day indulge in excessive revels, late-medieval culture often seems to border on the manic-depressive. But apparently such extreme reactions were necessary to help people cope with their fears.

The Prince of the World. A stone figure from the Church of St. Sebald, Nuremberg, from about 1330. From the front the man is smiling and master of all he surveys; from the rear he is crawling with vermin.

TRIALS FOR THE CHURCH AND HUNGER FOR THE DIVINE

The intense concentration on the meaning of death was also a manifestation of a very deep and pervasive religiosity. The religious enthusiasm of the High Middle Ages by no means flagged after 1300; if anything, it became more intense. But religious enthusiasm took on new forms of expression because of the institutional difficulties of the Church and the turmoils of the age.

After the humiliation and death of Pope Boniface VIII in 1303, the Church experienced a period of institutional crisis that was as severe and prolonged as the contemporary economic crisis. We may distinguish three phases: the so-called Babylonian Captivity of the papacy, 1305–1378; the Great Schism, 1378–1417; and the period of the Italian territorial papacy, 1417–1517. During the Babylonian Captivity the papacy was located in Avignon instead of Rome and was generally subservient to the interests of the French crown. There were several reasons for this: the most obvious was that since the test of strength between Philip the Fair and Boniface VIII had resulted in a clear victory for the French king, subsequent popes were unwilling to risk French royal ire. In fact, once the popes recognized that they could not give orders to the French kings, they found that they could gain certain advantages from currying their favor. One was a safe home in southern France, away from the tumult of Italy. Central Italy and the city of Rome in the fourteenth century had become so politically turbulent and rebellious that the pope could not even count on finding personal safety there, let alone sufficiently peaceful conditions to maintain orderly ecclesiastical administration. But no such danger existed in Avignon. Even though Avignon was not then part of the French kingdom—it was the major city of a small papal territory—French military might was close enough to guarantee the pope his much-needed security. Another advantage of papal subservience to French power was help from the French in pursuing mutually advantageous policies in Germany and

The Babylonian Captivity of the papacy

southern Italy. Perhaps most important was a working agreement whereby the French king would propose his own candidates to become bishops and the pope would then name them, thereby gaining sizable monetary payments. After 1305 the pro-French system became so entrenched that a majority of cardinals and all the popes until 1378 were themselves French.

The character of the Avignonese papacy

At Avignon the popes were more successful than ever in pursuing their policy of centralizing the government of the Church. For the first time they worked out a really sound system of papal finance, based on the systematization of dues collected from the clergy throughout Europe. The papacy also succeeded in appointing more candidates to vacant benefices than before (in practice often naming candidates proposed by the French and English kings), and they proceeded against heresy with great determination, indeed with ruthlessness. But whatever the popes achieved in power they lost in respect and loyalty. The clergy became alienated as a result of being asked to pay so much money, and much of the laity was horrified by the corruption and unbridled luxury displayed at the papal court: there the cardinals lived more splendidly than lords, dining off peacocks, pheasants, grouse, and swans, and drinking from elaborately sculptured fountains that spouted the finest wines. Most of the Avignonese popes themselves were personally upright and abstemious, but one, Clement VI (1342–1352), was worse than his cardinals. Clement was ready to offer any spiritual benefit for money, boasted that he would appoint even a jackass as bishop if political circumstances warranted, and defended his incessant sexual transgressions by insisting that he fornicated on doctors' orders.

The return to Rome

As time went on the pressures of informed public opinion forced the popes to promise that they would return to Rome. After one abortive attempt by Urban V in 1367, Pope Gregory XI finally did return to the Holy City in 1377. But he died a year later and then disaster struck. The college of cardinals, surrounded in Rome by clamoring Italians, yielded to local sentiment by naming an Italian as pope, who took the title of Urban VI. But most of the cardinals were Frenchmen and quickly regretted their decision, especially because Urban VI immediately began quarreling with them and revealing what were probably paranoid tendencies. Therefore, after only a few months, the French cardinals met again, declared the previous election void, and replaced Urban with one of their own number, who called himself Clement VII.

The Great Schism

Unfortunately, however, Urban VI did not meekly resign. On the contrary, he named an entirely new Italian college of cardinals and remained entrenched in Rome. Clement VII quickly retreated with his own party to Avignon and the so-called Great Schism ensued. France and other countries in the French political orbit—such as Scotland, Castile, and Aragon—recognized Clement, while the rest of Europe recognized Urban as the true pope. For three decades Christians looked on helplessly while the rival pontiffs hurled curses at each other and the international monastic orders became divided into Roman and Avignonese camps. The death of one or the other pope did not end the schism; each camp had its own set of cardinals which promptly named either a French or Italian successor. The desperateness of the situation led a council of prelates from both camps to meet in Pisa in 1409 to depose both popes and name a new one instead. But neither the Italian nor the French pope accepted the council's decision, and both had enough political support to retain some obedience. So after 1409 there were three rival claimants hurling curses instead of two.

The end of the Schism; conciliarism

The Great Schism was finally ended in 1417 by the Council of Constance, the largest ecclesiastical gathering in medieval history. This time the assembled prelates made certain to gain the crucial support of secular powers and also to eliminate the prior claimants before naming a new pope. After the council's election of Martin V in 1417, European ecclesiastical unity was thus fully restored. But a struggle over the nature of Church government followed immediately. The members of the Council of Constance challenged the prevailing medieval theory of papal monarchy by calling for balanced, "conciliar" government. In two momentous decrees they stated that a general council of prelates was superior in authority to the pope, and that such councils should meet regularly to govern the Church. Not surprisingly, subsequent popes—who had now returned to Rome—sought to nullify these decrees. When a new council met in Basel in 1431, in accordance with the principles laid down at Constance, the reigning pope did all he could to sabotage its activities. Ultimately he was successful: after a protracted struggle the Council of Basel dissolved in 1449 in abject failure, and the attempt to institute constitutional government in the Church was completely defeated. But the papacy won this victory over conciliarism only by gaining the support of the rulers of the European states. In separate concordats with kings and princes the popes granted the secular rulers much authority over the various local churches. The popes thus became assured of theoretical supremacy at the cost of surrendering much real power. To compensate for this they concentrated on consolidating their own direct rule in central Italy. Most of the fifteenth-century popes ruled very much like any other princes, leading armies, jockeying for alliances, and building magnificent palaces. Hence, although they did succeed for the first time in creating a viable political state, their reputation for disinterested piety remained low.

The decline of clerical prestige

While the papacy was undergoing these vicissitudes, the local clergy throughout Europe was undergoing a loss of prestige for several reasons. One was that the pope's greater financial demands forced the clergy to demand more from the laity, but such demands were bitterly resented, especially during times of prevailing economic crisis. Then too during outbreaks of plague the clergy sometimes fled their posts just like everyone else, but in so doing they lost whatever claim they had for being morally superior. Probably the single greatest reason for growing dissatisfaction with the clergy was the increase in lay literacy. The continued proliferation of schools and the decline in the cost of books—a subject we will treat later—made it possible for large numbers of lay people to learn how to read. Once that happened, the laity could start reading parts of the Bible, or, more frequently, popular religious primers. These made it clear that their local priests were not living according to the standards set by Jesus and the Apostles. In the meantime, the upheavals and horrors of the age drove people to seek religious solace more than ever. Finding the conventional channels of church attendance, confession, and submission to clerical authority insufficient, the laity sought supplementary or alternate routes to piety. These differed greatly from each other, but they all aimed to satisfy an immense hunger for the divine.

Lay devotional practices

The most widely traveled route was that of performing repeated acts of external devotion in the hope that they would gain the devotee divine favor on earth and salvation in the hereafter. People flocked to go on pilgrimages as never before and participated regularly in barefooted religious processions: the latter were often held twice a month and occasionally as often as once a week. Men and women also eagerly paid for thousands of masses to be said by full-time "Mass priests" for the souls of their dead relatives and left legacies for the reading of numerous requiem masses to save their own souls after death. Obsession with repeating prayers reached a peak when some pious individuals tried to compute the number of drops of blood that Christ shed on the cross so that they could say the same number of Our Fathers. The most excessive and repugnant form of religious ritual in the Later Middle Ages was flagellation. Some women who lived in communal houses beat themselves with the roughest animal hides, chains, and knotted thongs. A young girl who entered such a community in Poland in 1331 suffered extreme internal injuries and became completely disfigured within eleven months. Flailings were

A German Flagellant Procession. These penitents hoped they could ward off the Black Death by their mutually inflicted tortures.

not usually performed in public, but during the first onslaught of the Black Death in 1348 and 1349, whole bands of lay people marched through northern Europe chanting and beating each other with metal-tipped scourges in the hope of appeasing the apparent divine wrath.

Master Eckhart

An opposite route to godliness was the inward path of mysticism. Throughout the European continent, but particularly in Germany and England, male and female mystics, both clerical and lay, sought union with God by means of "detachment," contemplation, or spiritual exercises. The most original and eloquent late-medieval mystical theorist was Master Eckhart (c. 1260–1327), a German Dominican who taught that there was a power or "spark" deep within every human soul that was really the dwelling-place of God. By renouncing all sense of selfhood one could retreat into one's innermost recesses and there find divinity. Eckhart did not recommend ceasing attendance at church—he hardly could have because he preached in churches—but he made it clear that outward rituals were of comparatively little importance in reaching God. He also gave the impression to his lay audiences that they might attain godliness largely on their own volition. Thus ecclesiastical authorities charged him with inciting "ignorant and undisciplined people to wild and dangerous excesses." Although Eckhart pleaded his own doctrinal orthodoxy, some of his teachings were condemned by the papacy.

Diverse forms of mysticism

That Eckhart's critics were not entirely mistaken in their worries is shown by the fact that some lay people in Germany who were influenced by him did fall into the heresy of believing that they could become fully united with God on earth without any priestly intermediaries. But these so-called heretics of the Free Spirit were few in number. Much more numerous were later orthodox mystics, sometimes influenced by Eckhart and sometimes not, who placed greater emphasis on the divine initiative in the meeting of the soul with God and made certain to insist that the ministrations of the Church were a necessary contribution to the mystic way. Even they, however, believed that "churches make no man holy, but men make churches holy." Most of the great teachers and practitioners of mysticism in the fourteenth century were clerics, nuns, or hermits, but in the fifteenth century a modified form of mystical belief spread among lay people. This "practical mysticism" did not aim for full ecstatic union with God, but rather for an ongoing sense of some divine presence during the conduct of daily life. The most popular manual that pointed the way to this goal was the Latin *Imitation of Christ,* written around 1427, probably by the north German canon Thomas à Kempis. Because this was written in a simple but forceful style and taught how to be a pious Christian while still living actively in the world, it was particularly attractive to lay readers. Thus it quickly became translated into the leading European vernaculars. From then until today it has been more widely read by Christians than any other religious work outside of the Bible. The *Imitation* urges its readers to participate in one religious ceremony—the sacrament of the Eucharist—but otherwise it emphasizes inward piety. According to its teachings, the individual Christian is best able to become the "partner" of Jesus

Christ both by taking communion and also by engaging in biblical meditation and leading a simple, moral life.

John Wyclif and the Lollards

A third distinct form of late-medieval piety was outright religious protest or heresy. In England and Bohemia especially, heretical movements became serious threats to the Church. The initiator of heresy in late-medieval England was an Oxford theologian named John Wyclif (c. 1330–1384). Wyclif's rigorous adherence to the theology of St. Augustine led him to believe that a certain number of humans were predestined to be saved while the rest were irrevocably damned. He thought the predestined would naturally live simply, according to the standards of the New Testament, but in fact he found most members of the Church hierarchy indulging in splendid extravagances. Hence he concluded that most Church officials were damned. For him the only solution was to have secular rulers appropriate ecclesiastical wealth and reform the Church by replacing corrupt priests and bishops with men who would live according to apostolic standards. This position was obviously attractive to the aristocracy of England, who may have looked forward to enriching themselves with Church spoils and at least saw nothing wrong with using Wyclif as a bulldog to frighten the pope and the local clergy. Thus Wyclif at first received influential aristocratic support. But toward the end of his life he moved from merely calling for reform to attacking some of the most basic institutions of the Church, above all the sacrament of the Eucharist. This radicalism frightened off his influential protectors, and Wyclif probably would have been formally condemned for heresy had he lived longer. His death brought no respite for the Church, however, because he had attracted numerous lay followers—called Lollards—who zealously continued to propagate some of his most radical ideas. Above all, the Lollards taught that pious Christians should shun the corrupt Church and instead study the Bible and rely as far as possible on their individual consciences. Lollardy gained many adherents in the last two decades of the fourteenth century, but after the introduction in England of the death penalty for heresy in 1399 and the failure of a Lollard uprising in 1414 the heretical wave greatly receded. Nonetheless, a few Lollards did continue to survive underground, and their descendants helped contribute to the Protestant Reformation of the sixteenth century.

John Hus

Much greater was the influence of Wyclifism in Bohemia. Around 1400, Czech students who had studied in Oxford brought back Wyclif's ideas to the Bohemian capital of Prague. There Wyclifism was enthusiastically adopted by an eloquent preacher named John Hus (c. 1373–1415), who had already been inveighing in well-attended sermons against "the world, the flesh, and the devil." Hus employed Wyclifite theories to back up his own calls for the end of ecclesiastical corruption, and rallied many Bohemians to the cause of reform in the years between 1408 and 1415. Never alienating anyone as Wyclif had done by criticizing the doctrine of the Eucharist, Hus gained support from many different directions. The politics of the Great Schism prompted the king of Bohemia to lend Hus his protection, and influential aristocrats supported Hus for motives similar to those of their English counterparts. Above all, Hus gained a mass following because of his eloquence and concern for social justice. Accordingly, most of Bohemia was behind him when Hus in 1415 agreed to travel to the Council of Constance to defend his views and try to convince the assembled prelates that only thoroughgoing reform could save the Church. But although Hus had been guaranteed his personal safety, this assurance was revoked as soon as he arrived at the Council: rather than being given a fair hearing, the betrayed idealist was tried for heresy and burned.

The Hussite revolt

Hus's supporters in Bohemia were justifiably outraged and quickly raised the banner of open revolt. The aristocracy took advantage of the situation to seize Church lands, and poorer priests, artisans, and peasants rallied together in the hope of achieving Hus's goals of religious reform and social justice. Between 1420 and 1424 armies of lower-class Hussites, led by a brilliant blind general, John Zizka, amazingly defeated several invading forces of well-armed "crusading" knights from Germany. In 1434 more conservative, aristocratically dominated Hussites overcame the radicals, thereby ending attempts to initiate a purified new religious and social dispensation. But even the conservatives refused to return to full orthodoxy. Thus Bohemia never came back to the Catholic fold until after the Catholic Reformation in the seventeenth century. The Hussite declaration of religious independence was both a foretaste of what was to come one hundred years later with Protestantism and the most successful late-medieval expression of dissatisfaction with the government of the Church.

Political Crisis and Recovery

Progress in late-medieval politics despite turmoil

The story of late-medieval politics at first seems very dreary because throughout most of the period there was incessant strife. Almost everywhere neighbors fought neighbors and states fought states. But on closer inspection it becomes clear that despite the turmoil there was ultimate improvement in almost all the governments of Europe. In the course of the fifteenth century peace returned to most of the Continent, the national monarchies in particular became stronger, and the period ended on a new note of strength just as it had from the point of view of economics.

The political situation in Italy

Starting our survey with Italy, it must first be explained that the Kingdom of Naples in the extreme south of the Italian peninsula was sunk in endemic warfare or maladministration more or less without interruption throughout the fourteenth and fifteenth centuries. Otherwise, Italy emerged from the prevailing political turmoil of the Later Middle Ages earlier than any other part of Europe. The fourteenth century was a time of troubles for the Papal States, comprising most of central Italy, because forces representing the absent or divided papacy were seldom able to overcome the resistance of refractory towns and rival leaders of marauding military bands. But after the end of the Great Schism in 1417 the popes concentrated more on consolidating their own Italian territories and gradually became the strong rulers of most of the middle part of the peninsula. Farther north some of the leading city-states—such as Florence, Venice, Siena, and Genoa—had experienced at least occasional and most often prolonged social warfare in the fourteenth century because of the economic pressures of the age. But sooner or later the most powerful families or interest groups overcame internal resistance. By around 1400 the three leading cities of the north—Venice, Milan, and Florence—had fixed definitively upon their own different forms of government: Venice was ruled by a merchant oligarchy, Milan by a dynastic despotism, and Florence by a complex, supposedly republican system that was actually controlled by the rich. (After 1434 the Florentine republic was in practice dominated by the Medici banking family.)

Peace established in the fifteenth century

Having settled their internal problems, Venice, Milan, and Florence proceeded from about 1400 to 1454 to expand territorially and conquer almost all the other northern Italian cities and towns except Genoa, which remained prosperous and independent but gained no new territory. Thus, by the middle of the fifteenth century Italy was divided into five major parts: the states of Venice, Milan, and Florence in the north; the Papal States in the middle; and the backward Kingdom of Naples in the south. A treaty of 1454 initiated a half-century of peace between these states: whenever one threatened to upset the "balance of power," the others usually allied against it before serious warfare could break out. Accordingly, the last half of the fifteenth century was a fortunate age for Italy. But in 1494 a French invasion initiated a period of renewed warfare in which the French attempt at dominating Italy was successfully countered by Spain.

Germany: the triumph of the princes

North of the Alps political turmoil prevailed throughout the fourteenth century and lasted longer into the fifteenth. Probably the worst instability was experienced in Germany. There the virtually independent princes continually warred with the greatly weakened emperors, or else they warred with each other. Between about 1350 and 1450 near-anarchy prevailed, because while the princes were warring and subdividing their inheritances into smaller states, petty powers such as free cities and knights who owned one or two castles were striving to shake off the rule of the princes. Throughout most of the German west these attempts met with enough success to fragment political authority more than ever, but in the east after about 1450 certain stronger German princes managed to assert their authority over divisive forces. After they did so they started to govern firmly over middle-sized states on the model of the larger national monarchies of England and France. The strongest princes were those who ruled in eastern territories such as Bavaria, Austria, and Brandenburg, because there towns were fewer and smaller and the princes had earlier been able to take advantage of imperial weakness to preside over the colonization of large tracts of land. Especially the Habsburg princes of Austria and the Hohenzollern princes of Brandenburg—a territory joined in the sixteenth century with the easternmost lands of Prussia—would be the most influential powers in Germany's future.

France: causes of the Hundred Years' War

The great nation-states did not escape unscathed from the late-medieval turmoil either. France was strife-ridden for much of the period, primarily in the form of the Hundred Years' War between France and England. The Hundred Years' War was actually a series of conflicts that lasted for even more than one hundred years—from 1337 to 1453. There were several different causes for this prolonged struggle. The major one was the longstanding problem of French territory held by the English kings. At the beginning of the fourteenth century the English kings still ruled much of the rich southern French lands of Gascony and Aquitaine as vassals of the French crown. The French, who since the reign of Philip Augustus had been expanding and consolidating their rule, obviously hoped to expel the English, making war inevitable. Another cause for strife was that the English economic interests in the woolen trade with Flanders led them to support the frequent attempts of Flemish burghers to rebel against French rule. Finally, the fact that the direct Capetian line of succession to the French throne died out in 1328, to be replaced thereafter by the related Valois dynasty, meant that the English kings, who themselves descended from the Capetians as a result of intermarriage, laid claim to the French crown itself.

The course of the war: factors in the initial English success

France should have had no difficulty in defeating England at the start: it was the richest country in Europe and outnumbered England in population by some fifteen million to fewer than four million. Nonetheless, throughout most of the first three-quarters of the Hundred Years' War the English won most of the pitched battles. One reason for this was that the English had learned superior military tactics, using well-disciplined archers to fend off and scatter the heavily armored mounted French knights. In the three greatest battles of the long conflict—Crécy (1346), Poitiers (1356), and Agincourt (1415)—the outnumbered English relied on tight discipline and effective use of the longbow to inflict crushing defeats on the French. Another reason for English success was that the war was always fought on French soil. That being the case, English soldiers were eager to fight because they could look forward to rich plunder, while their own homeland suffered none of the disasters of war. Worst of all for the French was the fact that they often were badly divided. The French crown always had to fear provincial attempts to assert autonomy: especially during the long period of warfare, when there were several highly inept kings and the English encouraged internal French dissensions, many aristocratic provincial leaders took advantage of the confusion to ally with the enemy and seek their own advantage. The most dramatic and fateful instance was the breaking away of Burgundy, whose dukes from 1419 to 1435 allied with the English, an act that called the very existence of an independent French crown into question.

Joan of Arc

It was in this dark period that the heroic figure of Joan of Arc came forth to rally the French. In 1429 Joan, an illiterate but extremely devout peasant girl, sought out the uncrowned French ruler, Charles VII, to announce that she had been divinely commissioned to drive the English out of France. Charles was persuaded to let her take command of his troops, and her piety and sincerity made such a favorable impression on the soldiers that their morale was raised immensely. In a few months Joan had liberated much of central France from English domination and had brought Charles to Rheims, where he was crowned king. But in May 1430 she was captured by the Burgundians and handed over to the English, who accused her of being a witch and tried her for heresy. Condemned in 1431 after a predetermined trial, she was publicly burned to death in the market square at Rouen. Nonetheless, the French, fired by their initial victories, continued to move on the offensive. When Burgundy withdrew from the English alliance in 1435, and the English king, Henry VI, proved to be totally incompetent, there followed an uninterrupted series of triumphs for the French side. In 1453 the capture of Bordeaux, the last of the English strongholds in the southwest, finally brought the long war to an end. The English now held no land in France except for the Channel port of Calais, which they ultimately lost in 1558.

More than merely expelling the English from French territory, the Hundred Years' War resulted in greatly strengthening the powers of the French crown. Although many of the French kings during the long war had been ineffective personalities—one, Charles VI, suffered periodic bouts of insanity—the monarchy demonstrated remarkable staying power because it provided France with the strongest institutions it knew and therefore offered the only realistic hope for lasting stability and peace. Moreover, warfare emergencies allowed the kings to gather new powers, above all, the rights to collect national taxes and maintain a standing army. Hence after Charles VII succeeded in defeating the English, the crown was able to renew the high-medieval royal tradition of ruling the country assertively. In the reigns of Charles's successors, Louis XI (1461–1483) and Louis XII (1498–1515), the monarchy became ever stronger. Its greatest single achievement was the destruction of the power of Burgundy in 1477 when the Burgundian duke, Charles the Bold, fell in the battle of Nancy at the hands of the Swiss, whom Charles had been trying to dominate. Since Charles died without a male heir, Louis XI of France was able to march into Burgundy and reabsorb the breakaway duchy. Later, when Louis XII gained Brittany by marriage, the French kings ruled powerfully over almost all of what is today included in the borders of France.

Louis XI of France. A portrait by Fouquet.

Internal turmoil in England

Although the Hundred Years' War was fought on French instead of English soil, England also experienced great turmoil during the Later Middle Ages because of internal instability. Indeed, England was a hotbed of insurrection: of the nine English kings who came to the throne between 1307 and 1485, five died violently because of revolts or conspiracies. Most of these slain kings had proven themselves to be incapable rulers, but there were other reasons for England's political troubles as well. One was that the crown had been too ambitious in trying both to hold on to its territories in France and also to subdue Scotland. This policy often made it necessary to resort to heavy taxation and to grant major political concessions to the aristocracy. When English arms in France were successful, the crown rode the crest of popularity and the aristocracy prospered from military spoils and ransoms; but whenever the tides of battle turned to defeat, the crown became financially embarrassed and thrown on the political defensive. To make matters worse, the English aristocracy was particularly unruly throughout the period, not just because the aristocrats often had reason to distrust the inept kings, but also because the economic pressures of the age made them seek to enlarge their agricultural estates at the expense of each other. This led to factionalism, and factionalism often led to civil war.

The Wars of the Roses

After the English presence in France was virtually eradicated and the aristocracy could no longer hope to enrich itself on the spoils of foreign warfare, England's political situation became particularly desperate. As bad luck would have it, the reigning king, Henry VI (1422–1461), was one of the most incompetent that England has ever had. According to one authority, Henry "paralyzed and confused the whole process of English government with a royal irresponsibility and inanity which had no precedent." Henry's willfulness helped provoke the Wars of the Roses that flared on and off from 1455 to 1485. These wars received their name from the emblems of the two competing factions: the red rose of Henry's family of Lancaster and the white rose of the rival house of York. The Yorkists for a time gained the kingship, under such monarchs as Richard III, but in 1485 they were replaced by a new dynasty, that of the Tudors, who began a new period in English history. The first Tudor king, Henry VII, steadily eliminated rival claimants to the throne, avoided expensive foreign wars, built up a financial surplus, and gradually reasserted royal power over the aristocracy. When he died in 1509 he was therefore able to pass on to his son, Henry VIII (1509–1547), a royal power as great as it had ever been.

Henry VII. A 1505 portrait by M. Sittow.

The positive aspects of English political developments, 1307–1485

It is tempting to view the entire period of English history between 1307 and the accession of Henry VII in 1485 as one long, dreary interregnum that accomplished nothing positive. But that would not quite be doing justice to the time: in the first place, the fact that England did not entirely fall apart during the recurrent turbulence was an accomplishment in itself. Remarkably, the rebellious aristocrats of the Later Middle Ages never tried to proclaim the independence of any of their regions; only once, in 1405, did they seek unsuccessfully to divide the country between them. Discounting that insignificant exception, aristocratic rebels always sought to control the central government rather than destroy or break away from it. Thus when Henry VII came to the throne, he did not have to win back any English territories as Louis XI of France had had to win back Burgundy. More than that, the antagonisms of the Hundred Years' War had the ultimately beneficial effect of strengthening English national identity. From the Norman Conquest until deep into the fourteenth century, French was the preferred language of the English crown and aristocracy, but mounting anti-French sentiment contributed to the complete triumph of English by around 1400. The loss of lands in France was also ultimately beneficial because thereafter the crown was freed from the inevitability of war with the French. This freedom gave England more diplomatic maneuverability in sixteenth-century European politics and later helped strengthen England's ability to invest its energies in overseas expansion in America and elsewhere. Yet another positive development was the steady growth of effective governmental institutions; despite the shifting fortunes of kings, the central governmental administration expanded and became more sophisticated. Parliament too became stronger, largely because both the crown and the aristocracy believed that they could use it for their own ends. In 1307 Parliament had not yet become a regular part of the English governmental system, but by 1485 it definitely had. Later kings who tried to govern without it ran into severe difficulties.

The consolidation of royal power in Spain

While Louis XI of France and Henry VII of England were reasserting royal power in their respective countries, the Spanish monarchs, Ferdinand and Isabella, were doing the same on the Iberian peninsula. In the latter area there had also been incessant strife in the Later Middle Ages; Aragon and Castile had often fought each other, and aristocratic factions within those kingdoms had continually fought the crown. But in 1469 Ferdinand, the heir of Aragon, married Isabella, the heiress of Castile, and thereby created a union that laid the basis for modern Spain.

Ferdinand and Isabella

Although Spain did not become a fully united nation until 1716 because Aragon and Castile retained their separate institutions, at least warfare between the two previously independent kingdoms ended and the new country was able to embark on united policies. Isabella and Ferdinand, ruling respectively until 1504 and 1516, subdued their aristocracies, and, in the same year (1492), annexed Granada, the last Muslim state in the peninsula, and expelled all of Spain's Jews. Some historians believe that the expulsion of the Jews was motivated by religious bigotry, others that it was a cruel but dispassionate act of state that aimed to keep Spanish *conversos* (Jews who had previously converted to Christianity) from backsliding. Either way, the forced Jewish exodus led Ferdinand and Isabella to suppose that they had eliminated an internal threat to cohesive nationhood and emboldened them to initiate an ambitious foreign policy: not only did they turn to overseas expansion, as most famously in their support of Christopher Columbus, but they also entered decisively into the arena of Italian politics. Enriched by the influx of American gold and silver after the conquest of Mexico and Peru, and nearly invincible on the battlefields, Spain quickly became Europe's most powerful state in the sixteenth century.

The triumph of the national monarchies

Ultimately the clearest result of political developments throughout Europe in the Late Middle Ages was the preservation of basic high-medieval patterns. The areas of Italy and Germany that had been politically divided before 1300 remained politically divided thereafter. The emergence of middle-sized states in both of these areas in the fifteenth century brought more stability than had existed before, but events would show that Italy and Germany would still be the prey of the Western powers. The latter were clearly much stronger because they were consolidated around stronger national monarchies. The trials of the Later Middle Ages put the existence of these monarchies to the test, but after 1450 they emerged stronger than ever. The clearest illustration of their superiority is shown by the history of Italy in the years immediately following 1494. Until then the Italian states appeared to be relatively well governed and prosperous. They experimented with advanced techniques of administration and diplomacy. But when France and Spain invaded the peninsula the Italian states fell over like houses of cards. The Western monarchies could simply draw on greater resources and thus inherited the future of Europe.

The Formation of the Empire of Russia

Just as the half-century after 1450 witnessed the definitive consolidation of the power of the western European nation-states, so it saw the rise to prominence of the state that henceforth was to be the dominant power in the European East—Russia. But Russia was not at all like a Western nation-state; rather, by about 1500 Russia had taken the first decisive steps on its way to becoming Europe's leading Eastern-style empire.

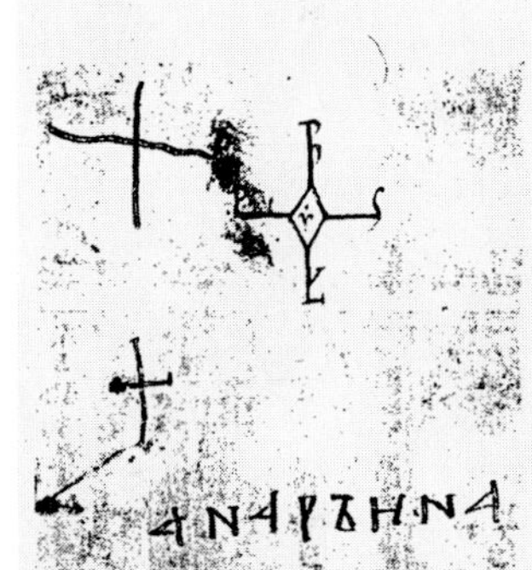

Signature of Anne of Kiev. The Kievan princess who became queen of France must have learned how to write her name in her native land, for the letters at the bottom of this document dating from 1063 spell out "Queen Anne" in the Russian (Cyrillic) alphabet. Her son Philip, however, could only make his "sign," as indicated at the top.

Had it not been for a combination of late-medieval circumstances, one or several east-Slavic states might well have developed along typical Western lines. Indeed, the founders of the first political entity located in the territories of modern-day Russia, Ukraine, and Belarus were themselves westerners—Swedish Vikings who in the tenth century established a principality centered around Kiev for the purposes of protecting their lines of trade between Scandinavia and Constantinople. Within two or three generations these Vikings became linguistically assimilated by their Slavic environment, but the Kievan state they founded remained until about 1200 very much part of the greater European community of nations. Since Kiev lay on the westernmost extremity of the Russian plain (today it is the capital of Ukraine), it was natural for the Kievan state of the High Middle Ages to maintain close and cordial diplomatic and trading relations with western Europe. For example, in the eleventh century King Henry I of France was married to a Kievan princess, Anne, and their son was consequently given the Kievan name of Philip, a christening that marked the introduction of this hitherto foreign first name into the West. Aside from such direct links with Western culture, Kievan government bore some similarity to Western limited monarchy inasmuch as the ruling power of the Kievan princes was limited by the institution of the *veche,* or popular assembly.

Reasons for retreat from the West: (1) the Mongol conquests in Russia

But after 1200 four epoch-making developments conspired to drive a wedge between Russia and western European civilization. The first was the conquest of most of the east-Slavic states by the Mongols, or Tartars,

Kievans Chasing Cumans. From a fifteenth-century Russian manuscript.

in the thirteenth century. As early as the mid-twelfth century Kiev had been buffeted by the incursions of an Asiatic tribe known as Cumans, but Kiev and other loosely federated Russian principalities ultimately managed to hold the Cumans at bay. The utterly savage Mongols, who crossed the Urals from Asia into Russia in 1237, however, were quite another matter. Commanded by Batu, a grandson of the dreaded Genghis Khan, the Mongols cut such swaths of devastation as they advanced westward that, according to one contemporary, "no eye remained open to weep for the dead." In 1240 the Mongols overran Kiev, and two years later they created their own state on the lower Volga River—the Khanate of the Golden Horde—that exerted suzerainty over almost all of Russia for

Western European View of the Mongols. When the first news of the Mongols reached the West, it was thought that they were an inhuman people who feasted on human flesh. Supposedly their horses were so rapacious that they devoured trees from the branches down.

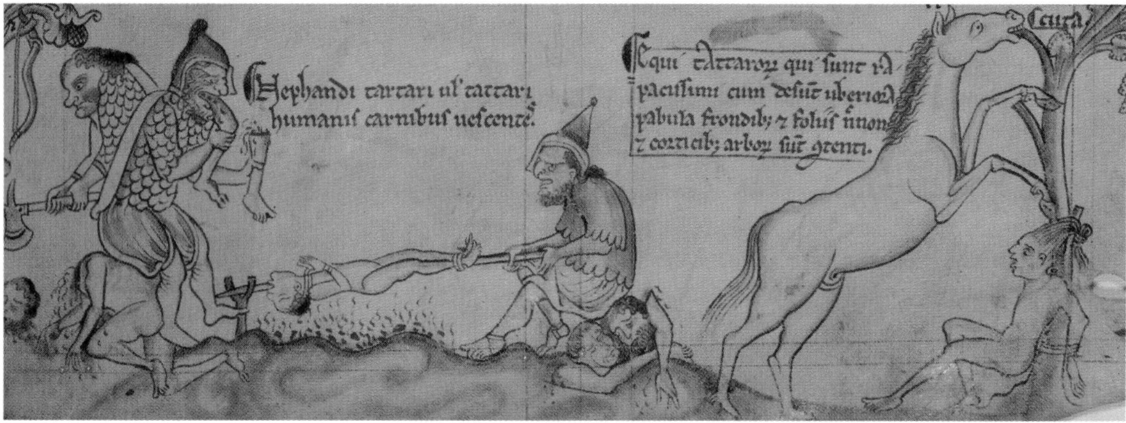

roughly the following two centuries. Unwilling or unable to institute governmental arrangements that would permit them to rule the vast expanses of Russia directly, the Mongol Khans instead tolerated the existence of several native Slavic states, from whom they demanded obeisance and regular monetary tribute. Under this "Tartar yoke," the normal course of Russian political development was inevitably impeded.

(2) The emergence of Moscow as a unifying force

The native principality that finally emerged to defeat the Mongols and unify much of Russia in the fifteenth century was the Grand Duchy of Moscow, situated deep in the northeastern Russian interior. Inasmuch as Moscow was located very far away from the Mongol power base on the lower Volga, the Muscovite dukes had greater freedom to consolidate their strength without Mongol interference than did some of their rivals, and when the Mongol Khans began to realize what was happening, it was too late to stem the Muscovite tide. But Moscow's remote location also placed it extremely far from western Europe: about 600 miles (often snow-covered) farther away from France or Italy than the distance separating those countries from Kiev. This added distance alone would have presented an appreciable obstacle to the establishment of close relations between Moscow and the West, but, to make matters far worse, the rise of Poland-Lithuania after 1386 and the fall of Constantinople in 1453 rendered cordial relations all but impossible.

(3) Resentment of Catholic Poland's expansion

Throughout most of the Middle Ages the Kingdom of Poland had been a second-rate power, usually on the defensive against German encroachments. But in the fourteenth century that situation changed dramatically, partly because German strength had by then become a ghost of its former self, and above all because the marriage in 1386 of Poland's reigning queen, Jadwiga, to Jagiello, grand duke of Lithuania, more than doubled Poland's size and enabled it to become a major expansionist state. Even before 1386 the Grand Duchy of Lithuania had begun to carve out an extensive territory for itself, not just on the shores of the Baltic where the present territory of Lithuania lies, but in Belarus and the Ukraine. Obviously, Lithuania's expansionist momentum increased after the union with Poland: in 1410 combined Polish-Lithuanian forces in the battle of Tannenberg inflicted a stunning defeat on the German military order of Teutonic Knights who ruled neighboring Prussia, and Poland-Lithuania extended its borders so far east in the early fifteenth century that the new power seemed on the verge of conquering all of Russia. But Poland-Lithuania subscribed to Roman Catholicism, whereas many of the Slavic peoples it had conquered were Eastern Orthodox who accordingly resented the sway of their new rulers. Eastern Orthodox Moscow was the obvious beneficiary of such discontent, becoming a center of religious resistance to Poland. Thus when Moscow was able to move on the offensive against Poland-Lithuania in the late fifteenth century, it appealed to religious as well as national sentiments. Prolonged warfare ensued, greatly exacerbating antagonisms, and since Poland-Lithuania stood in the Muscovites' minds for all the West, Moscow's attitude toward all of Western civilization became ever more etched by hostility.

(4) Impact of the fall of Constantinople

Finally, interrelated with this trend were the incalculable effects wrought by the fall of Constantinople to the Turks in 1453. We have seen in Chapter 9 that missionaries from the Byzantine Empire had been responsible for converting the Kievan Slavs to the Eastern Orthodox faith in the late tenth century. During the Kievan period Russia's commitment to Eastern Orthodoxy posed no barrier to cordial communications with western Europe because there was as yet no insuperable religious enmity between Orthodox Byzantium and the West. But embittered hatred is the only expression to describe Byzantine attitudes toward Rome after 1204 when the Western Fourth Crusaders sacked Constantinople. Eastern Orthodox Russians came to sympathize with their Byzantine mentors thereafter, and felt all the more that they had extraordinarily good reason to shun the "Roman infection" after the debacle of 1453. This was because in 1438 the Byzantines in Constantinople, sensing correctly that a mighty Turkish onslaught was in the offing, swallowed their pride and agreed to a submissive religious compromise with the papacy in the hope that this might earn them Western military support for their last-ditch stand. But despite this submission, no Western help was forthcoming and Constantinople fell to the Turks in 1453 without any Roman Catholic knight lifting a hand. Meanwhile, however, the Orthodox hierarchy of Moscow had refused to follow Byzantium in its religious submission for the obvious reason that Moscow was in no way threatened by the Turks. Once Constantinople fell, therefore, the Muscovites reached the conclusion that the Turkish victory was a divine chastisement for the Byzantines' religious perfidy, and the Muscovite state became the center of a particularly zealous anti-Roman ideology.

Ivan the Great

It is against this backdrop that we can examine the reign of the man who did the most to turn the Grand Duchy of Moscow into the nascent empire of Russia: Ivan III (1462–1505), customarily known as Ivan the Great. Ivan's immediate predecessor, Vasily II, had already gained the upper hand in Moscow's struggle to overthrow the domination of the Mongols, but Ivan was the one who completed this process by formally renouncing all subservience to the Mongol Khanate in 1480, by which time the Mongols were too awed by Muscovy's strength to offer any resistance. Concurrently, between 1462 and 1485, Ivan annexed one by one all the independent Russian principalities that remained between Moscow and Poland-Lithuania. And finally, as the result of two successive invasions of Lithuania (1492 and 1501), the mighty conqueror wrested away most of Belarus and the Ukraine along his western border. Thus when Ivan the Great died in 1505, it had become clear that Muscovy was a power to be reckoned with on the European scene.

Russia's isolation from the West

But it also would have been clear to any observer that Russian culture and government were now very non-Western. Having been divorced from the West for all practical purposes since about 1200, Russia had not kept up with the most basic Western intellectual and cultural developments. For example, there was virtually no secular literature, arithmetic was barely known, Arabic numerals were not used, and merchants made their

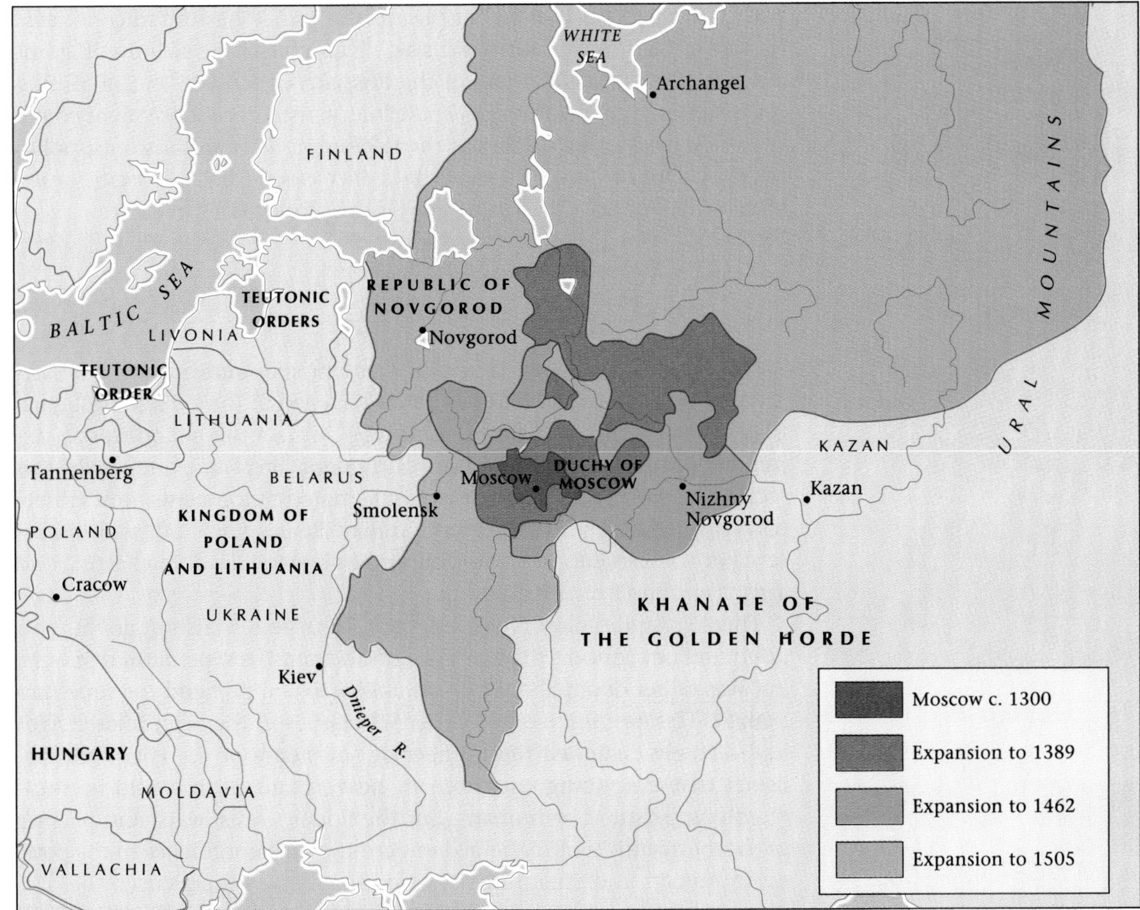

Russian Empire to 1505

calculations with the abacus. Nor were manners and customs comparable to those of the West. Women of the upper classes were veiled and secluded, and flowing beards and skirted garments were universal for men.

Toward political autocracy and imperialism

Perhaps most important, during the reign of Ivan III Russia was evolving in the direction of Eastern-style political autocracy and imperialism. This can be seen most clearly in Ivan's assumption of the title "tsar of all the Russias." The word *tsar* (sometimes spelled czar) is Russian for caesar, and Ivan's appropriation of it meant that he was claiming to be the successor of the defunct Byzantine emperors, who themselves had been heirs of the Roman caesars. To reinforce this claim, Ivan married the niece of the last Byzantine ruler, adopted as his insignia the Byzantine double-headed eagle, and rebuilt Moscow's fortified princely residence, the Kremlin, in magnificent style to display his imperial splendor. Ivan's appropriation of the Byzantine model was fateful for Russia's future political development because it enabled him and his successors to imitate the Byzantine emperors in behaving like Oriental despots who assumed without discussion that "what pleases the prince has the force of law." Moreover, as "tsar of all the Russias," Ivan conceived of himself as the autocratic potentate not just of the Russians of Moscow but of all Russians, and even of Belarussians and Ukrainians. As the subsequent course of events would show, this was the beginning of an expansionist policy by which future Russian tsars would incorporate both Russians and a wide variety of non-Russian peoples into Europe's largest empire.

Thought, Literature, and Art

Although it might be guessed that the extreme hardships of the Later Middle Ages in western Europe should have led to the decline or stagnation of intellectual and artistic endeavors, in fact the period was an extremely fruitful one in the realms of thought, literature, and art. In this section we will postpone treatment of certain developments most closely related to the early history of the Italian Renaissance, but will discuss some of western Europe's other important late-medieval intellectual and artistic accomplishments.

Crisis in theology and philosophy

Theology and philosophy after about 1300 faced a crisis of doubt. This doubt did not concern the existence of God and His supernatural powers, but was rather doubt about human ability to comprehend the supernatural. St. Thomas Aquinas and other Scholastics in the High Middle Ages had serenely delimited the number of "mysteries of the faith" and believed that everything else, both in heaven and earth, could be thoroughly understood by humans. But the floods, frosts, wars, and plagues of the fourteenth century helped undermine such confidence in the powers of human understanding. Once human beings experienced the universe as arbitrary and unpredictable, fourteenth-century thinkers began to wonder whether there was not far more in heaven and earth than could be understood by their philosophies. The result was a thoroughgoing reevaluation of the prior theological and philosophical outlook.

William of Ockham; nominalism

The leading late-medieval abstract thinker was the English Franciscan William of Ockham, who was born around 1285 and died in 1349, apparently from the Black Death. Traditionally, Franciscans had always had greater doubts than Dominicans like St. Thomas Aquinas concerning the abilities of human reason to comprehend the supernatural; Ockham, convinced by the events of his age, expressed these most formidably. He denied that the existence of God and numerous other theological matters could be demonstrated apart from scriptural revelation, and he emphasized God's freedom and absolute power to do anything. In the realm of human knowledge per se Ockham's searching intellect drove him to look for absolute certainties instead of mere theories. In investigating earthly matters he developed the position, known as *nominalism,* that only individual things, but not collectivities, are real, and that one thing therefore cannot be understood by means of another: to know a chair one has to see and touch it rather than just know what several other chairs are like. Ockham also formulated a logic that was based upon the assumption that words stood only for themselves rather than for real things. Such logic might not say much about the real world, but at least it could not be refuted, since it was as internally valid in its own terms as Euclidean geometry.

The significance of Ockham's thought

Ockham's outlook, which gained widespread adherence in the late-medieval universities, today often seems overly methodological and verging on the arid, but it had several important effects on the development of Western thought. Ockham's concern about what God *might* do led his followers to raise some of the seemingly absurd questions for which medieval theology has been mocked: for example, asking whether God can undo the past, or whether an infinite number of pure spirits can simultaneously inhabit the same place (the nearest medieval thinkers actually came to asking how many angels can dance on the head of a pin). Nonetheless, Ockham's emphasis on preserving God's autonomy led to a stress on divine omnipotence that became one of the basic presuppositions of sixteenth-century Protestantism. Further, Ockham's determination to find certainties in the realm of human knowledge ultimately helped make it possible to discuss human affairs and natural science without reference to supernatural explanations—one of the most important foundations of the modern scientific method. Finally, Ockham's opposition to studying collectivities and his refusal to apply logic to real things helped encourage *empiricism,* or the belief that knowledge of the world should rest on sense experience rather than abstract reason. This too is a presupposition for scientific progress: thus it is probably not coincidental that some of Ockham's fourteenth-century followers made significant advances in the study of physics.

Naturalism in late-medieval literature

Ockham's search for reliable truths finds certain parallels in the realm of late-medieval literature, although Ockham surely had no direct influence in that field. The major trait of the best late-medieval literature was *naturalism,* or the attempt to describe things the way they really are. This was more a development from high-medieval precedents—such as the explorations of human conduct pursued by Chrétien de Troyes, Wolfram von Eschenbach, and Dante—than a reaction against them. Furthermore, the steady growth of a lay reading public encouraged authors to avoid theological and philosophical abstractions and seek more to entertain by portraying people realistically with all their strengths and foibles. Another main characteristic of late-medieval literature, the predominance of composition in the European vernaculars instead of Latin, also developed out of high-medieval precedents but gained great momentum in the Later Middle Ages for two different reasons. One was that international tensions and hostilities, including the numerous wars of the age and the trials of the universal papacy, led to a need for security and a pride of self-identification reflected by the use of vernacular tongues. Probably more important was the fact that the continued spread of education for the laity greatly increased the number of people who could read in a given vernacular

Christine de Pisan. A leading writer of late-medieval vernacular prose literature, Christine de Pisan (1365–c. 1430) was intent on upholding the dignity of women. She is shown here writing about a gigantic Amazon warrior who could defeat men effortlessly in armed combat.

language but not in Latin. Hence although much poetry had been composed in the vernacular during the High Middle Ages, in the Later Middle Ages use of the vernacular was widely extended to prose. Moreover, countries such as Italy and England, which had just begun to cultivate their own vernacular literatures around 1300, subsequently began to employ their native tongues to the most impressive literary effect.

Boccaccio

The greatest writer of vernacular prose fiction of the Later Middle Ages was the Italian Giovanni Boccaccio (1313–1375). Although Boccaccio would have taken an honored place in literary history for some of his lesser works, which included courtly romances, pastoral poems, and learned treatises, by far the most impressive of his writings is the *Decameron,* written between 1348 and 1351. This is a collection of one hundred stories, mostly about love and sex, adventure, and clever trickery, supposedly told by a sophisticated party of seven young ladies and three men who are sojourning in a country villa outside Florence in order to escape the ravages of the Black Death. Boccaccio by no means invented all one hundred plots, but even when he borrowed the outlines of his tales from earlier sources he retold the stories in his own characteristically exuberant, masterful, and extremely witty fashion. There are many reasons why the *Decameron* must be counted as epochmaking from a historical point of view. The first is that it was the earliest ambitious and successful work of vernacular creative literature ever written in western Europe in narrative prose. Boccaccio's prose is "modern" in the sense that it is brisk, for unlike the medieval authors of flowery romances, Boccaccio purposely wrote in an unaffected, colloquial style. Simply stated, in the *Decameron* he was less interested in being "elevated" or elegant than in being unpretentiously entertaining. From the point of view of content, Boccaccio wished to portray men and women as they really are rather than as they ought to be. Thus when he wrote about the clergy he showed them to be as susceptible to human appetites and failings as other mortals. His women are not pallid playthings, distant goddesses, or steadfast virgins, but flesh-and-blood creatures with intellects, who interact more comfortably and naturally with men and with each other than any women in Western literature had ever done before. Boccaccio's treatment of sexual relations is often graphic, often witty, but never demeaning. In his world the natural desires of both women and men are not meant to be thwarted. For all these reasons the *Decameron* is a robust and delightful appreciation of all that is human.

Chaucer

Similar in many ways to Boccaccio as a creator of robust, naturalistic vernacular literature was the Englishman Geoffrey Chaucer (c. 1340–1400). Chaucer was the first major writer of an English that can still be read today with relatively little effort. Remarkably, he was both a founding father of England's mighty literary tradition and one of the four or five greatest contributors to it: most critics rank him just behind Shakespeare, and in a class with Milton, Wordsworth, and Dickens. Chaucer wrote several highly impressive works, but his masterpiece is unquestionably the *Canterbury Tales,* dating from the end of his career. Like the *Decameron,* this is a collection of stories held together by a frame, in Chaucer's case the device of having a group of people tell stories while on a pilgrimage from London to Canterbury. But there are also differences between the *Decameron* and the *Canterbury Tales*. Chaucer's stories are told in sparkling verse instead of prose, and they are recounted by people of all different classes—from a chivalric knight to a dedicated university student to a thieving miller with a wart on his nose. Lively women are also represented, most memorably the gap-toothed, oft-married "Wife of Bath," who knows all "the remedies of love." Each character tells a story that is particularly illustrative of his or her own occupation and outlook on the world. By this device Chaucer is able to create a highly diverse "human comedy." His range is therefore greater than Boccaccio's. And although he is as witty, frank, and lusty as the Italian, he is sometimes more profound.

Naturalism in late-medieval art

As naturalism was a dominant trait of late-medieval literature, so it was of late-medieval art. Already by the thirteenth century Gothic sculptors were paying far more attention than their Romanesque predecessors had to the way plants, animals, and human beings really looked. Whereas earlier medieval art had emphasized abstract design, the stress was now increasingly on realism: thirteenth-century carvings of leaves and flowers must have been done from direct observation and are the first to be clearly recognizable as distinct species. Statues of humans also gradually became more naturally proportioned and realistic in their portrayals of facial expressions. By around 1290 the concern for realism had become so great that a sculptor working on a tomb-portrait of the German emperor Rudolf of Habsburg allegedly made a hurried return trip to view Rudolf in person, because he had heard that a new wrinkle had appeared on the emperor's face.

Painting

In the next two centuries the trend toward naturalism continued in sculpture and was extended to manuscript illumination and painting. The latter was in certain basic respects a new art. Ever since the Ice Age, painting had been done on walls, but walls of course were not easily movable. The art of wall-painting continued to be cultivated in the Middle Ages and long afterward, especially in the form of *frescoes,* or paintings done on wet plaster. But in addition to frescoes, Italian artists in the thirteenth century first started painting pictures on pieces of wood or canvas. These were first done in tempera (pigments mixed with water and natural gums or egg-whites), but around 1400 painting in oils was introduced in the European north. These new technical developments created new artistic opportunities. Artists were now able to paint religious scenes on altarpieces for churches and for private devotions practiced by the wealthier laity at home. Artists also painted the first Western portraits, which were meant to gratify the self-esteem of monarchs and aristocrats. The earliest surviving example of a naturalistic, painted portrait is one of a French king, John the Good, executed around 1360. Others followed quickly, so that within a short time the art of portraiture done from life was highly developed. Visitors to art museums will notice that some of the most realistic and sensitive portraits of all time date from the fifteenth century.

The naturalistic style of Giotto

The most pioneering and important painter of the later Middle Ages was the Florentine Giotto (c. 1267–1337). He did not engage in individual portraiture, but he brought deep humanity to his religious images done on both walls and movable panels. Giotto was preeminently a naturalist, i.e., an imitator of nature. Not only do his human beings and animals look more natural than those of his predecessors, they seem to do more natural things. When Christ enters Jerusalem on Palm Sunday, boys climb trees to get a better view; when St. Francis is laid out in death, one onlooker takes the opportunity to see whether the saint had really received Christ's wounds; and when the Virgin's parents, Joachim and Anna, meet after a long separation, they actually embrace and kiss—perhaps the first deeply tender kiss in Western art. It was certainly not true, as one fanciful storyteller later reported, that an onlooker found a fly Giotto had painted so real that he attempted to brush it away with his hand, but Giotto in fact accomplished something more. Specifically, he was the first to conceive of the painted space in fully three-dimensional terms: as one art historian has put it, Giotto's frescoes were the first to "knock a hole into the wall." After Giotto's death a reaction in Italian painting set in. This was probably caused by a new reverence for the awesomely supernatural brought about by the horrors of the plague. Whatever the explanation, artists of the mid-fourteenth century briefly moved away from naturalism and painted stern, forbidding religious figures who seemed to float in space. But by around 1400 artists came back down to earth and started to build upon Giotto's influence in ways that led to the great Italian renaissance in painting.

The Flight into Egypt, by Giotto (c. 1267–1337). Giotto is regarded as the founder of the modern tradition in painting. A fresco in the Arena Chapel, Padua.

The Adoration of the Magi, by Giotto. The Star of Bethlehem is actually Halley's comet, which Giotto would have seen in the night skies in 1301; the fact that this fresco was executed in 1303 or 1304 indicates that Giotto must have made sketches from nature that he saved for future use.

The Marriage at Cana, by Giotto. The miracle in which Christ (seen blessing at the far left) turns water into wine.

The Meeting of Joachim and Anna at the Golden Gate, a fresco by Giotto. Note how the haloes merge: this old and barren couple will soon miraculously have a child, none other than Mary, the mother of Jesus.

The Virgin and Chancellor Rolin, by Jan van Eyck (1380–1441). The early Flemish painters loved to present scenes of piety in the sumptuous surroundings of wealthy burghers.

The Arnolfini Bethrothal, by van Eyck. A characteristic synthesis of everyday life and religious devotion. Scenes from Christ's passion surround the mirror. The artist himself appears reflected in the mirror as if to indicate that he is a witness to the betrothal. In addition, he wrote (above the mirror) "Johannes de eyck fuit hic" (Jan van Eyck was here).

Equestrian Knight (Guidoriccio da Fogliano), by Simone Martini (c. 1283–1344). One of the earliest western European depictions of a contemporary warrior on horseback. Earlier in the Middle Ages such a posture would have been shunned as exemplifying the sin of pride, whereas this painting was commissioned for public view in the communal palace in Siena.

Man with a Red Hat, by Hans Memling (c. 1430–1494).

The Flemish painters

In the north of Europe painting did not advance impressively beyond manuscript illumination until the early fifteenth century, but then it suddenly came very much into its own. The leading northern European painters were Flemish, first and foremost Jan van Eyck (c. 1380–1441), Roger van der Weyden (c. 1400–1464), and Hans Memling (c. 1430–1494). These three were the greatest early practitioners of painting in oil, a medium that allowed them to engage in brilliant coloring and sharp-focused realism. Van Eyck and van der Weyden excelled most at two things: communicating a sense of deep religious piety and portraying minute details of familiar everyday experience. These may at first seem incompatible, but it should be remembered that contemporary manuals of practical mysticism such as *The Imitation of Christ* also sought to link deep piety with everyday existence. Thus it was by no means blasphemous when a Flemish painter would portray behind a tender Madonna and Child a vista of contemporary life with people going about their usual business and a man even urinating against a wall. This union between the sacred and profane tended to fall apart in the work of Memling, who excelled in either straightforward religious pictures or secular portraits, but it would return in the work of the greatest painters of the Low Countries, Brueghel and Rembrandt.

Advances in Technology

Late-medieval technological achievements: (1) the weapons of war

No account of enduring late-medieval accomplishments would be complete without mention of certain epoch-making technological advances. Sadly, but probably not unexpectedly, treatment of this subject has to begin with reference to the invention of artillery and firearms. The prevalence of warfare stimulated the development of new weaponry. Gunpowder itself was a Chinese invention, but it was first put to particularly devastating uses in the late-medieval West. Heavy cannons, which made terrible noises "as though all the dyvels of hell had been in the way," were first employed around 1330. The earliest cannons were so primitive that it often was more dangerous to stand behind than in front of them, but by the middle of the fifteenth century they were greatly improved and began to revolutionize the nature of warfare. In one year, 1453, heavy artillery played a leading role in determining the outcome of two crucial conflicts: the Ottoman Turks used German and Hungarian cannons to breach the defenses of Constantinople—hitherto the most impregnable in Europe—and the French used heavy artillery to take the city of Bordeaux, thereby ending the Hundred Years' War. Cannons thereafter made it difficult for rebellious aristocrats to hole up in their stone castles, and thus they aided in the consolidation of the national monarchies. Placed aboard ships, cannons enabled European vessels to dominate foreign waters in the subsequent age of overseas expansion. Guns, also invented in the fourteenth century, were gradually perfected. Shortly after 1500 the most effective new variety of gun, the musket,

The Earliest Known Depiction of a Cannon. A fourteenth-century manuscript shows a primitive cannon firing an arrow rather than a cannonball.

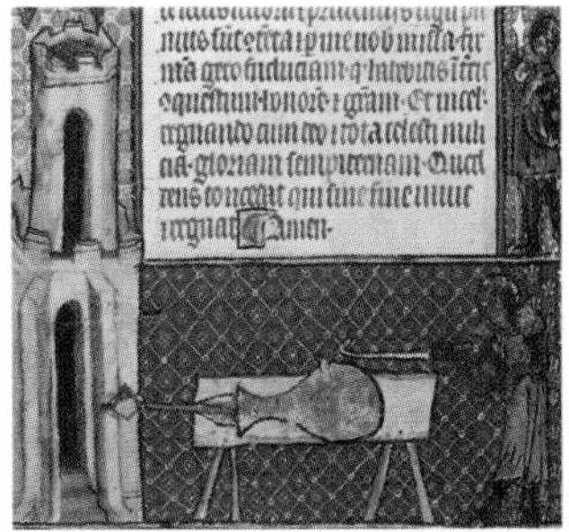

Siege of a City, c. 1470. The use of the cannon would soon put an end to traditional medieval fortifications.

allowed foot-soldiers to end once and for all the earlier military dominance of heavily armored mounted knights. Once lance-bearing cavalries became outmoded and fighting could more easily be carried on by all, the monarchical states that could turn out the largest armies completely subdued internal resistance and dominated the battlefields of Europe.

(2) Eyeglasses and navigational instruments

Other late-medieval technological developments were more life-enhancing. Eyeglasses, first invented in the 1280s, were perfected in the fourteenth century. These allowed older people to keep on reading when farsightedness would otherwise have stopped them. For example, the great fourteenth-century scholar Petrarch, who boasted excellent sight in his youth, wore spectacles after his sixtieth year and was thus enabled to complete some of his most important works. Around 1300 the use of the magnetic compass helped ships to sail farther away from land and venture out into the Atlantic. One immediate result was the opening of direct sea commerce between Italy and the North. Subsequently, numerous improvements in shipbuilding, map making, and navigational devices contributed to Europe's ability to start expanding overseas. In the fourteenth century the Azores and Cape Verde Islands were reached; then, after a long pause caused by Europe's plagues and wars, the African Cape of Good Hope was rounded in 1487, the West Indies reached in 1492, India reached by the sea route in 1498, and Brazil sighted in 1500. Partly as a result of technology the world was thus suddenly made much smaller.

Devil with Eyeglasses. Once spectacles became common they were even sported by devils in hell.

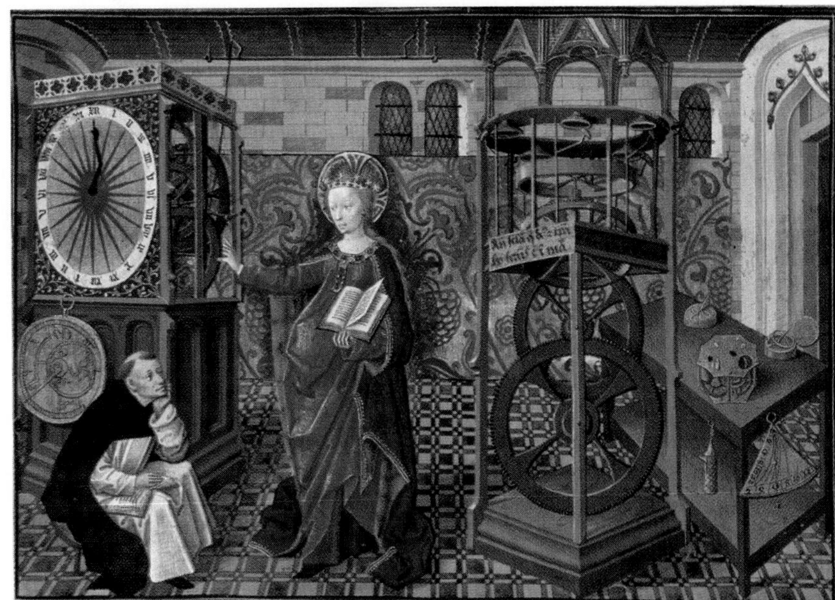

Horloge de Sapience (Lady Wisdom with Clocks). This miniature, from a French manuscript of about 1450, reflects the growing fascination with machines of all sorts and clocks in particular.

(3) Mechanical clocks

Among the most familiar implements of our modern life that were invented by Europeans in the Later Middle Ages were clocks and printed books. Mechanical clocks were invented shortly before 1300 and proliferated in the years immediately thereafter. The earliest clocks were too expensive for private purchase, but towns quickly vied with each other to install the most elaborate clocks in their prominent public buildings. These clocks not only told the time but showed the courses of sun, moon, and planets, and performed mechanical tricks on the striking of the hours. The new invention ultimately had two profound effects. One was the further stimulation of European interest in complex machinery of all sorts. This interest had already been awakened by the high-medieval proliferation of mills, but clocks ultimately became even more omnipresent than mills because after about 1650 they became quite cheap and were brought into practically every European home. Household clocks served as models of marvelous machines. Equally if not more significant was the fact that clocks began to rationalize the course of European daily affairs. Until the advent of clocks in the Later Middle Ages time was flexible. Men and women had only a rough idea of how late in the day it was and rose and retired more or less with the sun. People who lived in the country in particular performed different jobs at different rates according to the rhythm of the seasons. Even when hours were counted, they were measured at different lengths according to the amount of light in the different seasons of the year. In the fourteenth century, however, clocks first started relentlessly striking equal hours through the day and night. Thus they began to regulate work with new precision. People were expected to start and end work "on time" and many came to believe that "time is money." This emphasis on time-keeping brought new efficiencies but

Left: **Paper-Making at a Paper Mill.** Right: **A Printing Press.** From a title page of a Parisian printer, 1520.

also new tensions: Lewis Carroll's white rabbit, who is always looking at his pocket watch and muttering, "how late it's getting," is a telling caricature of time-obsessed Western man.

(4) Printing

The invention of printing with movable type was equally momentous. The major stimulus for this invention was the replacement of parchment by paper as Europe's primary writing material between 1200 and 1400. Parchment, made from the skins of valuable farm animals, was extremely expensive: since it was possible to get only about four good parchment leaves from one animal, it was necessary to slaughter between two to three hundred sheep or calves to gain enough parchment for a Bible! Paper, made from rags turned into pulp by mills, brought prices down dramatically. Late-medieval records show that paper sold at one-sixth the price of parchment. Accordingly, it became cheaper to learn how to read and write. With literacy becoming ever more widespread, there was a growing market for still-cheaper books, and the invention of printing with movable type around 1450 fully met this demand. By greatly saving labor, the invention made printed books about one-fifth as expensive as handwritten ones within about two decades.

The effects of printing

As soon as books became easily accessible, literacy increased even more and book culture became a basic part of the European way of life. After about 1500, Europeans could afford to read and buy books of all sorts—not just religious tracts, but instructional manuals, light entertainment, and, by the eighteenth century, newspapers. Printing ensured that ideas would spread quickly and reliably; moreover, revolutionary ideas could no longer be easily extinguished once they were set down in hundreds of copies of books. Thus the greatest religious reformer of the sixteenth century, Martin Luther, gained an immediate following throughout Germany by employing the printing press to run off pamphlets: had printing not been available to him, Luther might have died like Hus. The spread of books also helped stimulate the growth of cultural nationalism. Before printing, regional dialects in most European countries were often so diverse that people who supposedly spoke the same language often could barely understand each other. Such a situation hindered governmental centralization because a royal servant might be entirely unable to communicate with inhabitants of the provinces. Shortly after the invention of printing, however, each European country began to develop its own linguistic standards, which were disseminated uniformly by books. The "King's English" was what was printed in London and carried to Yorkshire or Wales. Thus communications were enhanced and governments were able to operate ever more efficiently.

Significance of clocks and books

In conclusion it may be said that clocks and books as much as guns and ocean-going ships helped Europe to dominate the globe after 1500. The habits inculcated by clocks encouraged Europeans to work efficiently and to plan precisely; the prevalence of books enhanced communications and the flow of progressive ideas. Once accustomed to reading books, Europeans communicated and experimented intellectually as no other peoples in the world. Thus it was not surprising that, after 1500, Europeans could start to make the whole world their own.

SUMMARY POINTS

- An economic depression (1300–1450) and the sudden onslaught of the Black Death (1347–1350) created a climate of insecurity and dislocation, prompting lower-class revolts and further social stratification. But drastically reduced population levels propelled greater agricultural specialization and the further development of urban life.
- The Catholic Church endured two institutional crises during the Later Middle Ages: the Babylonian Captivity of the papacy (1305–1378), when the pope resided in Avignon; and the Great Schism (1378–1417), during which rival popes divided the European Church.
- Politically, the monarchies in England, France, and Spain became strengthened in the late-medieval period while regional divisions

remained dominant in Germany and Italy. In the European East, the duke of Moscow, Ivan the Great, consolidated power and annexed numerous territories to forge the beginnings of the Russian Empire.

- Late-medieval art and literature continued the trend toward naturalism that had begun in the High Middle Ages. Writers such as Boccaccio and Chaucer created entertaining works in the vernacular, and artists such as Giotto and van Eyck explored perspective and human emotions in painting.
- Late-medieval inventions, including the cannon, the mechanical clock, and the printing press, fundamentally changed European civilization.

Selected Readings

Allmand, Christopher, *The Hundred Years War,* Cambridge, 1988. The standard account.

Breisach, Ernst, *Renaissance Europe, 1300–1517,* New York, 1973. The best college-level textbook.

Brucker, Gene A., *Renaissance Florence,* New York, 1969. An excellent introduction by one of America's foremost experts.

Bynum, Caroline W., *Holy Feast and Holy Fast: The Religious Significance of Food to Medieval Women,* Berkeley, 1987. A highly original study, full of rich insights into late-medieval religion and the place of women in society.

Cipolla, Carlo M., *Clocks and Culture, 1300–1700,* New York, 1977. Treats both technological developments and the importance of clocks as items of trade.

Cole, Bruce, *Giotto and Florentine Painting, 1280–1375,* New York, 1976. A clear and stimulating introduction.

Crummey, Robert O., *The Formation of Muscovy, 1304–1613,* New York, 1987. The standard detailed treatment.

Florinsky, Michael T., *Russia: A History and an Interpretation,* vol. I, New York, 1961. The best narrative in English of early Russian developments.

Geremek, Bronislaw, *The Margins of Society in Late Medieval Paris,* New York, 1987. A pioneering study of late-medieval "drifters," first published in Polish in 1971 by a historian who then helped lead Poland's breakaway from the Soviet Union.

Hanawalt, Barbara, *The Ties that Bound: Peasant Families in Medieval England,* New York, 1986. Indispensable for understanding late-medieval English rural society.

Herlihy, David, *Opera Muliebria: Women and Work in Medieval Europe,* New York, 1990. Proposes an original argument about a decline in vocational opportunities for women in the Later Middle Ages.

Hilton, R. H., and T. H. Aston, eds., *The English Rising of 1381,* Cambridge, 1984. A collection of articles that includes treatment of the *Jacquerie* and the *Ciompi.*

Huizinga, Johan, *The Waning of the Middle Ages,* New York, 1985. An evocatively written classic on forms of thought and art in the Low Countries.

Kaminsky, Howard, *A History of the Hussite Revolution,* Berkeley, 1967. Detailed and difficult but far and away the best treatment of the subject.

———, *Simon de Cramaud and the Great Schism,* New Brunswick, N.J., 1983. A brilliant materialist interpretation of the Schism and the activities of one of the foremost ecclesiastical politicians who helped bring it to a close.

Lerner, Robert E., *The Age of Adversity: The Fourteenth Century,* Ithaca, N.Y., 1968.

———, *The Heresy of the Free Spirit in the Later Middle Ages,* 2d ed., Notre Dame, 1991.

Lewis, P. S., *Later Medieval France: The Polity,* London, 1968.

McFarlane, K. B., *The Nobility of Later Medieval England,* Oxford, 1980. An excellent collection of essays by a late master of the field.

Meiss, Millard, *Painting in Florence and Siena after the Black Death,* Princeton, 1951. A stimulating attempt to relate art history to the spirit of an age.

Miskimin, Harry A., *The Economy of Early Renaissance Europe, 1300–1460,* Cambridge, 1975. The best short work on the subject.

Mollat, G., *The Popes at Avignon, 1305–1378,* London, 1963.

Mollat, Michel, and Philippe Wolff, *The Popular Revolutions of the Late Middle Ages,* London, 1973.

Oakley, Francis, *The Western Church in the Later Middle Ages,* Ithaca, N.Y., 1979.

Panofsky, Erwin, *Early Netherlandish Painting,* 2 vols., Cambridge, Mass., 1953. A brilliant specialized history by a master art historian.

Pernoud, R., *Joan of Arc,* New York, 1966. Joan viewed through the eyes of her contemporaries.

Smart, Alastair, *The Dawn of Italian Painting, 1250–1400,* Ithaca, N.Y., 1978. More detailed than Cole.

Vaughan, Richard, *Valois Burgundy,* London, 1975.

Waugh, Scott L., *England in the Reign of Edward III,* New York, 1991. The best introduction to life and politics in fourteenth-century England.

Source Materials

Allmand, Christopher. T., ed., *Society at War: The Experience of England and France During the Hundred Years War,* Edinburgh, 1973. An outstanding collection of documents.

Boccaccio, G., *The Decameron,* tr. M. Musa and P. E. Bondanella, New York, 1977.

Chaucer, G., *The Canterbury Tales.* (Many editions.)

Colledge, E., ed., *The Medieval Mystics of England,* New York, 1961.

Froissart, J., *Chronicles,* tr. G. Brereton, Baltimore, 1968. A selection from the most famous contemporary account of the Hundred Years' War.

Horrox, Rosemary, ed., *The Black Death,* New York, 1994. A fine collection of documents reflecting the impact of the Black Death, especially in England.

John Hus at the Council of Constance, tr. M. Spinka, New York, 1965. The translation of a Czech chronicle with an expert introduction and appended collection of documents.

Meister Eckhart, eds. E. Colledge and B. McGinn, 2 vols., New York, 1981–1986. A rich collection of Eckhart's basic works, expertly introduced and annotated.

Memoirs of a Renaissance Pope: The Commentaries of Pius II (abridged ed.), tr. F. A. Gragg, New York, 1959. A fascinating insight into the Renaissance papacy.

A Parisian Journal, 1405–1449, tr. J. Shirley, Oxford, 1968. A marvelous panorama of Parisian life recorded by an eyewitness.

PART FOUR

THE EARLY-MODERN WORLD

HISTORIANS TEND TO agree that the Middle Ages ended sometime roughly around 1500 and were followed by an "early-modern" period of European history that lasted until the concurrent outbreaks of the French and Industrial Revolutions at the very end of the eighteenth century. As early as about 1350 in Italy, representatives of a new cultural movement, usually called the Renaissance, began to challenge certain basic medieval assumptions and offer alternatives to medieval modes of literary and artistic expression. By around 1500 Renaissance ideals not only had triumphed fully in Italy, but also were spreading to northern Europe where they were reconceived to produce the highly influential movement of Christian humanism. At the same time, in the early sixteenth century western Europe lost much of its medieval appearance by expanding and dividing. Intrepid mariners and *conquistadores* ended Europe's millennium of geographical self-containment by venturing onto the high seas of the Atlantic and Indian Oceans and by planting Europe's flag throughout the world. Concurrently, however, Europe lost its religious uniformity as a result of the Protestant Reformation, which divided the continent up into hostile religious camps. Thereafter, from about 1560 to about 1660 western Europe experienced a period of grave economic, political, and spiritual crisis but emerged from this century of testing with renewed energy and confidence. A commercial revolution spurred the development of overseas colonies and trade and encouraged agricultural and industrial expansion. Although monarchs continued to meet with opposition from the various estates within their realms, they asserted their power as absolute rulers, stabilizing domestic unrest by continually expanding state bureaucracies. Warfare remained the chief instrument of their foreign policies; yet by the end of the period, the mutually recognized goal of those

Aristocratic Woman with Dog, by Jacopo da Pontormo (1494–1556).

policies was more often the maintenance of a general balance of power than the pursuit of unrestrained aggrandizement. Finally, in the later seventeenth century the scientific revolution, initiated earlier by Copernicus, was completed by Sir Isaac Newton and was followed during the eighteenth century by the "Enlightenment," or enthronement of a new secular faith in humanity's ability to master nature and better itself through its own efforts.

THE EARLY-MODERN WORLD

Politics	Philosophy and Science	Economics	Religion	Arts and Letters	
				Francis Petrarch (1304–1374)	
				Italian Renaissance (c. 1350–c. 1550)	
				Donatello (c. 1386–1466)	
	Civic humanism in Italy (c. 1400–c. 1450)				1400
				Masaccio (1401–1428)	
	Lorenzo Valla (1407–1457)				
				Botticelli (1445–1510)	
Renaissance popes (1447–1521)					
	Florentine Neoplatonism (c. 1450–c.1600)				
				Leonardo da Vinci (1452–1519)	
Constantinople falls to the Turks (1453)					
	Erasmus (c. 1469–1536)				
	Machiavelli (1469–1527)				
				Albrecht Dürer (1471–1528)	
	Nicholas Copernicus (1473–1543)				
				Ariosto (1474–1533)	
				Michelangelo (1475–1564)	
	Sir Thomas More (1478–1535)				
			Martin Luther (1483–1546)	Raphael (1483–1520)	
			Ulrich Zwingli (1484–1531)		
			Ignatius Loyola (1491–1556)		
French invade Italy (1494)				François Rabelais (c. 1494–1553)	
		Portugal gains control of East Indian spice trade (1498–1511)			
				Michelangelo's main work on Sistine Chapel (1508–1512)	1500
Henry VIII of England (1509–1547)			John Calvin (1509–1564)		
	Andreas Vesalius (1514–1564)				
			Letters of Obscure Men (1515)		

THE EARLY-MODERN WORLD

Politics	Philosophy and Science	Economics	Religion	Arts and Letters
			Erasmus's Greek New Testament (1516) Luther attacks indulgences (1517)	
Charles V, Holy Roman emperor (1519–1556)				
		Spain gains control of Central and South America (c. 1520–c. 1550)		
				Peter Brueghel (c. 1525–1569) Palestrina (c. 1525–1594)
Troops of Charles V sack Rome (1527)			Henry VIII of England breaks with Rome (1527–1534)	
Spanish gain supremacy in Italy (1529)				
	Jean Bodin (1530–1596) Michel de Montaigne (1533–1592)			
Counter-Reformation popes (1534–1590)			Anabaptists seize Münster (1534) Loyola's Society of Jesus approved by Pope Paul III (1540)	
			Calvin takes over Geneva (1541) Council of Trent (1545–1563)	El Greco (c. 1541–c. 1614)
				Cervantes (1547–1616)
		Introduction of tobacco to Europe (1550s)		
			Peace of Augsburg divides Germany into Lutheran and Catholic areas (1555)	
Philip II of Spain (1556–1598) Elizabeth I of England (1558–1603)			Elizabethan religious compromise in England (c. 1558–c. 1570)	
		Spanish silver from America floods into Europe (c. 1560–1600) "Price Revolution" in Europe (c. 1560–c. 1600)		

THE EARLY-MODERN WORLD

Politics	Philosophy and Science	Economics	Religion	Arts and Letters	
	Francis Bacon (1561–1626)				
	Galileo (1564–1642)			Shakespeare (1564–1616)	
Revolt of the Netherlands (1566–1609)					
				Claudio Monteverdi (1567–1643)	
	Johann Kepler (1571–1630)				
St. Bartholomew's Day massacre (1572)					
				Rubens (1577–1640)	
	William Harvey (1578–1657)				
Defeat of Spanish Armada (1588)	Thomas Hobbes (1588–1679)				
Henry IV of France (1589–1610)					
	René Descartes (1596–1650)				
Edict of Nantes (1598)				Bernini (1598–1680)	
				Velásquez (1599–1660)	
		Chartering of English East India Company (1600)			1600
		Chartering of Dutch East India Company (1602)			
James I of England (1603–1625)					
				Rembrandt (1606–1669)	
				John Milton (1608–1674)	
		Arrival of coffee in Vienna (1615)			
Thirty Years' War (1618–1648)					
	Bacon's *Novum Organum* (1620)				
				Molière (1622–1673)	
	Blaise Pascal (1623–1662)				
Supremacy of Richelieu in France (1624–1642)					
	John Locke (1632–1704)			Christopher Wren (1632–1723)	
	Descartes' *Discourse on Method* (1637)				

THE EARLY-MODERN WORLD

	Politics	Philosophy and Science	Economics	Religion	Arts and Letters
	Frederick William, Elector of Brandenburg (1640–1688)				
	English Civil War (1642–1649)	Isaac Newton (1642–1727)			
	Fronde revolts in France (1648–1653)				
	Commonwealth and Protectorate in England (1649–1660)				
			Height of mercantilism in Europe (1650–1750)		
	Louis XIV of France (1651–1715)				
	Leopold I, Habsburg emperor (1658–1705)				
	Restoration of Stuart dynasty in England (1660)				
	Charles II of England (1660–1685)				
			Colbert's economic reforms in France (1664–1683)		
	Peter the Great of Russia (1682–1725)				
					Antoine Watteau (1684–1721)
	Revocation of the Edict of Nantes (1685)				J. S. Bach (1685–1750)
					G. F. Handel (1685–1759)
	James II of England (1685–1688)				
		Newton's *Principia Mathematica* (1687)			
	"Glorious" Revolution in England (1688)				
	War of the League of Augsburg (1688–1697)				
		Montesquieu (1689–1755)			
	John Locke, *Two Treatises of Government* (1690)				
		Voltaire (1694–1778)	Founding of Bank of England (1694)		
1700			Introduction of maize and potato crops in Europe (c. 1700)		The Enlightenment (c. 1700–c. 1790)

THE EARLY-MODERN WORLD

Politics	Philosophy and Science	Economics	Religion	Arts and Letters
War of the Spanish Succession (1702–1714)				
			John Wesley (1703–1789)	
	Linnaeus (1707–1778)			Henry Fielding (1707–1754)
Jacques Bossuet, *Politics Drawn from the Very Words of Holy Scripture* (1708)				
	David Hume (1711–1776)			
	Rousseau (1712–1778)			
Treaty of Utrecht (1713)	Diderot (1713–1784)			
Frederick William I of Prussia (1713–1740)				
Louis XV of France (1715–1774)		Mississippi Bubble (1715)		
Ascendency of Robert Walpole as Britain's "first minister" (1720–1742)		South Sea Bubble (1720)		
		Last appearance of bubonic plague in western Europe (1720)		
	Immanuel Kant (1724–1804)			
		Enclosure movement in England (1730–1810)		
				Joseph Haydn (1732–1809)
				Edward Gibbon (1737–1794)
Frederick the Great of Prussia (1740–1786)				
Maria Theresa of Austria (1740–1780)				
	Condorcet (1743–1794)			
	Antoine Lavoisier (1743–1794)			
		General European population increase beginning (1750)		
	French *Encyclopedia* (1751–1772)			
Seven Years' War (1756–1763)				W. A. Mozart (1756–1791)
George III of Britain (1760–1820)				
Catherine the Great of Russia (1762–1796)				
Louis XVI of France (1774–1792)				

THE EARLY-MODERN WORLD					
	Politics	**Philosophy and Science**	**Economics**	**Religion**	**Arts and Letters**
					Jane Austen (1775–1817)
	War of American Independence (1776–1783)		Adam Smith, *The Wealth of Nations* (1776)		
	Joseph II of Austria (1780–1790)				
	Beginning of the French Revolution (1789)				
		Edward Jenner introduces vaccination (1796)			
1800					

CHAPTER 13

THE CIVILIZATION OF THE RENAISSANCE (c. 1350–c. 1550)

Now may every reflecting spirit thank God he has chosen to live in this new age, so full of hope and promise, which already exults in a greater array of nobly-gifted souls than the world has seen in the thousand years before.

—MATTEO PALMIERI, *On the Civil Life,* c. 1435

Whatever was done by man with genius and with a certain grace he held to be almost divine.

—L. B. ALBERTI, *Self-Portrait,* c. 1460

"A renaissance of the arts"

THE PREVALENT MODERN NOTION that a "Renaissance period" followed western Europe's medieval age was first expressed by numerous Italian writers who lived between 1350 and 1550. According to them, one thousand years of unrelieved darkness had intervened between the Roman era and their own times. During these "dark ages" the Muses of art and literature had fled Europe before the onslaught of barbarism and ignorance. Almost miraculously, however, in the fourteenth century the Muses suddenly returned, and Italians happily collaborated with them to bring forth a glorious "renaissance of the arts."

Limits of the term "renaissance"

Ever since this periodization was advanced historians have taken for granted the existence of some sort of "renaissance" intervening between medieval and modern times. Indeed, in the late nineteenth and early twentieth centuries many scholars went so far as to argue that the Renaissance was not just an epoch in the history of learning and culture but that a unique "Renaissance spirit" transformed all aspects of life—political, economic, and religious, as well as intellectual and artistic. Today, however, most experts no longer accept this characterization because they find it impossible to locate any truly distinctive "Renaissance" politics, economics, or religion. Instead, scholars tend to agree that the term "Renaissance" should be reserved to describe certain exciting trends in thought, literature, and the arts that emerged in Italy from roughly 1350 to 1550 and then spread to northern Europe during the first half of the sixteenth century. That is the approach that will be followed here: accordingly, when we refer to a "Renaissance" period in this chapter we mean to limit ourselves to an epoch in intellectual and cultural history.

Further qualifications

Granted this restriction, some further qualifications are still necessary. Since the word *renaissance* literally means "rebirth," it is sometimes thought that after about 1350 certain Italians who were newly cognizant of Greek and Roman cultural accomplishments initiated a classical cultural rebirth after a long period of "death." In fact, however, the High Middle Ages witnessed no "death" of classical learning. St. Thomas Aquinas, for example, considered Aristotle to be "the Philosopher" and Dante revered Virgil. Similarly, it would be completely false to contrast an imaginary "Renaissance paganism" with a medieval "age of faith" because however much most Renaissance personalities loved the classics, none went so far as to worship classical gods. And finally, all discussions of the post-medieval Renaissance must be qualified by the fact that there was no single Renaissance position on any given subject.

The continuing rediscovery and spread of classical learning

Nonetheless, in the realms of thought, literature, and the arts important distinguishing traits may certainly be found that make the concept of a "Renaissance" meaningful for intellectual and cultural history. First, regarding knowledge of the classics, there was indubitably a significant quantitative difference between the learning of the Middle Ages and that of the Renaissance. Medieval scholars knew many Roman authors, such as Virgil, Ovid, and Cicero, but in the Renaissance the works of others such as Livy, Tacitus, and Lucretius were rediscovered and made familiar. Equally if not more important was the Renaissance discovery of the literature of classical Greece. In the twelfth and thirteenth centuries Greek scientific and philosophical treatises were made available to westerners in Latin translations, but none of the great Greek literary masterpieces and practically none of the major works of Plato were yet known. Nor could more than a handful of medieval westerners read the Greek language. In the Renaissance, on the other hand, large numbers of Western scholars learned Greek and mastered almost the entire Greek literary heritage that is known today.

Renaissance Coin. This coin, struck about 1490, depicts King Ferrante of Naples. It is one of the earliest coins to return to the classical ideal of naturalistic portraiture and to use Roman capitals rather than Gothic lettering for the inscription.

Second, Renaissance thinkers not only knew many more classical texts than their medieval counterparts, but they used them in new ways. Whereas medieval writers tended to employ their ancient sources for the purposes of complementing and confirming their own preconceived Christian assumptions, Renaissance writers customarily drew on the classics to reconsider their preconceived notions and alter their modes of expression. Firm determination to learn from classical antiquity, moreover, was even more pronounced in the realms of architecture and art, areas in which classical models contributed most strikingly to the creation of fully distinct "Renaissance" styles.

A secular Renaissance culture

Third, although Renaissance culture was by no means pagan, it certainly was more secular in its orientation than the culture of the Middle Ages. The evolution of the Italian city-states in the fourteenth and fifteenth centuries created a supportive environment for attitudes that stressed the attainment of success in the urban political arena and living well in this world. Inevitably such secular ideals helped create a culture that was increasingly nonecclesiastical. To be sure, the Church retained its wealth and some of its influence, but it adjusted to the spread of secularity by becoming more secular itself.

Humanism

One word above all comes closest to summing up the most common and basic Renaissance intellectual ideals, namely *humanism.* This word has two different meanings, one technical and one general, but both apply to the cultural goals and ideals of a large number of Renaissance thinkers. In its technical sense humanism was a program of studies that aimed to replace the medieval Scholastic emphasis on logic and metaphysics with the study of language, literature, history, and ethics. Ancient literature was always preferred: the study of the Latin classics was at the core of the curriculum, and, whenever possible, the student was expected to advance to Greek. Humanist teachers argued that Scholastic logic was too arid and irrelevant to the practical concerns of life; instead, they preferred the "humanities," which were meant to make their students virtuous and prepare them for contributing to the public functions of the state. (Women, as usual, were generally ignored, but sometimes aristocratic women were given humanist training in order to make them appear more polished.) In a broader sense, humanism stressed the "dignity" of man as the most excellent of all God's creatures below the angels. Some Renaissance thinkers argued that man was excellent because he alone of earthly creatures could obtain knowledge of God; others stressed man's ability to master his fate and live happily in the world. Either way, Renaissance humanists had a firm belief in the nobility and possibilities of the human race.

The Italian Background

The erosion of distinctions between the aristocracy and upper bourgeoisie in Italy

The Renaissance originated in Italy for several reasons. The most fundamental was that Italy in the Later Middle Ages encompassed the most advanced urban society in all of Europe. Unlike aristocrats north of the Alps, Italian aristocrats customarily lived in urban centers rather than in rural castles and consequently became fully involved in urban public affairs. Moreover, since the Italian aristocracy built its palaces in the cities, the aristocratic class was less sharply set off from the class of rich merchants than in the north. Hence whereas in France or Germany there was never any appreciable variation from the rule that aristocrats lived off the income from their landed estates while rich town-dwellers (bourgeois) gained their living from trade, in Italy so many town-dwelling aristocrats engaged in banking or mercantile enterprises and so many rich mercantile families imitated the manners of the aristocracy that by the fourteenth and fifteenth centuries the aristocracy and upper bourgeoisie were becoming virtually indistinguishable. The noted Florentine family of the Medici, for example, emerged as a family of physicians (as the name suggests), made its fortune in banking, and rose imperceptibly into the aristocracy in the fifteenth century. The results of these developments for the history of education are obvious: not only was there a great demand for education in the skills of reading and counting necessary to become a successful merchant, but the richest and most prominent families sought above all to find teachers who would impart to their offspring the knowledge and skills necessary to argue well in the public arena. Consequently, Italy produced a large number of secular educators, many of whom not only taught students but demonstrated their learned attainments in the production of political and ethical treatises and works of literature. The schools of these educators, moreover, created the best-educated upper-class public in all of Europe and inevitably therewith a considerable number of wealthy patrons who were ready to invest in the cultivation of new ideas and new forms of literary and artistic expression.

The special appeal of the classical past

A second reason why late-medieval Italy was the birthplace of an intellectual and artistic renaissance lay in the fact that it had a far greater sense of rapport with the classical past than any other territory in western Europe. Given the Italian aristocratic commitment to an educational curriculum that stressed success in urban politics, the best teachers understandably sought inspiration from ancient Latin and Greek texts because politics and political rhetoric were classical rather than medieval arts. Elsewhere, resort to classical knowledge and classical literary style might have seemed intolerably antiquarian and artificial, but in Italy the classical past appeared most "relevant" because ancient Roman monuments were omnipresent throughout the peninsula and ancient Latin literature referred to cities and sites that Renaissance Italians recognized as their own. Moreover, Italians became particularly intent on reappropriating their classical heritage in the fourteenth and fifteenth centuries because Italians then were seeking to establish an independent cultural identity in opposition to a Scholasticism most closely associated with France. Not only did the removal of the papacy to Avignon for most of the fourteenth century and then the Great Schism from 1378 to 1417 heighten antagonisms between Italy and France, but during the fourteenth century there was an intellectual reaction against Scholasticism on all fronts which made it natural for Italians to prefer the intellectual alternatives offered by classical literary sources. Naturally, too, once Roman literature and learning became particularly favored in Italy, so did Roman art and architecture, for Roman models could help Italians create a splendid artistic alternative to French Gothicism just as Roman learning offered an intellectual alternative to French Scholasticism.

Patronage of the arts rooted in urban pride and private wealth

Finally, the Italian Renaissance obviously could not have occurred without the underpinning of Italian wealth. Oddly enough, the Italian economy as a whole was probably more prosperous in the thirteenth century than it was in the fourteenth and fifteenth. But late-medieval Italy was wealthier in comparison to the rest of Europe than it had been before, a fact that meant that Italian writers and artists were more likely to stay at home than seek employment abroad. Moreover, in late-medieval Italy unusually intensive investment in culture arose from an intensification of urban pride and the concentration of per capita wealth. Although these two trends overlapped somewhat, most scholars tend to agree that

Bernabò Visconti. The funeral monument of a magnificent lord who ruled Milan from 1354 to 1385.

a phase of predominantly public urban support for culture came first in Italy from roughly 1250 to about 1400 or 1450, depending on place, with the private sector taking over thereafter. In the first phase the richest cities vied with each other in building the most splendid public monuments and in supporting writers whose role was to glorify the urban republics in letters and speeches as full of magniloquent Ciceronian prose as possible. But in the course of the fifteenth century, when most Italian city-states succumbed to the hereditary rule of princely families, patronage was monopolized by the princely aristocracy. It was then that the great princes—the Visconti and Sforza in Milan, the Medici in Florence, the Este in Ferrara, and the Gonzaga in Mantua—patronized art and literature in their courts to glorify themselves, while lesser aristocratic families imitated those princes on a smaller scale. Not least of the great princes in Italy from about 1450 to about 1550 were the popes in Rome, who were dedicated to a policy of basing their strength on temporal control of the Papal States. Hence the most worldly of the Renaissance popes—Alexander VI (1492–1503); Julius II (1503–1513); and Leo X (1513–1521), son of the Florentine ruler Lorenzo de' Medici—obtained the services of the greatest artists of the day and for a few decades made Rome the unrivaled artistic capital of the Western world.

Pope Julius II, by Raphael. The acorns at the top of the throne posts are visual puns for the pope's family name, "della Rovere" (of the oak).

The Renaissance of Thought and Literature in Italy

Petrarch, the first humanist

In surveying the greatest accomplishments of Italian Renaissance scholars and writers it is natural to begin with the work of Francis Petrarch (1304–1374), the earliest of the humanists in the technical sense of the term. Petrarch was a deeply committed Christian who believed that Scholasticism was entirely misguided because it concentrated on abstract speculation rather than teaching people how to behave properly and attain salvation. Petrarch thought that the Christian writer must above all cultivate literary eloquence so that he could inspire people to do good. For him the best models of eloquence were to be found in the ancient literary classics, which he thought repaid study doubly inasmuch as they were filled with ethical wisdom. So Petrarch dedicated himself to searching for undiscovered ancient Latin texts and writing his own moral treatises in which he imitated classical style and quoted classical phrases. Thereby he initiated a program of "humanist" studies that was to be influential for centuries. Petrarch also has a place in purely literary history because of his poetry. Although he prized his own Latin poetry over the poems he wrote in the Italian vernacular, only the latter have proved enduring. Above all, the Italian sonnets—later called Petrarchan sonnets—which he wrote for his beloved Laura in the chivalrous style of the troubadours, were widely imitated in form and content throughout the Renaissance period.

Civic humanism

Because he was a very traditional Christian, Petrarch's ultimate ideal for human conduct was the solitary life of contemplation and asceticism. But in subsequent generations, from about 1400 to 1450, a number of Italian thinkers and scholars, located mainly in Florence, developed the alternative of what is customarily called *civic humanism.* Civic humanists like the Florentines Leonardo Bruni (c. 1370–1444) and Leon Battista Alberti (1404–1472) agreed with Petrarch on the need for eloquence and the study of classical literature, but they also taught that man's nature equipped him for action, for usefulness to his family and society, and for serving the state—ideally a republican city-state after the classical or contemporary Florentine model. In their view ambition and the quest for glory were noble impulses that ought to be encouraged. They refused to condemn the striving for material possessions, for they argued that the history of human progress is inseparable from mankind's success in gaining mastery over the earth and its resources. Perhaps the most vivid of the civic humanists' writings is Alberti's *On the Family* (1443), in which he argued that the nuclear family was instituted by nature for the well-being of humanity. Not surprisingly, however, Alberti consigned women to purely domestic roles within this framework, for he believed that "man [is] by nature more energetic and industrious," and that woman was created "to increase and continue generations, and to nourish and preserve those already born."

Leon Battista Alberti. A contemporary medal.

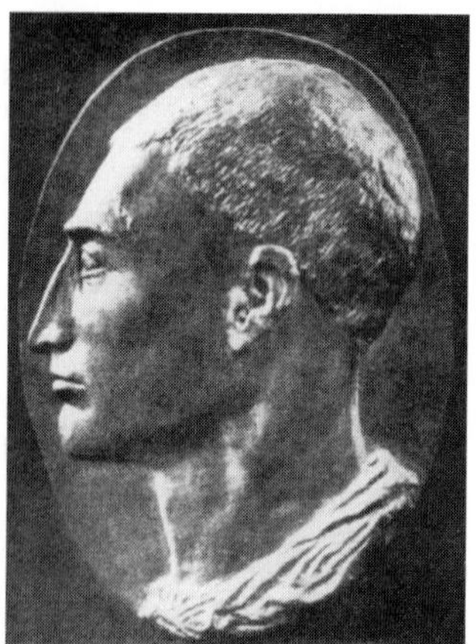

The civic humanists and classical Greek studies

In addition to differing with Petrarch in their preference for the active over the solitary or contemplative life, the civic humanists went far beyond him in their study of the ancient literary heritage. Some discovered important new Latin texts, but more important was their success in opening up the field of classical Greek studies. In this they were aided by several Byzantine scholars who had migrated to Italy in the first half of the fifteenth century and gave instruction in the Greek language. Coming to recognize the glories of ancient Greek literature, Italian scholars traveled to Constantinople and other Eastern cities in search of forgotten Greek masterpieces. In 1423 one Italian, Giovanni Aurispa, alone brought back 238 manuscript books, including works of Sophocles, Euripides, and Thucydides. Soon followed the work of translation into Latin, not word for word, but sense for sense in order to preserve the literary force of the original. In this way most of the Greek classics, particularly the writings of Plato, the dramatists, and the historians, were first made available to western Europe.

Lorenzo Valla and linguistic analysis

Related in his textual interests to the civic humanists, but by no means a full adherent of their movement, was the atypical yet highly influential Renaissance thinker Lorenzo Valla (1407–1457). Born in Rome and active primarily as a secretary in the service of the king of Naples, Valla had no inclination to espouse the ideas of republican political engagement as the Florentine civic humanists did. Instead, he preferred to advertise his skills as an expert in grammar, rhetoric, and the painstaking analysis of Greek and Latin texts by showing how the thorough study of language could discredit old verities. Most decisive in this regard was Valla's brilliant demonstration that the so-called Donation of Constantine was a medieval forgery. Whereas papal propagandists had argued ever since the early thirteenth century that the papacy possessed rights to temporal rule in western Europe on the grounds of a charter purportedly granted by the Emperor Constantine in the fourth century, Valla proved beyond dispute that the document in question was full of nonclassical Latin usages and anachronistic terms. Hence he concluded that the "Donation" was the work of a medieval forger whose "monstrous impudence" was exposed by the "stupidity of his language." This demonstration not only discredited a prize specimen of "medieval ignorance," but, more importantly, introduced the concept of anachronism into all subsequent textual study and historical thought. Valla also employed his skills in linguistic analysis and rhetorical argumentation to challenge a wide variety of philosophical positions, but his ultimate goals were by no means purely destructive, for he revered the literal teachings of the Pauline Epistles. Accordingly, in his *Notes on the New Testament* he applied his expert knowledge of Greek to elucidating the true meaning of St. Paul's words, which he believed had been obscured by St. Jerome's Latin Vulgate translation. This work was to prove an important link between Italian Renaissance scholarship and the subsequent Christian humanism of the north.

Renaissance Neoplatonism: Ficino and Pico

From about 1450 until about 1600 dominance in the world of Italian thought was assumed by a school of Neoplatonists, who sought to blend the thought of Plato, Plotinus, and various strands of ancient mysticism with Christianity. Foremost among these were Marsilio Ficino (1433–1499) and Giovanni Pico della Mirandola (1463–1494), both of whom were members of the Platonic Academy founded by Cosimo de' Medici in Florence. The academy was a loosely organized society of scholars who met to hear readings and lectures. Their hero was Plato: sometimes they celebrated Plato's birthday by holding a banquet in his honor, after which everybody gave speeches as if they were characters in a Platonic dialogue. Ficino's greatest achievement was the translation of Plato's works into Latin, thereby making them widely available to western Europeans for the first time. It is debatable whether Ficino's own philosophy may be called humanist because he moved away from ethics to metaphysics and taught that the individual should look primarily to the other world. In Ficino's opinion, "the immortal soul is always miserable in its mortal body." The same problem holds for Ficino's disciple Giovanni Pico della Mirandola, whose most famous work is the *Oration on the Dignity of Man.* Pico was certainly not a civic humanist since he saw little worth in mundane public affairs. But he did believe that there is "nothing more wonderful than man" because he believed that man is endowed with the capacity to achieve union with God if he so wills.

Pico della Mirandola. When the young nobleman Pico arrived in Florence at age nineteen he was said to have been "of beauteous feature and shape." This contemporary portrait may have been done by the great Florentine painter Botticelli.

Machiavelli

Hardly any of the Italian thinkers between Petrarch and Pico were really original: their greatness lay mostly in their manner of expression, their accomplishments in technical scholarship, and their popularization of different themes of ancient thought. The same, however, cannot be said of Renaissance Italy's greatest political philosopher, the Florentine Niccolò Machiavelli (1469–1527), who belonged to no school and stood in a class by himself. No one did more than Machiavelli to overturn all earlier views of the ethical basis of politics or to pioneer in the dispassionate direct observation of political life. Machiavelli's writings reflect the unstable condition of Italy in his time. At the end of the fifteenth century Italy had become the cockpit of international struggles. Both France and Spain had invaded the peninsula and were competing for the allegiance of the Italian city-states, which in many cases were torn by internal dissension making them easy prey for foreign conquerors. In 1498 Machiavelli became a prominent official in the government of the Florentine republic, set up four years earlier when the French invasion had led to the expulsion of the Medici. His duties largely involved diplomatic missions to other states. While in Rome he became fascinated with the achievements of Cesare Borgia, son of Pope Alexander VI, in cementing a solidified state out of scattered elements. He noted with approval Cesare's combination of ruthlessness with shrewdness and his complete subordination of morality to political ends. In 1512 the Medici returned to overthrow the republic of Florence, and Machiavelli was deprived of his position. Disappointed and embittered, he spent the remainder of his life at his country estate, devoting his time primarily to writing. In his *Discourses on Livy* he praised the ancient Roman republic as a model for all time. He lauded constitutionalism, equality, liberty (in the sense of freedom from outside interference), and subordination of religion to the interests of the state. But Machiavelli also wrote *The Prince,* in which he described the policies and practices of government, not in accordance with some lofty ideal, but as they actually were. The supreme obligation of the ruler, he avowed, was to maintain the power and safety of the country over which he ruled. No consideration of justice or mercy or the sanctity of treaties should be allowed to stand in his way. Cynical in his views of human nature, Machiavelli maintained that all men are prompted exclusively by motives of self-interest, particularly by desires for personal power and material prosperity. The head of the state should therefore not take for granted the loyalty or affection of his subjects. The one ideal Machiavelli kept before him in his later years was the unification of Italy. But this he believed could be achieved only through ruthlessness.

Castiglione's ideal courtier and court lady

Far more congenial to contemporary tastes than the shocking political theories of Machiavelli were the guidelines for proper aristocratic conduct offered in *The Book of the Courtier* (1516) by the diplomat and count Baldassare Castiglione. This cleverly written forerunner of modern handbooks of etiquette stands in sharp contrast to the earlier civic humanist treatises of Bruni and Alberti, for whereas they taught the sober "republican" virtues of strenuous service in behalf of the city-state and family, Castiglione, writing in an Italy dominated by magnificent princely courts, taught how to attain the elegant and seemingly effortless qualities necessary for acting like a "true gentleman." More than anyone else, Castiglione popularized the ideal of the "Renaissance man": one who is accomplished in many different pursuits and is also brave, witty, and "courteous," meaning civilized and learned. By no means ignoring the female sex, Castiglione, unlike Alberti, was silent about women's role in "hearth and home," but stressed instead the ways in which court ladies could be "gracious entertainers." Thereby he was one of the first European male writers to offer women an independent role outside of the household, a fact that should not be underrated even though he was offering such a role merely to the richest of the rich and even though his stress on "pleasing affability" today seems demeaning. Widely read throughout Europe for over a century after its publication, Castiglione's *Courtier* spread Italian ideals of "civility" to princely courts north of the Alps, resulted in the ever-greater patronage of art and literature by the European aristocracy, and gave currency to the hitherto novel proposition that some women other than nuns were not fated to be passive vessels of reproduction and nutrition.

Other sixteenth-century Italian literary achievements

Had Castiglione's ideal courtier wished to show off his knowledge of contemporary Italian literature, he would have had many works from which to choose, for sixteenth-century Italians were highly accomplished in the creation of imaginative prose and verse. Among the many impressive writers who might be mentioned, Machiavelli himself wrote a delightful short story, "Belfagor," and an engaging bawdy play, *Mandragola;* the great artist Michelangelo wrote many moving sonnets; and Ludovico Ariosto (1474–1533), the most eminent of sixteenth-century Italian epic poets, wrote a lengthy verse narrative called *Orlando Furioso* (The madness of Roland). Although woven substantially from materials taken from the medieval Charlemagne cycle, this work differed radically from any of the medieval epics because it introduced elements of lyrical fantasy and above all because it was totally devoid of heroic idealism. Ariosto wrote to make readers laugh and to charm them with felicitous descriptions of the quiet splendor of nature and the passions of love. His work represents the disillusionment of the late Renaissance, the loss of hope and faith, and the tendency to seek consolation in the pursuit of pleasure and aesthetic delight.

The Artistic Renaissance in Italy

Innovations in Renaissance painting

Despite numerous intellectual and literary advances, the most long-lived achievements of the Italian Renaissance were made in the realm of art. Of all the arts, painting was undoubtedly supreme. We have already seen that around 1300 very impressive beginnings were made in the history of Italian painting by the artistic genius of Giotto, but it was not until the fifteenth century that Italian painting began to attain its majority. One reason for this was that in the early fifteenth century the laws of linear perspective were discovered and first employed to give the fullest sense of three dimensions. Fifteenth-century artists also experimented with effects of light and shade (*chiaroscuro*) and for the first time carefully studied the anatomy and proportions of the human body. By the fifteenth century, too, increase in private wealth and the partial triumph of the secular spirit had freed the domain of art to a large extent from the service of religion. As we have noted above, the Church was no longer the only patron of artists. While subject matter from biblical history was still commonly employed, it was frequently infused with nonreligious themes. The painting of portraits for the purpose of revealing the hidden mysteries of the soul now became popular. Paintings intended to appeal primarily to the intellect were paralleled by others whose main purpose was to delight the eye with gorgeous color and beauty of form. The fifteenth century was characterized also by the introduction of painting in oil, probably from Flanders. The use of the new technique doubtless had much to do with the artistic advance of this period. Since oil does not dry as quickly as fresco pigment, the painter could now work more leisurely, taking time with the more difficult parts of the picture and making corrections if necessary as he went along.

The Expulsion of Adam and Eve from the Garden. Masaccio built on the artistic tradition established by Giotto in stressing emotion and psychological study. Until a recent restoration, Adam's genitalia were covered by fig leaves.

The majority of the great painters of the fifteenth century were Florentines. First among them was the precocious Masaccio (1401–1428). Although he died at the age of twenty-seven, Masaccio inspired the work of Italian painters for a hundred years. Masaccio's greatness as a painter is based on his success in "imitating nature," which became a primary value in Renaissance painting. To achieve this effect he employed perspective, perhaps most dramatically in his fresco of the Trinity; he also used chiaroscuro with originality, leading to a dramatic and moving outcome.

In the *Expulsion of Adam and Eve from the Garden,* he records the shame and guilt felt by the individuals in the biblical story.

The best known of the painters who directly followed the tradition begun by Masaccio was the Florentine Sandro Botticelli (1445–1510), who depicted both classical and Christian subjects. Botticelli's work excels in linear rhythms and sensuous depiction of natural detail. He is most famous for paintings that strike the eye as purely pagan because they display figures from classical mythology without any overt sign of a Christian frame of reference. His *Allegory of Spring* and *Birth of Venus* employ a style greatly indebted to the art of the Romans to display beautiful gods, goddesses, zephyrs, and muses moving gracefully in natural settings. Consequently these works used to be understood as the expression of "Renaissance paganism" at its fullest, a celebration of earthly delights breaking sharply with Christian asceticism. More recently, however, scholars have preferred to view them as allegories fully compatible with Christian teachings. According to this interpretation, Botticelli was addressing himself to learned aristocratic viewers, well-versed in the Neoplatonic theories of Ficino that considered ancient gods and goddesses to represent various Christian virtues. Venus, for example, might have stood for a species of chaste love. Although Botticelli's great "classical" works remain cryptic, two points remain certain: any viewer is free to enjoy them on their naturalistic sensuous level, and Botticelli had surely not broken with Christianity since he painted frescoes for the pope in Rome at just the same time.

Portrait of a Young Woman, by Sandro Botticelli (1445–1510).

Leonardo da Vinci

Perhaps the greatest of the Florentine artists was Leonardo da Vinci (1452–1519), one of the most versatile geniuses who ever lived. Leonardo

The Agony in the Garden, by Fra Angelico (1387–1455). Fra Angelico, a Dominican friar, drew on Masaccio's naturalism, emphasizing gentleness and restraint. In terms of content this fresco is noteworthy for introducing two female saints where they had no place in the original biblical account.

The Flagellation, by Piero della Francesca (c. 1420–1492). One of the finest and also one of the most puzzling paintings in the Western tradition. Among the many unresolved questions are why the flagellation of Christ is set in the background and why the men on the right appear in modern dress. It is certain, however, that Piero's attention to perspective and mathematical ratios was so exact that one could use his picture to buy and cut carpet for the entire floor.

The Birth of Venus, by Botticelli. Botticelli was a mystic as well as a lover of beauty, and the painting is most often interpreted as a Neoplatonic allegory.

was practically the personification of the "Renaissance man": he was a painter, architect, musician, mathematician, engineer, and inventor. The illegitimate son of a lawyer and a peasant woman, Leonardo set up an artist's shop in Florence by the time he was twenty-five and gained the patronage of the Medici ruler of the city, Lorenzo the Magnificent. But if Leonardo had any weakness, it was his slowness in working and difficulty in finishing anything. This naturally displeased Lorenzo and other Florentine patrons, who thought an artist was little more than an artisan, commissioned to produce a certain piece of work of a certain size for a certain price on a certain date. Leonardo, however, strongly objected to this view because he considered himself to be no menial craftsman but an inspired creator. Therefore in 1482 he left Florence for the Sforza court of Milan where he was given freer rein in structuring his time and work. He remained there until the French invaded Milan in 1499; after that he wandered about Italy, finally accepting the patronage of the French king, Francis I, under whose auspices Leonardo lived and worked in France until his death.

Lorenzo de' Medici, known as Lorenzo the Magnificent. A detail from *The Adoration of the Magi* by Benozzo Gozzoli showing the future Florentine ruler and patron of art.

The paintings of Leonardo da Vinci began what is known as the High Renaissance in Italy. His approach to painting was that it should be the most accurate possible imitation of nature. Leonardo was like a naturalist, basing his work on his own detailed observations of a blade of grass, the wing of a bird, a waterfall. He obtained human corpses for dissection—by which he was breaking the law—and reconstructed in drawing the minutest features of anatomy, which knowledge he carried over to his paintings. Leonardo worshiped nature, and was convinced of the essential divinity in all living things. It is not surprising, therefore, that he was a vegetarian, and that he went to the marketplace to buy caged birds, which he released to their native habitat.

Leonardo's masterpieces

It is generally agreed that Leonardo's masterpieces are the *Virgin of the Rocks* (which exists in two versions), the *Last Supper,* and the *Mona Lisa.* The first represents not only his marvelous technical skill but also his passion for science and his belief in the universe as a well-ordered place. The figures are arranged geometrically, with every rock and plant depicted in accurate detail. *The Last Supper,* painted on the walls of the refectory of Santa Maria delle Grazie in Milan, is a study of psychological reactions. A serene Christ, resigned to his terrible fate, has just announced to his disciples that one of them will betray him. The artist succeeds in portraying the mingled emotions of surprise, horror, and guilt in the faces of the disciples as they gradually perceive the meaning of their master's statement. The third of Leonardo's major triumphs, the *Mona Lisa,* reflects a similar interest in the varied moods of the human soul. Although it is true that the *Mona Lisa* is a portrait of an actual woman, the wife of Francesco del Giocondo, a Neapolitan, it is more than a mere photographic likeness. The distinguished art critic Bernard Berenson has said of it, "Who like Leonardo has depicted . . . the inexhaustible fascination of the woman in her years of mastery? . . . Leonardo is the one artist of whom it may be said with perfect literalness: 'Nothing that he touched but turned into a thing of eternal beauty.' "

The Annunciation, by Leonardo da Vinci (1452–1519). This early work, done around 1475 while Leonardo was an apprentice in the shop of the Florentine painter Verrocchio, is typical of the contemporary Florentine taste for sharply focused modeling and contrasts. (For another example see Botticelli's *Birth of Venus* on p. 426.) Yet one can see signs in the background of Leonardo's "hazy idealism": the remote mountains, half on earth, half hanging in the sky, could only have been painted by the independent-minded young genius.

The Virgin of the Rocks, by Leonardo da Vinci. This painting reveals not only Leonardo's interest in human physiognomy, but also his absorption in the atmosphere of natural settings.

Mona Lisa, by Leonardo da Vinci. Unlike most other Renaissance painters who sought to convey an understandable message, Leonardo created questions to which he gave no answer. Nowhere is this more evident than in the enigmatic countenance of Mona Lisa.

The Venetian painters

The beginning of the High Renaissance around 1490 also witnessed the rise of the so-called Venetian school, the major members of which were Giovanni Bellini (c. 1430–1516), Giorgione (1478–1510), and Titian (c. 1490–1576). The work of all these men reflected the luxurious life and the pleasure-loving interests of the thriving commercial city of Venice. Most Venetian painters had little of the concern with philosophical and psychological themes that characterized the Florentine school. Their aim was to appeal primarily to the senses rather than to the mind. They delighted in painting idyllic landscapes and gorgeous symphonies of color. For their subject matter they chose not merely the natural beauty of Venetian sunsets and the shimmering silver of lagoons in the moonlight but also the artificial splendor of sparkling jewels, richly colored satins and velvets, and gorgeous palaces. Their portraits were invariably likenesses of the rich and the powerful. In the subordination of form and meaning to color and elegance there were mirrored not only the sumptuous tastes of wealthy merchants, but also definite traces of Eastern influence that had filtered through from Byzantium during the Middle Ages.

The painters of the High Renaissance: Raphael

The remaining great painters of the High Renaissance all accomplished their most important work in the first half of the sixteenth century when Renaissance Italian art reached its peak. Rome was now the major artistic center of the Italian peninsula, although the traditions of the Florentine school still exerted a potent influence. Among the eminent painters of this period at least two must be given more than passing attention. One was Raphael (1483–1520), a native of Urbino, and perhaps the most beloved artist of the entire Renaissance. The lasting appeal of his style is due primarily to his ennobling humanism, for he portrayed the members of the human species as temperate, wise, and dignified beings. Although Raphael was influenced by Leonardo da Vinci and copied many features of his work, he cultivated a much more symbolical or allegorical approach. His *Disputà* symbolized the dialectical relationship between the Church in heaven and the Church on earth. In a worldly setting against a brilliant sky, theologians debate the meaning of the Eucharist, while in the clouds above, saints and the Trinity repose in the possession of a holy mystery. Raphael's *School of Athens* depicts a harmony between the Platonist and Aristotelian philosophies. Plato (painted as a portrait of Leonardo) is shown pointing upward to emphasize the spiritual basis of his world of Ideas, while Aristotle stretches a hand forward to exemplify his teaching that human life should be led in accordance with ethical moderation. Raphael is noted also for his portraits and Madonnas. To the latter, especially, he gave a softness and warmth that seemed to endow them with a sweetness and piety quite different from the enigmatic and somewhat distant Madonnas of Leonardo da Vinci.

Michelangelo's paintings

The last towering figure of the High Renaissance was Michelangelo (1475–1564) of Florence. If Leonardo was a naturalist, Michelangelo was an idealist; where the former sought to recapture and interpret fleeting natural phenomena, Michelangelo, who embraced Neoplatonism as a philosophy, was more concerned with expressing enduring, abstract

Young Knight in the Countryside, by Carpaccio (c. 1455–1526). A specimen of the delight in sumptuous color of the Venetian school of Renaissance painting.

St. Francis in the Desert, by Giovanni Bellini (c. 1430–1516)

The Madonna of the Dawn ("Alba Madonna"), by Raphael (1483–1520). Raphael's art was distinguished by warmth, serenity, and tenderness. Here, the artist emphasizes the humility of the Virgin Mary by having her seated on the ground. The fact that the child John the Baptist and the child Christ are holding a cross reminds the viewer of the Crucifixion to come.

The School of Athens, by Raphael

The Creation of Adam by Michelangelo (1475–1564). One of a series of frescoes on the ceiling of the Sistine Chapel in Rome. Inquiring into the nature of humanity, it represents Renaissance affirmativeness at its height.

truths. Michelangelo was a painter, sculptor, architect, and poet—and he expressed himself in all these forms with a similar power and in a similar manner. At the center of all of his paintings is the human figure, which is always powerful, colossal, magnificent. If humanity, and the potential of the individual, lay at the center of Italian Renaissance culture, then Michelangelo, who depicted the human, and particularly the male, figure without cease, is the supreme Renaissance artist.

Michelangelo's work in the Sistine Chapel

Michelangelo's greatest achievements in painting appear in a single location—the Sistine Chapel in Rome—yet they are products of two different periods in the artist's life and consequently exemplify two different artistic styles and outlooks on the human condition. Most famous are the sublime frescoes Michelangelo painted on the ceiling of the Sistine Chapel from 1508 to 1512, depicting scenes from the book of Genesis. All the panels in this series, including *God Dividing the Light from Darkness, The Creation of Adam,* and *The Flood,* exemplify the young artist's commitment to classical Greek aesthetic principles of harmony, solidity, and dignified restraint. Correspondingly, all exude as well a sense of sublime affirmation regarding Creation and the heroic qualities of mankind. But a quarter of a century later, when Michelangelo returned to work in the Sistine Chapel, both his style and mood had changed dramatically. In the enormous *Last Judgment,* a fresco done for the Sistine Chapel's altar wall in 1536, Michelangelo repudiated classical restraint and substituted a style that emphasized tension and distortion in order to communicate the older man's pessimistic conception of a humanity wracked by fear and bowed by guilt.

Renaissance sculpture

In the realm of sculpture the Italian Renaissance took a great step forward by creating statues that were no longer carved as parts of columns or doorways on church buildings or as effigies on tombs. Instead, Italian sculptors for the first time since antiquity carved free-standing statues "in the round." These freed sculpture from its bondage to architecture and established its status as a separate art frequently devoted to secular purposes.

The first great master of Renaissance sculpture was Donatello (c. 1386–1466). He emancipated his art from Gothic mannerisms and introduced a new vigorous note of individualism. His bronze statue of David triumphant over the body of the slain Goliath, the first free-standing nude since antiquity, established a precedent of glorifying the life-size nude. Donatello's *David,* moreover, represents a first step in the direction of imitating classical sculpture, not just in the depiction of a nude body, but also in the subject's posture of resting his weight on one leg. Yet this David is clearly a lithe adolescent rather than a muscular Greek athlete. Later in his career, Donatello more fully imitated ancient statuary in his commanding portrayal of the proud warrior Gattamelata—the first monumental equestrian statue in bronze executed in the West since the time of the Romans. Here, in addition to drawing very heavily on the legacy of antiquity, the sculptor most clearly expressed his dedication to immortalizing the earthly accomplishments of a contemporary secular hero.

Certainly the greatest sculptor of the Italian Renaissance—indeed, probably the greatest sculptor of all time—was Michelangelo. Believing with Leonardo that the artist was an inspired creator, Michelangelo pursued this belief to the conclusion that sculpture was the most exalted of the arts because it allowed the artist to imitate God most fully in recreating

David, by Donatello (c. 1386–1466). The first free-standing nude statue executed in the West since antiquity.

Gattamelata, by Donatello. Note the debt to the Roman equestrian statue of Marcus Aurelius, shown on p. 172.

human forms. Furthermore, in Michelangelo's view the most God-like sculptor disdained slavish naturalism, for anyone could make a plaster cast of a human figure, but only an inspired creative genius could endow his sculpted figures with a sense of life. Accordingly, Michelangelo subordinated naturalism to the force of his imagination and sought restlessly to express his ideals in ever more arresting forms.

As in his painting, Michelangelo's sculpture followed a course from classicism to anticlassicism, that is, from harmonious modeling to dramatic distortion. The sculptor's most distinguished early work, his *David,* executed in 1501, is surely his most perfect classical statue. Choosing, like Donatello, to depict a male nude, Michelangelo nonetheless conceived of his own *David* as a public expression of Florentine civic ideals, and hence as heroic rather than merely graceful. To this end he worked in marble—the "noblest" sculptural medium—and created a figure twice as large as life. Above all he employed classical style to depict a serenely confident young man at the peak of physical fitness, thereby representing the Florentine republic's own "fortitude" in resisting tyrants and upholding ideals of civic justice. The serenity seen in *David* is no longer prominent in the works of Michelangelo's middle period; rather, in a work such as his *Moses* of about 1515, the sculptor has begun to explore the use of anatomical distortion to create effects of emotional intensity—in this case, the biblical prophet's righteous rage. While such statues remained awesomely heroic, as Michelangelo's life drew to a close he experimented more and more with exaggerated stylistic mannerisms for the purpose of communicating moods of brooding pensiveness or outright pathos. The culmination of this trend in Michelangelo's statuary is his moving *Descent from the Cross,* a depiction of an old man resembling the sculptor himself grieving over the distended, slumping body of the dead Christ.

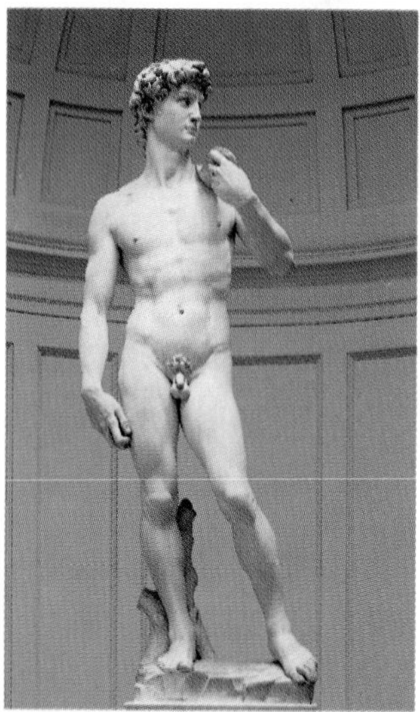

David, by Michelangelo. Over thirteen feet high, this serenely self-confident affirmation of the beauty of the human form was placed prominently by the Florentine government in front of Florence's city hall to proclaim the city's humanistic values.

Renaissance architecture

To a much greater extent than either sculpture or painting, Renaissance architecture had its roots in the past. The new building style was a compound of elements derived from the Middle Ages and from antiquity. It was not the Gothic, however, a style that had never found a congenial soil in Italy, but the Romanesque which provided the medieval basis for the architecture of the Italian Renaissance. The great architects of the Renaissance generally adopted their building plans from Romanesque churches and copied their decorative devices from the ruins of ancient Rome. The result was an architecture based on the cruciform floor plan of transept and nave and embodying the decorative features of the column and arch, or the column and lintel, the colonnade, and frequently the dome. Horizontal lines predominated. Renaissance architecture also emphasized geometrical proportion because Italian builders, under the influence of Neoplatonism, concluded that certain mathematical ratios reflect the harmony of the universe. A fine example of Renaissance architecture is St. Peter's Basilica in Rome, built under the patronage of Popes Julius II and Leo X and designed by some of the most celebrated architects of the time, including Donato Bramante (c. 1444–1514) and Michelangelo. Equally impressive are the artfully proportioned aristocratic country houses designed

Moses, by Michelangelo. Far less classical in style than Michelangelo's *David,* this statue stresses a sense of drama. (Moses was depicted with horns in medieval and Renaissance art on account of a faulty translation of a passage from the Book of Exodus.)

Descent from the Cross, by Michelangelo. This portrayal of tragedy was made by the sculptor for his own tomb. Note the distortion for effect exemplified by the elongated body and left arm of the figure of Christ. The figure in the rear is Nicodemus, but was probably intended to represent Michelangelo himself.

The Villa Rotonda, by Palladio. A highly influential Renaissance private dwelling near Vicenza. Note how Palladio drew for inspiration on the Roman Pantheon, pictured on p. 184.

by the northern Italian architect Andrea Palladio (1508–1580), who created secular miniatures of ancient temples such as the Roman Pantheon to glorify the aristocrats who dwelled within them.

The Waning of the Italian Renaissance

Political factors in the decline of the Italian Renaissance: the French invasion of 1494

Around 1550 the Renaissance in Italy began to decline after some two hundred glorious years. The causes of this decline were varied. Perhaps at the head of the list should be placed the French invasion of 1494 and the incessant warfare that ensued. The French king Charles VIII, who ruled the richest and most powerful kingdom in Europe, viewed Italy as an attractive prey for his grandiose ambitions. In 1494 he led an army of 30,000 well-trained troops across the Alps. Florence swiftly capitulated and within less than a year the French had promenaded down the peninsula and conquered Naples. By so doing, however, they aroused the suspicions of the rulers of Spain, who feared an attack on Sicily, which was their possession. An alliance among Spain, the Papal States, the Holy Roman Empire, Milan, and Venice finally forced Charles to withdraw from Italy. Yet upon his death his successor, Louis XII, launched a second invasion, and from 1499 until 1529 warfare in Italy was virtually uninterrupted. Alliances and counteralliances followed each other in bewildering succession, but they managed only to prolong the hostilities. The French won a great victory at Marignano in 1515, but they were decisively defeated by the Spanish at Pavia in 1525. The worst disaster came in 1527 when unruly Spanish and German troops, nominally under the command of the Spanish ruler and Holy Roman Emperor Charles V, but in fact entirely out of control, sacked the city of Rome, causing irreparable destruction. Only in 1529 did Charles finally manage to gain control over most of the Italian peninsula, putting the fighting to an end for a time. Once triumphant, Charles retained two of the largest portions of Italy for Spain—the Duchy of Milan and the Kingdom of Naples—and installed favored princes as the rulers of almost all the other Italian political entities except for Venice and the Papal States. These protégés of the Spanish crown continued to preside over their own courts, to patronize the arts, and to adorn their cities with luxurious buildings, but they were puppets of a foreign power and unable to inspire their retinues with a sense of vigorous cultural independence.

The waning of Italian prosperity

To the Italian political disasters was added a waning of Italian prosperity. Whereas Italy's virtual monopoly of trade with Asia in the fifteenth century had been one of the chief economic supports for the cultivation of Italian Renaissance culture, the gradual shifting of trade routes from the Mediterranean to the Atlantic region, following the overseas discoveries of around 1500, slowly but surely cost Italy its supremacy as the center of world trade. Since the incessant warfare of the sixteenth century also contributed to Italy's economic hardships, as did Spanish financial exactions in Milan and Naples, there was gradually less and less of a surplus to support artistic endeavors.

The Church asserts control over thought and art

A final cause of the decline of the Italian Renaissance was the Counter-Reformation. During the sixteenth century the Roman Church sought increasingly to exercise firm control over thought and art as part of a campaign to combat worldliness and the spread of Protestantism. In 1542 the Roman Inquisition was established; in 1564 the first Roman Index of

The States of Italy during the Renaissance, c. 1494

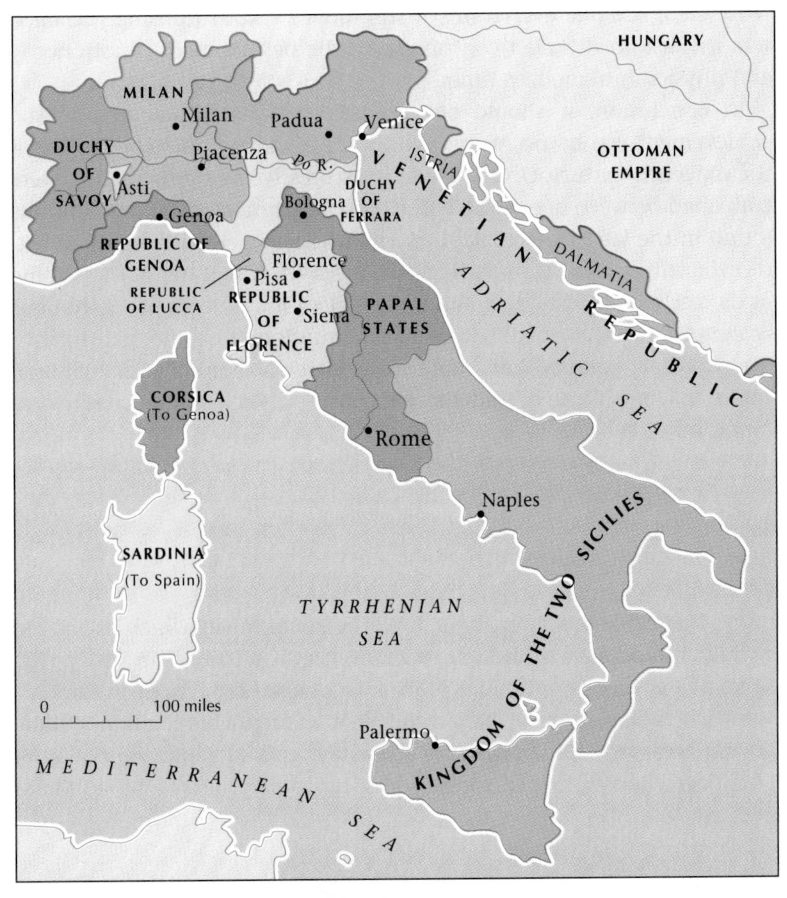

Prohibited Books was published. The extent of ecclesiastical interference in cultural life was enormous. For example, Michelangelo's great *Last Judgment* in the Sistine Chapel was criticized by some straitlaced fanatics for looking like a bordello because it showed too many naked bodies. Therefore, Pope Paul IV ordered a second-rate artist to paint in clothing wherever possible. (The unfortunate artist was afterward known as "the underwear-maker.") While this incident may appear merely grotesquely humorous, the determination of ecclesiastical censors to enforce doctrinal uniformity could lead to death, as in the case of the unfortunate Neoplatonic philosopher Giordano Bruno, whose insistence that there may be more than one world in contravention of the book of Genesis resulted in his being burned at the stake by the Roman Inquisition in 1600.

Giordano Bruno

The most notorious example of inquisitorial censorship of free intellectual speculation was the disciplining of the great scientist Galileo, whose achievements we will discuss in more detail later on. In 1616 the Holy Office in Rome condemned the new astronomical theory that the earth moves around the sun as "foolish, absurd, philosophically false, and formally heretical." Accordingly, the Inquisition proceeded immediately against Galileo when he published a brilliant defense of the heliocentric system in 1632. In short order the Inquisition made Galileo recant his "errors" and sentenced him to house arrest for the duration of his life. Galileo was not willing to face death for his beliefs, but after he publicly retracted his view that the earth revolves around the sun he supposedly whispered, "despite everything, it still moves." Not surprisingly, Galileo was the last great Italian contributor to the development of astronomy and physics until modern times.

Continued flourishing of Italian art and music

In conclusion, it should be emphasized that cultural and artistic achievement was by no means extinguished in Italy after the middle of the sixteenth century. On the contrary, impressive new artistic styles were cultivated between about 1540 and 1600 by painters who drew on traits found in the later work of Raphael and Michelangelo, and in the seventeenth century came the dazzling Baroque style, which was born in Rome under ecclesiastical auspices. Similarly, Italian music registered enormous accomplishments virtually without interruption from the sixteenth to the twentieth century. But whatever seemed threatening to the Church could not be tolerated, and the free spirit of Renaissance culture was found no more.

The Renaissance in the North

The diffusion of the Renaissance outside Italy

It was inevitable that after about 1500 the Renaissance, which originated in Italy, should have spread to other European countries. Throughout the fifteenth century a continuous procession of northern European students went to Italy to study in Italian universities such as Bologna or Padua, and an occasional Italian writer or artist traveled briefly north of the Alps. Such interchanges helped spread ideas, but only after around 1500 did most of northern Europe become sufficiently prosperous and politically stable to provide a truly congenial environment for the widespread cultivation of art and literature. Intellectual interchanges became much more extensive after 1494, when France and Spain started fighting on Italian battlefields. The result of this development was that more and more northern Europeans began to learn what the Italians had been accomplishing (Spain's forces came not just from Spain but also from Germany and the Low Countries). Then, too, leading Italian thinkers and artists, like Leonardo, began to enter the retinues of northern kings or aristocrats. Accordingly, the Renaissance became an international movement and continued to be vigorous in the north even as it started to wane on its native ground.

The religious roots of the northern Renaissance

The Renaissance outside Italy, however, was by no means identical to the Renaissance within Italy. Above all, the northern European Renaissance was generally less secular. The main explanation for this difference lies in the different social and cultural traditions Italy and northern Europe had inherited from the Middle Ages. As we have seen, late-medieval Italy's vigorous urban society fostered a secular educational system that led, in union with a revival of classicism, to the evolution of new and more secular forms of expression. The north, on the other hand, had a less mercantile and urban-oriented economy than did Italy and no northern cities ever attained the political dominance of their surrounding countrysides as did Florence, Venice, and Milan. Instead, political power was coalescing around the nation-states (or in Germany the princedoms), whose rulers were willing until about 1500 to acknowledge the educational and cultural hegemony of the clergy. Consequently, northern European universities tended to specialize in theological studies, and the most prominent buildings in almost all the leading northern European towns were cathedrals.

Northern Christian humanism

Simply stated, the northern Renaissance was the product of an engrafting of certain Italian Renaissance ideals upon preexisting northern traditions. This can be seen very clearly in the case of the most prominent northern Renaissance intellectual movement, *Christian humanism.* Agreeing with Italian humanists that medieval Scholasticism was too ensnarled in logical hair-splitting to have any value for the practical conduct of life, northern Christian humanists nonetheless looked for practical guidance from purely biblical, religious precepts. Like their Italian counterparts, they sought wisdom from antiquity, but the antiquity they had in mind was Christian rather than pagan—the antiquity, that is, of the New Testament and the early Christian fathers. Similarly, northern Renaissance artists were moved by the accomplishments of Italian Renaissance masters to turn their backs on medieval Gothic artistic styles and to learn instead how to employ classical techniques. Yet these same artists depicted classical subject matter far less frequently than did the Italians, and inhibited by the greater northern European attachment to Christian asceticism, virtually never dared to portray completely undressed human figures.

Erasmus

Any discussion of northern Renaissance accomplishments in the realm of thought and literary expression must begin with the career of

Desiderius Erasmus (c. 1469–1536), "the prince of the Christian humanists." The illegitimate son of a priest, Erasmus was born near Rotterdam in Holland, but later, as a result of his wide travels, became in effect a citizen of all northern Europe. Forced into a monastery against his will when he was a teenager, the young Erasmus found there little religion or formal instruction of any kind but plenty of freedom to read what he liked. He devoured all the classics he could get his hands on and the writings of many of the Church fathers. When he was about thirty years of age, he obtained permission to leave the monastery and enroll in the University of Paris, where he completed the requirements for the degree of bachelor of divinity. But Erasmus subsequently rebelled against what he considered the arid learning of Parisian Scholasticism. In one of his later writings he reported the following exchange: "Q. Where do you come from? A. The College of Montaigu. Q. Ah, then you must be bowed down with learning. A. No, with lice." Erasmus also never entered into the active duties of a priest, choosing instead to make his living by teaching and writing. Ever on the lookout for new patrons, he changed his residence at frequent intervals, traveling often to England, staying once for three years in Italy, and residing in several different cities in the Netherlands before settling finally toward the end of his life in Basel, Switzerland. By means of a voluminous correspondence that he kept up with learned friends he made wherever he went, Erasmus became the leader of a northern European humanist coterie. And by means of the popularity of his numerous publications, he became the arbiter of "advanced" northern European cultural tastes during the first quarter of the sixteenth century.

Erasmus's literary accomplishments

Erasmus's many-sided intellectual activity may best be appraised from two different points of view: the literary and the doctrinal. As a Latin prose stylist, Erasmus probably was unequaled since the days of Cicero. Extraordinarily learned and witty, he reveled in tailoring his mode of discourse to fit his subject, creating dazzling verbal effects when appropriate, and coining puns that took on added meaning if one knew Greek as well as Latin. Above all, Erasmus excelled in the deft use of irony, poking fun at all and sundry, including himself. For example, in his *Colloquies* (Latin for "discussions") he had a fictional character lament the evil signs of the times thus: "kings make war, priests strive to line their pockets, theologians invent syllogisms, monks roam outside their cloisters, the commons riot, and Erasmus writes colloquies."

Erasmus's "philosophy of Christ"

But although Erasmus's urbane Latin style and wit earned him a wide audience for purely literary reasons, he by no means thought of himself as a mere entertainer. Rather, he intended everything he wrote to propagate in one form or another what he called the "philosophy of Christ." The essence of Erasmus's Christian humanist convictions was his belief that the entire society of his day was caught up in corruption and immorality as a result of having lost sight of the simple teachings of the Gospels. Accordingly, he offered to his contemporaries three different categories of publication: clever satires meant to show people the error of their ways, serious moral treatises meant to offer guidance toward proper Christian behavior, and scholarly editions of basic Christian texts.

Knight, Death, and Devil, by Albrecht Dürer (1471–1528). This engraving of 1513 illustrates the ideal figure of Erasmus's *Handbook of a Christian Knight.* The Steadfast Knight is able to advance through the world on his charger, his loyal dog at his side, despite intimations of mortality and the snares of the devil.

The satires and moral treatises

In the first category belong the works of Erasmus that are still most widely read today—*The Praise of Folly* (1509), in which he pilloried Scholastic pedantry and dogmatism as well as the ignorance and superstitious credulity of the masses; and the *Colloquies* (1518), in which he held up contemporary religious practices for examination in a more serious but still pervasively ironic tone. In such works Erasmus let fictional characters do the talking, and hence his own views can be determined only by inference. But in his second mode Erasmus did not hesitate to speak clearly in his own voice. The most prominent treatises in this second genre are the quietly eloquent *Handbook of the Christian Knight* (1503), which urged the laity to pursue lives of serene inward piety, and the *Complaint of Peace* (1517), which pleaded movingly for Christian pacifism.

Erasmus's edition of the New Testament

Despite this highly impressive literary production, Erasmus probably considered his textual scholarship his single greatest achievement. Revering the authority of the early Latin fathers Augustine, Jerome, and Ambrose, he brought out reliable editions of all their works, and revering the authority of the Bible most of all, he applied his extraordinary skills as a student of Latin and Greek to producing a reliable edition of the New Testament. After reading Lorenzo Valla's *Notes on the New Testament* in 1504, Erasmus became convinced that nothing was more imperative than divesting the New Testament of the myriad errors in transcription and translation that had piled up during the Middle Ages, for no one could be a good Christian without being certain of exactly what Christ's message really was. Hence he spent ten years studying and comparing all the best early Greek biblical manuscripts he could find in order to establish an authoritative text. Finally appearing in 1516, Erasmus's Greek New Testament, published together with explanatory notes and his own new Latin translation, was one of the most important landmarks of biblical scholarship of all time.

Sir Thomas More and *Utopia*

One of Erasmus's closest friends, and a close second to him in distinction among the ranks of the Christian humanists, was the Englishman Sir Thomas More (1478–1535). Following a successful career as a lawyer and as speaker of the House of Commons, in 1529 More was appointed lord chancellor of England. He was not long in this position, however, before he incurred the wrath of his royal master, King Henry VIII, because More, who was loyal to Catholic universalism, opposed the king's design to establish a national church under subjection to the state. Finally, in 1534, when More refused to take an oath acknowledging Henry as head of the Church of England, he was thrown into the Tower, and a year later met his death on the scaffold as a Catholic martyr. Much earlier, however, in 1516, long before More had any inkling of how his life was to end, he published the one work for which he will ever be best remembered, the *Utopia*. Creating the subsequently popular genre of "utopian fiction," More's *Utopia* expressed an Erasmian critique of contemporary society. Purporting to describe an ideal community on an imaginary island, the book is really an indictment of the glaring abuses of the time—of poverty undeserved and wealth unearned, of drastic punishments, religious persecution, and the senseless slaughter of war. The inhabitants of Utopia hold all their goods in common, work only six hours a day so that all may have leisure for intellectual pursuits, and practice the natural virtues of wisdom, moderation, fortitude, and justice. Iron is the precious metal "because it is useful," war and monasticism are abolished, and toleration is granted to all who recognize the existence of God and the immortality of the soul. Although More advanced no explicit arguments in his *Utopia* in favor of Christianity, he clearly meant to imply that if the "Utopians" could manage their society so well without the benefit of Christian Revelation, Europeans who knew the Gospels ought to be able to do even better.

Ulrich von Hutten and the *Letters of Obscure Men*

Whereas Erasmus and More were basically conciliatory in their temperaments and preferred to express themselves by means of wry understatements, a third representative of the Christian humanist movement, Erasmus's German disciple Ulrich von Hutten (1488–1523), was of a much more combative disposition. Dedicated to the cause of German cultural nationalism, von Hutten spoke up truculently to defend the "proud and free" German people against foreigners. But his chief claim to fame was his collaboration with another German humanist, Crotus Rubianus, in the authorship of the *Letters of Obscure Men* (1515), one of the most stinging satires in the history of literature. This was written as part of a propaganda war in favor of a scholar named Johann Reuchlin who wished to pursue his study of Hebrew writings, above all, the Talmud. When Scholastic theologians and the German inquisitor general tried to have all Hebrew books in Germany destroyed, Reuchlin and his party strongly opposed the move. After a while it became apparent that direct argument was accomplishing nothing, so Reuchlin's supporters resorted to ridicule. Von Hutten and Rubianus published a series of letters, written in intentionally bad Latin, purportedly by some of Reuchlin's Scholastic opponents from the University of Cologne. These opponents, given such ridiculous names as Goatmilker, Baldpate, and Dungspreader, were shown to be learned fools who paraded absurd religious literalism or grotesque erudition. Heinrich Sheep's-mouth, for example, the supposed writer of one of the letters, professed to be worried that he had sinned grievously by eating on Friday an egg that contained the yolk of a chick. The author of another boasted of his "brilliant discovery" that Julius Caesar could not have written Latin histories because he was too busy with his military exploits ever to have learned Latin. Although immediately banned by the Church, the letters circulated nonetheless and were widely read, giving ever more currency to the Erasmian proposition that Scholastic theology and Catholic religious ritual had to be set aside in favor of the most earnest dedication to the simple teachings of the Gospels.

The decline of Christian humanism

With Erasmus, More, and von Hutten the list of energetic and eloquent Christian humanists is by no means exhausted, for the Englishman John Colet (c. 1467–1519), the Frenchman Jacques Lefèvre d'Étaples (c. 1455–1536), and the Spaniards Cardinal Francisco Ximénez de Cisneros (1436–1517) and Juan Luis Vives (1492–1540) all made signal contributions to the collective enterprise of editing biblical and early Christian texts and expounding Gospel morality. But despite a host of achievements, the Christian humanist movement, which possessed such an extraordinary degree of international solidarity and vigor from about 1500 to 1525, was thrown into disarray by the rise of Protestantism and subsequently lost its momentum. The irony here is obvious, for the Christian humanists' emphasis on the literal truth of the Gospels and their devastating criticisms of clerical corruption and excessive religious ceremonialism certainly helped pave the way for the Protestant Reformation initiated by Martin Luther in 1517. But, as will be seen in the following chapter, very few Christian humanists were willing to go the whole route with Luther in rejecting the most fundamental principles on which Catholicism was based, and the few who did became such ardent Protestants that they lost all the sense of quiet irony that earlier had been a hallmark of Christian humanist expression. Most Christian humanists tried to remain within the Catholic fold while still espousing their ideal of nonritualistic inward piety. But as time went on, the leaders of Catholicism had less and less tolerance for them because lines were hardening in the war with Protestantism and any internal criticism of Catholic religious practices seemed like giving covert aid to "the enemy." Erasmus himself, who remained a Catholic, died early enough to escape opprobrium, but several of his less fortunate followers lived on to suffer as victims of the Spanish Inquisition.

Northern Renaissance poetry

Yet if Christian humanism faded rapidly after about 1525, the northern Renaissance continued to flourish throughout the sixteenth century in primarily literary and artistic forms. In France, for example, the highly accomplished poets Pierre de Ronsard (c. 1524–1585) and Joachim du Bellay (c. 1522–1560) wrote elegant sonnets in the style of Petrarch, and in England the poets Sir Philip Sidney (1554–1586) and Edmund Spenser (c. 1552–1599) drew impressively on Italian literary innovations as well. Indeed, Spenser's *The Faerie Queene,* a long chivalric romance written in the manner of Ariosto's *Orlando Furioso,* communicates as well as any Italian work the gorgeous sensuousness typical of Italian Renaissance culture.

François Rabelais

More intrinsically original than any of the aforementioned poets was the French prose satirist François Rabelais (c. 1494–1553), probably the best loved of all the great European creative writers of the sixteenth century. Like Erasmus, whom he greatly admired, Rabelais began his career in the clergy, but soon after taking holy orders he left his cloister to study medicine. Becoming thereafter a practicing physician in Lyons, Rabelais interspersed his professional activities with literary endeavors of one sort or another. He wrote almanacs, satires against quacks and astrologers, and burlesques of popular superstitions. But by far his most enduring literary legacy consists of his five volumes of "chronicles" published under the collective title of *Gargantua and Pantagruel.*

Rabelais' affirmativeness

Rabelais' account of the adventures of Gargantua and Pantagruel, originally the names of legendary medieval giants noted for their fabulous size and gross appetites, served as a vehicle for his lusty humor and his penchant for exuberant narrative as well as for the expression of his philosophy of naturalism. To some degree, Rabelais drew on the precedents of Christian humanism. Thus, like Erasmus, he satirized religious ceremonialism, ridiculed Scholasticism, scoffed at superstitions, and pilloried every form of bigotry. But much unlike Erasmus, who wrote in a highly cultivated classical Latin style comprehensible to only the most learned readers, Rabelais chose to address a far wider audience by writing in an extremely down-to-earth French, often loaded with the crudest vulgarities. Likewise, Rabelais wanted to avoid seeming in any way "preachy" and therefore eschewed all suggestions of moralism in favor of giving the impression that he wished merely to offer his readers some rollicking good fun. Yet, aside from the critical satire in *Gargantua and Pantagruel,* there runs through all five volumes a common theme of glorifying the human and the natural. For Rabelais, whose robust giants were really life-loving human beings writ very large, every instinct of humanity was healthy, provided it was not directed toward tyranny over others. Thus in his ideal community, the utopian "abbey of Thélème," there was no repressiveness whatsoever, but only a congenial environment for the pursuit of life-affirming, natural human attainments, guided by the single rule of "do what thou wouldst."

Northern Renaissance architecture

Were we to imagine what Rabelais' fictional abbey of Thélème might have looked like, we would do best to picture it as resembling one of the famous sixteenth-century French Renaissance châteaux built along the River Loire, for the northern European Renaissance had its own distinctive architecture that often corresponded in certain essentials to its literature. Thus, just as Rabelais recounted stories of medieval giants in order to express an affirmation of Renaissance values, so French architects who

Chambord. Built in the early sixteenth century by an Italian architect in the service of King Francis I of France, this magnificent Loire Valley château combines Gothic and Renaissance architectural traits.

The West Side of the Square Court of the Louvre, by Pierre Lescot. The enlargement of the Louvre, begun by Lescot in 1546, took more than a century to complete. Drawing on the work of Bramante (see p. 434), he achieved a synthesis of the traditional château and the Renaissance palace.

constructed such splendid Loire châteaux as Amboise, Chenonceaux, and Chambord, combined elements of the late-medieval French flamboyant Gothic style with an up-to-date emphasis on classical horizontality to produce some of the most impressively distinctive architectural landmarks ever constructed in France. Yet much closer architectural imitation of Italian models occurred in France as well, for just as Ronsard and du Bellay modeled their poetic style very closely on Petrarch, so Pierre Lescot, the French architect who began work on the new royal palace of the Louvre in Paris in 1546, hewed closely to the classicism of Italian Renaissance masters in constructing a facade that emphasized classical pilasters and pediments.

Albrecht Dürer

It only remains to treat the accomplishments of northern Renaissance painting, another realm in which links between thought and art can be discerned. Certainly the most moving visual embodiments of the ideals of Christian humanism were conceived by the foremost of northern Renaissance artists, the German Albrecht Dürer (1471–1528). From the purely technical and stylistic points of view, Dürer's greatest significance lies in the fact that, returning to his native Nuremberg after a trip to Venice in 1494, he became the first northerner to master Italian Renaissance techniques of proportion, perspective, and modeling. Dürer also shared with

Left: **St. Jerome in his Study**, by Dürer. St. Jerome, a hero for both Dürer and Erasmus, represents inspired Christian scholarship. Note how the scene exudes contentment, even down to the sleeping lion, which seems rather like an overgrown tabby cat. Right: **The Four Apostles**, by Dürer. This painting in two separate panels is a moving statement of the artist's intense religious faith.

Self-Portrait, by Dürer. Dürer was the first major artist to paint self-portraits at different phases of his life. Here, aged twenty-eight, he makes himself seem Christlike. Note also the prominent initials "A.D." under the date of the painting at the upper left.

Erasmus, by Hans Holbein the Younger (1497–1543). This portrait is generally regarded as the most telling visual characterization of "the prince of the Christian humanists."

contemporary Italians a fascination with reproducing the manifold works of nature down to the minutest details and a penchant for displaying various postures of the human nude. But whereas Michelangelo portrayed his naked David or Adam entirely without covering, Dürer's nudes are seldom lacking their fig leaves, in deference to more restrained northern traditions. Moreover, Dürer consistently refrained from abandoning himself to the pure classicism and sumptuousness of much Italian Renaissance art because he was inspired primarily by the more traditionally Christian ideals of Erasmus. Thus Dürer's serenely radiant *St. Jerome* expresses the sense of accomplishment that Erasmus or any other contemporary Christian humanist may have had while working quietly in his study, his *Knight, Death, and Devil* (p. 441) offers a stirring visual depiction of Erasmus's ideal Christian knight, and his *Four Apostles* intones a solemn hymn to the dignity and penetrating insight of Dürer's favorite New Testament authors, Saints Paul, John, Peter, and Mark.

The portraits of Hans Holbein

Dürer would have loved nothing more than to have immortalized Erasmus in a major painted portrait, but circumstances prevented him from doing this because the paths of the two men crossed only once, and after Dürer started sketching his hero on that occasion his work was interrupted by Erasmus's press of business. Instead, the accomplishment of capturing Erasmus's pensive spirit in oils was left to the second greatest of northern Renaissance artists, the German Hans Holbein the Younger

(1497–1543). As good fortune would have it, during a stay in England Holbein also painted an extraordinarily acute portrait of Erasmus's friend and kindred spirit Sir Thomas More, which enables us to see clearly why a contemporary called More "a man of . . . sad gravity; a man for all seasons." These two portraits in and of themselves point up a major difference between medieval and Renaissance culture because, whereas the Middle Ages produced no convincing naturalistic likenesses of any leading intellectual figures, Renaissance culture's greater commitment to capturing the essence of human individuality created the environment in which Holbein was able to make Erasmus and More come to life.

Sir Thomas More, by Hans Holbein the Younger.

Renaissance Developments in Music

The evolution of music as an independent art

Music in western Europe in the fifteenth and sixteenth centuries reached such a high point of development that it constitutes, together with painting and sculpture, one of the most brilliant aspects of Renaissance endeavor. While the visual arts were stimulated by the study of ancient models, music flowed naturally from an independent evolution that had been in progress in medieval Christendom. As earlier, leadership came from men trained in the service of the Church, but secular music was now valued as well, and its principles were combined with those of sacred music to bring a decided gain in color and emotional appeal. The distinction between sacred and profane became less sharp; most composers did not restrict their activities to either field. Music was no longer regarded merely as a diversion or an adjunct to worship but came into its own as a serious independent art.

Different sections of Europe vied with one another for musical leadership. As with the other arts, advances were related to the generous patronage afforded by the prosperous cities of Italy and the northern European princely courts. During the fourteenth century a pre- or early Renaissance musical movement called *Ars Nova* (new art) flourished in Italy and France. Its outstanding composers were Francesco Landini (c. 1325–1397) and Guillaume de Machaut (1300–1377). The madrigals, ballads, and other songs composed by the Ars Nova musicians testify to a rich secular art, but the greatest achievement of the period was a highly complicated yet delicate contrapuntal style adapted for ecclesiastical motets. Machaut, moreover, was the first known composer to provide a polyphonic version for the singing of the Mass.

Fourteenth-Century Monks in Song. From a fresco by Simone Martini.

The fifteenth century was ushered in by a synthesis of French, Flemish, and Italian elements in the ducal court of Burgundy. This music was melodious and gentle, but in the second half of the century it hardened a little as northern Flemish elements gained in importance. As the sixteenth century opened, Franco-Flemish composers appeared in every important court and cathedral all over Europe, gradually establishing regional-national schools, usually in attractive combinations of Flemish with German, Spanish, and Italian musical cultures. The various genres thus created show a close affinity with Renaissance art and poetry. In the second half of the sixteenth century the leaders of the nationalized Franco-Flemish style were the Flemish Roland de Lassus (1532–1594), the most versatile composer of the age, and the Italian Giovanni Pierluigi da Palestrina (c. 1525–1594), who specialized in highly intricate polyphonic choral music written for Catholic church services under the patronage of the popes in Rome. Music also flourished in sixteenth-century England, where the Tudor monarchs Henry VIII and Elizabeth I were active in patronizing the arts. Not only did the Italian madrigal, imported toward the end of the sixteenth century, take on remarkable new life in England, but songs and instrumental music of an original cast anticipated future developments on the Continent. In William Byrd (1543–1623) English music produced a master fully the equal of the great Flemish and Italian composers of the Renaissance period. The general level of musical proficiency seems to have been higher in Queen Elizabeth's day than in ours: the singing of part-songs was a popular pastime in homes and at informal social gatherings, and the ability to read a part at sight was expected of the educated elite.

Renaissance Singers. A relief by Luca della Robbia.

The greatness of the Renaissance musical achievement

In conclusion, it may be observed that while accomplishments in counterpoint were already very advanced in the Renaissance period, our modern harmonic system was still in its infancy, and thus there remained much room for experimentation. At the same time one should realize that the music of the Renaissance constitutes not merely a stage in evolution but a magnificent achievement in itself, with masters who rank among the great of all time. The composers Lassus, Palestrina, and Byrd are as truly representative of the artistic triumph of the Renaissance as are the painters Leonardo, Raphael, and Michelangelo. Their heritage, long neglected, has within recent years begun to be appreciated, and is now gaining in popularity as interested groups of musicians devote themselves to its revival.

THE SCIENTIFIC ACCOMPLISHMENTS OF THE RENAISSANCE PERIOD

The nonscientific orientation of Renaissance humanism

Some crucial accomplishments were made in the history of science during the sixteenth and early seventeenth centuries, but these were not preeminently the achievements of Renaissance humanism. The educational program of the humanists placed a low value on science because it seemed irrelevant to their aim of making people more eloquent and moral. Science for humanists like Petrarch, Leonardo Bruni, or Erasmus was part and parcel of the "vain speculation" of the Scholastics, which they attacked and held up to ridicule. Accordingly, none of the great scientists of the Renaissance period belonged to the humanist movement.

Renaissance foundations of modern science: (1) Neoplatonism

Nonetheless, at least two intellectual trends of the period did prepare the way for great new scientific advances. One was the currency of Neoplatonism. The importance of this philosophical system to science was that it proposed certain ideas, such as the central position of the sun and the supposed divinity of given geometrical shapes, that would help lead to crucial scientific breakthroughs. Although Neoplatonism seems very "unscientific" from the modern perspective because it emphasizes mysticism and intuition instead of empiricism or strictly rational thought, it helped scientific thinkers to reconsider older notions that had impeded the progress of medieval science; in other words, it helped them to put on a new "thinking cap." Among the most important of the scientists who were influenced by Neoplatonism were Copernicus and Kepler.

(2) A mechanistic view of the universe

A second trend that contributed to the advance of science was very different: the growth in popularity of a *mechanistic* interpretation of the universe. Renaissance mechanism owed its greatest impetus to the publication in 1543 of the works of the great Greek mathematician and physicist Archimedes. Not only were his concrete observations and discoveries among the most advanced and reliable in the entire body of Greek science, but Archimedes taught that the universe operates on the basis of mechanical forces, like a great machine. Because his view was diametrically opposed to the occult outlook of the Neoplatonists, who saw the world as inhabited by spirits and driven by supernatural forces, it took some time to gather strength. Nonetheless, mechanism did gain some very important late Renaissance adherents, foremost among whom was the Italian scientist Galileo. Ultimately mechanism played an enormous role in the development of modern science because it insisted upon finding observable and measurable causes and effects in the world of nature.

(3) The integration of theory and practice

One other Renaissance development that contributed to the rise of modern science was the breakdown of the medieval separation between the realms of theory and practice. In the Middle Ages Scholastically trained clerics theorized about the natural world but never for a moment thought of tinkering with machines or dissecting corpses because this empirical approach to science lay outside the Scholastic framework. On the other hand, numerous technicians who had little formal education and knew little of abstract theories had much practical expertise in various aspects of mechanical engineering. Theory and practice began to come together in the fifteenth century. One reason for this was that the highly respected Renaissance artists bridged both areas of endeavor: not only were they marvelous craftsmen, but they advanced mathematics and science when they investigated the laws of perspective and optics, worked out geometric methods for supporting the weight of enormous architectural domes, and studied the dimensions and details of the human body. In general, they helped make science more empirical and practically oriented than it had been earlier. Other reasons for the integration were the decline in prestige of the overly theoretical universities and a growing interest in alchemy and astrology among the leisured classes. Thus although alchemy and astrology are today properly dismissed as unscientific superstitions, in the sixteenth and seventeenth centuries their vogue led some wealthy

Design for Machinery, by Leonardo da Vinci

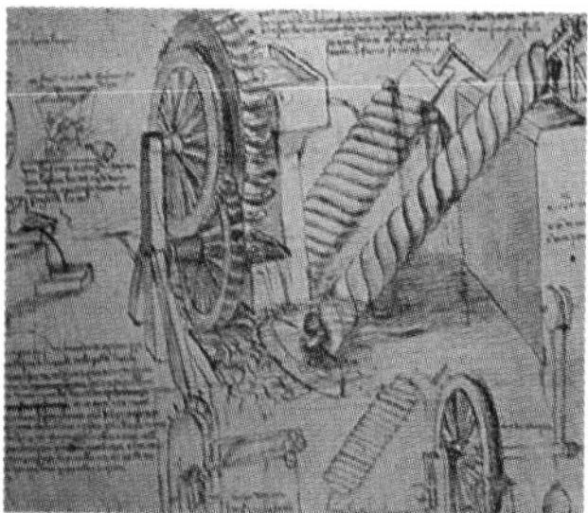

amateurs to start building laboratories and measuring the courses of the stars. Thereby scientific practice was rendered eminently respectable. When that happened modern science was on the way to some of its greatest triumphs.

The actual scientific accomplishments of the Renaissance period were international in scope. The achievement par excellence in astronomy—the formulation and proof of the heliocentric theory that the earth revolves around the sun—was primarily the work of the Pole Copernicus, the German Kepler, and the Italian Galileo. Until the sixteenth century the Ptolemaic theory that the earth stands still at the center of the universe went virtually unchallenged in western Europe. Nicholas Copernicus (1473–1543), a Polish clergyman who had absorbed Neoplatonism while studying in Italy, was the first to posit an alternative system. Copernicus made few new observations, but he thoroughly reinterpreted the significance of the old astronomical evidence. Inspired by the Neoplatonic assumptions that the sphere is the most perfect shape, that motion is more nearly divine than rest, and that the sun sits "enthroned" in the midst of the universe, "ruling his children the planets which circle around him," Copernicus worked out a new heliocentric theory. Specifically, in his *On the Revolutions of the Heavenly Spheres*—which he completed around 1530 but did not publish until 1543—he argued that the earth and the planets move around the sun in concentric circles. Copernicus's system itself was still highly imperfect: by no means did it account without difficulties for all the known facts of planetary motion. Moreover, it asked people to reject their common-sense assumptions: that the sun moves since they observe it moving across the sky and that the earth stands still since no movement can be felt. More serious, Copernicus contradicted passages in the Bible, such as the one wherein Joshua commands the sun to stand still. As a result of such problems, believers in Copernicus's heliocentric theory remained distinctly in the minority until the early seventeenth century.

The Ptolemaic System of the Universe

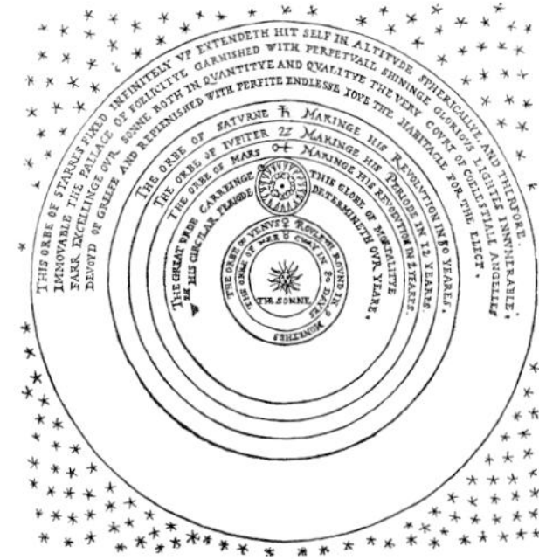
The Copernican System. A diagram devised by Copernicus himself. Note that the planetary orbits are still circular, as they were in the Ptolemaic system. It was Johann Kepler who proved that all the planets move in elliptical orbits.

It was Kepler and Galileo who ensured the triumph of Copernicus's revolution in astronomy. Johann Kepler (1571–1630), a mystical thinker who was in many ways more like a magician than a modern scientist, studied astronomy in order to probe the hidden secrets of God. His basic conviction was that God had created the universe according to mathematical laws. Relying on the new and impressively accurate astronomical observations of the Dane Tycho Brahe (1546–1601), Kepler was able to recognize that two assumptions about planetary motion that Copernicus had taken for granted were simply not in accord with the observable facts. Specifically, Kepler replaced Copernicus's view that planetary orbits were circular with his "First Law" that the earth and the other planets travel in elliptical paths around the sun, and he replaced Copernicus's belief in uniform planetary velocity with his own "Second Law" that the speed of planets varies with their distance from the sun. He also argued that magnetic attractions between the sun and the planets keep the planets in orbital motion. That approach was rejected by most seventeenth-century mechanistic scientists as being far too magical, but in fact it paved the way for the law of universal gravitation formulated by Isaac Newton at the end of the seventeenth century.

As Kepler perfected Copernicus's heliocentric system from the point of view of mathematical theory, so Galileo Galilei (1564–1642) promoted acceptance for it by gathering further astronomical evidence. With a telescope that he manufactured himself and raised to a magnifying power of thirty times, he discovered the moons of Jupiter and spots on the sun. He was also able to determine that the Milky Way is a collection of celestial bodies independent of our solar system and to form some idea of the enormous distances of the fixed stars. Though many held out against them, Galileo's discoveries gradually convinced the majority of scientists that the main conclusion of Copernicus was true. The final triumph of this idea is commonly called the *Copernican Revolution.* Few more significant events have occurred in the intellectual history of the world, for it overturned the medieval worldview and paved the way for modern conceptions of mechanism, skepticism, and the infinity of time and space. Some thinkers believe that it contributed also to the degradation of man, since it swept man out of his majestic position at the center of the universe and reduced him to a mere particle of dust in an endless cosmic machine.

Galileo

Leonardo da Vinci and Galileo as physicists

In the front rank among the physicists of the Renaissance were Leonardo da Vinci and Galileo. If Leonardo da Vinci had failed completely as a painter, his contributions to science would still entitle him to considerable fame. Not the least of these were his achievements in physics. Though he actually made few complete discoveries, his conclusion that "every weight tends to fall toward the center by the shortest way" contained the kernel of the law of gravity. In addition, he worked out the principles of an astonishing variety of inventions, including a diving board, a steam engine, an armored tank, and a helicopter. Galileo is especially noted as a physicist for his law of falling bodies. Skeptical of the traditional theory that bodies fall with a speed directly proportional to their weight, he taught that bodies dropped from various heights would fall at a rate of speed that increases with the square of the time involved. Rejecting the Scholastic notions of absolute gravity and absolute levity, he taught that these are purely relative terms, that all bodies have weight, even those which, like the air, are invisible, and that in a vacuum all objects would fall with equal velocity. Galileo seems to have had a broader conception of a universal force of gravitation than Leonardo da Vinci, for he perceived that the power that holds the moon in the vicinity of the earth and causes the satellites of Jupiter to circle around that planet is essentially the same as the force that enables the earth to draw bodies to its surface. He never formulated this principle as a law, however, nor did he realize all of its implications, as did Newton some fifty years later.

The record of Renaissance achievements in medicine and anatomy is also impressive. Attention must be called above all to the work of the German Theophrastus von Hohenheim, known as Paracelsus (1493–1541), the Spaniard Michael Servetus (1511–1553), and the Belgian Andreas Vesalius (1514–1564). The physician Paracelsus resembled Copernicus and Kepler in believing that spiritual rather than material forces governed the workings of the universe. Hence he was a firm believer in alchemy and astrology. Nevertheless, Paracelsus relied on observation for his knowledge of diseases and their cures. Instead of following the teachings of ancient authorities, he traveled widely, studying cases of illness in different environments and experimenting with many drugs. Above all, his insistence on the close relationship of chemistry and medicine foreshadowed and sometimes directly influenced important modern achievements in pharmacology and healing. Michael Servetus, whose major interest was theology but who practiced medicine for a living, discovered the pulmonary circulation of the blood. He described how the blood leaves the right chambers of the heart, is carried to the lungs to be purified, then returns to the heart and is conveyed from that organ to all parts of the body. But Servetus had no idea that the blood returned to the heart through the veins, a discovery that was made by the Englishman William Harvey in the early seventeenth century.

Michael Servetus. Over his subject's right shoulder, the portraitist has included a grim reminder of Servetus's fate: John Calvin ordered him burned at the stake in 1553.

Vesalius

Purely by coincidence the one sixteenth-century scientific treatise that came closest to rivaling in significance Copernicus's work in astronomy, Vesalius's *On the Structure of the Human Body,* was published in 1543, the same year that saw the issuance of Copernicus's *Revolutions of the Heavenly Spheres.* Vesalius was born in Brussels and studied in Paris but later migrated to Italy where he taught anatomy and surgery at the University of Padua. He approached his research from the correct point of view that much of ancient anatomical doctrine was in error. For him the ancient anatomy of Galen (so to speak, the Ptolemy of medicine) could be corrected only on the basis of direct observation. Hence he applied himself to frequent dissections of human corpses to see how various parts of the

Two Plates from Vesalius's *On the Structure of the Human Body.* On the left is a portrait of Vesalius himself displaying the sinews of the forearm. On the right we see "the human skeleton shown from the side." The presence of the sarcophagus with the Latin warning "we live by the spirit, all else will die" shows that scientific illustrations still had to be justified by moralistic sententiousness in the early-modern period.

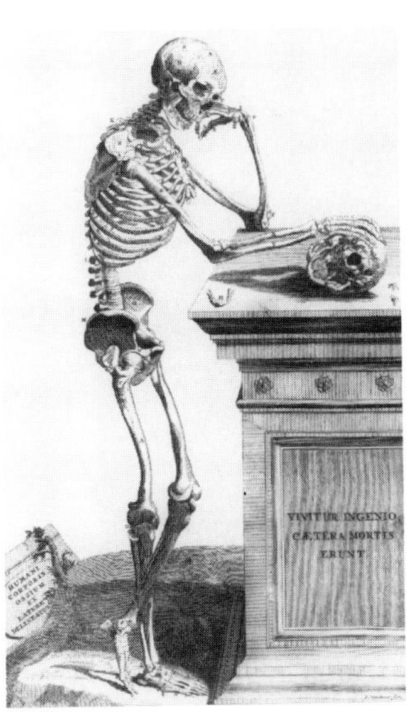

body actually appear when the skin covering is stripped away. Not content with merely describing in words what he saw, Vesalius then collaborated with an artist—Jan van Calcar, a fellow Belgian who had come to Italy to study under the Renaissance master Titian—in portraying his observations in detailed engravings. Art historians are uncertain as to whether van Calcar was directly inspired in executing his illustrations for Vesalius by knowledge of earlier anatomical drawings of Leonardo da Vinci, but even if he was not, he certainly relied on a cumulative tradition of expert anatomical depiction bequeathed to him by Italian Renaissance art. Gathered in Vesalius's *Structure of the Human Body* of 1543, van Calcar's plates offered a new map of the human anatomy just when Copernicus was laying out a new map of the heavens. Since Vesalius in the same work offered basic explanations of how parts of the body move and interact, in addition to discussing and illustrating how they look, he is often counted as the father of modern physiology as well as the father of modern anatomy. With his landmark treatise we come to a fitting end to our survey of Renaissance accomplishments inasmuch as his *Structure of the Human Body* represented the fullest degree of fruitful international intellectual exchange as well as the fullest merger of theory and practice, and art and science.

SUMMARY POINTS

- The Renaissance, a period of new trends in thought, literature, and the arts, first emerged in Italy from roughly 1350 to 1550, largely because of the relatively greater wealth and education of Italian society and Italy's stronger links with the Greek and Roman classical past.
- Renaissance thinkers and writers emphasized the importance of classical Greek and Roman works while developing more "modern" modes of thought and expression such as humanism.
- While many Italian Renaissance artists continued to create religious works for their Catholic patrons, some of them also celebrated naturalism, luxury, and, most notably, the beauty of the human form in purely secular works.
- Around 1500, intellectual exchanges and war brought Renaissance ideas to northern Europe. The northern European Renaissance was generally less secular, combining certain Italian Renaissance ideals with the social and cultural traditions of the North.
- The most prominent northern Renaissance authors and artists were Christian humanists who aimed to reform society by means of satire and advancing the ideals of the Gospels.

- Scientific advances made during the Renaissance period, especially the recognition that the earth and planets move around the sun and the mapping of human anatomy by means of dissection, became the basis for the development of modern science.

Selected Readings

Baker, Herschel, *The Image of Man: A Study of the Idea of Human Dignity in Classical Antiquity, the Middle Ages, and the Renaissance,* Cambridge, Mass., 1947. An engagingly written survey from the perspective of a modern liberal.

Baxandall, Michael, *Painting and Experience in Fifteenth Century Italy,* Oxford, 1972.

Benesch, Otto, *The Art of the Renaissance in Northern Europe,* rev. ed., New York, 1965.

Boas, Marie, *The Scientific Renaissance: 1450–1630,* New York, 1962. An excellent, straightforward survey.

Burckhardt, Jacob, *The Civilization of the Renaissance in Italy,* many eds. The nineteenth-century work that formulated the modern view of the Renaissance.

Burke, Peter, *Culture and Society in Renaissance Italy, 1420–1540,* New York, 1972.

Butterfield, Herbert, *The Origins of Modern Science,* rev. ed., New York, 1965. Clear and wide ranging. Shows how science developed from major changes in intellectual orientations.

Clark, Kenneth M., *Leonardo da Vinci,* 2d ed., Cambridge, 1952.

Crosby, Alfred W., *The Measure of Reality: Quantification and Western Society, 1250–1600,* New York, 1997. The most persuasive statement for an epochal shift that took place, roughly speaking, in the Renaissance period. Written with enormous verve and wit.

De Tolnay, Charles, *Michelangelo: Sculptor, Painter, Architect,* Princeton, 1975.

Fox, Alistair, *Thomas More: History and Providence,* Oxford, 1982.

Gilmore, Myron, *The World of Humanism, 1453–1517,* New York, 1952.

Gould, Cecil, *An Introduction to Italian Renaissance Painting,* London, 1957.

Hale, J. R., *Machiavelli and Renaissance Italy,* New York, 1960.

———, *Renaissance Europe: The Individual and Society, 1480–1520,* London, 1971. A different kind of survey that does not treat the great events but examines the quality of life.

Hay, Denys, ed., *The Renaissance Debate,* New York, 1965. A collection of readings on the question of how to define the Renaissance.

Herlihy, David, and Christiane Klapisch-Zuber, *Tuscans and Their Families,* New Haven, 1985. Best on the social context of Florentine culture.

Humfrey, Peter, *Painting in Renaissance Venice,* New Haven, 1995. The best introductory guide; useful for the student and tourist alike.

Kearney, Hugh, *Science and Change, 1500–1700,* New York, 1971. Argues that science progressed as the result of contributions made by three different "schools."

King, Margaret L., *Women of the Renaissance,* Chicago, 1991. Deals with women in all walks of life and in a variety of roles.

Kristeller, Paul O., *Eight Philosophers of the Italian Renaissance,* Stanford, 1964. Admirably clear.

———, *Renaissance Thought: The Classic, Scholastic, and Humanistic Strains,* New York, 1961. Very helpful in defining main trends of Renaissance thought.

Larner, John, *Culture and Society in Italy, 1290–1420,* New York, 1971.

Levey, M., *Early Renaissance (Style and Civilization),* Baltimore, 1967. Art history.

Panofsky, Erwin, *The Life and Art of Albrecht Dürer,* 4th ed., Princeton, 1955.

———, *Renaissance and Renascences in Western Art,* London, 1970. A difficult but rewarding attempt to distinguish the Italian Renaissance from its medieval predecessors.

Pope-Hennessy, John, *The Portrait in the Renaissance,* Princeton, 1966.

Ralph, Philip L., *The Renaissance in Perspective,* New York, 1973. Both a useful summary and a stimulus to thought.

Reese, Gustave, *Music in the Renaissance,* rev. ed., New York, 1959. The leading work on the subject.

Rice, Eugene F., Jr., *The Foundations of Early Modern Europe, 1460–1559,* 2d ed., New York, 1994.

———, *Saint Jerome in the Renaissance,* Baltimore, 1985. Employs a fascinating strategy for estimating Renaissance values.

Rocke, Michael, *Forbidden Friendships: Homosexuality and Male Culture in Renaissance Florence,* New York, 1996. Helps open a new area of study.

Seigel, Jerrold E., *Rhetoric and Philosophy in Renaissance Humanism,* Princeton, 1968. Treats a basic tension in the thought of early Renaissance thinkers.

Stechow, Wolfgang, *Northern Renaissance Art: 1400–1600,* Englewood Cliffs, N.J., 1966.

Tracy, James, *Erasmus: The Growth of a Mind,* Geneva, 1972. The best intellectual biography.

Whitfield, J. H., *A Short History of Italian Literature,* Baltimore, 1960.

Wittkower, Rudolf, *Architectural Principles in the Age of Humanism,* rev. ed., New York, 1965. An art-historical classic.

Source Materials

Alberti, Leon Battista, *The Family in Renaissance Florence,* tr. R. N. Watkins, Columbia, S.C., 1969.

Cassirer, Ernst, et al., eds., *The Renaissance Philosophy of Man,* Chicago, 1948. Leading works of Petrarch, Pico, etc.

Castiglione, B., *The Book of the Courtier,* tr. C. S. Singleton, New York, 1959.

Erasmus, D., *The Praise of Folly,* tr. J. Wilson, Ann Arbor, Mich., 1958.

———, *Ten Colloquies,* tr. C. R. Thompson, Indianapolis, 1957.

Kohl, Benjamin G., and Alison Andrews Smith, *Major Problems in the History of the Italian Renaissance,* Lexington, Mass., 1995. A good collection of readings that includes both documents and modern scholarly points of view.

Machiavelli, N., *The Prince,* tr. R. M. Adams, New York, 1976. In addition to Machiavelli's text, this edition provides related documents and an excellent selection of scholarly interpretations.

More, Sir Thomas, *Utopia,* tr. R. M. Adams, 2d. ed., New York, 1992. Provides background materials and selected scholarly interpretations as well as the text.

Rabelais, F., *Gargantua and Pantagruel,* tr. J. M. Cohen, Baltimore, 1955. A robust modern translation.

CHAPTER 14

EUROPE EXPANDS AND DIVIDES: OVERSEAS DISCOVERIES AND PROTESTANT REFORMATION

> Formerly we were at the end of the world, and now we are in the middle of it, with an unprecedented change in our fortunes.
>
> —HERNÁN PÉREZ DE OLIVA, addressing the city fathers of Cordova, Spain, 1524

> Since then your serene majesty and your lordships seek a simple answer, I will give it in this manner, neither horned nor toothed: unless I am convinced by the testimony of Scripture or by clear reason . . . I am bound by the Scripture I have quoted, and my conscience is captive to the Word of God. I cannot and I will not retract anything, since it is neither safe nor right to violate one's conscience. I cannot do otherwise, here I stand, may God help me. Amen.
>
> —MARTIN LUTHER, addressing the Diet of Worms, 1521

Overseas expansion of Spain and Portugal

MUCH AS THE CIVILIZATION of the Renaissance made fundamental contributions toward the shaping of the modern world, the two most dramatic developments in the transition from the Middle Ages to the early-modern period of western European history were the overseas ventures of Spain and Portugal and the Protestant Reformation. More or less overnight, these two developments changed the course of European history. Whereas European Christian civilization had been geographically self-contained throughout the thousand years of its prior history (excepting the relatively brief Crusade episode), in just a few decades, from 1488 to about 1520, Europeans sailed over the open seas to take commanding positions in Southeast Asia and lay claim to the whole Western Hemisphere. Ever since, the course of European history has been inseparable from interactions between events on the land mass of Europe and European engagements in the rest of the world.

The Protestant Reformation

But just when Europe was expanding it was also dividing. Up until the early sixteenth century, despite growing national differences, there remained a distinct European "Community of Christendom," presided over by the pope. Wherever one traveled one could hear the same Latin Mass, see infants baptized and couples wed according to the same ecclesiastical formulae, and receive blessings from priests who were all ordained by virtue of the same papal authority. As quickly as Europeans took hold of the world, however, they lost their spiritual unity. The Protestant Reformation initiated by Martin Luther in 1517, as well as the Catholic response to it, were both to have numerous progressive effects, but the most obvious immediate results were that Europe rapidly became divided along several different religious lines and that Europeans quickly started warring with one another in the name of faith.

A common theme of heroism

Although the overseas discoveries and Protestant Reformation were roughly contemporaneous, it is important to recognize that in their origins they had nothing directly to do with each other. The early explorers sailed prior to or in disregard of European religious dissensions, and the early Protestants gave little thought to the opening up of new trade routes or the discovery of continents. Yet there is warrant for treating the discoveries, the Protestant Reformation, and the Catholic Counter-Reformation all in the same chapter because their effects very quickly became interrelated, and also because all these movements were marked by incidents of great heroism. As Columbus sailed fearlessly into the unknown and Balboa viewed a new ocean, "silent, upon a peak in Darien," so Luther struggled fearlessly for a new understanding of "the justice of God" and the wounded soldier Ignatius Loyola found inspiration through inward "spiritual exercises," thereby opening up new vistas of their own.

The Overseas Discoveries and Conquests of Portugal and Spain

Western Europe seemingly on the defensive

At first glance the speed with which Europeans in the years around 1500 began to traverse the high seas appears bewildering and almost incomprehensible. With good reason most contemporaries perceived Christian civilization to be on the defensive, not the offensive, in the second half of the fifteenth century. In 1453 Constantinople, a hitherto impregnable barrier to Islamic advance, fell to the Turks, commanded by Sultan Muhammad II "the Conqueror"; Serbia was lost in 1459, and Albania followed in 1470. Most frightening of all to western Europeans was a Turkish landing on the Italian peninsula itself in 1480, which saw the city of Otranto occupied and half its inhabitants slaughtered. Only the death of Sultan Muhammad in 1481 caused the Turks to abandon their Italian foothold, but many feared that the "infidels" might soon return. In the midst of an unsuccessful attempt to organize united European resistance to the Turks, Pope Pius II (1458–1464) observed, "I see nothing good on the horizon."

Portuguese and Spanish conquests

Yet Pius II could hardly have been more wrong, for while Christians remained on the defensive against the Turks in eastern Europe until the later sixteenth century, Portuguese and Spanish sailing ships on the Atlantic horizon soon made Christians lords of much of the world. A few facts speak eloquently for themselves: in 1482 the Portuguese built a fortress at Elmina, in modern-day Ghana, which quickly dominated trade

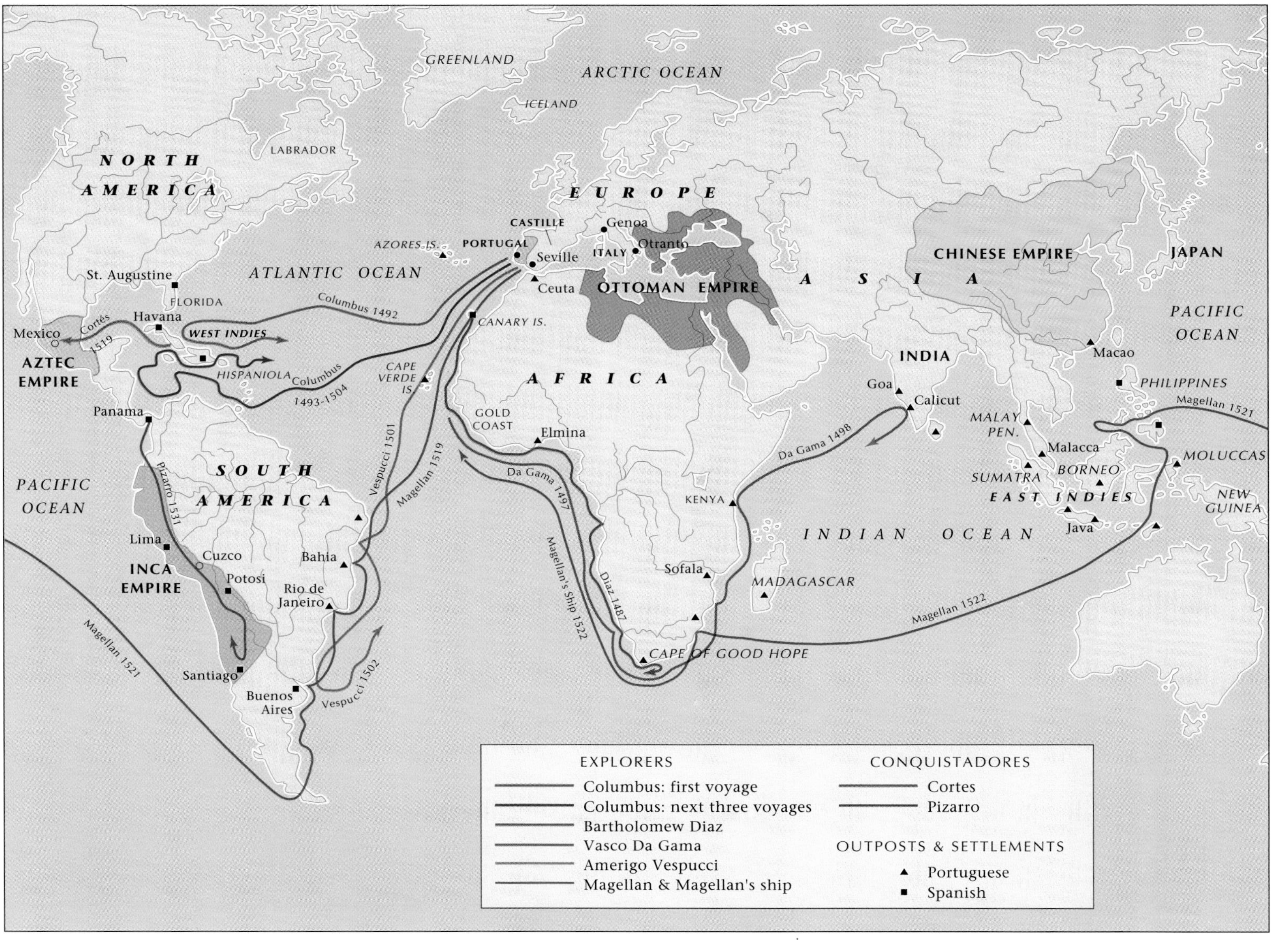

Overseas Exploration in the Fifteenth and Sixteenth Centuries

on the West African "Gold Coast"; in 1492 Columbus sighted the West Indies; in 1500 the Portuguese established their first trading base on the west coast of India; and in the two years from 1519 to 1521 the Spaniard Cortés seized hold of the Mexican empire of Montezuma.

Explanations for voyages: "Renaissance school"

How did this all happen so quickly? Two different schools of scholarly interpretation offer substantially different responses. Proponents of what may be called the "Renaissance school" point out that the Portuguese and Spanish voyages of discovery occurred at the same time as the spread of Renaissance civilization (Columbus was a direct contemporary of Leonardo da Vinci) and argue that European overseas expansion can only be explained as a manifestation of allegedly new Renaissance principles of curiosity and self-reliance in practical affairs. But this interpretation assumes falsely that medieval people were not curious and self-reliant. Proponents of the Renaissance school also call attention to the fact that many of the mariners who sailed for Portugal and Spain were Italian born, but here they dodge the reality that some Italian voyagers, like Columbus himself, came from Genoa, a city that hardly participated in Italian Renaissance civilization. More important, the Renaissance interpretation seems weak because the leading Italian Renaissance states did not patronize the voyages of discovery at all. Undeniably some bits of classical geographical knowledge acquired in Italy by Renaissance humanists strengthened the resolve of some explorers to pursue certain ocean routes, but otherwise the alternative to the Renaissance explanation, namely the view that the movement of overseas expansion came from medieval preparations, seems far preferable.

Medieval background to voyages: economic motives

Simply stated, the motives, the knowledge, and the wherewithal for the great discoveries were all essentially medieval. Certainly the single most dominant motive for the oceanic voyages was economic—the quest for Asiatic spices and other luxury goods. Pepper, cinnamon, nutmeg, ginger, and cloves could all be grown only in the tropical climates of South and Southeast Asia, and all were greatly prized throughout the High and Later Middle Ages because of their preservative qualities. (Imagine a civilization without refrigeration and one can easily understand why wealthy Europeans sought tangy spices to keep their food from putrifying and to relieve the monotony of salt.) In the Later Middle Ages, Asiatic spices, as well as luxury cloths and precious gems, reached European households by means of the enterprise of Arab, Venetian, and Genoese middlemen. But the costs were exorbitant, and a fortune was to be made by anyone who could go directly to the source by sea. (Land routes were out of the question because turbulent conditions in central Asia made them extremely unsafe; moreover, until the invention of railroads it normally was vastly more expensive to transport goods by land than by water.) Complementing the economic motives for overseas exploration were religious ones—hopes for converting unbaptized heathens and of finding imagined "lost Christians" in the East who might serve as allies against Islam. Needless to say, these hopes, like the lust for spices, flourished in the Middle Ages quite independently of the Italian Renaissance.

Medieval background to voyages: technology

Then too the most important knowledge that lay behind the great discoveries and also the technological means to execute them were as medieval as the motivations. The popular notion that Europeans before Columbus believed the earth to be flat is simply a mistake: it would have been impossible after the twelfth century to have found an educated person or a mariner who did not accept the fact that the earth is a sphere. Nor did this knowledge remain solely in the realm of theory. As early as 1291 two Genoese, the Vivaldi brothers, sailed out on the Atlantic with the aim of reaching the East Indies by a "westward route." Although the Vivaldis never came back, by the 1420s Portuguese mariners were sailing regularly back and forth on the Atlantic as far west as the Azores Islands. These Portuguese sailings offer proof that by about 1420 European shipbuilding and navigational technology were fully up to the challenge of reaching new continents. Since the Azores are one-third of the distance between Europe and America, from the strictly technological point of view any ship that could sail from Portugal to the Azores could have sailed all the way to the New World.

Timing of voyages of discovery

Why, then, was America not discovered much earlier than it actually was? Historians are at their greatest disadvantage in trying to explain things that did not happen, but two hypotheses may be offered. One relates to the fact that the fourteenth and fifteenth centuries were times of acute economic depression and political turmoil throughout western Europe. Since the major states of the Atlantic—France, England, and Castile (the dominant kingdom on the Spanish peninsula)—were all weakened by economic contraction and caught up in seemingly interminable wars, it is no wonder that none of them commissioned expensive and risky sailing ventures to the west. The second, less speculative hypothesis pertains to the change in routes pursued by Portugal, the one Atlantic state already deeply involved in ambitious seaward expeditions. After establishing colonies beginning around 1430 on the Atlantic islands of the Azores and Madeira that yielded a lucrative trade in sugar and wine, the Portuguese in the middle of the fifteenth century quite understandably turned their attention to exploring the coast of West Africa because Africa promised even greater wealth in gold and slaves. One Portuguese-African discovery led to another until the Cape of Good Hope was rounded in 1488 and the race for Asiatic spices that led to the most dramatic of European overseas exploits had begun. Thus seen from the perspective of late-medieval Portuguese sailing and trading history, the great discoveries look much less startlingly revolutionary than they do at first glance.

Portuguese voyages along African coastline

The fifteenth-century Portuguese voyages that served as the major connecting link to the dramatic achievements of the years around 1500 were commissioned by Portugal's Prince Henry "the Navigator" from 1418 until his death in 1460. Starting from an initial base of Ceuta in North Africa, Portuguese ships advanced steadily southward along the West African coastline, braving the ever-hotter sun and establishing forts and trading posts as they went. The extraordinary heroism of the sailors on

Prince Henry the Navigator, by a fifteenth-century Portuguese painter.

these ships can easily be appreciated from a mid-fifteenth-century account, according to which four galleys "were provisioned for several years and were away three years, but only one galley returned and even on that galley most of the crew had died. And those which survived could hardly be recognized as human. They had lost flesh and hair, the nails had gone from hands and feet. Their eyes were sunk deep in their heads and they were as black as Moors. They spoke of heat so incredible that it was a marvel that ships and crews were not burnt. They said also that they found no houses or land and they could sail no farther. The farther they sailed, so the sea became more furious and the heat grew more intense. They thought that the other ships had sailed too far and it was impossible that they should be able to return." But despite the terrifying tales that such crews told, new expeditions continually were sent out that ventured still farther.

Discovery of Cape of Good Hope

After Henry the Navigator's death in 1460 some slackening in the Portuguese enterprise ensued, but it regained vigor with the accession of King John II (1481–1495). Inasmuch as the Portuguese had already gained full control of the African Gold Coast and slave trade, they naturally began to set their sights on reaching the wealth of Asia. The literal as well as figurative turning point in this effort was the accidental rounding of the tip of southernmost Africa by the Portuguese captain Bartholomew Dias in 1488. Since Dias had accomplished this feat only by being caught in a gale, he pessimistically called this promontory the "Cape of Storms," but John II took a more optimistic view of the matter and renamed it the

Left: **The Tower of Belem.** Right: **A Portuguese Galleon.** The Tower of Belem, a fifteenth-century fort, stands at the beach where Vasco da Gama departed in 1497 to sail beyond the Cape of Good Hope to India. The galleon shown at the right is the sort of ship da Gama might have sailed in.

Cape of Good Hope. Furthermore, John resolved to organize a major naval expedition designed to travel beyond the cape all the way to India.

Vasco da Gama's voyage to India

After several delays John's successor, Manuel I (1495–1521), finally sent off a fleet in 1497 captained by Vasco da Gama which accomplished all that was planned. Da Gama's exploits were so heroic that they later became the basis for the Portuguese national epic, *The Lusiads.* After four months beyond sight of land the intrepid captain rounded Africa and sailed up Africa's east coast to Kenya. There he took on an Arab pilot and crossed the Indian Ocean to western India, where he loaded his ships with spices. Two years after his departure da Gama returned, having lost half of his fleet and one-third of his men. But his pepper and cinnamon were so valuable that they made his losses seem worthwhile. Now master of the quickest route to riches in the world, King Manuel swiftly capitalized on da Gama's accomplishment. After 1500, Portuguese trading fleets sailed regularly to India; by 1510 Portuguese arms had established full control of the western Indian coastline, and in 1511 Portuguese ships seized Malacca, a center of the spice trade on the Malay peninsula. The Cape of Good Hope thus had lived up to John II's prophetic name, and Europeans had arrived in Asia to stay.

Reasons for Columbus's westward voyage

The decision of the Spanish rulers to underwrite Columbus's famous voyage was directly related to the progress of the Portuguese ventures. Specifically, given the strong likelihood that the Portuguese would dominate the sea lanes leading to Asia by the east in the wake of Dias's successful return in 1488, the only alternative for Portugal's Spanish rivals was to finance someone bold enough to try to reach Asia by sailing west. The popular image of Christopher Columbus (1451–1506) as a visionary who struggled to convince hardened ignoramuses that the world was round does not bear up under scrutiny. In fact the sphericity of the earth was never in doubt. Rather the stubborn Genoese seaman who had settled in Spain erred in vastly underestimating the distance westward from Europe to Asia. Had Columbus known the actual circumference of the earth, even he would not have dared to set out because he would have realized that the distance to Asia, assuming no barriers lay between, was too great for ships of his day to traverse. America, then, was discovered as the result of a colossal error in reckoning, but when Columbus, with the financial backing of Queen Isabella of Castile, reached what we know today as the Bahamas and the island of Hispaniola in 1492 after only a month's sailing, he felt fully vindicated.

The "discovery" of America

Strictly speaking, it cannot be said that Columbus "discovered America" for two reasons. In the first place, experts now agree that the earliest Europeans to reach the Western Hemisphere were the Vikings, who touched on present-day Newfoundland, Labrador, and perhaps New England in voyages made around the year 1000. Second, Columbus did not "discover America" because he never knew what he found, dying in the conviction that all the new land he encountered was merely the outer reaches of Asia. Yet neither of these arguments diminishes Columbus's achievement because the Viking landings had been forgotten or ignored

Ferdinand and Isabella Worshiping the Virgin. A contemporary Spanish painting in which the royal pair are shown with two of their children in the company of saints from the Dominican order.

throughout Europe for hundreds of years, and if Columbus did not know what he had found, others, following immediately in his path, came to the realization soon thereafter. Although Columbus brought back no Asiatic spices from his voyage of 1492, he did return with some small samples of gold and a few natives who gave promise of entire tribes that might be enslaved. (Columbus and most of his contemporaries saw no conflict between converting heathen to Christianity and enslaving them.) This provided sufficient incentive for the Spanish monarchs, Ferdinand and Isabella, to finance three more expeditions by Columbus and many more by others. Soon the mainland was discovered as well as islands, and although Columbus refused until his death to accept the truth, the conclusion quickly became inescapable around 1500 that a new world had indeed been found. Since the recognition that Columbus had really stumbled upon a new world was most widely publicized by the Italian geographer Amerigo Vespucci (one of Vespucci's writings of 1504 was actually called *Mundus novus,* or "A new world"), the Western Hemisphere soon became known as "America" after Vespucci's first name.

The search for a "southwest passage" to Asia

One might well think that the discovery of a new world around 1500 would have delighted the Spanish rulers who had invested in it, but in fact it came as a disappointment, for with a major land mass standing between Europe and Asia, Spain hardly could hope to beat Portugal in the race for spices. Any remaining doubt that two vast oceans separated Europe from East Asia instead of one was completely removed when Vasco

Núñez de Balboa first viewed the Pacific from the Isthmus of Panama in 1513. Not entirely admitting defeat, Ferdinand and Isabella's grandson King Charles accepted Ferdinand Magellan's offer in 1519 to see whether a feasible route to Asia could be found by sailing around South America. But Magellan's voyage merely demonstrated that the perils of a journey around southern Argentina (to use the modern term) were simply too great: of five ships that left Spain, only one returned three years later, having been forced to circumnavigate the globe. Nor did Magellan himself live to tell this tale; instead, eighteen survivors out of an original crew of about two hundred and sixty-five reported that most of their comrades had died from scurvy or starvation and that their captain had been killed in a skirmish with East Indian natives. After this fiasco, all hope for an easy "southwest passage" came to an end.

The *conquistadores* plunder the New World for gold

But if it was disappointing that America loomed as a barricade to the East, it gradually became clear to the Spanish that the New World had much wealth of its own. From the start Columbus's gold samples, in themselves rather paltry, had nurtured hopes that somewhere in America gold might lie piled in ingots, and rumor fed rumor until a few Spanish adventurers really did strike it rich beyond their most avaricious imaginings. At first riches were seized by dint of astonishing feats of arms. In two years, from 1519 to 1521, the *conquistador* (Spanish for "conqueror") Hernando Cortés, commanding six hundred men, subjugated the Aztec empire of Mexico, which numbered a million, and carried off all of the Aztecs' fabulous wealth. Then in 1533 another conquistador, Francisco Pizarro, this time with a mere hundred eighty men, plundered the fabled

Left: **An Early Conception of the Encounter between Europeans and American Natives.** This sixteenth-century engraving shows how overseas voyaging was reconceived at home as a mixture of truth and fantasy. Note, for example, the small mermaid to the left of the ship in the foreground. Right: **The Silver Mines of Spanish America.** An engraving of 1602. Some of the miners work naked because of the heat.

gold of the Incas in conquering Peru. Cortés and Pizarro had the advantage of some cannon and a few horses, but they achieved their victories primarily by sheer courage, treachery, and cruelty. Never before or since have so few men won such great realms against such enormous odds, but seldom have men acted in so ruthless and repugnant a manner.

Economic rewards for Spain in the New World

Cortés, Pizarro, and their fellow conquistadores fought only for themselves, not for Spain, and knew only how to plunder, not produce, but by the middle of the sixteenth century the Spanish crown had taken governmental control of all Central and South America (except for Brazil, which was colonized by Portugal), and great quantities of bullion were being mined instead of stolen. Most important by far was the mining of silver. Gold, of course, was the more sought-after metal, but after quickly hauling off the stores of gold amassed for centuries by pre-Columbian native civilizations, the Spanish were able to mine only small quantities of gold on their own. On the other hand, however, they soon realized that in areas of Bolivia and Mexico they were sitting on some of the richest silver deposits in the world. By means of forced native labor and new refining techniques, Spanish overlords produced such vast quantities of silver bars by the second half of the sixteenth century that the relative lack of gold was hardly a disappointment. Since livestock farming and the production of sugar cane in sixteenth-century Spanish America also became highly remunerative, the Spanish crown could have had no regrets after all that Columbus had lighted on a new world instead of Asia.

Consequences of European expansion overseas

Subsequent chapters will pursue the continued development of European overseas expansion and colonization; here it may be said that the overall results of the initial achievements were extremely profound in their implications for at least three reasons. First of all, the emergence of Portugal and Spain as Europe's leading long-distance traders in the sixteenth century permanently moved the center of gravity of European economic power away from Italy and the Mediterranean toward the Atlantic. Deprived of their role as conduits of the spice trade, Genoa became Spain's banker and Venice gradually a tourist attraction, while Atlantic ports bustled with vessels and shone with wealth. Admittedly the prosperity of Portugal and Spain themselves was fleeting, but the other Atlantic states of England, Holland, and France quickly inherited their mantle as the preeminent economic powers of the world. Second, throughout Europe the increase in the circulation of imported goods and the sudden influx of bullion stimulated entrepreneurial ambitions. Simply stated, the opening of the seas around 1500 provided marvelous opportunities for people with ability and daring to make new fortunes, inspiring a sense that success could only lead to success. Thus not only were many enterprising individuals enriched overnight, but the entire sixteenth century was one of great overall economic growth for western Europe.

The human costs

Unfortunately, however, the enormous riches of America were gained only at an appalling cost in human life. Although exact figures are not available, of an estimated indigenous population of 250,000 on the island of Hispaniola in 1492, only about 500 remained in 1538. As for the

A Spaniard Kicking an Indian. As this sixteenth-century drawing makes clear, the Spanish treatment of the indigenous American population was brutal.

far larger population of Mexico, it declined by about 90 percent in the first century of Spanish rule. Not all this loss of life was due to conscious ruthlessness; on the contrary, huge numbers of natives died from epidemic diseases unwittingly introduced by the Europeans, for the natives had no biological resistance to such diseases as smallpox and measles. But countless innocent people also died as the result of merciless exploitation—literally worked so hard by their conquerors that they expired from exhaustion and lack of care. Thus, however much Europeans profited from their colonization of the New World, for the original inhabitants the appearance of the white man was an unmitigated disaster.

The Lutheran Upheaval

Impact of Martin Luther

While the Portuguese and Spanish were plowing new paths on the seas, a German monk named Martin Luther (1483–1546) was searching for a new path to the understanding of human salvation, and though his discoveries were made in the quiet of a monastic cell rather than in exotic tropical climes, their effects were no less momentous. Indeed, many Europeans felt the impact of Luther's activities much more immediately and directly than they did the results of the overseas discoveries, because once the German monk started attacking the institutions of the contemporary Roman Church he set off a chain reaction that rapidly resulted in the secession of much of northern Europe from the Catholic faith, thereby quickly affecting the religious practices of millions.

Martin Luther. A portrait by Lucas Cranach.

In searching for the causes of the Lutheran revolt in Germany, three main questions arise: (1) why Martin Luther instigated a break with Rome; (2) why large numbers of Germans rallied to his cause; and (3) why several ruling German princes decided to put the Lutheran Reformation into effect. Reduced to the barest essentials, the answers to these questions are that Luther broke with Rome because of his doctrine of justification by faith, that the German masses followed him primarily because they were swept away by a surge of religious nationalism, and that the princes were moved to institute Lutheranism particularly because of their quest for governmental sovereignty. Within a decade preacher, populace, and princes, so to speak, would all sing the same stirring Lutheran hymn, "A Mighty Fortress Is Our God," in the same church, but they arrived there by rather different paths.

Background to Luther's revolt: superstition

Many people think that Luther rebelled against Rome because he was disgusted with contemporary religious abuses—superstitions, frauds, and the offer of salvation for money—but that is only part of the story. Certainly abuses in Luther's day were grave and intensely upsetting to religious idealists. In a world beset by disease and disaster, frail mortals clutched at supernatural straws to seek health on earth and salvation in the hereafter. Some superstitious men and women, for example, believed that viewing the consecrated host during Mass in the morning would guard them from death throughout the day, and others neglected to swallow the consecrated wafer so that they could use it later either as a charm to ward off evil, an application to cure the sick, or a powder to fertilize their crops. Similarly, belief in the miraculous curative powers of saints was hard to distinguish from belief in magic. Every saint had his or her specialty: "for botches and biles, Cosmas and Damian; St. Clare for the eyes, St. Apolline for teeth, St. Job for pox. And for sore breasts, St. Agatha." Because alleged relics of Christ and the saints were thought to radiate marvelous healing effects, traffic in relics boomed. Even Luther's patron, the Elector Frederick the Wise of Saxony, had a collection in his castle church at Wittenberg of 17,000 relics, including a supposed remnant of Moses' burning bush, pieces of the holy cradle, shreds from Christ's swaddling clothes, and thirty-three fragments of the holy cross. As Mark Twain once sardonically observed, there were indeed enough splinters of the holy cross throughout Europe "to shingle a barn."

Background to Luther's revolt: sale of dispensations and indulgences

Superstitions and gross credulity were offensive enough to religious idealists of Luther's stamp, but worse still were the granting of dispensations and the promises of spiritual benefits for money. If a man wished to marry his first cousin, for example, he could usually receive an official religious dispensation allowing the marriage for a fee, and annulments of marriage—divorce being prohibited—similarly came for a price. Most malodorous to many, however, was the sale of indulgences. In Catholic theology, an indulgence is a remission by papal authority of all or part of the temporal punishment due for sin—that is, of the punishment in this life and in purgatory—after the guilt of sin itself is absolved by sacramental confession. As we have seen, the practice of granting indulgences began at the end of the eleventh century as an incentive for encouraging men to become Crusaders. Once it became accepted in the course of the High Middle Ages that the pope could dispense grace from a "Treasury of Merits" (that is, a storehouse of surplus good works piled up by Christ and the saints), it soon was taken for granted that the pope could promise people time off in purgatory as well. But indulgences originally granted for extraordinary deeds gradually came to be sold for money; by the fourteenth century, popes started granting indulgences to raise money for any worthy cause whatsoever, such as the building of cathedrals or hospitals; and finally, in 1476 Pope Sixtus IV (the patron of the Sistine Chapel) took the extreme step of declaring that the benefits of indulgences could be extended to the dead already in purgatory as well as to the living. Money, then, could not only save an individual from works of penance but could save his dearest relatives from eons of agonizing torments after death.

Luther's opposition to medieval Catholic theology

Certainly Luther was horrified by the traffic in relics and the sale of indulgences; indeed, the latter provided the immediate grounds for his revolt against Rome. But it was by no means the abuses of the late-medieval Church so much as medieval Catholic theology itself that he came to find thoroughly unacceptable. To this degree the term "Lutheran Reformation" is misleading, for Luther was no mere "reformer" who wanted to cleanse the current religious system of its impurities. Many Christian humanists of Luther's day were reformers in just that sense, but they shrank from breaking with Rome because they had no objections to the basic principles of medieval Catholicism. Luther, on the other hand, by no means would have been satisfied with the mere abolition of abuses because it was the entire Catholic "religion of works" that appalled him.

Augustinian and Thomistic theological systems

Simply stated, Luther preferred a rigorously Augustinian system of theology to a medieval Thomistic one. As we have seen, around the year 400 St. Augustine of Hippo had formulated an uncompromising doctrine of predestination which maintained that God alone determined human salvation and that His decisions concerning whom to save and whom to damn were made from eternity, without any regard to merits that given humans might show while sojourning on earth. This extreme view, however, left so little room for human freedom and responsibility that it was modified greatly in the course of the Middle Ages. Above all, during the twelfth and thirteenth centuries theologians such as Peter Lombard and St. Thomas Aquinas (hence the term "Thomistic") set forth an alternative belief system that rested on two assumptions: (1) since God's saving grace is not irresistible, humans can freely reject God's advances and encompass their own doom; and (2) since the sacramental ministrations of the Church communicate ongoing grace, they help human sinners improve their chances of salvation. Except in emergencies, none of the sacraments could be administered by persons other than priests. Having inherited this power from the Apostle Peter, the members of the clergy alone had the authority to cooperate with God in forgiving sins and in performing the miracle of the Eucharist, whereby the bread and wine were transubstantiated into the body and blood of the Saviour. In Luther's opinion, all of this amounted to saying that humans could be saved by the performance of "good works," and it was this theology of works that he became prepared to resist even unto death.

Luther's early life

Martin Luther may ultimately have been a source of inspiration for millions, but at first he was a terrible disappointment to his father. The elder Luther, who had risen from Thuringian German peasant stock and gained prosperity by leasing some mines, wanted his son Martin to rise still further. The father thus sent young Luther to the University of Erfurt to study law, but while there in 1505, possibly as the result of unconscious psychological rebellion against parental pressure, Martin shattered his father's ambitions by becoming a monk instead. Afterward, throughout his life Martin Luther was never to "put on airs." Even at the time of his greatest fame he lived simply and always expressed himself in the vigorous and sometimes earthy vernacular of the German peasantry.

Luther's search for religious solace

Like many great figures in the history of religion, Luther arrived at what he conceived to be the truth by a dramatic conversion experience. As a monk, young Martin zealously pursued all the traditional medieval means for achieving his own salvation. Not only did he fast and pray continuously, but he confessed so often that his exhausted confessor would sometimes jokingly say that his sins were actually trifling and that if he really wanted to have a rousing confession he should go out and do something dramatic like committing adultery. Yet, try as he might, Luther could find no spiritual peace because he feared that he could never perform enough good deeds to placate an angry God. But then, in 1513 he hit upon an insight that granted him relief and changed the course of his life.

Luther's "tower experience"

Luther's guiding insight pertained to the problem of the justice of God. For years he had worried that God seemed unjust in issuing commandments that He knew men would not observe and then in punishing them with eternal damnation for not observing them. But after becoming a professor of biblical theology at the University of Wittenberg (many members of his monastic order were expected to teach), Luther was led by the Bible to a new understanding of the problem. Specifically, while meditating on the words in the Psalms "deliver me in thy justice," it suddenly struck him that God's justice had nothing to do with His disciplinary power but rather with His mercy in saving sinful mortals through faith. As Luther later wrote, "At last, by the mercy of God, I began to understand the justice of God as that by which God makes us just in his mercy and through faith . . . and at this I felt as though I had been born again, and had gone through open gates into paradise." Since the fateful moment of truth came to Luther in the tower room of his monastery, it is customarily called his "tower experience."

Justification by faith

After that, everything seemed to fall into place. Lecturing on the Pauline Epistles in Wittenberg in the years immediately following 1513, Luther dwelled on the text of St. Paul to the Romans (1:17) "the just shall live by faith" to reach his central doctrine of "justification by faith alone."

Left: **Luther with Dove and Halo.** Right: **The Pope as a Donkey Playing Bagpipes.** Two specimens of Lutheran visual propaganda concerning "true" and "false" spiritual insight. While Luther was still a monk (before the end of 1522), the artist Hans Baldung Grien portrayed him as a saint whose insight into Scripture was sent by the Holy Spirit in the form of a dove. At right is a 1545 woodcut depicting Luther's view that "the pope can interpret Holy Scripture just as well as he can play the bagpipes."

By this he meant that God's justice does not demand endless good works and religious ceremonies, for no one can hope to be saved by his own works. Rather, humans are "justified"—that is, granted salvation—by God's saving grace alone, offered as an utterly unmerited gift to those predestined for salvation. Since this grace is manifested in humans in thoroughly passive faith, men and women are justified from the human perspective by faith alone. In Luther's view those who had faith would do good works anyway, but it was the faith that came first. Although the essence of this doctrine was not original but harked back to the predestinarianism of St. Augustine, it was new for Luther and the early sixteenth century, and if followed to its conclusions could only mean the dismantling of much of the contemporary Catholic religious structure.

The scandalous indulgence campaign

At first Luther remained merely an academic lecturer, teaching within the realm of theory, but in 1517 he was goaded into attacking some of the actual practices of the Church by a provocation that was too much for him to bear. The story of the indulgence campaign of 1517 in Germany is colorful but unsavory. The worldly Albert of Hohenzollern, archbishop of Mainz and youngest brother of the elector of Brandenburg, had sunk himself into enormous debt for several discreditable reasons. In 1513 he had to pay large sums for gaining dispensations from the papacy to hold the bishoprics of Magdeburg and Halberstadt concurrently, and for assuming these offices even though at twenty-three he was not old enough to be a bishop at all. Not satisfied, when the see of Mainz fell vacant in the next year, Albert gained election to that too, even though he knew full well that the costs of becoming archbishop of Mainz meant still larger payments to Rome. Obtaining the necessary funds by loans from the German banking firm of the Fuggers, he then struck a bargain with Pope Leo X (1513–1521): Leo proclaimed an indulgence in Albert's ecclesiastical territories on the understanding that half of the income raised would go to Rome for the building of St. Peter's Basilica, with the other half going to Albert so that he could repay the Fuggers. Luther did not know the sordid details of Albert's bargain, but he did know that a Dominican friar named Tetzel soon was hawking indulgences throughout much of northern Germany with Fugger banking agents in his train, and that Tetzel was deliberately giving people the impression that the purchase of an indulgence regardless of contrition in penance was an immediate ticket to heaven for oneself and one's dear departed in purgatory. For Luther this was more than enough because Tetzel's advertising campaign flagrantly violated his own conviction that people are saved by faith, not works. So on October 31, 1517, the earnest theologian offered to his university colleagues a list of ninety-five theses objecting to Catholic indulgence doctrine, an act by which the Protestant Reformation is conventionally thought to have begun.

Pope Leo X. Raphael's highly realistic portrait shows the pope with two of his nephews.

Luther's growing boldness

In circulating his theses within the University of Wittenberg, Luther by no means intended to bring his criticism of Tetzel to the public. Quite to the contrary, he wrote his objections in Latin, not German, and meant them only for academic dispute. But some unknown person translated and published Luther's theses, an event that immediately gained the hitherto obscure monk wide notoriety. Since Tetzel and his allies outside the university did not mean to let the matter rest, Luther was immediately called upon to withdraw his theses or defend himself. At that point, far from backing down, he became ever bolder in his attacks on the government of the Church. In 1519 in public disputation before throngs in Leipzig, Luther defiantly maintained that the pope and all clerics were merely fallible men and that the highest authority for an individual's conscience was the truth of Scripture. Thereupon Pope Leo X responded by charging the monk with heresy, and after that there was no alternative for Luther but to break with the Catholic faith entirely.

Theology of the new Lutheran faith

Luther's year of greatest creative activity came in 1520 when, in the midst of the crisis caused by his defiance, he composed three seminal pamphlets formulating the outlines of what was soon to become the new Lutheran religion. In these writings he put forth his three theological premises: justification by faith, the primacy of Scripture, and "the priesthood of all believers." We have already examined the meaning of the first. By the second he simply meant that the literal meaning of Scripture was always to be preferred to the accretions of tradition, and that all beliefs (such as purgatory) or practices (such as prayers to saints) not explicitly grounded in Scripture were to be rejected. As for "the priesthood of all believers," that meant that the true spiritual estate was the congregation of all the faithful rather than a society of ordained priests.

Practical implications

From these premises a host of practical consequences followed. Since works themselves had no intrinsic value for salvation, Luther discarded such formalized practices as fasts, pilgrimages, and the veneration of relics. Far more fundamentally, he recognized only baptism and the Eucharist as sacraments (in 1520 he also included penance, but he later changed his mind on this), denying that even these had any supernatural effect in bringing down grace from heaven. For Luther, Christ was really present in the consecrated elements of the Lord's Supper, but there was no grace in the sacrament as such; rather, faith was essential to render the Eucharist effective as a means for aiding the believer along the road to eternal life. To make the meaning of the ceremony clear to all, Luther proposed the substitution of German for Latin in church services, and, to emphasize that those who presided in churches had no supernatural authority, he insisted on calling them merely ministers or pastors rather than priests. On the same grounds there was to be no ecclesiastical hierarchy since neither the pope nor anyone else was a custodian of the keys to heaven, and monasticism was to be abolished since it served no purpose whatsoever. Finally, firm in the belief that no sacramental distinction existed between clergy and laity, Luther argued that ministers could marry, and in 1525 he took a wife himself.

The causes of Luther's success

Widely disseminated by means of the printing press, Luther's pamphlets of 1520 electrified much of Germany, gaining him broad and enthusiastic popular support. Because this response played a crucial role in determining the future success of the Lutheran movement—emboldening Luther to persevere in his defiance of Rome and soon encouraging some ruling princes to convert to Lutheranism themselves—it is appropriate before continuing to inquire into its causes. Of course, different combinations of motives influenced different people to rally behind Luther, but the uproar in Germany on Luther's behalf was above all a national religious revolt against Rome.

Susceptibility of Germany to religious rebellion

Ever since the High Middle Ages many people throughout Europe had resented the centralization of Church government because it meant the interference of a foreign papacy in local ecclesiastical affairs and the siphoning off of large amounts of ecclesiastical fees and commissions to the papal court. But certain concrete circumstances made Germany in the early sixteenth century particularly ripe for religious revolt. Perhaps greatest among these was the fact that the papacy of that time had clearly lost the slightest hint of apostolic calling but was demanding as much, if not more, money from German coffers as before. Although great patrons of the arts, successive popes of Luther's day were worldly scoundrels or

Pope Alexander VI: "Appearance and Reality." Even before Luther initiated the German Reformation, anonymous critics of the dissolute Alexander VI surreptitiously spread propaganda showing him to be a devil. By lifting a flap one can see Alexander transformed into a monster who proclaims "I am the pope."

sybarites. As Luther was growing up, the Borgia pope, Alexander VI (1492–1503), bribed the cardinals to gain the papacy, used the money raised from the jubilee of 1500 to support the military campaigns of his son Cesare, and was so lascivious in office that he was suspected of seeking the sexual favors of his own daughter Lucrezia. Alexander's scandals could hardly have been outdone, but his successor, Julius II (1503–1513), was interested only in enlarging the papal states by military means (a contemporary remarked that he would have gained the greatest glory had he been a secular prince), and Leo X, the pope obliged to deal with Luther's defiance, was a self-indulgent esthete who, in the words of a modern Catholic historian, "would not have been deemed fit to be a doorkeeper in the house of the Lord had he lived in the days of the apostles." Under such circumstances it was bad enough for Germans to know that fees sent to Rome were being used to finance papal politics and the upkeep of luxurious courts, but worse still to pay money in the realization that Germany had no influence in Italian papal affairs, for Germans, unlike the French or Spaniards, were seldom represented in the College of Cardinals and practically never gained employment in the papal bureaucracy.

Anti-Roman propaganda

In this overheated atmosphere, reformist criticisms voiced by both traditional clerical moralists and the new breed of Christian humanists exacerbated resentments. Ever since about 1400 prominent German critics of the papacy had been saying that the entire Church needed to be reformed "in head and members," and as the fifteenth century progressed, anonymous prophecies mounted to the effect, for example, that a future heroic emperor would reform the Church by removing the papacy from Rome to the Rhineland. Then in the early years of the sixteenth century, Christian humanists began to chime in with their own brand of satirical propaganda. Most eloquent of these humanists, of course, was Erasmus, who lampooned the religious abuses of his day with no mercy for Rome. Thus in *The Praise of Folly,* first published in 1511 and frequently reprinted, Erasmus stated that if popes were ever forced to lead Christlike lives, no one would be more disconsolate than themselves, and in his more daring pamphlet called *Julius Excluded,* published anonymously in Basel in 1517, the clever satirist imagined a dialogue held before the pearly gates in which Pope Julius II was locked out of heaven by Saint Peter because of his transgressions.

The role of German universities

In addition to the objective reality of a corrupt Rome and the circulation of anti-Roman propaganda, a final factor that made Germany ready for revolt in Luther's time was the belated growth of universities. All revolts need to have some general headquarters; universities were the most natural centers for late-medieval religious revolts because assembled there were groups of enthusiastic, educated young people accustomed to

Left: **The Seven-Headed Papal Beast.** Right: **The Seven-Headed Martin Luther.** Around 1530 a Lutheran cartoon was circulated in Germany which turned the papacy into the "seven-headed beast" of the Book of Revelation. The papacy's "seven heads" consist of pope, cardinals, bishops, and priests; the sign on the cross reads "for money, a sack full of indulgences"; and a devil is seen emerging from an indulgence treasure chest below. In response, a German Catholic propagandist showed Luther as Revelation's "beast." In the Catholic conception Luther's seven heads show him by turn to be a hypocrite, a fanatic, and "Barabbas"—the thief who should have been crucified instead of Jesus.

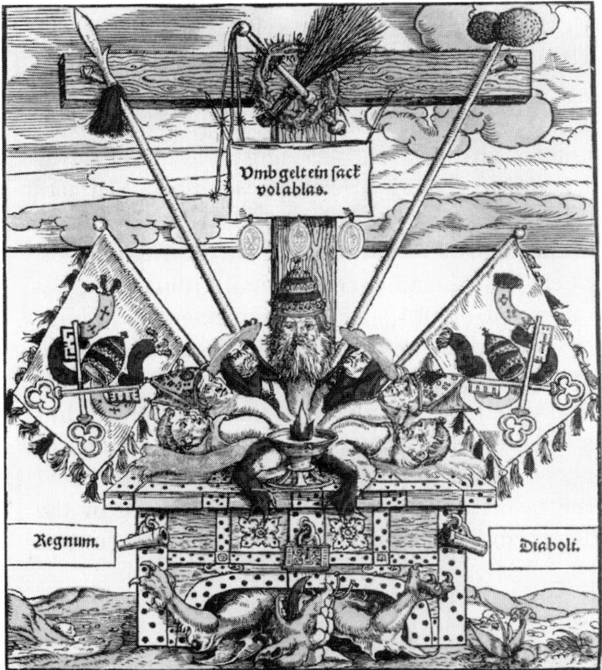

working together, who could formulate doctrinal positions with assurance, and who could turn out militant manifestoes at a moment's notice. There had hardly been any universities on German soil until a spate of new foundations between 1450 and 1517 provided many spawning grounds for cultural nationalism and religious resistance to Rome. Luther's own University of Wittenberg was founded as late as 1502, but soon enough it became the cradle of the Lutheran Reformation, offering immediate support to its embattled hero.

Luther's inflammatory pamphlets

Still, of course, there would have been no Lutheran Reformation without Luther himself, and the daring monk did the most to enflame Germany's dry kindling of resentment in his pamphlets of 1520, above all in one entitled *To the Christian Nobility of the German Nation*. Here, in highly intemperate colloquial German, Luther stated that "if the pope's court were reduced ninety-nine percent it would still be large enough to give decisions on matters of faith"; that "the cardinals have sucked Italy dry and now turn to Germany"; and that, given Rome's corruption, "the reign of Antichrist could not be worse." Needless to say, once this savage indictment was lodged, everyone wanted to read it. Whereas the average press run of a printed book before 1520 had been one thousand copies, the first run of *To the Christian Nobility* was four thousand, and these copies were sold out in a few days with many more thousands following.

Luther and his Wife, Katherine von Bora. Portraits done by Cranach for the couple's wedding in 1525.

Meanwhile, even as Luther's pamphlets were selling so rapidly, his personal drama riveted all onlookers. Late in 1520 the German rebel responded to Pope Leo X's bull ordering his recantation by casting not only the bull but all of Church law as well onto a roaring bonfire in front of a huge crowd. With the lines so drawn, events moved with great swiftness. Since in the eyes of the Church Luther was now a stubborn heretic, he was formally "released" to his lay overlord, the Elector Frederick the Wise, for proper punishment. Normally this would have meant certain death at the stake, but in this case Frederick was loath to silence the pope's antagonist. Instead, claiming that Luther had not yet received a fair hearing, he brought him early in 1521 to be examined by a "diet" (that is, a formal assembly) of the princes of the Holy Roman Empire convening in the city of Worms.

Luther vs. the Emperor Charles V

At Worms the initiative lay with the presiding officer, the newly elected Holy Roman emperor, Charles V. Charles was not a German; rather, as a member of the Habsburg family by his paternal descent, he had been born and bred in his ancestral holding of the Netherlands. Since he additionally held Austria, and as grandson of Ferdinand and Isabella by his maternal descent, all of Spain, including extensive Spanish possessions in Italy and America, the emperor had primarily international rather than national interests and surely thought of Catholicism as a sort of glue necessary to hold together all his far-flung territories. Thus from the start Charles had no sympathy for Luther, and since Luther fearlessly refused to back down before the emperor, declaring instead "here I stand," it soon became clear that Luther would be condemned by the power of state as well as by the Church. But just then Frederick the Wise

The Emperor Charles V. Two views by the Venetian painter Titian depict the emperor in a grandiose military pose, and the emperor as a sage ruler.

once more intervened, this time by arranging a "kidnapping" whereby Luther was spirited off to the elector's castle of the Wartburg and kept out of harm's way for a year.

Lutheranism triumphant

Thereafter Luther was never again to be in danger of his life. Although the Diet of Worms did issue an edict shortly after his disappearance proclaiming him an outlaw, the Edict of Worms was never properly enforced because, with Luther in hiding, Charles V soon left Germany to conduct a war with France. In 1522 Luther returned in triumph from the Wartburg to Wittenberg to find that all the changes in ecclesiastical government and ceremonial he had called for had spontaneously been put into practice by his university cohorts. Then, in rapid succession, several German princes formally converted to Lutheranism, bringing their territories with them. Thus by around 1530 a considerable part of Germany had been brought over to the new faith.

Importance of German princely support

At this point, then, the last of the three major questions regarding the early history of Lutheranism arises: why did German princes, secure in their own powers, heed Luther's call by establishing Lutheran religious practices within their territories? The importance of this question should by no means be underestimated, because no matter how much intense admiration Luther may have gained from the German populace, his cause surely would have failed had it not been for the decisive intervention and support of constituted political authorities. There had been heretics aplenty in Europe before, but most of them had died at the stake,

The Wartburg. The castle in central Germany where Luther was hidden after the Diet of Worms.

as Luther would have without the intervention of Frederick the Wise. And even had Luther lived, spontaneous popular expressions of support alone would not have succeeded in instituting Lutheranism because they could easily have been put down by the power of the state. In fact, although in the early years of Luther's revolt he was more or less equally popular throughout Germany, only in those territories where rulers formally established Lutheranism (mostly in the German north) did the new religion prevail, whereas in the others Luther's sympathizers were forced to flee, face death, or conform to Catholicism. In short, the word of the prince in religious matters was simply law.

Economic motives for adoption of Lutheranism

The distinction between populace and princes should not obscure the fact that the motivations of both for turning to Lutheranism were similar, with the emphasis on the princely side being the search for sovereignty. As little as common people liked the idea of money being pumped off to Rome, princes liked it less: German princes assembled at the Diet of Augsburg in 1500, for example, went so far as to demand the refund of some of the ecclesiastical dues sent to Rome on the grounds that Germany was being drained of its coin. Since such demands fell on deaf ears, many princes were quick to perceive that if Lutheranism were adopted, ecclesiastical dues would not be sent to support ill-loved foreigners and much of the savings would directly or indirectly wind up in their own treasuries.

Political motives

Yet the matter of taxation was only part of the larger issue of the search for absolute governmental sovereignty. Throughout Europe the major political trend in the years around 1500 was toward making the state dominant in all walks of life, religious as well as secular. Hence rulers sought to control the appointments of Church officials in their own realms and to limit or curtail the independent jurisdictions of Church courts. Because the papacy in this period had to fight off the attacks of internal clerical critics who wanted recognition of the "conciliarist" principle that general councils of prelates rather than popes should rule the Church (see Chapter 12), many popes found it advantageous to sign concordats with the most powerful rulers in the West—primarily the kings of France and Spain—whereby they granted the rulers much of the sovereignty they wanted in return for support against conciliarism. Thus in 1482 Sixtus IV conceded to the Spanish monarchs Ferdinand and Isabella the right to name candidates for all major Church offices. In 1487 Innocent VIII consented to the establishment of a Spanish Inquisition controlled by the crown, giving the rulers extraordinary powers in dictating religious policies. And in 1516, by the Concordat of Bologna, Leo X granted the choice of bishops and abbots in France to the French king, Francis I. In Germany, however, primarily because there was no political unity, princes were not strong enough to gain such concessions. Hence what they could not achieve by concordats some decided to wrest by force.

The princes seize their opportunity

In this determination they were fully abetted by Luther. Certainly as early as 1520 the fiery reformer recognized that he could never hope to institute new religious practices without the strong arm of the princes behind him, so he implicitly encouraged them to disappropriate the wealth of the Catholic Church as an incentive for creating a new order. At first the princes bided their time, but when they realized that Luther had enormous public support and that Charles V would not act swiftly to defend the Catholic faith, several moved to introduce Lutheranism into their territories. Motives of personal piety surely played their role in individual cases, but the common aim of gaining sovereignty by naming pastors, cutting off fees to Rome, and curtailing the jurisdiction of Church courts probably was the most decisive consideration. Given the added fact that under Lutheranism monasteries could be shut down and their wealth simply pocketed by the princes, the temptation to ordain the new faith regardless of any deeply felt religious convictions must have been overwhelming.

Luther's growing political and social conservatism

Once safely ensconced in Wittenberg as the protégé of princes, Luther began to express ever more vehemently his own profound conservatism in political and social matters. In a treatise of 1523, *On Temporal Authority*, he insisted that "godly" rulers must always be obeyed in all things and that even ungodly ones should never be actively resisted since tyranny "is not to be resisted but endured." Then, in 1525, when peasants throughout Germany rose up in economic revolt against their landlords—in some places encouraged by the religious radical Thomas Müntzer (c. 1490–1525), who urged the use of fire and sword against "ungodly" powers—Luther responded with intense hostility. In his vituperative pamphlet of 1525, *Against the Thievish, Murderous Hordes of Peasants*, he went so far as to urge all who could to hunt the rebels down like mad dogs, to "strike, strangle, stab secretly or in public, and remember that nothing can be more poisonous than a man in rebellion." Once the princes had ruthlessly put down the Peasants' Revolt of 1525, the firm alliance of Lutheranism with the powers of the state helped ensure social peace. In fact, after the bloody punishment of the peasant rebels there was never again to be a mass lower-class uprising in Germany.

Luther's last years

As for Luther himself, he concentrated in his last years on debating with younger, more radical religious reformers and on offering spiritual counsel to all who sought it. Never tiring in his amazingly prolific literary activity, he wrote an average of one treatise every two weeks for twenty-five years. To the end Luther was unswerving in his faith: on his deathbed in 1546 he responded to the question "Will you stand firm in Christ and the doctrine which you have preached?" with a resolute "Yes."

THE SPREAD OF PROTESTANTISM

Other forms of Protestantism

Originating as a term applied to Lutherans who "protested" an action of the German Imperial Diet of 1529, the word "Protestant" has come to mean any non-Catholic, non–Eastern Orthodox Christian. In fact, it was soon applied to non-Lutherans after 1529 because the particular form of Protestantism developed by Luther did not prove to be popular much beyond its native environment of Germany. To be sure, Lutheranism was instituted as the state religion of Denmark, Norway, and Sweden by official decrees of rulers made during the 1520s, and remains the religion of most Scandinavians today. But elsewhere early Protestantism spread in different forms. In England a break with Rome was introduced from above, just as in Germany and Scandinavia, but since Lutheranism appeared too radical for the reigning English monarch, a compromise variety of religious belief and practice, subsequently known as Anglicanism (in America, Episcopalianism), was worked out. On the other extreme, Protestantism spread more spontaneously in several cities of Switzerland and there soon took on forms that were more radical than Lutheranism.

Henry VIII, by Hans Holbein.

England's receptivity to Protestantism

Although the original blow against the Roman Church in England was struck by the head of the government, King Henry VIII (1509–1547), in breaking with Rome the English monarch had the support of most of his subjects. For this there were at least three reasons. First, in England, as in Germany, many people in the early sixteenth century had come to resent Rome's corruption and the siphoning off of the country's wealth to pay for the worldly pursuits of foreign popes. Second, England had already been the scene of protests against religious abuses voiced by John Wyclif's heretical followers, known as Lollards. The Lollards had indeed been driven underground in the course of the fifteenth century, but numbers of them survived in pockets throughout England, where they promulgated their anticlerical ideas whenever they could and enthusiastically welcomed Henry VIII's revolt from Rome when it occurred. Finally, soon after the outbreak of the Reformation in Germany, Lutheran ideas were brought into England by travelers and by the circulation of printed tracts. As early as 1520 a Lutheran group was meeting at the University of Cam-

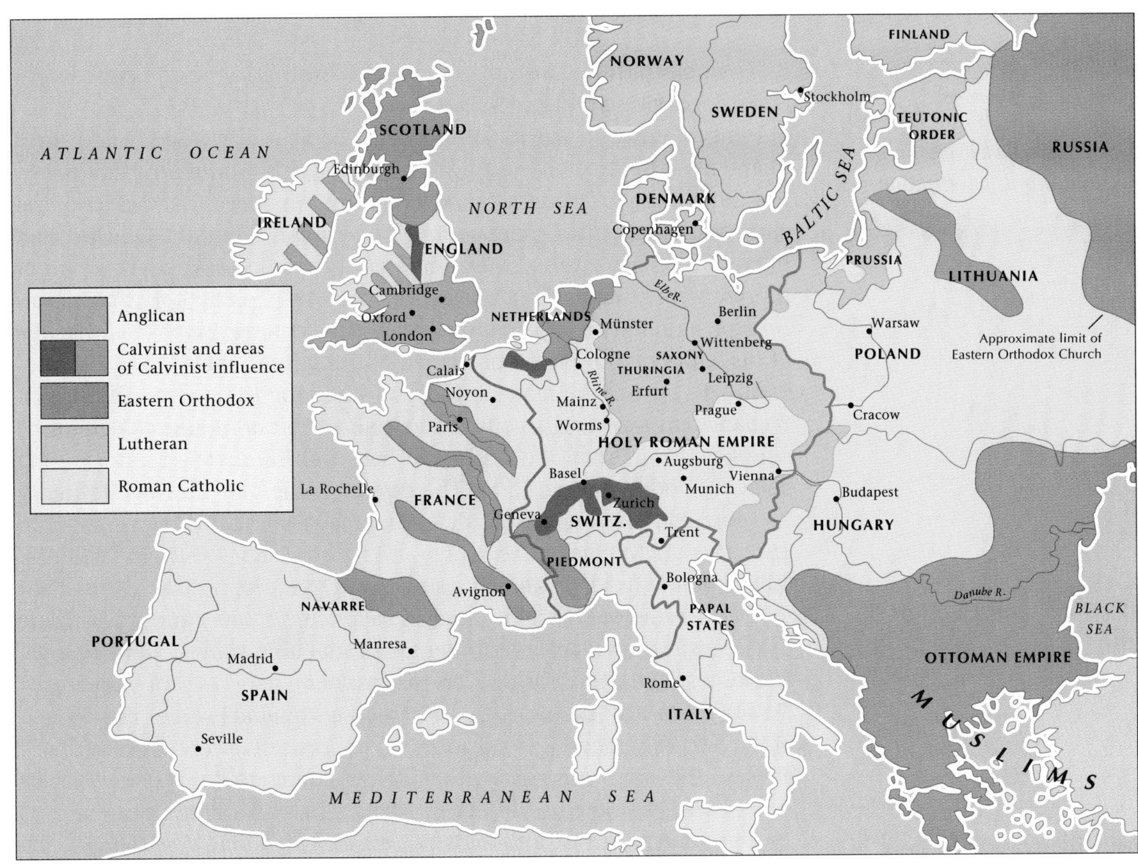

Religious Situation in Europe, c. 1560

bridge, and Lutheranism began to gain more and more clandestine strength as the decade progressed.

King Henry VIII's divorce suit

Despite all this, England would not have broken with Rome had Henry VIII not commanded it because of his marital difficulties. By 1527 the imperious Henry had been married for eighteen years to Ferdinand and Isabella's daughter, Catherine of Aragon, yet all the offspring of this union had died in infancy, save only Princess Mary. Since Henry needed a male heir to preserve the succession of his Tudor dynasty, and since Catherine was now past childbearing age, Henry had good reasons of state to break his marriage bonds, and in 1527 an immediate incentive arose when he became infatuated with the dark-eyed lady-in-waiting Anne Boleyn, who would not give in to his advances out of wedlock. The king hence appealed to Rome to allow the severance of his marriage to Catherine so that he could make Anne his queen. Although the law of the Church did not sanction divorce, it did provide that a marriage might be annulled if proof could be given that conditions existing at the time of the wedding had made it unlawful. Accordingly, the king's representatives, recalling that Queen Catherine had previously been married to Henry's older brother, who had died shortly after the ceremony was performed, rested their case on a passage from the Bible that pronounced it "an unclean thing" for a man to take his brother's wife and cursed such a marriage with childlessness (Leviticus 20:31).

Henry's break with Rome

Henry's suit put the reigning pope, Clement VII (1523–1534), in a quandary. If he rejected the king's appeal, England would probably be lost to Catholicism, for Henry was indeed firmly convinced that the Scriptural curse had blighted his chances of perpetuating his dynasty. On the other hand, if the pope granted the annulment he would provoke the wrath of the Emperor Charles V, Catherine of Aragon's nephew, for Charles was then on a military campaign in Italy and threatening the pope with a loss of his temporal power. There seemed nothing for Clement to do but procrastinate. At first he made a pretense of having the question settled in England, empowering his officials to hold a court of inquiry to determine whether the marriage to Catherine had been legal. Then, after a long delay, he suddenly transferred the case to Rome. But meanwhile Henry had lost patience and resolved to take matters into his own hands. In 1531 the king obliged an assembly of English clergy to recognize him as "the supreme head" of the English Church. Next he induced Parliament to enact a series of laws abolishing all payments to Rome and proclaiming the English Church an independent, national unit, subject alone to royal authority. With the passage of the parliamentary Act of Supremacy (1534), declaring "the King's highness to be supreme head of the Church of England [having] the authority to redress all errors, heresies, and abuses," the last bonds uniting the English Church to Rome had been cut.

The conservative nature of the Henrician Reformation

Yet these enactments did not yet make England a Protestant country. Quite to the contrary, although the break with Rome was followed by the dissolution of all of England's monasteries, with their lands and wealth being sold to many of the king's loyal supporters, the system of Church government by bishops (episcopalianism) was retained, and the English Church remained Catholic in doctrine. The Six Articles promulgated by Parliament in 1539 at Henry VIII's behest left no room for doubt as to official orthodoxy: oral confession to priests, masses for the dead, and clerical celibacy were all confirmed; moreover, the Catholic doctrine of the Eucharist was not only confirmed but its denial made punishable by death.

The consolidation of English Protestantism

Nonetheless, the influence of Protestantism in the country at large at this time was growing, and during the reign of Henry's son, Edward VI (1547–1553), Protestantism gained the ascendancy. Since the new king (born from Henry's union with his third wife, Jane Seymour) was only nine years old when he inherited the crown, it was inevitable that the policies of the government should be dictated by powers behind the throne. The men most active in this regard were Thomas Cranmer, archbishop of Canterbury, and the dukes of Somerset and Northumberland, who successfully dominated the regency. Inasmuch as all three had strong Protestant leanings, the creeds and ceremonies of the Church of England were soon drastically altered. Priests were permitted to marry; English was substituted for Latin in the services; the veneration of images was abolished; and new articles of belief were drawn up repudiating all sacraments except baptism and communion and affirming the Lutheran doctrine of justification by faith alone. Thus when the youthful Edward died in 1553 it seemed as if England had definitely entered the Protestant camp.

Popular resistance to Queen Mary's Catholicism

But Edward's pious Catholic successor, Mary (1553–1558), Henry VIII's daughter by Catherine of Aragon, thought otherwise. Because Mary associated the revolt against Rome with her mother's humiliations and her own removal from direct succession, upon coming to the throne she attempted to return England to Catholicism. Not only did she restore the celebration of the Mass and the rule of clerical celibacy, but she prevailed upon Parliament to vote a return to papal allegiance. Yet her policies ended in failure for several reasons. First of all, not only had Protestantism by then already sunk in among the English masses, but many of the leading families that had profited from Henry VIII's dissolution of the monasteries had become particularly committed to Protestantism because a restoration of Catholic monasticism would have meant the loss of their newly acquired wealth. Then too, although Mary ordered the burning of Cranmer and a few hundred Protestant extremists, these executions were insufficient to wipe out religious resistance—indeed, Protestant propaganda about "Bloody Mary" and the "fires of Smithfield" soon actually hardened resistance to Mary's rule, making her seem like a vengeful persecutor. But perhaps the most serious cause of Mary's failure was her marriage to Philip, Charles V's son and heir to the Spanish throne. Although the marriage treaty stipulated that in the event of Mary's death Philip could not succeed her, patriotic Englanders never trusted him. Hence when the queen allowed herself to be drawn by Philip into a war with France on Spain's behalf, in which England lost Calais, its last foothold on the European continent, many English people

The Burning of Archbishop Cranmer. In this Protestant conception an ugly Catholic, "Friar John," directs the proceedings, while the martyred Cranmer repeats Christ's words, "Lord, receive my spirit." John Foxe's *Book of Martyrs* (1563), in which this engraving first appeared, was an extraordinarily successful piece of English Protestant propaganda.

Philip of Spain and Mary Tudor. This double portrait was done on the occasion of the royal marriage.

became highly disaffected. No one knows what might have happened next because death soon after ended Mary's troubled reign.

The Elizabethan religious settlement

The question of whether England was to be Catholic or Protestant was thereupon settled definitively in favor of Protestantism by Elizabeth I (1558–1603). Daughter of Anne Boleyn and one of the most capable and popular monarchs ever to sit on the English throne, Elizabeth was predisposed in favor of Protestantism by the circumstances of her father's marriage as well as by her upbringing. But Elizabeth was no zealot, and wisely recognized that supporting radical Protestantism in England posed the danger of provoking bitter sectarian strife because some English people were still Catholic and others resisted extremism. Accordingly, she presided over what is customarily known as "the Elizabethan compromise." By a new Act of Supremacy (1559), Elizabeth repealed all of Mary's Catholic legislation, prohibited the exercise of any authority by foreign religious powers, and made herself "supreme governor" of the English Church—a more Protestant title than Henry VIII's "supreme head" insofar as most Protestants believed that Christ alone was the head of the Church. At the same time she accepted most of the Protestant ceremonial reforms instituted in the reign of her brother Edward. On the other hand, she retained Church government by bishops and left the definitions of some controversial articles of the faith, especially the meaning of the Eucharist, vague enough so that all but the most extreme Catholics and Protestants could accept them. Long after Elizabeth's death this settlement remained in effect. Indeed, as a result of the Elizabethan compromise, the Church of England today is broad enough to include such diverse elements as the "Anglo-Catholics," who differ from Roman Catholics only in rejecting papal supremacy, and the "low-church" Anglicans, who are as thoroughgoing in their Protestant practices as members of most other modern Protestant denominations.

Protestantism in Switzerland

If the Elizabethan compromise came about through royal decision-making, in Switzerland more spontaneous movements to establish Protestantism resulted in the victory of greater radicalism. In the early sixteenth century Switzerland was neither ruled by kings nor dominated by all-powerful territorial princes; instead, prosperous Swiss cities were either independent or on the verge of becoming so. Hence when the leading citizens of a Swiss municipality decided to adopt Protestant reforms no one could stop them, and Protestantism in Switzerland could usually take its own course. Although religious arrangements tended at first to vary in detail from city to city, the three main forms of Protestantism that emerged in Switzerland from about 1520 to 1550 were Zwinglianism, Anabaptism, and, most fateful for Europe's future, Calvinism.

Zwinglianism

Zwinglianism, founded by Ulrich Zwingli (1484–1531) in Zürich, was the most moderate form of the three. Although Zwingli was at first a somewhat indifferent Catholic priest, around 1516 he was led by close study of the Bible, as Luther was, to conclude that contemporary Catholic theology and religious observances conflicted with the Gospel. But he did not speak out until Luther set the precedent. Then, in 1522, Zwingli started attacking the authority of the Catholic Church in Zürich, and soon all Zürich and much of northern Switzerland had accepted his leadership in instituting reforms that closely resembled those of the Lutherans in Germany. Yet Zwingli did differ from Luther concerning the theology of the Eucharist: whereas Luther believed in the real presence of Christ's body, for Zwingli Christ was present merely in spirit. Thus for him the sacrament conferred no grace at all and was to be retained merely as a memorial service. This disagreement may seem trifling to many of us today, but at the time it was enough to prevent Lutherans and Zwinglians from uniting in a common Protestant front. Fighting independently, Zwingli fell in battle against Catholic forces in 1531, whereupon his successors in Zürich lost their leadership over Swiss Protestantism, and the Zwinglian movement was soon after absorbed by the far more radical Protestantism of John Calvin.

Anabaptism

Before that happened, however, the phenomenon of *Anabaptism* briefly flared up in Switzerland and also Germany. The first Anabaptists were members of Zwingli's circle in Zürich, but they quickly broke with him around 1525 on the issues of infant baptism and their conception of an exclusive Church of true believers. The name Anabaptism means "rebaptism," and stemmed from the Anabaptists' conviction that baptism should be administered only to adults because infants have no understanding of the meaning of the service. Yet this was only one manifestation of the Anabaptists' main belief that men and women were not born into any church. Although Luther and Zwingli alike taught the "priesthood of all believers," they still insisted that everyone, believer or not, should attend services and be part of one and the same officially instituted religious community. But the Anabaptists were sectarians or separatists, firm in the conviction that joining the true Church should be the product of an individual's inspired decision. For them, one had to follow the guidance of one's own "inner light" in opting for Church membership, and the rest of the world could go its own way. Since this was a hopelessly apolitical doctrine in an age when almost everyone assumed that Church and state were inextricably connected, Anabaptism was bound to be anathema to the established powers, both Protestant and Catholic. Yet in its first few years the movement did gain numerous adherents in Switzerland and Germany, above all because it appealed to sincere religious piety in calling for extreme simplicity of worship, pacifism, and strict biblical morality.

The turning point at Münster

Unhappily for the fortunes of Anabaptism, an unrepresentative group of Anabaptist extremists managed to gain control of the German city of Münster in 1534. These zealots combined sectarianism with millenarianism, or the belief that God wished to institute a completely new order of justice and spirituality throughout the world before the end of time. Determined to help God bring about this goal, the extremists attempted to turn Münster into a new Jerusalem. A former tailor named John of Leyden assumed the title of "King of the New Temple," proclaiming himself the successor of David. Under his leadership Anabaptist religious practices were made obligatory, private property was abolished, the sharing of goods was introduced, and even polygamy was instituted on the grounds

The Anabaptists' Cages, Then and Now. After the three Anabaptist leaders who had reigned in Münster for a year were executed in 1535, their corpses were prominently displayed in cages hung from a tower of the marketplace church. As can be seen from the photo on the right, the bones are now gone but the iron cages remain to this very day as a grisly reminder of the horrors of sixteenth-century religious strife.

of Old Testament precedents. Nonetheless, Münster succumbed to a siege by Catholic forces little more than a year after the Anabaptist takeover, and the new David, together with two of his lieutenants, was put to death by excruciating tortures. Given that Anabaptism had already been proscribed by many governments, this episode thoroughly discredited the movement, and all of its adherents were subjected to ruthless persecution throughout Germany, Switzerland, and wherever else they could be found. Among the few who survived were some who banded together in the Mennonite sect, named for its founder, the Dutchman Menno Simons (c. 1496–1561). This sect, dedicated to the pacifism and simple "religion of the heart" of original Anabaptism, has continued to exist until the present. Various Anabaptist tenets were also revived later by religious groups such as the Quakers and different Baptist and Pentecostal sects.

John Calvin

A year after events in Münster sealed the fate of Anabaptism, a twenty-six-year-old French Protestant named John Calvin (1509–1564), who had fled to the Swiss city of Basel to escape religious persecution, published the first version of his *Institutes of the Christian Religion,* a work that was soon to prove the most influential systematic formulation of Protestant theology ever written. Born in Noyon in northern France, Calvin originally had been trained for the law and around 1533 was studying the Greek and Latin classics while living off the income from a Church benefice. But then, as he later wrote, while he was "obstinately devoted to the superstitions of Popery," a stroke of light made him feel that God was extricating him from "an abyss of filth," and he thereupon opted for becoming a Protestant theologian and propagandist. Though some of these details resemble the early career of Luther, there was one essential difference: namely, whereas Luther was always a highly volatile personality, Calvin remained a cool legalist through and through. Thus, whereas Luther never wrote systematic theology but only responded to given problems as they arose or as the impulse struck him, Calvin resolved in his *Institutes* to set forth all the principles of Protestantism comprehensively, logically, and consistently. Accordingly, after several revisions and enlargements (the definitive edition appeared in 1559), Calvin's *Institutes of the Christian Religion* became the most theologically authoritative statement of basic Protestant beliefs and the nearest Protestant equivalent of St. Thomas Aquinas's *Summa Theologica.*

John Calvin. A recently discovered anonymous portrait.

Calvin's theology

The hallmark of Calvin's rigorous theology in the *Institutes* is that he started with the omnipotence of God and worked downward. For Calvin the entire universe is utterly dependent on the will of the Almighty, who created all things for His greater glory. Because of the original fall from grace, all human beings are sinners by nature, bound hand and foot to an evil inheritance they cannot escape. Nevertheless, the Lord for reasons of His own has predestined some for eternal salvation and damned all the rest to the torments of hell. Nothing that human beings may do can alter their fate; their souls are stamped with God's blessing or curse before they are born. But this does not mean, in Calvin's opinion, that Christians should be indifferent to their conduct on earth. If they are among the elect, God will implant in them the desire to live right. Upright conduct is a sign, though not an infallible one, that whoever practices it has been chosen to sit at the throne of glory. Public profession of faith and participation in the sacrament of the Lord's Supper are also presumptive signs of election to be saved. But most of all, Calvin required an active life of piety and morality as a solemn obligation resting upon members of the Christian commonwealth. For him, good Christians should conceive of themselves as chosen instruments of God with a mission to help in the fulfillment of His purposes on earth, striving not for their souls' salvation but for the glory of God. In other words, Calvin clearly did not encourage his readers to sit with folded hands, serene in the knowledge that their fate was sealed.

Calvin as Seen by His Friends and His Enemies. Above, an idealized contemporary portrait of Calvin as a pensive scholar. Below, a Catholic caricature in which Calvin's face is a composite made from fish, a toad, and a chicken drumstick.

Although Calvin always acknowledged a great theological debt to Luther, his religious teachings differed from those of the Wittenberg reformer in several essentials. First of all, Luther's attitude toward proper Christian conduct in the world was much more passive than Calvin's: for the former, the good Christian should merely endure the trials of this life in suffering, whereas for the latter the world was to be mastered in unceasing labor for God's sake. Second, Calvin's religion was more legalistic and more nearly an Old Testament faith than Luther's. This can be illustrated in the attitude of the two men toward Sabbath observance. Luther's conception of Sunday was similar to that which prevails among most Christians today. He insisted, of course, that his followers attend church, but he did not demand that during the remainder of the day they refrain from all pleasure or work. Calvin, on the other hand, revived the Jewish Sabbath with its strict tabus against anything faintly resembling worldliness. Finally, the two men differed explicitly on basic matters of Church government and ritual. Although Luther broke with the Catholic system of a gradated ecclesiastical hierarchy, Lutheran district superintendents were not unlike bishops, and Luther also retained a good many features of Catholic worship such as altars and vestments (special clothing for the clergy). In contrast, Calvin rejected everything that smacked to him of "popery." Thus he argued for the elimination of all traces of the hierarchical system, instead having congregational election of ministers and assemblies of ministers and "elders" (laymen responsible for maintaining proper religious conduct among the faithful) governing the entire Church. Further, he insisted on the barest simplicity in church services, prohibiting all ritual, vestments, instrumental music, images, and stained-glass windows. When these teachings were put into practice, Calvinist services became little more than "four bare walls and a sermon."

Not content with mere theory, Calvin was intent upon putting his teachings into practice. Sensing an opportunity to influence the course of events in the French-speaking Swiss city of Geneva, then in the throes of combined political and religious upheaval, he moved there late in 1536 and began preaching and organizing immediately. In 1538 his activities caused him to be expelled, but in 1541 he returned, with the city coming to be completely under his sway. Under Calvin's guidance Geneva's government became theocratic. Supreme authority in the city was vested in a "Consistory," made up of twelve lay elders and five ministers. (Although

Services in a Calvinist Church. "Four bare walls and a sermon."

Calvinist militancy

Calvin himself was seldom the presiding officer, he usually dominated the Consistory's decisions until his death in 1564.) In addition to passing on legislation submitted to it by a congregation of ministers, the Consistory had as its main function the supervision of morals. This activity was carried out not merely by the punishment of antisocial conduct but by a persistent snooping into the private life of every individual. Geneva was divided into districts, and a committee of the Consistory visited every household without warning to check on the habits of its members. Even the mildest forms of self-indulgence were strictly prohibited. Dancing, card-playing, attending the theater, working or playing on the Sabbath—all were outlawed as works of the devil. Innkeepers were forbidden to allow anyone to consume food or drink without first saying grace, or to permit any patron to stay up after nine o'clock. Needless to say, penalties were severe. Not only were murder and treason classified as capital crimes, but also adultery, "witchcraft," blasphemy, and heresy. During the first four years after Calvin gained control in Geneva, there were no fewer than fifty-eight executions out of a total population of only 16,000.

The spread of Calvinism

As reprehensible as such interference in the private sphere may seem today, in the middle of the sixteenth century Calvin's Geneva appeared as a beacon of thoroughgoing Protestantism to thousands throughout Europe. Calvin's disciple John Knox, for example, who brought Calvinism to Scotland, declared that Geneva under Calvin was "the most perfect school of Christ that ever was on earth since the days of the Apostles." Accordingly, many foreigners flocked to the "perfect school" for refuge or instruction, and usually returned home to become ardent proselytizers of Calvinism. Moreover, since Calvin himself thought of Geneva as a staging point for bringing Calvinism to France and the rest of the world, he encouraged the dispatching of missionaries and propaganda into hostile territories, with the result that from about the middle of the sixteenth century Geneva became the center of a concerted and militant attempt to spread the new faith far and wide. Soon Calvinists became a majority in Scotland, where they were known as Presbyterians; a majority in Holland, where they founded the Dutch Reformed Church; a substantial minority in France, where they were called Huguenots; and a substantial minority in England, where they were called Puritans. In addition, Calvinist preachers zealously tried to make converts in most other parts of Europe. But just as the Calvinists were fanning out through Europe, the forces of Catholicism were hardening in their determination to head off any further Protestant advances. The result, as we will see in the next chapter, was that many parts of a hitherto united Christendom became mired in bloody religious wars for decades after.

The Protestant Heritage

Inasmuch as Luther's revolt from Rome and the spread of Protestantism occurred after the height of the civilization of the Renaissance and before some particularly fundamental advances in modern European political, economic, and social development, it is tempting to think of historical events unfolding in an inevitably cumulative way: Renaissance, Reformation, "Triumphs of the Modern World." But history is seldom as neat as that. Although scholars will continue to disagree on points of detail, most agree that the Protestant Reformation inherited little from the civilization of the Renaissance, that indeed in certain basic respects Protestant principles were completely at odds with major assumptions of Renaissance humanists. As for the relationship between "Protestantism and Progress," the most apt formulation appears to be a statement from a book of that title by the great German religious historian Ernst Troeltsch, according to which "Protestantism has furthered the rise of the modern world . . . [but nowhere] does it appear as its actual creator."

Renaissance and Reformation

In considering the relationship between the Renaissance and the origins of the Protestant Reformation, it would admittedly be false to say that the one had absolutely nothing to do with the other. Certainly, criticisms of religious abuses by Christian humanists helped prepare Germany for the Lutheran revolt. Furthermore, close humanistic textual study of the Bible led to the publication of new, reliable biblical editions used by the Protestant reformers. In this regard a direct line ran from the Italian humanist Lorenzo Valla to Erasmus to Luther insofar as Valla's *Notes on the New Testament* inspired Erasmus to produce his own Greek edition and accompanying Latin translation of the New Testament in 1516, and that in turn enabled Luther in 1518 to reach some crucial conclusions concerning the literal biblical meaning of penance. For these and related reasons, Luther addressed Erasmus in 1519 as "our ornament and our hope."

The Christian humanists' opposition to Protestantism

But in fact Erasmus quickly showed that he had no sympathy whatsoever with Luther's first principles, and most other Christian humanists shunned Protestantism as soon as it became clear to them what Luther and other Protestant reformers actually were teaching. The reasons for this were that most humanists believed in free will while Protestants believed in predestination, that humanists tended to think of human nature as basically good while Protestants found it unspeakably corrupt, and that most humanists favored urbanity and tolerance while the followers of Luther and Calvin emphasized faith and conformity. Thus when Erasmus, for example, defended *The Freedom of the Will* in a treatise of 1524, Luther attacked it vehemently in his *Bondage of the Will* of the following year, insisting that original sin makes all humans "bound, wretched, captive, sick, and dead." And when Henry VIII introduced the Reformation into England, England's foremost Christian humanist, Sir Thomas More, resisted the break with Rome even unto martyrdom, mounting the scaffold with some stirring words about the primacy of the individual conscience.

Catholic and Protestant Views of a Cardinal. A genuine papal medal (top) depicted a cardinal (right-side up) merged with a bishop (upside down). In response, a Protestant replica (bottom), probably struck in the Netherlands, depicted a cardinal merged with a grinning fool.

If the Protestant Reformation, then, was by no means the natural outgrowth of the civilization of the Renaissance, it very definitely contributed to certain traits most characteristic of modern European historical development. Foremost among these was the rise of the untrammeled powers of the sovereign state. As we have seen, those German princes who converted to Protestantism were moved to do so primarily by the search for sovereignty, and the kings of Denmark, Sweden, and England followed suit for the same reasons. Not at all accidentally, the earliest act of the English Parliament announcing Henry VIII's break with Rome, the Act in Restraint of Appeals of 1533, put forth the earliest official statement that England is a completely independent country, "governed by one supreme head and king," possessed of "plenary, whole, and entire power . . . to render and yield justice and final determination to all manner of folk." Since Protestant leaders—Calvin as well as Luther—preached absolute obedience to "godly" rulers, and since the state in Protestant countries assumed direct control of the Church, the spread of Protestantism definitely resulted in the growth of state power. But, as we have also seen, the power of the state was growing anyway, and it continued to grow in Catholic countries like France and Spain where kings were granted most of the same rights over the Church that were forcibly seized by Lutheran German princes or Henry VIII.

Protestantism and nationalism

As for the growth of nationalism, a sense of national pride was already present in sixteenth-century Germany that Luther played upon in his appeals of 1520. But Luther himself then did the most to foster German cultural nationalism by translating the entire Bible into a vigorous German idiom. Up until then Germans from some regions spoke a language so different from that of Germans from other areas that they could not understand each other, but the form of German given currency by Luther's Bible soon became the linguistic standard for the entire nation. Religion did not help to unite the German nation politically because the non-German Charles V opposed Lutheranism and as a result Germany soon became politically divided into Protestant and Catholic camps. But elsewhere, as in Scotland and Holland, where Protestants fought successfully against Catholic overlords, Protestantism enhanced a sense of national identity. And perhaps the most familiar case of all is that of England, where a sense of nationhood had existed before the advent of

Protestantism even more markedly than it had in Germany, Scotland, or Holland, but where the new faith, as we shall see, helped underpin the greatest accomplishments of the Elizabethan Age.

Protestantism and modern economic development

The problem of Protestantism's relationship to modern commercial and industrial economic development is more controversial. Around 1900 the great German sociologist Max Weber, noticing that the economically advanced territories of England, Holland, and North America had all been Protestant, argued that Protestantism, particularly in its Calvinist forms, was especially conducive to acquisitive economic enterprise. According to Weber, this was because Calvinistic theology, as opposed to Catholicism, sanctified the ventures of profit-oriented traders and moneylenders, and gave an exalted place in its ethical system to the business virtues of thrift and diligence. But historians have found shortcomings in Weber's thesis. Although Calvin did indeed praise diligence and acknowledge that merchants could be "sanctified in their calling," he no more approved of exorbitant interest rates than Catholics did. Moreover Calvin argued vehemently that people should put their excess wealth at the service of the poor rather than piling up capital for the sake of gain or subsequent investment. Thus it appears that the "work ethic" necessary for economic success in commercial ventures did have some Calvinistic roots, but that Calvin's ideal merchant would by no means have been a great speculator or maker of fortunes. Bearing in mind that the European economy had already made great strides forward in the High Middle Ages and was advancing again in the early-modern period, not least because of the overseas ventures initiated by the Catholic powers of Portugal and Spain, Calvinism thus was at most just one of many contributory factors to the triumph of modern capitalism and the Industrial Revolution.

Protestantism's effects on relations between the sexes

Finally, there arises the subject of Protestantism's effects on social relationships, specifically those between the sexes. As opposed to the question of Protestantism and economic development, this topic is still relatively unstudied. What is certain is that Protestant men as individuals could be just as ambivalent about women as Catholics, heathens, or Turks. John Knox, for example, inveighed against the Catholic regent of Scotland, Mary Stuart, in a treatise called *The First Blast of the Trumpet Against the Monstrous Regiment of Women,* yet maintained deeply respectful relationships with women of his own faith. But if one asks how Protestantism as a belief system affected women's lot, the answer appears to be that it enabled women to become just a shade more equal to men, albeit still clearly within a framework of subjection. Above all, since Protestantism, with its stress on the primacy of Scripture and the priesthood of all believers, called on women as well as men to undertake serious Bible study, it sponsored primary schooling for both sexes and thus enhanced female as well as male literacy. But Protestant male leaders still insisted that women were naturally inferior to men and thus should always defer to men in case of arguments. As Calvin himself said, "let the woman be satisfied with her state of subjection and not take it ill that she is made inferior to the more distinguished sex." Both Luther and Calvin appear to have been happily married, but that clearly meant being happily married on their own terms.

CATHOLIC REFORM

Catholic reform before and after Luther

The historical novelty of Protestantism in the sixteenth century inevitably tends to cast the spotlight on such religious reformers as Luther and Calvin, but it must be emphasized that a powerful internal reform movement within the Catholic Church exercised just as profound an effect on the course of European history as Protestantism did. Historians differ about whether to call this movement the "Catholic Reformation" or the "Counter-Reformation." Some prefer the former term because they wish to show that significant efforts to reform the Catholic Church from within antedated the posting of Luther's theses and that therefore Catholic reform in the sixteenth century was no mere counterattack to check the growth of Protestantism. Others, however, insist quite properly that for the main part sixteenth-century Catholic reformers were indeed inspired primarily by the urgency of resisting what they regarded as heresy and schism. Fortunately the two interpretations are by no means irreconcilable, for they allude to two complementary phases: a Catholic Reformation that came before Luther and a Counter-Reformation that followed.

The Catholic Reformation

The Catholic Reformation beginning around 1490 was primarily a movement for moral and institutional reform inspired by the principles of Christian humanism and carried on with practically no help from the dissolute Renaissance papacy. In Spain around the turn of the fifteenth century, reform activities directed by Cardinal Francisco Ximénes de Cisneros (1436–1517) with the cooperation of the monarchy led to the imposition of strict rules of behavior for Franciscan friars and the elimination of abuses prevalent among the diocesan clergy. Although Ximénes aimed primarily at strengthening the Church in its warfare with Muslims, his work had some effect in regenerating Spanish Christian spiritual life. In Italy there was no similarly centralized reform movement, but a number of earnest clerics in the early sixteenth century labored on their own to make the Italian Church more worthy of its calling. The task was a difficult one on account of the entrenchment of abuses and the example of profligacy set by the papal court, but despite these obstacles, the Italian reformers did manage to establish some new religious orders dedicated to high ideals of piety and social service. Finally, it cannot be forgotten that such leading Christian humanists as Erasmus and Thomas More were in their own way Catholic reformers, for in criticizing abuses and editing sacred texts, men like these helped to enhance spirituality.

The Counter-Reformation popes

Once Protestantism began threatening to sweep over Europe, however, Catholic reform of the earlier variety clearly became inadequate to defend the Church, let alone turn the tide of revolt. Thus a second, more aggressive phase of reform under a new style of vigorous papal leadership gained momentum during the middle and latter half of the sixteenth century. The leading Counter-Reformation popes—Paul III (1534–1549), Paul IV (1555–1559), St. Pius V (1566–1572), and Sixtus V (1585–1590)—were collectively the most zealous crusaders for reform who had presided over the papacy since the High Middle Ages. All led upright personal lives. Indeed, some were so grimly ascetic that contemporaries were unsure whether they were not too holy: as a Spanish councillor wrote in 1567, "We should like it even better if the present Holy Father were no longer with us, however great, inexpressible, unparalleled, and extraordinary His Holiness may be." But in the circumstances of the Protestant onslaught, a pope's reputation for excessive asceticism was vastly preferable to a reputation for profligacy. More than that, becoming fully dedicated to activist revitalization of the Church, the Counter-Reformation popes reorganized their finances and filled ecclesiastical offices with bishops and abbots as renowned for austerity as themselves, and these appointees in turn set high standards for their own priests and monks.

The Council of Trent: doctrinal matters

These papal activities were supplemented by the actions of the Council of Trent, convoked by Paul III in 1545 and meeting at intervals thereafter until 1563. This general council was one of the most important in the history of the Church. After early debates about possible grounds for compromise, the Council of Trent without exception reaffirmed all the tenets challenged by the Protestant Reformers. Good works were held to be as necessary for salvation as faith. The theory of the sacraments as indispensable means of grace was upheld. Likewise, transubstantiation, the apostolic succession of the priesthood, the belief in purgatory, the invocation of saints, and the rule of celibacy for the clergy were all confirmed as essential elements in the Catholic system. On the question as to the proper source of Christian belief, the Bible and the traditions of apostolic teaching were held to be of equal authority. Not only was papal supremacy over every bishop and priest expressly maintained, but the supremacy of the pope over the Church council itself was taken for granted in a way that left the monarchical government of the Church undisturbed. The Council of Trent also reaffirmed the doctrine of indul-

Pope Paul III with His Nephews, by Titian (1488–1576). This painting emphasizes action far more than its forebear, Raphael's portrait of Pope Leo X with his nephews as shown on p. 472.

A Session of the Council of Trent. The pope is not present, but the cardinals who represent him are enthroned, facing the semicircle of bishops. The orator with a raised right hand is a theologian advancing an opinion.

gences that had touched off the Lutheran revolt, although it did condemn the worst scandals connected with the selling of indulgences.

The Council of Trent: practical reform and discipline

The legislation of Trent was not confined to matters of doctrine, but also included provisions for the elimination of abuses and for reinforcing the discipline of the Church over its members. Bishops and priests were forbidden to hold more than one benefice, so that absentees could not grow rich from a plurality of incomes. To address the problem of an ignorant priesthood, it was provided that a theological seminary must be established in every diocese. Toward the end of its deliberations the council decided upon a censorship of books to prevent heretical ideas from corrupting those who still remained in the faith. A commission was appointed to draw up an index, or list of writings that ought not to be read. The publication of this list in 1564 resulted in the formal establishment of the Index of Prohibited Books as a part of the machinery of the Church. Later, a permanent agency known as the Congregation of the Index was set up to revise the list from time to time. Altogether more than forty such revisions have been made. The majority of the books condemned have been theological treatises, and probably the effect in retarding the progress of learning has been slight. Nonetheless, the establishment of the Index must be viewed as a symptom of the intolerance that had come to infect both Catholics and Protestants.

St. Ignatius Loyola

In addition to the independent activities of popes and the legislation of the Council of Trent, a third main force propelling the Counter-Reformation was the foundation of the Society of Jesus, commonly known as the Jesuit order, by St. Ignatius Loyola (1491–1556). In the midst of a youthful career as a worldly soldier, the Spanish nobleman Loyola was

The Inspiration of St. Jerome, by Guido Reni. In 1546 the Council of Trent declared St. Jerome's Latin translation of the Bible, known as the Vulgate, to be the official version of the Catholic Church; then, in 1592, Pope Clement VIII chose one edition of the Vulgate to be authoritative above all others. Since Biblical scholars had known since the early sixteenth century that St. Jerome's translation contained numerous mistakes, Counter-Reformation defenders of the Vulgate insisted that even his mistakes had been divinely inspired and thus were somehow preferable to the original meaning of Scripture. The point is made visually in Guido Reni's painting of 1635.

The Society of Jesus as defenders of the faith and educators

wounded in battle in 1521 (the same year in which Luther defied Charles V at Worms), and while recuperating, he decided to change his ways and become a spiritual soldier of Christ. Shortly afterward he lived as a hermit in a cave near the Spanish town of Manresa for ten months, during which time, instead of reading the Bible as Luther or Calvin might have done, he experienced ecstatic visions and worked out the principles of his subsequent meditational guide, *The Spiritual Exercises*. This manual, completed in 1535 and first published in 1541, offered practical advice on how to master one's will and serve God by a systematic program of meditations on sin and the life of Christ. Soon made a basic handbook for all Jesuits, and widely studied by numerous Catholic lay people as well, Loyola's *Spiritual Exercises* had an influence second only to Calvin's *Institutes* of all the religious writings of the sixteenth century.

Nonetheless, St. Ignatius's founding of the Jesuit order itself was certainly his greatest single accomplishment. Originating as a small group of six disciples who gathered around Loyola in Paris in 1534 to serve God in poverty, chastity, and missionary work, Ignatius's Society of Jesus was formally constituted as an order of the Church by Pope Paul III in 1540, and by the time of Loyola's death it already numbered fifteen hundred members. The Society of Jesus was by far the most militant of the religious orders fostered by the Catholic reform movements of the sixteenth century. It was not merely a monastic society but a company of soldiers sworn to defend the faith. Their weapons were not to be bullets and spears but eloquence, persuasion, instruction in the right doctrines, and if necessary, more worldly methods of exerting influence. The organization was patterned after that of a military company, with a general as commander-in-chief and iron discipline enforced for all members. Individuality was suppressed, and a soldierlike obedience to the general was exacted of the rank and file. The Jesuit general, sometimes known as "the black pope" (from the color of the order's habit), was elected for life and was not bound to take advice offered by any other member. But he did have one clear superior, namely the Roman pope himself, for in addition to the three monastic vows of poverty, chastity, and obedience, all senior Jesuits took a "fourth vow" of strict obedience to the Vicar of Christ and were held to be at the pope's disposal at all times.

The activities of the Jesuits consisted primarily of proselytizing not just heathens but Christians, and establishing schools. Originally founded with the major aim of engaging in missionary work abroad, the early Jesuits by no means abandoned this goal, preaching to non-Christians in India, China, and Spanish America. For example, one of St. Ignatius's closest early associates, St. Francis Xavier (1506–1552), baptized thousands of natives and covered thousands of miles missionizing in South and East Asia. Yet, although Loyola had not at first conceived of his society as comprising shock troops against Protestantism, that is what primarily became of it as the Counter-Reformation mounted in intensity. Working by means of preaching and diplomacy—sometimes at the risk of their lives—Jesuits in the second half of the sixteenth century fanned out through Europe in direct confrontation with Calvinists. In many places the Jesuits succeeded in keeping rulers and their subjects loyal to Catholicism, in others they met martyrdom, and in some others—notably Poland and parts of Germany and France—they actually succeeded in regaining territory temporarily lost to the Protestant faith. Wherever they were allowed to settle, the Jesuits set up schools and colleges, for they firmly believed that a vigorous Catholicism could rest only on widespread literacy and education. Indeed their schools were often so efficient that, after the fires of religious hatred began to subside, upper-class Protestants would sometimes send their children to receive a Jesuit education.

Results of the Counter-Reformation

From the foregoing it should be self-evident that there is a "Counter-Reformation heritage" every bit as much as there is a Protestant one. Needless to say, for committed Catholics, the greatest achievement of sixteenth-century Catholic reform was the defense and revitalization of the faith. Without any question, Catholicism would not have swept over the globe and reemerged in Europe as the vigorous spiritual force it remains today had it not been for the determined efforts of the sixteenth-century reformers. But there were more practical results stemming from the Counter-Reformation as well. One was the spread of literacy in Catholic countries due to the educational activities of the Jesuits, and another was the growth of intense concern for acts of charity. Since Counter-Reformation Catholicism continued to emphasize good works as well as faith, charitable activities took on an extremely important role in the revitalized religion: hence spiritual leaders of the Counter-Reformation such as St. Francis de Sales (1567–1622) and St. Vincent de Paul (1581–1660) urged alms-giving in their sermons and writings, and a wave of founding of orphanages and houses for the poor swept over Catholic Europe.

Catholicism and a female religious elite

Two other areas in which the Counter-Reformation had less dramatic but still noteworthy effects were in the realm of women's history and intellectual developments. Whereas Protestantism encouraged female literacy for the purpose of making women just a little bit more like men in the ability to read the Bible, reinvigorated Catholicism pursued a different course. Most Catholic women were kept in a more subordinate position in the life of the faith than women under Protestantism, but Catholicism fostered a distinctive role for a female religious elite—countenancing the mysticism of a St. Teresa of Avila (1515–1582), or allowing the foundation of new orders of nuns such as the Ursulines and the Sisters of Charity. Under both Protestantism and Catholicism women remained subordinate, but in the latter model they were able to pursue their religious impulses more independently.

The Counter-Reformation and reason

Finally, it unfortunately cannot be said that the Counter-Reformation perpetuated the tolerant Christianity of Erasmus, for Christian humanists lost favor with Counter-Reformation popes and all of Erasmus's writings were immediately placed on the Index. But sixteenth-century Protestantism was just as intolerant as sixteenth-century Catholicism, and far more hostile to the cause of rationalism. Indeed, because Counter-Reformation theologians returned for guidance to the Scholasticism of St. Thomas Aquinas, they were much more committed to acknowledging the dignity of human reason than their Protestant counterparts who emphasized pure Scriptural authority and blind faith. Thus although a hallmark of the subsequent seventeenth-century scientific revolution was the divorce between spirituality of any variety and strict scientific work, it does not seem entirely coincidental that René Descartes, one of the founders of the scientific revolution, who coined the famous phrase "I think, therefore I am," was trained as a youth by the Jesuits.

SUMMARY POINTS

- Between 1488 and about 1520, Europeans in search of new trade routes to Asia traveled to, conquered, and established trading outposts in Central and South America, the West African coast, and South and Southeast Asia.
- Martin Luther developed Lutheranism between 1517 and 1522 as a rejection of many of the practices and teachings of the Catholic Church. By 1530 much of Germany had adopted Lutheranism, in part out of nationalistic sentiment and in part because German princes saw it as a way to assure their sovereignty independent of Rome.
- The Church of England was established between 1527 and 1559 as a result of Henry VIII's desire to divorce his wife. In Switzerland, Zwinglianism, Anabaptism, and Calvinism were developed between about 1520 and 1550 as rejections of the teachings and practices of the Catholic Church.
- Partly as a response to the criticisms of Protestantism and partly as an independent effort, the Catholic Church instituted reforms between about 1490 and 1590 that reaffirmed the doctrines of the Church but altered many practices that had been criticized. The effect of these reforms was to revitalize the Church.

Selected Readings

OVERSEAS EXPANSION

Boxer, C. R., *The Portuguese Seaborne Empire, 1415–1825,* New York, 1969. The standard work on the subject.

Elliott, J. H., *The Old World and the New, 1492–1650,* Cambridge, 1970. A superb short analysis of the many ways in which the discovery of the New World affected life in the Old.

Hale, J. R., *Renaissance Exploration,* New York, 1968. A scintillating brief introduction. Highly recommended as a point of departure.

Morison, Samuel Eliot, *Christopher Columbus, Mariner,* New York, 1955. A convenient abridgment of the master storyteller's definitive biography of Columbus, *Admiral of the Ocean Sea* (1942).

Parry, J. H., *The Age of Reconnaissance: Discovery, Exploration, and Settlement, 1450 to 1650,* London, 1963. Probably the best one-volume survey of the entire subject of early-modern European expansion; particularly strong on details of shipbuilding and navigation.

———, *The Spanish Seaborne Empire,* London, 1966. The counterpart to Boxer for the early Spanish colonial experience.

Phillips, J. R. S., *The Medieval Expansion of Europe,* Oxford, 1988. Makes the strongest case for continuity between medieval and Renaissance expansion.

PROTESTANT REFORMATION

Bainton, Roland H., *Here I Stand: A Life of Martin Luther,* Nashville, Tenn., 1950. The best introductory biography in English; absorbing and authoritative, though clearly partisan in Luther's favor.

———, *Women of the Reformation,* 3 vols., Minneapolis, 1970–1977. Full of interesting narrative, but little analysis.

Bouwsma, William, *John Calvin,* Oxford, 1988. Now the best biography available.

Brandi, Karl, *The Emperor Charles V,* New York, 1939. The standard narrative biography of the emperor who faced Luther and ruled much of Europe as well.

Davis, Natalie Z., *Society and Culture in Early Modern France,* Stanford, 1975. A collection of pioneering essays in historical anthropology, including a brilliant piece on the role of women in sixteenth-century religious movements.

Dickens, A. G., *The English Reformation,* 2d ed., University Park, Penn., 1991. The best introduction.

———, *Reformation and Society in Sixteenth-Century Europe,* London, 1966. A highly stimulating introductory survey, with the added advantage of being profusely illustrated.

Erikson, E. H., *Young Man Luther,* New York, 1958. A classic psychobiography that analyzes the young Luther's "identity crisis."

Grimm, Harold J., *The Reformation Era: 1500–1650,* 2d ed., New York, 1973. The best college-level text; consistently informative, balanced, and reliable.

Harbison, E. Harris, *The Age of Reformation,* Ithaca, N.Y., 1955. A fine elementary introduction by a master of the field.

———, *The Christian Scholar in the Age of the Reformation,* New York, 1956. Discusses the relationship between Christian humanism and early Protestantism.

Hillerbrand, Hans, *The World of the Reformation,* London, 1975. A stimulating overview.

McGrath, Alister, *The Intellectual Origins of the European Reformation,* New York, 1987. Concise and lucid exposition of complicated material.

McNeill, John T., *The History and Character of Calvinism,* New York, 1954. A basic, reliable, older work.

Monter, E. William, *Calvin's Geneva,* New York, 1967. Standard on the history of Calvin's Geneva.

Mullett, M., *Radical Religious Movements in Early Modern Europe,* London, 1980. Thematic analysis of some of the major effects of Protestantism, with as much attention given to the seventeenth as to the sixteenth century. Contains a particularly valuable annotated bibliography.

Hsia, R. Po-Chia, ed., *The German People and the Reformation,* Ithaca, N.Y., 1988. Essays representative of the most original and important work in this area.

Samuelsson, Kurt, *Religion and Economic Action,* New York, 1961. The standard critical evaluation of Max Weber's thesis that Calvinism fostered the modern "spirit of capitalism."

Scribner, R. W., *The German Reformation,* Atlantic Heights, N.J., 1986. A brief survey of recent work on Church reform in its social and cultural context. Includes superb bibliographies.

Skinner, Quentin, *The Foundations of Modern Political Thought: 2. The Age of Reformation,* Cambridge, 1978. The best analysis of Reformation and Counter-Reformation trends in political theory.

Smith, Lacey B., *Henry VIII: The Mask of Royalty,* Boston, 1971. A breathtaking interpretation of the last years of Henry VIII and the age in which he lived.

Spitz, Lewis W., *The Protestant Reformation: 1517–1559,* New York, 1985. A thorough survey.

Troeltsch, Ernst, *Protestantism and Progress,* New York, 1931. An enduring classic.

Wiesner, Merry E., *Women and Gender in Early Modern Europe,* Cambridge, Eng., 1993.

Williams, George H., *The Radical Reformation,* 3d ed., Kirksville, Mo., 1992. Detailed account of Anabaptism and the "left wing" of the Protestant Reformation.

CATHOLIC REFORM

Broderick, James, *The Origin of the Jesuits,* London, 1940. An older work, but still unsurpassed.

Delumeau, Jean, *Catholicism between Luther and Voltaire: A New View of the Counter-Reformation,* Philadelphia, 1977. A sympathetic account stressing the positive aspects of Reformed Catholicism.

Dickens, A. G., *The Counter-Reformation,* London, 1968. A splendid counterpart to Dickens's *Reformation and Society;* like its companion, profusely illustrated.

Janelle, Pierre, *The Catholic Reformation,* Milwaukee, 1949. A reliable brief introduction.

Jedin, Hubert, *A History of the Council of Trent,* 2 vols., London, 1957–1961. Authoritative and exhaustive.

Knowles, D., *From Pachomius to Ignatius: A Study in the Constitutional History of the Religious Orders,* Oxford, 1966. In less than one hundred masterful pages Knowles places the organizational principles of the Jesuits in historical perspective.

Marshall, Sherrin, ed., *Women in Reformation and Counter-Reformation Europe: Public and Private Worlds,* Bloomington, Ind., 1989.

SOURCE MATERIALS

Dillenberger, John, ed., *John Calvin: Selections from His Writings,* Garden City, N.Y., 1971.

———, *Martin Luther: Selections from His Writings,* Garden City, N.Y., 1961.

Hillerbrand, Hans J., ed., *The Protestant Reformation,* New York, 1967.

St. Ignatius Loyola, *The Spiritual Exercises,* tr. R. W. Gleason, Garden City, N.Y., 1964.

Ziegler, Donald J., *Great Debates of the Reformation,* New York, 1969.

CHAPTER 15

A CENTURY OF CRISIS FOR EARLY-MODERN EUROPE (c. 1560–c. 1660)

I do not wish to say much about the customs of the age in which we live. I can only state that this age is not one of the best, being a century of iron.
—R. MENTET DE SALMONET, *History of the Troubles in Great Britain* (1649)

What in me is dark
Illumine, what is low raise and support.
—JOHN MILTON, *Paradise Lost*

A massacre in Paris

ON THE NIGHT before St. Bartholomew's Day in August of 1572 the Catholic queen mother of France, Catherine de Medici, authorized the ambush of French Protestant leaders who had come to Paris to attend a wedding. Thereupon, during the hours after midnight, unsuspecting people were awakened and stabbed to death or thrown out of windows. Soon all the targeted Protestants were eliminated, but the killing did not stop because roving bands of Parisian Catholics seized the opportunity of licensed carnage to slaughter at will any enemies they happened upon, Protestant or otherwise. By morning the River Seine was clogged with corpses and scores of bodies hung from gibbets in witness to an event known ever since as the Massacre of St. Bartholomew's Day.

A century of crisis

Had this lamentable incident been an isolated event it hardly would be worth mentioning, but in fact throughout the hundred years from roughly 1560 to roughly 1660 outbreaks of religious mayhem—with Protestants the ruthless killers in certain cases as Catholics were in others—recurred in many parts of Europe. Moreover, to make matters far worse, economic hardships and prolonged wars accompanied religious riots to result in a century of pronounced crisis for European civilization. Granted that Europe's early-modern period of crisis was much less uniform in its nature and extent than the terrible times of the Later Middle Ages, seen from the broadest perspective the period from 1560 to 1660 was western Europe's "iron century"—an age of great turbulence and severe trials.

The St. Bartholomew's Day Massacre. A contemporary painting depicts the merciless slaughter of Huguenots in Paris. At the top left (in front of the large gate next to the Seine) the Queen Mother Catherine looks over a pile of naked dead bodies; to the right a Huguenot leader is being pushed out of a window.

Economic, Religious, and Political Tests

Impending crisis

Europe's time of troubles crept up on contemporaries unawares. For almost a century before 1560 most of the West had enjoyed steady economic growth, and the discovery of the New World seemed the basis of greater prosperity to come. Political trends too seemed auspicious, since most western European governments were becoming ever more efficient and providing more internal peace for their subjects. Yet around 1560 thunderclouds were gathering in the skies that would soon burst into terrible storms.

Soaring prices

Although the causes of these storms were interrelated, each may be examined separately, starting with the great price inflation. Nothing like the upward price trend that affected western Europe in the second half of the sixteenth century had ever happened before. The cost of a measure of wheat in Flanders, for example, tripled between 1550 and 1600, grain prices in Paris quadrupled, and the overall cost of living in England more than doubled during the same period. Certainly the twentieth century has seen much more dizzying inflations than this, but since the skyrocketing of prices in the later sixteenth century was a novelty, most historians agree on calling it a "price revolution."

If experts agree on the terminology, however, very few of them agree on the exact combination of circumstances that caused the price revolution, for early-modern statistics are patchy and many areas of economic theory remain under dispute. Nonetheless, for present purposes two explanations for the great inflation may be offered with confidence. The first is demographic. Starting in the later fifteenth century, Europe's population began to mount again after the plague-induced falloff: roughly estimated, there were about 50 million people in Europe around 1450 and 90 million around 1600. Since Europe's food supply remained more or less constant owing to the lack of any noteworthy breakthrough in agricultural technology, food prices inevitably were driven sharply higher by greater demand. Although the prices of manufactured goods did not rise as steeply because there was a greater match between supply and demand, the prices of manufactured items did rise, especially in cases where the supply of agricultural raw materials crucial to the manufacturing process remained relatively inelastic.

Causes of inflation: (1) population increase

Population trends explain much, but since Europe's population did not grow nearly as rapidly in the second half of the sixteenth century as prices, other explanations for the great inflation are still necessary. Foremost among these is the enormous influx of bullion from Spanish America. Around 1560 a new technique of extracting silver from ore made the working of newly discovered mines in Mexico and upper Peru highly practical, soon transforming the previous trickle of silver entering the European economy into a flood. Whereas in the five years from 1556 to 1560 roughly 10 million ducats worth of silver passed through the Spanish entry point of Seville, between 1576 and 1580 that figure had doubled, and between 1591 and 1595 it had more than quadrupled. Inasmuch as most of this silver was used by the Spanish crown to pay its foreign creditors and its armies abroad, or by private individuals to pay for imports from other countries, Spanish bullion quickly circulated throughout Europe, where much of it was minted into coins. This dramatic increase in the volume of money in circulation further fueled the spiral of rising prices. "I learned a proverb here," said a French traveler in Spain in 1603, "everything costs much here except silver."

(2) Influx of silver

Aggressive entrepreneurs and landlords profited most from the changed economic circumstances, while the masses of laboring people were hurt the worst. Obviously, merchants in possession of sought-after goods were able to raise prices at will, and landlords either could profit directly from the rising prices of agricultural produce or, if they did not farm their own lands, could always raise rents. But laborers in country and town were caught in a squeeze because wages rose far more slowly than prices, owing to the presence of a more-than-adequate labor supply. Moreover, because the cost of food staples rose at a sharper rate than the cost of most other items of consumption, poor people had to spend an ever-greater percentage of their paltry incomes on necessities. In normal years they barely managed to survive, but when disasters such as wars or poor harvests drove grain prices out of reach, some of the poor literally

Effects of inflation on the laboring poor

starved to death. The picture that thus emerges is one of the rich getting richer and the poor getting poorer—splendid feasts enjoyed amid the most appalling suffering.

Political results

In addition to these direct economic effects, the price inflation of the later sixteenth century had significant political effects as well because higher prices placed new pressures on the sovereign states of Europe. The reasons for this were simple. Since the inflation depressed the real value of money, fixed incomes from taxes and dues in effect yielded less and less. Thus merely to keep their incomes constant governments would have been forced to raise taxes. But to compound this problem, most states needed much more real income than previously because they were undertaking more wars, and warfare, as always, was becoming increasingly expensive. The only recourse, then, was to raise taxes precipitously, but such draconian measures incurred great resentment on the part of subject populations—especially the very poor who were already strapped more than enough by the effects of the inflation. Hence governments faced continuous threats of defiance and potential armed resistance.

Economic stagnation after 1600

Less need be said about the economic stagnation that followed the price revolution because it interfered little with most of the trends just discussed. When population growth began to ease and the flood of silver from America began to abate around 1600, prices soon leveled off. Yet because the most lucrative economic exploitation of the New World began only in the late seventeenth century and Europe experienced little new industrial development, the period from about 1600 to 1660 was at best one of very limited overall economic growth, even though a few areas—notably Holland—bucked the trend. Within this context the rich were usually able to hold their own, but the poor as a group made no advances since the relationship of prices to wages remained fixed to their disadvantage. Indeed, if anything, the lot of the poor in many places deteriorated because the mid-seventeenth century saw some particularly expensive and destructive wars, causing helpless civilians to be plundered by rapacious tax collectors or looting soldiers, or sometimes both.

Religious wars

It goes without saying that most people would have been far better off had there been fewer wars during Europe's iron century, but given prevalent attitudes, newly arisen religious rivalries made wars inevitable. Simply stated, until religious passions began to cool toward the end of the period, most Catholics and Protestants viewed each other as minions of Satan who could not be allowed to live. Worse, sovereign states attempted to enforce religious uniformity on the grounds that "crown and altar" offered each other mutual support and in the belief that governments would totter where diversity of faith prevailed. Rulers on both sides felt certain that religious minorities, if allowed to survive in their realms, would inevitably engage in sedition; nor were they far wrong since militant Calvinists and Jesuits were indeed dedicated to subverting constituted powers in areas where they had not yet triumphed. Thus states tried to extirpate all potential religious resistance, but in the process sometimes provoked civil wars in which each side tended to assume there could be no victory until the other was exterminated. And of course civil wars might become international in scope when one or more foreign powers resolved to aid embattled religious allies elsewhere.

Governmental crises

Compounding the foregoing problems were more strictly political ones: namely, while strapped by price trends and racked by religious wars, governments brought certain provincial and constitutional grievances down upon themselves. Regarding the provincial issue, most of the major states of early-modern Europe had been built up by conquests or dynastic unions with the result that many smaller territories had been subjected to rule by foreign governors. At first some degree of provincial autonomy was usually preserved and hence the inhabitants of such territories did not object too much to their annexation. But in the iron century, when governments were making ever-greater financial claims on all their subjects or trying to enforce religious uniformity, rulers customarily moved to destroy all remnants of provincial autonomy in order to implement their financial or religious policies. Naturally the province-dwellers were usually not inclined to accept total subjugation without a fight, so rebellions might break out on combined patriotic and economic or religious grounds. Nor was that all, since most governments seeking money and/or religious uniformity tried to rule their subjects with a firmer hand than before, and thus sometimes provoked armed resistance in the name of traditional constitutional liberties. Given this bewildering variety of motives for revolt, it is by no means surprising that the century between 1560 and 1660 was one of the most turbulent in all European history.

A Half-Century of Religious Wars

Religious wars in Germany until the Peace of Augsburg

The greatest single cause of warfare in the first half of Europe's iron century was religious rivalry. Indeed, wars between Catholics and Protestants began as early as the 1540s when the Catholic Holy Roman emperor Charles V tried to reestablish Catholic unity in Germany by launching a military campaign against several German princes who had instituted Lutheran worship in their principalities. At times thereafter it appeared as if Charles was going to succeed in reducing his German Protestant opponents to complete submission, but since he was also involved in fighting against France, he seldom was able to devote concerted attention to affairs in Germany. Accordingly, religious warfare sputtered on and off until a compromise settlement was reached in the Religious Peace of Augsburg (1555). This rested on the principle of *cuius regio, eius religio* ("as the ruler, so the religion"), which meant that in those principalities where Lutheran princes ruled, Lutheranism would be the sole state religion, and Catholicism for those with Catholic princes. Although the Peace of Augsburg was a historical milestone inasmuch as Catholic rulers for the first time acknowledged the legality of Protestantism, it boded ill for the future in assuming that no sovereign state larger than a free city (for which it made exceptions) could tolerate religious diversity.

Moreover, in excluding Calvinism it ensured that Calvinists would become aggressive opponents of the status quo.

Background of the French wars of religion

Even though wars in the name of religion were fought in Europe before 1560, those that raged afterward were far more brutal, partly because the combatants had become more fanatical (intransigent Calvinists and Jesuits customarily took the lead on their respective sides), and partly because the later religious wars were aggravated by political and economic resentments. Since Geneva bordered on France, since Calvin himself was a Frenchman who longed to convert his mother country, and since Calvinists had no wish to displace German Lutherans, the next act in the tragedy of Europe's confessional warfare was played out on French soil. Calvinist missionaries had already made much headway in France in the years between Calvin's rise to power in Geneva in 1541 and the outbreak of religious warfare in 1562. Of the greatest aid to the Calvinist (Huguenot) cause was the conversion of many aristocratic French women to Calvinism because such women often won over their husbands, who in turn maintained large private armies. The foremost example is that of Jeanne d'Albret, queen of the tiny Pyrenean kingdom of Navarre, who brought over to Calvinism her husband, the prominent French aristocrat Antoine de Bourbon, and her brother-in-law, the prince de Condé. Not only did Condé take command of the French Huguenot party when civil war broke out in 1562, but he later was succeeded in this capacity by Jeanne's son, Henry of Navarre, who came to rule all of France at the end of the century as King Henry IV. In addition to aristocrats, many people from all walks of life became Huguenots for a variety of motives, with Huguenot strength greatest in areas of the south that had long resented the dominance of northern rule from Paris. In short, by 1562 Calvinists comprised between 10 and 20 percent of France's population of roughly 16 million, and their numbers were swelling every day.

Jeanne D'Albret

French warfare: the St. Bartholomew's Day Massacre

Since both Catholics and Protestants assumed that France could have only a single *roi, foi,* and *loi* (king, faith, and law), civil war was inevitable, and no one was surprised when a struggle between the Huguenot Condé and the ultra-Catholic duke of Guise for control of the government during a royal minority led in 1562 to a show of arms. Soon all France was aflame. Rampaging mobs, often incited on either side by members of the clergy, ransacked churches and settled local scores. After a while it became clear that the Huguenots were not strong or numerous enough to gain victory, but they were also too strong to be defeated. Hence, despite intermittent truces, warfare dragged on at great cost of life until 1572. Then, during an interval of peace, the cultivated queen mother Catherine de Medici, normally a woman who favored compromise, plotted with members of the Catholic Guise faction to kill all the Huguenot leaders while they were assembled in Paris for the wedding of Henry of Navarre. In the early morning of St. Bartholomew's Day (August 24) most of the Huguenot chiefs were murdered in bed and two to three thousand other Protestants were slaughtered in the streets or drowned in the Seine by Catholic mobs. When word of the Parisian massacre spread to the provinces, some ten thousand more Huguenots were killed in a frenzy of blood lust that swept through France.

Henry IV establishes French religious peace

The St. Bartholomew's Day episode effectively broke the back of Huguenot resistance, but even then warfare did not cease because the neurotic King Henry III (1574–1589)* tried to play off Huguenots against the dominant Catholic Guise family and because die-hard Huguenots sometimes were able to ally with Catholics revolting against overburdensome taxes or inequities in tax assessments. Only when the politically astute Henry of Navarre succeeded to the French throne as Henry IV (1589–1610), initiating the Bourbon dynasty that would rule until 1792, did civil war finally come to an end. In 1593 Henry abjured his Protestantism in order to placate France's Catholic majority ("Paris is worth a Mass") and then, in 1598, he offered limited religious freedom to the Huguenots by the Edict of Nantes. According to the terms of this proclamation, Catholicism was recognized as the official religion, but Huguenot nobles were allowed to hold Protestant services privately in their castles, other Huguenots were allowed to worship at specified places (excluding Paris and all cities where bishops and archbishops resided), and the Huguenot party was permitted to fortify some towns, especially in the south and west, for military defense if the need arose. Thus, although the Edict of Nantes certainly did not countenance absolute freedom of worship, it nevertheless represented a major stride in the direction of toleration. With religious peace established, France quickly began to recover from decades of devastation, but Henry IV himself was cut down by the dagger of a Catholic fanatic in 1610.

Habsburg rule in the Netherlands

Contemporaneous with the religious warfare in France was equally bitter religious strife between Catholics and Protestants in the neighboring Netherlands, where national resentments gravely compounded religious hatreds. For almost a century the Netherlands (or Low Countries),

*Here, as elsewhere, dates following a ruler's name refer to dates of reign.

The Assassination of Henry IV. This contemporary engraving shows Henry seated in an open carriage without any concern for his personal danger while his assassin climbs on the spoke of the carriage wheel to attack him. The entire composition conveys a vivid impression of early-modern Paris.

Philip II of Spain. Titian's portrait shows Philip's resemblance to his father, Charles V, particularly in the protruding lower jaw of the Habsburgs (see p. 477).

comprising modern-day Holland in the north and Belgium in the south, had been ruled by the Habsburg family. Particularly the southern part of the Netherlands prospered greatly from trade and manufacture: southern Netherlanders had the greatest per capita wealth of all Europe, and their metropolis of Antwerp was northern Europe's leading commercial and financial center. Moreover, the half-century-long rule of the Habsburg Charles V (1506–1556) had been popular because Charles, who had been born in the Belgian city of Ghent, felt a sense of rapport with his subjects, and allowed them a large degree of local self-government.

Philip II and the Netherlands

But around 1560 the good fortune of the Netherlands began to ebb. When Charles V retired to a monastery in 1556 (dying two years later) he ceded all his vast territories outside of the Holy Roman Empire and Hungary—not only the Netherlands, but Spain, Spanish America, and close to half of Italy—to his son Philip II (1556–1598). Unlike Charles, Philip had been born in Spain, and thinking of himself as a Spaniard, made Spain his residence and the focus of his policy. Thus he viewed the Netherlands primarily as a potentially rich source of income necessary for pursuing Spanish affairs. (Around 1560 silver was only beginning to flood through Seville.) But in order to tap the wealth of the Netherlands Philip had to rule it more directly than his father had, and such attempts were naturally resented by the local magnates who until then had dominated the government. To make matters worse, a religious storm also was brewing, for after a treaty of 1559 ended a long war between France and Spain, French Calvinists had begun to stream over the Netherlandish border, making converts wherever they went. Soon there were more Calvinists in Antwerp than in Geneva, a situation that Philip II could not tolerate because he was an ardent Catholic who subscribed wholeheartedly to the goals of the Counter-Reformation. Indeed, as he wrote to Rome on the eve of conflict, "rather than suffer the slightest harm to the true religion and service of God, I would lose all my states and even my life a hundred times over because I am not and will not be the ruler of heretics."

Evidence of the complexity of the Netherlandish situation is found in the facts that the leader of resistance to Philip, William the Silent, was at first not a Calvinist and that the territories that ultimately succeeded in breaking away from Spanish rule were at first the most Catholic ones in the Low Countries. William "the Silent," a prominent nobleman with large landholdings in the Netherlands, was in fact very talkative, receiving his nickname from his ability to hide his true religious and political feelings when the need arose. In 1566, when still a nominal Catholic, he and other local nobles not formally committed to Protestantism appealed to Philip to allow toleration for Calvinists. But while Philip momentarily temporized, radical Protestant mobs proved to be their own worst enemy—ransacking Catholic churches throughout the country, methodically desecrating hosts, smashing statuary, and shattering stained-glass windows. Though local troops soon had the situation under control, Philip II nonetheless decided to dispatch an army of ten thousand com-

The Duke of Alva. The gaunt Spanish general who attempted in vain to extirpate Calvinism in the Netherlands.

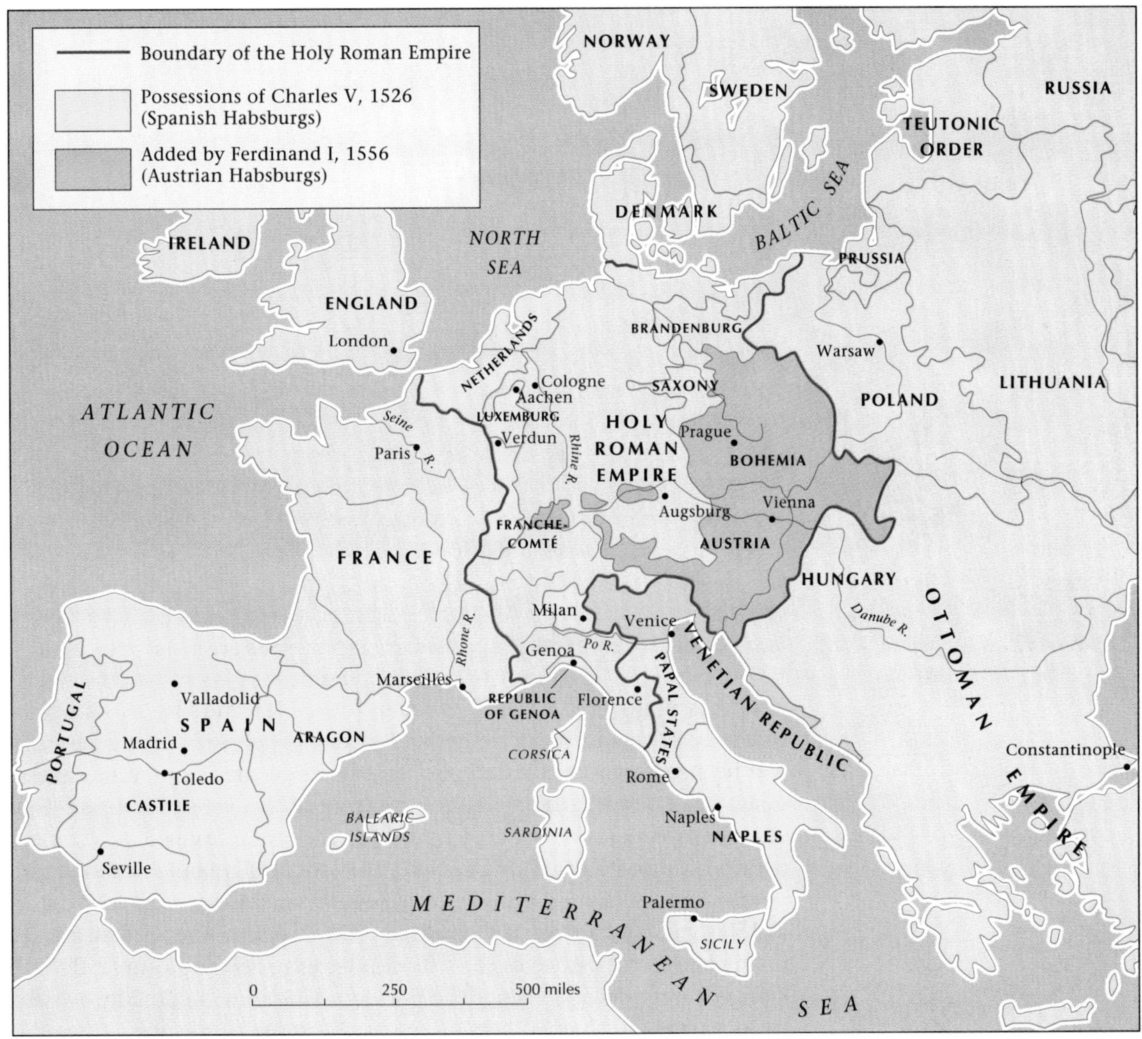

Europe, c. 1560

manded by the steely Spanish duke of Alva to wipe out Protestantism in the Low Countries forever. Alva's tribunal, the "Council of Blood," soon examined some twelve thousand persons on charges of heresy or sedition, of whom nine thousand were convicted and one thousand executed. William the Silent fled the country, and all hope for a free Netherlands seemed lost.

The revolt of the Netherlands

But the tide turned quickly for two related reasons. First, instead of giving up, William the Silent converted to Protestantism, sought help from Protestants in France, Germany, and England, and organized bands of sea rovers to harass Spanish shipping on the Netherlandish coast. And second, Alva's tyranny helped William's cause, especially when the hated Spanish governor attempted to levy a 10 percent sales tax. With internal

William the Silent seizes the northern Netherlands

Protestants Ransacking a Catholic Church in the Netherlands. The "Protestant fury" of 1566 was responsible for the large-scale destruction of religious art and statuary in the Low Countries, provoking the stern repression of Philip II.

disaffection growing, in 1572 William, for tactical military reasons, was able to seize the northern Netherlands even though the north until then had been predominantly Catholic. Thereafter geography played a major role in determining the outcome of the conflict. Spanish armies repeatedly attempted to win back the north, but they were stopped by a combination of impassable rivers and dikes that could be opened to flood out the invaders. Although William the Silent was assassinated by a Catholic in 1584, his son continued to lead the resistance until the Spanish crown finally agreed by a truce in 1609 to stop fighting and thus implicitly recognized the independence of the northern Dutch Republic. Meanwhile, the pressures of war and persecution had made the whole north Calvinistic, whereas the south—which remained Spanish—returned to uniform Catholicism.

Antagonism between England and Spain

Religious strife could thus take the form of civil war, as in France, or war for national liberation, as in the Netherlands. But it could also take the form of warfare between sovereign states, as in the case of the late-sixteenth-century struggle between England and Spain. After narrowly escaping domination by the Catholic Queen Mary and her Spanish husband Philip II, English Protestants rejoiced in the rule of Queen Elizabeth I (1558–1603) and naturally harbored great antipathy toward Philip II and the Counter-Reformation. Furthermore, English economic interests were directly opposed to those of the Spanish. A seafaring and trading people, the English in the later sixteenth century were steadily making inroads into Spanish naval and commercial domination, and were also determined to resist any Spanish attempt to block England's lucrative trade with the Low Countries. But the greatest source of antagonism lay in naval contests in the Atlantic, where English privateers, with the tacit consent of Queen Elizabeth, could not resist raiding silver-laden Spanish treasure ships. Beginning around 1570, and taking as an excuse the Spanish oppression of Protestants in the Netherlands, English admirals or pirates (the terms were really interchangeable) such as Sir Francis Drake and Sir John Hawkins began plundering Spanish vessels on the high seas. In a particularly dramatic sailing exploit lasting from 1577 to 1580, lust for booty and prevailing winds propelled Drake all the way around the world, to return with stolen Spanish treasure worth twice as much as Queen Elizabeth's annual revenue.

The defeat of the Spanish Armada

All this would have been sufficient provocation for Philip II to have retaliated against England, but because he had his hands full in the Netherlands he resolved to invade the island only after the English openly allied with the Dutch rebels in 1585. And even then Philip did not act without extensive planning and a sense of assurance that nothing could go wrong. Finally, in 1588 he dispatched an enormous fleet, confidently called the "Invincible Armada," to punish insolent Britannia. After an initial standoff in the English Channel, however, English fireships outmaneuvered the Spanish fleet, setting some Spanish galleons ablaze and forcing the rest to break formation. "Protestant gales" did the rest and a battered flotilla soon limped home with almost half its ships lost.

The salvation of Protestantism

The defeat of the Spanish Armada was one of the most decisive battles of Western history. Had Spain conquered England it is quite likely that the Spanish would have gone on to crush Holland and perhaps even to

Left: **The Defeat of the Spanish Armada.** Right: **Queen Elizabeth I.** The contemporary English oil painting of the great sea battle gives only a schematic idea of its turbulence. Note, however, the prominence of the papal insignia (tiara over crossed keys of St. Peter) on the ship in the middle foreground. Englishmen were convinced that had they not defeated the Spanish Armada in 1588 the pope would have planted his banner on their shores. At the right is a typically overblown portrait of Queen Elizabeth, known to her admiring subjects as "Gloriana," standing on a map of England.

destroy Protestantism everywhere. But, as it was, the Protestant day was saved, and not long afterward Spanish power began to decline, with English and Dutch ships taking ever-greater command of the seas. Moreover, in England itself patriotic fervor became intense. Popular even before then, "Good Queen Bess" was virtually revered by her subjects until her death in 1603, and England embarked on its golden "Elizabethan Age" of literary endeavor. War with Spain dragged on inconclusively until 1604, but the fighting never brought England any serious harm and was just lively enough to keep the English people deeply committed to the cause of their queen, their country, and the Protestant religion.

Years of Trembling

A new phase of turmoil

With the promulgation of the Edict of Nantes in 1598, the peace between England and Spain of 1604, and the truce between Spain and Holland of 1609, religious warfare tapered off and came to an end in the early seventeenth century. But in 1618 a major new war broke out, this time in Germany. Since this struggle raged more or less unceasingly until 1648 it bears the name of the Thirty Years' War. Far from returning to enduring peace, Spain and France became engaged in the conflict in Germany and in war with each other, and internal resentments in Spain, France, and England flared up in the decade of the 1640s in concurrent outbreaks of uprisings and civil turmoil. As an English preacher said in 1643, "these are days of shaking, and this shaking is universal." He might have added that while in some instances religion remained one of the contested issues, secular disputes about powers of government were now becoming predominant.

The Thirty Years' War

The clearest example is that of the Thirty Years' War, which began in a welter of religious passions as a war between Catholics and Protestants but immediately raised basic German constitutional issues and ended as an international struggle in which the initial religious dimension was almost entirely forgotten. Between the Peace of Augsburg in 1555 and the outbreak of war in 1618, Calvinists had replaced Lutherans in a few German territories, but the overall balance between Protestants and Catholics within the Holy Roman Empire had remained undisturbed. In 1618, however, when a Protestant uprising against Habsburg Catholic rule in Bohemia (not a German territory, yet part of the Holy Roman Empire) threatened to upset the balance, German Catholic forces ruthlessly counterattacked, first in Bohemia and then in Germany proper. Led by Charles V's Habsburg descendant Ferdinand II, who was archduke of Austria, king of Hungary, and from 1619 to his death in 1637, Holy Roman emperor, a German Catholic league seized the military initiative and within a decade seemed close to extirpating Protestantism throughout Germany. But Ferdinand, who was intent on pursuing political goals, imposed firm direct rule in Bohemia in order to build up the strength of his own Austro-Hungarian state, and attempted to revive the faded authority of the Holy Roman Empire in whatever ways he could.

Two Artistic Broadsides from the Thirty Years' War. On the left the German peasantry is ridden by the soldiery; on the right is an allegorical representation of "the monstrous beast of war."

The involvement of Sweden and France

Thus when the Lutheran king of Sweden, Gustavus Adolphus, the "Lion of the North," marched into Germany in 1630 to champion the nearly lost cause of Protestantism, he was welcomed by several German Catholic princes who preferred to see the former religious balance restored rather than stand the chance of surrendering their sovereignty to Ferdinand II. To make matters still more ironic, Gustavus's Protestant army was secretly subsidized by Catholic France, whose policy was then dictated by a cardinal of the Church, Cardinal Richelieu. This was because Habsburg Spain had been fighting in Germany on the side of Habsburg Austria, and Richelieu was determined to resist any possibility of France being surrounded by a strong Habsburg alliance on the north, east, and south. In the event, the military genius Gustavus Adolphus started routing the Habsburgs, but when he fell in battle in 1632, Cardinal Richelieu had little choice but to send ever-greater support to the remaining Swedish troops in Germany, until in 1635 French armies entered the war directly on Sweden's side. From then until 1648 the struggle was really one of France and Sweden against Austria and Spain, with most of Germany a helpless battleground.

The toll of warfare in Germany

The result was that Germany suffered more from warfare in the terrible years between 1618 and 1648 than it ever did before or after until the twentieth century. Several German cities were besieged and sacked nine or ten times over, and soldiers from all nations, who often had to sustain themselves by plunder, gave no quarter to defenseless civilians. With plague and disease adding to the toll of outright butchery, some parts of Germany lost more than half their populations, although it is true that others went relatively unscathed. Most horrifying was the loss of life in the final four years, when the carnage continued unabated even while

Gustavus Adolphus at the Battle of Leipzig. This engraving celebrates a victory won by the king of Sweden in 1631. One of the angels trumpets "German freedom," but the city of Leipzig is partly in flames and the Thirty Years' War would continue mercilessly for another seventeen years.

peace negotiators had already arrived at broad areas of agreement and were dickering over subsidiary clauses.

The Peace of Westphalia

Nor did the Peace of Westphalia, which finally ended the Thirty Years' War in 1648, do much to vindicate anyone's death, even though it did establish some abiding landmarks in European history. Above all, from the international perspective, the Peace of Westphalia marked the reemergence of France as the predominant power on the continental European scene, replacing Spain—a position France was to hold for two centuries more. In particular, France moved its eastern frontier directly into German territory by taking over large parts of Alsace. As for strictly internal German matters, the greatest losers were the Austrian Habsburgs, who were forced to surrender all the territory they had gained in Germany and to abandon their hopes of using the office of Holy Roman Emperor to dominate central Europe. Otherwise, something very close to the German status quo of 1618 was reestablished, with Protestant principalities in the north balancing Catholic ones in the south, and Germany so hopelessly divided that it could play no united role in European history until the nineteenth century.

The decline of Spain

Still greater losers from the Thirty Years' War than the Austrian Habsburgs were their Spanish cousins, for Spain had invested in the struggle vast sums it could not afford and ceased being a great power forever after. The story of Spain's swift fall from grandeur is almost like a Greek tragedy in its relentless unfolding. Despite the defeat of the "Invincible Armada" in 1588, around 1600 the Spanish empire—comprising all of the Iberian peninsula (including Portugal, which had been annexed by Philip II in 1580), half of Italy, half of the Netherlands, all of Central and South America, and even the Philippine Islands—was still the mightiest power

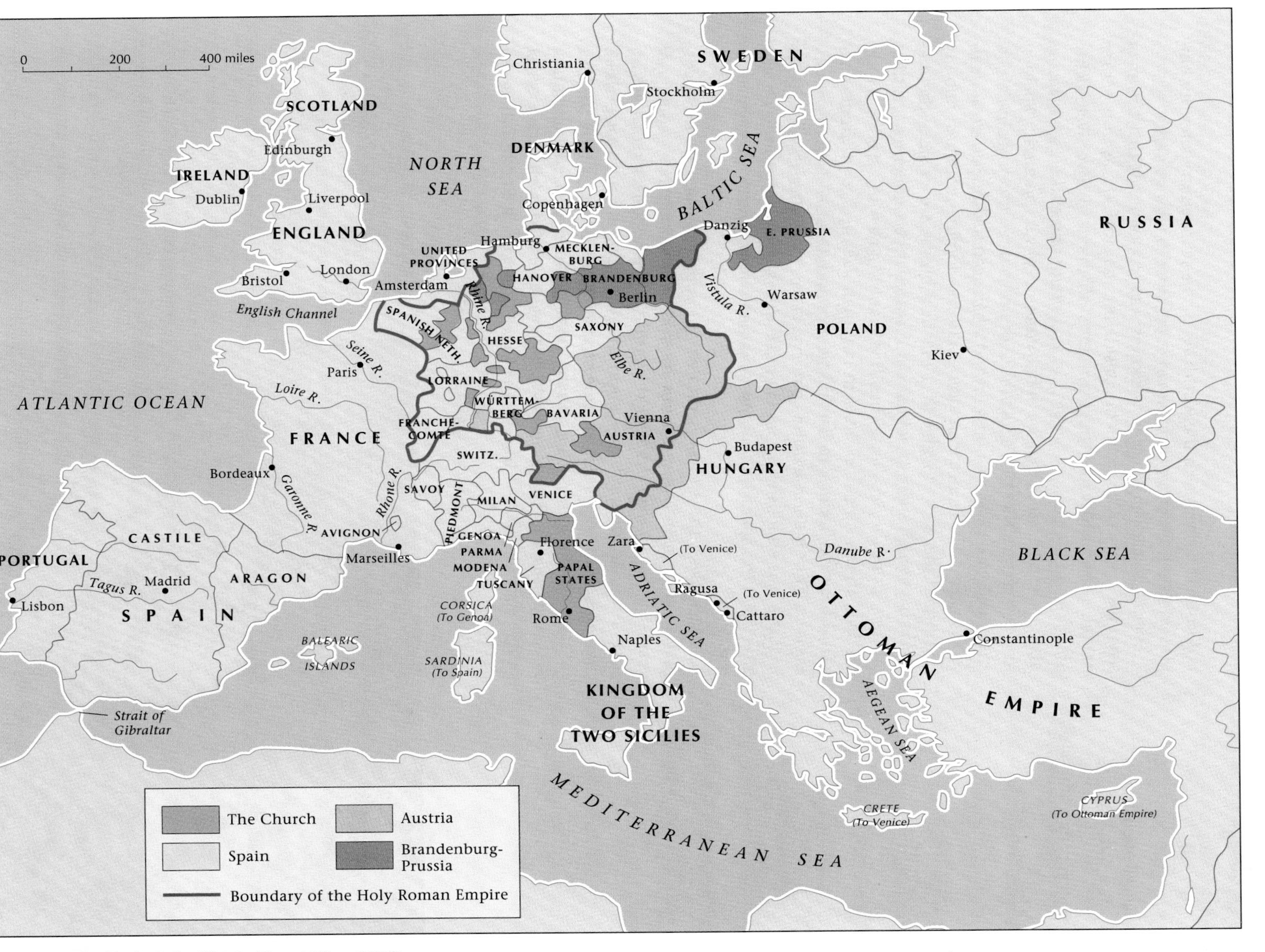

Europe at the End of the Thirty Years' War, 1648

not just in Europe but in the world. Yet a bare half-century later this empire on which the sun never set had come close to falling apart.

Economic causes of Spain's decline

Spain's greatest underlying weakness was economic. At first this may seem like a very odd statement considering that in 1600, as in the three or four previous decades, huge amounts of American silver were being unloaded on the docks of Seville. Yet as contemporaries themselves recognized, "the new world that Spain had conquered was conquering Spain in turn." Lacking either rich agricultural or mineral resources, Spain desperately needed to develop industries and a balanced trading pattern as its rivals England and France were doing. But the dominant Spanish nobility had prized ideals of chivalry over practical business ever since the medieval days when Spanish nobles were engaged in reconquering Christian territory from the Muslims. Thus the Spanish governing class was only too glad to use American silver to buy manufactured goods from other parts of Europe in order to live in splendor and dedicate itself to military exploits. Thus bullion left the country as soon as it entered, virtually no industry was established, and when the influx of silver began to decline after 1600 the Spanish economy remained with nothing except increasing debts.

Spain's continued aggressiveness

Nonetheless, the crown, dedicated to supporting the Counter-Reformation and maintaining Spain's international dominance, would not cease fighting abroad. Indeed, the entire Spanish budget remained on such a warlike footing that even in the relatively peaceful year of 1608 four million out of a total revenue of seven million ducats were paid for military expenditures. Thus when Spain became engaged in fighting France during the Thirty Years' War it overextended itself. The clearest visible sign of this was that in 1643 French troops at Rocroi inflicted a

The Recapture of Bahía. The Spanish constantly had to defend their overseas holdings from the Dutch. In 1625 a Spanish fleet recaptured the Brazilian port of Bahía, taken by the Dutch the year before. This Spanish propaganda painting combines realism and allegory by showing Spain's governing minister, the count of Olivares, proudly pointing to a painting of King Philip IV, while the returning inhabitants of Bahía nurse a wounded soldier.

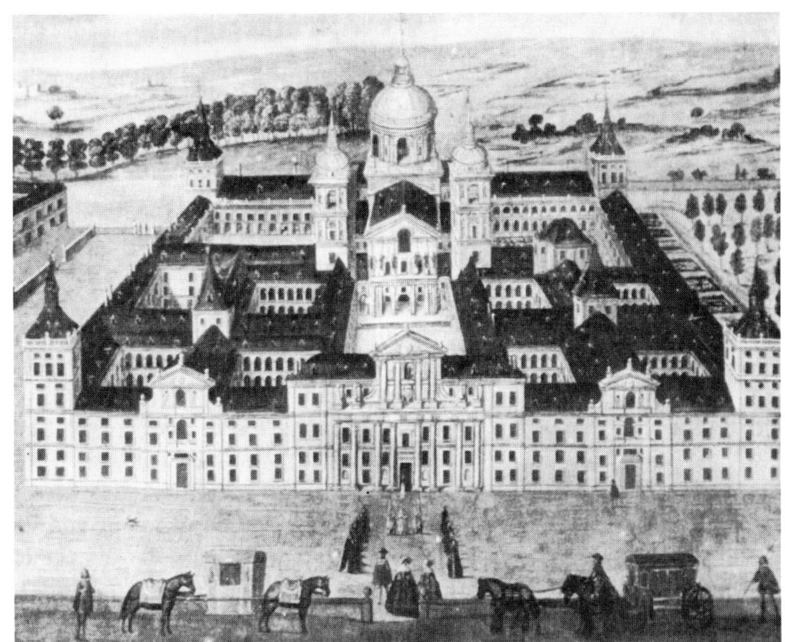

The Escorial. Philip II of Spain ordered the building between 1563 and 1584 of this somber retreat—part royal residence, part monastery—on an isolated spot, well removed from Madrid. Conceived on a grid-iron plan to honor the grid-iron martyrdom of St. Lawrence (on whose feast day Philip had won a decisive victory against the French), the Escorial symbolizes for many the Spanish crown's dedication to the ideals of the Counter-Reformation as well as its attempt to impose rationalized central government on the outlying provinces of the Spanish Empire. Some observers will note that it is the model for a racetrack in Kentucky—Churchill Downs.

stunning defeat on the famed Spanish infantry, the first time that a Spanish army had been overcome in battle since the reign of Ferdinand and Isabella. Worse still was the fact that by then two territories belonging to Spain's European empire were in open revolt.

Internal revolts against the Castilian government

In order to understand the causes of these revolts one must recognize that in the seventeenth century the governing power of Spain lay entirely in Castile. After the marriage of Isabella of Castile and Ferdinand of Aragon in 1469, geographically central Castile emerged as the dominant partner in the Spanish union, becoming even more dominant when Castile conquered the Muslim kingdom of Granada in southern Spain in 1492 and took over Portugal in 1580. In the absence of any great financial hardships, semi-autonomous Catalonia (the most fiercely independent part of Aragon) endured Castilian hegemony. But in 1640, when the strains of warfare induced Castile to limit Catalan liberties in order to raise more money and men for combat, Catalonia revolted and drove off Castilian governors. Immediately afterward the Portuguese learned of the Catalan uprising and revolted as well, followed by southern Italians who revolted against Castilian viceroys in Naples and Sicily in 1647. At that point only the momentary inability of Spain's greatest external enemies, France and England, to take advantage of its plight saved the Spanish Empire from utter collapse. Nothing if not determined, the Castilian government quickly put down the Italian revolts and by 1652 also brought Catalonia to heel. But Portugal retained its independence, and by the Peace of the Pyrenees, signed with France in 1659, Spain in effect conceded that it would entirely abandon its ambition of dominating Europe.

Spain and France compared

A comparison between the fortunes of Spain and France in the first half of the seventeenth century is highly instructive because some striking similarities existed between the two countries, but in the end differences turned out to be most decisive. Spain and France were of almost identical territorial extent, and both countries had been created by the same process of accretion. Just as the Castilian crown had gained Aragon in the north, Granada in the south, and then Portugal, so the kingdom of France had grown by adding on such diverse territories as Languedoc, Dauphiné, Provence, Burgundy, and Brittany. Since the inhabitants of all these territories cherished traditions of local independence as much as the Catalans or Portuguese, and since the rulers of France, like those of Spain, were determined to govern their provinces ever more firmly—especially when the financial stringencies of the Thirty Years' War made ruthless tax-collecting urgently necessary—a direct confrontation between the central government and the provinces in France became inevitable, just as in Spain. But France weathered the storm whereas Spain did not, a result largely attributable to France's greater wealth and the greater prestige of the French crown.

The reign of Henry IV

In good times most French people, including those from the outlying provinces, tended to revere their king. Certainly they had excellent reason to do so during the reign of Henry IV. Having established religious peace in 1598 by the Edict of Nantes, the affable Henry, who declared that there should be a chicken in every French family's pot each Sunday, set about to restore the prosperity of a country devastated by four decades of civil war. Fortunately France had enormous economic resiliency, owing primarily to its extremely rich and varied agricultural resources. Unlike Spain, which had to import food, France normally was able to feed itself, and Henry's finance minister, the duke of Sully, quickly saw to it that France could feed itself once more. Among other things, Sully distributed throughout the country free copies of a guide to recommended farming techniques and financed the rebuilding or new construction of roads, bridges, and canals to help expedite the flow of goods. In addition, Henry IV was not content to see France rest its economic development on agricultural wealth alone; instead he ordered the construction of royal factories to manufacture luxury goods such as crystal glass and tapestries, and he also supported the growth of silk, linen, and woolen cloth industries in many different parts of the country. Moreover, Henry's patronage allowed the explorer Champlain to claim parts of Canada as France's first foothold in the New World. Thus Henry IV's reign certainly must be counted as one of the most benevolent in all French history.

Cardinal Richelieu

Far less benevolent was Henry's *de facto* successor as ruler of France, Cardinal Richelieu (1585–1642), yet Richelieu fully managed to maintain France's forward momentum. The cardinal, of course, was never the real king of France—the actual title was held from 1610 to 1643 by Henry IV's ineffectual son Louis XIII. But as first minister from 1624 to his death in 1642 Richelieu governed as he wished, and what he wished most of all was to enhance centralized royal power at home and expand French influence in the larger theater of Europe. Accordingly, when Huguenots rebelled against restrictions placed on them by the Edict of Nantes, Richelieu put them down with an iron fist and emended the Edict in 1629 by depriving them of all their political and military rights. Since his armed campaigns against the Huguenots had been very costly, the cardinal then moved to gain more income for the crown by abolishing the semi-autonomy of Burgundy, Dauphiné, and Provence so that he could introduce direct royal taxation in all three areas. Later, to make sure all taxes levied were efficiently collected, Richelieu instituted a new system of local government by royal officials known as *intendants* who were expressly commissioned to run roughshod over any provincial obstructionism. By these and related methods Richelieu made French government more centralized than ever and managed to double the crown's income during his rule. But since he also engaged in an ambitious foreign policy directed against the Habsburgs of Austria and Spain, resulting in France's costly involvement in the Thirty Years' War, internal pressures mounted in the years after Richelieu's death.

Cardinal Richelieu. A contemporary portrait emphasizing the cardinal's austere bearing.

The *Fronde*

A reaction against French governmental centralization manifested itself in a series of revolts between 1648 and 1653 collectively known as "the slingshot tumults," or in French, the *Fronde.* By this time Louis XIII had been succeeded by his son Louis XIV, but because the latter was still a boy, France was governed by a regency consisting of Louis's mother, Anne of Austria, and her paramour Cardinal Mazarin. Considering that both were foreigners (Anne was a Habsburg and Mazarin originally an Italian adventurer named Giulio Mazarini), it is not surprising that many of their subjects, including some extremely powerful nobles, hated them. Moreover, nationwide resentments were greater still because the costs of war and several consecutive years of bad harvests had brought France temporarily into a grave economic plight. Thus when cliques of nobles expressed their disgust with Mazarin for primarily self-interested reasons, they found much support throughout the country, and uncoordinated revolts against the regency flared on and off for several years.

French absolutism triumphant

France, however, did not come close to falling apart. Above all, the French crown itself, which retained great reservoirs of prestige owing to a well-established national tradition and the undoubted achievements of Henry IV and Richelieu, was by no means under attack. On the contrary, neither the aristocratic leaders of the *Fronde* nor the commoners from all ranks who joined them in revolt claimed to be resisting the young king but only the alleged corruption and mismanagement of Mazarin. Some of the rebels, it is true, insisted that part of Mazarin's fault lay in his pursuit of Richelieu's centralizing, antiprovincial policy. But since most of the aristocrats who led the *Fronde* were merely "outs" who wanted to be "in," they often squabbled among themselves—sometimes even arranging agreements of convenience with the regency or striking alliances with France's enemy, Spain, for momentary gain—and proved completely unable to rally any unified support behind a common program. Thus when Louis XIV began to rule in his own name in 1651 and pretexts for revolting against "corrupt ministers" no longer existed, all opposition was soon silenced. As so often happens, the idealists and poor people paid the greatest price for revolt: in 1653 a defeated leader of popular resistance in Bordeaux was broken on a wheel, and not long afterward a massive new round of taxation was proclaimed. Remembering the turbulence of the *Fronde* for the rest of his life, Louis XIV resolved never to let his aristocracy or his provinces get out of hand again and ruled as the most effective royal absolutist in all of French history.

The case of England

Compared to the civil disturbances of the 1640s in Spain and France, those in England proved the most momentous in their results for the history of limited government. Whereas all that the revolts against Castile accomplished was the achievement of Portuguese independence and the crippling of an empire that was already in decline, and all that happened in France was a momentary interruption of the steady advance of royal power, in England a king was executed and barriers were erected against royal absolutism.

Henry VIII and Elizabeth I increase royal power

England around 1600 was caught up in a trend toward the growth of centralized royal authority characteristic of all western Europe. Not only had Henry VIII and Elizabeth I brought the English Church fully under royal control, but both monarchs employed so-called prerogative courts wherein they could proceed against subjects in disregard of traditional English legal safeguards for the rights of the accused. Furthermore, although Parliament met regularly during both reigns, members of Parliament were far less independent than they had been in the fifteenth century: any parliamentary representative who might have stood up to Henry VIII would have lost his head, and almost all parliamentarians admired Elizabeth enough to abide by her policies. Thus when the Stuart dynasty succeeded Elizabeth, the last of the Tudors, it was only natural that the Stuarts would try to increase royal power still more. And indeed they might have succeeded had it not been for their ineptness and an extraordinary combination of forces ranged against them.

James I. "The wisest fool in Christendom."

Lines of contention were drawn immediately at the accession of Elizabeth's nearest relative, her cousin James VI of Scotland, who in 1603 retained his Scottish crown but also became king of England as James I (1603–1625). Homely but vain, addled but erudite, James fittingly was called by Henry IV of France "the wisest fool in Christendom," and presented the starkest contrast to his predecessor. Whereas Elizabeth knew how to gain her way with Parliament without making a fuss about it, the schoolmasterish foreigner insisted on lecturing parliamentarians that he was semi-divine and would brook no resistance: "As it is atheism and blasphemy to dispute what God can do, so it is presumption and high contempt in a subject to dispute what a king can do." Carrying these sentiments further, in a speech to Parliament of 1609 he proclaimed that "kings are not only God's lieutenants on earth . . . but even by God Himself they are called gods."

That such extreme pretentions to divine authority would arouse strong opposition was a result even James should have been able to foresee, for the English ruling groups were still intensely committed to the theory of parliamentary controls on the crown. Yet not just theory was at stake, for the specific policies of the new king antagonized large numbers of his subjects. For example, James insisted upon supplementing his income by modes of money-raising that had never been sanctioned by Parliament, and when the leaders of that body remonstrated, he angrily tore up their protests and dissolved their sessions. Worse, he interfered with the freedom of business by granting monopolies and lucrative privileges to favored companies. And, worst of all in the eyes of most patriotic Englishmen, James quickly put an end to the long war with Spain and refused thereafter to become involved in any foreign military entanglements. Today many of us might think that James's commitment to peace was his greatest virtue; certainly his pacificism was justifiable financially since it spared the crown enormous debts. But in his own age James was hated particularly for his peace policy because it made him seem far too friendly with England's traditional enemy, Spain, and because "appeasement" meant leaving seemingly heroic Protestants in Holland and Germany in the lurch.

Causes of antagonism to James I

Although almost all English people (except for a small minority of clandestine Catholics) objected to James I's pacific foreign policy, those who hated it most were a group destined to play the greatest role in overthrowing the Stuarts, namely, the Puritans. Extremist Calvinistic Protestants, the Puritans believed that Elizabeth I's religious compromises had not broken fully enough with the forms and doctrines of Roman Catholicism. Called Puritans from their desire to "purify" the English Church of all traces of Catholic ritual and observance, they most vehemently opposed the English "episcopal system" of church government by bishops. But James I was as committed to retaining episcopalianism as the Puritans were intent on abolishing it because he viewed royally appointed bishops as one of the pillars of a strong monarchy: "No bishop, no king." Since the Puritans were the dominant faction in the House of Commons and many Puritans were also prosperous merchants who opposed James's monopolistic policies and money-raising expediencies, throughout his reign James remained at loggerheads with an extremely powerful group of his subjects for a combination of religious, constitutional, and economic reasons.

The Puritans

Nonetheless, James survived to die peacefully in bed in 1625, and had it not been for mistakes made by his son Charles I (1625–1649), England might have gone the way of absolutist France. Charles held the same inflated notions of royal power and consequently was quickly at odds with the Puritan leaders of Parliament. Soon after his accession to the throne Charles became involved in a war with France and needed revenue desperately. When Parliament refused to make more than the customary grants, he resorted to forced loans from his subjects, punishing those who failed to comply by quartering soldiers in their homes or throwing them into prison without a trial. In reaction to this, Parliament forced the Petition of Right on the king in 1628. This document declared all taxes not

Charles I

voted by Parliament illegal, condemned the quartering of soldiers in private houses, and prohibited arbitrary imprisonment and the establishment of martial law in time of peace.

The "eleven years' tyranny"

Angered rather than chastened by the Petition of Right, Charles I soon resolved to rule entirely without Parliament—and nearly succeeded. From 1629 to 1640 no Parliaments were called. During this "eleven years' tyranny," Charles's government lived off a variety of makeshift dues and levies. For example, the crown sold monopolies at exorbitant rates, revived highly antiquated medieval financial claims, and admonished judges to collect the stiffest of fines. Though technically not illegal, all of these expedients were deeply resented. Most controversial was the collection of "ship money," a levy taken on the pretext of a medieval obligation of English seaboard towns to provide ships (or their worth in money) for the royal navy. Extending the payment of ship money from coastal towns to the whole country, Charles threatened to make it a regular tax in contravention of the Petition of Right, and was upheld in a legal challenge of 1637 brought against him on these grounds by the Puritan squire John Hampden.

Charles I. This portrait by Van Dyck vividly captures the ill-fated monarch's arrogance.

By such means the king managed to make ends meet without the aid of taxes granted by Parliament. But he became ever more hated by most of his subjects, above all the Puritans, not just because of his constitutional and financial policies but also because he seemed to be pursuing a course in religion that came much closer to Catholicism than to Calvinism. Whether the English Puritans would have risen up in revolt on their own is a moot question, but they were ultimately emboldened to do so by a chain of events beginning with a revolt in Scotland. The uprising in Scotland of 1640 against the policy of an English king was not unlike those in Catalonia and Portugal of the same year against the Spanish crown except that the Scottish rising was not just nationalistic but also explicitly religious in nature. Like his father, Charles believed in the adage "no bishop, no king" and hence foolhardily decided to introduce episcopalian church government into staunchly Presbyterian Scotland. The result was armed resistance by Charles's northern subjects and the first step toward civil war in England.

The convening of Parliament

In order to obtain the funds necessary to punish the Scots, Charles had no other choice but to summon Parliament and soon found himself the target of pent-up resentments. Knowing full well that the king was helpless without money, the Puritan leaders of the House of Commons determined to take England's government into their own hands. Accordingly, they not only executed the king's first minister, the earl of Strafford, but they abolished ship money and the prerogative courts that ever since the reign of Henry VIII had served as instruments of arbitrary rule. Most significantly, they enacted a law forbidding the crown to dissolve Parliament and requiring the convening of sessions at least once every three years. After some indecision, early in 1642 Charles replied to these acts with a show of force. He marched with his guard into the House of Commons and attempted to arrest five of its leaders. All of them escaped, but an open conflict between crown and Parliament could no longer be avoided. Both parties collected troops and prepared for an appeal to the sword.

Civil war: the Cavaliers vs. the Roundheads

These events initiated the English Civil War, a conflict at once political and religious, which lasted from 1642 to 1649. Arrayed on the royal side were most of England's most prominent aristocrats and largest landowners, who were almost all "high-church" Anglicans. Opposed to them, the followers of Parliament included smaller landholders, tradesmen, and manufacturers, the majority of whom were Puritans. The members of the king's party were commonly known by the aristocratic name of Cavaliers. Their opponents, who cut their hair short in contempt for the fashionable custom of wearing curls, were derisively called Roundheads. At first the royalists, having obvious advantages of military experience, won most of the victories. In 1644, however, the parliamentary army was reorganized, and soon afterward the fortunes of battle shifted. The Cavalier forces were badly beaten, and in 1646 the king was compelled to surrender.

Charles I is beheaded

The struggle would now have ended had not a quarrel developed within the parliamentary party. The majority of its members, who had allied with the Presbyterian Scots, were ready to restore Charles to the throne as a limited monarch under an arrangement whereby a uniform Calvinistic Presbyterian faith would be imposed on both Scotland and England as the state religion. But a radical minority of Puritans, commonly known as Independents, distrusted Charles and insisted upon religious toleration for themselves and all other non-Presbyterian Protestants. Their leader was Oliver Cromwell (1599–1658), who had risen to command the Roundhead army. Taking advantage of the dissension within the ranks of his opponents, Charles renewed the war in 1648, but after a brief campaign was forced to surrender. Cromwell now resolved to end the life of "that man of blood," and, ejecting all the Presbyterians from Parliament by force of arms, obliged the remaining so-called Rump Parliament to vote an end to the monarchy. On 30 January 1649 Charles I was beheaded; a short time later the hereditary House of Lords was abolished, and England became a republic.

Oliver Cromwell

From republic to dictatorship

But founding a republic was far easier than maintaining one, and the new form of government, officially called a Commonwealth, did not last long. Technically the Rump Parliament continued as the legislative body, but Cromwell, with the army at his command, possessed the real power and soon became exasperated by the attempts of the legislators to perpetuate themselves in office and to profit from confiscating the wealth of their opponents. Accordingly, in 1653 he marched a detachment of troops into the Rump Parliament and saying "Come, I will put an end to your prating," ordered the members to disperse. Thereby the Commonwealth ceased to exist and was soon followed by the "Protectorate," or virtual dictatorship established under a constitution drafted by officers of the army. Called the Instrument of Government, this text was the nearest approximation of a written constitution England has ever had. Extensive powers were given to Cromwell as "lord protector" for life, and his office was made hereditary. At first a Parliament exercised limited authority in making laws and levying taxes, but in 1655 its members were abruptly dismissed by Cromwell. Thereafter the government became a thinly disguised autocracy, with Cromwell now wielding a sovereignty even more absolute than any the Stuart monarchs would have dared to claim.

The Stuart Restoration

Given the choice between a Puritan military dictatorship and the old royalist regime, when the occasion arose England unhesitatingly opted for the latter. Above all, years of Calvinistic austerities such as the prohibition of any public recreation on Sundays—then the worker's only holiday—had discredited the Puritans, making most people long for the milder Anglicanism of the original Elizabethan settlement. Thus not long after Cromwell's death in 1658, one of his generals seized power and called for elections for a new Parliament which met in the spring of 1660 and proclaimed as king Charles I's exiled son, Charles II. With the reign of Charles II (1660–1685) Anglicanism was immediately restored, but by no means the same was true for untrammeled monarchical power. Rather, stating with characteristic good humor that he did not wish to "resume his travels," Charles agreed to respect Parliament and observe the Petition of Right. Of greatest constitutional significance was the fact that all the legislation passed by Parliament immediately before the outbreak of the Civil War, including the requirement to hold Parliaments at least once every three years, remained as law. Thus in striking contrast to absolutist France, England became a limited monarchy. Putting its constitutional struggles behind it after one brief further test in the late seventeenth century, the realm of England would soon live up to the poet Milton's prediction of "a noble and puissant nation rousing herself like a strong man after sleep."

Quests for Light Out of Darkness

Caught up in economic uncertainty, religious rivalries, and political turmoil, many Europeans between 1560 and 1660 understandably cast about for emotional or intellectual resolutions of their most pressing problems. Sometimes, as in the case of the great witchcraft delusion, this quest led merely to an intensification of hysteria. But in the case of more dispassionate reflections, the search for ways of resolving Europe's crises led to some of the most enduring statements of moral and political philosophy of all time.

The origins of the witchcraft delusion

In seeking to explain belief in witchcraft, historians agree that the idea itself took shape toward the end of the Middle Ages. Peasant culture throughout the Middle Ages included belief in the possibilities of sorcery. In other words, most simple rural people assumed that certain unusual individuals could practice good, or "white" magic in the form of healing, divination for lost objects, and fortune-telling, or perhaps also evil, "black" magic that might, for example, call up tempests or ravage crops. Yet only in the fifteenth century did learned authorities begin to insist on theological grounds that black magic could be practiced only as a result of pacts with the devil. Naturally, once this belief became accepted, judicial officers soon found it urgent to prosecute all "witches" who practiced black magic because warfare against the devil was paramount to Christian society and "the evil one" could not be allowed to hold any sway. Accordingly, in 1484 Pope Innocent VIII ordered papal inquisitors to root out alleged witchcraft with all the means at their disposal, and the pace of witch hunts gained momentum in the following decades. Nor were witch trials curtailed in areas that broke with Rome, for Protestant reformers believed in the insidious powers of Satan just as much as Catholics did. Indeed, Luther himself once threw an inkpot at a supposed apparition of the devil, and Calvin saw Satan's evil workings wherever he looked. Thus both urged that alleged witches be tried more peremptorily and sentenced with less leniency than ordinary criminals, and persecutions of innocent people continued apace in Protestant as well as Catholic lands.

Witchcraft hysteria and the European crisis

Yet the outbreak of a real mania for catching and killing "witches" did not begin until about 1580. Therefore it can only be supposed that the witchcraft hysteria was connected in some way with Europe's general crisis—all the more since it continued for about as long as the age of crisis itself (until roughly 1660) and was most severe in just those localities where warfare or economic dislocation was most intense. In such places, whenever crops failed or cattle sickened people assumed that a "witch"—usually a defenseless old woman—was responsible, and rushed to put her to death. If not always old, the victims were most frequently women, no doubt in part because preachers had encouraged their flocks to believe that evil had first come into the world with Eve and in part because men

Supposed Witches Worshiping the Devil in the Form of a Billy-Goat. In the background other "witches" ride bareback on flying demons. This is one of the earliest visual conceptions of witchcraft, dating from around 1460.

Burning of Witches at Dernberg in 1555. From a sixteenth-century German pamphlet denouncing witchcraft.

in authority felt psychologically most ambivalent about members of the opposite sex. Pure sadism certainly cannot have been the original motive for such proceedings, but once trials began, horrendous sadism very often was unleashed. Thus old women, young girls, and sometimes even mere children might be brutally tortured by having needles driven under their nails, fires placed at their heels, or their legs crushed under weights until marrow spurted from their bones, in order to make them confess to having had filthy orgies with demons. The final death toll will never be known, but in the 1620s there was an average of one hundred burnings a year in the German cities of Würzburg and Bamberg, and around the same time it was said the town square of Wolfenbüttel "looked like a little forest, so crowded were the stakes."

The end of the hysteria

Why persecution quickly ended in the years immediately after 1660 will remain a matter for scholarly speculation. Aside from the fact that better times returned to most of Europe around then, probably the best explanation is that shortly after 1660 educated magistrates began to adhere to a mechanistic view of the universe. In other words, once the leaders of society came to believe that storms and epidemics arose from natural rather than supernatural causes, they ceased to countenance witch hunts.

Montaigne

Fortunately, other attempts of Europeans between 1560 and 1660 to master the darkness around them were not in themselves so dark. Indeed, one of the most "enlightened" of all European moral philosophers was the Frenchman Michel de Montaigne (1533–1592), who wrote during the height of the French wars of religion. The son of a Catholic father and a Huguenot mother of Jewish ancestry, the well-to-do Montaigne retired from a legal career at the age of thirty-eight to devote himself to a life of leisured reflection. The *Essays* that resulted were a new literary form originally conceived as "experiments" in writing (the French *essai* simply means "trial"). Because they are extraordinarily well written as well as being searchingly reflective, Montaigne's *Essays* ever since have ranked securely among the most enduring classics of French literature and thought.

Michel de Montaigne

Although the range of subjects of the *Essays* runs a wide gamut from "The Resemblance of Children to Their Fathers" to "The Art of Conversing," two main themes are dominant. One is a pervasive skepticism. Making his motto *"Que sais-je?"* (What do I know?), Montaigne decided that he knew very little for certain. According to him, "it is folly to measure truth and error by our own capacities" because our capacities are severely limited. Thus, as he maintained in one of his most famous essays, "On Cannibals," what may seem indisputably true and proper to one nation may seem absolutely false to another because "everyone gives the title of barbarism to everything that is not of his usage." From this Montaigne's second main principle followed—the need for tolerance. Since all people think they know the perfect religion and the perfect government, no religion or government is really perfect and consequently no belief is worth fighting for to the death.

Montaigne's fatalism

If the foregoing description makes Montaigne sound surprisingly modern, it must be emphasized that he was by no means a rationalist. On the contrary, he believed that "reason does nothing but go astray in everything," and that intellectual curiosity "which prompts us to thrust our noses into everything" is a "scourge of the soul." Moreover, concerning practical affairs Montaigne was a fatalist who thought that in a world governed by unpredictable "fortune" the best human strategy is to face the good and the bad with steadfastness and dignity. Lest people begin to think too highly of their own abilities, he reminded them that "sit we upon the highest throne in the world, yet we do sit upon our own behinds." Nonetheless, despite his passive belief that "fortune, not wisdom,

Rhinoceros and Unicorn. Sixteenth-century books of naturalism depicted "newly discovered" animals, some of which were real and others of which were figments of the imagination. (In fact a rhinoceros is hardly a less improbable creature than a unicorn.) Uncertain of absolute truth and falsity, Montaigne concluded that what seemed true one day might be cast into doubt tomorrow.

rules the life of mankind," the wide circulation of Montaigne's *Essays* did help combat fanaticism and religious intolerance in his own and subsequent ages.

Jean Bodin

If Montaigne sought refuge from the trials of his age in skepticism, tolerance, and resigned dignity, his contemporary, the French lawyer Jean Bodin (1530–1596), looked for more light to come out of darkness from the powers of the state. Like Montaigne, Bodin was particularly troubled by the upheavals caused by the religious wars in France—he had even witnessed the frightful St. Bartholomew's Day Massacre of 1572 in Paris. But instead of shrugging his shoulders about the bloodshed, he resolved to offer a political plan to make sure turbulence would cease. This he did in his monumental *Six Books of the Commonwealth* (1576), the earliest fully developed statement of governmental absolutism in Western political thought. According to Bodin, the state arises from the needs of collections of families, but once constituted should brook no opposition, for maintaining order is paramount. Whereas writers on law and politics before him had groped toward a theory of governmental sovereignty, Bodin was the first to offer a succinct definition; for him, sovereignty was "the most high, absolute, and perpetual power over all subjects," consisting principally in the power "to give laws to subjects without their consent." Although Bodin acknowledged the theoretical possibility of government by aristocracy or democracy, he assumed that the nation-states of his day would be ruled by monarchs and insisted that such monarchs could in no way be limited, either by legislative or judicial bodies, or even by laws made by their predecessors or themselves. Expressing the sharpest opposition to contemporary Huguenots who were saying (in contravention of the original teachings of Luther and Calvin) that subjects had a right to resist "ungodly princes," Bodin maintained that a subject must trust in the ruler's "mere and frank good will." Even if the ruler proved a tyrant, Bodin insisted that the subject had no warrant to resist, for any resistance would open the door "to a licentious anarchy which is worse than the harshest tyranny in the world." Since in his own day Bodin knew much "licentious anarchy" but had hardly any notion of how harsh the "harshest tyranny" could be, his position is somewhat understandable. Yet in the next century his *Commonwealth* would become the grounds for justifications of an increasingly oppressive French royal absolutism.

John Milton and the Levellers

Quite understandably, just as the French civil wars of the sixteenth century provoked a variety of responses, so did the English Civil War of the seventeenth. Drawing on a tradition of resistance to untrammeled state power expressed by French Huguenots and earlier English parliamentarians and Puritans, the great English Puritan poet John Milton enunciated a stirring defense of freedom of the press in his *Areopagitica* (1644). Similarly bold upholders of libertarianism were a party of Milton's Puritan contemporaries known as Levellers, the first exponents of democracy in the West since the ancient Greeks. Organizing themselves as a pressure group within Cromwell's army in the later 1640s when Charles I's monarchy seemed clearly doomed, the Levellers—who derived their name from their advocacy of equal political rights for all classes—agitated in favor of a parlimentary republic based on nearly universal male suffrage. For them, servants and other wage-laborers had no right to vote because they formed part of their employer's "family" and allegedly were represented by the family head. Moreover, the Levellers did not even deign to argue about women's rights. Otherwise, however, in the immortal words of one of their spokesmen, they argued that "the poorest He that is in England hath a life to live as the greatest He, and therefore . . . every man that is to live under a government ought first by his own consent to put himself under that government." But since Oliver Cromwell, who believed that the only grounds for suffrage was sufficient property, would have none of this, once Cromwell assumed virtually dictatorial powers the Leveller party disintegrated. More radical still were the communalist Diggers, so called from their attempts to cultivate common lands in 1649. Claiming to be "true Levellers," the Diggers argued that true freedom lies not in votes, but "where a man receives his nourishment," and hence argued for the redistribution of property. Cromwell, however, dispersed them quickly, and thus the Diggers have merely historical interest as vanguards of movements to come.

Far to the other extreme of the libertarian Puritans was the political philosopher Thomas Hobbes (1588–1679), whose reactions to the English Civil War led him to become the most forceful advocate of unrestrained state power of all time. Like Bodin, who was moved by the events of St. Bartholomew's Day to formulate a doctrine of political absolutism, Hobbes was moved by the turmoil of the English Civil War to do the same in his classic of political theory, *Leviathan* (1651). Yet Hobbes differed from Bodin in several respects. For one, whereas Bodin assumed that the absolute sovereign power would be a royal monarch, the more radical Hobbes, writing without any respect for tradition in Cromwell's England two years after the beheading of a king, thought the sovereign could be any ruthless dictator whatsoever. Then too, whereas Bodin defined his state as "the lawful government of families" and hence did not believe that the state could abridge private property rights because families could not exist without property, Hobbes's state existed to rule over atomistic individuals and thus was licensed to trample over both liberty and property.

The Title Page of Hobbes's *Leviathan*

Hobbes's pessimism

But the most fundamental difference between Bodin and Hobbes lay in the latter's uncompromisingly pessimistic view of human nature. Hobbes posited that the "state of nature" that existed before civil government came into being was a condition of "war of all against all." Since man naturally behaves as "a wolf" toward man and increasing fear of violent death in the state of nature makes human life "solitary, poor, nasty, brutish, and short," people for their own good at some purely theoretical point in time surrender their liberties to a sovereign ruler in exchange for his agreement to keep the peace. Having granted away their liberties, subjects have no right whatsoever to seek them back, and the sovereign can tyrannize as he likes—free to oppress his charges in any way other than to kill them, an act that would negate the very purpose of his rule. It is a measure of the relentless logic and clarity of Hobbes's abstract exposition that his *Leviathan* is widely regarded as one of the four or five greatest political treatises ever written, for practically nobody really likes what he says. Indeed, even in his own age Hobbes's views were vastly unpopular—libertarians detested them for obvious reasons, and royalists hated them as much because Hobbes was contemptuous of dynastic claims based on blood lineage and rationalized absolutist rule not on the grounds of powers granted from God, as most royalists did, but on powers surrendered by society. Yet because many important thinkers felt compelled to argue against Hobbes, he had enormous influence, if only in provoking the responses of others.

Perhaps the most moving attempt to bring light out of pervasive darkness was that of the seventeenth-century French moral and religious philosopher Blaise Pascal (1623–1662). Pascal began his career as a mathematician and scientific rationalist. A modern computer language has been named for him because he constructed the first calculating machine. (He did this when he was nineteen years old.) But at age thirty Pascal abandoned science as the result of a conversion experience and became a firm adherent of Jansenism, a puritanical faction within French Catholicism. From then till his death he worked on a highly ambitious philosophical-religious project meant to persuade doubters of the truth of Christianity by appealing simultaneously to their intellects and their emotions. Unfortunately, because of his premature death all that came of this was his *Pensées* (Thoughts), a collection of fragments and short informal pieces about religion written with great literary power. In these he argued that faith alone could show the way to salvation and that "the heart has its reasons of which reason itself knows nothing." Pascal's *Pensées* express the author's own sense of terror and anguish in the face of evil and eternity, but make the awe itself a sign of the existence of God. Individuals today will be moved by this work in varying degrees according to their own convictions, but few of any persuasion will dispute Pascal's proposition that "man knows he is wretched; he is therefore wretched because he is so; but he is very great because he knows it."

Blaise Pascal

Literature and the Arts

Grappling with the human condition

The combined wretchedness and greatness of humanity may be taken as the theme for the extraordinary profusion of towering works of literature and art produced during western Europe's period of crisis from 1560 to 1660. Of course not every single writing or painting of the era expressed the same message. During a hundred years of extraordinary literary and artistic creativity, works of all genres and sentiments were produced, ranging from the frothiest farces to the darkest tragedies, the serenest still lifes to the most grotesque scenes of religious martyrdom. Nonetheless, the greatest writers and painters of the period all were moved by a realization of the ambiguities and ironies of human existence not unlike that expressed in different ways by Montaigne and Pascal. They all were fully aware of the horrors of war and human suffering so rampant in their day, and all were directly or indirectly aware of the Protestant conviction that men are "vessels of iniquity," but they also inherited a large degree of Renaissance affirmativeness, and most of them accordingly preferred to view life on earth as a great dare.

Miguel de Cervantes

From the host of remarkable writers who flourished during what was probably the most extraordinary century in the entire history of western European poetry and drama, we may take the very greatest: Cervantes, the Elizabethan dramatists—Shakespeare to the fore—and John Milton. Although Miguel de Cervantes (1547–1616) was not strictly speaking either a poet or a dramatist, his masterpiece, the satirical romance *Don Quixote,* exudes great lyricism and drama. The plot recounts the adventures of a Spanish gentleman, Don Quixote of La Mancha, who has become slightly unbalanced by constant reading of chivalric epics. His mind filled with all kinds of fantastic adventures, he sets out at the age of fifty upon the slippery road of knight-errantry, imagining windmills to be glowering giants and flocks of sheep to be armies of infidels whom it is his duty to rout with his spear. In his distorted fancy he mistakes inns for castles and serving girls for courtly ladies on fire with love. Set off in contrast to the "knight-errant" is the figure of his faithful squire, Sancho Panza. The latter represents the ideal of the practical man, with his feet on the ground and content with the modest but substantial pleasures of eating, drinking, and sleeping. Yet Cervantes clearly does not wish to say that the realism of a Sancho Panza is categorically preferable to the "quixotic" idealism of his master. Rather, the two men represent different facets of human nature. Without any doubt, Don Quixote is a devastating satire on the anachronistic chivalric mentality that would soon help hasten Spain's decline. But for all that, the reader's sympathies remain with the protagonist, the man from La Mancha who dares to "dream the impossible dream."

Elizabethan drama

Directly contemporaneous with Cervantes were the English Elizabethan dramatists who collectively produced the most glorious age of theater known in the Western world. Writing after England's victory over the Spanish Armada, when national pride was at a peak, all exhibited great exuberance but none was by any means a facile optimist. In fact a strain of reflective seriousness pervades all their best works, and a few, like the tragedian John Webster (c. 1580–c. 1625), who "saw the skull beneath the skin," were if anything morbid pessimists. Literary critics tend to agree that of a bevy of great Elizabethan playwrights the most outstanding were Christopher Marlowe (1564–1593), Ben Jonson (c. 1572–1637), and, of course, William Shakespeare (1564–1616). Of the three, the fiery Marlowe, whose life was cut short in a tavern brawl before he reached the age of thirty, was the most youthfully energetic. In plays such as *Tamburlaine* and *Doctor Faustus* Marlowe created larger-than-life heroes who seek and come close to conquering everything in their path and feeling every possible sensation. But they meet unhappy ends because, for all his vitality, Marlowe knew that there are limits on human striving, and that wretchedness as well as greatness lies in the human lot. Thus though Faustus asks a reincarnated Helen of Troy, conjured up by Satan, to make him "immortal with a kiss," he dies and is damned in the end because immortality is not awarded by the devil or found in earthly kisses. In contrast to the heroic tragedian Marlowe, Ben Jonson wrote corrosive comedies that expose human vices and foibles. In the particularly bleak *Volpone* Jonson shows people behaving like deceitful and lustful animals, but in the later *Alchemist* he balances an attack on quackery and gullibility with admiration for resourceful lower-class characters who cleverly take advantage of their supposed betters.

William Shakespeare. Portrait made for the First Folio edition of his works, 1623.

Incomparably the greatest of the Elizabethan dramatists, William Shakespeare was born into the family of a tradesman in the provincial town of Stratford-on-Avon. His life is enshrouded in more mists of obscurity than the careers of most other great people. It is known that he left his native village, having gained little formal education, when he was about twenty, and that he drifted to London to find employment in the theater. How he eventually became an actor and still later a writer of plays is uncertain, but by the age of twenty-eight he had definitely acquired a reputation as an author sufficient to excite the jealousy of his rivals. Before he retired to his native Stratford about 1610 to spend the rest of his days in ease, he had written or collaborated in writing nearly forty plays, over and above 150 sonnets and two long narrative poems.

Shakespeare's three periods: (1) confidence

As everyone knows, Shakespeare's plays rank as a kind of secular Bible wherever the English language is spoken. The reasons lie not only in the author's unrivaled gift of expression, and in his scintillating wit, but most of all in his profound analysis of human character seized by passion and tried by fate. Shakespeare's dramas fall rather naturally into three groups. Those written during the playwright's earlier years are characterized by a sense of confidence. They include a number of history plays, which recount England's struggles and glories leading up to the triumph of the Tudor dynasty; the lyrical romantic tragedy *Romeo and Juliet;* and a wide variety of comedies including the magical *Midsummer Night's Dream* and Shakespeare's greatest creations in the comic vein—*Twelfth Night, As You Like It,* and *Much Ado about Nothing*. Despite the last-named title, few even of the plays of Shakespeare's early, lightest period are "much ado about nothing." Rather, most explore with wisdom as well as wit fundamental problems of psychological identity, honor and ambition, love and friendship. Occasionally they also contain touches of deep seriousness, as in *As You Like It,* when Shakespeare has a character pause to reflect that "all the world's a stage, and all the men and women merely players" who pass through seven "acts" or stages of life.

Such touches, however, never obscure the restrained optimism of Shakespeare's first period, whereas the plays from his second period are far darker in mood. Apparently around 1601 Shakespeare underwent a crisis during which he began to distrust human nature profoundly and to indict the whole scheme of the universe. The result was a group of dramas characterized by bitterness, frequent pathos, and a troubled searching into the mysteries of things. The series begins with the tragedy of indecisive idealism represented by *Hamlet,* goes on to the cynicism of *Measure for Measure* and *All's Well That Ends Well,* and culminates in the cosmic tragedies of *Macbeth* and *King Lear,* wherein characters assert that "life's but a walking shadow . . . a tale told by an idiot, full of sound and fury signifying nothing," and that "as flies to wanton boys are we to the gods; they kill us for their sport." Despite all this gloom, however, the plays of Shakespeare's second period generally contain the dramatist's greatest flights of poetic grandeur.

(2) Crisis

Although *Macbeth* and *Lear* suggest an author in the throes of deep depression, Shakespeare managed to resolve his personal crisis and end his dramatic career with a third period characterized by a profound spirit of reconciliation. Of the three plays (all idyllic romances) written during this final period, the last, *The Tempest,* is the greatest. Here ancient animosities are buried and wrongs are righted by a combination of natural and supernatural means, and a wide-eyed, youthful heroine rejoices on first seeing men with the words "O brave new world, that has such people in it!" Here, then, Shakespeare seems to be saying that for all humanity's trials life is not so unrelentingly bitter after all, and the divine plan of the universe is somehow benevolent and just.

(3) Reconciliation

Though less versatile than Shakespeare, not far behind him in eloquent grandeur stands the Puritan poet John Milton (1608–1674). The leading publicist of Oliver Cromwell's regime, Milton wrote the official defense of the beheading of Charles I as well as a number of treatises justifying Puritan positions in contemporary affairs. But he was also a man full of contradictions who loved the Greek and Latin classics at least as much as the Bible. Hence he could write a perfect pastorial elegy, *Lycidas,* mourning the loss of a dear friend in purely classical terms. Later, when forced into retirement by the accession of Charles II, Milton, though now blind, embarked on writing a classical epic, *Paradise Lost,* out of material found in Genesis concerning the creation of the world and the fall of man. This magnificent poem, which links the classical tradition to Christianity more successfully than any literary work written before or since, is surely one of the greatest epics of all time. Setting out to "justify the ways of God to man," Milton in *Paradise Lost* first plays "devil's advocate" by creating the compelling character of Satan, who defies God with boldness and subtlety. But Satan is more than counterbalanced in the end by the real "epic hero" of *Paradise Lost,* Adam, who learns to accept the human lot of moral responsibility and suffering, and is last seen leaving Paradise with Eve, the world "all before them."

John Milton. From the first edition of his poems, 1645.

Portrait of a Young Man, by Bronzino (1503–1572). Bronzino was a Florentine Mannerist painter who preferred the "objective" representation of oddities. Notice the carefully chiseled grotesques at the bottom and the young man's wandering left eye. The numerous contrasts between light and shade and the large number of vertical surfaces in the background contribute to a sense of surrealism.

"Mannerism": Pontormo and Bronzino

The ironies and tensions inherent in human existence also were portrayed with eloquence and profundity by several immortal masters of the visual arts who flourished during the "century of crisis." The dominant goal in Italian and Spanish painting during the first half of this period, the years between about 1540 and 1600, was to fascinate the viewer with special effects. This goal, however, was achieved by means of two entirely different styles. (Confusingly, both styles are sometimes referred to as "Mannerism.") The first was based on the style of the Renaissance master Raphael but moved from that painter's gracefulness to a highly self-conscious elegance bordering on the bizarre and surreal. Representatives of this approach were the Florentines Pontormo (1494–1557) and Bronzino (1503–1572). Their sharp-focused portraits are flat and cold, yet strangely riveting.

Fray Felix Hortensio Paravicino, by El Greco (c. 1541–1614). More restrained in composition than most of the artist's other work, this portrait nonetheless communicates a sense of deep spiritual intensity.

The other extreme was theatrical in a more conventional sense—highly dramatic. Painters who followed this approach were indebted to Michelangelo but went much farther than he did in emphasizing shadowy contrasts, restlessness, and distortion. Of this second group, the two most outstanding were the Venetian Tintoretto (1518–1594) and the Spaniard El Greco (c. 1541–1614). Combining aspects of Michelangelo's style with the traditionally Venetian taste for rich color, Tintoretto produced an enormous number of monumentally large canvases devoted to religious subjects that still inspire awe with their broodingly shimmering light and gripping drama. More emotional still is the work of Tintoretto's disciple, El Greco. Born Domenikos Theotokopoulos on the Greek island of Crete, this extraordinary artist absorbed some of the stylized elongation

The Crucifixion, by Tintoretto (1518–1594). This Venetian master of Mannerism combined typically Venetian richness of color with an innovative concern for movement and emotion.

Saint Andrew and St. Francis, by El Greco. A striking exemplification of the artist's penchant for elongation as well as his profound psychological penetration.

The Laocoön, by El Greco. An extreme example of Manneristic stress on restlessness and distortion. Note that the Spanish painter here drew for inspiration on the famous Hellenistic sculpture group shown on p. 145.

"Mannerism": Tintoretto and El Greco

characteristic of Greco-Byzantine icon painting before traveling to Italy to learn color and drama from Tintoretto. Finally he settled in Spain, where he was called "El Greco"—Spanish for "the Greek." El Greco's paintings were too strange to be greatly appreciated in his own age, and even now they appear so unbalanced as to seem the work of one almost deranged. Yet such a view slights El Greco's deeply mystical Catholic fervor as well as his technical achievements. Best known today is his transfigured landscape, the *View of Toledo,* with its somber but awesome light breaking where no sun shines. But equally inspiring are his swirling religious scenes and several of his stunning portraits in which gaunt, dignified Spaniards radiate a rare blend of austerity and spiritual insight.

The Baroque style

The dominant artistic school of southern Europe from about 1600 until the early 1700s was that of the Baroque, a school not only of painting but of sculpture and architecture. The Baroque style retained aspects of the dramatic and the irregular (the word "Baroque" itself comes from the Portuguese for a rough pearl), but it avoided seeming bizarre or overheated and aimed above all to instill a sense of the affirmative. The main reason for this was that Baroque art in all genres was most often propagandistic. Originating in Rome as an expression of the ideals of the Counter-Reformation papacy and the Jesuit order, Baroque architecture in particular aimed to gain adherence for a specific worldview. Similarly, Baroque painting often was done in the service of the Counter-Reformation Church, which at its high tide around 1620 seemed everywhere to be on the offensive. When Baroque painters were not celebrating Counter-

View of Toledo, by El Greco. Light breaks where no sun shines. One of the most awesomely mysterious paintings in the entire Western tradition.

The Calling of St. Matthew, by Caravaggio (1565–1609). Among the earliest of the great Baroque painters, Caravaggio specialized in contrasts of light and shade (*chiaroscuro*), and preferred to conceive of religious scenes in terms of everyday life. Here Christ (extreme right), whose halo is the only supernatural detail in the composition, enters a tavern to call St. Matthew (pointing doubtfully at himself) to his service.

Left: **David**, by Bernini (1598–1680). Whereas the earlier conceptions of David by the Renaissance sculptors Donatello and Michelangelo were reposeful (see pp. 433 and 434), the Baroque sculptor Bernini chose to portray his young hero at the peak of physical exertion. Right: **The Ecstasy of St. Theresa**, by Bernini. As David is seen at the peak of bodily exertion, St. Theresa is shown at the peak of spiritual transport.

Reformation ideals, most of them worked in the service of monarchs who sought their own glorification.

Indubitably the most imaginative and influential figure of the original Roman Baroque was the architect and sculptor Gianlorenzo Bernini (1598–1680), a frequent employee of the papacy who created one of the most magnificent celebrations of papal grandeur in the sweeping colonnades leading up to St. Peter's Basilica. Breaking with the serene Renaissance classicism of Palladio, Bernini's architecture retained the use of classical elements such as columns and domes, but combined them in ways meant to express both aggressive restlessness and great power. In addition Bernini was one of the first to experiment with church facades built "in depth"—building frontages not conceived as continuous surfaces but that jutted out at odd angles and seemingly invaded the open space in front of them. If the purpose of these innovations was to draw the viewer emotionally into the ambit of the work of art, the same may be said for Bernini's aims in sculpture. Harking back to the restless motion of Hellenistic statuary—particularly the Laocoön group—and building on tendencies already present in the later sculpture of Michelangelo, Bernini's statuary emphasizes drama and incites the viewer to respond to it rather than serenely to observe.

The Church of S. Carlo alle Quattro Fontane, Rome. Built by Bernini's contemporary Francesco Borromini in 1665, the facade of S. Carlo well exemplifies the frontage "in depth" characteristic of Baroque architecture.

Since most Italian Baroque painters lacked Bernini's artistic genius, to view the very greatest masterpieces of southern European Baroque painting one must look to Spain and the work of Diego Velázquez (1599–1660). Unlike Bernini, Velázquez, a court painter in Madrid just when Spain hung on the brink of ruin, was not an entirely typical exponent of the Baroque style. Certainly many of his canvases display a characteristically Baroque delight in motion, drama, and power, but Velázquez's best work is characterized by a more restrained thoughtfulness than is usually found in the Baroque. Thus his famous *Surrender of Breda* shows muscular horses and splendid Spanish grandees on the one hand, but un-Baroque humane and deep sympathy for defeated, disarrayed troops on the other. Moreover, Velázquez's single greatest painting, *The Maids of Honor,* done around 1656 after Spain's collapse, radiates thoughtfulness rather than drama and is one of the most probing artistic examinations of illusion and reality ever executed.

Brueghel

Southern Europe's main northern rival for artistic laurels in the "iron century" was the Netherlands, where three extremely dissimilar painters all explored the theme of the greatness and wretchedness of man to the fullest. The earliest, Peter Brueghel (c. 1525–1569), worked in a vein related to earlier Netherlandish realism. But unlike his predecessors, who favored quiet urban scenes, Brueghel exulted in portraying the busy, elemental life of the peasantry. Most famous in this respect are his rollicking *Peasant Wedding* and *Peasant Wedding Dance,* and his spacious *Harvesters,* in which guzzling and snoring fieldhands are taking a well-deserved break from their heavy labors under the noon sun. Such vistas give the impression of uninterrupted rhythms of life, but late in his career Brueghel became appalled by the intolerance and bloodshed he witnessed during

Pope Innocent X, by Velázquez (1599–1660). A trenchant portrait with an evident debt to Raphael's Julius II (see p. 419).

The Surrender of Breda, by Velázquez. Celebrating a Spanish victory over the Dutch in an early phase of the Thirty Years' War, the Spanish lances point proudly skyward in contrast to the desolate Dutch smoke, but the Spanish commander displays magnanimity for the defeated enemy.

The Maids of Honor, by Velázquez. The artist himself is at work on a double portrait of the king and queen of Spain (who may be seen in the rear mirror), but reality is more obvious in the foreground in the persons of the delicately impish princess, her two maids, and a misshapen dwarf. The twentieth-century Spanish artist Picasso gained great inspiration from this work.

The Massacre of the Innocents, by Brueghel (c. 1525–1569). This painting shows how effectively art can be used as a means of social commentary. Many art historians believe that Brueghel was tacitly depicting the suffering of the Netherlands at the hands of the Spanish in his own day.

The Harvesters, by Brueghel. Brueghel chose to depict both the hard work and the recreation of the peasantry.

the time of the Calvinist riots and the Spanish repression in the Netherlands and expressed his criticism in an understated yet searing manner. In *The Blind Leading the Blind,* for example, we see what happens when ignorant fanatics start showing the way to each other. More powerful still is Brueghel's *Massacre of the Innocents,* which from a distance looks like a snug scene of a Flemish village buried in snow. In fact, however, heartless soldiers are methodically breaking into homes and slaughtering babies, the simple peasant folk are fully at their mercy, and the artist—alluding to a Gospel forgotten by warring Catholics and Protestants alike—seems to be saying "as it happened in the time of Christ, so it happens now."

Rubens

Vastly different from Brueghel was the Netherlandish Baroque painter Peter Paul Rubens (1577–1640). Since the Baroque was an international movement closely linked to the spread of the Counter-Reformation, it should offer no surprise that Baroque style was extremely well represented in just that part of the Netherlands which, after long warfare, had been retained by Spain. In fact, Rubens of Antwerp was a far more typical Baroque artist than Velázquez of Madrid, painting literally thousands of robust canvases that glorified resurgent Catholicism or exalted second-rate aristocrats by portraying them as epic heroes dressed in bearskins. Even when Rubens's intent was not overtly propagandistic he customarily reveled in the sumptuous extravagance of the Baroque manner, being perhaps most famous today for the pink and rounded flesh of his well-nourished nudes. But unlike a host of lesser Baroque artists, Rubens was not entirely lacking in subtlety and was a man of many moods. His gentle portrait of his son Nicholas catches unaffected childhood in a moment of repose, and though throughout most of his career Rubens had celebrated martial valor, his late *Horrors of War* movingly portrays what he himself called "the grief of unfortunate Europe, which, for so many years now, has suffered plunder, outrage, and misery."

Rubens's Portrait of his Son Nicholas.

Rembrandt

In some ways a blend of Brueghel and Rubens, the greatest of all Netherlandish painters, Rembrandt van Rijn (1606–1669), defies all attempts at facile characterization. Living across the border from the Spanish Netherlands in staunchly Calvinistic Holland, Rembrandt belonged to a society that was too austere to tolerate the unbuckled realism of a Brueghel or the fleshy Baroque pomposity of a Rubens. Yet Rembrandt managed to put both realistic and Baroque traits to new uses. In his early career he gained fame and fortune as the painter of biblical scenes that lacked the Baroque's fleshiness but retained its grandeur in their swirling forms and stunning experiments with light. In this early period too Rembrandt was active as a realistic portrait painter who knew how to flatter his self-satisfied subjects by emphasizing their Calvinistic steadfastness, to the great advantage of his purse. But gradually his prosperity faded, apparently in part because he grew tired of flattering and definitely because he made some bad investments. Since personal tragedies also mounted in the painter's middle and declining years his art inevitably became far more pensive and sombre, but it gained in dignity, subtle lyricism, and

The Horrors of War, by Rubens (1577–1640). The war god Mars here casts aside his mistress Venus and threatens humanity with death and destruction. In his old age Rubens took a far more critical view of war than he did for most of his earlier career.

The Triumph of the Eucharist, by Rubens. A typical Baroque work, this painting proclaims the victory of the Cross and the Eucharistic Chalice, symbols of Counter-Reformation Catholicism.

The Polish Rider, by Rembrandt (1606–1669). Unlike Titian's equestrian Charles V (see p. 477), Rembrandt's rider is reflective and hence more humane.

Aristotle Contemplating the Bust of Homer, by Rembrandt. One of the greatest painters' view of one of the greatest of philosophers caught up by the aura of one of the greatest poets.

Self-Portrait, by Judith Leyster (1609–1660). Leyster was a Dutch contemporary of Rembrandt who pursued a successful career as an artist during her early twenties, before she married. Respected in her own day, she was all but forgotten for centuries thereafter.

awesome mystery. Thus his later portraits, including those of himself, are imbued with introspective qualities and a suggestion that only the half is being told. Equally moving are explicitly philosophical paintings such as *Aristotle Contemplating the Bust of Homer,* in which the supposedly earthbound philosopher seems spellbound by the otherworldly luminous radiance of the epic poet, and *The Polish Rider,* in which realistic and Baroque elements merge into a higher synthesis portraying a pensive young man setting out fearlessly into a perilous world. Like Shakespeare, Rembrandt knew that life's journey is full of perils, but his most mature paintings suggest that these can be mastered with poetry and courage.

SUMMARY POINTS

- Economic hardships, prolonged wars, and religious riots combined to produce a century of pronounced crisis in Europe from about 1560 to about 1660.
- Dramatic price inflation, caused in part by growing populations and influx of silver from Spanish South America, devastated the laboring poor and reduced the resources of governments.
- Conflicts between Catholics and Protestants led to civil war in France and England, a war for the independence of the Netherlands, and a war on the high seas between England and Spain.

The Thirty Years' War was at first a religious war between Catholics and Protestants in Germany but gradually turned into an international struggle for hegemony in Europe in which France replaced Spain as the mightiest European power.

- Political philosophers responded to the turmoil of the age with prescriptions for government that ranged from the libertarianism sought by some Huguenots and Puritans to the absolutism advocated by Jean Bodin and Thomas Hobbes.
- Extraordinary works of literature and art were produced between 1560 and 1660, including the plays of William Shakespeare, the poems of John Milton, and the paintings of El Greco, Brueghel, and Rembrandt.

Selected Readings

Aston, T. H., ed., *Crisis in Europe: 1560–1660,* London, 1965. A collection of highly valuable essays.

Braudel, Fernand, *The Mediterranean and the Mediterranean World in the Age of Philip II,* 2 vols., New York, 1972. One of the most brilliant history books of our age. Treats life in the Mediterranean regions in the second half of the sixteenth century with particular emphasis on how geography determines the course of human history.

Chute, Marchette, *Shakespeare of London,* New York, 1949. The best popular biography.

Dean, Leonard F., ed., *Shakespeare: Modern Essays in Criticism,* rev. ed., New York, 1967. A variety of scholarly appraisals.

Dunn, Richard S., *The Age of Religious Wars, 1559–1715,* 2d ed., New York, 1979. The best college-level text on this period. Extremely well written.

Elliott, John H., *Imperial Spain, 1469–1716,* London, 1963. A splendid work of synthesis.

———, *Europe Divided: 1559–1598,* London, 1968. An extremely lucid narrative of complex events.

———, *Richelieu and Olivares,* New York, 1984. Brilliant comparative history setting off similarities and differences between seventeenth-century France and Spain.

Elton, G. R., *England under the Tudors,* 3d ed., London, 1991. Engagingly written and authoritative.

Frame, Donald, *Montaigne: A Biography,* New York, 1965. By far the best study in English.

Fraser, Lady Antonia, *Cromwell: The Lord Protector,* London, 1973. A popular biography.

Held, Julius S., and Donald Posner, *17th and 18th Century Art: Baroque Painting, Sculpture, Architecture,* New York, 1979. The most complete introductory review of the subject in English.

Hibbard, Howard, *Bernini,* Baltimore, 1965. The basic study in English of this central figure of Baroque artistic activity.

Hill, Christopher, *The Century of Revolution: 1603–1714,* 2d ed., New York, 1982. A valuable survey of English developments that holds narrative to a minimum and stresses economic and social trends.

Hirst, Derek, *Authority and Conflict: England, 1603–1658,* London, 1986. Integrates recent interpretations. The best survey out of several available.

Kahr, Madlyn M., *Velázquez: The Art of Painting,* New York, 1976.

Kamen, Henry, *The Iron Century: Social Change in Europe, 1559–1660,* rev. ed., New York, 1976. One of the most detailed and persuasive statements of the view that there was a "general crisis" in many different aspects of European life.

Le Roy Ladurie, Emmanuel, *Carnival in Romans,* New York, 1979. A close-up view of social turmoil in France in 1580.

Levack, Brian P., *The Witch-Hunt in Early Modern Europe,* 2d ed., New York, 1995.

Mattingly, Garrett, *The Armada,* Boston, 1959. Fascinating narrative; thoroughly reliable and reads like a novel.

Monter, E. William, ed., *European Witchcraft,* New York, 1969. Selected readings with fine introductions by one of the world's leading experts.

Parker, Geoffrey, *The Dutch Revolt,* rev. ed., Ithaca, N.Y., 1989. The standard survey in English on the revolt of the Netherlands.

———, *Europe in Crisis: 1598–1648,* Brighton, Sussex, 1980. A primarily political narrative of war and revolution in Europe exclusive of England.

Pennington, D. H., *Seventeenth-Century Europe,* London, 1970. An extremely thorough and reliable survey that follows the conventional periodization of treating a century bounded by the round numbers 1600 and 1700.

Pierson, Peter, *Philip II of Spain,* London, 1975. An absorbing attempt to study Philip's personality and actions in terms of the dominant assumptions of his age.

Rabb, Theodore K., *The Struggle for Stability in Early Modern Europe,* New York, 1975. A stimulating essay arguing that a shift from crisis to stability took place around 1660.

Roots, Ivan, ed., *Cromwell, A Profile,* New York, 1973. A collection of readings on problems in interpretation; complements Fraser.

Rosenberg, Jakob, *Rembrandt: Life and Work,* rev. ed., Ithaca, N.Y., 1980.

Russell, Conrad, *The Crisis of Parliaments: English History, 1509–1660,* New York, 1971. The best survey covering this broad range of time.

Shearman, John, *Mannerism,* Baltimore, 1967. Treats trends in late-sixteenth-century architecture and sculpture as well as Manneristic painting.

Steinberg, S. H., *The Thirty Years' War and the Conflict for European Hegemony, 1600–1660,* New York, 1966. The best scholarly account.

Stone, Lawrence, *The Causes of the English Revolution, 1529–1642,* New York, 1972. A judicious analysis by one of the foremost social historians of our age.

Thomas, Keith, *Religion and the Decline of Magic,* London, 1971. A marvelously insightful broad-gauged study of popular belief in England.

Walzer, Michael, *The Revolution of the Saints: A Study in the Origins of Radical Politics,* Cambridge, Mass., 1965. An attempt by a political scientist to demonstrate that English Puritanism was the earliest incarnation of modern political radicalism.

Wedgwood, C. V., *William the Silent,* London, 1944. A laudatory and urbanely written biography.

Cervantes, Miguel de, *Don Quixote,* tr. Walter Starkie, New York, 1957.
Hobbes, Thomas, *Leviathan,* abridged by F. B. Randall, New York, 1964.
Montaigne, Michel de, *Essays,* tr. J. M. Cohen, Baltimore, 1958.
Pascal, Blaise, *Pensées,* French-English ed., H. F. Stewart, London, 1950.
Sprenger, Jakob, and H. Kramer, *The Malleus Maleficarum,* tr. M. Summers, 2d ed., London, 1948. A frightful yet fascinating work, the *Malleus* ("The Hammer of Witches") was the most frequently used handbook of early-modern witchcraft prosecutors.

CHAPTER 16

THE ECONOMY AND SOCIETY OF EARLY-MODERN EUROPE

> We ought to esteem and cherish those trades which we have in remote or far countries, for besides the increase in shipping and mariners thereby, the wares also sent thither and received from thence are far more profitable unto the kingdom than by our trades near at hand.
>
> —THOMAS MUN, *England's Treasure by Foreign Trade,* 1630

> In nearly every state in Europe citizens are divided into the three orders of nobles, clergy, and people. . . . Even Plato, although he intended all his citizens to enjoy an equality of rights and privileges, divided them into the three orders of guardians, soldiers and labourers. All this goes to show that there never was a commonwealth, real or imaginary, even if conceived in the most popular terms, where citizens were in truth equal in all rights and privileges. Some always have more, some less than the rest.
>
> —JEAN BODIN, *Six Books of the Commonwealth,* 1570

Economic change

ANY STUDY of early-modern European society must concern itself with change, with the factors that in the two hundred years after 1600 were powerful enough to produce the political upheaval of the French Revolution and the economic stimulus for the Industrial Revolution. Arguably, the most profound change during that period was economic. By the latter part of the eighteenth century, the freebooting overseas expansionism that had begun in the sixteenth century with the Spanish *conquistadores* had ended with Europe at the center of a vast system of worldwide trade. Commerce on this increasingly global scale had given birth to institutions fashioned for its support, and had altered patterns of living among those caught up in its overpowering dynamic. Banks and joint-stock companies financed international commercial ventures. New urban workshops responded to the intensified demand for manufactured goods. As international banking developed into a highly sophisticated profession, its practitioners became powerful. As urban workshops imposed new conditions and habits, the urban artisan was forced to bend uncomfortably to unfamiliar demands.

New economic realities and old social forms

European society as a whole found bending no more comfortable. Change was imposed upon national communities that, in many cases, were still defined according to the hierarchies of the Middle Ages: landlord and peasant, nobleman and serf. Each order was expected to acknowledge its inherent obligations and responsibilities, as each was assumed to be part of an organic and divinely sanctioned communal whole. Where, within this preordained structure, was the independent commercial entrepreneur or the dispossessed laborer supposed to fit? Tension of this sort between old forms and new realities was further exacerbated by the general crisis that we analyzed in the preceding chapter. Change produced by economic expansion and dislocation occurred against the background of civil and religious turmoil that tore much of Europe to pieces in the seventeenth century, and against an equally disruptive cycle of demographic swings caused by warfare and disease, by good weather one year, bad weather—and hence famine—the next. Those were the changes closest to the lives of most Europeans, the men and women still bound to the land, for whom, as the French historian Pierre Goubert has observed, "death was at the center of life, just as the graveyard was at the center of the village." The concerns of this chapter are thus both the economic and social circumstances that produced change over a period of almost two hundred years, and the habits and traditions that were making change complex and difficult.

Life and Death: Patterns of Population

No facts better illustrate the degree to which the two hundred years of European history between 1600 and 1800 were subject to chance and change than those having to do with life and death—patterns of population, as they imprinted themselves across the early-modern period.

The threat of famine

The pattern of life for most Europeans centered on the struggle to stay alive. They lived and worked within a subsistence economy, considering themselves extremely fortunate if they could grow or earn what it took to survive. In most instances their enemy was not an invading army, but famine; it is not surprising that one's well-being was measured simply by one's girth. At least once a decade, climatic conditions—usually a long period of summer rainfall—would produce a devastatingly bad harvest, which in turn would result in widespread malnutrition often leading to serious illness and death. A family might survive for a time by eating less, but eventually, with its meager stocks exhausted and the cost of grain high, the human costs would mount. The substitution of grass, nuts, and tree bark for grain on which the peasants depended almost entirely for nourishment was as inadequate for them as it appears pathetic to us.

Population crises

Widespread crop failures occurred at fairly regular intervals—the worst in France, for example, about every thirty years (1597, 1630, 1662, 1694). They helped to cause the series of population crises that are the outstanding feature of early-modern demographic history. Poor harvests and the high prices produced by a scarcity of grain meant not only undernourishment and possible starvation, but increasing unemployment: with fewer crops to be harvested, more money was spent on food and, consequently,

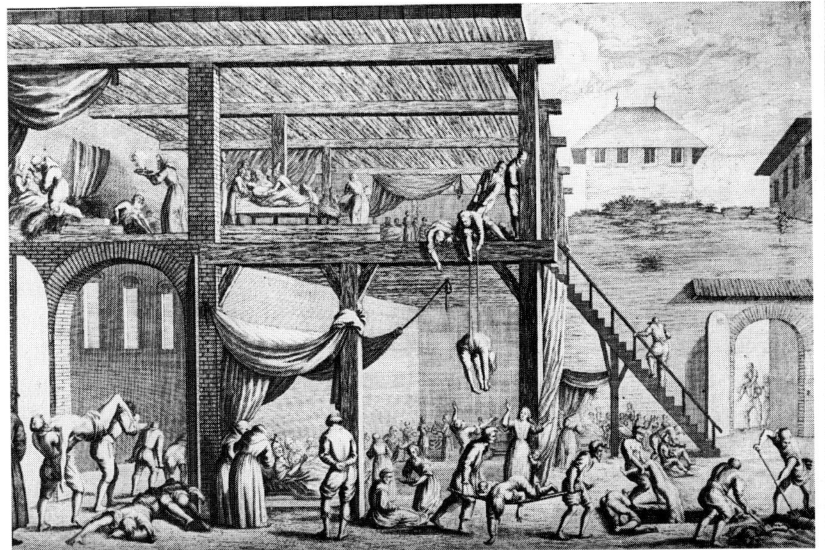

Left: **A Plague Hospital in Vienna.** The efforts to contain outbreaks of plague by gathering the sick in establishments such as this and burying the dead on the site proved unsuccessful. Right: **A Physician's Mask.** This German device containing smelling salts in its curved beak was designed to combat the plague, which physicians incorrectly believed was spread by poisonous vapors.

less on manufactured goods. The despair such conditions could easily breed would in turn contribute to a postponement of marriage and of births, and thus to a population decline. The patterns of marriages and births revealed in local parish registers indicate that throughout Europe the populations of individual communities rose and fell dramatically in rhythm with the fortunes of the harvest.

Health and sanitation

An undernourished population is a population particularly susceptible to disease. Bubonic plague ravaged seventeenth-century Europe. Severe outbreaks occurred in Seville in 1649, in Amsterdam in 1664, and in London the following year. By 1700 it had all but disappeared; it last appeared in western Europe in a small area of southern France in 1720, though Moscow suffered an outbreak as late as 1771. Despite the gradual retreat of the plague, however, other diseases took a dreadful toll, in an age when available medical treatment was little more than crude guesswork, and in any event, beyond the reach of the poor. Epidemics of dysentery, smallpox, and typhus occurred with savage regularity. As late as 1779, more than 100,000 people died of dysentery in the French province of Brittany. Most diseases attacked rich and poor impartially. Water supplies in towns and in the country were contaminated by heedless disposal of human waste and by all manner of garbage and urban filth. Bathing, feared at one time as a method of spreading disease, was by no means a weekly habit, whatever the social status of the household. Samuel Pepys, a prosperous servant of the crown in seventeenth-century London, recorded in his diary that his housemaid was in the habit of picking the lice from his scalp, that he took his first bath only after his wife had taken hers and

"Summer Amusement: Bugg Hunting." In this joking treatment of one of the facts of everyday life the bedbugs meet sudden death in a full chamber pot.

experienced the pleasures of cleanliness, and that he had, on occasion, thought nothing of using the fireplace in his bedroom as a toilet, the maid having failed to provide him with a chamberpot. If such was Pepys's attitude toward hygiene and sanitation, imagine that of the poverty-stricken peasant, and the threat to health implicit in such attitudes.

The precariousness of life helped encourage most men and women in early-modern Europe to postpone marriage until their mid- to late twenties, by which time they hoped not only to have survived but also to have accumulated sufficient resources to establish a household. Young couples lived on their own, and not, as in societies elsewhere, as part of "extended" families of three generations. Since a son could not inherit until his father died, he was compelled to establish himself independently, and to postpone starting his own family until he had done so. Though historians have failed to find a clear explanation for this pattern of later marriages, it may have resulted from a growing desire on the part of younger men and women for a higher standard of living. Late marriage helped to control the birth rate. Once married, however, a couple generally produced their first child within a year. Although subsequent children appeared with annual or biennial regularity, long periods of breastfeeding, which tends to reduce the mother's fertility, and near poverty went some way toward limiting childbirth.

Population growth

Until the middle of the eighteenth century, populations continued to wax and wane according to the outbreak of warfare, famine, and disease. From about 1750 on, however, there was a steady and significant population increase, with almost all countries experiencing major growth. In Russia, where territorial expansion added further to the increases, the population rate may have tripled in the second half of the eighteenth century. Gains elsewhere, while not usually as spectacular, were nevertheless significant. The population of Prussia doubled; Hungary's more than

Eighteenth-Century Sanitation. "Nightmen" moved through city streets after dark emptying the refuse of privies.

tripled; and England's population, which was about 5.5 million in 1700, reached 9 million in 1800. France, already in 1700 the most heavily populated country in Europe (about 20 million), added another 6 million before 1790. Spaniards multiplied from 7.6 million in 1717 to 10.5 million in 1797. Although reasons for the population increase remain something of a mystery, historians are inclined to agree that it was the cumulative result of a decrease in infant mortality and a very gradual decline in the death rate, due in large measure to an equally gradual increase in the food supply. Better transportation facilitated the shipment of food over greater distances. Land clearances, particularly in England, and in Prussia and Russia, where territories were opened to colonization, provided an essential ingredient for increased production. New staples—the potato and maize—supplemented the diets of the very poor. And although evidence here is only fragmentary, it appears that whereas the climate of seventeenth-century Europe was abnormally bad, that of the succeeding hundred years was on the whole favorable.

New problems and attitudes

Population increase brought with it new problems and new attitudes. For example, in France, it meant pressure on the land, as more peasants attempted to wring survival from an overpopulated countryside. The consequence was migration from the country to the city. The decline in the death rate among infants—along with an apparent increase in illegitimacy at the end of the eighteenth century—created a growing population of unwanted babies among the poor. Some desperate women resorted to infanticide, though since children murdered at birth died without benefit of baptism, the crime was stigmatized as especially heinous by the Church as well as by society in general. More often, babies were abandoned at the doors of foundling hospitals. As an English benefactor of several such institutions, Jonas Hanway, remarked in 1766, "it is much less difficult to the human heart and the dictates of self-preservation to drop a child than to kill it." In Paris during the 1780s from seven to eight thousand children were being abandoned out of a total of thirty thousand new births. Paradoxically, some historians now argue that during this same period the decrease in infant and child mortality encouraged many parents to lavish care and affection on their offspring in a way that they had not when the repeated early deaths of their sons and daughters had taught them the futility of that emotional bond.

The "rise" of towns and cities

Although somewhere between 80 and 90 percent of the population lived in small rural communities, towns and cities were coming to play an increasingly important role in the life of early-modern Europe. One must speak of the "rise" of towns and cities with caution, however, since the pace of urbanization varied greatly across the Continent. Russia remained almost entirely rural: only 2.5 percent of its population lived in towns in 1630, and that percentage had risen by only 0.5 percent by 1774. In Holland, on the other hand, 59 percent of the population was urban in 1627 and 65 percent in 1795.

Shifts in urban population

The total number of urban dwellers did not vary markedly after the end of the sixteenth century, when there were approximately 200 cities in Europe with a population of over 10,000. What did change between 1600 and 1800 was, first, the way in which those cities were distributed across the map, concentrated increasingly in the north and west; and second, the growing proportion of very large cities to the whole. The patterns of trade and commerce had much to do with these shifts. Cities like Hamburg in Germany, Liverpool in England, Toulon in France, and Cadiz in Spain grew by about 250 percent between 1600 and 1750. Amsterdam, the hub of early-modern international commerce, increased from 30,000 in 1530 to 115,000 in 1630 and 200,000 by 1800. Naples, the busy Mediterranean port, went from a population of 300,000 in 1600 to nearly half a million by the late eighteenth century. Where goods were traded, processed, and manufactured, fleets built and provisioned, people flocked to work. An eighteenth-century commentator noted that the laborers in Paris were "almost all foreigners"—that is, men and women born outside the city: carpenters from Savoy, water carriers from Auvergne, porters from Lyons, stonecutters from Normandy, wigmakers from Gascony, shoemakers from Lorraine.

Ebb and flow of urban growth

As some cities expanded, others stagnated or declined as a result of commercial changes. Norwich, in England, grew at the expense of older industrial centers on the English Channel when the manufacture of woolen goods shifted north. The population of the important German market center of Frankfurt declined during and after the Thirty Years' War, when difficulties of communication and the general instability caused by frequent military campaigns diverted much of its former business to Amsterdam.

Growth of administrative centers

The most spectacular urban population growth occurred in the administrative capitals of the increasingly centralized nations of Europe. By the middle of the eighteenth century, Madrid, Berlin, and St. Petersburg all had populations of over 100,000. London grew from 674,000 in 1700 to 860,000 a century later. Paris, a city of approximately 180,000 in 1600, increased to over half a million by 1800. Berlin grew from a population of 6,500 in 1661, to 60,000 in 1721, to 140,000 in 1783. Its increase was due in part to the fact that successive Prussian rulers undertook to improve its position as a trade center by the construction of canals that linked it with Breslau and Hamburg. Its population rose as well, however, because of the marked increase in Prussian army and bureaucratic personnel based in the capital city. Of the 140,000 citizens of Berlin in 1783, approximately 65,000 were state employees or members of their families.

The Dynamics of Agriculture and Industry

Traditional techniques yield to innovation

The dramatic shifts in population we have been tracing were in some cases the cause, in others the effect, of equally important changes occurring in agriculture and industry. Throughout most of the two-hundred-year period under review, agricultural production was generally carried on according to traditional techniques that kept the volume of produc-

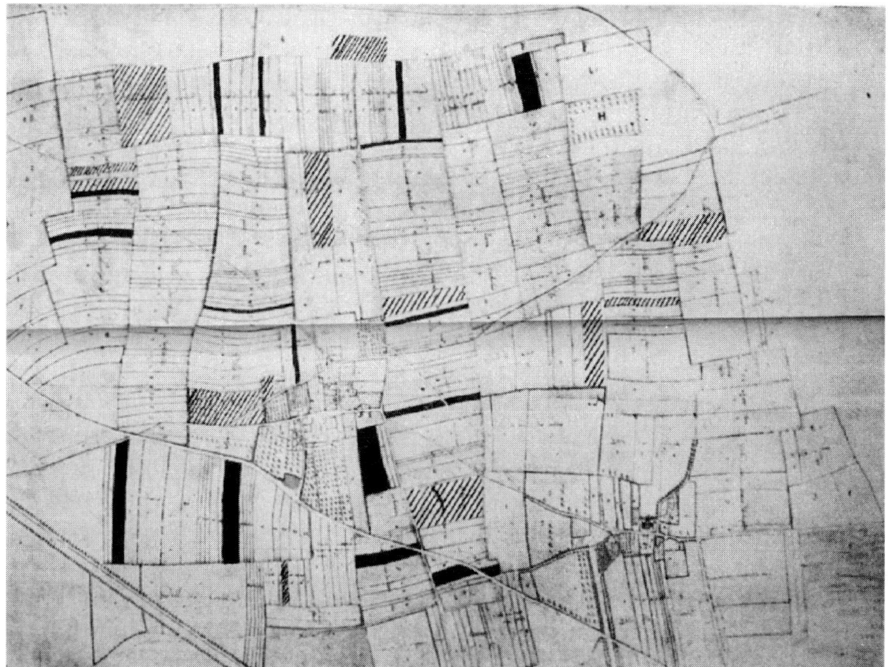

The Open-Field System in Northern France, 1738. Note the subdivision of large tracts into narrow strips, often owned by different proprietors.

tion low; yet by the end of the eighteenth century, tradition in some areas had yielded to innovation, with the result that production was increasing dramatically.

The open-field system

Most of the agricultural regions of seventeenth-century Europe consisted of open fields. In the north, these fields were usually large sections of land, divided into long, narrow strips; in the south, the strips tended to reflect the more irregular shape of local landscapes. Although one or two rich proprietors might own as much as three-fourths of the land in an open-field village, that land did not make up one solid block. Instead it was made up of a great many plots, seldom contiguous, within the various open fields that surrounded the village. Landholding was further complicated by local usage. In France, for example, a *seigneur* might own a group of estates (*seigneury*) whose boundaries were not contiguous with any one parish. A parish, in turn, might be dependent on more than one *seigneur.* A property owner's *desmesne*—which he worked with hired laborers for his own direct profit—and his tenant farms—those that he leased out to peasants—all consisted of bits and pieces of land that lay alongside other bits and pieces that belonged to other landowners—very often small peasant proprietors. Each large open field thus resembled a patchwork quilt. Under these circumstances, in order for the fields to be cultivated with any degree of efficiency, all the "patches" had to be planted with the same crop, and sown, cultivated, and harvested together.

The inefficiency inherent in the management of a multitude of plots by many farmers was a price small peasant proprietors were willing to pay in return for the social utility of communal decision-making and the right to graze livestock on common land. Once landlords, particularly in England and Holland, began to compete for markets as capitalist agricultural entrepreneurs, however, they looked for ways to overcome the inefficiency of traditional practices, so as to improve the yield on their land.

Enclosure

By the end of the eighteenth century a great many English and Dutch landlords had resolved the problem of low production by adopting a full range of innovative farming techniques, the most drastic of which was the enclosure of open fields to allow for more systematic and therefore more productive farming. "Enclosure" was the term for land reorganization within a traditional village community. The earliest enclosures in England took place in the fifteenth and sixteenth centuries and entailed the conversion of lands into fenced-off sheep meadows. Because of the great profits to be accrued from wool, some landlords converted common pastures that hitherto had supported peasant livestock into their own preserves for sheep-raising, thus threatening the livelihood of entire peasant communities.

Absolute vs. common property rights

Enclosure was more easily accomplished in those countries—England most notably—where there was a system of absolute property rights and wage labor. Where the tradition of "common" rights to grazing and foraging was strong, as in France, landlords found it far more difficult to impose a new economic order. In France, as well, a large peasantry owned small plots of land outright, adding up to approximately one-third of all agricultural land. It had neither an interest in nor the financial capacity for change. Monarchs tended to oppose enclosure since it promised to enrich further a rival noble class. In seventeenth-century France the monarchy needed an economically stable peasantry to support its expanding tax programs, and therefore worked to secure peasants in the customary tenure of their farms. Thus defended, the peasants were better able to resist effectively attempts at enclosure launched by large landholders. English property owners were more fortunate, taking advantage of the absence of royal opposition during the Cromwellian period to enclose on a broad scale.

Scientific farming

The really dramatic enclosure movement in England took place, however, at the end of the early-modern period, between 1710 and 1810. Landlords began to engage in the practice of "scientific farming." They realized that by introducing new crops and farming methods they could reduce the amount of land kept fallow and bring in higher yields and thus higher profits. The most important new crops with which landowners experimented were clover, alfalfa, and related varieties of leguminous plants. These reduced fertility much less than cereal grains and helped to improve the quality of the soil by gathering nitrogen and making the ground more porous. Another new crop that had a similar effect was the turnip. The greatest propagandist for the planting of this unattractive vegetable was Viscount Charles Townshend (1674–1738), a prominent aristocrat and politician, who toward the end of his life gained the nickname of "Turnip" Townshend because of his dedication to the use of the turnip in new crop-rotation systems.

Clover, alfalfa, and turnips not only helped do away with fallow lands; they also provided excellent winter food for animals, thereby aiding the production of more and better livestock. More livestock also meant more manure. Accordingly, intensive manuring became another way in which scientific farmers could eliminate the need for fallow land. Other improvements in farming methods introduced in the period were more intensive hoeing and weeding, and the use of the seed drill for planting grain. The latter eliminated the old wasteful method of sowing grain by hand, much of it remaining on top to be eaten by birds.

THE

Englifh Farrier,

OR,

Countrey-mans Treafure.

Shewing approved Remedies to cure all Difeafes, Hurts, Maimes, Maladies, and Griefes in Horfes: and how to know the feverall Difeafes that breed in them; with a defcription of every Veine; how, and when to let them blood, according to the nature of their Difeafes.

With directions to know the feverall Ages of them.

Faithfully fet forth according to Art and approved experiment, for the benefit of Gentlemen, Farmers, Inholders, Husbandmen, and generally for all.

Improved Farming. The title page of one of many agricultural tracts available to farmers interested in improving their output.

Enclosure was a change that had major social consequences where it occurred. Village life under the open-field system was communal to the extent that decisions as to which crops were to be grown where and when had to be arrived at jointly. Common land afforded the poor not only a place to tether a cow, to fish, or to gather firewood, but to breathe at least a bit of the air of social freedom. Enclosure cost villagers their modest freedoms, as well as the traditional right to help determine how the community's subsistence economy was to be managed. Cottagers (very small landholders) and squatters, who had over generations established a customary right to the use of common lands, were reduced to the rank of landless laborers.

The increasingly capitalistic basis of European agriculture

On the Continent, except for Holland, there was nothing comparable to the English advance in scientific farming. Nor, with the notable exception of Spain, was there a pronounced enclosure movement as in England and the Low Countries. Yet despite that fact, European food production became increasingly capitalistic in the seventeenth and eighteenth centuries. Landlords leased farms to tenants and reaped profits as rent. Often they allowed tenants to pay rent in the form of half their crops. This system of sharecropping was most prevalent in France, Italy, and Spain. Farther east, in Prussia, Poland, Hungary, and Russia, landowners continued to rely on unpaid serfs to till the land. But wherever the scale of production and marketing was altered to increase profits, it brought change in its wake.

Introduction of maize and potatoes

The eighteenth century saw the introduction of two crops from the New World, maize (Indian corn) and the potato, which eventually resulted in the provision of a more adequate diet for the poor. Since maize can be grown only in areas with substantial periods of sunny and dry weather, its cultivation spread through Italy and the southeastern part of the Continent. Whereas an average ear of grain would yield only about four seeds for every one planted, an ear of maize would yield about seventy or eighty. That made it a "miracle" crop, filling granaries where they had been almost empty before. The potato was an equally miraculous innovation for the European North. Its advantages were numerous: potatoes could be grown on the poorest, sandiest, or wettest of lands where nothing else could be raised; they could be fitted into the smallest of patches. Raising potatoes even in small patches was profitable because the yield of potatoes was extraordinarily abundant. Finally, the potato provided an inexpensive means of improving the human diet. It is rich in calories and contains many vitamins and minerals. Northern European peasants initially resisted growing and eating potatoes. Clergymen taught them to fear the plant because it is not mentioned in the Bible. Some claimed that it transmitted leprosy. Still others insisted that it was a cause of flatulence, a property acknowledged by a French authority on diet in 1765, although the writer added, "What is a little wind to the vigorous organs of the peasants and workers?" Yet in the course of the eighteenth century the poor grew accustomed to the potato, although sometimes after considerable pressure. Frederick the Great compelled Prussian peasants to cultivate potatoes until the crop achieved acceptance and became a staple throughout much of northern Germany. By about 1800 the average north German peasant family ate potatoes as a main course at least once a day.

Rural manufacturing: the putting-out system

Agriculture was not the only commercial enterprise in early-modern rural Europe. Increasingly, manufactured goods—particularly textiles—were being produced in the countryside, as entrepreneurs battled to circumvent artisanal and guild restrictions that limited production in urban manufacturing centers. Unfettered rural industry was a response to the constantly growing demand of new markets created by the increase in regional, national, and international commerce. Entrepreneurs made use of the so-called putting-out system to address this demand and to reap large profits. Unhampered by guild regulations, which in medieval times had restricted the production and distribution of textiles to maintain price levels, merchants would buy up a stock of raw material, most often wool or flax, which they would then "put out," or supply, to rural workers for carding (combing the fibers) and spinning. Once spun, the yarn or thread was collected by the merchant and passed to rural weavers, who wove it into cloth. Collected once more, the material was processed by other workers at bleaching or dyeing shops and collected for a final time by the entrepreneur who then sold it either to a wholesaler or directly to retail customers.

Regional specialization

Although the putting-out phenomenon—or, as it is often referred to, the process of *proto-industrialization*—occurred throughout Europe, it was usually concentrated regionally. Most industrial areas specialized in the production of particular commodities, based on the availability of raw materials. Flanders was a producer of linens; Verviers (in present-day Belgium) of woolens; Silesia of linens. As markets—regional, national, and international—developed, these rural manufacturing areas grew accordingly. Industries employed homeworkers by the thousands. A major mid-eighteenth-century textile firm in Abbeville, France, provided work to 1,800 in central workshops but to 10,000 in their own homes. One of the largest woolen manufacturers in Linz, Austria, in 1786 was employing 35,000, of whom more than 29,000 were domestic spinners.

Rural workers accepted this system of manufacture as a means of staving off poverty or possible starvation in years of particularly bad harvests. Domestic textile production involved the entire family. Even the youngest children could participate in the process of cleaning the raw wool. Older children carded. Wives and husbands spun or wove. Spinning, until the invention of the jenny at the end of the eighteenth century (see p. 729), was a far more time-consuming process than weaving, which had been speeded considerably by the Englishman John Kay's early-eighteenth-century invention of the fly-shuttle, a mechanical device that automatically returned the shuttle to its starting place after it had been "thrown" across the loom.

Family production

In addition to providing extra income, the putting-out system brought other advantages to rural homeworkers. They could regulate the pace of their labor to some degree, and could abandon it altogether when farm work was available during the planting and harvest seasons. Their ability to work at home was a mixed blessing, however, for conditions in cottages that were wretchedly built and poorly ventilated were often exceedingly cramped and unpleasant, especially when workers were compelled to accommodate a bulky loom within their already crowded living quarters. But domestic labor, however unpleasant, was preferable to work away from home in a shop, where conditions might be even more oppressive under the watchful eye of an unsympathetic master. There were also advantages for the merchant-entrepreneur, who benefited not only

Advantages of putting-out

Left: "**Rustic Courtship.**" This detail from an etching (1785) by the English satirist Thomas Rowlandson suggests the advantages of doorstep domestic industry: natural lighting, improved ventilation, and a chance to converse with visitors. Work under these self-paced conditions, though usually long and hard, was carried on to a personal rhythm. Right: **Artisan and Family,** by Gerard ter Borch. This seventeenth-century wheelwright, though a skilled artisan, is nevertheless depicted as living in a house whose condition suggests near-poverty. Sickness, a bad harvest, unemployment—any of these might easily drive him and his family over the edge.

from the absence of guild restrictions, but from the fact that none of his capital was tied up in expensive equipment. (Spinners usually owned their spinning wheels; weavers either owned or rented their looms.) Governments appreciated the advantages of the system too, viewing it as one way to alleviate the ever-present problem of rural poverty. The French abolished the traditional privileges of urban manufacturers in 1762, acknowledging by law what economic demand had long since established: the widespread practice of unrestricted rural domestic production. By that time, proto-industrialization prevailed not only in northern France, but in the east and northeast of England, in Flanders, and in much of northern Germany—all areas where a mixed agricultural and manufacturing economy made economic sense to those engaged in it as entrepreneurs and producers.

Quality of life under the family system

Later generations, looking back nostalgically on the putting-out system, often compared it favorably to the factory system that displaced it. Life within the system's "family economy" was seldom other than hard, however. While workers could set their own pace to some extent, they remained subject to the demands of small, often inexperienced entrepreneurs who, misjudging their markets, might overload spinners and weavers with work at one moment, then abandon them for lack of orders the next. Though it often kept families from starvation, the system did little to mitigate the monotony and harshness of their lives. Its pressures are crudely if eloquently expressed in an English ballad in which the weaver husband responds to his wife's complaint that she has no time to sit at the "bobbin wheel," what with the washing and baking and milking she must do. No matter, the husband replies. She must "stir about and get things done./ For all things must aside be laid,/ when we want help about our trade."

Other rural manufacturing activities

Textiles were not the only manufactured goods produced in the countryside. In France, for example, metal-working was as much a rural as an urban occupation, with migrant laborers providing a work force for small, self-contained shops. In various parts of Germany, the same sort of unregulated domestic manufacturing base prevailed: in the Black Forest for clock-making, in Thuringia for toys. English production of iron grew fivefold from the mid-sixteenth to the late seventeenth century. The phenomenon of proto-industrialization increased demand for raw materials. Pressure on timber reserves for fuel led to widespread deforestation, with a resulting exploitation of coal reserves, particularly in the Rhineland, England, and the south Netherlands. In 1550 the English mined 200,000 tons of coal. By 1800 that figure had risen to 3 million.

Rudimentary transportation systems

Rural industry flourished despite the fact that for most of the early-modern period transportation systems remained rudimentary. In all but a very few cases, roads were little more than ill-defined tracks, full of holes as much as four feet deep, and all but impassable in the rain, when carts and carriages might stay mired in deep ruts for days. One of the few paved roads ran from Paris to Orléans, the main river port of France, but that was a notable exception. In general, no one could travel more than

Outside an Inn, by Thomas Rowlandson. Coaching inns brought the outside world into the lives of isolated villagers. Note the absence of any clearly defined roadway.

12 miles an hour—"post haste" at a gallop on horseback—and speed such as that could be achieved only at the expense of fresh horses at each stage of the ride. In the late seventeenth century, a journey of 60 miles over good roads could be accomplished in twenty-four hours, provided that the weather was fair. To travel by coach from Paris to Lyons, a distance of approximately 250 miles, took ten days. Merchants ran great risks when they shipped perishable goods. Breakables were not expected to survive for more than 15 miles. Transportation of goods by boat along coastal routes was far more reliable than shipment overland, though in both cases the obstacle of excessive tolls was frequently inhibiting. In 1675, English merchants calculated that it was cheaper to ship coal 300 miles by water than to send it 15 miles overland, so impassable were the roads to heavy transport. Madrid, without a river, relied upon mules and carts for its supplies. By the mid-eighteenth century, the city required the services of over half a million mules and 150,000 carts, all forced to labor their way into town over rugged terrain. In 1698, a bronze statue of Louis XIV was sent on its way from the river port of Auxerre, southeast of Paris, to the town of Dijon. The cart in which it was dispatched was soon stuck in the mud, however, and the statue remained marooned in a wayside shed for twenty-one years, until the road was improved to the point that it could continue its belated journey.

Transportation improvements

Gradually in the eighteenth century transportation improved. The French established a Road and Bridge Corps of civil engineers, with a separate training school, in 1747. Work began in the 1670s on a series of canals that eventually linked the English Channel to the Mediterranean. In England, private investors, spearheaded by that inveterate canal-builder the duke of Bridgewater, constructed a network of waterways and turnpikes tying provincial towns to each other and to London. With improved roads came stagecoaches, feared at first for their speed and recklessness much as automobiles were feared in the early twentieth century.

The Duke of Bridgewater Canal

People objected to being crowded into narrow carriages designed to reduce the load pulled by the team of horses. "If by chance a traveller with a big stomach or wide shoulders appears," an unhappy passenger lamented, "one has to groan or desert." But improvements such as stagecoaches and canals, much as they might increase the profits or change the pattern of life for the wealthy, meant little to the average European. Barges plied the waterways from the north to the south of France, but most men and women traveled no farther than to their neighboring market town, on footpaths or on rutted cart tracks eight feet wide, which had served their ancestors in much the same way.

Urban manufacturing centers

That industry flourished to the extent it did, despite the hazards and inefficiencies of transport, is a measure of the strength of Europe's ever-increasing commercial impulse. Rural proto-industrialization did not prevent the growth of important urban manufacturing centers. In northern France, many of the million or so men and women employed in the textile trade lived and worked in cities such as Amiens, Lille, and Rheims. The eighteenth-century rulers of Prussia made it their policy to develop Berlin as a manufacturing center, taking advantage of an influx of French Protestants to establish the silk-weaving industry there. Even in cities, however, work was likely to be carried out in small shops, where anywhere from five to twenty journeymen labored under the supervision of a master to manufacture the particular products of their craft. Despite the fact that manufacturing was centered in homes and workshops, by 1700 these industries were increasing significantly in scale as many workshops grouped together to form a single manufacturing district. Textile industries led this trend, but it was true as well of brewing, distilling, soap and candle-making, tanning, and the manufacturing of various chemical substances for the bleaching and dyeing of cloth. These and other industries might often employ several thousand men and women congregated together into towns—or larger communities of several towns—all dedicated to the same occupation and production.

New machinery and techniques

Techniques in some crafts remained much as they had been for centuries. In others, however, inventions changed the pattern of work as well as the nature of the product. Knitting frames, simple devices to speed the manufacture of textile goods, made their appearance in England and Holland. Wire-drawing machines and slitting mills, the latter enabling nailmakers to convert iron bars into rods, spread from Germany into England. Mechanically powered saws were introduced into shipyards and elsewhere across Europe in the seventeenth century. The technique of calico printing, the application of colored designs directly to textiles, was imported from the Far East. New and more efficient printing presses appeared, first in Holland and then elsewhere. The Dutch invented a machine called a "camel," by which the hulls of ships could be raised in the water so that they could be more easily repaired.

Adverse reaction to changing machinery and processes

Innovations of this kind were not readily accepted by workers. Laborsaving machines such as mechanical saws threw men out of work. Artisans, especially those organized into guilds, were by nature conservative, anxious to protect not only their restrictive "rights," but the secrets of their trade. Often, too, the state would intervene to block the widespread use of machines if they threatened to increase unemployment. The Dutch and some German states, for example, prohibited the use of what was described as a "devilish invention," a ribbon-loom capable of weaving sixteen or more ribbons at the same time. Sometimes the spread of new techniques was curtailed by states in order to protect the livelihood of powerful commercial interest groups. On behalf of both domestic textile manufacturers and importers of Indian goods, calico printing was for a time outlawed in both France and England. The cities of Paris and Lyons and several German states banned the use of indigo dyes because they were manufactured abroad.

The human implications of change

Changes that occurred in trade, commerce, agriculture, and industry, though large-scale phenomena, nevertheless touched individual men and women directly. Enclosure stripped away customary rights. An English cottager by 1780 might well have lost his family's age-old right to tether a cow on the common, which was now an enclosed and "scientifically" manured corn field. Markets developed to receive and transmit goods from around the world altered the lives of those whose work now responded to their rhythms. A linen weaver in rural Holland in 1700, whose peasant father had eked out a meager living from his subsistence farm, now supplemented his income by working for an Amsterdam entrepreneur, and paid progressively less for his food as a result of the cheap grain imported to the Low Countries across the Baltic Sea from eastern Europe. A carpenter in an early-eighteenth-century Toulon shipyard lost his job when his employer purchased a mechanical saw that did the work of five men. A sailor on one of the ships built in that Toulon shipyard died at sea off the French colony of Martinique, an island of which he had never heard, at a distance so far from home as to be inconceivable to those who mourned his death when they learned of it months later. Meanwhile, in vast areas of southern and eastern Europe, men and women led lives that followed the same patterns they had for centuries, all but untouched by the changes taking place elsewhere. They clung to the life they knew, a life which, if harsh, was at least predictable.

The Commercial Revolution

Capitalism defined

Hand in hand with changes in agriculture and industry came an alteration in the manner in which commerce was organized and trade conducted. So extensive were changes in these areas over the course of two hundred years that it is accurate to speak of them as comprising a commercial revolution. The early-modern world of commerce and industry grew increasingly to be governed by the assumptions of capitalism and mercantilism. Reduced to its simplest terms, *capitalism* is a system of production, distribution, and exchange, in which accumulated wealth is invested by private owners for the sake of gain. Its essential features are private enterprise, competition for markets, and business for profit. Generally it involves the wage system as a method of payment of workers—that is, a mode of payment based not on the amount of wealth workers create, but rather upon their willingness to compete with one another for jobs. Capitalism represented a direct challenge to the semi-static economy of the medieval guilds, in which production and trade were—in theory, at least—conducted for the benefit of society and with only a reasonable charge for the service rendered, instead of unlimited profits. Capitalism is a system designed to encourage commercial expansion beyond the local level, on a national and international scale. Guildmasters had neither the money (capital) to support nor the knowledge to organize and direct commercial enterprises beyond their own towns. Activity on that wider scale demanded the resources and expertise of wealthy and experienced entrepreneurs. The capitalist studied patterns of international trade. He knew where markets were and how to manipulate them to his advantage.

The medieval origins of mercantilism

Capitalism is a system designed to reward the individual. In contrast, *mercantilist* doctrine emphasized direct governmental intervention in economic policy to enhance the general prosperity of the state and to increase political authority. Mercantilism was by no means a new idea. It was in fact a variation on the medieval notion that the populace of any particular town was a community with a common wealth, and that the economic well-being of such communities depended on the willingness of that populace to work at whatever task God or their rulers assigned them to benefit the local community as a whole. The mercantilism of the seventeenth and eighteenth centuries translated this earlier concept of community as a privileged, but regimented, economic unit from the level of towns to the level of the entire state. The theory and practice of mercantilism reflected the expansion of state power. Responding to the needs of war, rulers enforced mercantilist policies, often by increasingly autocratic methods, certain that the needs of the state must take precedence over those of individuals.

Mercantilism in theory

Mercantilist theory held that a state's power depended on its actual, calculable wealth. The degree to which a state could remain self-sufficient, importing as little as necessary while exporting as much as possible, was the clearest gauge not only of its economic prosperity but of its power. This doctrine had profound effects on state policy. First, it led to the establishment and development of overseas colonies. Colonies, mercantilists reasoned, would, as part of the national community, provide it with raw materials, including precious metals in some instances, which would otherwise have to be obtained outside the community. Second, the doctrine of mercantilism inspired state governments to encourage industrial production and trade, both sources of revenue that would increase the state's income.

Mercantilism in practice

Although most western European statesmen were prepared to endorse mercantilist goals in principle, the degree to which their policies reflected those goals varied according to national circumstance. Spain, despite its insistence on closed colonial markets and its determination to amass a fortune in bullion, never succeeded in attaining the economic self-sufficiency that mercantilist theory demanded. But mercantilism, which appealed at least in theory to the rulers in Madrid, had little attraction for the merchants of Amsterdam. The Dutch recognized that the United Provinces were too small to permit them to achieve economic self-sufficiency. Throughout the seventeenth and eighteenth centuries the Dutch remained dedicated in principle and practice to free trade, often investing, contrary to mercantilist doctrine, in the commercial enterprises of other countries and promoting national prosperity by encouraging the rest of Europe to rely upon Amsterdam as a hub of international finance and trade.

Effects of capitalism and mercantilism on individuals

Capitalism and mercantilism represented a coming together of theories and practices imposed often sporadically and seldom systematically by entrepreneurs and governments during the early-modern period. The result over time, however, produced important consequences for individuals as well as for nations and regions. Laboring men and women frequently found themselves the victims of the policies and programs of those who, either as individuals or state functionaries, managed and controlled dynamic, expansionist national economies. For example, capitalists could afford to invest in large quantities of manufactured goods, and if necessary, hold them unsold until they could command a high price, favorable to them but damaging to the budget of humbler consumers. Mercantilism persuaded policy-makers to discourage domestic consumption, since goods purchased on the home market reduced the goods available for export. Government policy was thus to keep wages low, so that laborers would not have more money to spend than it took to provide them with basic food and shelter.

International centers and commercial routes

Together, governments and entrepreneurs designed new institutions that facilitated the expansion of global commerce during the seventeenth and eighteenth centuries to effect the commercial revolution of early-modern Europe. While local and regional markets continued to flourish, international centers such as Antwerp, Amsterdam, and London became hubs for a flourishing and complex system of international trade. An increasing number of European men and women grew dependent upon the commerce that brought both necessities and luxuries into their lives. The eighteenth-century essayist Joseph Addison sang the praises of the beneficient merchant prince: "There are not more useful members in the Commonwealth," he wrote. "They distribute the gifts of nature, find work for the poor, and wealth to the rich, and magnificence to the great."

Elements of the commercial revolution: (1) increased capital

Enterprise on this new scale depended on the availability of capital for investment. And that capital was generated primarily by a long-term, gradual increase in agricultural prices throughout much of the period. Had that increase been sharp, it would probably have produced enough hunger and suffering to retard rather than stimulate economic growth. Had there been no increase, however, the resulting stagnation produced by marginal profits would have proved equally detrimental to expansion. Agricultural entrepreneurs had surplus capital to invest in trade; bankers put that surplus to use to expand their commercial enterprises. Together, capitalist investors and merchants profited.

(2) The rise of banking

Banks played a vital role in the history of this expansion. Strong religious and moral disapproval of lending money at interest meant that banking had enjoyed a dubious reputation in the Middle Ages. Because the Church did come to allow profit-making on commercial risks, however, banks in Italy and Germany were organized during the fourteenth and fifteenth centuries, most notably by the Medici family in Florence and the Fugger family in Augsburg. The rise of these private financial

A Square in Seventeenth-Century Amsterdam. This contemporary painting emphasizes the central role independent merchants, consumers, and trade played in Dutch city life.

houses was followed by the establishment of government banks, reflecting the mercantilist goal of serving the monetary needs of the state. The first such institution, the Bank of Sweden, was founded in 1657. The Bank of England was established in 1694, at a time when England's emergence as a world commercial power guaranteed that institution a leading role in international finance. The growth of banking was necessarily accompanied by the adoption of various aids to financial transactions on a large scale, further evidence of a commercial revolution. Credit facilities were extended and payment by check introduced, thereby encouraging an increase in the volume of trade, since the credit resources of the banks could now be expanded far beyond the actual amounts of cash in their vaults.

(3) Changes in business organization: (a) regulated companies

International commercial expansion called forth larger units of business organization. The prevailing unit of production and trade in the Middle Ages was the workshop or store owned by an individual or a family. Partnerships were also quite common, in spite of the grave disadvantage of unlimited liability of each of its members for the debts of the entire firm. Obviously neither of these units was well adapted to business involving heavy risks and a huge investment of capital. The attempt to devise a more suitable business organization resulted in the formation of *regulated companies,* which were associations of merchants banded together for a common venture. Members did not pool their resources but agreed merely to cooperate for their mutual advantage and to abide by certain definite regulations.

(b) joint-stock companies

The commercial revolution was facilitated in the seventeenth century when the regulated company was largely superseded by a new type of organization at once more compact and broader in scope. This was the *joint-stock company,* formed through the issuance of shares of capital to a considerable number of investors. Those who purchased the shares might or might not take part in the work of the company. Whether they did or not, they were joint owners of the business and therefore entitled to share in its profits in accordance with the amount they had invested. The joint-stock company of the early-modern period is best understood not so much as a conscious precursor of capitalist endeavor but as a pragmatic attempt at commercial expansion by both individuals and the state, its structure dictated by present opportunity and circumstance. Initially, for example, the Dutch United East India Company, one of the earliest joint-stock ventures, had expected to pay off its investors ten years after its founding in 1602, much as regulated companies had. Yet when that time came, the directors recognized the impossibility of the plan. By 1612, the company's assets were scattered—as ships, wharves, warehouses, and cargoes—across the globe. As a result, the directors urged those anxious to realize their profits to sell their shares on the Amsterdam exchange to other eager investors, thereby ensuring the sustained operation of their enterprise and, in the process, establishing a practice of continuous financing that was soon to become common.

(c) chartered companies

While most of the early joint-stock companies were founded for commercial ventures, some were organized later in industry. A number of the

The Lyons Stock Exchange. Built in 1749, the stylish and impressive facade of the structure bespeaks the prominent role of commerce in French society.

outstanding trading combinations were also *chartered companies.* They held charters from the government granting a monopoly of the trade in a certain locality and conferring extensive authority over the inhabitants, and were thus an example of the way capitalist and mercantilist interests might coincide. Through a charter of this kind, the British East India Company undertook the exploitation of vast territories on the Indian subcontinent, and remained virtual ruler there until the end of the eighteenth century.

(d) partnership between state and commerce

In most European countries, and particularly in France, government and commerce generally worked to promote each other's interests. The exception was the Dutch, who almost exclusively put their capital to work not for the state but for the rest of Europe. In time of war, governments called upon commercial capitalists to assist in the financing of their campaigns. When England went to war against France in 1689, for example, the government had no long-range borrowing mechanism available to it; during the next quarter-century the merchant community, through the Bank of England, assisted the government in raising over £170 million and in stabilizing the national debt at £40 million. In return, trading companies used the war to increase long-distance commercial traffic at the expense of their French enemy, and exerted powerful pressure on the government to secure treaties that would work to their advantage.

(4) A money economy

A final important feature of the commercial revolution was the development of a more efficient money economy. Money had been used widely since the revival of trade in the eleventh century. Nevertheless, there were few coins with a value that was recognized other than locally; no country could be said to have had a uniform monetary system. The growth of trade and industry in the commercial revolution accentuated the need for more stable and uniform monetary systems. The problem was solved by the adoption by every important state of a standard system of money to be used for all transactions within its borders. Much time elapsed, however, before the reform was complete.

Inflation caused by increased availability of silver

The economic institutions just described never remained static, but rather existed in a continuously volatile state of development. This volatility, in turn, had a direct effect on the lives of individual men and women. One major result of overseas expansion, for example, was the severe inflation caused by the increase in the supply of silver that plagued Europe at the end of the sixteenth century. Price fluctuations, in turn, produced further economic instability. Businessmen were tempted to expand their enterprises too rapidly; bankers extended credit so liberally that their principal borrowers, especially noblemen, often defaulted on loans. In both Spain and Italy, wages failed to keep pace with rising prices, which brought severe and continuing hardships to the lower classes. Impoverishment was rife in the cities, and bandits flourished in the rural areas.

The South Sea Bubble

Speculative greed could, and sometimes did, threaten to bring a nation to its knees. Though feverish speculation characterized the early-modern period as a whole, the most notorious bouts of that particular economic disease occurred in the early eighteenth century. The so-called South Sea Bubble was the result of deliberate inflation of the value of stock of the South Sea Company in England, whose offer to assume the national debt led to unwarranted confidence in the company's future. When buoyant hopes gave way to fears, investors made frantic attempts to dispose of their shares for whatever they would bring. The crash that came in 1720 was the inevitable result.

The Mississippi Bubble

During the years when the South Sea Bubble was being inflated in England, the French were engaged in a similar wave of speculative madness. In 1715 a Scotsman by the name of John Law persuaded the regent of France to adopt his scheme for paying off the national debt through the issuance of paper money and to grant him the privilege of organizing the Mississippi Company for the colonization and exploitation of Louisiana. As happened in England, stock prices soared in response to an alluring but basically unrealistic scheme. Stories were told of butchers and tailors who made fortunes from their few initial shares. Ultimately, however, panic set in, and in 1720 the Mississippi Bubble burst in a wild panic.

Colonization and Overseas Trade

Spanish colonization

The institutions of the commercial revolution—banks, credit facilities, joint-stock companies, monetary systems—were designed specifically to assist both capitalist entrepreneurs and mercantilist policy-makers in the development and exploitation of trade. Despite the existence of increasingly profitable European commercial routes and centers, the most visible evidence of the economic expansionism of early-modern Europe were the overseas colonies and trading posts developed and exploited during the seventeenth and eighteenth centuries. Following the exploits of the *conquistadores,* the Spanish established colonial governments in Peru and in Mexico, which they controlled from Madrid in proper mercantilist fashion by a Council of the Indies. The governments of Philip II and his successors were determined to defend their monopoly in the New World. They issued trading licenses only to Spanish merchants; exports and imports passed only through the port of Seville (later the more navigable port of Cadiz), where they were registered at the government-operated Casa de Contratación, or customs house. In their heyday, Spanish traders circled the globe. Because of the lucrative market for silver in East Asia, they found it well worth their while to establish an outpost in far-off Manila in the Philippines, where Asian silk was exchanged for South American bullion. The silk was then shipped back to Spain by way of the Mexican ports of Acapulco and Veracruz. The search for gold and silver was accompanied by the establishment of permanent colonies in Central and South America and on the east and west coasts of North America in what are now the states of Florida and California.

Challenges to Spanish predominance

Spain's predominance did not deter other countries from attempting to win a share of the treasure for themselves. Probably the boldest challengers were the English, and their leading buccaneer the "sea dog" Sir Francis Drake, who three times raided the east and west coasts of Spanish America and who, in 1587, the year before the Armada set sail on its ill-fated voyage north, "singed the beard of the Spanish king" by attacking the Spanish fleet at its anchorage in Cadiz harbor. Yet despite dashing heroics of that sort, the English could do no more than dent the Spanish trade.

English colonization

English colonists sought profits elsewhere by establishing agricultural settlements in North America and the Caribbean basin. Their first permanent, though ultimately unsuccessful, colony was Jamestown, in Virginia, founded in 1607. Over the next forty years, 80,000 English emigrants sailed to over twenty autonomous settlements in the New World. In this instance, however, religious freedom, as well as economic gain, was often the motive of the settlers. The renowned band of "pilgrim fathers" that landed on the New England shores in 1620 was but one of a large number of dissident groups, both Protestant and Catholic, that sought to escape attempts to impose religious conformity. Religion also played a role in the efforts of the Spanish to colonize Central and South America, and of the French to penetrate the hinterlands of North America. Roman Catholic Jesuit missionaries, intent upon the conversion of native Americans to Christianity, joined fur traders in journeys across the continent to the Great Lakes and the Mississippi.

The growth of English colonial regulation

Both England and France were quick to extract profit from their expanding colonial empires. England's agricultural colonies were producing crops in high demand throughout Europe. The success of colonial planters encouraged the governments of both Oliver Cromwell and

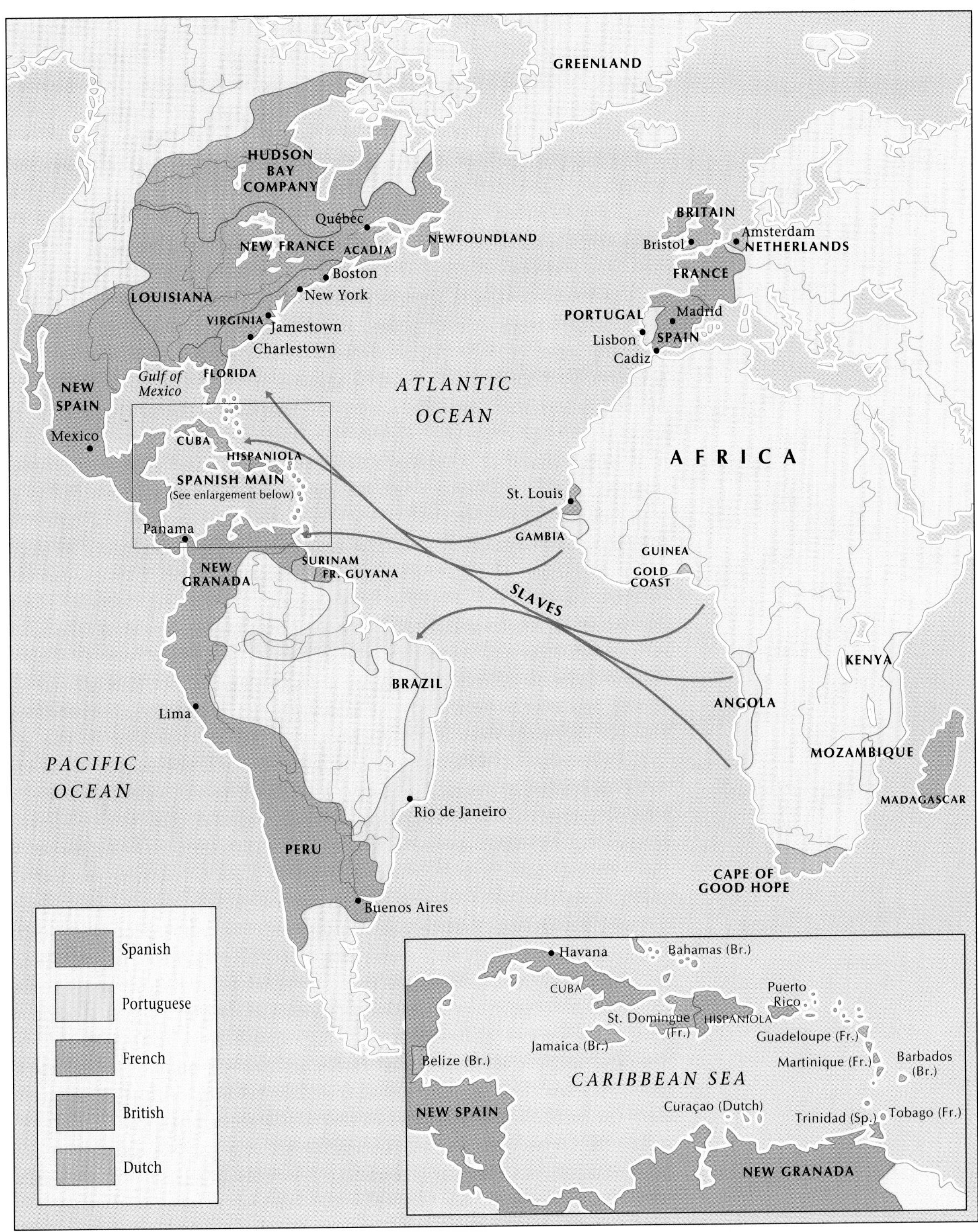

The Atlantic World in 1713

Charles II to intervene in the management of their overseas economy. Navigation acts, passed in 1651 and 1660, and rigorously enforced thereafter, decreed that all exports from English colonies to the mother country be carried in English ships, and forbade the direct exporting of certain "enumerated" products directly from the colonies to Continental ports.

Sugar and tobacco

The most valuable of those products were sugar and tobacco. Sugar, virtually unknown in Europe earlier, had become a popular luxury by the end of the sixteenth century. Where once it had been considered no more than a medicine, one observer now noted that the wealthy were "devouring it out of gluttony." Sugarcane was grown in the West Indies after 1650 in ever-larger amounts. In the eighteenth century, the value of the sugar that England imported from its small island colonies there—Barbados, Jamaica, St. Kitts, and others—exceeded the value of its imports from the vast subcontinents of China and India. Although the tobacco plant was imported into Europe by the Spaniards about fifty years after the discovery of America, another half-century passed before Europeans took up the habit of smoking. At first the plant was believed to possess miraculous healing powers and was referred to as "divine tobacco" and "our holy herb nicotian." (The word "nicotine" derives from the name of the French ambassador to Portugal, Jean Nicot, who brought the tobacco plant to France.) The practice of smoking was popularized by English explorers, especially by Sir Walter Raleigh, who had learned to smoke while living among the Indians of Virginia. It spread rapidly through all classes of European society. Governments at first joined the Church in condemning the use of tobacco because of its socially and spiritually harmful effects, but by the end of the seventeenth century, having realized the profits to be made from its production, they were encouraging its use.

The French in America

French colonial policy matured during the administration of Louis XIV's mercantilist finance minister, Jean Baptiste Colbert (1619–1683), who perceived of overseas expansion as an integral part of state economic policy. He organized joint-stock companies to compete with those of the English. He encouraged the development of lucrative sugar-producing colonies in the West Indies, the largest of which was St. Domingue (present-day Haiti). France also dominated the interior of the North American continent. Frenchmen traded furs and preached Christianity to the Indians in a vast territory that stretched from Acadia and the St. Lawrence River in the northeast to Louisiana in the west. Yet the financial returns from these lands were hardly commensurate with their size. Furs, fish, and tobacco were exported to home markets, but not in sufficient amounts to match the profits from the sugar colonies of the Caribbean or from the line of trading posts the French maintained in India.

The Dutch in the Far East

The Dutch were even more successful than the English and the French in establishing a flourishing commercial empire in the seventeenth century. They succeeded in establishing a colony on the southern tip of Africa at the Cape of Good Hope. Far more important, however, were their commercial adventurings in South Asia. Their joint-stock East India Company, founded in 1602, rivaled its English counterpart in Asia, gain-

The Dutch East India Company Warehouse and Timber Wharf at Amsterdam. The substantial warehouse, the stockpiles of lumber, and the company ship under construction in the foreground illustrate the degree to which overseas commerce could stimulate the economy of the mother country.

ing firm control of Sumatra, Borneo, and the Moluccas, or Spice Islands, and driving Portuguese traders from an area where they had heretofore enjoyed an undisturbed commercial dominion. The result was a Dutch monopoly in pepper, cinnamon, nutmeg, mace, and cloves. The Dutch also secured an exclusive right to trade with the Japanese, and maintained outposts in China and India as well. In the Western Hemisphere, their achievements were less spectacular. Following a series of trade wars with England, they surrendered their North American colony of New Amsterdam (subsequently renamed New York) in 1667, retaining Surinam, off the northern coast of South America, as well as the islands of Curaçao and Tobago in the West Indies in compensation.

The decline of the Spanish commercial empire

The fortunes of these commercial empires rose and fell in the course of the seventeenth and eighteenth centuries. The Spanish, mired in persistent economic stagnation and embroiled in a succession of expensive wars and domestic rebellions, were powerless to prevent losses to their empire. Their merchant marine, once a match for cunning pirate-admirals like Drake, was by the middle of the seventeenth century unable to protect itself from attack by its more spirited commercial rivals. In a war with Spain in the 1650s, the English captured not only the island of Jamaica but treasure ships lying off the Spanish harbor of Cadiz. Further profit was obtained by bribing Spanish customs officials on a grand scale. During the second half of the century, two-thirds of the imported goods sold in Spanish colonies were smuggled in by Dutch, English, and French traders. By 1700, though Spain still possessed a colonial empire, it was one that lay at

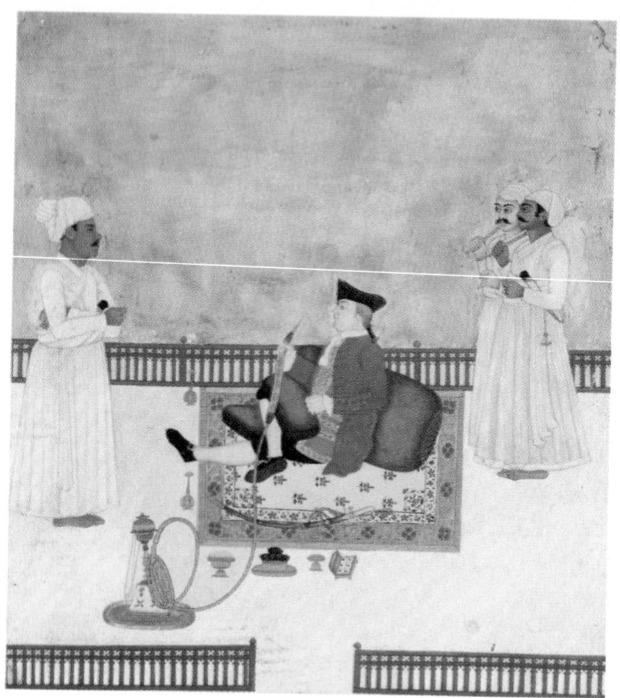

The Rewards of Commercial Exploitation. An English employee of the East India Company enjoying his ease and his opium, as depicted by an eighteenth-century Indian artist.

the mercy of its more dynamic rivals. A brief revival of its fortunes under more enlightened leadership in the mid-eighteenth century did nothing to prevent its ultimate eclipse.

English trade with Portugal and its colonies

Portugal, too, found it impossible to prevent foreign penetration of its colonial economies. The English worked diligently and successfully to win commercial advantages there. They obtained concessions to export woolens duty-free into Portugal itself in return for similar preferential treatment for Portuguese wines. (The notorious affection of the English upper class for port wine dates from the signing of the Treaty of 1703.) English trade with the mother country led in time to English trade with the Portuguese colony of Brazil, and indeed to the opening of commercial offices in Rio de Janeiro.

Anglo-French rivalry

During the eighteenth century, however, a growing Anglo-French rivalry in India stole the commercial spotlight from the Dutch spice monopoly in the Far East. The French and English East India Companies employed mercenaries to establish and expand trading areas such as Madras, Bombay, and Pondichéry. By exploiting indigenous industries, European capitalists continued to increase the flow of fine cotton textiles, tea, and spices, which passed through these commercial depots on their way to Europe. The struggle for worldwide economic dominance reached a peak in the mid-eighteenth century (see pp. 628–629). At that time the Anglo-French rivalry in India was resolved in England's favor. As a sign of France's defeat, in 1769 the French East India Company was dissolved.

Despite the commercial importance of India, however, patterns of world trade came increasingly to be dominated by western routes that had developed in response to the lucrative West Indian sugar industry, and to the demand for slaves from Africa to work the plantations in the Caribbean. Here England again eventually assumed the lead. Typically, a ship might begin its voyage from New England with a consignment of rum and sail to Africa, where the rum would be exchanged for a cargo of slaves. From the west coast of Africa the ship would then cross the South Atlantic to the sugar colonies of Jamaica or Barbados, where slaves would be traded for molasses, which would make the final leg of the journey to New England, where it would be made into rum. A variant triangle might see cheap manufactured goods move from England to Africa, where they would be traded for slaves. Those slaves would then be shipped to Virginia and exchanged for tobacco, which would be shipped to England and processed there for sale in Continental markets. Other eighteenth-century trade routes were more direct: the Spanish, French, Portuguese, and Dutch all engaged in the slave trade between Africa and Central and South America; the Spanish attempted, in vain, to retain a mercantilist monopoly on direct trade between Cadiz and their South American colonies; others sailed from England, France, or North America to the Caribbean and back again. And of course trade continued to flourish between Europe and the Near and Far East. But the triangular western routes, dictated by the grim economic symbiosis of sugar and slaves, remained dominant.

Increasing dominance of western trade routes

The cultivation of sugar and tobacco depended on slave labor, and as demand for those products increased, so did the traffic in black slaves, without whose labor those products could not be raised or harvested. At the height of the Atlantic slave trade in the eighteenth century, somewhere between 75,000 and 90,000 blacks were shipped across the Atlantic yearly: 6 million in the eighteenth century, out of a total of over 9 million for the entire history of the trade. About 35 percent went to English and French Caribbean plantations, 5 percent (roughly 450,000) to North America, and the rest to the Portuguese colony of Brazil and to Spanish colonies in South America. Although run as a monopoly by various governments in the sixteenth and early seventeenth centuries, in its heyday the slave trade was open to private entrepreneurs who operated ports on the West African coast. Traders exchanged cheap Indian cloth, metal goods, rum, and firearms with African slave merchants in return for their human cargo. Already disoriented and degraded by their capture at the hands of rival tribes, black men, women, and children were packed by the hundreds into the holds of slave ships for the gruesome "middle passage" across the Atlantic (so called to distinguish it from the ship's voyage from Europe to Africa, and from the slave colony back to Europe again). Shackled to the decks, without sanitary facilities, the black "cargo" suffered horribly; the mortality rate, however, remained at about 10 or 11 percent, not much higher than the rate for a normal sea voyage of one hundred days or more. Since traders had to invest as much as £10 per slave in their enterprise, they ensured that their consignment would reach its destination in good enough shape to be sold for a profit.

The slave trade

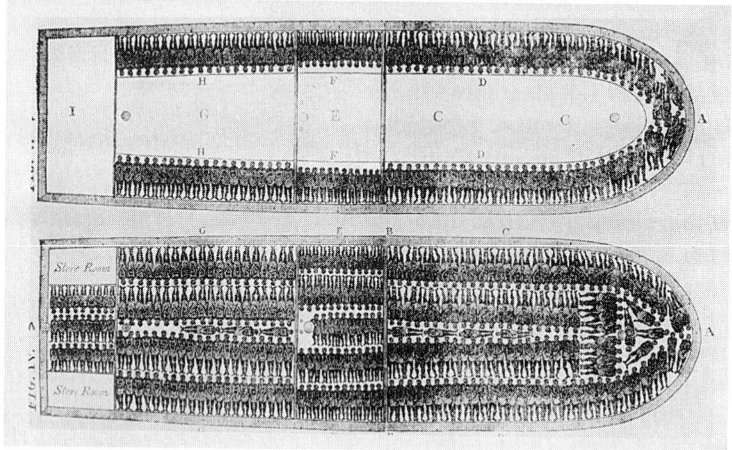

How Slaves Were Stowed Aboard Ship during the Middle Passage. Men were "housed" on the right; women on the left; children in the middle. The human cargo was jammed onto platforms six feet wide without sufficient headroom to permit an adult to sit up. This diagram is from evidence gathered by English abolitionists and depicts conditions on the Liverpool slave ship *Brookes*.

High profits from slaves

The trade was risky, dependent on a good wind and fair weather, and competition was increasingly keen. Yet profits could run high, occasionally as much as 300 percent. Demand for slaves remained constant throughout the eighteenth century. By the 1780s, there were more than 500,000 slaves on the largest French plantation island, St. Domingue, and 200,000 or more on the English counterpart, Jamaica. Those numbers reflected the expanding world market for slave-grown crops. As long as there was a market for the crops cultivated by slaves—as long as the economy relied to the extent it did upon slave labor—governments would remain unwilling to halt the system that, as one Englishman wrote in 1749, provided "an unexhaustible fund of wealth to this nation."

Apologists for the slave trade argued that though there was reason to rejoice that slavery had been banished from the continent of Europe (forgetting, apparently, the extent to which it continued to exist east of the Elbe in the form of serfdom), it remained a necessity in other parts of the world. Not until the very end of the eighteenth century did Europeans begin to protest the ghastly traffic. Public pressure, first from Quakers and then from others motivated by either religious or humanitarian zeal, helped put an end to the trade in England in 1807, and to slavery itself in British colonies in 1833. Slavery in French colonies was abolished in 1793, but only after slaves had risen in massive revolt on St. Domingue. Elsewhere, in Latin and North America, slavery lasted well into the nineteenth century—in the United States, until the Civil War of 1861–1865. The racism it promulgated has lasted until the present day.

Female Slave Being Whipped. After capture by rival tribes, black men, women, and children could expect further suffering, both during the middle passage and after reaching their final destinations.

The slave trade was an integral part of the history of the dramatic rise of English and French commerce during the eighteenth century. French colonial trade, valued at 25 million livres in 1716, rose to 263 million livres in 1789. In England, during roughly the same period, foreign trade increased in value from £10 million to £40 million, the latter amount more than twice that for France. These figures suggest the degree to which statecraft and private enterprise were bound to each other. If merchants depended on their government to provide a navy to protect and defend their overseas investments, governments depended equally on entrepreneurship, not only to generate money to build ships, but to sustain the trade upon which national power had come to rely so heavily.

Life within a Society of Orders

Orders, privilege, and freedom

Despite the economic and demographic shifts that were occurring in early-modern Europe, society remained divided into traditional orders or ranks. The changes we have been concerned with occurred against the continuity of long-accepted social divisions based upon birth and occupation. As circumstances altered, the fluid patterns of economic reorganization clashed with older, rigid assumptions about the place of men and women within a preordained—to many, a divinely ordained—social hierarchy. Jean Bodin, the French philosopher, wrote in 1570 that the division of the citizenry into "the three orders of nobles, clergy and people" was no more than natural. "There never was a commonwealth, real or imaginary, where citizens were in truth equal in all rights and privileges. Some always have more, some less than the rest." And some had none.

The meaning of "freedom"

Most would have recognized infinitely subtle subdivisions among and between the three orders Bodin specified. Ranks were demarcated by rights and privileges. "Freedom" was understood as one such privilege, as a benefit, bestowed not upon all men and women but upon special groups whose position "freed" them to do certain things others could not do, or freed them from the burden of doing certain things that were required of others. An English landowner was, because of the position his property conferred upon him, privileged, and therefore "free," to participate directly in the election of his government. A French nobleman was privileged, and therefore "free," to avoid the heavy burden of taxation levied upon the unprivileged orders. A German tailor who had served out his seven-year apprenticeship was free to set up his own shop for profit, something an unapprenticed man was not traditionally "at liberty" to do, no matter what his degree of skill with needle and thread. The master tailor's position conferred his freedom, just as the position of aristocrat and property owner conferred theirs.

The theater of a society of orders

The members of the higher orders attempted at all times to live their lives in a particular style that accorded with their rank. The nobility was taught from birth to consider itself above and apart from the rest of society. Merchants and manufacturers were just as insistent upon maintaining the traditional marks of privilege that separated them from artisans and peasants. Sumptuary laws decreed what could be worn and by whom. An edict promulgated in the German principality of Brunswick in 1738, for example, forbade servant girls to use silk dress materials, to wear gold or silver ornaments, or shoes of anything but plain black leather. A similar seventeenth-century law in the Polish city of Posen prohibited the wives of burghers from wearing capes or long hair. Style was not simply a matter of current whim. It was a badge of status and was carefully adhered to as such. An aristocratic lady powdered her hair and rouged her cheeks as a

Middle-Class Fashion. In this seventeenth-century portrait of a Dutch burgomaster and his family, the patriarch and his wife are wearing the costume of an earlier generation, while the children are clothed in the current style. All display the opulence characteristic of their prosperous class.

sign that she was an aristocrat. Life within a society of orders demanded a certain degree of theatricality, especially from those at the top of the social hierarchy. Aristocrats "acted" their part in a calculatedly self-conscious way. Their manner of speech, their dress, the ceremonial sword they were privileged to wear, the title by which they were addressed—these were the props of a performance that constantly emphasized the distinctions between those above and those below. Noble families lived in castles, chateaux, or country houses whose size and antiquity were a further proclamation of superiority. When they built new mansions, as the *nouveau riche* capitalist English gentry did in the eighteenth century, they made certain their elaborate houses and spacious private parks declared their newfound power. The English politician Robert Walpole had an entire village moved to improve the view from his grand new residence.

The nobility

The vast majority of men and women defined and understood social hierarchy in terms of the rural communities in which they lived. At the head of those communities, in all likelihood, stood a representative of the noble elite. The nobility probably numbered about 3 percent of the total population of Europe. The percentage was higher in Russia, Poland, Hungary, and Spain; lower in Germany, France, and England. Ownership of a landed estate was proof of one's elevated rank. Generally speaking, the more land one possessed, the higher one stood within the social hierarchy. In Hungary, five noble families owned about 14 percent of the entire country; the greatest of these, Prince Esterházy, controlled the lives of more than half a million peasants. Most noblemen were not nearly so

Gala Dinner at Schoenbrunn Palace in Vienna. Given on the occasion of Joseph II's wedding, this banquet was an example of the extravagance this Hapsburg monarch believed suitable to the occasion.

rich and powerful. Some, indeed, could rely on little more than inherited privilege to distinguish themselves from peasants.

Nobility and commerce

Tradition had it that noble service meant military service; yet, as we shall see, that tradition—like so many others—was increasingly breached during the early-modern period. Noble title was granted by a monarch, in theory for service to the state. But such service was more and more frequently defined as nonmilitary, as support, financial and political, for the expanding apparatus of local and central government. The pattern of noble life varied considerably from country to country. In England and Prussia, the nobility tended to reside on its estates; in south and west Germany, and in France, they were more likely to leave the management of their estates to stewards and to live at the royal court or in cities. Despite the traditional assumption that noblemen need not, and therefore must not, soil their aristocratic reputation by commercial dealing, by the end of the eighteenth century they were involving themselves in increasing numbers in a variety of entrepreneurial enterprises. Some exploited mineral deposits on their estates; others invested in overseas trade. In France, two of the four largest coal mines were owned and operated by noblemen, while the duke of Orléans was an important investor in the newly established chemical dye industry. In eastern Europe, because there were few middle-class merchants, noblemen frequently undertook to market their agricultural produce themselves.

An "open" nobility

In no country was the nobility a completely closed order. Men who proved of use to the crown as administrators or lawyers, men who amassed large fortunes as a consequence of judicious—and often legally questionable—financial transactions, moved into the ranks of the nobility with increasing frequency during the late seventeenth and eighteenth centuries. Joseph II of Austria was making financiers into noblemen by the dozen in the late eighteenth century. In France, it was possible to attain nobility through the purchase of expensive offices from the crown. Membership could be purchased in the legal nobility of the "robe," headed by members of the thirteen provincial *parlements* whose function it was to record, and thereby sanction, the laws of the kingdom, and to adjudicate cases appealed from lower courts.

The peasantry

Land ownership brought the nobility into direct relationship with the peasants and laborers who worked the land and over whose lives their masters exercised dominion. The status of the peasantry varied greatly across the face of rural Europe. In the east—Russia, Poland, Hungary, and in parts of Germany beyond the Elbe—the desire for profit in agriculture and the collusion of the state with the nobility led to the growth of a "second serfdom," a serf system much stronger than that which had existed during the Middle Ages. In East Prussia, serfs often had to work from three to six days a week for their lord, and some had only late evening or night hours to cultivate their own lands.

Peasant subordination in eastern Europe

Peasants throughout eastern Europe found their destinies controlled in almost all respects by their masters. Noble landlords dispensed justice in manorial courts and even ruled in cases to which they were themselves interested parties. These men were a combination of sheriff, chief magistrate, and police force in one, able to sentence their "subjects" to corporal punishment, imprisonment, exile, or in many cases death, without right of appeal. Peasants could not leave their land, marry, or learn a trade unless permitted to do so by their lord. In Russia, where half the land was owned by the state, peasants were bound to work in mines or workshops if their masters so ordered, and could be sold to private owners. Although Russian peasant serfs were said to possess a "legal personality" that distinguished them from slaves, the distinction was obscured in practice. They lived as bound to their masters as had their great-grandfathers.

The position of the peasantry

In western Europe, the position of the peasantry reflected the fact that serfdom had all but disappeared by the sixteenth century. Peasants might theoretically own land, although the vast majority were either tenants or laborers. Hereditary tenure was in general more secure than in the east; peasants could dispose of their land and had legal claim to farm buildings and implements. Although far freer than their eastern European counterparts, the peasantry of western Europe still lived to a great degree under the domination of landowners. They were in many cases responsible for the payment of various dues and fees: an annual rent paid to landlords by those who might otherwise own their land outright; a special tax on recently cleared land; a fee, often as much as one-sixth of the assessed value of the land, collected by the manorial lord whenever peasant property changed hands; and charges for the use of the lord's mill, bakery, or wine press. In France, peasants were compelled to submit to the *corvée,* a requirement that they labor for several weeks a year maintaining local roads. Even access to the often questionable justice meted out in the manorial courts, which endured throughout the early-modern period in almost all of western Europe, was encumbered with fees and commissions. To many peasants, however, the most galling badge of their inferiority was their inability to hunt within the jurisdiction of their landlord's manor. The slaughter of game was a privilege reserved to the nobility, a circumstance generating sustained resentment on the part of a population that looked upon deer and pheasant not as a symbol of aristocratic status but as a necessary supplement to its meager diet. Noble landlords rarely missed an opportunity to extract all the money they could from their peasants while constantly reminding them of the degree to which their destiny was controlled by the lord of the manor.

A French Peasant. Tattered and overworked, this peasant farmer is shown feeding his livestock as the tax collector at his door relieves him of all of his profits.

Despite their traditional subservience, however, western European peasants found themselves caught up directly in the process of economic change. The growth of centralized monarchies intensified the states' need for income, with the result that peasants were more burdened than ever with taxes and required services. They responded by accepting a new role as wage-earners in an expanding market economy, some as agricultural day laborers on enclosed estates, others as part of the work force in expanding rural industries. A few were genuinely independent, literate, influential members of the communities where they lived, owning not only land but considerable livestock. In France, some acted as intermediaries between their landlords, from whom they leased several large farms, and the sharecroppers who actually worked the land. Most, however, were far less fortunate. Those with claim to a small piece of property usually worked it into infertility in the course of one or two generations as they scrambled to make it produce as much as possible.

Peasant bread and board

Poor peasants often lived, contrary to the biblical injunction, by bread alone—two pounds a day if they were lucky, the dark dough a mixture of wheat and rye flour. According to region, bread was supplemented by peas and beans, beer, wine, or, far less often, skimmed milk. Peasant houses usually contained no more than one or two rooms, and were constructed of wood, plastered with mud or clay. Roofs were most often thatched with straw, which was used as fertilizer when replaced, and provided fodder for animals at times of scarcity. Furnishings seldom consisted of more than a table, benches, pallets for sleeping, a few earthenware plates, and simple tools—an axe, a wooden spade, a knife.

Peasant women

Peasant women tended livestock and vegetables, and managed the dairy, if there was one. Women went out as field workers, or worked at home knitting, spinning, or weaving in order to augment the family income. A popular seventeenth-century poem has a laborer's wife lamenting her lot with a refrain that has echoed down the ages: ". . . my labor is hard,/ And all my pleasures are debarr'd;/ Both morning, evening, night and noon,/ I am sure a woman's work is never done."

Market Scene, by Jean Michelin. Peasant women and children bringing produce to a nearby market town.

Urban living conditions

The spread of proto-industrialization broke down the previously sharp demarcations between town and country, between the life lived inside a city's medieval walls and that lived outside. Suburbs merged urban and rural existence. In some, textile workers labored. In others, families of fashion took their ease, creating an environment "where the want of London smoke is supplied by the smoke of Virginia tobacco," as one Englishman remarked wryly. Houses in areas inhabited by the wealthy were increasingly built of brick and stone, which replaced the wood, lath, and plaster of the Middle Ages. This change was a response to the constant danger of fire. The great fire of London in 1666, which destroyed three-quarters of the town—12,000 houses—was the largest of the conflagrations that swept cities with devastating regularity. Urban dwellings of the laboring poor remained firetraps. Workers' quarters were badly overcrowded; entire families lived in one-room accommodations in basements and attics that were infested with bugs and fleas.

Urban society: the bourgeoisie

Urban society was, like its rural counterpart, a society of orders. In capital cities, noble families occupied the highest social position, as they did in the countryside, living a parasitic life of conspicuous consumption. The majority of cities and towns were dominated by a nonnoble *bourgeoisie*. That French term originally designated a burgher or townsman who was a long-term, resident property owner or leaseholder and taxpayer. By the eighteenth century it had come to mean a townsman of some means who aspired to be recognized as a person of local importance and evinced a willingness to work hard, whether at counting-house or government office, and a desire to live a comfortable, if by no means extravagant, existence. A bourgeois gentleman might derive his income from rents; he might, as well, be an industrialist, banker, merchant, lawyer, or physician.

If he served in the central bureaucracy, he would consider himself the social superior of those provincials whose affairs he administered. Yet he would himself be looked down upon by the aristocracy, many of whom enjoyed thinking of the bourgeoisie as a class of vulgar social climbers, often conveniently forgetting their own commercial origins a generation or two previously. The French playwright Molière's comedy *The Bourgeois Gentleman* (1670) reflected this attitude, ridiculing the manners of those who were trying to ape their betters. "Bourgeois," another French writer observed, "is the insult given by noblemen to anybody they deem slow-witted or out of touch with the court." The bourgeoisie usually constituted about 20 to 25 percent of a town's population. As its economic elite, these men were almost always its governing elite as well.

Throughout the early-modern period, there was considerable movement into and out of the urban bourgeoisie. Prosperous tradesmen and successful small-time commercial entrepreneurs might see their offspring rise in station, particularly if they married well. At the same time, those who made their money in trade could purchase land, and by paying fees to their king, gain the right to an ennobling office. In seventeenth-century Amiens, a major French textile center, the upper bourgeoisie deserted trade and derived the majority of its income from land or bonds. Where the bourgeoisie thrived, it more often than not did so as the result of a burgeoning state or regional bureaucracy.

The "Bon Ton." This English cartoon mocks the rage for French fashion and illustrates the affluence of a middle class able to afford the changing dictates of fashion.

Urban society: shopkeepers and artisans

Next within the urban hierarchy was a vast middle range of shopkeepers and artisans. Many of the latter continued to learn and then to practice their crafts as members of guilds, which in turn contained their own particular ascending order of apprentice, journeyman, and master, thus preserving the pervasive principle of hierarchy. Throughout the early-modern period, however, commercial expansion threatened the rigid hierarchy of the guild structure. The expense and curtailed output resulting from restrictive guild practices met with serious opposition in big cities such as Paris and London, and in the industrial hinterlands of France and Germany, where expanding markets called for cheaper and more readily available goods. Journeymen tailors and shoemakers in increasing numbers set up shops without benefit of mastership and produced cheaper coats and shoes in defiance of guild regulations. In the silk workshops of Lyons, both masters and journeymen were compelled to labor without distinction of status for piece rates (wages paid per finished article, rather than per hour) set by merchandising middlemen and far below an equitable level in the opinion of the silk workers. Artisans like these, compelled to work for low wages at the behest of profiteering middlemen, grew increasingly restive. In France and Germany, journeymen's associations had originated as social and mutual-aid organizations for young men engaged in "tramping" the country to gain experience in their trade. In some instances, however, these associations fostered the development of a trade consciousness that led to strikes and boycotts against masters and middlemen over the issues of wages and working conditions. An imperial law passed in Germany in 1731 deprived the associations of their right to organize, and required journeymen to carry a certificate of identification as testimony of their respectability during their travels.

Urban society: the poor

At the bottom of urban society was a mass of semi-skilled and unskilled workers: carters and porters; stevedores and dockers; water carriers and sweepers; seamstresses, laundresses, cleaners, and domestic servants. These men and women, like their rural counterparts, lived on the margins of life, constantly battling the trade cycles, seasonal unemployment, and epidemics that threatened their ability to survive. A number existed in shanties on the edge of towns and cities. In Genoa, the homeless poor were sold as galley slaves each winter. In Venice, the poor lived on decrepit barges under the city's bridges. A French ordinance of 1669 ordered the destruction of all houses "built on poles by vagabonds and useless members of society." Deprived of the certainty of steady work, these people were prey not only to economic fluctuations and malevolent "acts of God," but to a social system that left them without any "privilege" or "freedom" whatsoever.

Attitudes toward poverty

Attitudes toward poverty varied from country to country. Most localities extended the concept of orders to include the poor: "the deserving"—usually orphans, the insane, the aged, the infirm; and "the undeserving"—able-bodied men and women who were out of work or who, even though employed, could not support themselves and their families. The authorities tended to assume in the latter case that poverty was the result of personal failings; few made a connection between general economic circumstances and the plight of the individual poor. For the deserving, private charitable organizations, such as those in France founded by the order of St. Vincent de Paul and by the Sisters of Charity, provided assistance. For the undeserving, there was harsh treatment at the hands of the state whose concern to alleviate extreme deprivation arose more from a desire to avert public disorder than from motives of human charity. Food riots were common occurrences. In times of scarcity the French government frequently intervened to reduce the price of grain, hoping thereby to prevent an outbreak of rioting. Yet riots nevertheless occurred. When property damage resulted, the ringleaders were generally severely punished, usually by hanging. The remainder of the crowd was often left untouched by the law, a fact suggesting the degree to which governments were prepared to tolerate rioting itself as a means of dealing with the chronic consequences of poverty.

The treatment of paupers

Poverty remained a central and intractable problem for the governments of all European countries. Poor vagrants were perceived as a serious threat to social tranquillity. They were therefore frequently rounded up at harvest time to keep them from plundering the fields. Vagrants and other chronically unemployed persons were placed in poorhouses where conditions were little better than those in prisons. Often the very young, the very old, the sick, and the insane were housed together with hardened criminals. Poor relief in England was administered parish by parish in accordance with a law passed in 1601. Relief was tied to a "law of settlement," which stipulated that paupers might receive aid only if still resid-

Hanging Thieves. This seventeenth-century engraving is designed to teach a lesson. Troops stand by and priests bless the condemned criminals as they are executed by the dozen. "At last," the engraver's caption reads, "these infamous lost souls are hung like unhappy fruit."

ing in the parish of their birth. An unemployed weaver who had migrated fifty miles in search of work could thus expect assistance only if he returned home again. In the late eighteenth century, several European countries established modest public works programs in an attempt to relieve poverty by reducing unemployment. France, for example, undertook road-building projects in the 1770s under the auspices of its progressive finance minister, Turgot. But generally speaking, indigence was perceived not as a social ill for which a remedy might be sought, but as an indelible stigma demarking those at the bottom of society.

Education in a society of orders: the nobility

European social institutions reflected the patterns of hierarchy. Nowhere was this more apparent than in the field of education. One barrier—a knowledge of Latin—separated nobles and a fair number of scholars and professionals from the commercial middle ranks; a second—the ability to read and write—separated the middle from the rest. Noblemen were generally educated by private tutors; though they might attend university for a time, they did so not in preparation for a profession but to receive further educational "finishing." Indeed during the late seventeenth and eighteenth centuries, universities more or less surrendered intellectual leadership to various academies established with royal patronage by European monarchs to enhance their own reputations as well as to encourage the advancement of science and the arts: the Royal Society of London, founded by Charles II in 1660; the French Academy of Sciences, a project upon which Louis XIV lavished a good deal of ostentatious attention; and the Berlin Royal Academy of Science and Letters, patronized by Frederick the Great of Prussia in the eighteenth century. Few noblemen had the interest or the intelligence to participate in the activities of these august organizations, which were not, in any case, teaching institutions. Far better suited to their needs and inclinations was "the grand tour," often of many months' duration, which led the nobleman through the capitals of Europe, and during which he was expected to acquire a kind of international *politesse.* One observer, commenting on the habits of young English noblemen abroad, remarked, "they game; purchase pictures, mutilated statues, and mistresses to the astonishment of all beholders."

Training for government service

Endowed, fee-charging institutions for the training of a governmental elite existed in France (the *collège*) and Spain (the *colegio mayor*) and in Germany and Austria (the *gymnasium*). Here the emphasis was by no means on "practical" subjects such as modern language or mathematics, but on the mastery of Greek and Latin translation and composition, the intellectual badge of the educated elite. An exception was the Prussian University of Halle, designed to teach a professional elite; a contemporary described that institution as teaching only what was "rational, useful, and practical."

Education for the middle orders

Male children from the middle orders destined to enter the family business or profession as a rule attended small private academies where the curriculum included the sort of "useful" instruction ignored in the *collèges* and *gymnasia.* Female children, from both the upper and the middle orders, were almost invariably educated at home, receiving little more than rudimentary instruction in gentlewomanly subjects such as modern language, belles lettres, and music, if from the noble ranks; and a similar, if slightly more practical training, if from the bourgeoisie.

Education for the poor

No European country undertook the task of providing primary education to all its citizens until the middle of the eighteenth century, when Frederick the Great in Prussia and the Habsburg monarchs Maria Theresa and her son Joseph II in Austria instituted systems of compulsory attendance. Available evidence suggests that their results fell far short of expectation. An early-nineteenth-century survey from the relatively enlightened Prussian province of Cleves revealed dilapidated schools, poorly attended classes, and an incompetent corps of teachers. Educational conditions were undoubtedly worse in most other European communities.

Increasing literacy

Though modern scholars can make no more than educated guesses, it appears certain that literacy rates increased considerably in the seventeenth and eighteenth centuries; in England, from one in four males in 1600 to one in two by 1800; in France, from 29 percent of the male population in 1686 to 47 percent in 1786. Literacy among women increased as well, though their rate of increase generally lagged behind that of men: only 27 percent of the female population in France was literate in 1786. Naturally, such rates varied according to particular localities and circumstances, and from country to country. Literacy was higher in urban areas that contained a large proportion of artisans. In rural eastern Europe, literacy remained extremely low (20–30 percent) well into the nineteenth century. Notwithstanding state-directed efforts in Prussia and Austria, the rise in literacy was largely the result of a growing determination on the part of religiously minded reformers to teach the poor to read and write as a means of encouraging obedience to divine and secular authority. A

Establishing the French Academy of Sciences and the Foundation of the Observatory, by Henri Testelin. This painting, which shows Louis XIV as patron, testifies to his enthusiastic support of the Academy.

Sunday-school movement in eighteenth-century England and similar activities among the Christian Brotherhood in France are clear evidence of this trend.

Popular culture

Though the majority of the common people were probably no more than barely literate, they possessed a flourishing culture of their own. Village life, particularly in Roman Catholic countries, centered about the church, to which men and women would go on Sundays not only to worship but to socialize. Much of the remainder of their day of rest would be devoted to participation in village games. Religion provided the opportunity for association and for a welcome break from the daily work routines. Pilgrimages to a nearby shrine, for example, would include a procession of villagers led by one of their number carrying an image of the village's patron saint and accompanied by drinking, dancing, and picnicking. In towns, Catholics joined organizations called "confraternities" in France, Italy, Austria, and the Netherlands, which provided mutual aid and a set of common rituals and traditions centered upon a patron saint. Religious community was expressed as well in popular Protestant movements that arose in the eighteenth century: Pietism on the Continent and Methodism in England. Both emphasized the importance of personal salvation through faith and the potential worth of every human soul regardless of station. Both therefore appealed particularly to people whose position within the community had heretofore been presumed to be without

Vauxhall Gardens, by Thomas Rowlandson. This London scene suggests the degree to which men and women from different social orders came together for sport, drinking, and adventure.

any value. Though Methodism's founder, John Wesley (1703–1791), preached obedience to earthly authority, his willingness to rely on working men and women as preachers and organizers gave them a new sense of personal importance.

Carnival and other amusements

Popular culture often combined in one event traditions that were part religious, part secular, and, indeed, part pagan. One such occasion was Carnival, that vibrant pre-Lenten celebration indigenous not only to Mediterranean Europe but to Germany and Austria as well. Carnival represented an opportunity for common folk to cast aside the burdens and restraints imposed upon their order by secular authority. Performances and processions celebrated a "world turned upside down," a theme popular throughout much of Europe from the Later Middle Ages, which appealed to commoners for a variety of ambiguous psychological reasons, but in large part, certainly, as a way of avenging symbolically the economic and social oppression under which they lived. For a few days, the oppressed played the role of the oppressor and rulers were made to look like fools and knaves. In parades, men dressed as kings walked barefoot while peasants rode on horseback or in carriages; the poor threw pretend money to the rich. These occasions, although emphasizing social divisions, worked to hold communities to a common cultural center, since, through most of the early-modern period, both rich and poor celebrated together, as they did on major religious holidays. Annual harvest festivals, once sponsored by the Church, were increasingly secular celebrations of release from backbreaking labor, punctuated by feasting, drinking, sporting, and lovemaking. Fairs and traveling circuses brought something of distant places and people into lives bound to one spot. The

French Tavern. Often located outside the city limits so as to avoid the payment of municipal taxes, taverns such as this provided a gathering place for workers to drink, gossip, and relax after the day's labors. The tavern also served as a convenient place for public readings and for airing common grievances.

drudgery of everyday life was also relieved by horse races, cock fights, and bear baiting. Taverns played an even more constant role in the daily life of the village, providing a place for men to gather over tobacco and drink and indulge in gossip and gambling.

Laboring men and women depended on an oral tradition of myth, legend, and superstition to steady their lives and give them point and purpose. Stories in books sold at fairs by peddlers were passed on by those who could read. They told of heroes and saints, and of kings like Charlemagne whose paternal concern for his common subjects led him into battle against his selfish nobility. Belief in villains matched belief in heroes. Witchcraft, as we have seen, was a reality for much of the period. So was Satan. So was any supernatural force, whether for good or evil, that could help them make sense of a world in which they, more than any, were victims of events beyond their control.

Stability and change

Though increasingly secularized, popular customs, celebrations, and beliefs remained a stabilizing force in early-modern Europe. They were the cultural expression of that social order to which the vast majority of Europeans belonged. Popular culture in the main tended to reinforce the traditions and assumptions of order and hierarchy. Peasants and urban workers worshiped saints and venerated heroic rulers, thereby accepting the authority of the established, ordered society of which they were a part. They were seldom satisfied with their lot, yet they were as seldom willing to question the social structure they saw as a bulwark against the swift changes so often surrounding them. Popular culture helped to bind men and women to what civilization had been, as capitalism and mercantilism impelled them in the direction of what it would become.

SUMMARY POINTS

- Until the mid-eighteenth century, warfare, famine, and disease curbed population growth. After about 1750, however, most western European countries saw steady and significant population growth, particularly in cities where trade, commerce, and administration attracted laborers.
- Agriculture and industry saw gradual technical improvements in the seventeenth and eighteenth centuries, such as scientific farming and the "putting-out" system of craft production, that improved efficiency and increased output.
- Commerce and industry grew increasingly capitalistic and mercantilistic in the 1600s and 1700s. Cooperation between businesses and governments allowed national economies to expand and international trade to flourish.
- The overseas colonies and trading posts developed by European powers during the seventeenth and eighteenth centuries were evidence of economic expansion and mercantilist policies. The Spanish, French, English, and Dutch competed for trading advantages in North, Central, and South America, the Caribbean, and the Far East. Agricultural industries in the Americas fueled demand for African slaves.
- Early-modern European society was rigidly ordered, giving rights and privileges to those of higher social rank and very little to those of lower rank. Popular customs, celebrations, and beliefs reinforced the traditions of hierarchy.

SELECTED READINGS

Blum, Jerome, *Lord and Peasant in Russia,* Princeton, 1961. A good study of Russian society.

Braudel, F., *The Structures of Everyday Life: The Limits of the Possible,* New York, 1981. A survey of the material conditions of life; profusely illustrated.

Burke, Peter, *Popular Culture in Early Modern Europe,* London, 1978. Synthesizes work on the period between 1500 and 1800; fascinating.

M. L. Bush, ed., *Social Orders and Social Classes in Europe since 1500,* New York, 1992. Essays on a broad range of subjects, including the Church, tenant rights, and the concept of class.

Cipolla, Carlo M., *Before the Industrial Revolution: European Society and Economy, 1000–1700,* 3d ed., New York, 1994. Wide-ranging and full of deft observations.

Darnton, Robert, *The Great Cat Massacre and Other Episodes in French Cultural History,* New York, 1984. Fascinating explorations into early-modern French mentalities.

———, *The Literary Underground of the Old Regime,* Cambridge, 1982. An examination of the world of popular writers, sellers of illegal books, and the literary underworld of eighteenth-century Paris.

Davis, David Brion, *The Problem of Slavery in Western Culture,* Ithaca, N.Y., 1966. A brilliant analysis of Western attitudes and assumptions.

Davis, Natalie Z., *Society and Culture in Early Modern France,* Stanford, 1975. Eight scintillating essays by a pioneer in the use of anthropological methods for the study of early-modern European history.

Davis, Ralph, *The Rise of the Atlantic Economies,* Ithaca, N.Y., 1973. A thorough analysis of early-modern trade and commerce.

De Vries, Jan, *The Economy of Europe in an Age of Crisis, 1600–1750,* New York, 1976. A survey of the emerging capitalist economies of early-modern Europe.

Doyle, William, *The Old European Order, 1660–1800,* 2d ed., New York, 1992. An excellent general survey with chapters on population, trade, social orders, and public affairs.

Forster, Robert, *The Nobility of Toulouse in the Eighteenth Century,* Baltimore, Md., 1960. A careful analysis of the extent and nature of aristocratic power.

Foucault, M., *The History of Sexuality: An Introduction,* Vol. I, New York, 1978. Useful material on the early-modern period.

Fraser, Antonia, *The Weaker Vessel,* New York, 1984. Includes discussion of the role of women in the English Civil War.

Gibson, Wendy, *Women in Seventeenth-Century France,* New York, 1989. A thorough survey of women's lives and work.

Houston, R. A., *Literacy in Early Modern Europe: Culture and Education, 1500–1800,* New York, 1988. A valuable analysis of the various types of educational institutions and who did—and did not—attend them.

Hufton, Olwen H., *The Poor of Eighteenth-Century France, 1750–1789,* Oxford, 1974. One of the first studies of a preindustrial "underclass."

Inikori, Joseph E., and Stanley Engerman, eds., *The Atlantic Slave Trade: Effects on Economies, Societies, and Peoples in Africa, the Americas, and Europe,* Durham, N.C., 1992. An outstanding collection of thoughtful and well-researched essays emphasizing the complexity and enormity of the slave trade and its wide and profound effects.

Kaplow, Jeffry, *The Names of Kings: The Parisian Laboring Poor in the Eighteenth Century,* New York, 1972. A valuable study of the urban poor.

Laslett, Peter, *The World We Have Lost,* 2d ed., New York, 1971. Analyzes the nature of rural society in early-modern England.

Le Roy Ladurie, Emmanuel, *The Peasants of Languedoc,* Urbana, Ill., 1974. A classic on peasant life and demography.

Levine, David, *Family Formation in an Age of Nascent Capitalism,* New York, 1977. A thoughtful treatment of patterns of social formation.

Lougee, Carolyn C., *Le Paradis des Femmes: Women, Salons, and Social Stratification in Seventeenth-Century France.* Princeton, 1976. Women's role in the intellectual life of the old regime.

Mousnier, R., *Peasant Uprisings in Seventeenth-Century France, Russia and China,* New York, 1970. A comparative analysis.

Parry, J. H., *The Age of Reconnaissance,* Berkeley, 1981. The role of the colonies in the economy and politics of early-modern Europe.

Postma, Johannes, *The Dutch in the Atlantic Slave Trade, 1600–1815,* New York, 1990. A thoroughly documented examination of the critical Dutch role in the expansion of the Atlantic slave trade from a small undertaking to a trade with global dimensions.

Ranum, Orest, *Paris in the Age of Absolutism,* New York, 1968. A useful view of urban life.

Rich, E. E., and C. H. Wilson, eds., *The Cambridge Economic History of Europe:* Volume 5, *The Economic Organization of Early Modern Europe,* New York, 1977. An indispensable guide to the study of the period's economy and society.

Roche, Daniel, *The People of Paris: An Essay in Popular Culture in the Eighteenth Century,* Dover, N.H., 1986. Livelihood and concerns of ordinary Parisians.

Sabean, David, *Power in the Blood: Popular Culture and Village Discourse in Early-Modern Germany,* New York, 1984. A reconstruction of the collective mind of a German village over the course of two centuries.

Schama, Simon, *The Embarrassment of Riches: An Interpretation of Dutch Culture in the Golden Age,* New York, 1988. A full-bodied analysis of the God-fearing yet materially inclined Dutch.

Stone, Lawrence, *The Family, Sex and Marriage in England, 1500–1800,* New York, 1977. An important, controversial book that argues important changes in attitudes over the course of three centuries.

Wilson, Charles, *England's Apprenticeship, 1603–1763,* 2d ed., London, 1984. A reliable economic survey.

Wrigley, E. A., *Population and History,* New York, 1969. A good introduction to family history.

Source Materials

Barnett, G. E., ed., *Two Tracts by Gregory King,* Baltimore, 1936. An introduction to the work of the modern world's first real statistician.

Goubert, Pierre, *The Ancien Régime: French Society, 1600–1750,* London, 1973. Particularly strong in its descriptions of rural life. Includes selections from illuminating documents.

Ménétra, Jacques Louis, *Journal of My Life,* trans. Arthur Goldhammer, intr. Daniel Roche, 1986. The autobiography of a Parisian glazier who played checkers with Rousseau and was an eyewitness to the Revolution.

Northrup, David, ed., *The Atlantic Slave Trade,* Lexington, Mass., 1994. A judicious collection of primary and secondary source materials that examines the entire sweep of the trade, from beginnings to the fight for abolition.

Young, Arthur, *Travels in France during the Years 1787, 1788, 1789,* London, various editions. Vivid observations by an English traveler.

CHAPTER 17

THE AGE OF ABSOLUTISM (1660–1789)

There are four essential characteristics or qualities of royal authority.
First, royal authority is sacred.
Second, it is paternal.
Third, it is absolute.
Fourth, it is subject to reason.
—JACQUES BOSSUET, *Politics Drawn from the Very Words of Holy Scripture*

Absolutism defined

THE PERIOD FROM the assumption of personal rule by Louis XIV of France (1661) until the French Revolution (1789) is known as the age of absolutism. The label is accurate if we define *absolutism* as the conscious attempt by state sovereigns—sometimes successful; more often not—to extend their legal and administrative power over their subjects, and over the vested interests of the social and economic orders in which those subjects were ranked. The dates are suggestive in that for the period as a whole the activities of French monarchs most clearly expressed the intentions of absolutist government. Yet both the dates and the label need to be treated with some caution. We have already noted that from about 1500 on, a general trend to make the state more powerful had manifested itself in England and on the Continent. Sixteenth-century kings saw in Protestantism a way of asserting the sovereignty of their states over the power of the papacy and the aristocracy. And political thinkers such as Jean Bodin were championing absolutist theory in their writings well before Louis XIV assumed personal rulership of France. By establishing the French monarchs as prototypical early-modern rulers, we risk ignoring other modes of centralized government instituted by the rulers of Prussia, Russia, and Austria. And we exclude the crucially important exception of England, where after 1688, absolutist tendencies gave way to oligarchy.

Absolutism qualified

The term "absolutism" needs qualification. As practiced by western European eighteenth-century rulers, absolutism was not despotism. They did not understand it as a license for untrammeled and arbitrary rule, such as that practiced by Oriental potentates. Despite the best efforts of these European monarchs to consolidate their authority, they could not issue irresponsible decrees and achieve lasting compliance. Aristocrats, churchmen, merchants, and entrepreneurs remained strong enough within their respective orders to ensure that kings and queens would need to justify the actions they took. Moreover, rulers tended to respect not only the strength of their political adversaries but the processes of law; they quarreled openly and broke with tradition only under exceptional circumstances. No matter how "absolute" monarchs might wish to be, they were limited as well by rudimentary systems of transportation and communication from interfering with any degree of consistency and efficiency in the daily lives of their subjects.

The relationship between state power and economic innovation

Although the emphasis in this chapter is largely upon political, diplomatic, and military events, absolutism cannot be fully understood without relating it to the commercial and industrial trends we have just analyzed. Tariff legislation, industrial regulations, wars of trade, currency manipulation, tax laws—all were useful tools in the construction of a new economic order. And all were tools that could be employed only by a strongly centralized state. Governments might take active steps to manage production and exportation, as the English did when they imposed the Navigation Acts in 1660, which restricted imports to material transported on English ships or those of their country of origin, and required colonial goods to pass through English ports before being sold elsewhere. Other governments (the French, for example), in their determination to finance expanding bureaucratic and military establishments, imposed new taxes and exacted an increasingly high price for the privileges they meted out. The state's expanding financial demands placed considerable pressure on both urban middle orders and peasantry to make more money. And the result of that pressure, in turn, was entrepreneurship and wage labor.

Bearing in mind, then, the important symbiotic relationship between state power and economic innovation, we shall, in this chapter, measure the extent of royal power throughout Europe in the late seventeenth and eighteenth centuries, examine the varieties of absolutism as instituted and practiced by different monarchs, and take note of the way in which the centralization of power contributed to the rise of an international state system.

The Appeal and Justification of Absolutism

Absolutism's appeal

Absolutism appealed to many Europeans for the same reason that mercantilism did. In theory and practice, it expressed a desire for an end to the constant alarms and confusions of Europe's "iron century." The French religious wars, the Thirty Years' War in Germany, and the English Civil War all had produced great turbulence. The alternative, domestic order, absolutists argued, could come only with strong, centralized government. Just as mercantilists maintained that economic stability would result from regimentation, so absolutists contended that social and political harmony would be realized when subjects recognized their duty to obey their divinely sanctioned rulers.

The duties of the monarch

Absolutist monarchs insisted, in turn, upon *their* duty to teach their subjects, even against their will, how to order their domestic affairs. As Margrave Karl Friedrich, eighteenth-century ruler of the German principality of Baden, expressed it: "We must make them, whether they like it or not, into free, opulent and law-abiding citizens." Looking back to the seventeenth-century wars that had torn Europe apart, rulers can be excused for believing that absolutism's promise of stability and prosperity—"freedom and opulence"—presented an attractive as well as an imperative alternative to disorder. Louis XIV of France remembered the *Fronde* as a threat to the welfare of the nation that he had been appointed by God to rule wisely and justly. When marauding Parisians entered his bedchamber one night in 1651 to discover if he had fled the city with Mazarin, Louis saw the intrusion as a horrid affront not only to his own person, but to the state. Squabbles among the nobility and criticisms of royal policy in the Paris Parlement during his minority left him convinced that he must exercise his powers and prerogatives rigorously if France was to survive and prosper as a great European state.

Goals of absolute monarchs: army, administration, and revenue

In order to achieve that objective, absolutist monarchs worked to control the disposition of the state's armed forces, the administration of its legal system, and the collection and distribution of its tax revenues. This ambitious goal required an efficient bureaucracy that owed its primary allegiance not to some social or economic order with interests antithetical to the monarchy, but to the institution of the monarchy itself. One hallmark of absolutist policy was its determination to construct a set of institutions strong enough to withstand, if not destroy, the privileged interests that had hindered royal power in the past. The Church and the nobility, the semiautonomous regions, and the would-be independent representative bodies (the English Parliament and the French Estates-General) were all obstacles to the achievement of strong, centralized monarchical government. And the history of absolutism is, as much as anything, the history of the attempts of various rulers to bring these institutions to heel.

Absolutism and the control of the Church and its clergy

In those major European countries where Roman Catholicism still remained the state religion—France, Spain, and Austria—successive monarchs throughout the eighteenth century made various attempts to "nationalize" the Church and its clergy. We have already noted the way in which in the fifteenth and sixteenth centuries popes had conceded certain powers to the temporal rulers of France and Spain. Later absolutists, building on those earlier precedents, wrested further power from the Church in Rome. Even Charles III, the devout Spanish king who ruled from 1759 to 1788, pressed successfully for a papal concordat granting the state control over ecclesiastical appointments, and established his right to sanction the proclamation of papal bulls.

Absolutism and the control of the noble orders

Powerful as the Church was, it did not rival the nobility as an opponent of a centralized state. Monarchs combatted the noble orders in various ways. Louis XIV attempted to control the ancient French aristocracy by depriving it of political power while increasing its social prestige. Peter the Great, the talented and erratic tsar of early eighteenth-century Russia, co-opted the nobility into government service. Later in the century, Catherine II struck a bargain whereby in return for the granting of vast estates and a variety of social and economic privileges such as exemption from taxation, the Russian nobility virtually surrendered the administrative and political power of the state into the empress's hands. In Prussia under Frederick the Great, the army was staffed by nobles; here again, as in Peter's Russia, was a case of co-option. Yet in late-eighteenth-century Austria, the Emperor Joseph II adopted a policy of confrontation rather than accommodation, denying the nobility exemption from taxation and deliberately blurring the distinctions between nobles and commoners.

Struggle between local and central power

These struggles between monarchs and nobles had implications for the additional struggle between local privileges and centralized power. Absolutists in France waged a constant and never entirely successful war against the autonomy of provincial institutions, often headed by nobles, much as Spanish rulers in the sixteenth century had battled independent-minded nobles in Aragon and Catalonia. Prussian rulers intruded into the governance of formerly "free" cities, assuming police and revenue powers over their inhabitants. These various campaigns, constantly waged and usually successful for a time, were evidence of the nature of absolutism and of its continuing success.

Theoretical apologists for absolutism

Absolutism had its theoretical apologists as well as its able practitioners. In addition to the political philosophies of men such as Bodin, defenders of royal power could rely on treatises such as Bishop Jacques Bossuet's *Politics Drawn from the Very Words of Scripture* (1708), written during the reign of Louis XIV, to sustain the case for extended monarchical control. Bossuet argued that absolute government was not the same as arbitrary government, since God, in whom "all strength and all perfection were united," was united as well with the person of the king. "God is holiness itself, goodness itself, and power itself. In these things lies the majesty of God. In the image of these things lies the majesty of the prince." It followed that the king was answerable to no one but God himself, and that the king was as far above other mortals as God was above the king. "The prince, as prince, is not regarded as a private person; he is a public personage, all the state is in him. . . . As all perfection and all strength are united in God, all the power of individuals is united in the Person of the prince. What grandeur that a simple man should embody so much." What grandeur indeed! Bossuet's treatise was the most explicit and extreme statement of the theory of the divine right of kings, the doctrine that James I had tried to foist upon the English. Unlikely as it may sound to modern ears, the political philosophy of Bossuet was comforting to men and women in the upper orders of society who craved peace and stability after a century or more of international and domestic turmoil, who found themselves embarked upon bold economic adventures that required a strong and stable polity, and who realized that absolutism might well require their collaboration and therefore bring them gain.

Bishop Jacques Bossuet

The Château of Versailles. Dramatically expanded by Louis XIV in the 1660s from a hunting lodge to the principal royal residence and the seat of government, the château became a monument to the international power and prestige of the Grand Monarch.

THE ABSOLUTISM OF LOUIS XIV

Absolutism as theater: Louis XIV

Examine a portrait of Louis XIV (1643–1715) in court robes; it is all but impossible to discern the human being behind the facade of the absolute monarch. That facade was carefully and artfully constructed by Louis, who recognized, perhaps more clearly than any other early-modern ruler, the importance of theater as a means of establishing authority. Well into the eighteenth century, superstitious commoners continued to believe in the power of the king's magic "touch" to cure disease. Louis and his successors manipulated the theater of their sovereignty so as to enhance their position as divine-right rulers endowed with God-like powers and far removed from common humanity.

Louis XIV's opulence

The advantages of strategic theater were expressed most clearly in Louis's palace at Versailles, the town outside of Paris to which he moved his court. The building itself was a stage upon which Louis attempted to mesmerize the aristocracy into obedience by his performance of the daily rituals of absolutism. The main facade of the palace was a third of a mile in length. Inside, tapestries and paintings celebrated French military victories and royal triumphs. In the vast gardens outside, statues of Apollo, god of the sun, recalled Louis's claim to be the "Sun King" of the French. Noblemen vied to attend him when he arose from bed, ate his meals (usually stone-cold, having traveled the distance of several city blocks from royal kitchen to royal table), strolled in his gardens, or rode to the hunt. As Louis called himself the Sun King, so his court was the epicenter of his royal effulgence. Its glitter, in which France's leading nobles were required by their monarch to share, was deliberately manufactured so as to blind them to the possibility of disobedience to the royal will. Instead of plotting some sort of minor treason on his estate, a marquis enjoyed the pleasure of knowing that on the morrow he was to be privileged to engage the king in two or three minutes of vapid conversation as the royal party made its stately progress through the vast palace halls (whose smells were evidence of the absence of sanitation facilities and of the seamy side of absolutist grandeur).

Louis XIV on his duties

Louis understood this theater as part of his duty as sovereign, a duty that he took with utmost seriousness. Though far from brilliant, he was hard-working and conscientious. Whether or not he actually remarked *"L'état, c'est moi"* (I am the State), he believed himself personally responsi-

One of the Fountains in the Gardens at Versailles. The grounds as well as the palace were part of the backdrop for the theater of absolutism.

Louis XIV, the Sun King. This portrait by Rigaud illustrates the degree to which absolute monarchy was defined in terms of studied performance.

ble for the well-being of his subjects. "The deference and the respect that we receive from our subjects," he wrote in a memoir he prepared for his son on the art of ruling, "are not a free gift from them but payment for the justice and the protection that they expect from us. Just as they must honor us, we must protect and defend them."

The administration of French absolutism: intendants and revenue

Louis defined this responsibility in absolutist terms: as a need to concentrate royal power so as to produce general domestic tranquillity. While taming the nobility, he conciliated the upper bourgeoisie by enlisting its members to assist him in the task of administration. He appointed them as intendants, responsible for the administration and taxation of the thirty-six *generalités* into which France was divided. Intendants usually served outside the region where they were born, and were thus unconnected with the local elites over which they exercised authority. They held office at the king's pleasure, and were clearly "his" men. Other administrators, often from families newly ennobled as a result of administrative service, assisted in directing affairs of state from Versailles. These men were not actors in the theater of Louis the Sun King; they were the hard-working assistants of Louis the royal custodian of his country's welfare. Much of the time and energy of Louis's bureaucrats were expended on the collection of taxes, necessary above all in order to finance the large standing army on which France's ambitious foreign policy depended. Absolutism, it must never be forgotten, was a mechanism designed to assist ambitious monarchs in their determination to increase their power through conquest. In addition to the *taille,* or land tax, which increased throughout the seventeenth century and upon which a surtax was levied as well, the government introduced a *capitation* tax (head tax), payable by all, and pressed successfully for the collection of indirect taxes such as those on salt (the *gabelle*) and on wine and tobacco. Since the nobility was exempt from the *taille,* its burden fell most heavily on the peasantry, whose periodic local revolts Louis easily crushed.

Curbing regional power

Regional opposition—and indeed regionalism generally—was curtailed, but by no means eliminated, during Louis's reign. Although intendants and lesser administrators came from afar, did not speak the local dialect, and ignored local custom, they were generally obeyed. The semiautonomous outer provinces of Brittany, Languedoc, and Franche-Comté (several of the territories known collectively as the *pays d'états*) suffered the crippling of their provincial Estates. To put an end to the power of regional *parlements,* Louis decreed that members of those bodies that refused to register his laws would be summarily exiled. The Estates-General, the national French representative assembly last summoned in 1614 during the troubled regency that followed the death of Henry IV, did not meet again until 1789.

Louis XIV's religious policies

Louis was equally determined, for reasons of state and of personal conscience, to impose religious unity upon the French. That task proved to be difficult and time-consuming. The Huguenots were not the only source of theological heterodoxy. Quietists and Jansenists—both claiming to represent the "true" Roman faith—battled among themselves for adherents to their particular brand of Catholicism. Quietists preached retreat into personal mysticism that emphasized a direct relationship between God and the individual human heart. Such doctrine, dispensing as it did with the intermediary services of the Church and of the orthodox authority those services represented, was suspect in the eyes of absolutists wedded to the doctrine of *un roi, une loi, une foi* (one king, one law, one faith). Jansenism—a movement named for its founder Cornelius Jansen, a seventeenth-century bishop of Ypres—challenged the authority of the state church with an unorthodox doctrine of predestination, proclaiming the salvation of no more than an elected few. Louis persecuted Quietists and Jansenists, offering them the choice of recanting or of prison and exile. Against the Huguenots he waged an even sterner war. Protestant churches and schools were destroyed; Protestant families were forced to convert. In 1685, Louis revoked the Edict of Nantes, the legal foundation of the toleration Huguenots had enjoyed since 1598. French Protestants were thereafter denied civil rights, and their clergy was exiled. Thousands of religious refugees fled France for England, Holland, the Protestant states of Germany, and America, where their particular professional and artisanal skills made a significant contribution to economic prosperity. (The silk industries of Berlin and of Spitalfields, an urban quarter of London, were established by Huguenots.)

Colbert's economic policies

Louis's drive for unification and centralization was assisted by his ability to rely upon increased revenues. Those revenues were largely the result of policies and programs initiated by Jean Baptiste Colbert (1619–1683), the country's finance minister from 1664 until his death. Colbert was an energetic and committed mercantilist who believed that until France could put its fiscal house in order it could not achieve economic greatness. He tightened the process of tax collection, and he eliminated wherever possible the practice of tax farming, the system whereby collection agents were permitted to withhold a certain percentage of what they gathered for themselves. When Colbert assumed office, only about 25 percent of the taxes collected throughout the kingdom was reaching the treasury. By the time he died, that figure had risen to 80 percent.

Jean Baptiste Colbert

Colbert's efforts were not limited to managing the public debt and wringing the inefficiencies out of the tax system, however. During this period the state also merchandised government positions and privileges on an increasing scale. Judgeships, mayoralities, and other public offices were sold, and guilds purchased the right to enforce trade regulations. The state extracted direct profit from every office it created and every privilege it controlled, demonstrating once again the way in which economy and politics were inextricably intertwined.

Colbert as mercantilist

As a mercantilist, Colbert did all he could to increase the nation's income by means of protection and regimentation. Tariffs he imposed in 1667 and 1668 were designed to discourage the importation of foreign goods into France. He invested in the improvement of France's roads and waterways. And he used state money to promote the growth of national industry, in particular the manufacture of goods such as silk, lace, tapestries, and glass, which had long been imported. Yet Colbert's efforts to achieve national economic stability and self-sufficiency could not withstand the insatiable demands of Louis XIV's increasingly expensive wars. Indeed, by the end of Louis's reign, the limitations of his absolutist ambitions were strikingly evident. As we shall see, his aggressive foreign policy lay in ruins. The country's finances were enfeebled by the economic demands that policy exacted. Colbert himself foreshadowed Louis's ultimate failure when he lectured him in 1680, "Trade is the source of public finance and public finance is the vital nerve of war. . . . I beg your Majesty to permit me only to say to him that in war as in peace he has never consulted the amount of money available in determining his expenditures."

Absolutism in Central and Eastern Europe, 1660–1720

Absolutism and national unity

Whatever success Louis XIV did enjoy as an absolute monarch was in part the result of his own abilities, and of those of his advisers. Yet it was due as well to the fact that he could claim to stand as the supreme embodiment of the will of all of his people. Despite its internal division into territories and orders that continued to claim some right to independence, France was already unified before the accession of Louis XIV and possessed a sense of itself as a nation. In this, it differed from the empires, kingdoms, and principalities to the east, where rulers faced an even more formidable task than did Louis as they attempted to weld their disparately constructed monarchies into a united, centralized whole. The Thirty Years' War had delivered a final blow to the pretensions of the Holy Roman Empire, which the French philosopher Voltaire dubbed neither holy, Roman, nor an empire. Power, in varying degrees, passed to the over three hundred princes, bishops, and magistrates who governed the assorted states of Germany throughout the remainder of the seventeenth and eighteenth centuries.

Absolutism in the German states

Despite the minute size of their domains, many of these petty monarchs attempted to establish themselves as absolutists in miniature, building lesser versions of Louis XIV's Versailles. They remodeled cities to serve as explicit expressions of their power. Broad avenues led to monumental squares and eventually to the grand palace of the monarch. Medieval cities had masked the inequalities of the social order in their crowded, twisted streets and passageways, where different social ranks often lived jumbled together in close physical proximity. Absolutist capital cities, in contrast, celebrated inequality, their planning and architecture purposely emphasizing the vast distance separating the ruler from the ruled. European absolutists followed the French example by maintaining standing armies and paying for their expensive pretensions by tariffs and tolls that severely hampered the development of any sort of economic unity within the region as a whole. Although these rulers often prided themselves on their independence from imperial control, in many instances they were client states of France. A sizable portion of the money Louis devoted to the conduct of foreign affairs went to these German princelings. States like Saxony, Brandenburg-Prussia, and Bavaria, which were of a size to establish themselves as truly independent, were not averse to forming alliances against their own emperor.

The absolutism of Frederick William of Brandenburg

Most notable among these middle-sized German states was Brandenburg-Prussia, whose emergence as a power of consequence during this period was the result of the single-minded determination of its rulers, principally Frederick William, elector of Brandenburg from 1640 to 1688, whose abilities have earned him the title of "Great Elector." The rise of Brandenburg-Prussia from initial insignificance, poverty, and devastation in the wake of the Thirty Years' War resulted from three basic achievements that can be credited to the Great Elector. First, he pursued an adroit foreign policy that enabled him to establish effective sovereignty over the widely dispersed and underdeveloped territories under his rule: Brandenburg, a large but not particularly productive territory in north-central Germany; Prussia, a duchy to the east that was dangerously exposed on three sides to Poland; and a sprinkling of tiny states—Cleves, Mark, and Ravensberg—to the west. By siding with Poland in a war against Sweden in the late 1650s, the Great Elector obtained the Polish king's surrender of nominal overlordship in East Prussia. And by some crafty diplomatic shuffling in the 1670s, he secured his western provinces from French interference by returning Pomerania, captured in a recent war, to France's Swedish allies.

The establishment of a large standing army

Frederick William's second achievement was the establishment of a large standing army, the primary instrument of his diplomatic successes. By 1688, Brandenburg-Prussia had 30,000 troops permanently under arms. That he was able to sustain an army of this size in a state with comparatively limited resources was a measure of the degree to which the army more than repaid its costs. It ensured the elector and his successors absolute political control by fostering obedience among the populace, an obedience they were prepared to observe if their lands might be spared the devastation of another Thirty Years' War.

Taxation and bureaucracy: bargaining with the Junkers

The third factor contributing to the emergence of the Great Elector's state as an international power was his imposition of an effective system of taxation and his creation of a government bureaucracy to administer it. Here he struck an important bargain with the powerful and privileged landlords (*Junkers*) without whose cooperation his programs would have had no chance of success. In return for an agreement that allowed them to reduce their peasant underlings to the status of serfs, the Junkers gave away their right to oppose a permanent tax system, provided, of course, that they were made immune from the payment of taxes themselves. (As in other European countries, taxes in Prussia fell most heavily on the peasantry.)

The Junkers and the army

Henceforth, the political privileges of the landlord class diminished; secure in their right to manage their own estates as they wished, the Junkers were content to surrender management of the Hohenzollern possessions into the hands of a centralized bureaucracy. Its most important department was a military commissariat, whose functions included not only the dispensing of army pay and matériel, but the development of industries to manufacture military equipment. Frederick William's success

Prussians Swearing Allegiance to the Great Elector at Königsberg, 1663. The occasion upon which the Prussian estates first acknowledged the overlordship of their ruler. This ceremony marked the beginning of the centralization of the Prussian state.

was due primarily to his ability to gain the active cooperation of the Junker class, something he needed even more than Louis XIV needed the support of the French nobility. Without it, Frederick William could never have hammered together a state from the disparate territories that were his political raw material. To obtain it, he used the army, not only to maintain order, but as a way of co-opting Junker participation. The highest honor that could befall a Brandenburg squire was commission and promotion as a military servant of the state.

The Habsburg Empire

Like the Prussian rulers, the Habsburg monarchs were confronted with the task of transforming four different regions into a cohesive state. In the case of Austria, this effort was complicated by the fact that these areas were ethnically and linguistically diverse: the southernmost Germanic lands that roughly make up the present-day state of Austria; the northern Czech- (Slavic-) speaking provinces of Bohemia and Moravia; the German-speaking Silesia, inherited in 1527; and Hungary (where the Magyar population spoke a non-Slavic, Finno-Ugric language), also acquired in 1527 but largely lost to Turkish invasion just a few years afterward. For the next 150 years the Habsburgs and the Turks vied for control of Hungary. Until 1683 Turkish pashas ruled three-fourths of the Magyar kingdom, extending to within eighty miles of the Habsburg capital of Vienna. In 1683 the Turks beseiged Vienna itself, but were repulsed by the Austrians, assisted by a mixed German and Polish army under the command of King John Sobieski of Poland. This victory was a prelude to the Habsburg reconquest of virtually all of Hungary by the end of the century.

Bargaining with Bohemia and Moravia

The task of constructing an absolutist state from these extraordinarily varied territories was tackled with limited success by the seventeenth-century Habsburg emperors Ferdinand III (1637–1657) and Leopold I (1658–1705). Most of their efforts were devoted to the establishment of productive agricultural estates in Bohemia and Moravia, and to taming the independent nobility there and in Hungary. Landlords were encouraged to farm for export and were supported in this effort by a government decree that compelled peasants to provide three days of unpaid *robot* service per week to their masters.* For this support, Bohemian and Moravian landed elites exchanged the political independence that had in the past expressed itself in the activities of their territorial legislative Estates.

Problems with the Hungarian nobility

Habsburg rulers tried to effect this same sort of bargain in Hungary as well. But there the tradition of independence was stronger and died harder. Hungarian (or Magyar) nobles in the west claimed the right to elect their king, a right they eventually surrendered to Leopold in 1687. But the central government's attempts to reduce the country further by administering it through the army, by granting large tracts of land to German aristocrats and settlers, and by persecuting non-Catholics were an almost total failure. The result was a powerful nobility that remained fiercely determined to retain its traditional constitutional and religious

*The English usage of the term *robot* derives from the Czech designation of a serf.

"liberties." The Habsburg emperors could boast that they too, like absolutists elsewhere, possessed a large standing army and an educated (in this case, German-speaking) bureaucracy. But the exigencies imposed by geography and ethnicity kept them at some distance from the absolutist goal of a unified, centrally controlled and administered state.

Russian absolutism

Undoubtedly the most dramatic episode in the history of early-modern absolutist rule was the dynamic reign of Tsar Peter I of Russia (1682–1725). Peter's accomplishments alone would clearly have earned him his history-book title, Peter the Great. But his imposing height—he was nearly seven feet tall—as well as his mercurial personality—jesting one moment, raging the next—certainly helped. Peter is best remembered as the tsar whose policies brought Russia into the world of western Europe. Previously the country's rulers had set their faces firmly against the West, disdaining a civilization at odds with the Eastern Orthodox culture that was their heritage, while laboring to keep the various ethnic groups—Russians, Ukrainians, and a wide variety of nomadic tribes—within their ever-growing empire from destroying not only each other but the tsarist state itself. Since 1613 Russia had been ruled by members of the Romanov dynasty, who had attempted with some success to restore political stability following the chaotic "time of troubles" that had occurred after the death of the bloodthirsty, half-mad Tsar Ivan (the Terrible) in 1584. Tsar Alexis I (1645–1676) took a significant step toward unification in 1654 when he secured an agreement with the Ukrainians to incorporate that portion of the Ukraine lying east of the Dneiper River into the Muscovite state. But the early Romanovs were faced with a severe threat to this unity and their rule between 1667 and 1671, when a Cossack leader (the Russian Cossacks were semiautonomous bands of peasant cavalrymen) named Stenka Razin led much of southeastern Russia into rebellion. Stenka Razin's uprising found widespread support from serfs who had been oppressed by their masters as well as from non-Russian tribes in the lower Volga area who longed to cast off the domination of Moscow. But ultimately Tsar Alexis and the Russian nobility whose interests were most at stake were able to raise an army capable of defeating Razin's zealous but disorganized bands. Before the rebellion was finally crushed, more than 100,000 rebels had been slaughtered.

Peter the Great. An eighteenth-century mosaic.

These campaigns were but a prelude to the deliberate and ruthless drive to absolutist power launched by Peter after he overthrew the regency of his half-sister Sophia and assumed personal control of the state in 1689. Within ten years he had scandalized nobility and clergy alike by traveling to Holland and England to recruit highly skilled foreign workers and to study the craft of shipbuilding. Upon his return he distressed them still further by declaring his intention to Westernize Russia and initiating this campaign by cutting off the "Eastern" beards and flowing sleeves of leading noblemen at court. Determined to "civilize" the nobility, he published a book of manners which forbade spitting on the floor and eating with one's fingers, and encouraged the cultivation of the art of polite conversation between the sexes.

Peter Cutting a Nobleman's Beard. In this Russian woodcut Peter the Great is portrayed as a diminutive pest.

Peter as above the law

Much as Peter wished to consider himself a westerner, his particular brand of absolutism differed from that of other contemporary monarchs. As we have seen, the autocracy imposed by Ivan III in the fifteenth century had a decidedly Eastern cast. Peter was the willing heir to much of that tradition. He considered himself above the law and thus his own absolute master to a degree that was alien to the absolutist theories and traditions of the Habsburgs and Bourbons. Autocrat of all the Russias, he ruled despotically, with a ferocious individual power that western European rulers did not possess. Armed with such arbitrary power in theory, and intent on realizing its full potential in practice, Peter set out to turn Russia toward the West and to modernize his state. He would brook no opposition.

The suppression and reconstruction of the army

Confronted with a rebellion among the *streltsy,* the politically active, elite corps of the army who were most opposed to his innovations and who favored the restoration of his half-sister to the throne, Peter reacted with a savagery that astonished his contemporaries. Roughly 1,200 suspected conspirators were summarily executed, many of them gibbeted outside the walls of the Kremlin, where their bodies remained for months as a graphic reminder of the fate awaiting those who would dare to challenge his absolute authority. Applying a lesson from the West, Peter proceeded to create a large standing army recruited from the ranks of the peasantry and scrupulously loyal to the tsar. One of every twenty males was conscripted for lifelong service. He financed his army, as did other absolutists, by increasing taxes, with their burden falling most heavily on the peasantry. To equip his new military force, he fostered the growth of the iron and munitions industries. Factories were built and manned by peasant laborers whose position was little better than that of slaves. Serfs

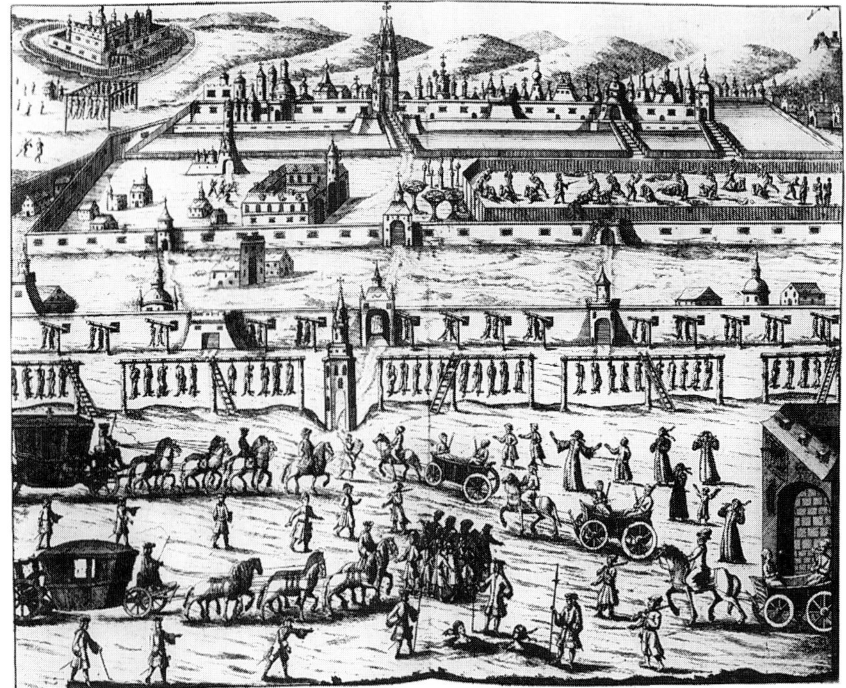

Peter the Great's Execution of the Streltsy. This contemporary print shows scores of corpses gibbeted outside the walls of the Kremlin. Peter kept the rotting bodies on display for months to discourage his subjects from opposing his efforts to Westernize Russian society.

were also commandeered for other public works projects, such as road and canal building, necessary for the modernization of the state.

Absolutism and the new bureaucracy

In an effort to further consolidate his absolute power, he replaced the Duma—the nation's rudimentary national assembly—with a rubber-stamp senate, and appointed a procurator, or agent, dependent directly on him, to manage the affairs of the tradition-bound Russian Orthodox Church, which essentially became an extension of the state. At the same time, Peter was fashioning new, larger, and more efficient administrative machinery to cope with the demands of his modernization program. Although he preferred to draw into the bureaucracy "new" men, whose loyalty to the tsar would be unerring, he was compelled to rely upon the services of the noble—or *boyar*—class as well, rewarding them by increasing their control over their serfs. Nevertheless, membership in his new bureaucracy did not depend on birth. One of his principal advisers, Alexander Menshikov, began his career as a cook and finished as a prince. Bureaucratic status replaced noble rank as the key to power. The administrative machinery devised by Peter furnished Russia with its ruling class for the next two hundred years.

The influence of foreign policy

Peter the Great's Eurocentric worldview also manifested itself in his foreign policy, as witnessed by his bold drive to gain a Russian outlet on the Baltic Sea. Previous battles with the Turks to secure a port on the Black Sea, and thus a southern passage to the West, had failed. Now he engaged in a war with Sweden's meteoric soldier-king Charles XII (1697–1718), who devoted most of his reign to campaigns in the field against the Danes, the Poles, and the Russians. By defeating Charles decisively at the battle of Poltava in 1709, Peter was able to secure his window to the West. He promptly outdid his absolutist counterparts in Europe, who had moved their courts to the outskirts of their capital cities, by moving the Russian capital from Moscow to an entirely new city on the Gulf of Finland. An army of serfs was employed to erect the baroque city of St. Petersburg around a palace intended to imitate and rival Louis XIV's Versailles.

Peter's successors

Not surprisingly, Peter's drastic programs met with concerted resistance. Resentment smoldered under his imposing hand, even within the palace. His son Alexis, who had dared to declare himself opposed to his father's innovations, became a rallying point for the forces of resistance to the tsar and his policies, and died under torture inflicted at his father's command in 1718. Upon Peter's death in 1725, *boyar* determination to undo his reforms surfaced during the succession struggle. There followed a series of ineffective tsars, creatures of the Palace Guard, thus allowing the resentful nobles to rescind many of his reforms. In 1762, the crown passed to Catherine II, a ruler whose ambitions and determination were equal to those of her august predecessor.

The failure of absolutism to take root elsewhere

Peter the Great of Russia, Leopold I of Austria, Frederick William of Brandenburg-Prussia, and above all Louis XIV of France: these were the "great" seventeenth-century absolutists. Elsewhere, the fortunes of absolutism fared far less well. The ineffectual, weak-minded Spanish monarch

The St. Petersburg Palaces. This first of six versions of the Winter Palace (left) was erected in 1711. It quickly proved to be too modest for Peter's needs. Within a decade he had created a far more elaborate complex called Peterhof (right), complete with fountains fashioned after those of Versailles.

Charles II found himself besieged by rebellions in Portugal and Sicily. In 1668, after years of fighting, he was forced to recognize Portuguese independence. In Sweden, Charles X and Charles XI managed to extend their territories at the expense of the Danes and to quell the independence of the aristocracy by confiscating their fiefdoms. During the reign of Charles XII, however, that legacy was dissipated by an adventurous but ultimately unproductive foreign policy. In Poland, the opposition of the landed gentry—or *szlachta*—to any form of centralized government produced a political stalemate that amounted to little more than anarchy. Foreign powers took advantage of this situation to intervene in Polish affairs and, in the eighteenth century, to carve up the country and distribute it among themselves.

The English Exception

The policies of Charles II

But what of England, which had experienced a taste of absolutist centralization under the Tudors and early Stuarts, and indeed under Oliver Cromwell, but which possessed in its Parliament the longest tradition and most highly developed form of representative government in western Europe? England's political history in the late seventeenth century provides the most striking contrast to Continental absolutism. Charles II (son of the beheaded Charles I), who returned from exile and ascended the throne in 1660, was initially welcomed by most English men and women. He pledged himself not to reign as a despot, but to respect Parliament and to observe Magna Carta and the Petition of Right, for he admitted that he was not anxious to "resume his travels." His delight in the unbuttoned moral atmosphere of his court and the culture it supported (risqué plays, dancing, and marital infidelity) mirrored a public desire to forget the restraints of the puritan past. The wits of the time suggested that Charles, "that known enemy to virginity and chastity," played his role as the father of his country to the fullest. However, as Charles's admiration of things French grew to include the absolutism of Louis XIV, he came to be regarded as a threat to more than English womanhood by a great many powerful Englishmen. However anxious to restore the monarchy, they were not about to surrender their traditional rights to another Stuart autocrat. By the late 1670s, the country found itself divided politically into those who supported the king (called by their opponents "Tories," a popular nickname for Irish Catholic bandits) and those opposed to him (called by their opponents "Whigs," a similar nickname for Scottish Presbyterian rebels).

Charles suspends Clarendon Code

As the new party labels suggest, religion remained an exceedingly divisive national issue. Charles was sympathetic to Roman Catholicism, even to the point of a deathbed conversion in 1685. He therefore opposed the stiff code of ecclesiastical regulations, known as the Clarendon Code, which had reestablished Anglicanism as the official state religion and which penalized Catholics and Protestant dissenters. In 1672, Charles suspended the Clarendon Code, although the public outcry against this action compelled him to retreat. This controversy, and rising opposition to the probable succession of Charles's ardent Roman Catholic brother James, led to a series of Whig electoral victories between 1679 and 1681. But Charles found that increased revenues, plus a secret subsidy he was receiving from Louis XIV, enabled him to govern without resort to Parliament, to which he would otherwise have had to go for money. In addition to ignoring Parliament, Charles further infuriated and alarmed Whig politicians by arranging the execution of several of their most prominent leaders on charges of treason, and by remodeling local government in

Charles II of England

such a way as to make it more dependent on royal favor. Charles died in 1685 with his power enhanced, but he left behind him a political and religious legacy that was to be the undoing of his successor.

James II as religious zealot

James II was the very opposite of his brother. A zealous Catholic convert, he alienated his Tory supporters, all of whom were of course Anglicans, by dismissing them in favor of Roman Catholics, and by once again suspending the penal laws against Catholics and dissenters. His stubbornness, as one historian has remarked, made it all but impossible for him to take "yes" for an answer. Whereas Charles had been content to defeat his political enemies, James was determined to humiliate them. Like Charles, James interfered in local government, but his appointments were so personally distasteful and so mediocre as to arouse active opposition. James made no attempt to disguise his Roman Catholicism. He publicly declared his wish that all his subjects might be converted, and paraded papal legates through the streets of London. When, in June 1688, he ordered all Anglican clergymen to read his decree of toleration from their pulpits, seven bishops refused and were clapped into prison on charges of seditious libel. At their trial, however, they were declared not guilty, to the vast satisfaction of the English populace.

The succession question

The trial of the bishops was one event that brought matters to a head. The other was the birth of a son in 1688 to James and his second wife, the Roman Catholic daughter of the duke of Modena. This male infant, who was to be raised a Catholic, replaced James's much older Protestant daughter Mary as heir to the British throne. Despite a rumor that the baby boy was an imposter smuggled into the royal bedchamber in a warming pan, political leaders of both parties were prepared not only to believe in the legitimacy of the child but to take active steps to prevent the possibility of his succession. A delegation of Whigs and Tories crossed the Channel to Holland with an invitation to Mary's husband William of Orange, the *stadholder* or chief executive of the United Provinces and the great-grandson of William the Silent. William was asked to cross to England with an invading army to restore English religious and political freedom. As leader of a Continental coalition determined to thwart Louis XIV's expansionist policies, he accepted, welcoming the chance such a move represented to bring England into active opposition to the French (see p. 614).

William III

William and Mary: joint sovereigns of England

William's "conquest" was a bloodless coup. James fled the country in 1688, thereby allowing Parliament to declare the throne vacant and clearing the way for the accession of William and Mary as joint sovereigns of England. A Bill of Rights, passed by Parliament and accepted by the new king and queen in 1689, reaffirmed English civil liberties such as trial by jury, habeas corpus (guaranteeing the accused a speedy trial), and the right of petition and redress, and established that the monarchy was subject to the law of the land. An Act of Toleration, passed in 1689, granted dissenters the right to worship, though not the right to full political protection. In 1701, with the son of the exiled James II now reaching maturity in France, an Act of Succession ordained that the English throne was to pass first to Mary's childless sister Anne, who ruled from 1702 to 1714, and then to George, elector of the German principality of Hanover, who was the great-grandson of James I. The connection was a distant one, but the Hanoverian dynasty was Protestant, and George reputed to be a capable enough ruler. The act was further evidence of the degree to which Parliament could dictate its terms. Henceforth, all English sovereigns were to be communicants of the Church of England. If foreign born, they could not engage England in the defense of their native land, nor leave the country, without Parliamentary consent.

A "glorious" revolution?

The events of 1688 and 1689 were soon referred to by the English as "the Glorious Revolution." Glorious for the English in that it occurred without bloodshed (although James is reputed to have been suffering from a nosebleed at the moment of crisis). Glorious, too, for defenders of Parliamentary prerogative. Although William and Mary and their royal successors continued to enjoy a large measure of executive power, after 1688 no king or queen attempted to govern without Parliament, which met annually from that time on. Parliament strengthened its control over the collection and expenditure of public money. Future sovereigns were henceforth unable to conduct the country's business without recourse to the House of Commons for the funds to do so. Glorious, finally, for advocates of the civil liberties now guaranteed within the Bill of Rights.

1688 as a defense of status quo

Yet 1688 was not all glory. It was a revolution that consolidated the position of large property holders, local magnates whose political and economic power base in their rural constituencies and on their estates had been threatened by the interventions of Charles II and James II. If it was a revolution, it was one designed to restore the *status quo* on behalf of a wealthy social and economic order that would soon make itself even wealthier as it drank its fill of government patronage and war profits. And it was a revolution that brought nothing but misery to the Roman Catholic minority in Scotland, which joined with England and Wales in the union of Great Britain in 1707, and the Catholic majority in Ireland where, following the Battle of the Boyne in 1690, repressive military forces imposed the exploitive will of a self-interested Protestant minority upon the Catholic majority.

Defense of 1688: the political theories of John Locke

Although the "Glorious Revolution" was an expression of immediate political circumstance, it was a reflection as well of anti-absolutist theories that had risen in the late seventeenth century to challenge the ideas of writers such as Bodin, Hobbes, and Bossuet. Chief among these opponents of absolutism was the Englishman John Locke (1632–1704), whose *Two Treatises of Civil Government,* written prior to the revolution, though published in 1690, was used to justify the events of the previous two years. Locke maintained that originally all humans had lived in a theoretical state of nature in which absolute freedom and equality prevailed, and in which there was no government of any kind. The only law was the law of nature, which individuals enforced for themselves in order to protect their natural rights to life, liberty, and property. It was not long, however, before they began to perceive that the inconveniences of the state of nature greatly outweighed its advantages. With individuals attempting to enforce their own rights, confusion and insecurity were the unavoidable results. Accordingly, the people agreed among themselves to establish a civil society, to set up a government, and to surrender certain powers to it. But they did not make that government absolute. The only power they conferred upon it was the executive power of the law of nature. Since the state was nothing but the joint power of all the members of society, its authority could "be no more than those persons had in a state of nature before they entered into society, and gave it up to the community." All powers not expressly surrendered were reserved to the people themselves. If the government exceeded or abused the authority explicitly granted in the political contract, it became tyrannical; the people then had the right to dissolve it or to rebel against it and overthrow it.

Locke and limited sovereignty

Locke condemned absolutism in every form. He denounced despotic monarchy, but he was no less severe in his strictures against the absolute sovereignty of parliaments. Though he defended the supremacy of the law-making branch, with the executive primarily an agent of the legislature, he nevertheless refused to concede to the representatives of the people an unlimited power. Arguing that state government was instituted among people for the preservation of property, he denied the authority of any political agency to invade the natural rights of a single individual. The law of nature, which embodied these rights, was an automatic limitation upon every branch of the government. Locke's theoretical defense of political liberties emerged in the late eighteenth century as an important element in the intellectual background of the American and French Revolutions. In 1688, however, it served a far less radical purpose. The landed magnates responsible for the exchange of James II for William and Mary could read Locke as an apologia for their conservative revolution. James II, rather than protecting their property and liberties, had encroached upon them; hence they had every right to overthrow the tyranny he had established and to replace it with a government that would, by ensuring their rights, defend their interests.

John Locke

Warfare and Diplomacy: The Emergence of a State System

The emergence of new state interests

To the extent that absolute monarchs succeeded in attaining their goals of unification and centralization, their states took shape as individual, identifiable political and economic entities. Often, it is true, the interests of a monarch might clash with those of the country over which he ruled. Bourbon kings and Habsburg emperors worried about the future of their family dynasties to the detriment of the future of France or Austria. And religion, the factor that had torn Europe apart in the preceding century, remained an international issue in 1700. But increasingly, both dynasty and religion were superseded by newer "interests"—commerce and international balance and stability.

Emergence of state system

The result was the emergence of a state system. Although the achievements of various monarchs were limited, they were significant enough to encourage diplomats to speak more commonly than in the past of the "interests" of a particular state, as if that state somehow had a corporate personality of its own, and of the way in which those interests might coincide or conflict with the interests of another state. What followed was a significant redefinition of the aims and calculations of diplomacy and warfare.

The growth of diplomacy

The organization of diplomatic bureaucracies was a major accomplishment of absolutist monarchies. Had most foreign ministers and ambassadors read the Dutchman Hugo Grotius's treatise on *The Law of War and Peace* (1625), they would have agreed with him about the necessity of establishing a body of rules that would help to bring reason and order to relations between governments. In practice, of course, reason and order gave way to bribery and improvisation. Yet the rationalization of diplomatic processes and the establishment of foreign ministries and embassies in European capitals, with their growing staffs of clerks and ministers, reflected a desire to bring order out of the international chaos that had gripped Europe during the early seventeenth century. International relations in the late 1600s was, among other things, a history of diplomatic coalitions, an indication of the degree to which negotiation was now a weapon in the armory of the absolutist state.

The growth of professional armies

Warfare, however, continued to play an integral and almost constant role in the international arena. The armies of the period grew dramatically. When Louis XIV acceded to power in 1661, the French army numbered 20,000 men; by 1688, it stood at 290,000; by 1694, 400,000. These armies were increasingly professional organizations, controlled directly by the state, and under the command of trained officers recruited from

The Capture of Cambrai by Louis XIV in 1677. This print illustrates the tactics of siege warfare as practiced by early-modern armies. Louis is shown receiving an emissary from the city, whose walls have been breached by siege guns.

the nobility. In Prussia, common soldiers were mostly conscripts; in other European countries they were volunteers, either native or foreign, though often "volunteers" in no more than name, having been coerced or tricked into service. Increasingly, however, enlistment was perceived by common soldiers as an avenue to a career, one that included the possibility of promotion to corporal or sergeant, and in the case of France, the promise of a small pension at the end of one's service. However recruited, common soldiers became part of an increasingly elaborate and efficient fighting force. Above all, they were made to understand the dire consequences of disobedience, breaking rank, or desertion. Soldiers were expected to obey instantly and unquestioningly. Failure to do so resulted in brutal punishment, often flogging, sometimes execution. Drill, not only on the battlefield but on the parade ground, in brilliant, elaborate uniforms and intricate formations, was designed to reduce individuals to automaton-like parts of an army whose regiments were moved across battlefields as a chess player moves pawns across the board—and with about the same concern for loss of human life.

The foreign policies of Louis XIV

The patterns of international relations during the period from 1660 to 1715 show European monarchs making use of the new machinery of diplomacy and warfare to resolve the conflicting interests of dynasty, stability, and commerce. At the center of that pattern, as at the center of Europe, stood Louis XIV. From 1661 until 1688, in a quest for glory, empire, and even revenge, he waged war across his northern and eastern frontiers on the pretext that the lands in question belonged both to the Bourbons and to the French by tradition, by former treaty, or by dynastic inheritance. His aggressively expansionist policies, alarming to other European rulers, led William of Orange, in 1674, to form an anti-French coalition with Austria, Spain, and various smaller German states. Yet Louis continued to push his frontiers eastward, invading territories that had been Germanic for centuries, and capturing Strassburg in 1681 and Luxembourg in 1684. Louis's seizure of Strassburg (subsequently called Strasbourg by the French), completing the conquest of the German-speaking province of Alsace begun in 1634 by Richelieu, irreversibly incorporated the seeds of a Franco-German animosity centered on this region that would bear bitter fruit in the great wars of the nineteenth and twentieth centuries. A second coalition, the so-called League of Augsburg (1686), which comprised Holland, Austria, Sweden, and further German allies, was only somewhat more successful than the first.

Europe on the verge of war

These allies were concerned above all to maintain some sort of European balance of power. They feared an expansionist France would prove insatiable, as it pressed its boundaries farther and farther into Germany and the Low Countries. Louis, mistakenly expecting that William would be forced to fight an English army under James to establish his right to his new throne and would therefore be too preoccupied to devote his full attention to developments on the Continent, kept up the pressure. In September 1688 he invaded the Palatinate and occupied the city of Cologne. The following year the French armies crossed the Rhine and continued their eastward drive, burning Heidelberg and committing numerous atrocities throughout the middle Rhine area. Aroused at last to effective action, the League of Augsburg, led by William and now including in addition to its original members both England and Spain, engaged Louis in a war that was to last until 1697.

War of the League of Augsburg

The major campaigns of this War of the League of Augsburg were fought in the Low Countries. William managed to drive an army under his predecessor, James II, from Ireland in 1690; from that point on, he took command of the allied forces on the Continent. By 1694 Louis was pressed hard, not only by his allied foes, but by a succession of disastrous harvests that crippled France. Fighting remained stalemated until a treaty was signed at Ryswick in Holland in 1697, which compelled Louis to return most of France's recent gains, except for Alsace, and to recognize William as the rightful king of England.

The problem of the Spanish Succession

Ryswick did nothing, however, to resolve the dynastic tangle known as the Spanish Succession. Since Charles II of Spain had no direct heirs, and since he appeared to be on his deathbed in 1699, European monarchs and diplomats were obsessed by the question of who would succeed to the vast domain of the Spanish Habsburgs: not only Spain itself, but also its overseas empire, as well as the Spanish Netherlands, Naples, Sicily, and other territories in Italy. Both Louis XIV and Leopold I of Austria were married to sisters of the decrepit, unstable Charles; and both, naturally, eyed the succession to the Spanish inheritance as an exceedingly tempting dynastic plum. Yet it is a measure of the degree to which even absolutists were willing to keep their ambitions within bounds that both Leopold and Louis agreed to William's suggestion that the lion's share of the Habsburg lands should go to six-year-old Joseph Ferdinand, the prince of Bavaria, who was Charles II's grandnephew. Unfortunately, in 1699 the child died. Though the chances of war increased, William and Louis were prepared to bargain further and arranged a second treaty that divided the Spanish empire between Louis's and Leopold's heirs. Yet at the same time, Louis's diplomatic agents in Madrid persuaded Charles to sign a will in which he stipulated that the entire Spanish Habsburg inheritance should pass to Louis's grandson Philip of Anjou. This option was welcomed by many influential Spaniards, willing to endure French hegemony in return for the protection France could provide to the Spanish empire. For a time, Louis contemplated an alternative agreement that would have given France direct control of much of Italy. When Charles finally died in November 1700, Louis decided to accept the will. As if this was not enough to drive his former enemies back to war, he sent troops into the Spanish Netherlands and traders to the Spanish colonial empire, while declaring the late James II's son—the child of the warming-pan myth—the legitimate king of England.

War: the battle of Blenheim

Once it was clear to the allies that Louis intended to treat Spain as if it were his own kingdom, they again united against him in the cause of balance and stability. William died in 1702, just as the War of the Spanish Succession was beginning. His position as first general of the coalition passed to two brilliant strategists, the Englishman John Churchill, duke of Marlborough, and his Austrian counterpart Prince Eugene of Savoy, an upper-class soldier of fortune who had been denied a commission by Louis. Under their command the allied forces engaged in battle after fierce battle in the Low Countries and Germany, including an extraordinary march deep into Bavaria, where the combined forces under Marlborough and Eugene smashed the French and their Bavarian allies decisively at Blenheim (1704). While the allies pressed France's armies on land, the English navy captured Gibraltar and the island of Minorca, thus establishing a strategic and commercial foothold in the Mediterranean, and helping to open a fourth major military theater in Spain itself.

Military stalemate

The War of the Spanish Succession was a "professional" war that tested the highly trained armies of the combatants to the fullest. At the battle of Malplaquet in northeastern France in 1709, 80,000 French soldiers faced 110,000 allied troops. Though Marlborough and Eugene could claim to have won that battle, in that they forced the French to retreat, they suffered 24,000 casualties, twice those of the French. Neither Malplaquet nor other such victories brought the allies any closer to their final goal, which now appeared to be not the containment, but the complete destruction of the French military force. Queen Anne of England (Mary's sister and William's successor), once Marlborough's staunchest defender, grew disillusioned with the war and fired her general.

Dynastic changes and the pursuit of peace

More than war weariness impelled the combatants toward negotiation, however. The War of the Spanish Succession had begun as a conflict about the balance of power in Europe and the world. Yet dynastic changes had by 1711 compelled a reappraisal of allied goals. Leopold I had died in 1705. When his elder son and successor Joseph I died in 1711, the Austrian monarchy fell to Leopold's youngest son, the Archduke Charles, who had been the allies' candidate for the throne of Spain. With Charles now the Austrian and the Holy Roman Emperor as Charles VI (1711–1740), the prospect of his accession to the Spanish inheritance conjured up the ghost of Charles V and threatened to give him far too much power. International stability therefore demanded an end to hostilities and diplomatic negotiation toward a solution that would reestablish some sort of general balance.

The Treaty of Utrecht

The Treaty of Utrecht settled the conflict in 1713 by redistributing territory and power in equitable portions. No one emerged a major winner or loser. Philip, Louis's grandson, remained on the throne of Spain, but Louis agreed that France and Spain would never be united under the same ruler. Austria gained territories in the Netherlands and Italy. The Dutch, victims of French aggression during the war, were guaranteed protection of their borders against future invasion. The English retained Gibraltar and Minorca, as well as territory in America (Newfoundland, Acadia, Hudson Bay) and in the Caribbean (St. Kitts). Perhaps most valuable of all, the English extracted the *asiento* from Spain, which gave them the right to supply Spanish America with African slaves. The settlement reflected the degree to which new interests had superseded old. Balance of power and stability among states were the major goals of the negotiations, goals that reflected a departure from the world of seventeenth-century turmoil when religion had been a major factor in international conflict. The eventual "winners" were undoubtedly the English, whose dynastic concerns were limited to a general acceptance of the Hanoverian settlement, and who could therefore concentrate their efforts on amassing overseas territories that would contribute to the growth of their economic prosperity and hence their international power.

Enlightened Absolutism and Limited Monarchy in the Eighteenth Century

"Enlightened" absolutism

Eighteenth-century absolutism was a series of variations on the dominant themes composed in the previous century by Louis XIV. That it has earned itself the historical distinction of "enlightened" absolutism suggests that those variations were of some consequence. Eighteenth-century rulers backed their sovereign claims not in the language of divine right, but in terms of their determination to act, as Frederick the Great of

The Age of Absolutism

Louis XV

Prussia declared, as "first servant of the state." That phrase meant not so much service to the people as it did service to the goal of further strengthening the authority of the state over institutions that sought to challenge its corporate well-being. Enlightened rulers moved to curtail the privileges of old institutions. The Roman Catholic Church, for example, was compelled to suffer the expulsion of the Jesuits from most Catholic countries. Customary laws benefiting particular orders or interests were reformed. To strengthen the state community, innovative policies in the areas of taxation, economic development, and education were instituted. As we shall see in Chapter 18, rational schemes of this sort reflected the spread of Enlightenment ideals as manifested in the writings of thinkers such as Beccaria, Diderot, and Voltaire. (The last was, in fact, a guest at Frederick's court for several years.) Assisting enlightened "first servants" in the implementation of these changes was a growing cadre of lesser servants: bureaucrats, often recruited from the nobility, but once recruited, expected to declare primary allegiance to their new master, the state. Despite innovation, "enlightened" absolutists continued to insist, as their predecessors had, that state sovereignty rested with the monarchy. Authority remained their overriding concern, and to the extent that they combatted efforts by the estates of their realms to dilute that authority, they declared their descent from their seventeenth-century forebears.

Louis XIV's successors

Louis XIV's successors, his great-grandson Louis XV (1715–1774) and that monarch's grandson Louis XVI (1774–1792), were unable to sustain the energetic drive toward centralization that had taken place under the Sun King. Indeed, during his last years, while fighting a desperate defensive war against his allied enemies, Louis XIV had seen his own accomplishments begin to crumble under the mounting pressure of military expenses. His heir was only five years old when he assumed the throne. As he grew up, Louis XV displayed less single-minded determination than had his great-grandfather to act the role of Sun King. The heroic, Baroque grandeur of the main palace at Versailles yielded to the Rococo grace of the Grand and Petit Trianons, pleasure pavillions built by Louis XV in the palace gardens.

Resurgence of the *parlements*

During the minority of Louis XV, the French *parlements,* those courts of record responsible for registering royal decrees, enjoyed a resurgence of power which they retained throughout the century. No longer tame adjuncts of absolutist governmental machinery as they had been under Louis XIV, these bodies now proclaimed themselves the protectors of French "liberties." In 1770, encouraged by his chancellor René Maupeou, Louis XV issued an edict effectively ending the right of *parlements* to reject decrees. Protest on the part of the magistrates resulted in their imprisonment or banishment. The *parlements* themselves were replaced by new courts charged not only with the responsibility of rubber-stamping legislation but also with administering law more justly and less expensively. When Louis XVI ascended the throne in 1774, his ministers persuaded him to reestablish the *parlements* as a sign of his willingness to conciliate his trouble-making aristocracy. This he did, with the result that government—particularly the management of finances—developed into a stalemated battle.

Stalemate was what the Prussian successors to Frederick William, the Great Elector, were determined to avoid. Frederick I (1688–1713), the Great Elector's immediate successor, enhanced the appearance and cultural life of Berlin. As the Roman numeral by his name attests, he also succeeded in bargaining his support to the Austrians during the War of the Spanish Succession in return for the coveted right to style himself king. (The Austrian monarch was the Holy Roman Emperor and therefore had the right to create kings.)

The achievements of Frederick I of Prussia

Frederick William I (1713–1740), cared little for the embellishments his father had made to the capital city. His overriding concern was the building of a first-rate army. So single-minded was his attention to the military that he came to be called "the sergeant king." Military display became an obsession. His private regiment of "Potsdam Giants" was composed exclusively of soldiers over six feet in height. The king traded musicians and prize stallions for such choice specimens and delighted in marching them about his palace grounds. Frederick William I's success as the builder of a military machine can be measured in terms of numbers: 30,000 men under arms when he came to the throne; 83,000 when he died twenty-seven years later, commander of the fourth-largest army in Europe, after France, Russia, and Austria. Since he could hardly count on volunteers, most of his soldiers were conscripts, drafted from the peasantry for a period of years and required to attend annual training exercises lasting three months. Conscription was supplemented by the kidnapping of forced recruits in neighboring German lands. To finance his army, Frederick William I increased taxes and streamlined their collection through the establishment of a General Directory of War, Finance, and Domains. In 1723, he instituted a system of administration by boards, hoping thereby to eliminate individual inefficiency through collective responsibility and surveillance. In addition, he created an inspectorate to uncover and report to him the mistakes and inefficiencies of his officialdom. Even then, he continued to supervise personally the implementation of state policy while shunning the luxuries of court life; for him, the "theater" of absolutism was not the palace but the office, which placed him at the helm of the state and the army. Perceiving the resources of the state to be too precious to waste, he pared costs at every turn to the point where, it was said, he had to invite himself to a nobleman's table in order to enjoy a good meal.

Frederick William I builds first-rate army

Frederick William I

A hard, unimaginative man, Frederick William I had little use for his son, whose passion was not the battlefield but the flute, and who admired French culture as much as his father disdained it. Not surprisingly, young Frederick rebelled; in 1730, when he was eighteen, he ran away from court with a friend. Apprehended, the companions were returned to the king, who welcomed the fledgling prodigal with something other than a fatted calf. Before Frederick's eyes, he had the friend executed. The grisly lesson took. Thenceforward Frederick, though he never surrendered

The apprenticeship of Frederick the Great

Frederick the Great and Voltaire. Although Frederick offered asylum to the French philosophe, this "enlightened despot" did not permit his intellectual pursuits to interfere with matters of state.

his love of music and literature, bound himself to his royal duties, living in accordance with his own image of himself as "first servant of the state," and earning himself history's title of Frederick the Great.

The seizure of Silesia

Frederick William I's zealous austerity and his compulsion to build an efficient army and administrative state made Prussia a strong state. Frederick the Great (1740–1786), building on the work of his father, raised his country to the status of a major power. As soon as he became king in 1740, Frederick mobilized the army his father had never taken into battle and occupied the poorly protected Austrian province of Silesia to which Prussia had no legitimate claim. Although he had earlier vowed to make morality rather than expediency the hallmark of his reign, he seemingly had little difficulty in sacrificing his youthful idealism in the face of an opportunity to make his Prussian state a leading power. The remaining forty-five years of his monarchy were devoted to the consolidation of this first bold stroke.

The nobility in the army and the bureaucracy

Such a daring course required some adjustments within the Prussian state. The army had to be kept at full strength, and to this end, Frederick staffed its officer corps with young noblemen. In expanding the bureaucracy, whose financial administration kept his army in the field, he relied on the nobility as well, reversing the policy of his father, who had recruited his civil servants according to merit rather than birth. But Frederick was not one to tolerate mediocrity; he fashioned the most highly professional and efficient bureaucracy in Europe. The degree to which both army and bureaucracy were staffed by the nobility is a measure of his determination to secure the unflagging support of the most privileged order in his realm, in order to ensure a united front against Prussia's external foes.

Frederick the Great as an enlightened absolutist

Frederick's domestic policies reflected that same strategy. In matters where he ran no risk of offending the nobility, he followed his own rationalist bent, prohibiting the torture of accused criminals, putting an end to the bribing of judges, and establishing a system of elementary schools. He encouraged religious toleration, declaring that he would happily build a mosque in Berlin if he could find enough Muslims to fill it. (Yet he was strongly anti-Semitic, levying special taxes on Jews and making efforts to close the professions and the civil service to them.) On his own royal estates he was a model "enlightened" monarch. He abolished capital punishment, curtailed the forced labor services of his peasantry, and granted them long leases on the land they worked. He fostered scientific forestry and the cultivation of new crops. He opened new lands in Silesia and brought in thousands of immigrants to cultivate them. When wars ruined their farms, he supplied the peasants with new livestock and tools. Yet he never attempted to extend these reforms to the estates of the Junker elite, since to have done so would have alienated that social and economic group upon which Frederick was most dependent.

Charles VI and the "pragmatic sanction"

Although the monarchs of eighteenth-century Austria eventually proved themselves even more willing than Frederick the Great to undertake significant social reform, the energies of Emperor Charles VI (1711–1740) were concentrated on guaranteeing the future dynastic and territorial integrity of the Habsburg lineage and domain. Without a male heir, Charles worked to secure the right of his daughter Maria Theresa to succeed him as eventual empress. By his death in 1740 Charles had managed to persuade not only his subjects but all the major European powers to accept his daughter as his royal heir—a feat known as the "pragmatic sanction." Yet his painstaking efforts were only partially successful. As we have seen, Frederick the Great used the occasion of Charles's death to seize Silesia. The French, unable to resist the temptation to grab what they could, joined the coalition against the new empress, Maria Theresa (1740–1780).

Maria Theresa of Austria. The empress was a formidable monarch and a match for Frederick the Great.

Maria Theresa: adversity and centralization

With most of her other possessions already occupied by her enemies, Maria Theresa appealed successfully to the Hungarians for support. The empress was willing to play the role of the wronged woman when, as on this occasion, it suited her interests to do so. Hungary's vital troops combined with British financial assistance enabled her to battle Austria's enemies to a draw, although she never succeeded in regaining Silesia. The experience of those first few years of her reign persuaded Maria Theresa, who was both capable and tenacious, to reorganize her dominions along the tightly centralized lines characteristic of Prussia and France. Ten new administrative districts were established, each with its own "war commissar" appointed by and responsible to the central administration in Vienna—an Austrian equivalent of the French intendant. Property taxes were increased to finance an expanded army, which was modernized and professionalized so as to remain on a par with the military establishments of the other great powers. Centralization, finances, army: once more those three crucial elements in the formula of absolute rule came into play.

Joseph II's reforms

Reform did not stop there, however. Together Maria Theresa and her son Joseph II, with whom she ruled jointly from 1765 to 1780, and who then succeeded her for another ten years, instituted a series of significant social reforms. Although both mother and son were devout Roman Catholics, they moved to assert their control over the Church, removing the clergy's exemption from taxation and decreeing the state's ability to block the publication of papal bulls in Austria. In 1773, following the papal suppression of the Jesuits, they used the order's assets to finance a program of state-wide primary education. Although the General Schools Ordinance of 1774 never achieved anything like a universally literate population, it did succeed in educating hundreds of thousands, and in financing not only schools for children but schools as well for those who taught the children. Joseph followed these reforms with an "Edict on Idle Institutions" in 1780, which resulted in the closing of hundreds of monastic houses, whose property went to support charitable institutions now under state control. These reforms and others—liberalization of punishment for criminal offenses, a relaxation of censorship, the abolishing of serfdom and feudal dues, and an attempt to eradicate superstition by curbing the practice of pilgrimages and celebration of saint's days—made Joseph more enemies than friends, among both the noble elite and the common people. "Enlightened" though Joseph II was, how-

Edict of Tolerance. An illustration from a pamphlet depicting Joseph II of Austria as an enlightened monarch.

ever, he nevertheless remained a staunch absolutist, as concerned with the maintenance of a strong army and an efficient bureaucracy as with the need to educate his peasantry. Joseph's brother Leopold II, who succeeded him in 1790, attempted to maintain the reformist momentum. His death two years later and the accession of his reactionary son Francis II (1792–1835) put an end to liberalizing experiments.

Catherine as an "enlightened" monarch

Unlike Joseph II, Catherine the Great of Russia (1762–1796) felt herself compelled to curry the favor of her nobility by involving them directly in the structure of local administration, by exempting them from military service and taxation, and probably most important, by granting them absolute control over the serfs on their estates. Her policy grew out of her strong ties to powerful nobles and her involvement in the conspiracy that led to the assassination of her husband, Tsar Peter III, the last of a series of weak rulers who followed Peter the Great. Catherine was herself a German, and prided herself on her devotion to Western principles of government. Ambitious to establish a reputation as an intellectual and enlightened monarch, she corresponded with French philosophers, wrote plays, published a digest of William Blackstone's *Commentaries on the Laws of England,* and began a history of Russia. Her contributions to social reform did not extend much beyond the founding of hospitals and orphanages, and the expression of a pious hope that someday the serfs might be liberated. Although she did summon a commission in 1767 to codify Russian law, its achievements were modest: a minor extension of religious toleration, a slight restriction of the use of torture by the state. Catherine's interest in theories of reform did, however, stimulate the development of a social conscience among certain gentry intellectuals, foreshadowing a more widespread movement in the nineteenth century.

Catherine the Great

The Pugachev rebellion

Any plans Catherine may have had for improving the lot of the peasants, however, were abruptly cancelled after their frustration with St. Petersburg's centralization efforts erupted in a violent peasant-serf rebellion in 1773–1774. Free peasants in the Volga valley region found themselves compelled to provide labor services to nobles sent by the crown to control them, Cossacks were subjected to taxation and conscription for the first time, and factory workers and miners were pressed into service in the state's industrial enterprises. These and other disparate but dissatisfied groups, including serfs, united under the rebel banner of Emelyan Pugachev, an illiterate Cossack who claimed to be the late Tsar Peter III. The hapless Peter, who had spoken as a reformer in life, in death became a larger-than-life hero for those opposed to the determined absolutism of his successor. As Pugachev marched, he encouraged his followers to strike out not only against the empress but also against the nobility and the church. More than 1,500 landlords and priests were murdered, and the ruling classes were terrified as the revolt spread. While Catherine's forces initially had little success against the rebel army, the threat of famine plagued Pugachev's advance and finally led to disarray among his troops. Betrayed in 1774, he was captured and taken in an iron cage to Moscow, where he was tortured and killed. Catherine responded to this uprising

Emelyan Pugachev Shackled and Encaged after His Capture

with further centralization and tightening of aristocratic authority over the peasantry.

The significance of Catherine the Great

The brutal suppression and punishment of the rebels reflected the ease with which the German-born Catherine took to the despotic authoritarianism that characterized Russian absolutism. At the same time, Catherine continued the work of Peter the Great in introducing Russia to Western ideas; she came to terms with the nobility in a way that brought stability to the state; and she made the country a formidable power in European affairs by extending its boundaries to include not only most of Poland but also lands on the Black Sea.

The absolutist worldview

Eighteenth-century monarchs shared a desire to pursue policies that would mark their regimes as befitting a world that was leaving obscurantism and fanaticism behind. They were determined to press ahead with the task, begun by their seventeenth-century predecessors, of building powerful, centralized states by continuing to attempt the elimination or harnessing of the ancient privileges of still-powerful noble orders and provincial estates. The notion of a limited monarchy, in which power was divided between local and central authorities and shared by monarchs, nobles, and legislative assemblies, struck them as a dangerous anachronism. Yet as the century progressed, they found that conviction challenged by the emergence of England, under limited monarchy, as the world's leading commercial and naval power.

The Hanoverian succession in Britain

England (or Britain, as the country was called after its union with Scotland in 1707) prospered as a state in which power was divided between the king and Parliament. This division of political power was guaranteed by a constitution which, though unwritten, was grounded in common law and strengthened by precedent and by particular legal settlements such as those that had followed the restoration of the Stuarts in 1660 and the overthrow of James II in 1688. The Hanoverians George I (1714–1727) and his son George II (1727–1760) were by no means political nonentities. Though George I could not speak English, he could converse comfortably enough with his ministers in French. The first two Georges made a conscientious and generally successful effort to govern within their adopted kingdom. They appointed the chief ministers who remained responsible to them for the creation and direction of state policy. Yet because Parliament, after 1688, retained the right to legislate, tax, and spend, its powers were far greater than those of any European parlement, estate, or diet. During the reign of the first two Hanoverians, politics was on most occasions little more than a struggle between factions within the Whig party, composed of wealthy—and in many cases newly rich—landed magnates who were making fortunes in an expanding economy based on commercial and agricultural capitalism.

George I of Britain

The Tories, because of their previous association with the Stuarts, remained political "outs" for most of the century. To the Whigs, national politics was no longer a matter of clashing principles. Those principles had been settled—to their satisfaction—in 1688. Nor was politics a matter of legislating in the national interest. Britain was governed locally, not

The House of Commons. Despite its architectural division into two "sides," the House was composed of men of property whose similar economic interests encouraged them to agree on political fundamentals.

from the center as in an absolutist state. Aristocrats and landed gentry administered the affairs of the particular counties and parishes in which their estates lay, as lords lieutenant, as justices of the peace, as overseers of the poor, unhampered, to a degree unknown on the Continent, by legislation imposed uniformly throughout the kingdom. The quality of local government varied greatly. Some squires were as "allworthy" as Henry Fielding's fictional character of that name in the novel *Tom Jones*. Others cared for little beyond the bottle and the hunt. A French traveler noted in 1747 that the country gentleman was "naturally a very dull animal" whose favorite after-dinner toast was "to all honest fox hunters in Great Britain." These men administered those general laws that did exist—the Poor Law, game laws—which were drawn in such a way as to leave their administrators wide latitude, a latitude that they exercised in order to enhance the appearance of their own local omnipotence. Thus in Britain there was no attempt to pass a law establishing a state-wide system of primary education. Centralizing legislation of that sort, the hallmark of absolutist states, was anathema to the British aristocracy and gentry. They argued that education, if it was to be provided, should be provided at their expense, in village schoolrooms by schoolmasters in their employ. Those instructors would make it their business to teach their pupils not only rudimentary reading, writing, and figuring, but the deferential behavior that bespoke the obligation of the poor to their rich benefactors.

Local government

As the Church of England catechism had it, they were "to do their duty in that station of life unto which it shall please God to call them."

Robert Walpole as chief minister

Politics, then, was neither first principles nor national legislation. It was "interest" and "influence," the weaving of a web of obligations into a political faction powerful enough to secure jobs and favors—a third secretaryship in the foreign office from a minister, an Act of Enclosure from Parliament. The greatest master of this game of politics was Robert Walpole (1676–1745), who was Britain's leading minister from the early 1720s until 1742. Walpole is sometimes called Britain's first prime minister, a not entirely accurate distinction, since officially that position did not exist until the nineteenth century. Prime minister or not, he wielded great political power. He took advantage of the king's frequent absences in Hanover to assert control over the day-to-day governance of the country. He ruled as chief officer of his cabinet, a small group of like-minded politicians whose collective name derived from the room in which they met. In time the cabinet evolved into the policy-making executive arm of the British political system; Britain is governed today by cabinet and Parliament, the cabinet being composed of leading politicians from the majority party in Parliament.

Walpole and the nature of British politics

Walpole was a member of a Norfolk gentry family who had risen to national prominence on the fortune he amassed while serving as paymaster-general to the armed forces during the War of the Spanish Succession. Adept at bribery and corruption, he used his ability to reward his supporters with appointments to ensure himself a loyal political following. By the end of his career, grossly fat and stuffed seemingly with the profits of his years in office, he was being depicted by cartoonists and balladeers as Britain's most accomplished robber. "Little villains must submit to Fate,"

Left: **Sir Robert Walpole with Members of His Cabinet.** Right: **A Portrait of Walpole**

lamented a typical lampoon, "while great ones do enjoy the world in state." Walpole was no more corrupt, however, than the political process over which he presided. Most seats in Parliament's lower House of Commons were filled by representatives from boroughs that often had no more than two or three dozen electors. Hence it was a relatively simple task to buy votes, either directly or with promises of future favors. Walpole cemented political factions together into an alliance that survived for about twenty years. During that time, he worked to ensure domestic tranquillity by refusing to press ahead with any legislation that might arouse national controversy. He withdrew what was perhaps his most innovative piece of legislation—a scheme that would increase excise taxes and reduce import duties as a means of curbing smugglers—in the face of widespread popular opposition.

George III: the battle over prerogative

Other Whig politicians succeeded Walpole in office in the 1740s and 1750s, but only one, William Pitt, later elevated to the House of Lords as the earl of Chatham, commanded public attention as Walpole had. George III (1760–1820), who came to the throne as a young man in 1760, resented the manner in which he believed his royal predecessors had been treated by the Whig oligarchy. Whether or not, as legend has it, his mother fired his determination with the constant injunction "George, be king!" he began his reign convinced that he must assert his rightful prerogatives. He dismissed Pitt and attempted to impose ministers of his own choosing on Parliament. King and Parliament battled this issue of prerogative throughout the 1760s. In 1770, Lord North, an aristocrat satisfactory to the king and with a large enough following in the House of Commons to ensure some measure of stability, assumed the position of first minister. His downfall occurred a decade later, as a result of his mismanagement of the overseas war that resulted in Britain's loss of its original thirteen North American colonies. A period of political shuffling was followed by the king's appointment, at the age of twenty-three, of another William Pitt, Chatham's son, and this Pitt directed Britain's fortunes for the next twenty-five years—a political reign even longer than Walpole's. Although the period between 1760 and 1780 witnessed a struggle between crown (as the king and his political following were called) and Parliament, it was a very minor skirmish compared with the titanic constitutional struggles of the seventeenth century. Britain saw the last of absolutism in 1688. What followed was the mutual adjustment of the two formerly contending parties to a settlement both considered essentially sound.

War and Diplomacy in the Eighteenth Century

The Seven Years' War

The history of European diplomacy and warfare after 1715 is one in which the twin goals of international stability and economic expansion remained paramount. The fact that those objectives often conflicted with each other set off further frequent wars, in which the ever-growing standing armies of absolutist Europe were matched against each other and in which the deciding factor often turned out to be not Continental military strength, but British naval power. The major conflict at mid-century, known as the Seven Years' War in Europe and the French and Indian War in North America, reflects the overlapping interests of power balance and commercial gain. In Europe, the primary concern was balance. Whereas in the past France had seemed the major threat, now Prussia loomed—at least in Austrian eyes—as a far more dangerous interloper. Under these circumstances, in 1756 the Austrian foreign minister, Prince Wenzel von Kaunitz, effected the so-called diplomatic revolution, which put an end to the enmity between France and Austria, and resulted in a formidable threat to the Prussia of Frederick the Great. Frederick, meanwhile, was taking steps to protect his flanks. While anxious not to arouse his French ally, he nevertheless signed a neutrality treaty with the British, who were concerned with securing protection for their sovereign's Hanoverian domains. The French read Frederick's act as a hostile one, and thus fell all the more readily for Kaunitz's offer of an alliance. The French indeed perceived a pressing need for trustworthy European allies, since they were already engaged in an undeclared war with Britain in North America. By mid-1756 Kaunitz could count France, Russia, Sweden, and several German states as likely allies against Prussia. Rather than await retribution from his enemies, Frederick invaded strategic but neutral Saxony and then Austria itself, thus once again playing the role of aggressor.

Shifting power balances

The configurations in this diplomatic gavotte are undoubtedly confusing. They are historically important, however, because they indicate the way in which the power balance was shifting, and the attempts of European states to respond to those shifts by means of new diplomatic alliances. Prussia and Britain were the volatile elements: Prussia on the Continent; Britain overseas. The war from 1756 to 1763 in Europe centered upon Frederick's attempts to prevent the dismemberment of his domain at the hands of the French-Austrian-Russian alliance. Time and again the Prussian army's superiority and Frederick's own military genius frustrated his enemies' attacks. Ultimately, Prussia's survival against these overwhelming odds—"the miracle of the House of Brandenburg"—was ensured by the death of the Tsarina Elizabeth (1741–1762), daughter of Peter the Great, and by the accession of Peter III (1762), whose admiration for Frederick was as great as was his predecessor's hostility. Peter withdrew from the war, returning the conquered provinces of East Prussia and Pomerania to his country's erstwhile enemy. The peace that followed, though it compelled Frederick to relinquish Saxony, recognized his right to retain Silesia, and hence put an end to Austria's hope of one day recapturing that rich prize.

The British navy as key to victory

Overseas, battles occurred not only in North America but in the West Indies and in India, where Anglo-French commercial rivalry had resulted in sporadic, fierce fighting since the 1740s. Ultimate victory would go to that power possessing a navy strong enough to keep its supply routes

The Battle of Québec, 1759. Most often remembered for the fact that the British and French commanders, Generals Wolfe and Montcalm, were killed on the bluffs above the St. Lawrence River (the Plains of Abraham), this battle was most notable for the success of the British amphibious assault, a measure of Britain's naval superiority.

open—that is, to Britain. Superior naval forces resulted in victories along the North American Great Lakes, climaxing in the Battle of Québec in 1759 and the eventual surrender of all of Canada to the British. By 1762 the French sugar islands, including Martinique, Grenada, and St. Vincent, were in British hands. Across the globe in India, the defeat of the French in the Battle of Plassey in 1757 and the capture of Pondichéry four years later made Britain the dominant European presence on the subcontinent. In the Treaty of Paris in 1763, which brought the Seven Years' War to an end, France officially surrendered Canada and India to the British, thus affording them an extraordinary field for commercial exploitation.

"Taxation without representation . . ."

The success of the British in North America in the Seven Years' War was itself a major cause of the war that broke out between the mother country and her thirteen North American colonies in 1775. To pay for the larger army the British now deemed necessary to protect their vastly expanded colonial possessions, they imposed unwelcome new taxes on the colonists. The North Americans protested that they were being taxed without representation. The home government responded that, like all British subjects, they were "virtually" if not actually represented by the present members of the House of Commons. Colonists thundered back that the present political system in Britain was so corrupt that no one but the Whig oligarchs could claim that their interests were being looked after.

The American Revolution

Meanwhile the British were exacting retribution for rebellious acts on the part of colonists. East India Company tea shipped to be sold in

Boston at prices advantageous to the company was dumped in Boston Harbor. The port of Boston was thereupon closed, and representative government in the colony of Massachusetts curtailed. The British garrison clashed with colonial civilians. Colonial "minutemen" formed a counterforce. By the time war broke out in 1775, most Americans were prepared to sever ties with Britain and declare themselves an independent nation, which they did the following year. Fighting continued until 1781 when a British army surrendered to the colonists at Yorktown to the tune of a song entitled "A World Turned Upside Down." The French, followed by Spain and the Netherlands, determined to do everything possible to inhibit the further growth of Britain's colonial empire, had allied themselves with the newly independent United States in 1778. A peace treaty signed in Paris in 1783 recognized the sovereignty of the new state. Though the British lost direct control of their former colonies, they reestablished their transatlantic commercial ties with America in the 1780s. Indeed, the brisk trade in raw cotton between the slave-owning southern states and Britain made possible the industrial revolution in textiles that began in the north of England at this time, and that carried Britain to worldwide preeminence as an economic power in the first half of the nineteenth century. This ultimately profitable arrangement lay in the future. At the time, the victory of the American colonists seemed to contemporary observers to right the world balance of commercial power, which had swung so far to the side of the British. In this instance, independence seemed designed to restore stability.

Poland and the balance of power in eastern Europe

In eastern Europe, however, the very precariousness of Poland's independence posed a threat to stability and to the balance of power. As an independent state, Poland functioned, at least in theory, as a buffer among the major central European powers—Russia, Austria, and Prussia. Poland was the one major central European territory whose landed elite had successfully opposed introduction of absolutist centralization and a consequent curtailment of its "liberties." The result, however, had not been anything like real independence for either the Polish nobility or the country as a whole. Aristocrats were quite prepared to accept bribes from foreign powers in return for their vote in elections for the Polish king. And their continued exercise of their constitutionally guaranteed individual veto (the *liberum veto*) in the Polish Diet meant that the country remained in a perpetual state of weakness that made it fair game for the land-hungry absolutist potentates who surrounded it.

The first partition of Poland

In 1764 Russia intervened to influence the election of King Stanislaus Poniatowski, an able enough nobleman who had been one of Catherine the Great's lovers. Thereafter Russia continued to meddle in the affairs of Poland—and of Turkey as well—often protecting both countries' Eastern Orthodox Christian minority. When war finally broke out with Turkey in 1769, resulting in large Russian gains in the Balkans, Austria made known its opposition to further Russian expansion, lest it upset the existing balance of power in eastern Europe. In the end Russia was persuaded to acquire territory in Poland instead, by joining Austria and Prussia in a gen-

Dividing the Royal Cake. A contemporary cartoon showing the monarchs of Europe at work carving up a hapless Poland.

eral partition of that country's lands. Though Maria Theresa opposed the dismemberment of Poland, she reluctantly agreed to participate in the partition in order to maintain the balance of power, an attitude that prompted a scornful Frederick the Great to remark, "She weeps, but she takes her share." According to the agreement of 1772, Poland lost about 30 percent of its kingdom and about half of its population.

The second and third partitions of Poland

Following this first partition, the Russians continued to exercise virtual control of Poland. King Stanislaus, however, took advantage of a new Russo-Turkish war in 1788 to press for a more truly independent state with a far stronger executive than had existed previously. A constitution adopted in May 1791 established just that; but this rejuvenated Polish state was to be short-lived. In January 1792, the Russo-Turkish war ended, and Catherine the Great pounced. Together the Russians and Prussians took two more enormous bites out of Poland in 1793, destroying the new constitution in the process. A rebellion under the leadership of Thaddeus Kosciuszko, who had fought in America, was crushed in 1794 and 1795. A final swallow by Russia, Austria, and Prussia in 1795 left nothing of Poland at all. After this series of partitions of Poland, each of the major powers was a good deal fatter; but on the international scales by which such things were measured, they continued to weigh proportionately the same.

European upheaval

The final devouring of Poland occurred at a time when the Continent was once again engaged in a general war. Yet this conflict was not just another military attempt to resolve customary disputes over commerce or problems of international stability. It was the result of violent revolution that had broken out in France in 1789, that had toppled the Bourbon dynasty there, and that threatened to do the same to other monarchs across Europe. The second and third partitions of Poland were a final bravura declaration of power by monarchs who already feared for their heads. Henceforth, neither foreign nor domestic policy would ever again be dictated as they had been in absolutist Europe by the convictions and determinations of kings and queens alone. Poland disappeared as Europe fell to pieces, as customary practice gave way to new and desperate necessity.

Absolutism's legacy

Though absolutism met its death in the years immediately after 1789, the relevance of its history to that of the modern world is greater than it might appear. First, centralization provided useful precedents to nineteenth-century state-builders. Modern standing armies—be they made up of soldiers or bureaucrats—are institutions whose origins rest in the age of absolutism. Second, absolutism's centripetal force contributed to an economic climate that gave birth to industrial revolution. Factories built to produce military matériel, capitalist agricultural policies designed to provide food for burgeoning capital cities, increased taxes that drove peasants to seek work in rural industries: these and other programs pointed to the future. Third, in their constant struggle to curb the privileges of nobility and oligarchy, absolute monarchs played out one more act in a drama that would continue into the nineteenth century. French nobles, Prussian junkers, and Russian boyars all bargained successfully to retain their rights to property and its management while surrendering to some degree their role as governors. But as long as their property rights remained secure, their power was assured. The French Revolution would curb their power for a time, but they were survivors. Their adaptability, whether as agricultural entrepreneurs or as senior servants of the state, ensured their order an important place in the world that lay beyond absolutism.

SUMMARY POINTS

- Absolutism, in part a response to the turmoil and insecurity of the late sixteenth and early seventeenth centuries, was instituted by the European monarchs Louis XIV of France, Peter the Great of Russia, Leopold I of Austria, and Frederick William of Brandenburg-Prussia through such means as the development of bureaucracies beholden to the crown, the co-optation of the nobility, and the weakening of the Church and local institutions.
- In England, the system of limited monarchy and representative government survived royal attempts to rule absolutely.

- The European balance of power became the preeminent international issue in the late 1600s and the early 1700s. Concerns over the expanding power of the French and Spanish rulers led to the War of the League of Augsburg (1688–1697) and the War of the Spanish Succession (1702–1714).
- The "enlightened absolutists" of the eighteenth century made some gestures toward more lenient policies, but they nevertheless ruled as absolutists, increasing their own power by raising large standing armies.
- Shifting power balances and the imperatives of economic expansion set off increasingly frequent wars between the Western powers, including the Seven Years' War (1756–1763), which established Britain as the preeminent naval and commercial power in Europe, and the Russo-Turkish War (1769–1792), during and after which Poland was divided among several powers.

Selected Readings

Anderson, M. S., *Peter the Great,* 2d ed., London, 1995. A good, thorough biography.

———, *War and Society in Europe of the Old Regime, 1618–1789,* New York, 1988. An extensive survey that addresses the relationships between war and the societies of early-modern Europe.

Avrich, Paul, *Russian Rebels, 1600–1800,* New York, 1972. A study of revolts against absolutist power.

Baxter, Stephen, *William III and the Defense of European Liberty, 1650–1702,* New York, 1966. The best study of the Dutchman who became England's king.

Beales, Derek, *Joseph II,* New York, 1987. Now the standard biography of this "enlightened" despot.

Brewer, John, *Party Ideology and Popular Politics at the Accession of George III,* New York, 1976. A revisionist interpretation of political alignments and party.

Briggs, Robin, *Early Modern France, 1560–1715,* 2d ed., New York, 1997. A survey that includes sections on social and cultural, as well as political, history.

Burke, Peter, *The Fabrication of Louis XIV,* New Haven, Conn., 1992. A study of the manner in which the king created his self-image.

Carsten, F. L., *The Origins of Prussia,* Westport, Conn., 1954. The standard account of Prussia's rise and of the achievement of the Great Elector.

Churchill, Winston S., *Marlborough,* New York, 1968. An abridged edition of Churchill's magnificently written biography of his ancestor.

Corvisier, André, *Armies and Societies in Europe, 1494–1789,* Bloomington, Ind., 1979. Focuses on the French army.

Dukes, Paul, *The Making of Russian Absolutism: 1613–1801,* 2d ed., New York, 1990. A survey that focuses on the increasing power of the state.

Dunn, Richard S., *The Age of Religious Wars, 1559–1715,* 2d ed., New York, 1979. A detailed and up-to-date survey, useful for the history of late seventeenth- and early eighteenth-century absolutism.

Fraser, Antonia, *Royal Charles: Charles II and the Restoration,* New York, 1979. A readable, reliable life of the king and his times.

Goubert, Pierre, *Louis XIV and Twenty Million Frenchmen,* New York, 1972. A valuable study, the starting point for an understanding of the Sun King's reign.

Hatton, Ragnhild, *Europe in the Age of Louis XIV,* New York, 1969. Thoughtful interpretation of the period; excellent illustrations.

Herr, Richard, *The Eighteenth Century Revolution in Spain,* Princeton, 1958. The best introduction to Spain in this period.

Holborn, Hajo, *The Age of Absolutism,* New York, 1964. The best survey for Germany. Second volume of Holborn's *History of Modern Germany.*

Hufton, Olwen H., *Europe: Privilege and Protest, 1730–1789,* Ithaca, N.Y., 1980. Focuses on the growth of central state power.

Lewis, W. H., *The Splendid Century: Life in the France of Louis XIV,* New York, 1953. A delightfully written survey.

Mettam, Roger, *Power and Faction in Louis XIV's France,* Cambridge, 1988. A study that discusses the powers that Louis did not control at court.

Palmer, R. R., *The Age of the Democratic Revolution: A Political History of Europe and America, 1760–1800,* Vol. I, Princeton, 1964. Argues in favor of a general European aristocratic reaction prior to 1789.

Plumb, John H., *Sir Robert Walpole,* 2 vols., Boston, 1956, 1961. A well-written, sympathetic biography of England's leading eighteenth-century politician.

Riasanovsky, Nicholas V., *A History of Russia,* 5th ed., Oxford, 1993. A useful introduction.

Ritter, Gerhard, *Frederick the Great: A Historical Profile,* Berkeley, 1968. A readable biography.

Rudé, George, *Europe in the Eighteenth Century: Aristocracy and the Bourgeois Challenge,* New York, 1972. A survey that stresses social stratification and tension.

Speck, W. A., *Stability and Strife: England, 1714–1760,* Cambridge, Mass., 1977. A good survey.

Vierhaus, Rudolph, *Germany in the Age of Absolutism,* New York, 1988. A synthesis of recent historiography on the growth and spread of absolutism.

Wangermann, Ernst, *The Austrian Achievement, 1700–1800,* London, 1973. A suggestive introductory survey.

Wolf, John B., *Louis XIV,* New York, 1968. The standard biography in English.

Woloch, Isser, *Eighteenth-Century Europe: Tradition and Progress, 1715–1789,* New York, 1982. A thoughtful, well-organized survey.

Source Materials

Locke, John, *Two Treatises of Government.* (Many editions.) The argument against absolutism.

Saint-Simon, Louis, *Historical Memoirs.* (Many editions.) A brilliant source for evidence about life at the court of Louis XIV.

Rulers of Principal States

THE CAROLINGIAN DYNASTY

Pepin of Heristal, Mayor of the Palace, 687–714
Charles Martel, Mayor of the Palace, 715–741
Pepin III, Mayor of the Palace, 741–751; King, 751–768
Charlemagne, King, 768–814; Emperor, 800–814
Louis the Pious, Emperor, 814–840

Middle Kingdoms

Lothair, Emperor, 840–855
Louis (Italy), Emperor, 855–875
Charles (Provence), King, 855–863
Lothair II (Lorraine), King, 855–869

West Francia

Charles the Bald, King, 840–877; Emperor, 875–877
Louis II, King, 877–879
Louis III, King, 879–882
Carloman, King, 879–884

East Francia

Ludwig, King, 840–876
Carloman, King, 876–880
Ludwig, King, 876–882
Charles the Fat, Emperor, 876–887

HOLY ROMAN EMPERORS

Saxon Dynasty

Otto I, 962–973
Otto II, 973–983
Otto III, 983–1002
Henry II, 1002–1024

Franconian Dynasty

Conrad II, 1024–1039
Henry III, 1039–1056
Henry IV, 1056–1106
Henry V, 1106–1125
Lothair II (Saxony), 1125–1137

Hohenstaufen Dynasty

Conrad III, 1138–1152
Frederick I (Barbarossa), 1152–1190
Henry VI, 1190–1197
Philip of Swabia, 1198–1208 } Rivals
Otto IV (Welf), 1198–1215 }
Frederick II, 1220–1250
Conrad IV, 1250–1254

Interregnum, 1254–1273

Emperors from Various Dynasties

Rudolf I (Habsburg), 1273–1291
Adolf (Nassau), 1292–1298
Albert I (Habsburg), 1298–1308
Henry VII (Luxemburg), 1308–1313
Ludwig IV (Wittelsbach), 1314–1347
Charles IV (Luxemburg), 1347–1378
Wenceslas (Luxemburg), 1378–1400
Rupert (Wittelsbach), 1400–1410
Sigismund (Luxemburg), 1410–1437

Habsburg Dynasty

Albert II, 1438–1439
Frederick III, 1440–1493
Maximilian I, 1493–1519
Charles V, 1519–1556
Ferdinand I, 1556–1564
Maximilian II, 1564–1576
Rudolf II, 1576–1612
Matthias, 1612–1619
Ferdinand II, 1619–1637
Ferdinand III, 1637–1657
Leopold I, 1658–1705
Joseph I, 1705–1711
Charles VI, 1711–1740
Charles VII (not a Habsburg), 1742–1745
Francis I, 1745–1765
Joseph II, 1765–1790
Leopold II, 1790–1792
Francis II, 1792–1806

RULERS OF FRANCE FROM HUGH CAPET

Capetian Dynasty

Hugh Capet, 987–996
Robert II, 996–1031
Henry I, 1031–1060
Philip I, 1060–1108
Louis VI, 1108–1137
Louis VII, 1137–1180
Philip II (Augustus), 1180–1223
Louis VIII, 1223–1226
Louis IX (St. Louis), 1226–1270
Philip III, 1270–1285
Philip IV, 1285–1314
Louis X, 1314–1316
Philip V, 1316–1322
Charles IV, 1322–1328

Valois Dynasty

Philip VI, 1328–1350
John, 1350–1364
Charles V, 1364–1380
Charles VI, 1380–1422
Charles VII, 1422–1461
Louis XI, 1461–1483
Charles VIII, 1483–1498
Louis XII, 1498–1515
Francis I, 1515–1547
Henry II, 1547–1559
Francis II, 1559–1560
Charles IX, 1560–1574
Henry III, 1574–1589

Bourbon Dynasty

Henry IV, 1589–1610
Louis XIII, 1610–1643
Louis XIV, 1643–1715
Louis XV, 1715–1774
Louis XVI, 1774–1792

After 1792

First Republic, 1792–1799
Napoleon Bonaparte, First Consul, 1799–1804
Napoleon I, Emperor, 1804–1814
Louis XVIII (Bourbon dynasty), 1814–1824
Charles X (Bourbon dynasty), 1824–1830
Louis Philippe, 1830–1848
Second Republic, 1848–1852
Napoleon III, Emperor, 1852–1870
Third Republic, 1870–1940
Pétain regime, 1940–1944
Provisional government, 1944–1946
Fourth Republic, 1946–1958
Fifth Republic, 1958–

RULERS OF ENGLAND

Anglo-Saxon Dynasty

Alfred the Great, 871–899
Edward the Elder, 899–924
Ethelstan, 924–939
Edmund I, 939–946
Edred, 946–955
Edwy, 955–959
Edgar, 959–975
Edward the Martyr, 975–978
Ethelred the Unready, 978–1016
Canute, 1016–1035 (Danish Nationality)
Harold I, 1035–1040
Hardicanute, 1040–1042
Edward the Confessor, 1042–1066
Harold II, 1066

House of Normandy

William I (the Conqueror), 1066–1087
William II, 1087–1100
Henry I, 1100–1135
Stephen, 1135–1154

House of Plantagenet

Henry II, 1154–1189
Richard I, 1189–1199
John, 1199–1216
Henry III, 1216–1272
Edward I, 1272–1307
Edward II, 1307–1327
Edward III, 1327–1377
Richard II, 1377–1399

House of Lancaster

Henry IV, 1399–1413
Henry V, 1413–1422
Henry VI, 1422–1461

House of York

Edward IV, 1461–1483
Edward V, 1483
Richard III, 1483–1485

House of Tudor

Henry VII, 1485–1509
Henry VIII, 1509–1547
Edward VI, 1547–1553
Mary, 1553–1558
Elizabeth I, 1558–1603

House of Stuart

James I, 1603–1625
Charles I, 1625–1649

Commonwealth and Protectorate, 1649–1659

House of Stuart Restored

Charles II, 1660–1685
James II, 1685–1688
William III and Mary II, 1689–1694
William III alone, 1694–1702
Anne, 1702–1714

House of Hanover

George I, 1714–1727
George II, 1727–1760
George III, 1760–1820
George IV, 1820–1830
William IV, 1830–1837
Victoria, 1837–1901

House of Saxe-Coburg-Gotha

Edward VII, 1901–1910
George V, 1910–1917

House of Windsor

George V, 1917–1936
Edward VIII, 1936
George VI, 1936–1952
Elizabeth II, 1952–

RULERS OF AUSTRIA AND AUSTRIA-HUNGARY

*Maximilian I (Archduke), 1493–1519
*Charles V, 1519–1556
*Ferdinand I, 1556–1564
*Maximilian II, 1564–1576
*Rudolf II, 1576–1612
*Matthias, 1612–1619
*Ferdinand II, 1619–1637
*Ferdinand III, 1637–1657
*Leopold I, 1658–1705
*Joseph I, 1705–1711
*Charles VI, 1711–1740
Maria Theresa, 1740–1780
*Joseph II, 1780–1790

*also bore title of Holy Roman Emperor

*Leopold II, 1790–1792
*Francis II, 1792–1835 (Emperor of Austria as Francis I after 1804)
Ferdinand I, 1835–1848
Francis Joseph, 1848–1916 (after 1867 Emperor of Austria and King of Hungary)
Charles I, 1916–1918 (Emperor of Austria and King of Hungary)
Republic of Austria, 1918–1938 (dictatorship after 1934)
Republic restored, under Allied occupation, 1945–1956
Free Republic, 1956–

RULERS OF PRUSSIA AND GERMANY

*Frederick I, 1701–1713
*Frederick William I, 1713–1740
*Frederick II (the Great), 1740–1786
*Frederick William II, 1786–1797
*Frederick William III, 1797–1840
*Frederick William IV, 1840–1861
*William I, 1861–1888 (German Emperor after 1871)
Frederick III, 1888
*William II, 1888–1918
Weimar Republic, 1918–1933
Third Reich (Nazi Dictatorship), 1933–1945
Allied occupation, 1945–1952
Division into Federal Republic of Germany in west and German Democratic Republic in east, 1949–1991
Federal Republic of Germany (united), 1991–

*Kings of Prussia

RULERS OF RUSSIA

Ivan III, 1462–1505
Vasily III, 1505–1533
Ivan IV, 1533–1584
Theodore I, 1584–1598
Boris Godunov, 1598–1605
Theodore II, 1605
Vasily IV, 1606–1610
Michael, 1613–1645
Alexius, 1645–1676
Theodore III, 1676–1682
Ivan V and Peter I, 1682–1689
Peter I (the Great), 1689–1725
Catherine I, 1725–1727
Peter II, 1727–1730
Anna, 1730–1740
Ivan VI, 1740–1741
Elizabeth, 1741–1762
Peter III, 1762
Catherine II (the Great), 1762–1796
Paul, 1796–1801
Alexander I, 1801–1825
Nicholas I, 1825–1855
Alexander II, 1855–1881
Alexander III, 1881–1894
Nicholas II, 1894–1917
Soviet Republic, 1917–1991
Russian Federation, 1991–

RULERS OF SPAIN

Ferdinand { and Isabella, 1479–1504
and Philip I, 1504–1506
and Charles I, 1506–1516 }
Charles I (Holy Roman Emperor Charles V), 1516–1556
Philip II, 1556–1598
Philip III, 1598–1621
Philip IV, 1621–1665
Charles II, 1665–1700
Philip V, 1700–1746
Ferdinand VI, 1746–1759
Charles III, 1759–1788
Charles IV, 1788–1808
Ferdinand VII, 1808
Joseph Bonaparte, 1808–1813
Ferdinand VII (restored), 1814–1833
Isabella II, 1833–1868
Republic, 1868–1870
Amadeo, 1870–1873
Republic, 1873–1874
Alfonso XII, 1874–1885
Alfonso XIII, 1886–1931
Republic, 1931–1939
Fascist Dictatorship, 1939–1975
Juan Carlos I, 1975–

RULERS OF ITALY

Victor Emmanuel II, 1861–1878
Humbert I, 1878–1900
Victor Emmanuel III, 1900–1946
Fascist Dictatorship, 1922–1943 (maintained in northern Italy until 1945)
Humbert II, May 9–June 13, 1946
Republic, 1946–

PROMINENT POPES

Silvester I, 314–335
Leo I, 440–461
Gelasius I, 492–496
Gregory I, 590–604
Nicholas I, 858–867
Silvester II, 999–1003
Leo IX, 1049–1054
Nicholas II, 1058–1061
Gregory VII, 1073–1085
Urban II, 1088–1099
Paschal II, 1099–1118
Alexander III, 1159–1181
Innocent III, 1198–1216
Gregory IX, 1227–1241
Innocent IV, 1243–1254
Boniface VIII, 1294–1303
John XXII, 1316–1334
Nicholas V, 1447–1455
Pius II, 1458–1464
Alexander VI, 1492–1503
Julius II, 1503–1513
Leo X, 1513–1521
Paul III, 1534–1549
Paul IV, 1555–1559
Sixtus V, 1585–1590
Urban VIII, 1623–1644
Gregory XVI, 1831–1846
Pius IX, 1846–1878
Leo XIII, 1878–1903
Pius X, 1903–1914
Benedict XV, 1914–1922
Pius XI, 1922–1939
Pius XII, 1939–1958
John XXIII, 1958–1963
Paul VI, 1963–1978
John Paul I, 1978
John Paul II, 1978–

Illustration Credits

Volume One
Frontispiece, ii, Tate Gallery, London/Art Resource, NY
Part One: xviii, cliché Bibliothèque Nationale de France, Paris
Chapter 1: 7 (top left), Ralph Morse, Life Magazine © Time Inc.; **7 (bottom)**, Sygma Photo News; **7 (top right)**, Neg. no. 15509, Courtesy Dept. of Library Services, American Museum of Natural History; **8 (both)**, Courtesy Dept. of Library Services, American Museum of Natural History; **9**, Ankara Arkeologi Muzesi, Ankara; **11**, Courtesy of The Oriental Institute of The University of Chicago; **12**, Hirmer Fotoarchiv; **13 (top and bottom left)**, from *The Origins of War*, by Arthur Ferrill, published by Thames and Hudson Inc., New York; **13 (bottom right)**, from *Four Thousand Years Ago*, by Geofrey Bibby, 1961. Courtesy Alfred A. Knopf, Inc.; **15**, The Peabody Museum, Harvard University

Chapter 2: 18, Hirmer Fotoarchiv; **19**, © Photo RMN, Paris/Chuzeville; **20**, from *The Origins of War*, by Arthur Ferrill, published by Thames and Hudson Inc., New York; **21 (left)**, Staatliche Museen zu Berlin—Preußischer Kulturbesitz, Vorderasiatisches Museum; **21 (right)**, Ashmolean Museum; **22 (top left)**, © by the Ashmolean Museum, Oxford; **22 (top right)**, Courtesy of the British Museum; **22 (bottom left)**, R.M.N., Paris; **22 (bottom right)**, Hirmer Fotoarchiv; **23**, Courtesy of the Oriental Institute of The University of Chicago; **24**, from *Women's Work*, by Elizabeth Wayland Barber; **26**, The Nelson Trust, The Nelson-Atkins Museum of Art, Kansas City, Missouri (49-15); **27**, Hirmer Fotoarchiv; **28**, The Pierpont Morgan Library, New York; **30**, Hittite Sculpture © by The Metropolitan Museum of Art; **32**, Courtesy of The Oriental Institute of The University of Chicago; **33 (both)**, Hirmer Fotoarchiv; **36**, Staatliche Museen zu Berlin—Preußischer Kulturbesitz, Vorderasiatisches Museum/bpk; **37**, Staatliche Museen zu Berlin—Preußischer Kulturbesitz, Vorderasiatisches Museum

Chapter 3: 42, from *The Origins of War*, by Arthur Ferrill, published by Thames and Hudson, Inc., New York; **45**, Vanni/Art Resource, NY; **46**, The Metropolitan Museum of Art, Rogers Fund, 1942 (42.2.3) © by The Metropolitan Museum of Art; **47 (top)**, Egyptian. Papyri. Funerary papyrus of the songress of Amun Nany (30.4.31) © by The Metropolitan Museum of Art; **47 (bottom)**, Erich Lessing/Art Resource, NY; **48 (top)**, Staatliche Museen zu Berlin—Preußischer Kulturbesitz, Agyptisches Museum; **48 (bottom)**, Giraudon/Art Resource, NY; **49**, Lee Boltin; **51**, Erich Lessing/Art Resource, NY; **52 (top)**, Erich Lessing/Art Resource, NY; **52 (bottom)**, Courtesy Museum of Fine Arts, Boston; **53 (both)**, Museum Expedition/Courtesy, Museum of Fine Arts, Boston; **54**, Staatliche Museen zu Berlin—Preußischer Kulturbesitz, Agyptisches Museum; **55 (top)**, Boltin Picture Library; **55 (bottom)**, Egyptian paintings—copies. Menna with family fishing and fowling (30.4.48) © by The Metropolitan Museum of Art; **56**, Egyptian paintings—copies. Making bricks. (30.4.77) © by The Metropolitan Museum of Art

Chapter 4: 60, Courtesy of The Oriental Institute of The University of Chicago; **63**, American Numismatic Society; **64**, Biblical Archaeological Society; **67**, Alinari/Art Resource, NY; **69**, Biblical Archaeological Society; **73 (top)**, Greek, coin showing the labyrinth; obverse: head of the goddess Hera, minted in Knossos, Crete, silver drachem, 350/220 B.C.E., diam: 1.8 cm, Martin A. Ryerson collection, 1922.4914. Photograph © 1997, The Art Institute of Chicago. All rights reserved; **73 (bottom)**, Courtesy of The Oriental Institute of The University of Chicago; **74 (top)**, Alison Frantz; **74 (bottom)**, National Museum of Greece; **75**, from *Women's Work*, by Elizabeth Wayland Barber; **76 (both)**, from *Women's Work*, by Elizabeth Wayland Barber; **77 (top)**, Hirmer Fotoarchiv; **77 (bottom)**, Scala/Art Resource, NY; **78**, Lee Boltin; **79**, Hirmer Fotoarchiv

Part Two: 82, Werner Forman/Art Resource, NY

Chapter 5: 88, Art Resource, NY; **89 (top left and right)**, Scala/Art Resource, NY; **89 (bottom)**, Acropolis Museum, Athens (AM 624); **90 (both)**, Deutschen Archaologischen Instituts; **91**, Art Resource, NY; **93**, Hirmer Fotoarchiv; **95**, Acropolis Museum; **96 (top)**, Hirmer Fotoarchiv; **96 (bottom)**, Staatliche Antikensammlungen und Glyptothek München; **97**, American School of Classical Studies at Athens: Agora Excavations; **98**, R.M.N., Paris; **99**, Scala/Art Resource, NY; **102**, Staatliche Antikensammlungen und Glyptothek München; **103**, Staatliche Museen zu Berlin—Bildarchiv Preußisher Kulturbesitz: Antikensammlung; **105**, Greek vases, black-figured. Amphora. Men weighing merchandise (47.11.5 Side B) © by The Metropolitan Museum of Art; **108**, Erich Lessing/Art Resource, NY; **109**, Deutschen Archaologischen Instituts; **110**, Scala/Art Resource, NY; **114**, Staatliche Antikensammlungen und Glyptothek München; **115 (bottom left)**, The Warder Collection, NY; **115 (bottom right)**, George P. Brockway; **117 (top)**, Inv. no. Chrviii 967, The National Museum, Copenhagen, Dept. of Classical and Near Eastern Antiquities; **117 (bottom)**, Museo Nazionale Romano; **118 (left)**, Hartwig Koppermann; **118 (center)**, R.M.N., Paris; **118 (right)**, Nimatallah/Art Resource, NY; **119 (both)**, Scala/Art Resource, NY; **120**, Art Resource, NY; **121**, University Prints

Chapter 6: 126, Hirmer Fotoarchiv; **127**, American Numismatic Society; **128**, Courtesy of The Oriental Institute of The University of Chicago; **129**, ANE. Metalwork: Gold. Vessel in form of lion pro-tome. (54.3.3) © by The Metropolitan Museum of Art; **131 (both)**, Courtesy of The Oriental Institute of The University of Chicago; **132**, from *The Origins of War*, by Arthur Ferrill, published by Thames and Hudson Inc., New York; **134**, The Warder Collection, NY; **136**, Hirmer Fotoarchiv; **137**, Greek, Syria, Coin showing Antiochus I Soter; reverse: Apollo seated with bow and arrow, silver tetradrachem, Reign 281–261 B.C.E., diam: 2.9 cm, Gift of William F. Dunham, 1920.725. Photograph © 1997, The Art Institute of Chicago. All rights reserved; **138**, Erdmut Lerner; **140**, Arkeoloji Müzesi, Istanbul; **142**, Alinari/Art Resource, NY; **143 (top)**, Greek sculpture: Old Market Woman (09.39) © by The Metropolitan Museum of Art; **143 (bottom)**, University Prints; **144 (top)**, Scala/Art Resource, NY; **144 (bottom)**, Alinari/Art Resource, NY; **145 (top)**, Giraudon/Art Resource, NY; **145 (bottom)**, Nimatallah/Art Resource, NY; **146 (top)**, The Metropolitan Museum of Art, Rogers Fund, 1923 (23.160.20) © by The Metropolitan Museum of Art; **146 (bottom)**, The Metropolitan Museum of Art, Bequest of Mrs. H. O. Havemeyer, 1929, The H. O. Havemeyer Collection. (29.100.377) © by The Metropolitan Museum of Art; **148**, Arkeoloji Müzesi, Istanbul

Chapter 7: 152 (left), Scala/Art Resource, NY; **152 (right)**, Nimatallah/Art Resource, NY; **153 (top)**, © Photo R.M.N., Paris/Hervé Lewandowski; **153 (bottom)**, Villa Giulia Museum, Rome/The Warder Collection, NY; **154 (top)**, Scala/Art Resource, NY; **154 (center)**, Scala/Art Resource, NY; **154 (bottom)**, Photo by Aaron M. Levin; **158**, Photo by Zindman/Fremont; **159 (both)**, American Numismatic Society; **164 (top)**, Ny Carlsberg Glyptotek; **164 (bottom)**, Scala/Art Resource, NY; **165 (both)**, American Numismatic Society; **168**, Scala/Art Resource, NY; **169**, Scala/Art Resource, NY; **171 (top)**, Roman, coin showing the Emperor Trajan; reverse: Trajan and officers on platform facing three kings; minted in Rome, gold aureus, A.D. 115/117, diam: 1.8 cm, Gift of Martin A. Ryerson, 1922.4871. Photograph © 1997, The Art Institute of Chicago. All rights reserved; **171 (bottom)**, The Warder Collection, NY; **172**, Scala/Art Resource, NY; **173**, Vat. Lat. 3867, fol. 3v. Foto Biblioteca Vaticana; **174**, Scala/Art Resource, NY; **175**, Roman mosaic: rabbit with mushrooms and lizard (17.193.233) © by The Metropolitan Museum of Art; **176**, Art Resource, NY; **177 (top)**, Roman, Coin showing Empress Julia Domna; reverse: Pietas (piety) offers incense at altar, minted in Rome, gold aureus, A.D. 199–207, diam: 2 cm, Gift of Martin A. Ryerson, 1922.4883. Photograph © 1997, The Art Institute of Chicago. All rights reserved; **177 (bottom)**, John Ross/Art Resource, NY; **178**, Italian State Tourist Office; **180 (top)**, Scala/Art Resource, NY; **180 (bottom)**, Art Resource, NY; **181 (top)**, Photo by Zindman/Fremont; **181 (bottom)**, Scala/Art Resource, NY; **184**, Alinari/Art Resource, NY; **185**, SEF/Art Resource, NY

Chapter 8: 191, Ny Carlsberg Glyptotek; **192 (top)**, The Warder Collection, NY; **192 (bottom)**, R.M.N., Paris; **193 (left)**, The Warder Collection, NY; **193 (right)**,

Scala/Art Resource, NY; **195**, Art Resource, NY; **196**, Art Resource, NY; **197**, The Warder Collection, NY; **198 (top)**, Scala/Art Resource, NY; **198 (bottom)**, Cleveland Museum of Art, John L. Severance Fund; **200**, Sculpture—reliefs. Early Christian. Sarcophagus lid with Last Judgment (24.240) © by The Metropolitan Museum of Art; **202**, The Warder Collection, NY; **203 (both)**, The Warder Collection, NY; **204**, Akademische Druck/The Warder Collection, NY; **205**, Biblioteca Medicea Laurenziana, Florence; **208**, American Numismatic Society; **210 (both)**, The Warder Collection, NY; **213**, Houghton Library, Harvard University; **214**, The Warder Collection, NY; **215**, By permission of the British Library; **216**, Utrecht University Library (x fol 4 rariora, fol.16r); **218**, Scala/Art Resource, NY; **219**, Scala/Art Resource, NY; **220 (top)**, Scala/Art Resource, NY; **220 (bottom)**, Scala/Art Resource, NY

Part Three: 224, Robert E. Lerner
Chapter 9: 234 (top), Metalwork—gold. Byzantine. Chalice with repousse design (17.190.1710 View #1) © by The Metropolitan Museum of Art; **234 (bottom)**, American Numismatic Society; **235**, Biblioteca Nacionale, Madrid; **236**, cliché Bibliothèque Nationale de France, Paris; **239**, Dumbarton Oaks, Washington, D.C. © 1995; **240**, Scala/Art Resource, NY; **242 (top)**, Giraudon/Art Resource, NY; **242 (bottom)**, The Warder Collection, NY; **243**, The Warder Collection, NY; **244**, Anderson Art Reference Bureau/Art Resource, NY; **246**, Arab Information Bureau; **248**, E. U. L. Or. Ms. 20, fol. 45v: used with permission of the Edinburgh University Library; **249 (left)**, Scala/Art Resource, NY; **249 (right)**, Erich Lessing/Art Resource, NY; **256**, Bodleian Library, University of Oxford, Division of Oriental Manuscripts, MS Marsh 144; **258**, Scala/Art Resource, NY; **259**, Daniel Aubry; **261**, Koninklijke Bibliothek, Brussels; **262**, Scala/Art Resource, NY; **263**, Kunsthistorisches Museum, Vienna; **264**, Scala/Art Resource, NY; **266**, cliché Bibliothèque Nationale de France, Paris; **267**, Vatican Library: MS. Reg. Ret. 762, fol. 82r, written at Tours 800 A.D. Detail; **269**, Courtesy of the British Museum; **270**, cliché Bibliothèque Nationale de France, Paris; **271 (top)**, cliché Bibliothèque Nationale de France, Paris; **271 (bottom left)**, Utrecht University Library, HS 32, fol 76v **271 (bottom right)**, Staatliche Museen zu Berlin—Preußischer Kulturbesitz, Staatsbibliothek, Bamberg

Chapter 10: 278, Biblioteca Riccardiana, Florence, Manuscript Ricc. 492 c. 18, with the permission of the Ministero per I Beni Culturali e Ambientali; **279**, Pierpont Morgan Library, New York/Art Resource, NY; **280 (top)**, Utrecht University Library (F qu 348 rariora, fol. A6v); **280 (bottom)**, Bodleian Library, Division of Western Manuscrips, University of Oxford, MS. Boldl. 264, fol 81r; **281**, By permission of the British Library; **283**, The Warder Collection, NY; **284 (top)**, By permission of the British Library; **284 (bottom)**, cliché Bibliothèque Nationale de France, Paris; **285**, Pierpont Morgan Library, New York/Art Resource, NY; **286**, cliché Bibliothèque Nationale de France, Paris; **287**, cliché Bibliothèque Nationale de France, Paris; **288**, Staatliche Museen zu Berlin—Preußischer Kulturbesitz, Bayerisches Hauptstaatsarchiv; **290 (top)**, Photo by Zindman/Fremont; **290 (bottom)**, The Bettmann Archive; **291**, cliché Bibliothèque Nationale de France, Paris; **292 (top)**, Commision Régionale d'Alsace; **292 (bottom)**, Diebold Schilling, Official Bernese Chronicle, vol. 1, Burgerbibliothek, Berne, Mss.h.h.l.l., p. 289; **293**, Service Photographique des Archives Nationales; **294**, French Government Tourist Office; **297 (top)**, Staatliche Museen zu Berlin—Preußischer Kulturbesitz, Schloßkirche Cappenberg; **297 (bottom)**, MS. Pal. Lat. 1071, fol. 1v, Foto Biblioteca Vaticana; **302**, Giraudon/Art Resource, NY; **303**, The Walters Art Gallery, Baltimore; **304**, cliché Bibliothèque Nationale de France, Paris; **305**, Scheide Library, Princeton University; **309 (top)**, Giraudon/Art Resource, NY; **309 (bottom)**, cliché Bibliothèque Nationale de France, Paris; **311**, Museo del Prado, Madrid

Chapter 11: 320, The Bettmann Archive; **321**, Scala/Art Resource, NY; **322**, The Warder Collection, NY; **326**, Bayerische Staatsbibliothek, München; **327**, MS W. 139 F244, detail, The Walters Art Gallery, Baltimore; **329**, The Warder Collection, NY; **330**, Courtesy of Thames and Hudson; **331**, Bayerische Staatsbibliothek, München; **332**, © 1997 Artists' Rights Society (ARS), N.Y./ADAGP, Paris; **333**, Giraudon/Art Resource, NY; **335**, Scala/Art Resource, NY; **336**, Scala/Art Resource, NY; **337 (left)**, cliché Bibliothèque Nationale de France, Paris; **337 (right)**, Negativ aus dem Bildarchiv der Österreicheschen Nationalbibliothek, Wien; **339**, Teresa Gross-Diaz; **341**, The Walters Art

Gallery, Baltimore; **342**, The Bettmann Archive; **343 (top)**, Fitzwilliam Museum; **343 (bottom)**, Minatur 59v, Codex poet., Württembergische Landesbibliothek, Stuttgart; **344**, Österreichesche Nationalbibliothek, Wien; **345 (top)**, Bibliothèque Sainte-Geneviève; **345 (bottom)**, The Warder Collection, NY; **346**, Giraudon/Art Resource, NY; **349**, Foto Marburg/Art Resource, NY; **350 (top)**, Bayerische Staatsbibliothek, München; **350 (bottom)**, The Pierpont Morgan Library, New York; **351 (top)**, Montpelliar, Faculté de Medicine; **351 (bottom)**, The Bodleian Library, Oxford: MS Bodley. 264, fol. 81v (detail); **352 (top)**, cliché Bibliothèque Nationale de France, Paris; **352 (bottom)**, Erich Lessing/Art Resource, NY; **353**, Badische Landesbibliothek; **354 (both)**, Richard List/Corbis; **355**, Giraudon/Art Resource, NY; **356**, The Warder Collection, NY; **357**, Giraudon/Art Resource, NY

Chapter 12: 362, The Warder Collection, NY; **363**, The Walters Art Gallery, Baltimore; **364**, R.M.N., Paris; **366 (top)**, Art Resource, NY; **366 (bottom)**, Stadtbibliothek Nürnberg, Amb. 317.2°, f. 10r; **369**, Kath. Pfarramt; **370**, cliché Bibliothèque Nationale de France, Paris; **371**, Giraudon/Art Resource, NY; **372 (top)**, The Walters Art Gallery, Baltimore; **372 (bottom left)**, cliché Bibliothèque Nationale de France, Paris; **372 (bottom right)**, The Warder Collection, NY; **373 (both)**, Foto Marburg/Art Resource, NY; **376**, Bayerische Staatsbibliothek, München; **382**, Wildenstein & Company, Inc./private collection; **383**, By courtesy of the National Portrait Gallery, London; **385**, The Warder Collection, NY; **386 (top)**, Erich Lessing/Art Resource, NY; **386 (bottom)**, CCC Ms. 16, fol. 166r, detail, Courtesy of the Master and Fellows of Corpus Christi College, Cambridge; **392**, By permission of the British Library; **395 (top left)**, Scala/Art Resource, NY; **395 (top right)**, Scala/Art Resource, NY; **395 (bottom left)**, Scala/Art Resource, NY; **395 (bottom right)**, Scala/Art Resource, NY; **396 (top)**, R.M.N., Paris; **396 (bottom)**, Reproduced by courtesy of the Trustees, The National Gallery, London. Photograph © The National Gallery, London; **397**, Erich Lessing/Art Resource, NY; **398**, Städelsches Kunstinstitut Frankfurt/© Ursula Edelmann, Artothek; **399 (top)**, Christ Church, University of Oxford; **399 (bottom)**, Pierpont Morgan Library, NY/Art Resource, NY; **400**, Bayerische Staatsbibliothek, München; **401**, © Bibliothèque Royale Albert 1er, Bruxelles, ms. 11209, fol. 3 recto; **402 (left)**, The New York Public Library: Astor, Lenox, and Tilden Foundations; **402 (right)**, Gutenberg Museum

Part Four: 406, Photo Artothek/ © by Städelsches Kunstinstitut Frankfurt
Chapter 13: 416, Photo by Zindman/Fremont; **419 (top)**, Milan, Sforza Castle Museums; **419 (bottom)**, Art Resource, NY; **420**, National Gallery of Art, Washington, D. C., Kress Collection; **422**, © Photo RMN, Paris; **424**, Scala/Art Resource, NY; **425 (top)**, Staatliche Museen zu Berlin—Preußischer Kulturbesitz, Gemäldgalerie; **425 (bottom)**, Scala/Art Resource, NY; **426 (top)**, Scala/Art Resource, NY; **426 (bottom)**, Erich Lessing/Art Resource, NY; **427**, Scala/Art Resource, NY; **428 (top)**, Scala/Art Resource, NY; **428 (bottom left and right)**, R.M.N., Paris; **430 (top)**, Erich Lessing/Art Resource, NY; **430 (bottom)**, © The Frick Collection, New York; **431 (top)**, Andrew W. Mellon Collection, © 1997 Board of Trustees, National Gallery of Art, Washington, c. 1510, oil on panel transferred to canvas, diameter: .945 (37¼); framed: 1.372 × 1.359 (54 × 53½); **431 (bottom)**, Scala/Art Resource, NY; **432**, Scala/Art Resource, NY; **433 (top)**, Nimatallah/Art Resource, NY; **433 (bottom)**, Scala/Art Resource, NY; **434**, Scala/Art Resource, NY; **435 (top)**, Scala/Art Resource, NY; **435 (bottom)**, Erich Lessing/Art Resource, NY; **436**, Scala/Art Resource, NY; **438**, The Hulton Deutsch Collection; **441**, Harvey D. Parker Fund/Courtesy Museum of Fine Arts, Boston; **445 (top)**, Vanni/Art Resource, NY; **445 (bottom)**, R.M.N., Paris; **446 (left)**, Dürer, St. Jerome in His Study. © by The Metropolitan Museum of Art; **446 (center and right)**, Alte Pinakothek, Munich; **447 (left)**, Alte Pinakothek, Munich; **447 (right)**, R.M.N., Paris; **448 (top)**, © The Frick Collection, New York; **448 (bottom)**, Giraudon/Art Resource, NY; **449**, Scala/Art Resource, NY; **450**, Art Resource, NY; **451 (top)**, By permission of the British Library; **451 (bottom)**, By permission of the Folger Shakespeare Library; **452**, Scala/Art Resource, NY; **453 (top)**, The Hulton Deutsch Collection; **453 (bottom left)**, The New York Public Library: Astor, Lenox, and Tilden Foundations; **453 (bottom right)**, Vesal, A.: Humani corporis fabrico. Basel 1543 Herzog August Bibliothek Wolfenbuettel: 3 Phys. fol.

Chapter 14: 462 (top), José Pessoa, Arquivo Nacional de Fotografia, Instituto Português de Museus; **462 (bottom left)**, The Warder Collection, NY; **462 (bottom right)**, National Maritime Museum, London; **464**, Museo del Prado, Madrid; **465 (left)**, Vespucci, A.: Das sind die gefunden Menschen. 1505. Herzog August Bibliothek Wolfenbuettel: QUH26 (5); **465 (right)**, cliché Bibliothèque Nationale de France, Paris; **467**, Det kongelige Bibliotek: Gl. kgl Saml. 2232. Side 527; **468**, Scala/Art Resource, NY; **471 (both)**, By permission of the British Library; **472**, Alinari/Art Resource, NY; **474 (both)**, Staatsbibliothek, Bern; **475 (left)**, Staatliche Museen zu Berlin—Preußischer Kulturbesitz, Kupferstichkabinett; **475 (right)**, By permission of the British Library; **476 (both)**, Oeffentliche Kunstsammlung Basel, Kunstmuseum/ Photo: Martin Buhler; **477 (left)**, Museo del Prado, Madrid; **477 (right)**, Alte Pinakothek, Munich; **478**, New China Photos/Eastfoto; **480**, National Trust/Art Resource, NY; **483**, John R. Freeman & Co.; **484**, By kind permission of the Marquess of Tabistock and Trustees of the Bedford Estate; **486 (both)**, The Warder Collection, NY; **487**, Erich Lessing/Art Resource, NY; **488 (top)**, Giraudon/Art Resource, NY; **488 (bottom)**, The Warder Collection, NY; **489**, Inv. nr. HB 17566, Germanisches Nationalmuseum, Nürnberg; **491 (both)**, Courtesy of the British Museum; **494**, The Nelson Trust, The Nelson-Atkins Museum of Art, Kansas City, Missouri; **495**, Negativ aus dem Bildarchiv der Österreicheschen Nationalbibliothek, Wien; **496**, Kunsthistorisches Museum, Vienna

Chapter 15: 502, François Dubois, La St. Barthélemy, 1572, oil on wood. 94 × 154 cm. photo: J.-C. Ducret, Musée des Beaux-Arts, Lausanne; **506**, Giraudon/Art Resource, NY; **507**, Photo Bulloz, Musée Carnavalet; **508 (top)**, Museo del Prado, Madrid; **508 (bottom)**, Courtesy of the Hispanic Society of America, New York; **510**, The New York Public Library: Astor, Lenox, and Tilden Foundations; **511 (left)**, National Maritime Museum, London; **511 (right)**, By courtesy of the National Portrait Gallery, London; **513 (both)**, John R. Freeman & Co.; **514**, The Hulton Deutsch Collection; **516**, Museo del Prado, Madrid; **517**, Ampliaciones Y Reproducciones, MAS; **519**, Giraudon/Art Resource, NY; **520**, By courtesy of the National Portrait Gallery, London; **522**, Photo Bulloz; **523**, Scala/Art Resource, NY; **525**, Bibliothèque Royale, Brussels; **526**, The Mansell Collection, London; **527 (top)**, Photo Bulloz; **527 (bottom)**, Urb. Lat. 276, fol. 41r, Foto Biblioteca Apostolica Vaticana; **529**, cliché Bibliothèque Nationale de France, Paris; **530**, Photo Bulloz; **531**, Art Resource, NY; **532**, By permission of the Folger Shakespeare Library; **533**, The Warder Collection, NY; **534 (top)**, The Metropolitan Museum of Art. Bequest of Mrs. H. O. Havemeyer, 1929. The H. O. Havemeyer Collection (29.100.16); **534 (bottom)**, Isaac Sweetser Fund/Courtesy Museum of Fine Arts, Boston; **535 (top)**, Erich Lessing/Art Resource, NY; **535 (bottom)**, Museo del Prado, Madrid; **536**, El Greco, Laocoön, Samuel H. Kress Collection, © Board of Trustees, National Gallery of Art, Washington; **537**, Paintings. Spanish. El Greco: View of Toledo (29.100.6) © by The Metropolitan Museum of Art; **538 (all)**, Scala/Art Resource, NY; **539**, Scala/Art Resource, NY; **540 (top left)**, Scala/Art Resource, NY; **540 (top right)**, Museo del Prado, Madrid; **540 (bottom)**, Museo del Prado, Madrid; **541 (top)**, Erich Lessing/Art Resource, NY; **541 (bottom)**, Bruegel: The Harvesters (July) (19.164) © by The Metropolitan Museum of Art; **542**, Art Resource, NY; **543 (top)**, Nimatallah/Art Resource, NY; **543 (bottom)**, Museo del Prado, Madrid; **544 (top)**, © The Frick Collection, New York; **544 (bottom)**, Paintings. Dutch. Rembrandt: Aristotle with a Bust of Homer (61.198) © by The Metropolitan Museum of Art; **545**, Gift of Mr. and Mrs. Robert Woods Bliss, © 1997 Board of Trustees, National Gallery of Art, Washington, c. 1630, oil on canvas, .746 × .657 (29⅜ × 25⅞); framed: .975 × .876 × .092 (38⅜ × 34½ × 3⅝)

Chapter 16: 551 (left), Negativ aus dem Bildarchiv der Österreicheschen Nationalbibliothek, Wien; **551 (right)**, Inv. nr. HB 13157, Germanisches Nationalmuseum, Nürnberg; **552 (top)**, Bridgeman Art Library; **552 (bottom)**, St. Bartholomew's Hospital, London; **555**, Routledge, Inc.; **557**, The New York Public Library: Astor, Lenox, and Tilden Foundations; **559 (left)**, Bridgeman Art Library; **559 (right)**, Staatliche Museen zu Berlin—Preußischer Kulturbesitz, Gemäldgalerie/bpk; **561**, Bridgeman Art Library; **562**, John R. Freeman & Co.; **566**, Giraudon/Art Resource, NY; **568**, cliché Bibliothèque Nationale de France, Paris; **573**, John R. Freeman & Co.; **574**, Victoria & Albert Museum, London/Art Resource, NY; **576 (top)**, The Warder Collection, NY; **576 (bottom)**, The Hulton Deutsch Collection; **578**, Roger Viollet; **579**, Erich

Lessing/Art Resource, NY; **581**, Giraudon/Art Resource, NY; **582**, Giraudon/Art Resource, NY; **583**, Courtesy of the British Museum; **585**, The New York Public Library: Astor, Lenox, and Tilden Foundations; **587**, Giraudon/Art Resource, NY; **588**, Victoria & Albert Museum, London/Art Resource, NY; **589**, cliché Bibliothèque Nationale de France, Paris

Chapter 17: 596, Erich Lessing/Art Resource, NY; **597**, Giraudon/Art Resource, NY; **598**, Giraudon/Art Resource, NY; **599**, Erich Lessing/Art Resource, NY; **601**, Paintings. French. Champaigne: Jean Baptiste Colbert (51.34) © by The Metropolitan Museum of Art; **603**, by Friedrich Wilhelm Kurfürst von Brandenburg/Ullstein; **605 (top)**, Erich Lessing/Art Resource, NY; **605 (bottom)**, Staatliche Museen zu Berlin—Preußischer Kulturbesitz; **606**, By permission of the British Library; **608 (left)**, Society for Cultural Relations with the Soviet Union; **608 (right)**, Roger Viollet; **609**, Victoria & Albert Museum, London/Art Resource, NY; **610**, Bridgeman Art Library; **612**, Bridgeman Art Library; **613**, Photo Bulloz, Valciennes; **618**, Photo Bulloz, Petit Palais; **619**, Bridgeman Art Library; **620**, cliché Bibliothèque Nationale de France, Paris; **621**, Erich Lessing/Art Resource, NY; **622**, Erich Lessing/Art Resource, NY; **623 (top)**, Giraudon/Art Resource, NY; **623 (bottom)**, The Warder Collection, NY; **624**, By courtesy of the National Portrait Gallery, London; **625**, By courtesy of the National Portrait Gallery, London; **626 (left)**, Courtesy of the British Museum; **626 (right)**, Victoria & Albert Museum, London/Art Resource, NY; **629**, Courtesy of the Director, National Army Museum, London; **631**, Giraudon/Art Resource, NY

INDEX

Guide to Pronunciation

The sounds represented by the diacritical marks used in this Index are illustrated by the following common words:

āle	ēve	ıce	ōld	ūse	
ăt	ĕnd	ĭll	ŏf	ŭs	fo͝ot
câre			fôrm	ûrn	
ärm					

Vowels that have no diacritical marks are to be "neutral," for example: Aegean = ȧ-je'an, Basel = bäz' el, Basil = ba' zil, common = kŏm' on, Alcaeus = ăl-sē' us. The combinations *ou* and *oi* are pronounced as in "out" and "oil."